James Forde
Portadown.
_____

From Belle.

Christmas 1984.

A Commentary
on Isaiah

A Commentary
on Isaiah

with Emphasis on the Messianic Hope

Homer Hailey

BAKER BOOK HOUSE
Grand Rapids, Michigan 49506

To those fine young men and women
who in my classes were first introduced to the prophets
and there learned to appreciate and love
these men and their writings,
this volume is affectionately dedicated

Contents

World Judgment and Deliverance of God's People (24–27)   195

Jerusalem-Zion: Warnings and Promises (28–35)   225

Historical Link (36–39)   299

PART TWO   Hope for Troublous Times (40–66)

Introduction (40)   327

The Contest Between Jehovah and the Idols
(41–48)   341

The Servant and the Glory of Zion (49–57)   405

National Sins, Redemption by Jehovah, and Future
Glory (58–66)   471

Appendixes   531

Bibliography   541

Foreword

Homer Hailey writes for the common man who is interested in serious Bible study. His commentaries on the Minor Prophets and Revelation have been enthusiastically received because they bridge the gap between technical, scholarly writings and popular devotional studies on these books of the Bible. And now he has produced a similar commentary on Isaiah. This is a monumental accomplishment of a difficult task, and we are the beneficiaries of Hailey's painstaking labor. I believe it is his best work ever.

Isaiah is a majestic book that portrays the tense conditions in Judah during the Assyrian invasions in a vivid and gripping way. It contrasts the faith of the few who trusted in the Lord with the unbelief of the many who feared the king of Assyria. It also contrasts the gloom of Judah's present sinful condition with the glory of its future restoration from captivity and the eventual establishment of the messianic kingdom.

Many scholars have been baffled by the strong predictive element in Isaiah and, as George L. Robinson puts it, have performed "a sort of reckless surgery" on the book. But, certainly, a prophet who could transcend the limitation of space and see "the Holy One of Israel" on His throne in heaven could overcome the limitation of time and peer into the distant future to describe the fall of Babylon, the return of the remnant, and the suffering of the messianic Servant. Homer Hailey accepts the organic unity of Isaiah and interprets its messianic prophecies in the light of the apostle John's statement that Isaiah "saw" [Christ's] glory; and he spake of him" (John 12:41).

I have had the privilege of being both a student and colleague of Homer Hailey. He has exerted a profound influence on my life as he has on thousands of others. I cherish his long-term helpfulness more than words can express, but I honor his love for the Bible even more. He has been preaching and teaching the message of Isaiah for over fifty years. For a long, long time, he had planned to write a commentary on the book. But he never rushes into anything. He studied, taught, argued, sought advice, wrote, and rewrote until his dream became a reality. In fact, a biography of the life of Homer Hailey could easily revolve around all the episodes which have led to the eventual publication of this commentary. Consequently, this commentary is distinctively his own, sprinkled throughout with his own fresh ideas. As a commentator, Hailey is cautious but confident, and he is always thoroughly conservative.

All who read this book will profit immensely from it. Having read it carefully in installments as it was being written, I heartily recommend it to every Bible student. The study of it will prove to be a joy, not "a weariness of the flesh" (Eccles. 12:12). Homer Hailey has paid the high price of "weariness of the flesh" through much study; as a result, all the Bible student has to do to reap the joy of knowing the Book of Isaiah is to spend a little bit of time with Hailey's commentary. I congratulate Homer Hailey, therefore, on a job well done, and on behalf of the Bible students who will be using this book I convey to him heartfelt thanks.

Melvin D. Curry
Florida College
Temple Terrace, Florida

Preface

For many years the Book of Isaiah has held a special fascination for me, challenging me to spend long hours in the study of it and affording many pleasant hours of teaching. I recognize that many scholars have written excellent commentaries explaining the mission and message of Isaiah, the dean of all Old Testament prophets. However, wishing to provide a book written in simple language which might help others to appreciate this grand prophecy and to see more clearly the messianic hope held by the ancient Hebrews, I undertook the writing of this commentary.

In writing I have kept in view the average person, the so-called common man, for such people make up the greater part of most congregations. My aim has been to help the reader not only to understand what Isaiah is saying, but also to grasp something of his insight into the glory and majesty of Jehovah God, to envision His absolute holiness, to appreciate His infinite love for the people whom He chose, but who had forsaken Him, and to see the working out of His purpose for the redemption of people from among all nations, gathering them into one great family. I also hope that the reader will be impressed with the terrible emptiness, failure, and consequences of idolatry; the exceeding sinfulness of sin; and the inevitable judgment these bring upon unbelievers.

In the midst of the national and individual rebellion, the sin, and the darkness of impending judgment so evident throughout the Book of Isaiah, there shines in splendor the immortal and glorious hope of deliverance by Jehovah. The Servant in whom this hope would one day be realized is more fully set forth in Isaiah's prophecy than in any other. This aspect of the prophet's message is emphasized in the commentary before you. The hope of the people of Isaiah's day was to be found in the Servant who would come; ours, similarly, must be in the Servant who has come. Though rooted in the history of that period, the Book of Isaiah is a book for all time.

Among those writers to whom I owe a special debt of gratitude for their help are James Addison Alexander, Franz Delitzsch, H. C. Leupold, George Rawlinson, George Adam Smith, and Edward J. Young, to name a few. Besides these conservative commentators, I am indebted to scholars of different and more liberal views, whose writings forced a fresh investigation and the rethinking of positions formerly held. However, the challenge they presented only confirmed my conservative view of the Book of Isaiah. Admittedly, portions of the prophecy are difficult, defying and testing the most profound biblical scholars, who must at times acknowledge their uncertainty as to the prophet's meaning. At such points I can only venture to state what is the most probable meaning, leaving the reader to draw his own conclusion.

In writing a book such as this, one finds himself indebted not only to those writers who preceded him, but also to friends who helped and encouraged him. I am grateful to my friend and former student, Melvin D. Curry, head of the Division of Bible, Florida College,

Temple Terrace, Florida, for reading the manuscript and making a number of valuable recommendations, and to my long-time friend, Clinton D. Hamilton, executive vice-president, Broward Community College, Fort Lauderdale, Florida, for several helpful suggestions. I am especially indebted to two sisters in Christ for their immeasurable help and for their valuable time so unselfishly devoted to the project: Mrs. Margie Garrett of Florida College, who carefully corrected the sentence structure where needed, and to Mrs. Ruby Stroup of Tucson, Arizona, who painstakingly typed the manuscript and provided valuable suggestions as we worked together. My profound thanks go to these two women for unsparingly giving of their time and rendering great help.

I have purposely avoided footnotes, keeping their number to a bare minimum. When quoting from an author I have included (usually within parentheses) an abbreviation of the source; one may check the bibliography for the full title. To limit the length of the commentary I have not quoted verses before commenting on them, though often the text or portions of it are quoted in italics in the comments. I suggest that you have your Bible open when studying this book. The text used is the American Standard Version, 1901. I sincerely wish that the book will fulfill the hope of both the reader and myself.

Homer Hailey

Introduction

Israel and Judah

In many respects the conditions characterizing Israel and Judah in the eighth century B.C. were similar to those which characterize our own society in the twentieth century. In their prosperity, Israel and Judah forgot God and fell into corruption and decay. Under the leadership of Jeroboam II (782–753 B.C.) Israel's borders had been largely restored, and the period was characterized by a prosperity unknown there since the days of Solomon. In Judah the capable and skillful Uzziah (767–740 B.C.) in a large measure restored the borders of that country, and prosperity reached a peak not enjoyed since Solomon's day. In both nations this material affluence produced the

17

ills that so often accompany wealth. The people forgot God and ascribed their prosperity and well-being to the idols to which they had turned.

Idolatry was rampant in Israel. Since Solomon's death (931 B.C.), when the northern kingdom separated from Judah, Israel worshiped Jehovah through the symbol of the two golden calves which had been set up at Bethel and Dan by their first king, Jeroboam I. All succeeding kings had followed him in honoring these two calves. Added to this form of idolatry was Baal worship, a national cult established through the influence of Jezebel, the wife of Ahab, who reigned from 874 to 853 B.C. Thus cursed with two forms of idolatry—Jehovah worship under the symbol of the calves and Baal worship, a purely pagan cult—the nation plunged into depths of apostasy from which it never recovered. This rejection of Jehovah by the northern kingdom was accompanied by political corruption, social decay, and moral depravity, all of which brought the judgment of God upon the nation.

However, before this judgment was carried out by the Lord, God raised up two prophets whom He sent to cry out against the sins of the day and to plead with the people to return to Jehovah. Amos, a bold, rugged, and courageous shepherd of the arid section about Tekoa south of Jerusalem, was the first (755 B.C.). He described the corrupt condition of Israel in vivid, graphic, and often picturesque language. Judgment, he said, was on its way, and, as Isaiah later described the danger posed by Assyria, "It shall be nought but terror to understand the message" (28:19). Amos warned that the palaces would be plundered (3:11) and that the luxury-loving people who sat on silken cushions of their couches or beds would be so decimated that what would remain might well be compared to two legs (of a sheep) or a piece of an ear rescued by a shepherd from the mouth of a lion (3:12). Their winter and summer houses, together with their ivory-inlaid furniture, would all perish (3:15). The women of Samaria, wives of the lords, described as "kine [cattle] of Bashan," fattened as for slaughter, would be cut off and cast out of the land, led away into captivity with hooks (4:1–3). Luxury and extravagance, gained at the expense of the poor (6:1–6), would all be brought to nought, and the revelers would be carried away captive (6:7–11). "Therefore thus will

I do unto thee, O Israel; and because I will do this unto thee, prepare to meet thy God, O Israel" (4:12).

Contemporary with Amos, but prophesying a few years later, was Hosea (750–725 B.C.). Unlike Amos, Hosea was apparently a native of Israel, the land to which he was sent. Although Hosea shows a tender and sympathetic feeling toward the wicked and sinful nation—words like "mercy" occur over and over as he appeals to and pleads with the people to return unto Jehovah—he is nonetheless severe in his denunciation of Israel's idolatry, the evil fruits of which were so evident in everyday life.

Hosea uses the word *whoredom* to describe Israel's apostasy from Jehovah and worship of heathen gods. This word and the phrase "play the harlot" recur time and again. To Hosea all false worship was spiritual whoredom; he compares the people who served idols to a harlot who serves the lusts of men for the pay she receives.

Hosea also calls the nation to a court of law to be tried before Jehovah, "because there is no truth, nor goodness, nor knowledge of God in the land" (4:1). In contrast to what he did not find, the prophet points out that which faced him on every hand: "There is nought but swearing and breaking faith, and killing, and stealing, and committing adultery; they break out, and blood toucheth blood" (4:2). This sounds remarkably like the headlines of a modern daily paper! Because of these evil conditions, "the land [shall] mourn, and every one that dwelleth therein shall languish, with the beasts of the field and the birds of the heavens" (4:3).

Israel's idols, made of silver and gold which God had given them, would be cut off together with the calves which they fashioned and worshiped in Bethel and Dan (Hos. 8:4–5). "For they sow the wind, and they shall reap the whirlwind" (8:7). Jehovah had written for Ephraim, which here represents Israel, "the ten thousand things of [his] law; but they are counted as a strange thing" (8:12). Israel had forgotten her Maker and built palaces, and Judah had multiplied fortified cities—activities contrary to simple faith and life in God. But God would send a fire upon His cities to devour the castles thereof (8:14). The real reason for God's inflicting punishment was clearly summarized by the prophet Hosea when he said, "For thou hast

19

played the harlot, departing from thy God; thou hast loved hire upon every grain-floor" (9:1); this was spiritual whoredom.

Because of Israel's guilt in rebelling against God, Hosea said, "They shall fall by the sword; their infants shall be dashed in pieces, and their women with child shall be ripped up" (13:16). From where would such a judgment come? Jehovah did not leave the people to wonder: He would make it known. This was the bitter day laid up for them, but there would be a better day beyond this judgment when they would return to Jehovah and have their iniquity taken away (ch. 14).

Isaiah and Micah clearly show that the moral and spiritual conditions in Judah were little better than they were in Israel. We will look at those conditions in our study of Isaiah.

While Israel and Judah were basking in the luxury and profligacy of their recently acquired prosperity, there were rumblings of invasion as the clouds of war loomed ominously in the north and east. Once more Assyria had her eyes upon the west as she flexed her military muscles and made threats of world conquest. Amos had been no more specific than to say, "An adversary there shall be, even round about the land" (3:11), and "A nation . . . shall afflict you from the entrance of Hamath unto the brook of the Arabah" (6:14), indicating only the direction from which the affliction would come and the limit to which it would extend. A few years later Hosea specifically identified the adversary, saying, "They [the people of Israel] shall eat unclean food in Assyria" (9:3). Speaking of the calf at Bethel, he said, "It also shall be carried unto Assyria for a present to king Jareb" (10:6). In addition, since Israel had rejected Jehovah as their God and King, "they shall not return into the land of Egypt; but the Assyrian shall be their king, because they refused to return to me" (11:5). The very word *Assyria* struck terror in the hearts of those who heard it, bringing to mind the terrible nature of the judgment described by Hosea (13:16).

Assyria

A brief summary of Assyria's rise to power will serve as a background to the Book of Isaiah. Little is known of the early period of

Assyria's history, except that it dates back to the middle of the third millennium B.C. Its earliest population was culturally inferior to that of Babylon but superior in energy and military spirit. Assyria's earliest history already reveals its commercial interest and influence. Trading colonies were established wherever the people felt strong enough to protect them. These colonies flourished in the first quarter of the second millennium B.C., and during this time several rulers strengthened the growing nation.[1] It seems, however, that the Assyrians were brought under the power of the Babylonian Hammurabi, who ruled from 1728 to 1686 B.C.[2]

During the five-hundred-year period, 1500–1000 B.C., several strong rulers contributed greatly to the development of the growing nation. Foremost in importance among these kings, and particularly interesting to us, is Tiglath-pileser I (c. 1116–1078 B.C.), who led the nation to new heights of military power and conquest. His policy was to show no mercy to his enemies; reports of his cruelty struck terror in the hearts of those whom he set out to conquer. This policy was also adopted by his successors, and Assyria's cruelty became the scourge of the world until its capital city, Nineveh, fell in 612 B.C. But Tiglath-pileser was not only a great warrior; he was also a great builder of palaces, cities, and strongholds.

With the death of Tiglath-pileser Assyria's power began to wane, but it was restored by Ashur-dan II (932–910 B.C.) and his son Adad-nirari II (909–889 B.C.). Under the reign of the latter numerous neighboring powers were conquered. Adad-nirari continued the policy of excessive cruelty, showing no mercy to the conquered peoples, burning their cities, beheading thousands, and flaying many alive. Knowing this about the Assyrians helps us to understand the terror which Hosea's prophecy of impending judgment (13:16) must have struck in the hearts of the people of Israel.

The next Assyrian ruler of interest to our study is Ashur-nasir-pal II (883–859 B.C.), who built the Assyrian army into the greatest war

---

1. Siegfried J. Schwantes, *A Short History of the Ancient Near East* (Grand Rapids: Baker, 1965), chs. 18–20.

2. Joseph P. Free, *Archaeology and Bible History* (Wheaton, Ill.: Van Kampen, 1950), p. 33, n. 54; see also p. 81.

machine known up to that time. Though he was also a wise ruler of his people, he was an exceedingly cruel warrior and conqueror, surpassing even his forebears. His cruelty is heart-sickening: he is reported to have built a tower covered with the skins of flayed enemies, to have walled up his opponents, leaving them to die, and to have impaled countless others on poles about the city. His conquest stopped at the Mediterranean Sea, in which he ceremoniously washed his weapons as conqueror of all. This brought him near to the land of the Hebrews, but there is no record of his having entered it.

His successor, Shalmaneser III (859–824 B.C.), not only faced the task of making further conquests, but also that of retaining the territory conquered by his father, Ashur-nasir-pal. His conquests brought him closer to Israel than any of his predecessors had been; in his own account of the battle at Qarqar on the Orontes River just northwest of Hamath, he claims to have defeated twelve kings. Among this number are listed Ahab of Israel and Benhadad of Damascus.[3] The fact that Shalmaneser did not follow up on this victory leaves its completeness in question. The battle was probably a draw.

Writing of a later period (781–746 B.C.), Schwantes says, "Assyria underwent another period of weakness. . . . A contributing cause to Assyrian impotence at this time was a terrible plague which devastated the country."[4] It was during this period that Jeroboam II, king of Israel, restored the border of Israel" (II Kings 14:25). It was also during this time that God sent Jonah to Nineveh to preach to that heathen city. No doubt this period of Assyrian weakness, coupled with the plague, contributed to the readiness with which both the king and people of Nineveh listened to Jonah's message.

In 745 B.C. an Assyrian general revolted and usurped the throne, called himself Tiglath-pileser III, after the name of one of the former great rulers. He reigned from 745 to 727 B.C., and it is at this point that the history of Israel and Judah touches that of Assyria, with a most significant consequence for God's people. During his reign Tiglath-pileser III began the conquest of northern Israel and Sa-

---

3. George A. Barton, *Archaeology and the Bible*, 7th ed. (Philadelphia: American Sunday-School Union, 1937), p. 458.

4. Schwantes, *Short History*, p. 122.

maria. The judgment announced by the prophets was now on its way. Had the people of Israel listened to the prophets whom God sent to them, destruction could have been averted. Indeed, in Judah a sufficient number did listen to the prophets Isaiah and Micah. Heeding their messages and influenced by good King Hezekiah, Judah averted captivity at this time.

It now seems evident that Tiglath-pileser III is the Pul of biblical history—"Pul the king of Assyria" to whom Menahem, king of Israel, paid tribute (II Kings 15:19). However, a question is raised by the chronicler's remark that "the God of Israel stirred up the spirit of Pul king of Assyria, and the spirit of Tiglath-pilneser [pileser] king of Assyria" (I Chron. 5:26). Were these two different kings, or are they two names for the same king? Kraeling says that the identity of Pul as Tiglath-pileser was established long ago by the cuneiform inscriptions "which showed that Pul (Pulu) was the name given him as king of Babylonia."[5] Free quotes Joseph Horner's translation, "And the God of Israel stirred up the spirit of Pul king of Assyria, *even Tiglath-pileser* king of Assyria, and he [singular] carried them away," thus indicating that the two names refer to one king.[6]

Tiglath-pileser and the three kings who succeeded him greatly affected the history of Israel and Judah. These kings and their relationship to Israel and Judah will be dealt with in greater detail in the body of this book. The four Assyrian kings and the years of their rule are:

Tiglath-pileser III, 745–727 B.C.

Shalmaneser V, 727–722 B.C.

Sargon II, 721–705 B.C.

Sennacherib, 705–681 B.C.

Tiglath-pileser III began the conquest of Israel by carrying into captivity part of the northern tribes of Zebulun and Naphtali (Isa.

---

5. Emil G. H. Kraeling, *Rand McNally Bible Atlas* (Chicago: Rand McNally, 1957), p. 294.

6. Free, *Archaeology*, p. 196.

9:1–2). When besieged by the combined forces of King Pekah of Israel and King Rezin of Syria, King Ahaz of Judah "sent messengers to Tiglath-pileser king of Assyria, saying, I am thy servant and thy son: come up, and save me out of the hand of the king of Syria, and out of the hand of the king of Israel" (II Kings 16:7). The king of Assyria gladly responded to this request, though at great cost to Judah and Ahaz.

Shalmaneser V, another military general, succeeded his father Tiglath-pileser to the throne of Assyria and began the siege against Samaria which resulted in that city's fall. There is a question, however, as to whether the city fell under his direction of the siege and before his death, or under the leadership of his successor, Sargon II. This question raises a second one: Did Samaria fall to the Assyrians in 722 or 721 B.C.? In a number of his chronicles Sargon claims that it was he who destroyed the city. Also, according to his record, 27,290 Israelites were deported to Assyria, while captives from other countries were brought into the conquered land of Israel. These newcomers and the remaining Israelites intermarried; the Samaritans of Jesus' day were their descendants. It has been suggested that Sargon may have been the general who directed the siege in its latter days. He then claimed the honor of its conquest when Shalmaneser died. At any rate we can conclude that Samaria fell toward the close of 722 or in the early part of 721. Hosea's prophecy was thus dramatically fulfilled.

Upon the death of Sargon (705 B.C.), his son Sennacherib inherited the throne. He is described by historians as a gifted military commander but an arrogant character who inspired the hatred of all. Indeed, he so alienated two of his sons that they slew him while he was worshiping in the house of his god (Isa. 37:38). It was Sennacherib who besieged Jerusalem (701 B.C.) only to have 185,000 of his men destroyed by Jehovah at the gates of the city (Isa. 37:36).

Before the invasion of any of these kings, God raised up Amos and Hosea to preach in Israel, and Isaiah (740–700 B.C.) and Micah (735–700 B.C.) to try to turn Judah back to Himself. Isaiah seems to have done his preaching in Jerusalem, whereas Micah, sometimes called the village or country prophet, confined his efforts largely to the smaller towns northwest and southwest of Jerusalem.

In 612 B.C. the Assyrian capital of Nineveh fell to the Babylonians, who were assisted by the Medes. The final battle between the Assyrians and Babylonians was fought at Haran (609 B.C.), bringing to an end the rule of one of the cruelest nations in history. The fall of Nineveh is graphically described in the prophecy of Nahum. Let it be said to the Assyrians' credit, however, that they served as a buffer state to the threat of invasion from barbaric hordes of the north and that they encouraged the development of architecture, certain sciences, literature, and sculpture. The tragedy of their civilization was that their greatest advances were in military skills which were used for the conquest and ruthless destruction of neighboring peoples.

Isaiah, the Man

It was in the midst of this background of uncertain times and international turmoil that Isaiah grew up. King Uzziah, one of the best rulers to reign in Judah, gave able leadership to the people, encouraging trade, agriculture, development of the natural resources of the land, and building programs. However, as indicated earlier, this prosperity brought with it the attendant profligacy of an affluent society. Religious apostasy and the worship of idols were accompanied by political corruption, greed, social laxity, and moral decay. Isaiah, a man of strong character, deep faith in God, courage, and conviction, was the man of the hour whom the Lord selected to carry the torch of truth in the midst of spiritual darkness. Able to deal with any class, Isaiah was effective in court circles, among false religious leaders, and among the common people. He had the mission of turning the people back to Jehovah, thereby averting captivity by the Assyrians. He proved true to this call. Jan Valeton the Younger says of him: "Never perhaps has there been another prophet like Isaiah, who stood with his head in the clouds and his feet on the solid earth, with his heart in the things of eternity and his mouth and hands in the things of time, with his spirit in the eternal counsel of God and his body in the very definite moment of history."[7] Truly, Isaiah may be called the dean of all the prophets.

---

7. Quoted in George L. Robinson, *The Book of Isaiah* (Grand Rapids: Baker, 1954 reprint), p. 22.

Little is known of Isaiah's personal life. What we do know is derived from the book which bears his name and a few references in the historical books of the Bible. His name means "salvation of the Lord," or "the Lord is salvation," and indicates that his mission was to point the people to the Lord, the only source of salvation. We know that he was married and that his wife was a prophetess (Isa. 8:3). He had at least two sons who had prophetic names. Shear-jashub ("a remnant shall return"), the elder of the two, was old enough to accompany his father when he met King Ahaz at the end of the conduit of the upper pool (7:3). The name of Isaiah's second son was Maher-shalal-hash-baz ("the spoil speedeth, the prey hasteth," 8:3).

All the prophets of God stood in close relationship to their times; they did not speak or write abstractly. They dealt with real-life situations and wrote, first of all, for their own generation, but also for succeeding generations, the people of all ages who would face similar economic, political, and moral issues. Though he addressed himself to the Jews of the day, Isaiah can be called the prophet of the future, for he constantly pointed to events to come. The future tense and the prophetic perfect, which refers to coming events as if they have already occurred, characterize his writing throughout. He saw clearly the future of Judah, the destruction of the heathen nations, and the coming of a King, the Messiah, who would rule in righteousness.

From the book itself we learn that Isaiah was not only a prophet but also a great statesman with a keen insight into the world affairs of his day. It is said that Edmund Burke, the great English statesman of the eighteenth century, habitually read from Isaiah before attending Parliament and held the prophet in the highest esteem. The prophet was advisor to kings, meeting them on an equal level before God and not fearing to condemn the wrong and point to the right. Not only were there internal conditions to deal with, along with the rising power of Assyria, but there was also the problem of Egypt, the great crocodile to the southwest, which was determined not to give up the glory of her past world domination without a struggle. This led to the development of three political parties in Judah during the time of Isaiah: an Egyptian party, which advocated an alliance with Egypt against Assyria; an Assyrian party, which would capitulate to Assyria; and a

"Jehovah" or nationalist party led by Isaiah, who urged loyalty to the Lord as the only way to salvation.

Isaiah was likewise a great reformer who condemned the errors of the people and pointed to Jehovah as the source of all right conduct. It was only by returning to Jehovah, rejecting all idolatry, and building on the solid rock of truth as revealed by God, that Judah could avert destruction. Idols, corruption in the political realm, and immorality of every kind must go. The people must learn to "wait for Jehovah," letting Him lead them instead of listening to the voices of false leaders.

As a theologian (if we may use the word with regard to his study of and insight into the true nature and character of God), Isaiah was without a peer. He saw the Lord as King, high and exalted above all creation and absolute in holiness and righteousness, and he constantly emphasized Jehovah's control over the nations and their destiny. The words *righteousness* and *justice*, the principles on which God always acts, occur repeatedly in Isaiah's message. The true character and nature of God would someday be revealed in the coming of Immanuel ("God with us"). The exalted and lofty concept of Jehovah which would be revealed in the one to come is the predominant thought and emphasis in this book. Although all of the prophets who wrote of the latter days and the events of that period told of and presented certain aspects of the Messiah who was to come, Isaiah had by far the deepest insight into and clearest concept of the Redeemer. This is by no means to disparage any of the other prophets, but simply to note that God singled out Isaiah for that purpose and so inspired him (I Peter 1:10–12; II Peter 1:21).

From II Chronicles we know that in addition to his prophecy Isaiah wrote an account of the acts of Uzziah; apparently these acts are not recounted in the historical books of the Bible nor in the book bearing the prophet's name (II Chron. 26:22). We also know that Isaiah recorded a "vision" in which he detailed "the rest of the acts of Hezekiah, and his good deeds" (II Chron. 32:32). We have no account of Isaiah's death; neither do we know whether he lived at all beyond the time of Hezekiah and into the period of Manasseh's reign. There is a tradition that he was sawed asunder on the order of Manasseh. This is apparently based on an apocryphal book, *The Ascen-*

sion of Isaiah. Moreover, Justin Martyr in his dialogue with Trypho reproaches the Jews with the accusation, "whom [Isaiah] you sawed asunder with a wooden saw."[8] But there is no solid evidence of this. Though we would like to know more of the details of Isaiah's personal life, they have not been revealed. The prophet instead placed his emphasis on "the Holy One of Israel" and His control of the destiny of men and nations. At least we know that Isaiah's lot was happier than that which befell most prophets, for he lived to see the fruit of his labors—the hand of God spared his people from defeat by the Assyrians.

Isaiah, the Book

Because of the number of chapters, the Book of Isaiah is generally thought to be the longest of all prophetic books; but page for page (in the ASV), it is slightly shorter than Jeremiah and roughly equivalent to Ezekiel. The contents of the book are not always in chronological order, a fact which at times presents difficulties to the student. For example, the call of the prophet to his work appears in chapter 6 rather than at the beginning of the book. An adequate explanation for this may not be possible, but at the proper time we shall make an attempt to explain it. It is quite possible that the materials in the book may have been written in sections according to subject matter and later gathered into the whole. Remember that the prophet prophesied under varying circumstances over a forty-year period.

One of the strong points of the book is its emphasis on salvation by faith, for it was on the basis of faith in God that the people would be saved from their guilt and its consequences. George L. Robinson calls the book the Epistle to the Romans of the Old Testament,[9] and this well describes its message. The people are urged and encouraged to wait for the Lord, to wait earnestly, to expect, to hope in faith.

The book also emphasizes that the Messiah would bring in the Gentiles together with the Jews. The coming one would be a light,

---

8. Justin Martyr *Dialogue with Trypho* 120, in *Ante-Nicene Fathers* (New York: Scribner, 1903), vol. 1, p. 259.

9. Robinson, *Isaiah*, p. 14.

bringing salvation to the peoples of all nations. Both Jews and Gentiles would be part of one great spiritual kingdom, universal in its scope, ruled by a King of righteousness. Why the Jews could not see and accept this great purpose of Jehovah as set forth by Isaiah and fulfilled in the Christ who came has long been a mystery. The prophet, however, had an explanation for it: the Jews closed their eyes, stopped their ears, and hardened their hearts so that they could not accept the truth.

The unitary authorship of the Book of Isaiah has been under attack by critics for over a century; some claim there were two Isaiahs (the writer of chs. 1–39 and the writer of chs. 40–66), some three, and others claim the book is a composite of numerous unknown writers. It is not within the scope or nature of this volume to enter into a discussion of this question, but suffice it to say that to all conservative scholars and students of Isaiah the evidence of the critics is inconclusive. Robinson points to the fact that the expression "the Holy One of Israel" occurs twenty-five (actually twenty-six) times in Isaiah, twelve times in chapters 1–39, thirteen (actually fourteen) times in chapters 40–66, and only six times elsewhere. [10] In none of the twenty-one passages in the New Testament where the writer or speaker quotes Isaiah and appeals to the prophet by name is there any hint of suspicion that more than one Isaiah wrote the book bearing that title. That the New Testament quotations are drawn from both divisions of the book is an effective witness to its unity. In addition, the complete manuscript of Isaiah discovered at Qumran in 1947 and believed by all scholars (as far as I know) to date back to the second century before Christ has no break between chapters 39 and 40. This is strong evidence that the transcribers knew of only one author of the book. The historical section, chapters 36–39, serves as a conclusion to the first section of the book and as an introduction to the second, thus uniting the two. I accept and defend the unity of authorship of Isaiah.

---

10. Ibid. On this point of unity let the student consult conservative introductions. Two short books are suggested: Oswald T. Allis, *The Unity of Isaiah* (Philadelphia: Presbyterian and Reformed, 1950); Edward J. Young, *Who Wrote Isaiah?* (Grand Rapids: Eerdmans, 1958).

Scope of the Book

Isaiah was the man of the hour. Brought up in the city of Jerusalem during the prosperous reign of Uzziah, he was thoroughly acquainted with the political and social conditions of the day. Not only did he have a spiritual depth and insight into the true character of Jehovah such as few men have ever possessed, but he also had a broad comprehension of the historical movements of his time. The prophet watched as the powerful Assyrian Empire, destined to become the scourge of the earth, swept across the world of that day and cast its ominous shadow over the nations.

Within his own kingdom Isaiah saw the results of apostasy from God: political, moral, and social decay. He saw Assyria, a nation from afar, as the instrument in God's hand to chasten His people in an attempt to save a remnant. Isaiah opened his prophecy with a description of Judah's apostasy, God's call to come and reason together, and His offer of pardon (ch. 1). This was followed by a vision of the latter days in which God's ideal for His city of Zion would be realized (2:1–4). Immediately drawn back to the present condition in Judah, the prophet denounced the ungodly rulers and judges, the false prophets and the wanton women who contributed their part to the immorality of the nation (2:5–4:1). But it would not always be this way; through the purging effects of judgment God would eventually have a purified remnant who would rejoice in Him (4:2–6). Isaiah then proceeded to pronounce woes upon various segments of society and to warn of impending judgment (ch. 5). At this point we read that upon the death of Uzziah, the prophet received his call from Jehovah to carry God's message of doom and hope to the people (ch. 6).

There had been both good and bad rulers in Judah, but even among the best there were serious flaws. David had committed adultery, and then had tried to cover his sin by murder. Solomon, the wise king who ruled in peace, had introduced idolatry into the nation as he set up altars to the gods of his many wives. Uzziah, one of the best of Judah's kings, had been prompted by pride to enter the sanctuary and burn incense to Jehovah, an act limited by law to the priests only. Even Hezekiah, in many ways one of the best of the kings, was tempted to lean on Egypt rather than on Jehovah for aid against

Assyria. Later he allowed himself to be lifted by pride to show his treasures to ambassadors sent from Babylon to congratulate him on his recovery from illness. For this sin of Hezekiah, Judah would be carried into captivity in Babylon at some future date (Isa. 39).

In the light of this failure on the part of the kings who ruled over God's people, Isaiah announces that the Lord will raise up a King who will rule in righteousness. This becomes the major theme of Isaiah (chs. 7–12). The King will be born of a virgin, a sign to the house of David (ch. 7); this event will be preceded by the scourge of the Assyrians (ch. 8), bringing darkness to Israel. But eventually those who sit in darkness will see light, the light of a new King, kingdom, and glory (9:1–7). Severe judgments are then pronounced upon Ephraim and Judah (9:8–10:4); these are followed by the announcement that Assyria will invade the land and in turn be destroyed (10:5–34). The prophet reaches a climax with prophecies of the coming of the Branch from Jesse's roots and His rule (ch. 11) and a song of thanksgiving (ch. 12).

Before the coming of this spiritual King and His kingdom, all the heathen nations of that time, from the greatest to the least, must be judged and brought to an end (chs. 13–23). With their destruction the kingdom of God will stand out all the more glorious. This proclamation of the judgment of the heathen nations is followed by a prophecy of world judgment; Jehovah is again revealed as Judge of the nations and especially the great world-city, which will be left a waste and desolation. This foreshadows the fall of the Babylon of Revelation 17 and 18. In this world judgment Jehovah will protect those who put their trust in Him (chs. 24–27). Ephraim, Judah, and Jerusalem are given more warnings and threats from Jehovah, with special emphasis on the danger of alliances with Egypt. There is assurance, however, of Jehovah's eventual gracious reign over His people (chs. 28–33). The futures of Edom (symbol of the world) and of Zion (symbol of the spiritual people) are then contrasted (chs. 34–35). The first of the two major parts of Isaiah closes with a historical section. Divine intervention thwarts Assyria's effort to take Jerusalem. Faith wins the battle! This is followed by the account of Hezekiah's sickness and recovery and his showing of the treasures of the kingdom to

31

Merodach-baladan's messengers, whereupon Jehovah pronounces that Judah will be carried off to Babylon (chs. 36–39).

With the victory over Assyria, and the assurance by Jehovah of Babylonian captivity at some future date, the prophet's work now was to prepare the people for that captivity and assure them of the return of a remnant. The second major part of the book is the record of this phase of Isaiah's work. The prophet entered into an all-out war against the idols, setting forth the Lord as sole deity (chs. 40–48). He named Cyrus as the deliverer whom God would raise up (44:28–45:7). Amid words of encouragement, assurances of deliverance, indications of inclusion of the Gentiles in God's plan, and songs of the Messiah-Servant who was to come, Isaiah gave warnings as to the consequences of further sins against Jehovah. With the coming of the Servant there would also appear His glorious kingdom, which would extend far beyond the borders of the former (chs. 49–57). Again the glorified Zion is described and salvation is assured. The old order would pass and there would be new heavens and a new earth where, after a complete victory, the saints would behold the dead bodies of their enemies (chs. 58–66).

Thus it was given to Isaiah to see the hand of God in the affairs of his day and to behold Him working out His purpose in history. Through judgment upon judgment, as wave follows wave, the prophet was able to see an emerging remnant of faithful, purified saints through whom Jehovah would bring forth His righteous King, Immanuel ("God with us"), and His indestructible kingdom which would fill the earth from sea to sea. The coming of the Servant-King and His kingdom, an event which perfectly fulfilled Isaiah's prophecy, stands as a Gibraltar of evidence sustaining the word of God and as a timeless condemnation of Jews who refuse to believe and of Gentiles who refuse to listen.

PART ONE

The Assyrian Period: Conflict and Victory (1–39)

Discourses and Prophecies Centering in Jerusalem and Judah (1–12)

CHAPTER 1

Isaiah's Personal Introduction to His Book

Whether we view chapter 1 as a court scene in which Jehovah calls the nation to a trial (Leupold, Smith, Robinson, and others), or view it otherwise (Young), it seems clear that Jehovah is calling His nation and His children to an accounting for their conduct and behavior toward Him, pointing to the consequences of their course of life. Although it may not have been the first part of the book to have been written, the content of chapter 1 serves well as an introduction to the book. The conditions set forth well describe the state of affairs at the time of Sennacherib's invasion of the land (701 B.C.). The chapter may have been written then and placed at the beginning of the book

35

when the prophet brought his prophecies together in one volume. If this be so, it helps us to understand why the account of Isaiah's call does not occur at the beginning of the book (it is recorded in ch. 6). Chapter 1 may be divided as follows:

1. The sin-sick and rebellious nation (vv. 2–9).
2. Corruption and hypocritical worship (vv. 10–15).
3. God's call to reformation of life (vv. 16–20).
4. The lament over Jerusalem (vv. 21–23).
5. Redemption through purging (vv. 24–31).

Here the prophet points out the sins of the people, calls them to reformation, declares judgment, and reveals Jehovah as their only hope of salvation. Salvation, whether at that time or in the future, must come from God; He alone can make the provision.

1 The prophet introduces himself as Isaiah, which means "Jehovah saves" or "Jehovah is salvation." His name is the epitome of his entire message to the people. He is the *son of Amoz* (not the prophet Amos), a man otherwise unknown. The *vision* which he saw is equivalent to *the word* which he saw (2:1). It is the message which God revealed or gave to him; it is of divine origin. The vision pertains not only to chapter 1 but to the entire book; a prophet from God spoke the word which God gave him (Deut. 18:18–19).

Although the vision was *concerning Judah and Jerusalem,* it included the northern tribes of Israel (9:1–10:9) and the heathen nations of that day as they affected the fortunes and welfare of the people of God (chs. 13–23; 24–27, etc.). The focus of the prophecy is indicated by the frequent occurrence of the names *Judah* and *Jerusalem. Judah* occurs twenty-nine times in the book, twenty-five in Part One (chs. 1–39) and four in Part Two (chs. 40–66); *Jerusalem* occurs forty-nine times, thirty in the first section and nineteen in the second. Thus Jerusalem occupies the more important role in the vision.

In the days of Uzziah—Uzziah, who was also known as Azariah (II Kings 15), was one of the outstanding kings of Judah; his death is usually dated 740 B.C.[1] *Jotham*, son of Uzziah, was coregent with his father from the time Uzziah became a leper until his death. Jotham followed his father's policies, striving to carry out his projects and meeting with almost equal success. *Ahaz*, with whom we shall deal later, was a wicked man with little, if any, faith in God. *And Hezekiah*, one of the best kings Judah ever had, played a major role in the history and salvation of the nation. Part One of the Book of Isaiah closes with Sennacherib's defeat at the hands of Jehovah (701 B.C.), the illness and recovery of Hezekiah, and the visit of Merodach-baladan's ambassadors, when Jehovah foretold the captivity in Babylon.

Inasmuch as the prophet says that his vision includes the period of Uzziah, but later says that he received the call to the prophetic office in the year that King Uzziah died (ch. 6), it must be concluded that he began his work in the closing period of the king's life. We are not told whether Isaiah lived into the reign of Manasseh; but if he did, it was probably a period of retirement in which he devoted his energies to other work, perhaps to writing, for he is credited with writing "the rest of the acts of Uzziah, first and last" (II Chron. 26:22), and "the acts of Hezekiah, and his good deeds, . . . in the book of the kings of Judah and Israel" (II Chron. 32:32).

The Sin-sick and Rebellious Nation (vv. 2–9)

2 As Moses, in his farewell speech to the nation just before his death (Deut. 32:1), had called upon the heavens to hear and the earth to give ear to his words, so Isaiah, standing midway between Moses and the Christ, now calls upon these two permanent parts of God's creation to give ear. In Deuteronomy 31:28–29 Moses explained the significance of his calling heaven and earth to witness: "For I know

---

1. For a discussion of the dates of these kings see Edwin R. Thiele, *A Chronology of the Hebrew Kings* (Grand Rapids: Zondervan, 1978), pp. 40–42, 77–78. According to Thiele, Uzziah's rule of fifty-two years (II Kings 15:2) included a twenty-four-year coregency with his father; the coregency ended in 767 with the latter's death and Uzziah continued to reign until his own death in 740. Jotham was coregent with Uzziah from 750 to 740 and then sole ruler until 735. Ahaz reigned from 735 to 715 and Hezekiah from 715 to 686. For a different view, see Edward J. Young, *The Book of Isaiah* (Grand Rapids: Eerdmans, 1972), vol. 2, pp. 540–42.

that after my death ye will utterly corrupt yourselves, and turn aside from the way which I have commanded you." What Moses said would come to pass was being fulfilled in Isaiah's day. Accordingly, Isaiah now calls to the same *heavens* and *earth* to bear witness to the corruption of the nation. God had *brought up children*, but they had *rebelled* against Him. The Hebrew word used here indicates a breach of relationship.

3   To illustrate the stupidity of the nation, Isaiah introduces as metaphors the *ox* and the *ass*, neither of which is noted for its breadth of intelligence. However, the ox knows its owner and the ass knows its crib; they know that their food and shelter are both provided by their master. But God's people give neither thought nor consideration to these matters.

4   God's people are weighted down with iniquity; as the seed of evil, they breed evil wherever they go; they deal corruptly. They have both forsaken and despised (lightly esteemed) Jehovah, *the Holy One of Israel*. He has not forsaken them, but they Him, and even now He is trying to reach them and turn them back to Himself. They have gone backward, degenerating into a sinful nation, alienating themselves from Jehovah.

5   The nation is *sick* with a loathsome disease which grows worse and worse. The *whole head*, the seat of intelligence and knowledge, is sick; the whole *heart*, the fountainhead of affection and love, is faint, having no courage or conviction. When the mind is corrupt, it is impossible to restore the heart to health, for one cures the affection by knowing goodness and truth.

6   The people are sin-sick from *head* to *foot*; there is *no soundness* or spiritual health in them. Old *wounds* are full of pus, *bruises* are clearly visible, and the welts of *stripes* stand out. The people have done nothing to heal themselves by turning to Jehovah, but their condition continues to fester and grow more putrid. What a terrible picture of the spiritual condition of the nation!

7–9   The prophet then turns from metonymy to reality. The country was *desolate*; the cities were burned with fire; foreigners had consumed the produce of the land in the presence of the helpless populace. Instead of being the stronghold of God in the midst of a land flowing with milk and honey, the people of Zion stood desolate as a frail booth in the midst of a vineyard, weak and shaken by the wind, or as a temporary hut in a cucumber garden—as a besieged city! This description harmonizes with that of Micah 6:13–16, and corresponds with the curses of Leviticus 26 and Deuteronomy 28. *Except Jehovah of hosts had left unto us a very small remnant, we should have been as Sodom*—so completely destroyed that there was no trace of her former existence—or as Gomorrah, likewise waste and desolate and destroyed by fire. But even in the midst of spiritual desolation like unto *Sodom* and *Gomorrah* the mercy of God had spared a *remnant.* Although Judah would go into captivity, a remnant would return (10:20–21); likewise under the Messiah a remnant will be saved (Rom. 9:29) according to the election of divine grace (Rom. 11:5). Jehovah will bring about the salvation of the redeemed and rescued of every age. Note, however, that they always comprise only a remnant—a small portion—never the whole.

Corruption Hiding Behind Hypocritical Worship (vv. 10–15)

10–13 The prophet calls upon the *rulers* of this immoral Sodom and the people of this unspiritual Gomorrah to hear the word of Jehovah. It is not the man Isaiah who is speaking, but it is God speaking through him: *Hear the word of Jehovah . . . give ear unto the law*—the teaching—*of our God.* While the nation might plead that they are the people of God and that sacrifices and worship are in abundance at the temple, such factors are nothing to God if they are hypocritical, representing only a formal and empty show. Jehovah uses strong language when He says that such offerings are *vain* and *an abomination,* that which He abhors or loathes. The sacrifices of the people are only attempts to hide behind the sham of formalism. This has always been and continues to be a favorite refuge for those who are unfit to come before Jehovah in spirit and truth and who know not the true character of God. Who has commanded such of you? Not I, says the Lord; for I cannot tolerate such. As we would say, "I cannot stomach it."

14 Jehovah also repudiated the way in which the people observed the festivals: the weekly Sabbaths, the monthly New Moons, and the three annual solemn assemblies (Passover, Pentecost, and the Feast of Tabernacles). *I am weary of bearing them,* enduring or tolerating them, says the Lord. He hates such hypocritical sham. This is not to say that God had repudiated the festivals themselves, for He had instituted them through Moses. He delighted in His divinely appointed worship, but only when it was offered in the proper spirit and for the appointed purpose. What He hated and despised was the hypocrisy of the worshipers (see also Amos 5:21–23, where the same indictment is made against Israel).

15 God would hide His eyes when the people *spread* or lifted their *hands* toward Him in order to be filled from His bounty in answer to their prayers, or when they lifted their hands as if filled with offerings of praise. Why? Their hands were *full of blood*—the blood of men murdered by the worshipers, or the blood of those who died because they had been robbed of their sustenance by the nobles' greed. In either instance, the worshipers were guilty of social crimes. Vain, empty, hypocritical worship cannot hide the crimes of a nation, then or now.

God's Call to Reformation of Life (vv. 16–20)

16 Jehovah now calls for a reformation of life which must proceed from genuine repentance, a change of will. Acceptable worship and fellowship with God can come only from a clean heart and life; therefore three commands are issued which deal with sins: (1) *Wash you, make you clean;* this must be taken in a spiritual sense, for ceremonial washings which do not involve the heart cannot avail. This is a command to the people which they must obey. If man repents and changes his life, God forgives and blots out sin. (2) *Put away the evil of your doings from before mine eyes;* abolish idolatry and sham worship and all the attendant evils that accompany such practices. (3) *Cease to do evil.* With the putting away of the evils of false worship, God commanded a putting away of all moral evil, in worship and toward one's fellow men. All three commands are essential.

17 The prophet now enumerates five positive demands, all essential to acceptance with God. These are ethical or social directives: (1) *Learn to do well.* This demand indicates that man does not inher-

ently know what is right; he must be taught. Isaiah is saying that by their evil practices the people have so confused their knowledge of right that they must now be taught what is well and good in God's sight. (2) *Seek justice* in all things, especially in dealings at court, at all times. (3) *Relieve the oppressed*, for oppression had grown out of the corrupt judicial system; indifference was displayed towards the rights of others. (4) *Judge the fatherless*. (5) *Plead for the widow*. Those who had no father or husband to safeguard their rights should be protected by the judges. These groups had been neglected by the rulers and judges, for there was no profit in spending time in their behalf. Such practical reforms must follow the cleansing God demanded.

18 Verses 18–20 have long been a favorite quotation among Bible students, but there are diverse views as to its significance. Is it a call to a court trial, or is it a call to bring the controversy to an end? Thomas Cheyne translates, "Let us bring our dispute to an end" (quoted by Rawlinson). Smith accepts this interpretation, though he acknowledges that Cheyne later withdrew it (I. 13). Smith says that though he calls this chapter "a trial-at-law," it is "far more a *personal* than a *legal* controversy. . . . It is not Judah and the Law that are confronted; it is Judah and Jehovah" (I. 8–9). Delitzsch says, "Jehovah here challenges Israel to a formal trial." But Young contends, "It is not a legal trial which is here described. It is rather a command to be judged in the light of God's law (i.e., to reason together) and repent." Barnes says, "Here it [the phrase, "Let us reason together"] denotes the kind of contention, or argumentation, which occurs in a court of justice, where the parties reciprocally state the grounds of their cause." God first states the charge and then the grounds on which He will pardon (I. 71–72). Leupold suggests that Isaiah's stinging rebuke in the earlier verses brought a reaction from the hearers that led Jehovah to soften His attitude and say, "Let us reach an adjustment," or "Let us settle our differences," or even "Let us adjust our misunderstanding" (I. 64). Leupold endorses Smith's translation ("Let us bring our reasoning to a close") on the grounds that after one has been reasoning a point for some time he does not add, "Come, let us reason together"; rather, one would say, "Let us settle the matter" (I. 66).

41

Regardless of how one translates the passage, the exhortation *Come* carries with it the force of a command: *let us reason together,* or reach an adjustment, or settle our difference. God is very definitely offering pardon to His people: *though your sins be as scarlet, they shall be as white as snow; though they be red like crimson, they shall be as wool.* The two colors, scarlet and crimson, very nearly the same, refer to the deep-dyed or double-dyed condition wrought by sin. Scarlet is the color of blood, the harlot's garments (Rev. 17:4), and the beast on which she will ride (v. 3). Here it describes the deep-seated nature of Judah's sins. But though the nation be so deeply stained with sins, Jehovah promises that they shall become as white as snow or wool, completely forgiven and cleansed.

19–20   But the promise is conditional: *If ye be willing and obedient* (the will must be obedient!), *ye shall eat the good of the land,* the bounty of its produce. *But if ye refuse and rebel, ye shall be devoured with the sword.* Be obedient and eat; rebel and be eaten (the sword is a devouring instrument). This promise is absolutely sure, for it is the word of God—*for the mouth of Jehovah hath spoken it.* As at the beginning of the nation's history (Deut. 30:15, 19), life and death are once more set before the people.

The Lament over Jerusalem (vv. 21–23)

21   The prophet now contrasts the city of his day with what it had once been: *How is the faithful city become a harlot!* The picture is that of a wife who in her youth was devoted to her husband, faithful to him in every way; but now she is selling herself to others as a harlot. Judah had reacted toward Jehovah in the same manner. The same charge was leveled against Israel by Hosea: "Rejoice not, O Israel, for joy, like the peoples; for thou hast played the harlot, departing from thy God; thou hast loved hire upon every grain-floor" (Hos. 9:1). God had predicted this when He said to Moses, "And this people will rise up, and play the harlot [go a whoring, King James] after the strange gods of the land . . . and will forsake me" (Deut. 31:16). Whereas Judah had been full of justice, and righteousness had lodged in her, she was now a land of murderers. The words *justice* and *righteousness* occur many times in the Book of Isaiah. Although a clear distinction between the two is sometimes difficult, the basic idea of *justice* is fair and equitable decisions and actions by the judicial branch of government; that of *righteousness* is conformity to an ethical or moral standard. Both were being sorely perverted.

22 Although our own nation is not chosen of Jehovah as was Israel, the same charge could be made against it today. Israel's *silver*, a symbol of purity, had become as the scum or slag thrown off from molten metal. Her *wine* that cheered the heart was diluted with water, and therefore greatly weakened.

23 From metonymy the prophet again turns to reality. The princes or leaders were rebellious against God and His righteousness; instead of associating with Jehovah and the faithful, they were companions of thieves. Each loved bribes and sought rewards: *they judge not the fatherless, neither doth the cause of the widows come unto them.* They had no time for helping the powerless, for there was no pay to be derived from such services.

Redemption Through Purging (vv. 24–31)

24 Jehovah had called the people to reason with Him, to resolve the difference, and had promised to cleanse them (vv. 18–20); but they had refused to give heed. He now speaks as *the Lord, Jehovah of hosts,* the Lord of all forces heavenly and earthly. He is *the Mighty One of Israel,* to whom they are answerable. He will ease Himself of his adversaries, that is, He will be comforted by relieving Himself of those who have distressed or troubled Him. And He will avenge Himself of His enemies by vindicating His own holiness and the righteousness of His rejected law. This he will accomplish by bringing judgment upon those hostile to Him.

25 As one purifies metal in a fiery furnace, so in the furnace of judgment Jehovah will *turn* His hand upon the apostate people to *thoroughly purge* the *dross,* the scum, all the impurities that contaminate the true or pure metal.

26 When this is done, He will restore judges and counsellors who give righteous guidance and advice. Jerusalem will again be called *The city of righteousness, a faithful town.*

27 Through this divine judgment there will be a purging and a restoration of a right relationship with Jehovah, bringing forth a new spiritual Israel. They will be redeemed by the very justice and righteousness which they have rejected, for *Zion shall be redeemed with justice*—divine justice—*and her converts* ("they that return to her," margin) *with righteousness*. This divine justice will exercise judgment upon sin and sinners, and the righteousness of God will effect righteousness in the converts.

28   The Lord now turns to the idolaters who refuse to be turned or changed. Those who forsake Jehovah, the *transgressors and sinners* together, shall be destroyed—*consumed* in the fire of judgment.

29   Those who trust in their idols will be ashamed when they realize the folly of such trust. Apparently the *oaks* (or terebinths) represent either the wood from which the idol is made or the grove in which it is worshiped, probably the latter. And *the gardens* which God's enemies favor, seemingly the places especially developed for idolatrous devotion and worship (see Isa. 65:3; 66:17), will someday bring confusion and shame to those who have chosen them.

30   Idolaters will become like the grove and garden in which they worship. They will be *as an oak* that is dead and whose leaves are dried, or *as a garden* which for lack of water is parched by the sun; both ignite speedily and burn briskly.

31   A third figure is added. The *strong* men will be like the refuse of flax, dry and ignitable by a *spark*. The work of the strong man—the idol—will be the igniting spark; both the strong man and the idol, which is the work of his hand, will burn together. Since Jehovah has issued this decree, there is no power to hinder the burning or to quench the fire once it is ignited.

As we hinted earlier, the date of this chapter is uncertain. The only two recorded events during Isaiah's time of prophesying that fit the conditions described are the Syro-Ephraimitic war of Ahaz's day (ch. 7) and the Assyrian invasion under Sennacherib (701 B.C.) in the days of Hezekiah (chs. 36–37). Neither of these suggestions seems completely satisfactory, but regardless of our uncertainty as to the exact date, the chapter certainly does present an excellent summary of the entire book. The themes of idolatry, the sins of the rulers and the people, corruption in all areas of social life, and Jehovah's responses—condemnation, judgment, and destruction as well as exhortation and the provision of redemption and salvation—recur throughout the great Book of Isaiah.

CHAPTER 2
Jerusalem: The Ideal and the Real

From the dark picture of Zion as a forsaken shed in the midst of desolation (1:8) and as an unfaithful wife who had become a harlot (1:21), the prophet turns to the future and sees Zion glorified above all cities and nations (2:1–4). He is then called back to reality once more and sees the city in its present condition, polluted with sin, the fruit of idolatry (2:5–4:1). The glorious ideal can be reached only through judgment and cleansing by Jehovah (4:2–6). Smith well describes the picture in this section as "the three Jerusalems": Jerusalem the ideal (2:1–4); Jerusalem the real (2:5–4:1); and Jerusalem the redeemed (4:2–6).

Although the Messiah Himself is not mentioned in the first of these passages (2:1–4), it clearly pertains to the messianic period. The Messiah, referred to as the Branch of Jehovah, appears in chapter 4. In chapters 2 and 3 the emphasis is on Jerusalem (Mount Zion), the center of divine government, both its future glory and present shame. It is to this divinely appointed capital of God's spiritual kingdom that the Messiah is to come.

1 Isaiah again introduces himself. Unlike 1:1, however, where he spoke of *the vision* which he saw concerning Judah and Jerusalem, here it is *the word* that he sees. In each, the vision and the word, Judah and Jerusalem are in the forefront. To see the word is to comprehend and understand its message. When John on Patmos heard a voice as of a trumpet, he "turned to see the voice that spake with [him]" (Rev. 1:12); and having turned, he saw the source of it. So Isaiah saw the vision, the word, and understood both it and its source; the vision and the word came from God.

Jerusalem the Ideal (vv. 2–4)

2 Delitzsch says that the expression *the latter days* "never refers

45

to the course of history immediately following the time being, but invariably indicates the furthest point in the history of this life—the point which lies on the outermost limits of the speaker's horizon" (I. 113). This raises the question as to what is the furthest point in the history of this life—the point which lies on the outermost limits of the speaker's horizon.

Approximately 150 years after Isaiah, Daniel used the same phrase, *the latter days,* in reference to the same future period: God through a dream "hath made known to the king Nebuchadnezzar what shall be in the latter days" (Dan. 2:28). The prophet then proceeded to interpret the image in the king's dream as a picture of four world empires and events to transpire during the last of them. The four empires were the Babylonian, Medo-Persian, Macedonian, and the Roman. The Roman Empire, then, represented the furthest point, "the point which lies on the outermost limits of the speaker's horizon." Therefore, the events of *the latter days* were events that would occur during the period of the Roman Empire.

In the New Testament there is corroboration of this understanding of the phrase "the latter days." Peter interpreted the word "afterward" in Joel 2:28 as equivalent to "the last days" (Acts 2:17). He then continued, "Yea and on my servants and on my handmaidens in those days [the last days] will I pour forth my Spirit; and they shall prophesy" (Acts 2:18). In his next sermon Peter said, "Yea and all the prophets from Samuel and them that followed after, as many as have spoken, they also told of these days" (Acts 3:24). Peter obviously regarded his own time as being "the latter days" of which the prophets spoke. Therefore, *the latter days* spoken of by the prophet Isaiah (the "these days" of Peter) are in fact the present dispensation.

Furthermore, we read in the New Testament that Christ was manifested "at the end of the times" (I Peter 1:20—literally, "in the last times"), and that through Him God hath "in these last days" spoken unto us (Heb. 1:2, King James). Therefore, *the latter days* spoken of by Isaiah are to be understood as that period in which God would make known His law through Jesus Christ and send it forth from Jerusalem and from Zion. Isaiah was speaking of that which began on Pentecost and continues now. We are living in "the last times"; these are *the latter days.*

That which would come to pass in the latter days was the establishment of Jehovah's house *on the top of the mountains*; it would be *exalted above the hills* and universal in scope—*all nations shall flow unto it.* The Holy Spirit has not left us to wonder or guess at the meaning of the expression *the mountain of Jehovah's house,* for we read in Zechariah 8:3: "Thus saith Jehovah: I am returned unto Zion, and will dwell in the midst of Jerusalem: and Jerusalem shall be called The city of truth; and the mountain of Jehovah of hosts, The holy mountain." The glory of this mountain would surpass and exceed all others.

Physical Zion was the steep hill in the southeastern section of Jerusalem on which David had built his fortress and on which Solomon later built the temple. It became a symbol of an impregnable stronghold against enemies and the dwelling place of God among His people. The word *Zion* came to be used in prophecy to refer to the spiritual Zion to come, that is, the dwelling place of God among His redeemed people where they find security and peace. Later in the Book of Isaiah this point will be emphasized and become clear. Zion, as the mountain of God's house and people, was the place from which the law would go forth and from which the people would be ruled by His word.

From Jehovah's cry against Babylon in Jeremiah 51:25 it is evident that "mountain" signifies a government or a seat of government: "Behold, I am against thee, O destroying mountain, saith Jehovah, which destroyest all the earth; and I will stretch out my hand upon thee, and roll thee down from the rocks, and will make thee a burnt mountain." Babylon was a mountain (nation) of destruction which would become a burnt mountain; God's mountain, by contrast, would be a government or nation of refuge, peace, and salvation—a holy mountain *exalted above* others, or, as some translate, "at the head of" all others.

It is unto this mountain that the Christians addressed in the Book of Hebrews had come: "For ye are not come unto a mount that might be touched [Sinai] . . . but ye are come unto mount Zion, and unto the city of the living God, the heavenly Jerusalem . . . [the] church of the firstborn who are enrolled in heaven" (Heb. 12:18–23), which is "the house of God" (I Tim. 3:15). Delitzsch well says, "What God

47

commenced at Sinai for Israel, would be completed at Zion [Jerusalem] for all the world" (I. 116). Consider again the words of Zechariah: "Jerusalem shall be called The city of truth; and the mountain of Jehovah of hosts, The holy mountain." It was this mountain that Jehovah said would be established in the latter days, and it was unto this mount and city that the Hebrew Christians had come. Hence, the *mountain* of Isaiah is the kingdom, the church of God of the new covenant, for the writer of Hebrews concludes his argument, "Wherefore, receiving a kingdom that cannot be shaken, let us have grace" (12:28).

This mountain would be established and exalted above all other mountains; it would transcend all the kingdoms of the world in greatness and grandeur. In a vision Ezekiel was brought into the land of Israel and set "down upon a very high mountain, whereon was as it were the frame of a city on the south" (Ezek. 40:2). The stone that was cut out without hands and smote the image in Nebuchadnezzar's dream became a great mountain filling the whole earth (Dan. 2:35). All three passages are speaking of the same mountain—the kingdom of the new covenant. *And all nations shall flow unto it.* In this ideal city of God, not just the one nation of the Jews, but all nations (plural), all races from among the Gentiles, would be included. The picture is that of a large stream of peoples flowing into the city.

3 *And many peoples shall go and say, Come ye, and let us go up to the mountain of Jehovah, to the house of the God of Jacob; and he will teach us of his ways, and we will walk in his paths: for out of Zion shall go forth the law* (teaching or instruction), *and the word of Jehovah from Jerusalem.* The *many peoples* (plural) of this verse is equivalent to the *all nations* of verse 2. Not only is it a great multitude, but it includes individuals from among all races and tribes of the Gentiles. As these flow or stream into the city, they invite others to join them, saying, *he will teach us of his ways, and we will walk in his paths.* Instead of deafness and rebellion as in Isaiah's day, there will be a readiness to hear and a willingness to walk in God's paths. Teaching always precedes proper conduct. Isaiah later said, "And all thy children shall be taught of Jehovah; and great shall be the peace of thy children" (54:13). Jesus repeatedly emphasized this point (John 6:44–

45; Matt. 28:18–20). So from the spiritual center of divine government the law and the word of God will go forth to all the world.

4 *And he will judge between* (among) *the nations, and will decide concerning many peoples:* God will be the final arbiter or judge in all matters. Since the nations will come to Zion to learn His law and to walk in His ways, God's word will be the standard by which all matters are judged. This principle is clearly taught throughout the New Testament. Also, God will continue to judge and execute vengeance on the heathen nations that hearken neither to His word nor to His divinely appointed ruler (Ps. 2; Mic. 5:15). God will judge who is and who is not in the kingdom (see also Heb. 12:23). The prophet points to the character of the citizens of the kingdom: *they shall beat their swords into plowshares, and their spears into pruning-hooks; nation shall not lift up sword against nation, neither shall they learn war any more.* Here the prophet is certainly not speaking of the world, for its people will war continually, but rather of the *all nations* and *many peoples* who will come to the mountain of Jehovah's house. He is describing the character of the citizens of the new kingdom. In the holy mountain they will learn war no more. "They shall not hurt nor destroy in all my holy mountain" (11:9). Isaiah is not describing a future situation in which the nations of the world will not fight wars; wars will always be fought. He is describing the character of the kingdom of *the latter days,* the one to which the Hebrew saints had come (Heb. 12:18–29), and to which men of all the nations may and do come today.

Through Zechariah, a prophet about two centuries after Isaiah, God said, "Rejoice greatly, O daughter of Zion: shout, O daughter of Jerusalem: behold, thy king cometh unto thee." In this prophecy we see the King, whom we shall consider later, coming to the city described by Isaiah. "He is just, and having salvation; lowly, and riding upon an ass, even upon a colt the foal of an ass. And I will cut off the chariot from Ephraim, and the horse from Jerusalem; and the battle bow shall be cut off; and he shall speak peace unto the nations: and his dominion shall be from sea to sea, and from the River to the ends of the earth" (Zech. 9:9–10; cf. Hos. 2:18). Zechariah 9:9 is quoted by Matthew (21:5) and applied to Christ's triumphal entry into the city of Jerusalem. It was, therefore, in His kingdom that the implements of war would be cut off; He would speak peace to the nations. This He did, as recorded in the Gospels and by Paul: "He came and preached peace to you that were far off, and peace to them that were nigh" (Eph. 2:17). Both Isaiah and Zechariah describe the character of the kingdom of God under Christ, contrasting it with the kingdom under the old economy. The new kingdom would not be extended or defended by weapons of carnal warfare; its weapons are spiritual (II Cor. 10:3–5; Eph. 6:10–17).

Corruption: The People Have Forsaken Jehovah (vv. 5–11)

5   As if smitten by the hard fist of reality, the prophet looks from the ideal of Israel's future glory to the corruption of his days. Since in the ideal age the Gentiles shall say, "Come ye, and let us go up to the mountain of Jehovah . . . [and] walk in his paths" (v. 3), it is altogether fitting now to say, *O house of Jacob, come ye, and let us walk in the light of Jehovah.* Only in this way could the ideal ever be attained.

6   With an abrupt change in the person(s) being addressed—from the Jews to God—Isaiah notes that God has forsaken His people, casting them off and leaving them to their own devices. Isaiah then declares that the reason for this rejection is the corruption found in the land. He sets forth this state of decay by using the word *full* (or *filled*) four times: (1) The people of Jacob *are filled with* pagan *customs from the east*, from the Euphrates through Arabia to Elath, the seaport town on the Gulf of Aqaba. Abandoning Jehovah and His word, God's chosen people had become *soothsayers*—a word of uncertain meaning, but associated with some form of idolatry forbidden by the Lord (Lev. 18:26; Deut. 18:10–12)—*like the Philistines*, their heathen neighbors to the southwest. That *they strike hands with* ("please themselves in," King James) *the children of foreigners* indicates that they find pleasure in associating with foreigners and enjoy heathen ways rather than their own divinely appointed isolation.

7   (2) *Their land is full of silver and gold* and the treasures which these can purchase. (3) It is *full of horses* and *chariots*, which had been forbidden in the law (Deut. 17:16). All of this accumulation of mate-

rial wealth and power had led the Jews to forget their dependence on God.

8   (4) Most tragic of all, *their land also is full of idols*; they worship the creations of their own hands (for the folly of this, see the comments on 44:9–20). All four of these conditions were in direct violation of the law; for this reason Jehovah had cast off His people.

9   The sins leading to these conditions would bring judgment upon all; both the ordinary man of low degree and the man of high degree would be abased, brought low, humbled greatly. The situation was so bad that the prophet cries, *Forgive them not*, for he can see no hope for a change.

10   In view of this impending judgment, the prophet urges the people to take refuge in caves among the rocks, or to go underground, that they may escape from the *terror* of God's presence and the brightness or excellency of His *majesty*.

11   Because of their idolatry, their pride and arrogancy, their accumulation of wealth, and the consequent removal of God from their thoughts, the people must be brought low; the nation must be debased. In the humbling of these vain and haughty people, *Jehovah alone shall be exalted in that day*. What a lesson this should be to the godless, materialistic world of today!

Judgment: A Day of Jehovah (vv. 12–22)

12   Pride and arrogancy must go, but it will take *a day of Jehovah* to accomplish this. It will be a day chosen by the Lord, a day of judgment, the execution of God's wrath upon the wicked and the deliverance of the righteous from that which destroys the way of the Lord. When that day comes, *all that is lifted up shall be brought low*, cast down.

13–16   The prophet proceeds to enumerate four pairs of the high things that will be brought low when the day of the Lord shall fall: (1) *the cedars of Lebanon* and *the oaks of Bashan*; (2) *the high mountains* and *the hills that are lifted up*; (3) *every lofty tower* and *every fortified wall*; (4) *all the ships of Tarshish* and *all pleasant imagery* (or articles of art brought from far countries). Commentators are uncertain as to how these objects to be brought low are to be interpreted. Are they

51

symbolic figures of speech (metonymies), or are they to be taken literally? It is plausible to interpret the first two pairs as symbols of great men and lofty kingdoms, but the second two pairs are difficult to interpret figuratively. Consequently, most commentators interpret these objects literally: the cedars of Lebanon and oaks of Bashan, greatly prized by the ancients, will suffer destruction in the judgment; the mountains and hills will be denuded in the process. The lofty towers and fortified cities will be literally destroyed, as will be the mighty ships that ply the sea as far west as Tarshish in Spain. Leupold's suggestion may not be far amiss: "We may well have here a kind of half-figurative description in which the literal and figurative blend inextricably" (I. 83).

17–18 The four pairs we have discussed may well be pointing to a fifth pair to be brought low by the judgment of God: *And the loftiness of man shall be bowed down, and the haughtiness of men shall be brought low*. All that man has looked to and prized as mighty and lofty, together with his own pride and haughtiness, will be abased. For the second time the prophet says, *And Jehovah alone shall be exalted in that day* (cf. v. 11)—the day of Jehovah. When everything that man exalts, including himself, is brought to nought, God, the only eternal and permanent verity, and His word, the absolute truth, shall stand out clearly. *And the idols shall utterly pass away*; the gods they represent are thus demonstrated to be nonexistent figments of the imagination, helpless to save.

19 In the terror of the "day of Jehovah" men will seek hiding places in *the caves of the rocks* and in *the holes of the earth*—any place that offers refuge from the wrath of God (cf. Hos. 10:8; Luke 23:30; Rev. 6:16–17). In view here are temporal judgments. The shaking of the earth refers to a shaking of the world of the wicked, not to literal earthquakes.

20–21 When God shakes the earth, the people will cast even their most expensive idols to the *moles and the bats* which hide in burrows beneath the ground or in caves. Those idols will be a hindrance to panicked sinners as they seek refuge from the terror of Jehovah and His exalted majesty.

22 There is one final exhortation: *Cease ye from man* and from the creation of his hands, for he is mortal and his works are vanity.

What way of salvation can he offer? He must look to one higher than himself for help—and that one is Jehovah God.

CHAPTER 3
Political and Social Confusion

Isaiah's closing exhortation in the second chapter was, "Cease ye from man, whose breath is in his nostrils; for wherein is he to be accounted of?" (v. 22). His breath can be cut off at any moment. In chapter 3 Isaiah proceeds to show the folly of relying on man and the utter confusion that results from such confidence, for the destiny of man and nations rests in the hands of God. Both Jerusalem—the political, economic, and social center of the nation—and the nation of Judah itself are in a state of almost total collapse, for they have relied on man, and Jehovah is about to take away all that in which they have put their trust.

The Wages of Sin! (vv. 1–12)

1   The proclamation of judgment breaks forth afresh upon Jerusalem and Judah, for *the Lord, Jehovah of hosts*, is in control. The name *Lord (Adonai)* indicates ownership, complete possession; He is the owner and master of all. *Jehovah (Yahweh)* is the personal name of the supreme God, the name by which He was known to Israel; He is the eternally existent one. The phrase *of hosts* at times signifies the heavenly bodies and beings; at other times it denotes armies which Jehovah controls and directs to accomplish His purpose. The title *Jehovah of hosts* tells us that He is supreme commander of all forces. There follows a list of twelve specific things on which the people depended and which the Lord will take away (vv. 1–3). (1) He will take away the whole *stay and staff* of food and water, the support of life upon which all people depend and without which they cannot survive. These shall be taken away by the Lord, for they are His.

2–3   The Lord also declares that He will take away the various classes of men on whom Judah depended, men who constituted the stay and support of the nation: (2) *the mighty man,* heroes of the people, men of exploits whom they praised; (3) *the man of war,* those on whom the nation depended for its defense; (4) *the judge,* the governor or ruler to whom the people looked for justice; (5) *the prophet,* the spokesman representing Jehovah (though there were also false prophets); (6) *the diviner,* the one who practiced sorcery or witchcraft, forms of occult art; (7) *the elder,* an elderly person or member of the city council; (8) *the captain of fifty,* a military leader; (9) *the honorable man,* one of such worthy character that he is looked up to, possibly one close to the king; (10) *the counsellor,* one to whom the people looked for wise guidance and good advice; (11) *the expert artificer,* one skilled in the art of engraving, whether metal or wood; (12) *the skilful enchanter,* a professional who practices magic and divination. All these, who were looked upon as props to the nation, protecting and sustaining it, will be taken away.

4   Instead of wise rulers, Jehovah will give the nation rulers who are irrational, immature, irresponsible youths who are in turn dominated by a self-serving aristocracy.

5   The populace will become like the leaders, each one oppressing his neighbor and oppressed by his neighbor. All feeling of concern for and interest in others will vanish. Contrary to the law of God (Lev. 19:32), children will dishonor the elderly, and base men will have no regard for the honorable.

6   The nation will reach such a state of oppression and general degradation that no one will want to be ruler. A man will meet his brother in his father's house and, on the grounds that the brother has a coat to wear, insist that he become ruler, saying, *Let this ruin be under thy hand.* (That possession of a coat distinguishes a man from others and qualifies him for office indicates the desperateness of the situation.)

7   But the brother will refuse, saying, *I will not be a healer,* that is, a surgeon or binder of wounds (recall the condition described in 1:6). He will say that he does not have the means by which to meet the needs of the people, denying that he has either bread or clothing, even the coat which his brother claims he has. He probably demonstrates unusual wisdom when he refuses to be made ruler.

8–9   The prophet now declares that *Jerusalem is ruined* (has

54

stumbled), *and Judah is fallen* (morally and spiritually); but of course total collapse comes later. The reason for this condition is that their words *(their tongue)* and their deeds *(their doings)* are against Jehovah; they utterly refuse to listen to or obey Him. By their conduct they *provoke the eyes of his glory.* God sees what man does, and what He sees provokes Him to action. The impudence of the inhabitants of Jerusalem and Judah is stamped upon their faces, witnessing against them. As did the Sodomites (Gen. 19), these people openly and shamelessly declare their sin; there is no effort to hide it. Therefore, *Woe unto their soul!* Woe to their lives, their whole beings, for they have done evil unto themselves in sinning against God.

10–11 A divine principle running throughout the Bible is now announced: As a man sows, so shall he reap. The righteous shall eat or partake of the fruits of their righteousness, but *woe unto the wicked!* As he has done so shall it be done unto him. Obadiah expresses the same principle (Obad. 15), as does Paul (Gal. 6:7–8). To reap the blessings of righteousness, man must act righteously; if he prefers to live wickedly, he must be prepared to bear the consequence. It is ever that simple.

12 The prophet returns to a consideration of the rulers and their influence on the people: *As for my people, children are their oppressors, and women rule over them.* Inexperienced and immature rulers who act like boys and are controlled by dominating women cannot give a people sound leadership. Rather, they become oppressors of the people, causing them to err and go astray from God's paths. Here the Lord has in view the political leaders, but not to the exclusion of the false prophets who led the people into error. Micah well describes how easy it is for a false prophet to lead the people astray: "If a man walking in a spirit of falsehood do lie, saying, I will prophesy unto thee of wine and strong drink; he shall even be the prophet of this people" (Mic. 2:11). The same principle can be observed today. Our country is on the verge of political and economic ruin because of unsound leadership; and the church has experienced apostasy and spiritual chaos because of the leadership of elders, preachers, and teachers who regard not the Lord's way but follow their own. However, this does not excuse the people, for they have chosen to follow.

Judgment of the Rulers (vv. 13–15)

13 Jehovah, who stands ready to judge the peoples (the nations), is also ready to enter into a court of judgment with the rulers of His own people. In using the plural here *(peoples)* the prophet is not focusing his attention on a universal judgment of the nations. Rather, he is saying that even as Jehovah is the Judge of nations, so He is also the Judge of His own nation.

14 The judgment is directed toward the elders and princes—the ruling class. They are charged with having eaten up God's vineyard, that is, His people (see ch. 5). Spoils from the poor are found in the houses of the rulers, testifying that they have been corrupt in their judging and have robbed the people.

15 In a tone of hot indignation Jehovah asks through the prophet, "What do you mean by this? Do you think you can get away with such behavior?" He then uses two strong words: the rulers *crush* the people as with a heavy load or hammer, and *grind* them like grain under a millstone. These are God's people whom the rulers so mistreat; their conduct stands condemned by *the Lord, Jehovah of hosts* (v. 1). They must answer to Him.

Indictment of Vain and Worldly Women (vv. 3:16–4:1)

16–17 Suddenly the prophet breaks off from censoring the rulers to hurl a lightning bolt of judgment against the proud and haughty women of Jerusalem. He regards these vain and wanton women as a contributing factor in the corruption and fall of Judah, for women exercise a tremendous force in the making or breaking of a nation. Jehovah charges these women with being haughty, proud, and arrogant. These traits are revealed by their *outstretched necks and wanton eyes*, their proud posture and seductive looks. They seek attention by the way they walk, affecting a daintiness or youthful appearance by tripping along and wearing anklets with bells that tinkle. *Therefore*—always consider a *therefore* for it focuses attention on consequences or what is to follow—*Therefore the Lord will smite with a scab the crown of the head of the daughters of Zion, and Jehovah will lay bare their secret parts.* To their shame and humiliation, the sexual features to which they would attract attention will be laid bare in the hands of crude, rough, barbarous captors.

18–23 *In that day*—the day that the Lord smites the haughty women (v. 17)—He will take away their ornaments of beauty and vanity; that is, their adornments will be carried away as booty by the conquerors. The prophet enumerates twenty-one items prized by the women of the day, from anklets to headtires (headbands), from perfume boxes to mirrors, from various garments to the ornaments with which they were bedecked. Neither the prophet nor Peter (I Peter 3:1–5) condemns women for adorning themselves. What he does condemn is that which he sees beneath all the vanity and external show, the character which clothing and ornamentation cannot hide. Beneath the glitter and tinsel, the worldly ostentation, he sees selfish, proud, and sensuous lives patterned after the world with its lust and lascivious ways. The picture is one of conduct and character that are contrary to the holiness and righteousness of Jehovah. In their pride and lewdness these women are leading the nation to ruin by exerting a far-reaching influence on its life and destiny. Why cannot today's Christian women, with the ideal of Christ's standard before them, see the inconsistency of patterning their conduct and dress after the world?

24 The character and conduct of the haughty women of Judah will bring a complete change in their fortunes. *Instead of sweet spices there shall be rottenness*, the odor of decay; *instead of a girdle, a rope* about the waist by which they will be led into captivity; *instead of well set hair*, the crown of a woman's beauty and glory, there will be *baldness*, a manifestation of degradation; *instead of a robe*, the festival robe (v. 22) worn at fashionable and gala affairs, there will be *a girding of sackcloth*, a coarse, rough garment worn next to the body as a symbol of anguish and grief; and *branding instead of beauty*, that is, branding as a slave or captive. All this will come to pass because the women of Judah have turned to the way of the idolatrous world, forsaking Jehovah, the God of their fathers, the God of mercy and love who had redeemed and blessed them so richly.

25–26 God's judgment on Judah is climaxed with a dark picture of death and destruction: the men of Judah *shall fall by the sword*; the valorous and mighty shall be destroyed in the war. The gate of the city, where people congregated in former times, will be vacated—a symbol of grief and lamentation. The city will be desolate and empty, and the once proud Zion will sit upon the ground in prostration and humiliation, thus receiving the wages of sin.

CHAPTER 4
Jerusalem the Redeemed

1　The first verse of chapter 4 is actually a continuation of the message of chapter 3. In the midst of desolation the women of Judah will do what is contrary to the standard of social ethics; *seven women,* the number of completion or perfection, *shall take hold of one man in that day, saying, We will eat our own bread, and wear our own apparel: only let us be called by thy name; take thou away our reproach.* The men will have been so decimated by war that the women, in an effort to escape the shame of having no husband and of being childless, will be willing to share a husband with other women so their reproach might be removed, thus substituting one shame for another. They will be willing to assume the husband's normal responsibility of providing their food and clothing if only they can be called by his name. Ah, the ugly fruit of sin! This is the fate of Jerusalem which loomed so vividly before the prophet.

The Branch of Jehovah (v. 2)

We have reached the end of the cycle which began in chapter 2—from Jerusalem the ideal to Jerusalem the real to Jerusalem the redeemed. The prophet began with a picture of Jerusalem-Zion as Jehovah purposed it (2:2–4). He then described the Jerusalem that he saw in his own time, with its sin, decay, and corruption. He singled out the rulers and the haughty women (2:5–4:1). And now, beyond the inevitable judgment that must come, he sees Jerusalem the redeemed, cleansed and purified (4:2–6). In the first section Jerusalem-Zion is set forth as the center of God's rule, the capital of His spiritual kingdom, from which will go forth His word and law and to which the nations (the Gentiles) will come. The nature of this kingdom and its people is declared to be nonmilitary, thus completely different from the nations of earth. The second section sets forth the failure of the people under their present order; they are proud and put their trust in the arm of flesh. Their wickedness must be purged by judgment. In the third section the emphasis is on the new Jerusalem-Zion made glorious by the presence of the Branch and of Jehovah. The new order will be divinely created; a cleansing will be effected by Jehovah. As chapter 1 served as an introduction to the entire book, chapters 2–4 serve as a preview of the remainder of the book—the ideal, the reality, and redemption. Jehovah is working out His eternal purpose.

2 The phrase *in that day* always refers to the time indicated by the context. In 2:2 "the latter days" pointed to the time of Jehovah's mountain in the messianic age, which would follow the judgment of Judah and the sweeping away of the filth of Zion. Hence, *in that day* is to be understood as the latter days when judgment will have been executed and Jerusalem-Zion redeemed. At that time *shall the branch of Jehovah be beautiful and glorious.* Isaiah introduces the word *branch*; its special meaning here is later developed both by Isaiah and by two of the prophets who followed him. With regard to the reading of the margin, "shoot or sprout," Leupold comments: "'Sprout,' 'shoot,' or 'branch' are all inadequate [translations of the Hebrew word]. It is not only a part of a tree (branch). It is more than a little beginning of growth (shoot or sprout). It is the 'growing thing,' with the connotation of abundant vitality and fresh life. . . . It is best understood in this connection as being the great work of salvation which Yahweh has undertaken for the good of mankind" (I. 102). God's people were not to lose sight of the promise made by Jehovah to the serpent (Gen. 3:15), to Abraham (Gen. 12:3; 22:18), to Isaac and Jacob, to Judah (Gen. 49:9–10), and to David (II Sam. 7:11–16). David said that his own salvation depended on that promise: God "hath made with me an everlasting covenant,/Ordered in all things, and sure:/For it is all my salvation, and all my desire,/Although he maketh it not to grow" (II Sam. 23:5). The promise is not forgotten; it is still alive. And when *the branch* comes forth, it *shall be beautiful and glorious*—characterized by true beauty and divine glory, in contrast to the false beauty and worldly glory described in chapter 3.

The idea of *the branch* is further developed by Isaiah in 11:1, where he identifies it as coming out of the stock of Jesse, David's father, and in 11:10, where he refers to it as the ensign around which the nations will gather. About one hundred years after Isaiah, Jeremiah said, "Behold, the days come, saith Jehovah, that I will raise unto David a righteous Branch, and he shall reign as king and deal wisely, and shall execute justice and righteousness [these words frequently recur in Isaiah] in the land" (Jer. 23:5). Jeremiah repeated this promise in slightly different form: Jehovah will "cause a Branch of righteousness to grow up unto David" (33:15). And Zechariah, one of the last prophets, proclaimed, "I [Jehovah] will bring forth my servant the Branch" (Zech. 3:8). Zechariah advanced still another step, making "Branch" a personal name: "Behold, the man whose name is the Branch: and he . . . shall sit and rule upon his throne; and he shall be a priest upon his throne" (Zech. 6:12–13). Here the offices of King and Priest are combined.

And the fruit of the land shall be excellent and comely, majestic and beautiful, pleasing to the eye. Although other explanations are given of the fruit of the land ruled over by the Branch, it seems out of context to interpret it any way other than as spiritual fruit. We have seen that the mountain of Jehovah and Zion-Jerusalem are actually the spiritual kingdom under the Messiah, and the Branch is the Messiah who will come to Zion in the latter days; so why should not the fruit of the land, the mountain to which the peoples will come, be of a spiritual nature? Jeremiah said that the Branch will "execute justice and righteousness in the land"; hence the fruit of the land will be the spiritual fruit of those who submit to His rule of righteousness. This fruit will be *for them that are escaped of Israel,* that is, the remnant.

The Escaped of Israel—The Remnant (vv. 3–4)

3 *And it shall come to pass, that he that is left in Zion, and he that remaineth in Jerusalem, shall be called holy, even every one that is written among the living in Jerusalem.* Here Isaiah has in view the remnant "according to the election of grace" (Rom. 11:5). The primary emphasis is on the word *holy*; for whereas in the old Jerusalem the emphasis has been on rank (3:2–3, 14), in the new Jerusalem it will be on holiness of life. The fact that the remnant *shall be called holy* unto the Lord, set apart and consecrated unto Him, presupposes that they have a personal character of holiness and righteousness. They are set apart from the common or profane; they belong to the sphere of the sacred. They are those found in the register of God, His book of life.

4 The remnant shall be called holy *when the Lord shall have washed away the filth of the daughters of Zion.* The finery so highly esteemed by the women of Zion (3:16–23) is called *filth* by the Lord. Instead of being *holy,* they are covered with defilement and corruption which will be washed away by the judgment of Jehovah. At the same time the Lord *shall have purged the blood of Jerusalem from the midst thereof.* This refers to blood shed by murderers (1:15), or to those who died because the rulers deprived them of the necessities of life (3:14–15). Both the filth of the women and the blood shed by the nobility must be purged. This would be done *by the spirit of justice, and by the spirit of burning*—by a blast emanating from the throne of Jehovah. An unnamed psalmist wrote, "Righteousness and justice are the foundation of his throne./A fire goeth before him, and burneth up his adversaries round about" (Ps. 97:2–3). This spirit or breath from Jehovah, the fire that goes forth from His throne, will purge the city of its filth and blood.

Protection and Guidance for the New Zion (vv. 5–6)

5 To illustrate the protection to be granted the new Zion, the prophet draws on Israel's experience in their departure from Egypt and their wanderings in the wilderness, when Jehovah both led and protected them by cloud and by fire. *And Jehovah will create over the whole habitation of mount Zion, and over her assemblies, a cloud and smoke by day, and the shining of a flaming fire by night.* The word *create* in this verse is the word used in Genesis of the original creation of heaven and earth; hence it refers to a new creation. In Isaiah 65:17–18 the same word is used three times. Jehovah says, "I create new heavens and a new earth. . . . Be ye glad and rejoice for ever in that which I create; for, behold, I create Jerusalem a rejoicing, and her people a joy." An unnamed psalmist said, "And a people which shall be created shall praise Jehovah" (Ps. 102:18). The new order will come about by a divine creation of something that did not exist before. This manifestation of Jehovah's presence will be not only over the hill of Zion itself, but also over the whole habitation and over her assemblies, wherever the people may be when they come together for worship. This thought foreshadows the idea of independent congregations of the Lord's people, all of which are in turn an integral part of the new spiritual Zion. It seems that the cloud of smoke and the fire cover all the glory of the new Zion, indicating Jehovah's constant presence, both to direct and to protect (see Heb. 13:5–6; Phil. 4:5).

6   In contrast to the forsaken and desolate booth or hut (1:8), there shall be in the new Zion *a pavilion for a shade in the day-time from the heat, and for a refuge and for a covert from storm and from rain*. Here is a place for protection from searing heat and the storms of life, the broiling heat of persecution and the pelting hail of the world forces of evil. God has provided a shield of protection, a place where each of His children may be near Him.

The latter days have come; the mountain of Jehovah's house has been established above the hills, and all nations have been flowing unto it for nearly two millennia. God judges as He translates the saved into the kingdom of His Son. Zion's wickedness and the fruits of her idolatry have been judged by Jehovah and purged and cleansed by a fire from His presence, leaving her redeemed and made fit as a dwelling place for Jehovah. And the beautiful Branch has appeared, bringing glory to the city of spiritual Jerusalem. It is the only kingdom on earth sustained and extended by a spiritual rather than physical sword; it is the only place where true peace can be found.

CHAPTER 5
The Vineyard and Its Fruits

The exact time of the prophecy in this chapter is unknown; it is thought to have been spoken either in the latter days of Jotham or the early period of the reign of Ahaz. The chapter presents the dark and ugly picture of a people who had sown the seeds of profligacy and lust and who were now reaping the evil fruits and consequences of their deeds. To a people who boasted of their special favor in the eyes of Jehovah and who looked upon their material prosperity under the reigns of Uzziah and Jotham as an expression of that favor, Isaiah's words must have appeared as the rankest of heresy. The chapter contains no promise or expression of the divine grace of God except the favor He had shown in planting the vineyard.

The prophecy falls into three sections: (1) the song of the Beloved and His vineyard (vv. 1–7); (2) the harvest—wild or rotten grapes (vv. 8–23); and (3) a terrifying judgment (vv. 24–30).

The Song of the Beloved and His Vineyard (vv. 1–7)

1   Here the prophet changes his approach to the problem of the nation and its sins; he assumes the role of a poet or singer, teaching through a poetic parable which he sings. He presents a beautiful, tender, picturesque scene of a loving Husbandman who with affectionate hands prepares and plants a vineyard. *Let me sing for* (of, or about) *my well-beloved a song of my beloved touching his vineyard. My well-beloved had a vineyard in a very fruitful hill.* Imagine yourself standing on a lofty elevation looking down on a beautifully landscaped hill, rich and fertile and open to the sun on all sides—an idyllic dream. The prophet would have his hearers envision a vineyard on just such a site. Yet anyone who has visited the land of Palestine is aware that many rocks cover the hilly landscape. It would require a prodigious amount of work to create a vineyard there. In addition to the vineyard itself, the emphasis seems to be on the *Beloved,* Jehovah, the prophet's friend.

2   *And he digged it, and gathered out the stones thereof, and planted it with the choicest vine, and* (with the stones he) *built a tower in the midst of it* from which to keep watch over it. Anticipating an abundant harvest, the Husbandman hewed out of a rock a winepress in which to tread the vintage. He then looked for a rich harvest of luscious and delectable grapes; but, instead, the vineyard brought forth wild, sour, harsh grapes. What a disappointment!

63

3   Isaiah turns from the foregoing scene of beauty to a song of lament and eventually of judgment. He first addresses the inhabitants of Jerusalem because, as the capital of the nation, it was also the leader in the apostasy. Next he addresses the men of Judah, for the people of the nation were equally guilty. Speaking for Jehovah, the prophet calls upon the people to *judge . . . betwixt me and my vineyard.*

4   What more could the Beloved have done to enhance the beauty and productivity of the vineyard than He had done? And why, when He looked for a rich harvest, to which He most certainly was entitled, did He find only wild, worthless grapes? Something had gone awry.

5   The Husbandman now proceeds to tell the hearers what He will do with the vineyard. Inasmuch as He had exerted the labor to make it fertile, removing the stones, digging the soil, planting the vines and caring for them, He has a perfect right to abandon it to destruction should He see fit. He will take away the hedge and tear down the wall which protect the vineyard. Let it be eaten and trampled by the beasts!

6   Left to itself, unpruned and untilled, the vineyard will soon be overrun with briers and thorns. Furthermore, the Beloved will command the clouds not to come up, leaving the vineyard without rain. Here judgment is exerted through divine control over the elements; they are subject to the will of their Creator.

7   At this point the prophet abandons the poetic device of direct speech by Jehovah. Isaiah plainly tells his hearers what he has been talking about. *For the vineyard of Jehovah of hosts is the house of Israel, and the men of Judah his pleasant plant.* He then makes a play upon words (paronomasia) which loses its significance in the translation: *he looked for justice* ("mishpat," Hebrew), *but, behold, oppression* (or bloodshed) ("mispah," Hebrew); *for righteousness* ("sedakah," Hebrew), *but, behold, a cry* ("seakah," Hebrew). Planted and cared for by Jehovah, the people enjoyed a special place in His purpose and providence; but because they had utterly failed in the mission to which they had been called, they would lose that place of favor. As Job said, "Jehovah gave, and Jehovah hath taken away; blessed be the name of Jehovah" (Job 1:21).

The Harvest: Wild Grapes! Six Woes! (vv. 8–23)

With the pronouncement of six woes and in vivid and harsh descriptions, the prophet sets forth the features of a corrupt civilization. Modern nations that have reached a high degree of so-called civilization can read this chapter and see their own image reflected. Greed and avarice as well as alcoholism and sensuous entertainments characterize a people so laden with iniquity that they can no longer discern between good and evil. They have become so wise in their own conceit that they feel no dependence whatever upon God. But God is not mocked; such behavior brings down upon itself judgment and destruction.

Woe to greedy land-barons (vv. 8–10)

8　The first woe is pronounced against greed, avarice, covetousness, and selfish ambition. Woe unto the rich landowners who buy up or otherwise acquire the land of the less fortunate until the original owners are crowded out. In the city, house touches house; all of them are now owned by the rich, who subject the poor to squalid conditions. In the country the rich dwell alone in the midst of their vast possessions of land. Micah, Isaiah's contemporary, is even more vivid in his description of the conditions: "They covet fields, and seize them; and houses, and take them away: and they oppress a man and his house, even a man and his heritage" (2:2). Smith suggests that Isaiah is not dealing with problems caused by state regulation of land, but with the sins of men, their greed and avarice (I. 41).

9　Jehovah reveals to the prophet what the judgment shall be. *In mine ears*, the ears of Isaiah, Jehovah reveals what shall follow such greed and oppression of one's fellow men, one's brethren. The houses thus acquired shall be left desolate, without inhabitant, falling into a state of decay.

10　And likewise the land, whether ravished by war or drought, or untilled because the inhabitants have moved to the cities, will be unproductive. Moses had assured the people that the rejection of God's laws would bring a curse upon the land. It would not yield its increase, and the trees would yield no fruit (Lev. 26:20; Deut. 28:16–19). This divine judgment will now come to pass. The phrase *ten acres of vineyard* is thought to indicate the area that one yoke of oxen could plow in ten days. This large area will produce a quantity of wine only slightly in excess of eight gallons; and *a homer of seed shall yield but an ephah,* which is one-tenth the amount sowed (an ephah is one-tenth of a homer). Greed fails to reap the fruit of expectation, for somehow God has a way of bringing unholy ambitions to nought.

Woe to heavy drinkers (vv. 11–17)

11 Generally men rise early in the morning to pursue worthy occupations, but not the people of Judah. They *rise up early in the morning, that they may follow strong drink.* This is not an occasional thing, but a daily practice; drinking has become a way of life with the people. Strong drink includes not only wine from the grape but also intoxicants from various other sources, especially "wines made artificially from fruit, honey, raisins, dates, etc., including barley-wine or beer" (Delitzsch). Moreover, the drinking continues *late into the night, till wine inflame them.*

12 Drinking seems always to have been the curse of the affluent and prosperous. Every so-called civilized nation of today has its alcohol-related problems of crime, accidents, broken homes, maimed children, and souls so seared by its use that the spiritual appeals of the Lord are ignored and ridiculed (cf. ch. 28). Revelry and debauchery are companions to drinking—*and the harp and the lute, the tabret and the pipe, and wine, are in their feasts* ("is their feast," Delitzsch). While the people of Judah feast and revel, the inflaming stimulation of wine and the provocative music arouse sensuous excesses. We are reminded of our own generation, which is cursed by the same plague of drinking, oftentimes to excess. The difference today is that in addition to consuming alcohol, the youth of the nation are wasting away on drugs and narcotics. And the abominable "rock concerts," which epitomize the hedonistic morality of a socially depraved nation, have become the current feasts of thousands of young men and women who are to be the parents and leaders of tomorrow.

But they regard not the work of Jehovah, neither have they considered the operation of his hands. The people of that day, who had succumbed to the evils of *strong drink*, were not concerned with the purpose God was working out through His chosen people, nor were they worried about the consequent judgment that was bound to come. How few learn that they who sow the wind shall reap the whirlwind (Hos. 8:7)—the tornado of divine wrath, the work of God's hands. "Look not thou upon the wine when it is red,/When it sparkleth in the cup,/When it goeth down smoothly:/At the last [there will always be an 'at the last,' a day of recompense] it biteth like a serpent,/ And stingeth like an adder" (Prov. 23:31–32).

13 *Therefore* (the word introduces a conclusion, in this case the consequence of Judah's conduct) *my people are gone into captivity for lack of knowledge.* The captivity is so certain that the prophet can speak of it as if it has already taken place. In reality the people are in captivity to their own sins and passions, the result of leaving God out of their thinking: "Israel doth not know, my people doth not consider" (1:3); like their brethren to the north, they "are destroyed for lack of knowledge" (Hos. 4:6). They are unaware of the judgment hanging over them. Their rich or honorable men—men of position who have feasted on the gratification of fleshly lusts—and the multitude who have satiated their desire for wine and strong drink by extending their drinking bouts long into the night, will find themselves famished for food and parched from thirst.

14 Another *therefore* indicates that the judgment is not yet complete. *Sheol hath enlarged its desire, and opened its mouth without measure.* Sheol, translated "grave," "pit," or "hell" in the King James, probably means the grave or tomb which ultimately receives all the dead: "The wicked shall be turned back unto Sheol [i.e., the grave or the unseen],/Even all the nations that forget God" (Ps. 9:17); and "Sheol and Abaddon [destruction] are never satisfied [never full]" (Prov. 27:20). Sheol greedily opens its mouth as a ravenous, devouring beast into which descends a multitude of people, along with their glory, pomp, and reveling. All the things in which the people glory will be destroyed; the nation will be carried into captivity, their Sheol, or grave, where they will abide unseen as far as their land and its blessings are concerned.[2]

---

2. For a discussion of the word *Sheol* see *Theological Wordbook of the Old Testament*, ed. R. Laird Harris (Chicago: Moody, 1980), vol. 2, p. 892; and *Zondervan Pictorial Encyclopedia of the Bible*, ed. Merrill C. Tenney (Grand Rapids: Zondervan, 1975), vol. 5, p. 395.

15–16   Whereas the mean man and the great man will be bowed and humbled (cf. 2:9, 11, 17), Jehovah will be exalted in realization of the justice of His judgment. In contrast to the disregard in which the people now hold Him, He will be sanctified, acknowledged as holy, for justice and righteousness are the foundation of His throne (Ps. 89:14; 97:2).

17   And when Jehovah is exalted, instead of the voluptuous feasts and drunken carousals of the earlier period, lambs will find pasture, and the mature ones will find food amidst the rubble of the devastated city and country. The land which once was coveted and seized by the rich will be grazing places for the sheep of wandering nomads.

Woe to them who are enslaved to sin (vv. 18–19)

18   In a graphic and vivid picture the prophet presents the third woe, which describes men drawing (pulling) iniquity with cords of falsehood. We see men harnessed in the falsehoods of their idolatry and their misconceptions of Jehovah, drawing their sins after them (some think "unto" them) like heavily loaded wagons. They pull their sin after them, as with a heavy rope with which one might draw a wagon or loaded cart. Their entanglement in sin and iniquity has made them slaves.

19   But the disposition and attitude that these men demonstrate toward the Lord is even worse than the entanglement described in verse 18. They make a mockery of Isaiah's warning of judgment by saying, *Let him* (the Lord) *make speed, let him hasten his work, that we may see it.* Speaking in a light and sneering tone, they would walk by sight and not by faith. But when judgment comes, "it shall be nought but terror to understand the message" (28:19). Then in a mock piety they employ lightly the name so often used by Isaiah: *and let the counsel of the Holy One of Israel draw nigh and come, that we may know it!* It is so easy to be light and flippant when things are normal; but when the earth quakes, the lightning flashes, and the terrifying thunder rolls, it is a different story. Terrified, they will seek caves and holes in which to hide themselves (2:19).

Woe to those who confuse moral distinctions (v. 20)

20   *Woe unto them that call evil good, and good evil; that put* *darkness for light, and light for darkness; that put bitter for sweet, and sweet for bitter!* The spirit that ridicules God and His word leads to a confusion of moral distinctions in which the people cannot discern between true and false values. Sin's harmful effects upon the heart and soul are finding full expression in the thinking and life of the society of the day. The fourth woe is pronounced against this moral perversity caused by spiritual blindness and deafness.

The distinction between good and evil is clearly fixed in the moral character of God and is made known in His revelation to man; therefore, calling good evil, and evil good, does not make it so or alter eternal principles. The confusing of light and darkness in the mind of man leads to moral chaos; in the end the darkness cannot overcome the light; light will be the victor (John 1:5). However hard man may try to avoid the consequences, the momentary sweetness of sin must inevitably bear the bitter fruit of remorse and grief.

Today the general reaction to moral sins has been so toned down that there is no distinction between good and evil in the average mind. The conditions condemned by Isaiah's fourth woe seem to be the expression of our society today. Drinking is equated with a good time; as in pagan cultures adultery and fornication are considered simply the gratification of a natural or normal urge; rebellion against constituted authority (including the destruction of property) is looked upon as a normal phase through which one passes. But it is ever true that sin is defiance against God, rebellion against His will, and an effort to overthrow His moral standards; it is the substitution of the will of man, motivated by lust, the desires of the flesh and mind.

Woe to the self-deceived (v. 21)

21 When man ridicules the word of God and His prophets (v. 19), and confuses the principles of good and evil (v. 20), he becomes dependent upon his own fallible wisdom which, since it is apart from God, is fatal in its consequence. The prophet addresses himself to such a state of affairs: *Woe unto them that are wise in their own eyes, and prudent in their own sight.* In his quest for the source of true wisdom, Job concludes, "Behold, the fear of the Lord, that is wisdom; and to depart from evil is understanding" (Job 28:28). Both the people and the rulers of the nation had fallen into a sorry trap;

69

they had forsaken Jehovah, the source of true wisdom, and trusted in
their own.

Woe to the perverters of justice (vv. 22–23)

22–23   The sixth woe is pronounced against the rulers whose
addiction to strong drink prevented them from ruling with keen
minds. The prophet here returns to the principle of the second woe
(vv. 11–17): *Woe unto them that are mighty to drink wine, and men of
strength to mingle strong drink.* What follows in verse 23 indicates
that those under consideration were judges who, instead of being
adept at rendering right judgments, were experts at mixing strong
drinks; this was their claim to renown.

These judges accepted bribes and took away the righteousness due
the righteous; they did not recognize and deal justly with those who
were right before God. Hosea's word to northern Israel was just as
applicable to their brethren in the south: "Whoredom and wine and
new wine take away the understanding." Forsaking the true wisdom
and relying on their own, "My people ask counsel at their stock, and
their staff declareth unto them; for the spirit of whoredom hath
caused them to err, and they have played the harlot, departing from
under their God" (Hos. 4:11–12).

A Terrifying Judgment (vv. 24–30)

24   Instead of pronouncing a seventh woe, the prophet bursts
forth with an explosive declaration of judgment. *Therefore* introduces
a consequence based on conditions previously discussed. With this
word the prophet had introduced judgments in verses 13 and 14; now
two "therefores" (vv. 24 and 25) introduce additional pictures of judgment. By using two similes from nature Isaiah describes the calami-
tous judgment: a roaring fire, either a prairie fire (as in early
American history) or a great forest fire (as experienced today), and a
devastating earthquake which leaves the streets strewn with corpses.

As a fire devours the stubble of a field or a dry forest, the burning
material melts down to the ground. The root, which supplies
moisture and hence life to the plant, shall be as rottenness (i.e., there
will be no life); and the flower that produces the fruit shall go up as

dust, ashes carried away with the updraft. All this destruction is traced to one ultimate cause: *They have rejected the law of Jehovah of hosts, and despised the word of the Holy One of Israel.* Only Israel had the law and the word of Jehovah; therefore, much was expected of them. Having looked with loathing and contempt upon His word, they had rejected that law. The severity of judgment would be equal to that of their sin.

25 This picture of destruction by fire is followed by a second *therefore,* which likewise looks back to the cause of judgment, Judah's forsaking and despising of the law and word of Jehovah. Divine punishment is now seen in a terrible earthquake. His anger kindled, Jehovah stretches out His hand against His people and smites them with such mighty force that the mountains tremble or shake. Consequently, instead of the usual accumulated filth which litters Oriental cities, dead bodies fill the streets. Yet, in spite of these destructive judgments, the people had not repented. *For all this his anger is not turned away, but his hand is stretched out still.* There are more judgments to come!

What was in the prophet's mind, and what was before him as he uttered this prophecy? Is he saying that the fires of the people's own lusts, their inward rottenness of moral character, would destroy them? Is the earthquake of which Isaiah speaks the one mentioned by Amos and Zechariah (Amos 1:1; Zech. 14:5); or is the prophet referring to calamities like those described by Amos when he spoke of the "cleanness of teeth," the withholding of rain, the "blasting and mildew," the pestilence and the sword by which Israel's cities had been overthrown (Amos 4:6–11)? Perhaps Isaiah is speaking figuratively of the destruction wrought in Judah by the kings of Syria and Israel in the days of Ahaz when thousands perished and other thousands were carried into captivity by Israel (II Chron. 28:5–8). All of these are possibilities; one cannot be certain as to exactly what is in Isaiah's mind. But regardless of what the prophet has in mind, he emphasizes the basic principle that because there has been no repentance, God's hand is still held out in judgment against His people.

26 A more terrible judgment is on its way. Jehovah will lift an ensign—a flag, cloth, or some other symbol—upon a pole to the nations afar, and will hiss or whistle for them to come *with speed swiftly*. This army will be well prepared, fresh and strong.

27   In response to Jehovah's call, the nations will come in haste, neither sleeping nor slumbering (drowsing off). Their attire for battle will be complete, carefully assembled, lacking nothing.

28–30   The nations' *arrows are sharp, and all their bows bent; their horses' hoofs shall be accounted as flint, and their wheels as a whirlwind*. They are ready for immediate conflict. Iron shoes for horses were unknown at that time, so the reference to hoofs like flint may be to a special breed of horses whose speed would not be impeded by tender feet. The wheels of the chariots would stir up a whirlwind of dust as they came roaring like a lioness or like young lions bent on prey. They would roar like a lion that lays hold on its prey and carries it off to be consumed at a safe distance where there is no other beast to take it away. The whole terrifying scene is climaxed with this invading army's being likened to the roaring of an overflowing sea which engulfs a land, as in a hurricane or tidal wave that leaves utter destruction in its wake (cf. 8:5–8). As land is overflowed by such a sea, one beholds only darkness and distress; as the clouds of judgment approach, the light is gradually extinguished until total darkness encompasses the land.

Some seven hundred years prior to the period of Isaiah, Moses had forewarned Israel that if they hearkened not to the voice of Jehovah and if they turned to the gods of the nations, "Jehovah will bring a nation against thee from far, from the end of the earth, as the eagle flieth; a nation whose tongue thou shalt not understand; a nation of fierce countenance, that shall not regard the person of the old nor show favor to the young . . . [a nation that] shall besiege thee in all thy gates, until thy high and fortified walls come down" (Deut. 28:49–52). That prophecy was now to be fulfilled. Although at this point Isaiah does not name the invaders called by Jehovah to execute His wrath, he later identifies them as Assyria (7:17; 8:7; 10:5; etc.). However, due to the diligent efforts of Isaiah and Micah, and the influence of the good King Hezekiah, when the Assyrian attack actually came, Jehovah spared Judah and Jerusalem from destruction, turning the Assyrian army which came against Jerusalem into a sea of the dead (37:36–38). Though Judah and Jerusalem were spared at that time, Jehovah said through Isaiah that the day would come when the people would be carried away into Babylon (ch. 39). Habakkuk describes the swift and terrible approach of the Chaldeans in language equally as graphic as that used by Isaiah in describing the coming of the Assyrians (Hab. 1:5–11). Through the campaigns of foreign invaders against Israel, Judah, and Jerusalem, Jehovah fulfilled the predictions of Moses in Leviticus 26 and Deuteronomy 28, where the terrible consequence of sin and idolatry is clearly spelled out as a warning to all nations for all time.

Three distinct prophecies are now before us: (1) Corruption and sin-sickness from head to foot would bring upon the people the judgment of divine wrath. But out of this judgment God, through His grace, would spare a remnant (ch. 1). (2) Though the real Zion in Isaiah's time was rebellious and sin-cursed, the ideal Zion would come forth in the latter days through chastening, washing, and purification in the fires of affliction (chs. 2–4). (3) The Beloved's vineyard had produced only the sour fruit of sin, bringing on the approaching dark and terrible judgment (ch. 5). Though this judgment would not bring the nation to repentance, out of it would come a chastened and purged remnant. Again and again we read of God's grace: it will not be utterly wasted! These three prophecies set the pattern for the rest of the book, and they serve as an introduction to the whole of Isaiah's work.

The Vision and Call of Isaiah

After reading many expositions of Isaiah, one is left with the feeling that there is no clear explanation as to why chapter 6 appears where it does instead of at the beginning of the book. The opinions of various writers leave us with the impression that their efforts are basically guesses, with no real foundation in fact or revelation. Young suggests that unlike Jeremiah, whose personality stands out throughout his book, Isaiah the man recedes into the background while the message stands predominant. What we know about Isaiah himself is learned primarily through his preaching and message. He begins with an introduction to his message (chs. 1–5). The first chapter appears to be the logical place to begin. There he names all the kings during whose reigns he prophesied and introduces the topics of Judah's sins and the fundamental message God has for the nation. When Isaiah comes to his own call he works it in without disruption, making it coincide with chapter 1, an effective literary device. He introduces himself and his right to speak, having been called by Jehovah to the office of prophet. Since Isaiah's call is found at this juncture, we proceed with our study in the assurance that its position is not haphazard or accidental but according to the purpose of God and His prophet. We are content in the confidence that we do not need to know the final answer, for it rests in the mind of God.

Chapter 6 falls into three divisions: (1) Isaiah's vision of the mighty Jehovah (vv. 1–5); (2) the prophet's consecration to his mission (vv. 6–7); and (3) his commission from Jehovah (vv. 8–13).

Isaiah's Vision of the Lord (vv. 1–5)

1   The year of King Uzziah's death is usually placed somewhere in the period 748–734 B.C.; 740–739 (Thiele) is the date most often accepted. The death of this great king brought an end to an era in the history of Judah. As mentioned earlier, Uzziah's reign had been one of prosperity and affluence not experienced since the days of Solomon; however, with it came the sins we have described. Although Judah was to experience three more good kings, Jotham, Hezekiah, and Josiah, the history of the nation during this period was one of decline; her days of glory were gone. This decline, conflict and ultimate captivity, the return of a remnant, and the coming of the Servant of Jehovah who would redeem the people from a greater bondage, constitute the themes of the prophet's message.

It was in the crucial year of King Uzziah's death that Jehovah revealed Himself in a vision to Isaiah. The prophet states, *I saw the Lord sitting upon a throne, high and lifted up; and his train filled the temple.* We are not told where the prophet was when he saw the vision; but it is easy to imagine him worshiping in the temple when the whole of the temple melted away and in its stead he found himself in heaven, the true temple of Jehovah, beholding the Lord of glory. Quoting from this chapter, John says, "These things said Isaiah, because he saw his glory; and he spake of him [Jesus]" (John 12:41), who is the "effulgence of his glory, and the very image of his substance" (Heb. 1:3). Apparently this is *the Lord* whom the prophet saw, "since no man hath seen God at any time" (John 1:18), nor, for that matter, can any man see Him (I Tim. 6:16). The majestic train or skirt, the glorious robe of His apparel, filled the temple, covering the total floor area about Him.

2 About the throne are the seraphim, who appear to be hovering above Him who is seated on the throne, their feet not touching the floor, which is covered by the train of His robe. The *seraphim* appear only here. The word (which is the plural form of "seraph") seems to indicate "fiery beings," a special class of angels not to be identified or confused with the cherubim of Ezekiel. They have wings, faces, feet, and voices with which they praise Him who sits on the throne—an indication that they are spiritual entities or personalities. Each seraph has six wings: two cover his feet, two are used to fly, and two cover his face because he is in the presence of the majestic Lord of the universe. The number of these glorious beings is not stated, but the context seems to indicate a host.

3 As each seraph cries, *Holy, holy, holy,* there seems to be a responsive cry from another. Because three is the number of divinity, the threefold recital of "holy" probably indicates the absolute holiness of Him who sits on the throne; He is absolutely separate from all sin or uncleanness. Contrary to pantheism, which holds that God is identical with the universe, Isaiah sees Him as separate from and above His creation (cf. Eph. 4:6). *The whole earth is full of his glory;* the whole creation reveals and expresses the glory of its Creator. See also Psalm 19.

4 As the seraph cried, the thunder of his voice caused the foundations of the thresholds on which the prophet stood to shake and tremble, *and the house was filled with smoke.* The source of the smoke is uncertain. Did it come from the song of the seraphim as they praised the Lord, from the altar of incense which is ever before the throne, or from the smoke of the Lord's wrath against sin (Ps. 18:8; II Sam. 22:9), wrath which was soon to be poured out upon the wicked? In a similar vision John saw the seven angels with the seven bowls of wrath about to be poured out upon a wicked world. Then "the temple was filled with smoke from the glory of God, and from his power; and none was able to enter into the temple, till the seven plagues of the seven angels should be finished" (Rev. 15:8). It seems likely, then, that the smoke should be identified with God's wrath, but the reader is left to make his own decision as to the source.

5   In the presence of such glory and absolute holiness, and possibly the smoke of God's holy wrath, the prophet becomes conscious of his own sinfulness and cries out, *Woe is me! for I am undone.* He is lost, ruined, doomed to die. In chapter 5 the prophet had pronounced six woes upon the wicked and ungodly world. This, the seventh woe, he pronounces upon himself, for in a world of sin "there is none righteous, no, not one" (Rom. 3:10, quoting Ps. 14:1). The prophet offers two reasons for his doom: *I am a man of unclean lips, and I dwell in the midst of people of unclean lips.* Having been brought face to face with the King, Jehovah of hosts, who is absolute in holiness, the prophet realized that even the purest person is unclean when measured by the divine standard. In addition, unintentionally, and possibly unconsciously, one becomes tainted with uncleanness when surrounded by the unclean; he invariably takes on some of the impurities of his environment.

The Consecration of the Prophet (vv. 6–7)

6   Upon this cry of the prophet, who recognized his own sinfulness in the presence of God, one of the seraphs separated himself from the rest. Taking a live coal or stone from the altar, he flew to the prophet, touching his lips with the coal. Whether the seraph took the coal from the altar with the tongs and then transferred it to his hand, or continued to hold it with the tongs, seems inconsequential. The altar is no doubt the altar of incense, not the altar of burnt-offering; for the former is the altar located before the throne (Exod. 30:1–10; Rev. 8:3).

7   Touching the mouth of the prophet with the coal, the seraph said, *Lo, this hath touched thy lips; and thine iniquity is taken away, and thy sin forgiven.* Sin and the guilt of sin must be removed—

blotted out—if one is to be an acceptable servant of the Lord (cf. David's words in Ps. 51:10, 14); and since all sin is ultimately against God (Ps. 51:4), only God can forgive it. It is not the hot coal or the seraph that forgives and abolishes sin; we have in the vision a symbolic picture of Isaiah's recognition and acknowledgment of his own sins and God's forgiveness of those sins. True, no sacrifice is indicated or referred to; but inasmuch as John recognized the Christ in this scene of divine glory (John 12:41), it is not beyond reason to conclude that it is through Him and His future sacrifice that Isaiah's sins were forgiven. The prophet was now ready to respond to the Lord's need of someone whom He could send and through whom He could reveal in future visions and revelations the Servant of Jehovah, through whom all forgiveness and redemption would be accomplished.

The Prophet's Commission from Jehovah (vv. 8–13)

8   Having been cleansed from his sin and having had his iniquity taken away, Isaiah is now in a position to hear and respond to the Lord's call. He hears the voice of the Lord, asking, *Whom shall I send, and who will go for us?* In the use of the plural "us," the Lord is probably referring to His court, not to the Trinity, though this is possible. The purpose of the vision was to prepare someone to be sent to the people. The prophet is ready with a willing and immediate response, *Here am I; send me.*

9   The prophet is now commissioned to go, with instruction to preach a message that *this people,* no longer "my people" (3:12; 5:13) or "his people" (5:25), will refuse to hear or heed. Though the people will hear the prophet's words, in their frame of mind they will neither understand nor perceive the truth and application of his message.

10   In preaching Isaiah will make the heart of this people fat, their ears heavy, and their eyes shut, *lest they see with their eyes, and hear with their ears, and understand with their heart, and turn again, and be healed.* The Lord is telling the prophet what will come to pass as a result of his preaching: his words, which should accomplish one end, will, in fact, result in another. What could and should produce repentance and salvation will end in total apostasy. To think that God is here decreeing that His word will be rejected independent of the

77

will of the people themselves is contrary to both the nature of God and His own statement. His invitation is, "Come now, and let us reason together." If the people hearken, their sins will be as snow and wool; if they are willing and obedient, they will eat the good of the land. But if they refuse to hear and rebel, they will be destroyed by the sword (1:18–20). The point of the Lord's word to the prophet is that the preaching is intended by the Lord to harden the people completely if they do not listen. The issue now rests with the people themselves. But from His knowledge of the people's history and His own divine insight, the Lord knows what the reaction will be. The hardening will be complete; and it will, in fact, be accomplished by preaching that is actually intended to save.

The question might be raised as to why the Lord, knowing that hardening would be the result, would preach to the people at all. Note that it is the nation, "this people," that will completely reject the message. But out of the nation God had said there will be left a remnant (1:9); the individuals who make up this remnant will hear. Jehovah never loses sight of the individuals who will hear His voice and do His will.

11–12 The prophet responds with a question, *Lord, how long?* Is Isaiah asking how long it will be until the nation is completely hardened, or how long he should continue to preach, seeing the people will not hearken? He probably is asking when the hardening will be complete. But whatever the exact meaning of the question may have been, the answer would be the same, for Isaiah is to continue preaching until the hardening is complete. Jehovah's answer is heartrending. The hardness of heart, dullness of ears, and blindness of eyes will lead to total destruction. Isaiah should continue preaching, then, *until cities be waste without inhabitant,* destroyed by invaders; until *houses be without man,* vacant, the people having been driven out of their homes; until *the land become utterly waste,* untilled and trampled under foot, no longer productive; until *Jehovah have removed men far away,* carrying them captive into a foreign land, far removed from their beloved homeland; and until *the forsaken places be many in the midst of the land*—a fulfillment of the predictions of Moses (Lev. 26; Deut. 28) and of the prophet himself (1:7–8).

13 Dark and bleak as the picture may be, the Lord allows a ray of light to break through the menacing storm clouds; there will be a remnant that will escape. Though a tenth, a small remnant, escape, even it in turn will be eaten up until those that remain will be but a remnant of the remnant. As a terebinth or oak tree is felled, with only the stump or stock remaining, *so the holy seed is the stock* (or substance, life) *thereof.* The thought is that out of the small remnant escaping will come a smaller remnant; even the whole remnant shall not endure. This smaller remnant, the stock or substance of the remnant, is what Paul had in view when he said, "Even so then at this present time also there is a remnant according to the election of grace" (Rom. 11:5; see also 9:27–28). This is the remnant of the remnant; the smallness of its number is also attested by Ezekiel's illustration of the few hairs bound in his skirts (see Ezek. 5:1–4).

CHAPTER 7

The Syro-Ephraimitic Uprising

Beginning with this chapter, we will be considering not only prophecies concerning coming oppressions, but also the "Immanuel consolations." These consolations, which occur throughout chapters 7–12, are a crucial part of the discourses centering on Jerusalem and Judah (chs. 1–12).

Five years before Uzziah's death (740 B.C.), Tiglath-pileser III, a general in the Assyrian army, seized the throne of that nation; he ruled from 745 to 727 B.C. Immediately making his bid for world domination, he thrust westward, striking terror in the hearts of the kings of Syria and Israel. In times past these two nations had warred against each other; but now, with a common enemy, they formed an alliance for protection against the approaching Assyrians. Apparently they sought to involve Jotham, and later Ahaz, in a coalition with them. Evidently Jotham refused, for they came up against him (II Kings 15:37); but nothing more is known of this effort.

The full force of the determination of King Rezin of Syria and King Pekah of Israel to make an alliance with Judah came in the days of Ahaz, who ruled from 735 to 715 B.C. (II Kings 16; II Chron. 28).

79

It is difficult to determine at just what point in Ahaz's reign the events of Isaiah 7 occurred, but apparently it was in the early period before his idolatrous practices had fully matured (II Kings 16:3–4), because Isaiah speaks to him of "Jehovah thy God" (v. 11).

The Syria-Israel Confederacy (vv. 1–2)

1–2 The prophet introduces this section with the simple statement that *it came to pass in the days of Ahaz* that Rezin the king of Syria and Pekah the son of Remaliah, king of Israel, *went up to Jerusalem to war against it; but could not prevail against it;* that is, they could not take the city. Next we read that Ahaz was informed that *Syria is confederate with Ephraim.* A literal translation of the Hebrew would be, "Syria rests upon Ephraim." Alternate translations have it that Syria "encamped with" Ephraim. In modern terminology we would say that Syria and Ephraim became "allies." When the faithless Judean King Ahaz became aware of the situation, he was greatly agitated. In the words of Isaiah, *his heart trembled, and the heart of his people, as the trees of the forest tremble with the wind.* Never would this have been said of David or Uzziah, men of faith in Jehovah, for the power of Syria and Ephraim could not compare to the power of the mighty God of Israel. Perfect love and trust cast out fear, but Ahaz and the people had neither.

Confrontation Between Belief and Unbelief (vv. 3–9)

3 To test the king, Jehovah sent Isaiah and his son Shear-jashub to meet him *at the end of the conduit of the upper pool, in the highway of the fuller's field.* The exact location of this conduit and pool is uncertain, but it is thought that the pool is what was known as the Upper Pool or the Pool of Shiloah (New Testament Siloam). Located below Zion in the southeast section of Jerusalem, it was slightly north of the Old Pool. *The conduit* probably refers to a watercourse that emptied into the pool or issued from it. *The fuller's field* was a hard-surfaced area where cloth was made clean and soft by kneading it or treading it in cold water. The lad's name meant "A remnant shall return"; that is, a remnant shall be spared by being converted and returning to Jehovah. The very presence of a boy with this name should have sent a signal to the king concerning Jehovah's intention. It should have caused him to heed Isaiah's message. Israel would be driven from their land, but even then a remnant would return to Jehovah. If Ahaz proved unfaithful, neither he nor the house of David would "be established" (v. 9), that is, continue to exist; judgment would come upon them. But even so, there would always be a remnant (1:9).

4   The prophet's attitude stands in stark contrast to that of the king: Isaiah displayed courageous faith, whereas Ahaz was filled with terror and trembling. The prophet's first word was a command from Jehovah: *And say unto him, Take heed* (be warned, look out, be careful) *and be quiet* (keep calm, be at rest, do not be hasty; look to the Lord and let Him lead); *fear not* (a command from Jehovah—a person with faith has nothing to fear), *neither let thy heart be faint* (weak, lacking in courage). Ahaz's faintheartedness was the consequence of fear, and his fear was the result of lack of faith in God. Jehovah refers to Rezin and Remaliah's son (Pekah, whom He disdains even to name), the cause of Ahaz's fear, as *two tails of smoking firebrands*. Their fierceness is burned out; they are like the ends of two burnt sticks or stumps, smoking after the fire, with their power gone. They are nothing to be afraid of.

5–6   Rezin and Pekah had purposed evil against Ahaz. They intended to provoke, disturb, and arouse Judah to anger, to make a breach in the city, remove Ahaz, and set up their own king, the son of Tabeel, apparently a Syrian, though Young offers evidence from Albright that he may have been a son of Uzziah (I. 16, n. 45).

7   However, Rezin and Pekah (like Ahaz) had not reckoned with Jehovah, who now says concerning the evil scheme, *It shall not stand, neither shall it come to pass*. Jehovah would thwart their plan to overthrow Ahaz, for he represented the lineage of David. Ahaz should have accepted God at His word.

8–9   Jehovah further declares, *For the head of Syria is Damascus*, that is, Syria is all that Damascus will rule; *and the head of Damascus is Rezin*, that is, his headship shall not extend beyond Syria. Within sixty-five years *shall Ephraim be broken in pieces, so that it shall not be a people*. This prophecy looked not only to the fall of Samaria and

81

the Assyrian captivity which occurred a few years later (721 B.C.), but beyond. It looked to the time when Ephraim *shall not be a people*. This was fulfilled after the captivity, when the king of Assyria brought foreigners into the land (II Kings 17:24). This king was Esar-haddon (Ezra 4:2), who ruled Assyria from 681 to 668 B.C. When these colonists were brought in and intermarried with the remnant, Ephraim came to an end. The sixty-five years extended from the days of Ahaz to some point during the reign of Esar-haddon.

Jehovah now says the same thing about Ephraim and Remaliah's son (Pekah) that He said about Syria and Rezin: *The head of Ephraim is Samaria*, that is, Ephraim is to be the extent of Samaria's headship; *and the head of Samaria is Remaliah's son*—that shall be the extent of his rule. Neither Damascus nor Samaria shall be the head of Judah or Jerusalem; for God is Jerusalem's head, and Ahaz rules it for the Lord. This word from Jehovah should have assured the king, but he was in no mood to listen. In a final word God says, *If ye will not believe, surely ye shall not be established*. Basically, to believe is to be assured, to hold a firm conviction regarding a matter; to *be established* (the Hebrew word comes from the same root) is to be made firm. Without faith Ahaz has no stability. The continued existence of Ahaz and his court—the house of David and its rule—is conditional on faith. If Judah's king would not believe, then he would not be established. Faith in Jehovah was requisite to the nation's continued existence.

Several points in this confrontation merit our attention. First, the policy of quiet confidence advocated by Isaiah. *Take heed, and be quiet; fear not*, is instruction to Ahaz to be of a tranquil spirit which rests in Jehovah, and to adopt a policy of trustful waiting on Jehovah to provide deliverance. The prophet continued to advocate quiet trust in God throughout the entire period of Judah's conflict with Assyria. Second, God assured Ahaz that within sixty-five years, about the lifetime of a man, Ephraim would be broken and destroyed as a nation. This should have warned the king against an alliance with Assyria, for Pekah's alliance with a foreign power (Rezin) would end in the total destruction of Ephraim. Third, Ahaz had to exhibit faith if Jehovah was to establish the king and give deliverance to the people. Ahaz should have realized that, in spite of all odds against the believer, a quiet, fearless faith in Jehovah gives the victory, for it puts one on God's side.

The Sign of Immanuel (vv. 10–17)

10–11 To assure Ahaz that he had nothing to fear from the two kings, Jehovah spoke through the prophet, saying, *Ask thee a sign of Jehovah thy God; ask it either in the depth, or in the height above.* A sign may be either miraculous or natural; in this instance it probably would be supernatural. The extent of God's offer is unlimited: whatever Ahaz might ask as a sign that God would carry out His purpose and that Ephraim would no longer be a foe—be it an earthquake or lightning, be it something in the sea or in the stellar spaces of the heavens, be it something sensational or something simple—God would give it.

12 But the faithless king refused, saying, *I will not ask, neither will I tempt Jehovah.* Ahaz did not want a sign because he did not want to believe; his mind was already made up. Either he had already appealed to Tiglath-pileser for help or he was planning to appeal to him shortly. In either case he was rejecting Jehovah. His reply was hypocritical and unbelieving. He feigned respect for Jehovah's word, "Ye shall not tempt Jehovah your God" (Deut. 6:16), but at the same time he rejected Him and His offer. One is not tempting God when one does what God commands or directs.

13 This expression of unbelief called forth an indignant retort from the prophet: *Hear ye now, O house of David: Is it a small thing for you to weary men, that ye will weary my God also?* The king represented the whole house of David, and through the house of David the entire nation of Judah was involved. When Ahaz refused to ask for a sign, thereby rejecting Jehovah, he involved not only himself and those ruling with him, but also the destiny of those who would follow him on the throne. The matter is now taken out of the hand of Ahaz, for the prophet addresses not the unbelieving king, but the house of David. The sign would now be given to the house of David and through it to the nation. Ahaz not only wearied men and the prophet, but he also grieved and offended Jehovah. It is worthy of note that in verse 11 the prophet says, *thy God,* and in verse 13, *my*

God, indicating that Isaiah could no longer speak of Jehovah as Ahaz's God, for the king had rejected Him.

14 *Therefore the Lord himself will give you a sign: behold, a virgin shall conceive, and bear a son, and shall call his name Immanuel.* *Therefore,* in view of the king's rejection of Jehovah's offer, *the Lord,* the master of all forces and power whom Isaiah had seen at his call, "high and lifted up" (6:1), *will give you* (plural, the house of David, and through it the nation) *a sign.* The word *behold* rouses attention. The prophet is going to announce an unusual birth of a special child who will be the sign to the house of David and of Israel. Controversy has long existed over the term *virgin—a* ("the," Hebrew) *virgin shall conceive.* The Revised Standard Version translates the Hebrew as "a young woman" and places "virgin" in the margin; even if both translations are allowable, "virgin" should be the reading in the text proper. The word in the Hebrew is *almah.* It occurs six times in addition to the passage before us, and in each instance refers to an unmarried, chaste maiden. In Genesis 24:43 Rebekah is called a "maiden" *(almah);* in Genesis 24:16 she is called "a virgin" *(bethulah),* whom no man had known. In Exodus 2:8 Miriam, as she watched over her brother, is called "the maiden" *(almah).* She must have been quite young at the time, although her age is nowhere stated. In Psalm 68:25 we are told of "damsels" who played timbrels in the sanctuary; they would certainly have been of chaste character. The word occurs twice in the Song of Solomon; it refers to a chorus of young women (1:3) and to a group distinguished from Solomon's "queens" and "concubines" (6:8). In Proverbs 30:19 it refers to a maiden in contrast to an adulterous woman (v. 20). In each case it appears that the word is used to indicate a virgin of marriageable or premarriageable age, a young woman who was neither married nor had known a man. Additional evidence that the emphasis in Isaiah is on a special unmarried chaste maiden is the use of the definite article in both the Hebrew and Septuagint texts—*the* virgin. Despite the attempt to prove otherwise, the word seems never to be used of a married woman or of an immoral woman.

Much has been written on the identity of this virgin or young woman and the son born to her. (1) In Justin Martyr's (A.D. 100–165) *Dialogue with Trypho,* Trypho, a Jew, contends that she is only a "young woman" who gave birth to Hezekiah.[3] (2) In his commentary, Clements expresses the belief that she is Isaiah's wife, and that the child is his own (pp. 86, 88). (3) Willis thinks she is a young pregnant wife known to Ahaz and his court (pp. 160–61). Other views maintain that (4) she symbolizes a number of young women of that day; (5) she is a particular virgin or young woman known to Isaiah and Ahaz; (6) she is "a symbol of the Jewish community of Isaiah's day, about to give birth to the next generation" (quoted from Willis, p. 160). It appears certain that *a sign* so momentous that only Jehovah could give it must have involved far more than any of these explanations. Furthermore, there is no evidence for any of them, and they contradict Matthew and Luke, who taught otherwise.

A second question concerns the son and his identity; none of the understandings of the virgin which we have just mentioned offers a satisfactory answer. Correlate passages in the Old Testament give strong support to the position that the prophet is speaking of a virgin who will conceive miraculously and give birth to an exceptional child (the sign). Immediately after the first sin, God promised that the seed of the woman would bruise Satan's head (Gen. 3:15). Jehovah assured David, "When . . . thou shalt sleep with thy fathers, I will set up thy seed after thee . . . and I will establish the throne of his kingdom for ever. I will be his father, and he shall be my son" (II Sam. 7:12–14). It is clear that the prophecy addressed to David had an immediate fulfillment in Solomon (I Chron. 28:6–7); but it is equally clear that it had a more far-reaching application in Christ, God's Son whom He would set upon His throne (Ps. 2:6; Heb. 1:5). If the seed of David were to be God's Son in an extraordinary manner or sense, it would require a special means of entrance into the world. Micah, Isaiah's contemporary, said of the Ruler to come: "[His] goings forth are from of old, from everlasting" (Mic. 5:2), thus identifying Him as preexistent to His earthly birth. Isaiah calls the Child who is to come *a son given*; His name will be called *Mighty God* (9:6). Thus Isaiah identifies Immanuel with the Deity. For someone who is kin equally to man and God—a human-divine being—to dwell among us would

---

3. Justin Martyr, *Dialogue with Trypho* 67, in *Ante-Nicene Fathers* (New York: Scribner, 1903), vol. 1, p. 231.

necessitate a miraculous entrance into the world. So, "virgin" is the correct rendering of the word *almah*, and the Messiah is the Son who fulfilled the promise. If the prophet were speaking of the birth of an ordinary child, it would not be a sign.

And (the virgin) *shall call his name Immanuel*, which means "God with us," a further indication that the Son will be a special divine being. Twice more the prophet uses the wonderful name (8:8, 10). When Jehovah reveals to Isaiah that the Assyrians will overrun Israel as a mighty river overflows its bounds, inundating and devastating the land and reaching even unto the head, He addresses Immanuel (8:5–8). And when the prophet taunts the nations to make an uproar, to gird themselves and take counsel together, only to be broken in pieces and destroyed, he again cries out, *Immanuel*—"God is with us" (8:9–10). The prophet looks to Him who is to come as though He were already on earth.

Delitzsch translates the passage, "The virgin conceives, and bears a son, and [the virgin] calls his name Immanuel," indicating that the virgin names the child. Young is equally specific: "and she shall call his name Immanuel." In the Old Testament there are records of fathers naming their sons. Could the naming of the Son by the virgin indicate that He had no earthly father, and that only she could know with certainty that He was divinely begotten? The thought is intriguing, though not expressed.

A brief review of the prophet's overall plan will help us understand what he is saying at this point. He has already introduced God's ideal Jerusalem, spiritual Zion (2:2–4). In his description of the cleansing and purifying through which Jerusalem will be redeemed (4:2–6), he introduced "the branch of Jehovah," who will be beautiful and glorious (4:2). Isaiah has also said that a remnant will be called holy (v. 3). Further, this remnant will be of the stock of Israel (6:13). In chapter 7 the revelation of God's purpose advances a step to the announcement of the coming of the Branch of Jehovah to accomplish His work.

In future prophecies Isaiah will present the Ruler as "Mighty God, Everlasting Father, Prince of Peace." The government of God's kingdom will rest on His shoulder (9:6–7). This one to come will be the Branch of Jesse (hence a descendant of David), and on Him the Spirit

86

of Jehovah will rest. As the Branch of Jehovah (4:2) and Branch of Jesse (11:1), He will be both God and man—the rallying point of both Jews and Gentiles (ch. 11). Further, He will be the Servant of Jehovah, God's spiritually chosen one, a light to the Gentiles, and a covenant (a personal bond) between Jehovah and His people (49:1–13). As Jehovah's Suffering Servant, He will be exalted as the Redeemer of mankind (52:13–53:12).

As this point, then, Isaiah introduces this special one as *God with us*. Bringing into the world someone who is both God and man necessitates a special means of entrance. How this can be done is solved by a miraculous conception in the womb of a woman, in this case a virgin. The miraculous conception and birth are clearly set forth in the Gospels of Matthew and Luke, where the Son of the virgin is identified as the Messiah. In Luke's account, an angel appears to Mary, a virgin, telling her what will come to pass; in Matthew's account an angel appears to Joseph, who will be the foster father of the Immanuel of Isaiah's prophecy. In the evangelists' accounts of the birth of Jesus, and especially in Matthew's appeal (1:23) to Isaiah's prophecy, there is evidence that in Isaiah 7:14 we have a prophecy of Christ.

Some theologians of the liberal school have endeavored to dismiss the doctrine of the virgin birth as a myth of Jewish origin. This effort has been thoroughly refuted by J. Gresham Machen in his excellent book *The Virgin Birth of Christ*. [4] Opponents of the conservative view must produce some evidence that the idea of a virgin birth evolved among the Jewish traditions. To this date, no such evidence has been produced. It seems clear that the Jews themselves did not look upon Isaiah 7:14 as grounds to expect that the Messiah would be virgin-born.

To briefly summarize Machen's argument: The Jewish concept of the transcendence of God, which is found in the Old Testament and in their traditions, precluded the idea of God's producing a Son through a woman. The New Testament narratives preserve this lofty concept of God's transcendence as they inform us that Jesus was

---

4. J. Gresham Machen, *The Virgin Birth of Christ* (New York: Harper and Brothers, 1930), pp. 280–316.

conceived by the creative, life-giving power of the Holy Spirit, power which overshadowed the virgin. The crass heathen idea of gods cohabiting with human persons is nowhere to be found. Indeed, such an idea is repugnant to both the Jewish and Christian concept of God. The Jewish expectation that the Messiah would be of the house of David did not involve a virgin birth. They looked for a Messiah from the fleshly lineage of David, but there is no evidence that they expected anything other than natural procreation by two fleshly parents.

The only passage in the Old Covenant on which such an idea could have rested is the one under consideration. The only other text to which appeal might be made is Psalm 2:7: "Thou art my son;/This day have I begotten thee." But this does not refer to the Son's physical birth, but to His entering into His rule by resurrection from the dead (cf. Acts 13:33). It seems that there is no evidence that the virgin birth was a Jewish idea.

What, then, is the source of the doctrine of the virgin birth? The source is the New Testament accounts of one miraculously conceived in the womb of a virgin, conceived by the Holy Spirit in fulfillment of an inspired prophecy which was not (and could not have been) understood until it was fulfilled. Young has well summarized the orthodox position on Isaiah 7:14 and what it has to say concerning Christ's coming: (1) His birth would be in the form of a wondrous sign; (2) the mother would be a chaste virgin; (3) the very presence of the Child would bring God to His people; (4) the prophecy can be correctly interpreted only in the light of Jesus' birth. All those who hold to the divine inspiration of Scripture acknowledge this: the Messiah to come was to be born through a miraculous conception in the womb of a virgin, thus coming into the world as the Son of God and the Son of man. Only the birth of Jesus fulfills this prediction.

15–16 Now comes one of the most perplexing problems faced by commentators on the Book of Isaiah—the problem of how the promise of a sign applied to the immediate situation. There can be no question that the Messiah is the Son who would be brought forth, for Matthew, an apostle selected by the Lord and inspired by the Holy Spirit, so interpreted the passage (Matt. 1:22–23). Another obvious point is that the sign is not given to Ahaz, for he had been given an opportunity to receive a sign and had rejected it. The sign is promised to the house of David (v. 13). Furthermore, it is evident that verses 15 and 16 apply to the Son promised in verse 14, but with what significance? Before we attempt an explanation, let us consider the verses themselves.

Butter, more properly, "curds" (margin) or solidified milk, *and honey shall he eat, when he knoweth to refuse the evil and choose the good.* Having rejected Jehovah, the house of David and of Israel will experience evil days, not good. The child's food will not be royal food (as thought by some commentators) or the food of plenty and prosperity (as thought by others) but of scarcity (cf. vv. 21–22). His childhood, the interval from infancy to the age when he can make a choice of the good over evil, is a brief period, a short measure of time before *the land whose two kings thou* (Ahaz) *abhorrest shall be forsaken.* The kingdoms of Syria and Ephraim, fearing which the faithless king had rejected Jehovah, shall soon come to nought; for already the fire of their raging is burned out.

17   The prophet continues to address Ahaz. Since the king had rejected Jehovah and would appeal to Assyria, Jehovah would give him Assyria. He had feared the devastation of Pekah and Rezin, but their invasion is not to be compared to that of the king of Assyria. *Jehovah will bring upon thee* (Ahaz), *and upon thy people,* the people who followed him in unbelief, *and upon thy father's house,* the ruling house of David, days such as had not been known since *Ephraim departed from Judah.* The tragic separation of Ephraim (and the nine other northern tribes) from Judah and Benjamin had dealt a fatal blow to the united kingdom. Assyria would now strike an additional blow against Judah and the fleshly house of David, which would eventually result in final destruction by the Babylonians a century later.

At this point we return to the promise of Immanuel. Because of his unbelief the king cannot be established (v. 9). To Ahaz Jehovah will give the king of Assyria, who will bring upon the people and house of David days such as they have not previously experienced. What, then, will happen to the purpose and promises of God concerning the seed of David, God's Son, who is to rule upon the throne of David (II Sam. 7:11–16) and Jehovah (Ps. 2:6)?

To think, as several conservative scholars do, that Isaiah saw in vision the coming of Immanuel is not without foundation. The prophet began with the words: *The vision of Isaiah the son of Amoz, which he saw concerning Judah and Jerusalem in the days. . . of Ahaz . . ."* (1:1). He then spoke *the word* that he *saw concerning Judah and Jerusalem* (2:1). The apostle John comments: "These things said Isaiah, because he saw his [Christ's] glory; and he spake of him" (John 12:41); and Paul says, "Well spake the Holy Spirit through Isaiah the prophet unto your fathers" (Acts 28:25). We conclude that in vision the prophet saw what was coming to the nation and beyond that the glory of the Messiah; he saw the word of God and spoke by the Holy Spirit. He saw and spoke by divine revelation. Fully aware of the trying days to come at the hands of Assyria and Babylon, when the house of David as a political entity would be brought to nought, the prophet made known that the promise and hope would be preserved in Immanuel the Branch, the Servant who would be born of a virgin.

The Devastation from Assyria (vv. 18–25)

18   The remainder of chapter 7 is devoted to a description of the devastation of the land by the Assyrians, that which Jehovah will bring upon Ahaz. The introductory words, *And it shall come to pass in that day,* refer to the day of the Assyrian invasion, which was mentioned in verse 17. The *fly* or poisonous insect of Egypt, possibly the tsetse fly, and the *bee,* the stinging bee of Assyria, refer to the armies of the two nations. Rawlinson observes that the figures are well taken, for the armies of Egypt were numerous as swarms of flies, but not as well disciplined as those of Assyria, whose armies were well trained and ever ready for war. The *rivers of Egypt* is a reference to the Nile and its numerous canals. The *fly* and the *bee* would both come at the bidding of Jehovah.

19   These armies will fill the desolate or waste valleys, take refuge in the clefts of the rocks, rest upon the hedges, and trample the pastures. In the decades to come these two forces, and later Chaldea, will use the occupied land of Judah as a staging ground, and it will

often be a battleground as well. Some of the invasions and battles will be discussed in the chapters to follow.

20   The phrase *in that day,* as in verse 18, looks back to verse 17, the day of Assyria's invasion. The Euphrates was *the River* from beyond which the Assyrian army would come. As Ahaz had sought to hire by tribute the king of Assyria to shave clean the land of Israel and Syria, so Jehovah would use the Assyrian to shave Judah. Judah is here likened to a man stripped of his garments, ready to be shaved from his feet to his head. To be thus humiliated would be a shame to any man, and so it would be to the land of Judah, which would be completely denuded of its people and its wealth.

21–22   The same period of time is again indicated by the use of *in that day.* The coming of the Assyrians will so devastate the land that a man will be fortunate to have even a young cow or two sheep. And as has already been indicated (v. 15), butter and honey will be the individual's only food, since the fields and vineyards will have been devastated and the land turned to pasture. The animals will supply an abundance of milk, and the flowers will provide nectar for the bees. The prophet is not referring to a land "flowing with milk and honey," so often spoke of in earlier days, but to the desolation which was brought on that same good land by the unbelief and sins of Ahaz and the people.

23–25   For the fourth time the prophet introduces his thought with the phrase *in that day,* thereby relating his four prophecies back to verse 17 and the coming of the king of Assyria. Further desolation is described: In place of the beautiful vineyards, so prized by their owners, there will be briers and thorns; men will come there to hunt, a return to the primitive life of former years, because the land will be fit only for wild animals and the more venturesome domesticated ones. Where the people formerly had no fear of walking in the well-terraced vineyards and fields, they will fear the thorns and briers. Oxen and sheep might venture there, but not men. The total picture is one of desolation and ruin brought on by the nation's unbelief and rejection of Jehovah and His way. Ahaz could have averted this ruin had he but looked to Jehovah, the God of Israel. Let it be clearly noted that the judgment is from Jehovah; it is He who will hiss for the fly and bee to come.

CHAPTER 8
Assyria: The Overwhelming Flood

In chapter 7, the prophet and his son Shear-jashub ("a remnant shall return") had met Ahaz and appealed to him not to fear the Israel-Syria alliance. He refused to listen to the prophet; therefore a sign, Immanuel ("God with us"), was given to the house of David, and the king of Assyria would be given to Ahaz. In this chapter the prophet turns to the people, giving them a word of warning accompanied by a sign, Maher-shalal-hash-baz; but, like Ahaz, they refuse to listen. The prophet then tells them of the Assyrian flood about to come upon them. He builds his hope of the remnant on the few faithful disciples gathered about him. The prophet earlier looked from the political house of David to the Immanuel to come; now he looks from the decadent nation to the few faithful individuals. It is in these, Immanuel and the faithful few, that God will eventually accomplish His purpose. In Immanuel darkness will be transformed to light (9:1–7).

The Sign: Maher-shalal-hash-baz (vv. 1–4)

1 Jehovah instructed the prophet to take a great tablet (it is not revealed whether it was of wood, stone, or animal skin) and to write upon it *with the pen of a man*, that is, in simple letters which could be read by the common people. Apparently the tablet was to be set up in a prominent place where it could be seen by all. On the tablet was to be written, *For Maher-shalal-hash-baz*, which means "the spoil speedeth, the prey hasteth." No explanation was made to the people; they were left to determine the meaning of the message for themselves.

2 Jehovah continues to speak: *I will take unto me faithful witnesses to record*, that is, to testify that Isaiah had written this prophecy long before it was fulfilled. *Uriah the priest* is probably the priest who built a replica of the Damascene altar for Ahaz (II Kings 16:10–13), but Zechariah is unknown. As a friend or ally of Ahaz, rather than of Isaiah, Uriah's testimony would carry all the more weight.

3 The prophet *went unto the prophetess; and she conceived, and*

bare a son. The woman was Isaiah's wife. She is called a prophetess because of her relationship to Isaiah; there is no indication that she herself prophesied, although this is entirely possible. To the son was given the name *Maher-shalal-hash-baz,* so that in addition to the great tablet bearing these words, there was a living sign or witness that *the spoil speedeth, the prey hasteth* (margin).

4   The imminence of this impending calamity is declared by the prophet: *For before the child shall have knowledge to cry, My father, and, My mother, the riches of Damascus and the spoil of Samaria shall be carried away before the king of Assyria.* This reference to the child's age at the time of the calamity limits the intervening period to two or three years. At some time during the reign of Pekah, son of Remaliah, Tiglath-pileser carried the people of northern Israel into captivity (II Kings 15:29). After dispensing with Pekah, the Assyrian monarch besieged Damascus, taking it in 732 B.C. and carrying away large quantities of booty. Truly, when this prophecy was uttered, "the spoil was speeding, the prey hastening," for the booty of Israel and Syria was soon to be carried away to Assyria. Thus, just as Jehovah had given Ahaz personal assurance that Assyria would be upon Israel and Syria within a short period (ch. 7), so He also gave the people a sign to the same effect—Maher-shalal-hash-baz. As one can sense, these were momentous times!

The Overwhelming Flood: Assyria (vv. 5–8)

5–6   There was no reason to rejoice or to relax, for Ahaz's effort to court the favor of Assyria would fail. Instead of saving the land, Ahaz's move would bring only further ruin and misery to the people. Now a direct word from Jehovah to the prophet tells the people what to expect. Two reasons are given for the overflowing judgment to come: First, *this people* (Judah) *have refused the waters of Shiloah that go softly, and,* second, they *rejoice in Rezin and Remaliah's son. The waters of Shiloah* refers either to the place where Isaiah met Ahaz (7:3), or to a small stream that issued from beneath the temple area and flowed south into the southeastern section of the city. The expression cannot refer to the conduit of Hezekiah which connected the Gihon Spring with the Pool of Shiloah, for that had not yet been tunneled. This stream, ever so clear and pure, representing Jehovah's presence, purity, and power, did not compare in size with the great river Euphrates; hence, the people disdained it. It is of course true that the waters of Shiloah and the nation of Judah seemed insignificant when compared to the Euphrates and Assyria, but Jehovah's presence and concern for His land made all the difference in the world. The phrase *rejoice in Rezin and Remaliah's son* probably refers to the people's rejoicing over the spoil made of these two by Assyria. That jubilance would be short-lived, for the very power that had overrun Israel and Syria would soon overflow Judah.

7   The Lord is the one whom the people should fear and respect, for upon the land He will bring the king of Assyria and all the glory of his great army like a mighty raging river that overflows its banks and inundates the lands about it.

8   *It shall sweep onward into Judah; it shall overflow and pass through; it shall reach even to the neck*—that is, the Assyrian flood shall reach even unto Jerusalem, but shall not engulf it. The prophet envisions the river overflowing its banks and covering the land just as a great bird of prey in swooping down completely overshadows the land with its outstretched wings. But the land inundated by the surging waves is Immanuel's land—*thy land, O Immanuel*. It is the land in which the virgin's Son will be born (Mic. 5:2), the land in which He will appear as light, making it glorious "in the latter time" (Isa. 9:1–2). The head that extends above the neck and thus escapes the flood is Jerusalem-Zion, to which Immanuel will come as the great Redeemer (59:20). Thus, neither the land nor the city will be completely destroyed, for the God who has promised the birth of Immanuel (7:14) will preserve the land in which He will be born and the Zion to which He will come. Assyria and all the military powers to follow it cannot thwart Jehovah's purpose.

Only Jehovah Shall Be Your Fear (vv. 9–15)

9–10   With confidence and assurance that God is with him and His faithful few and that Immanuel will come, the prophet cries out with a taunting challenge to the heathen nations, the enemies of God's land and people: *Make an uproar, O ye peoples, and be broken in pieces; and give ear, all ye of far countries: gird yourselves and be broken in pieces.* All the nations of the world who oppose Jehovah are here brought together as one group (those nations in view in v. 7 and all others of the same spirit), and their destiny is clearly announced: they shall be broken in pieces; their uproar shall die out like the echo of an empty boast. They shall take counsel together, but it shall be brought to nought. They will speak their word, plotting the fall and destruction of God's land; but *it* (their word) *shall not stand: for God is with us.* In this instance "Immanuel" is not a personal name but simply a declaration of the source of victory for God's people and the source of the defeat of the heathen plans. Judah shall prevail, *for God is with us.* There is no question but that He who is ever the deliverer and power of God's people, the Divine Presence of 7:14 and 8:8, is in view here.

11   Isaiah now says that Jehovah spoke to him *with a strong hand,* or "with strength of hand" (Hebrew). The message was one of restraint, instruction, and assurance. God *instructed* Isaiah *not to walk in the way of this people,* thus restraining him from being influenced either by their actions or by their charges against him.

12   Jehovah's instruction was, *Say ye not, A conspiracy, concerning all whereof this people shall say, A conspiracy; neither fear ye their fear, nor be in dread thereof.* Isaiah's opposition to alliance with Assyria would be considered by the people as treason against Ahaz, a conspiracy to thwart his purposes as king. But Isaiah was to fear neither the people's unjust accusations nor that which they feared. Isaiah was not in opposition to the king, but he was against the king's unbelief and infidelity, which were leading the nation to destruction. Further, he was not speaking for himself, but for Jehovah; God had given him the words to speak. The charge that the prophet was guilty of conspiracy or treason was false; he was not to be afraid of it. Nor was he to fear what the people feared, for it would come to nought.

13   Instead of being afraid to take a position opposite to that of the populace and those in authority, thus risking a charge of treason, Isaiah is exhorted to recognize the holiness of the Lord: *Jehovah of hosts, him shall ye sanctify* (set apart as holy); *and let him be your fear, and let him be your dread.* Here is the word of assurance. Jehovah had long ago established fear of and respect for Himself as an inviolable

principle for His people. Through Moses He had said, "Thou shalt fear Jehovah thy God; and him shalt thou serve" (Deut. 6:13—note that in Matt. 4:10 Jesus quotes this text). If Jehovah is held in the reverential awe to which He is entitled one need fear no other. Unfortunately, this principle has too often been ignored. Young has well said, "Throughout the history of the church, those who have sought to call the church back to her God-given mission and away from her man-made 'programs' have been treated as troublemakers" (I. 310).

14–15 As the *fear* and *dread* of the faithful, Jehovah *shall be for a sanctuary,* a refuge (cf. 4:6), even as the prophet Nahum said later, "Jehovah is good, a stronghold in the day of trouble; and he knoweth them that take refuge in him" (Nah. 1:7). But for the unbelievers who reject Him and His word, He shall be *for a stone of stumbling and for a rock of offence to both the houses of Israel,* both Ephraim and Judah, and *for a gin and for a snare to the inhabitants of Jerusalem.* Israel and Judah are here thought of as one, for had it not been for sin they would be one. Instead of being a refuge or place of safety, Jehovah will be to them a stumbling block on which they fall and are broken in pieces (cf. I Peter 2:8). He will be to Jerusalem a gin or snare in which unbelievers will be caught like a bird and consumed. Consider the consequences of rejecting this sanctuary! The prophet lists five: *And* (1) *many shall stumble thereon, and* (2) *fall, and* (3) *be broken, and* (4) *be snared, and* (5) *be taken.* An inevitable total destruction awaits the people who follow their own human delusions to the rejection of divine truth.

Bind Up the Testimony (vv. 16–18)

16–17 The preaching and exhortation of the prophet had fallen on deaf ears; it was ignored. Therefore, the command follows, *Bind thou up the testimony, seal the law* (teaching) *among my disciples.* Who is the speaker? Three interpretations have been offered:

1. In verse 16 God is addressing the prophet; in verse 17 the Messiah is the speaker. This position is strengthened by the quoting of verse 18 in Hebrews 2:13, where the words are put in the mouth of the Messiah. Young very cautiously inclines to this view.
2. In verse 16 God is the speaker, commanding that for a time Isaiah cease his prophetic activity; then in verse 17 the prophet responds. Leupold, Alexander, and Rawlinson hold this view.
3. The prophet speaks, instructing his disciples to bind and seal up the testimony for some future time; in verse 18 he speaks of himself and his family as signs. Delitzsch, Erdman, and Barnes hold this view of the passage.

Since there are divergent views, it would be exceedingly unwise to be dogmatic. It seems that the prophet is speaking or, rather, Jehovah is speaking through him, instructing those taught by the prophet—his disciples—either to bind the teaching of this chapter in a roll and lay it aside, or to bind it in their hearts. The prophet then says, *I will wait for Jehovah, that hideth his face from the house of Jacob, and I will look for him.* With his message rejected by the house of Jacob, he will now wait for Jehovah, looking for Him to act in His own time. With judgment already under way, it might be a long time before Jacob's glory is revealed.

18   The prophet seems to be speaking to his disciples as he continues, *Behold, I and the children whom Jehovah hath given me are for signs and for wonders in Israel from Jehovah of hosts, who dwelleth in Mount Zion.* A sign need not necessarily be a miracle. The names given to Isaiah and his sons were signs or pledges of Jehovah regarding something to be accomplished by Him in the future. Isaiah's name ("Jehovah saves" or "Salvation is of Jehovah") pointed to the fact that the people must look to Jehovah for salvation. The name of the elder son, Shear-jashub, signified that a remnant would return to Jehovah even then, and that at some future time a remnant would turn to Him and become His people. And the name of the second son, Maher-shalal-hash-baz, pointed to the defeat and captivity of Israel and Syria by the Assyrians. These names were a sign and a wonder—an assurance from Jehovah that He would act and produce wonder and

97

awe in the eyes of the beholders when that which the names signified was fulfilled. These signs were from Jehovah of hosts, *who dwelleth in Mount Zion.* As surely as Jehovah had chosen Zion to be His dwelling place among His people, He would just as surely carry out His purpose. Immanuel (the coming Messiah) would ultimately fulfill God's purpose, which always seems to be on Isaiah's mind.

To the Law and to the Testimony (vv. 19–22)

19   Isaiah mentioned earlier that the people had turned to idolatrous worship and strange practices (1:21; 2:6, 20; 3:2–3). He now asks his disciples not to yield when unbelievers attempt to persuade the faithful to seek knowledge from those who have familiar spirits— persons who claim that the dead speak through them—and from wizards. The prophet warns that no clear message can come from those who merely *chirp and mutter.* Finally he thrusts a sword to the heart of the matter: *Should not a people seek unto their God? on behalf of the living should they seek unto the dead?*

20   Let the people return to God! If they would be instructed, then let them hear Jehovah the loving God: *To the law and to the testimony!* This should be the watchword of the faithful. Here, not among the dead, is where men shall find the truth and direction for the living; here they shall find light even in the hours of national calamity. *If they speak not according to this word*—the word of the law and the testimony, divine revelation and instruction—*surely there is no morning for them.* There will be no dawning light, but only stygian darkness and despair, void of all hope, for those who reject God's truth. What a tragedy, when it could have been otherwise! This principle has not changed; it is operative now as then.

21   When the Assyrian invasion comes, the people, having rejected God and His word, *shall pass through it, sore distressed and hungry,* stumbling blindly along. There shall be no food for them and their children; the ravages of war will be evident on every hand. *They shall fret themselves, and curse by their king and by their God, and turn their faces upward.* The reading of the margin is preferable, "They shall curse their king and their God." They will work themselves into such a rage that they will lose all sense of what is right.

Eager to blame someone other than themselves for their condition, they will curse their king for his failure, and they will even curse God. Thus, when they look upward, they will find a great empty void instead of help.

22 Ah, the terror of the day! after peering into the empty heavens the people look to the earth; but, *behold, distress and darkness, the gloom of anguish; and into thick darkness they shall be driven away.* This is the bleak and dark picture of a people who, having forsaken their God, reap the wages of sin. Every planting brings its own harvest and every harvest is the reaping of a planting. Creatures endowed with the gift of freedom persist in evil to their own ruin. Truly the wages of sin is death.

CHAPTER 9
The Dawning Light

Dark days followed the prophecies spoken to Ahaz (ch. 7) and to the people (ch. 8), the days when the king of Assyria devastated the land. The invasion of Tiglath-pileser (734–732 B.C.) brought distress and hunger, darkness, and the gloom of anguish. But judgment does not always bring repentance or effect conversion; more often it only hardens (see 8:19–22). The darkness the people experienced consisted not only of the hopelessness of their physical condition, but also of the darkness of sin and ignorance, for they had rejected Jehovah and were serving gods of wood and of stone. This darkness was far worse than that of material loss or economic uncertainty; it had come upon Israel just as Isaiah later said it would come upon the nations: "For, behold, darkness shall cover the earth, and gross darkness the peoples" (60:2). Sin was the cause of their bitter lot.

Light Shines in the Darkness (vv. 1–3)

1–2 It would not always be this way, however. For though gloom and anguish, distress, and thick darkness would fill the land of Zebulun and Naphtali, these trials would eventually be done away with. These two northern tribes were the first to bear the brunt of Assyria's cruel invasion and destruction. Located as they were in the territory later known as "upper" and "lower" Galilee, they would also be the first to see a great light break forth to dispel the long night of bitter prostration: *But there shall be no gloom to her that was in anguish.* The prophet projects himself into the future—beyond the time when the Assyrian inflicted distress and darkness, and into the period when the shame of the vanished tribes would be taken away. *In the former time he brought into contempt the land of Zebulun and the land of Naphtali; but in the latter time hath he made it glorious, by the way of the sea, beyond the Jordan, Galilee of the nations.* From the vantage point of the future, the prophet views his own present as long past. He uses the Hebrew prophetic perfect, "declaring the end from the beginning, and from ancient times things that are not yet done" (46:10), to describe events to come as if they were already accomplished.

Instead of darkness and death, light and life appear. Through the Spirit of prophecy Isaiah sees that which is yet to come almost as clearly as Matthew saw it when it was fulfilled in Jesus (Matt. 4:12–16). After John the Baptist was delivered up, Jesus withdrew into Galilee to begin His work in the borders of Zebulun and Naphtali. Jesus, "the light of the world" (John 8:12), was "the true light, even the light which lighteth every man, coming into the world" (John 1:9). His life was "the light of men" (John 1:4), and in Him the sun of righteousness arose "with healing in its beams" (Mal. 4:2, margin). This light began to shine in the land of Zebulun and Naphtali where the gloom had first settled centuries earlier. The people of God's nation who once walked in darkness now had a great light burst upon them. Yet, as Delitzsch well put it, "the great light should not come till Israel reached its blackest night."

3 *Thou hast multiplied the nation, thou hast increased their joy: they joy before thee according to the joy in harvest, as men rejoice when they divide the spoil.* The nation was multiplied, the new Israel extended, as the Gentiles were brought in, for, as Isaiah prophesied, "all nations shall flow unto it" (2:2), and Jehovah will give "a light of the Gentiles" (42:6). With the nation multiplied, joy would be increased, for all in the new holy nation would exult in the joy of their

salvation. The prophet uses two figures to illustrate his point: men rejoicing in harvest when the barns are full and the vats overflow, and victors rejoicing when they divide the spoils of war. The fullness of spiritual life would belong to the nation, and they would share in a complete victory and triumph over the adversary.

The Basis of This Joy (vv. 4–7)

4 In spelling out the reasons for joy the prophet introduces each of the next three verses with the word *for*. *For the yoke of his burden, and the staff of his shoulder, the rod of his oppressor, thou hast broken as in the day of Midian.* Here is cause for rejoicing! The burden of bondage, the staff applied to the back or shoulder, and the rod of the slave driver have been removed from the oppressed. This relief is offered to the whole nation, though accepted by only a remnant. Those who rejoice in the light will be delivered from the bondage of sin, the yoke of the law, and the enslavement of idolatry. They will walk in the glorious light of their freedom (John 8:31–36; Gal. 4:8–9; 5:1), *as in the day of Midian.* Israel had served Midian for seven years. Finally, the foreign oppressor was completely routed and driven out of the land. The deliverance was not achieved by the hand of man, nor was Midian overthrown by the force of an army. By the power of God working through a handful of faithful men Midian had been defeated and destroyed (Judg. 7–8). In like manner would Jehovah now rout the enemy.

5 *For all the armor of the armed man in the tumult, and the garments rolled in blood, shall be for burning, for fuel of fire.* "Every boot of the booted warrior" (margin), every blood-stained garment of the invading armies, will be burned, destroyed. Military accouterments will not be a part of the new Israel's strength; rather, they shall be done away with (Isa. 2:2–4; Hos. 2:18; Zech. 9:10). The new Israel will be a spiritual kingdom, each citizen clothed in a spiritual armor befitting the nature of the new conflict (Eph. 6:10–20).

6 The third *for* brings the prophet's hearers to the real basis and cause of their joy: *For unto us a child is born, unto us a son is given.* The Child born, the Son given, is the Immanuel, "God with us," of 7:14. There He was a sign given by the Lord; here He is a Ruler who

101

brings salvation and deliverance to His people. The prophet continues to speak of events to come as if they have already occurred—*a child is born, a son is given*—so certain is Isaiah that the promise will be fulfilled. *And the government shall be upon his shoulder*—He shall rule. Government, the seat of authority, is often likened to a key—it has the power to bind or to loose, to open or to shut. Later on, Jehovah says to Shebna the treasurer, "I will commit thy government into [Eliakim's] hand. . . . And the key of the house of David will I lay upon his shoulder; and he shall open, and none shall shut; and he shall shut, and none shall open" (Isa. 22:21–22). The government and key now belong to the Child, the Son. Jesus Himself claims to have the key of David (Rev. 3:7).

The real glory of the one to be born and His relationship to deity are revealed in the names by which He will be called. In the ancient world one's name was viewed as a reflection of all that one was, including qualities of character, whether good or bad, strong or weak. *And his name shall be called Wonderful, Counsellor, Mighty God, Everlasting Father, Prince of Peace.* In Isaiah 7:14 the mother names the Child, but here another names Him. Here He is named by Jehovah, for only God could designate names which reflect the Child's very character and being. Is He here given four or five descriptive titles? Leupold and Young list four, uniting the first two into one, "Wonderful-Counsellor," whereas Alexander, Delitzsch, and Rawlinson hold to five, following the wording in the American Standard Version. The prophet does not mean to say that the Child will actually wear these five titles or appellations, but that they are descriptive of who and what He is. Of course, only Jesus Himself knows fully all that His name implies.

The first title, *Wonder* or *Wonderful*, describes the Child as the marvel of the ages, the full revelation of the Father. He has mighty power over Satan and sin; His mission is one of redemption and an expression of infinite love; the summation of all spiritual and moral truth is found in Him. The wonder of His person and work would startle many nations (52:15). He excites awe in the heart of the honest beholder.

As King over His kingdom and director of its war of conquest, He is the *Counsellor* of all His subjects. Angels and ministering spirits may serve, but the counsel of peace belongs to Him and to Him alone. It is in His two offices of Priest and King that He administers this counsel (Zech. 6:13). In Him are summed up all the treasures of wisdom and knowledge (Col. 2:3). He is the true Counsellor in whom all may find words of wisdom by which to be guided and by which to solve the problems of life and to understand its principles.

The name *Mighty God* identifies the Child with the Godhead, both in deity and in power. He is equal with God. Indeed, this very title is applied to Jehovah in Isaiah 10:21: "A remnant shall return, even the remnant of Jacob, unto the mighty God." The psalmist had written of the Son as God: His throne is forever and He wields the scepter of uprightness over His kingdom (Ps. 45:6); Jeremiah says of Him, "He shall be called: Jehovah our righteousness" (Jer. 23:6). In His work He exerted the power of the almighty God.

The title *Everlasting Father* or "Eternal Father" clearly places the Child outside the pale of created beings; as God, He is eternal. He already existed at the beginning: "In the beginning was the Word" (John 1:1); "For in him were all things created . . . and he is before all things" (Col. 1:16–17). As *Father*, He is not only the Creator, but He is also the Protector and Sustainer of the new creation. Joseph had been made "a father to Pharaoh" (Gen. 45:8), a protector and sustainer of the ruler and his empire; likewise Eliakim was made "a father . . . to the house of Judah" (Isa. 22:21). But since the Child is eternal, there never was a time when He was not a Father in the sense of Protector.

As *Prince of Peace* the child comes as a mighty Prince who conquers not by the sword, but by the message of peace directed to the hearts of men. He establishes and maintains true peace, not the peace the world gives, but peace which is a result of spiritual fullness, companionship with God, and a right relationship with man. This peace comes when sin, the cause of strife, is banished from an individual's life; sin must be removed, forgiven, blotted out. Micah calls the Child "our peace" (5:5). "He shall speak peace unto the nations" (Zech. 9:10). Paul says, "He came and preached peace to you that were far off, and peace to them that were nigh" (Eph. 2:17). Young has accurately said, "In active vigor He is the true David and in love of peace the real Solomon."

103

7 *Of the increase of his government and of peace there shall be no end.* Political governments usually grow through war or intrigue, only to weaken amid corruption, debt, and internal decay until they succumb and fall prey to the hand of another. But the government of this Prince shall grow to include people of all nations, for "his dominion shall be from sea to sea, and from the River to the ends of the earth" (Zech. 9:10). All of this will be accomplished through the power of peace. Micah adds his testimony, "And he shall stand, and shall feed his flock in the strength of Jehovah, in the majesty of the name of Jehovah his God: and they shall abide; for now shall he be great unto the ends of the earth. And this man shall be our peace" (5:4–5a). His kingdom will ever increase, for His message will spread to bring men from all the world under His reign.

This Son shall sit *upon the throne of David, and upon his kingdom, to establish it.* We are told that Solomon "sat upon the throne of David his father" (I Kings 2:12), that he "sat upon the throne of Jehovah as king instead of David his father" (I Chron. 29:23), and that he sat upon "his [own] throne" (I Kings 1:37, 47). Clearly, there was but one throne; the throne of Jehovah, the throne of David, the throne of Solomon are all one. David and Solomon reigned over God's temporal kingdom; the Child-Son now reigns over God's spiritual kingdom. There is still but one throne, the throne of David, that is, the throne of Jehovah; and Christ sits upon it.

The Child upholds or sustains His kingdom *with justice and with righteousness from henceforth even for ever.* Justice and righteousness are the foundation of God's throne (Pss. 89:14; 97:2). The words *justice* and *righteousness* occur over and over in the Book of Isaiah. *Justice* is rightness and fairness in making decisions. It is rooted in the character of God. *Righteousness* is basically conformity to an ethical or moral standard established by the Lord. It is by these attributes that the Child now upholds the kingdom and will uphold it till the end of time.

The zeal of Jehovah of hosts will perform this. The zeal of Jehovah is His jealousy for His name and for His people. Delitzsch suggests that it is "a glowing fire," the fire of God's love and the fire of His wrath, the jealousy of absolute love. From before His throne of righteousness and justice go forth "lovingkindness and truth" (Ps. 89:14), yet at the same time "A fire goeth before him,/And burneth up his adversaries round about" (Ps. 97:3).

The night came, captivity engulfed both nations, and the throne of David fell into disrepute (Amos 9:11). Then the Child was born, the Son was given; He came radiating a divine light. It was given to Him to sit upon the throne of David, establish the kingdom of peace, and uphold it with justice and righteousness *from henceforth, even for ever*. The angel Gabriel (Luke 1:26–38), Matthew (Matt. 4:12–16), Peter (Acts 2:29–36), and Paul (Acts 13:32–39) clearly declare that Christ fulfilled this prophecy. Let all people recognize this today and enter into and share the peace of His glorious spiritual kingdom.

The Arrogance of Ephraim (vv. 8–12)

In 9:8–10:4 the prophet once again turns to the theme of Jehovah's anger and the coming judgment. The basic pattern in this section has already been set in 5:24–30. After a description of destruction by fire and by earthquake the prophet declared, "For all this his anger is not turned away, but his hand is stretched out still" (v. 25). There followed an account of the bringing in of a nation from afar, which could be none other than the terrible invasion by Assyria (vv. 26–30).

In the present section, after a beautiful and glorious picture of light, redemption, and rule by the Messiah, a picture of hope (9:1–7), the prophet delivers four strophes or stanzas of judgment. Each stanza closes with the refrain of 5:25, "For all this his anger is not turned away, but his hand is stretched out still" (9:12, 17, 21; 10:4). These four stanzas declaring that because of the people's rejection of Jehovah His hand is still outstretched against them in judgment are followed by a description of the coming Assyrian invasion and of that nation's subsequent destruction at the hand of Jehovah (10:5–34). How much of God's judgment had already been sent by this time upon Israel and Judah cannot be determined accurately. If there is any connection between this proclamation of God's judgment and His continued anger and the judgment of chapter 5, it is not revealed. Smith considers the present passage to be out of place and would insert the whole, 9:8–10:4, between verses 25 and 26 of chapter 5 (I. 47). However, other than the similarity of pattern and likeness of the content of the two sections, there seems to be no basis for such an arrangement, especially no textual basis.

8 Although the name *Jacob* at times refers to both Ephraim and Judah and at other times to only one of them, it seems that when the prophet says, *The Lord sent a word into Jacob, and it hath lighted upon Israel,* he has Ephraim in mind. The word sent forth is that which follows. When it lights, it will be like a time-bomb exploding (Leupold) or a thunderbolt (Young). God's word brings His deeds to pass (cf. John 14:10).

9–10 When the word is fulfilled, the people shall understand that God is executing judgment against Ephraim's boast made in pride and in stoutness of heart: *The bricks are fallen, but we will build with hewn stone; the sycomores are cut down, but we will put cedars in their place.* It is not known whether this boast followed some natural catastrophe, such as an earthquake, or came after partial destruction by some warring enemy. Neither can it be determined whether this was an actual boast or simply the prophet's summation of the people's arrogant and proud thoughts, but the meaning is clear. Whatever the calamity had been, the people did not learn from it. The houses which had been built of sun-dried bricks would be rebuilt with hewn stones, which were far more costly and luxurious. The valuable sycomore trees which flourished in the area would be replaced with cedar trees, which were more precious and highly esteemed. In later years Edom made a similar boast (Mal. 1:4). Men have always been slow learners, especially when fighting against God.

11–12 Jehovah responds to this arrogant and boastful spirit: *Therefore Jehovah will set up on high against him the adversaries of Rezin,* who can be none other than the Assyrians. The next phrase, *and will stir up his enemies,* is more difficult to interpret. Is Isaiah referring to the enemies of Israel or of Rezin? The sentence structure seems to indicate the enemies of Rezin, *the Syrians before* ("on the east," margin), *and the Philistines behind* ("on the west," margin). However, this interpretation presents a problem. Who are the Syrians on the east who would be enemies of Rezin, the king of Syria? They would have to be Syrians who were taken by the Assyrians, became enemies of Rezin, and now threaten Ephraim. On the other hand, if "his enemies" is interpreted as the enemies of Ephraim, the reference to the Philistines presents a problem. In II Chronicles 28:18–19 there is an account of the Philistines coming against Judah in the days of Ahaz, but there is no record of their coming against Ephraim. Of course, it is possible that victory in the south encouraged the Philistines to continue north into the territory of Ephraim. But whether the Syrians and Philistines are the enemies of Ephraim or of Rezin, the result of the attack is clear: *And they shall devour Israel with open mouth,* cruelly and completely. Sad to say, however, the cruelty of the enemies moves neither Ephraim to repentance nor Jehovah to retract: *For all this his anger is not turned away, but his hand is stretched out still.* There is more to come.

Israel to Be Cut Off, Head and Tail (vv. 13–17)

13 Even though God's hand is outstretched in judgment, *yet the people have not turned unto him that smote them, neither have they sought Jehovah of hosts.* It had been Jehovah who smote the people, chastening them in an effort to turn them back to Himself, but to no avail. They had not sought Him; they had not turned to Him as their God and only source of help. To turn unto the Lord denotes a true conversion, a complete reversal of heart and absolute trust in Him.

14 *Therefore Jehovah will cut off from Israel head and tail, palmbranch and rush, in one day.* The prophet uses two figures: one from the animal realm *(head and tail)* and the other from the vegetable world *(palm-branch and rush).* The head directs while the tail merely wags; the palm-branch is at the top of the stately palm, whereas the rush is a marsh grass, lowly and abased. To cut them off in one day indicates the suddenness of the destruction.

15 The prophet explains the first of the two metaphors, but leaves the people to make their own interpretation of the second. *The elder and the honorable man,* the leaders and guides of the people, *he is the head; and the prophet that teacheth lies,* he who speaks in the name of Jehovah, but speaks not from Him, *he is the tail.* The precise phrase "false prophet" does not occur in the Old Testament, but is a New Testament term. However, this idea of the false prophet occurs over and over in the Old. As the tail of a dog wags its fawning approval of its master, so the prophet of lies hypocritically approves the ungodly decisions and actions of the leaders. Both prophet and leaders will perish; both will be cut off.

16 *For they that lead this people cause them to err; and they that are led of them are destroyed.* Both political leaders and religious teachers bear a tremendous responsibility, for the thinking and conduct of a people are largely molded by these two groups. There is no indication that the false prophets shared with the elders in ruling the people except by their sanctioning and supporting of false standards by their false assertions. Echoing Isaiah's judgment concerning political leaders, Jesus said regarding the Pharisees of His day: "Let them alone: they are blind guides. And if the blind guide the blind, both shall fall into a pit" (Matt. 15:14).

17 *Therefore the Lord will not rejoice over their young men,* whom He ordinarily used in war to destroy His enemies; but rather He would use foreigners to destroy Israel's young men. *Neither will he have compassion on their fatherless and widows,* whom He had formerly protected—"He [God] doth execute justice for the fatherless and widow" (Deut. 10:18). But like the nations Jehovah had thrust out, destroying young and old, His own people had now reached the point where they were no longer fit to live. The cause of this rejection by Jehovah is set forth in three charges against the people: (1) *every one is profane,* polluted by false and hypocritical conduct—a godless person; (2) every one is *an evil-doer,* one who forsakes Jehovah and does evil to his fellow man (cf. 1:4); *and* (3) *every mouth speaketh folly*—disregarding moral and spiritual values, all the people speak of disgraceful and sinful things. They were guilty of both doing and speaking evil—expressions of an evil heart. Through His prophets God continued to call, but in the stubbornness of their hearts the people refused to hear. Therefore, the deadly refrain occurs again: *For all this his anger is not turned away, but his hand is stretched out still.* Through these experiences of Israel and God's reaction to the people, we should learn something of the nature and character of God. His anger and judgment are as absolute and as much an expression of Himself as are His love and mercy.

The Devouring Fire: Wickedness and Civil War (vv. 18–21)

18 Wickedness had lighted the flame of destruction in the north-

ern kingdom, and it *burneth as the fire;* beginning in the underbrush, *it devoureth the briers and thorns,* that which is most easily ignited. From there the fire proceeds to the larger combustible materials: *yea, it kindleth in the thickets of the forest, and they roll upward in a column of smoke,* billowing heavenward. The fire begins with the wickedness of individuals; soon the whole forest or nation is destroyed. Anyone familiar with the great forest fires of the West senses the terror of the picture.

19   This consuming of the land by the wickedness of the people is an expression of the wrath of Jehovah—*Through the wrath of Jehovah of hosts is the land burnt up; and the people are as the fuel of fire.* Wickedness carries within its bosom the fire of its own destruction. Jehovah had warned of this when He said of the man who walks in stubbornness of heart, "Then the anger of Jehovah and his jealousy will smoke against that man, and all the curse that is written in this book shall lie upon him" (Deut. 29:20). Of God's deliverance of him from his enemies, David said, "There went up a smoke out of his nostrils,/And fire out of his mouth devoured:/Coals were kindled by it" (Ps. 18:8). Moreover, "A fire goeth before him,/And burneth up his adversaries round about" (Ps. 97:3). What was now taking place should have come as no surprise, for God had given forewarning. *No man spareth his brother,* for wickedness turns men against even their brothers whom they should endeavor to help.

20–21   There was not only the threat of destruction from foreigners—Assyria, Syria, and Philistia—but also the northern tribes were being torn by the internal destruction of civil war. Each was snatching what he could from his neighbor on the right hand and on the left; *they shall eat every man the flesh of his own arm,* consuming themselves. But even then they will not be satisfied; each will experience the gnawing of an insatiable hunger. This wicked indifference to the finer feelings of brotherhood and the mutual bearing of each other's burdens led to civil war between two tribes that should have been closest—Ephraim and Manasseh were the sons of Joseph. But not so; each was against the other, devouring and being devoured with an enmity and mutual bitterness that was exceeded only by their hatred for Judah, their brethren to the south. And *for all this*—their wickedness, hatred among themselves, and rejection of Jehovah—*his* *anger is not turned away, but his hand is stretched out still.* There is still more to come.

CHAPTER 10
The Use and Doom of Assyria

Visitation and Desolation! (vv. 1–4)

1–2 The prophecy of these verses is directed against the unrighteous judges and lawyers who serve not the cause of right but their own wicked greed. The first three of Isaiah's four stanzas of judgment were directed primarily against Samaria and the kingdom of the north; this one is against the rulers in Jerusalem. The sinners and their sins are first described: *Woe unto them that decree unrighteous decrees, and to the writers that write perverseness.* The judges issue oppressive decrees and then put them in willfully unjust writings. The woe is followed by a pointing out of the twofold effect upon the people: the wicked judges (1) *turn aside the needy from justice*, not allowing them an opportunity at the courts where justice should be established, and (2) *rob the poor of my people of their right*, not only refusing their right at the court, but deliberately robbing the poor of the little they have. The poor and needy are the special prey of dishonest and powerful judges; but to enrich themselves they go even further in their evils, *that widows may be their spoil, and that they may make the fatherless their prey!* Those who are helpless, wholly dependent on the fairness of the judges, are their choice victims. This brings these perverse men under the curse of God, for He had long since said, "Cursed be he that wresteth the justice due to the sojourner, fatherless, and widow. And all the people shall say, Amen" (Deut. 27:19). That curse is now about to fall, for all court judgment should be executed in righteousness (Lev. 19:15).

3 Isaiah now raises three questions which should stir most serious thinking: First, *And what will ye do in the day of visitation, and in the desolation which shall come from far?* Although a time or day of visitation may be one of mercy, the term is almost always used in the

110

Old Testament to denote a day of judgment and calamity. The prophet leaves no question here as to his meaning, for he describes the day of visitation as *the desolation which shall come from far.* Although Isaiah does not here reveal the name of the nation which shall come from far, in the next section Jehovah makes known that it is the terrible nation of Assyria. A second question is posed, *To whom will ye flee for help?* The people had rejected Jehovah the only true help, and He, as a result, will bring the Assyrians upon them. Therefore they will be left in a helpless, hopeless condition. Then comes the final question, *And where will ye leave your glory?* To whom will you entrust it for safekeeping? The glory of the people was their political position, which they would lose, and their wealth, which would be carried away as booty by the conquering nation into their own land. There would be no place to entrust it for safekeeping.

4   What shall be the end of the judges themselves? They shall be put in cells and either bow down or through weakness fall at the feet of other prisoners. Or through weakness they might fall at the feet of other prisoners on the long trek to the foreign land. Or they might even fall amidst the slain in battle, becoming covered with others slain in the conflict. Since none of these judgments bring repentance, the striking refrain is uttered for the final time: *For all this his anger is not turned away, but his hand is stretched out still.* What a terrible end for a people who had had every blessing and assurance of life from the great and mighty God to whom they belonged. But they had refused and rejected all this, and by their conduct they had asked for the judgment they would now receive.

Assyria: Jehovah's Rod (vv. 5–11)

The people refused to turn to Jehovah, continuing in their rebellion against Him; therefore, His hand was against them still. The Assyrian whom God would bring from afar is now declared to be the instrument of divine wrath. This word of the prophet makes clear Jehovah's use of heathen nations to accomplish His purpose. He raises up nations, uses them, and then destroys them. Not only did He use Assyria against Ephraim and Judah at this time, but later He also raised up Babylon to destroy Assyria and to carry Judah into captivity (Hab. 1:5–11). Afterward He would raise up the Medes against Babylon, to be His arrows (Isa. 13:17; 44:28–45:7; Jer. 51:11, 28). When the Medes had accomplished His purpose, He would bring Alexander of Macedonia against the Medo-Persian power to destroy it (Dan. 8). And so the providence of God worked among the heathen nations to prepare the way for the establishing of His spiritual kingdom and the ultimate consummation of His eternal purpose.

The coming of the Messiah has not been forgotten by the prophet; the judgments in 9:8–10:34 form a block that fits into the messianic pattern of chapters 7–12. Israel and Judah must be made to realize that the people are not ready for Him to come. Wickedness must be judged by the Lord, and the heathen nations must be destroyed before the spiritual kingdom is brought in. Upon the ruin of world powers, epitomized in the Assyrian Empire, would rise the great power of Immanuel, the Son of God and son of David. God would be with His people in the mighty shoot of Jesse (ch. 11).

5   As the prophet had pronounced woes upon Judah (ch. 5), upon himself (6:5), and upon the unrighteous judges of the land (10:1), so he now pronounces woe upon the Assyrian nation which Jehovah will use against Israel and Judah. *Ho* (woe) *Assyrian, the rod of mine anger, the staff in whose hand is mine indignation!* Since the nation is being personified, no one king is in the prophet's mind; the spirit and character of the whole people are before him. Assyria is the rod in Jehovah's hand to be employed against His own people. In turn, Jehovah's indignation is in the hand of the Assyrian to be exercised against Judah.

6   Jehovah Himself will send the Assyrian power against *a profane nation*, a nation which is polluted by idolatry and wickedness and refuses to distinguish between the holy and the unholy, the godly and the godless. *Against the people of my wrath*, Jehovah's own people, *will I give him a charge.* Assyria is charged by Jehovah *to take the spoil, and to take the prey.* The carrying away of the booty of conquest will be by the direction and will of God, who determines who shall be the conqueror and who shall be the conquered. Assyria is charged *to tread them* (Judah) *down like the mire of the streets.* To the modern generation, accustomed to paved roads and streets and rarely venturing into byways, this may not mean much; but to the

older generation who remember what it was like to tread through slushy, miry, muddy streets, the picture is meaningful indeed. In such a quagmire of filth and slime the people would be trodden down.

7   It was not the Assyrian's intention to serve God's purpose, for the Lord says, *Howbeit he meaneth not so, neither doth his heart think so; but it is in his heart to destroy, and to cut off nations not a few*—to cut them off in quantity. How shall we harmonize this statement of the prophet with Rabshakeh's proud boast, "Am I now come up without Jehovah against this place [Jerusalem] to destroy it? Jehovah said unto me, Go up against this land, and destroy it" (II Kings 18:25)? It is very doubtful that Sennacherib had received a message from Jehovah by dream or otherwise. It is more probable that having heard of the prophecies of Judean prophets that Assyria would come against the land, he was playing on these prophecies to frighten the people. For Isaiah says plainly that the Assyrian did not think he was being used of the Lord. Actually, however, God was using him as the instrument of judgment because it was in the Assyrian's heart to conquer and rule the world.

8–9   The Assyrian boasts that his princes are all kings, and no doubt there were kings of many conquered peoples in his army, serving as his military commanders. He probably thought that by comparison his military leaders were as superior to those of other countries as kings are to ordinary military captains. Having boasted of the superiority of his leaders, he continues by boasting of his conquests and achievements. He enumerates six conquered cities, beginning from the north and moving southward, ever nearer Judah and Jerusalem. *Is not Calno as Carchemish?* Calno was a Syrian city whose location is uncertain. Carchemish was an ancient Hittite city located on the banks of the Euphrates River 250 to 300 miles west of Ninevah. *Is not Hamath as Arpad?* Arpad, also a city of Syria, was located southwest of Carchemish. Hamath, located on the Orontes River, was the center of an independent kingdom which at one time was controlled by Judah but was apparently lost to Israel, for it was recovered by Jeroboam II (II Chron. 8:3–4; II Kings 14:28). *Is not Samaria as Damascus?* Both had been conquered by the Assyrians. These rhetorical questions raise another question concerning the

113

date of this prophecy. Of these cities conquered by Assyria, Young says, "Calno was taken in 738 B.C., Carchemish on the Euphrates in 717, Hamath on the Orontes in 720, Arpad in 740 and 720, Samaria in 722 and Damascus in 732" (I. 362). Delitzsch places the prophecy in the first three years of Ahaz's reign, suggesting that the king of Assyria is speaking of coming conquests as if they were already accomplished. But this seems improbable. Since Samaria fell in 722 or 721 B.C. and Sennacherib besieged Judah and Jerusalem in 702–701, it seems more probable that Isaiah spoke this prophecy between those two dates, possibly around 717 when Sargon was active in the west subduing Carchemish.

10–11   Oriental monarchs looked upon their victories or defeats as expressions of the strength or weakness of the nation's gods. The Assyrian king continued his boast, saying, *As my hand hath found the kingdoms of the idols, whose graven images did excel them of Jerusalem and of Samaria; shall I not, as I have done unto Samaria and her idols, so do to Jerusalem and her idols?* The idols of the conquered cities excelled those of Samaria and Jerusalem in exquisite design and workmanship, as well as in number. Having easily taken Samaria, the king thought that the taking of Jerusalem would be easy. His boast was blasphemous, for it put Jehovah, the mighty God, in the category of the heathen idols, which were empty vanities.

The Assyrian's Boast and Jehovah's Response (vv. 12–19)

12   Jehovah will not let the blasphemy of the Assyrian pass unnoticed, but the time is not yet; the Lord has further work for him. *Wherefore it shall come to pass, that, when the Lord hath performed his whole work upon mount Zion and on Jerusalem, I will punish the fruit of the stout heart of the king of Assyria, and the glory of his high looks.* God's *whole work* is His complete judgment upon the wickedness of His people. This done, the Lord will punish the *fruit of the stout heart of the king*, a fitting term to describe the complete product of his arrogant, proud, blasphemous heart—his self-glorification.

13   The king's arrogance is evident in his use of *my* and *I*. *For he hath said, By the strength of my hand I have done it, and by my wisdom; for I have understanding; and I have removed the bounds of*

the peoples, and have robbed their treasures, and like a valiant man I have brought down them that sit on thrones. However, his wisdom was folly and his strength weakness, for he was boasting of his power against the God who would bring him down. In reality, it was not he who had removed the bounds of the peoples, transferring the people of a nation he had conquered to another country and bringing others into the conquered land. He did not realize that it was Jehovah who "set the bounds of the peoples" (Deut. 32:8), "having determined their [the nations'] appointed seasons, and the bounds of their habitation" (Acts 17:26). Nor did he realize that it was God who brought down them that sat on thrones—"The Most High ruleth in the kingdom of men, and giveth it to whomsoever he will, and setteth up over it the lowest of men" (Dan. 4:17). This principle has never been abrogated; rulers of today still need to learn it.

14 As he continues his boast, the Assyrian king claims that his *hand hath found as a nest the riches of the peoples.* The world was like a nest forsaken by the mother bird so that there was no resistance. All he had to do was gather the riches as one would gather (scoop up) eggs in a basket and carry them away. There was no resistance from the baby birds in the nest; they neither *moved the wing* nor *opened the mouth* nor *chirped.* Like the relentless tide of an overflowing river, the Assyrian's great war machine swept everything before it.

15 But it was not by his power alone that the heathen king conquered. Jehovah raises several simple but penetrating questions: *Shall the axe boast itself against him that heweth therewith?* Which uses which? Does the axe use the hewer or the hewer the axe? The same question is asked concerning a saw: *Shall the saw magnify itself against the carpenter,* or does the carpenter operate the saw? A third metaphor follows: *as if a rod shall wield them that lift it up, or as if a staff should lift up him that is not wood.* The Assyrian has nothing of which to boast, for Jehovah is using him as one would use an axe, a saw, or a rod; he is Jehovah's staff that accomplishes His purpose. So are all nations today.

16 Therefore, when Jehovah finishes His work with the Assyrian, He will *send among his fat ones leanness; and under his glory there shall be kindled a burning like the burning of fire,* which will consume the arrogant nation. Disease and want will consume the fat

115

of the well-fed army and nation, and a crackling fire will devour their glory as it does a forest.

17   The prophet declares the source of the fire: *And the light of Israel will be for a fire, and his Holy One for a flame*—God will be the fire of Assyria's destruction. Through Moses Jehovah had said, "Jehovah thy God is a devouring fire" (Deut. 4:24), and Isaiah speaks later of Jehovah as the people's "everlasting light" (60:19). This fire will begin in the lower stratum of the Assyrian army, for the fire *will burn and devour his thorns and his briers in one day*, probably a reference to the destruction of the army before Jerusalem in one night (37:36).

18–19   Here the prophet speaks of the beginning of the end of Assyria's glory. *He* (Jehovah) *will consume the glory of his forest*, his valiant army, *and of his fruitful field*, the nation, *both soul and body*, that is, completely. As soul and body stand for the whole man, so shall the whole of Assyria be destroyed. *And it shall be as when a standard-bearer fainteth*, or "as when a sick man pineth away" (margin). Like a man who has become ill and weak, the nation will be brought to nought. The trees of the Assyrian's glorious forest, the army and nation, will become so few that a lad can walk among them and count them.

A Remnant Shall Return (Shear-jashub) (vv. 20–23)

20–21   In contrast to the total destruction of Assyria for seeking to destroy the house of Jacob, a remnant of the house of Israel will escape. This remnant will not lean upon a heathen nation as had Ahaz, who sent "unto the kings of Assyria to help him"; they came unto Ahaz, "but strengthened him not" (II Chron. 28:16, 20). In order to bolster his sagging power, Ahaz "sacrificed unto the gods of Damascus which smote him. . . . But they were the ruin of him, and of all Israel" (II Chron. 28:23). Unlike Ahaz, the remnant *shall lean upon Jehovah, the Holy One of Israel, in truth*. Whereas the nation under Ahaz had trusted in the lies of idolatry and false leadership, the remnant will rely upon the truth as it is found in God alone. Their hope will be in God, not in a world power. *A remnant shall return, even the remnant of Jacob, unto the mighty God*. In this *remnant* is fulfilled the promise expressed in the name of Isaiah's son Shear-jashub (7:3); *the mighty God* points to the Child to be born, the Son to be given, who will be called Mighty God (9:6). Thus a remnant will escape the Assyrian destruction, and then a remnant of this remnant will be saved under the Child, the Mighty God (cf. 1:9; 6:13).

22   That those who return will be but a small number in contrast to the entire nation is clearly indicated by Isaiah: *For though thy people, Israel, be as the sand of the sea, only a remnant shall return.* Jehovah never promised that all the descendants of Abraham would be saved; those who would be saved were always spoken of as a remnant. Paul quoted this passage and applied it to Jews saved under Christ: though the nation be brought to a full end, a remnant shall be saved (Rom. 9:27). *A destruction is determined, overflowing with righteousness.* Not only will the Assyrians be destroyed, but there will also be a complete destruction of the old Jewish nation. That destruction will be *overflowing with righteousness*—it will be a righteous judgment. Just as the judgment executed by the Assyrians will come as an overflowing river (8:7–8), so likewise the ultimate destruction of the nation, brought about by righteous judgment, will come as an overwhelming flood.

23   *For a full end, and that determined, will the Lord, Jehovah of hosts, make in the midst of all the earth.* Not only will there be a complete end of the Assyrians, but there will also be a full end of all heathen powers and of the Jewish nation; this will occur under Jehovah's direction, not by human determination. This prophecy does not refer to the final judgment described in the New Testament, but to a world judgment in time, *in the midst of all the earth.* This general world judgment is described in Isaiah 24–27, following the judgment of the heathen nations described in chapters 13–23.

Be Not Afraid! Though on His Way, the Assyrian Shall Be Brought Low (vv. 24–34)

24   With words of assurance that a remnant will be saved, the prophet urges the people that dwell in Zion, where God resides among them, not to be afraid of the Assyrian; for though he smite and afflict them as did Egypt, the affliction will not last forever. Egypt

117

afflicted the people with the harsh labor of slavery, whereas the Assyrians will destroy them with the rod and staff of war.

25 True, the indignation against Zion will be severe while it lasts, but *yet a very little while, and the indignation against thee shall be accomplished, and mine anger shall be directed to his destruction.* Though the period between the assaults of Tiglath-pileser and the defeat of Sennacherib will be some thirty years, that is a very short time in the whole history of the nation. When Jehovah determines that the time has come, He will provide the means for Assyria's destruction.

26 Jehovah will stir up against the Assyrian a scourge, an affliction both painful and destructive, which shall be *as in the slaughter of Midian at the rock of Oreb.* As the destruction of the Midianites by the faithful few under Gideon had been by the hand of Jehovah, so will the destruction of the Assyrians be a work of God (see Judg. 7). A second illustration is drawn from history: *his rod will be over the sea, and he will lift it up after the manner of Egypt.* Jehovah will lift up His rod, just as it was lifted by Moses at the Red Sea, providing escape for His people when they went through the sea on dry land. Jehovah will destroy the enemy, as He did the Egyptians when the waters closed in on them.

27 The phrase *in that day* identifies the work of deliverance spoken of in this verse with what has just preceded. The Lord's work of deliverance is now described as the removing of a burden and the breaking of a yoke, a further reminder of the deliverance from Egypt. *And it shall come to pass in that day, that his burden shall depart from off thy shoulder, and his yoke from off thy neck.* The next phrase, *and the yoke shall be destroyed by reason of fatness,* is more difficult to interpret. Several commentators suggest that Isaiah is saying that like an ox which grows so large and strong that it breaks its yoke, Israel cannot be destroyed by her enemies.

28–32 The Assyrian is on his way! In moving language the prophet paints a graphic picture of the Assyrian army drawing near to Jerusalem. Since the Assyrians came against the city from the southwest, the prophet is not describing the actual coming but an approach that would strike terror in the hearts of the towns he mentions. Of the twelve towns or cities named, the site of eight (possibly ten) can be identified with a fair degree of certainty. Aiath, possibly Ai, located

118

about twelve or fifteen miles to the north of Jerusalem, is the most distant of the group. The Assyrians have already passed through Migron; and at Michmash, important in the days of Saul (I Sam. 13), they laid up their baggage, possibly in the realization that they would encounter difficulty in crossing over the pass. The army is now lodging at Geba. The people of Ramah are terrified; and the inhabitants of Gibeah, the ancient city of King Saul, have fled from their homes. The people of Gallim are called upon to cry out because of the approaching terror, and Laishah is told to listen to the shriek of anguish in her sister city. *O thou poor Anathoth!* This village, about three miles northeast of Jerusalem and the birthplace of Jeremiah, stirs Isaiah's pity to a high pitch. Madmenah and the inhabitants of Gebim flee from before the face of the enemy. Nob, a Levitical city, is the nearest of the group to Jerusalem, only two miles away. It is probably from Nob, within sight of Jerusalem, that the Assyrian will pause and shake his fist at Zion. Jerusalem will soon be his—so he thinks!

33   But the Lord has other thoughts. The prophet returns to the figure of a forest (cf. v. 19) to describe the terror to be inflicted by Jehovah: *Behold, the Lord, Jehovah of hosts, will lop the boughs with terror*—He will trim the haughty and mighty king of his glory, substituting terror in its stead. *And the high of stature shall be hewn down, and the lofty shall be brought low.* Jehovah is able to strike down the most arrogant and mighty of earth, cutting them down to size, for they are as mortal as the most lowly.

34   Here stands the mountain of Lebanon, the symbol of all that is powerful on earth, over against Mount Zion, the city of God and the symbol of His presence and power. The result is devastating: *And he will cut down the thickets of the forest with iron, and Lebanon shall fall by a mighty one*—the Mighty God. The destruction is complete. Both the mighty cedars and the thickets and underbrush will fall by the hand of God (cf. 9:18). Therefore, fear not; there are better things ahead for the people of Zion—God's faithful remnant.

CHAPTER 11
The King, His Subjects, and the Remnant

Assyria would invade the land; Samaria would fall and Israel would be carried into captivity. By Jehovah's hand Jerusalem and Judah would be smitten with the rod and brought very low. Assyria would be destroyed like a forest, with only dead stumps left, never to rise again. Its military and political power, which relied on humans rather than God, would utterly fail; the destruction of the Assyrians would be complete and final. In the midst of these dark and gloomy prophecies Jehovah held out a beam of light to encourage and sustain His faithful ones. A remnant would endure throughout the trying times of captivity and would return. Out of the remnant would come God's spiritual kingdom. A virgin would conceive and bring forth a Son, Immanuel, God with us (7:14), and on His shoulder would rest the government of the kingdom (9:6–7). He would come forth like a twig from roots in the Davidic stump which were apparently dead yet still alive.

The prophet now gives the people a fuller description of the descendant of David who had been promised to that illustrious king (II Sam. 7:11–16); both His character and the nature of His rule are set forth (vv. 1–5). Neither the Branch nor His kingdom would be identical in nature with the old Davidic order. From the beginning the old physical or political kingdom and its kings had within them the seeds of their own failure and destruction. Anything human is destined to corruption and decay. The new spiritual kingdom and its divine King (7:14; 9:6–7) would be subject to neither. The physical kingdom would pass away; the spiritual would endure. Next, Isaiah describes the character of the King's subjects (vv. 6–9), a topic which had been introduced in an earlier prophecy (2:2–4). The prophet then proceeds to reintroduce (cf. 1:9; 10:20–22) and enlarge upon the subject of the remnant, which would include peoples from among the Gentiles (vv. 10–16). Jehovah's redemption of the remnant is followed by a song of praise and thanksgiving for their redemption (ch. 12).

The Shoot of Jesse (vv. 1–5)

1   The house of David will fall into such a state of dishonor and disrepute (cf. Amos 9:11) that the prophet here does not refer to it by its proper name, but by the name of David's father—the stock of Jesse.

And there shall come forth a shoot out of the stock of Jesse, and a branch out of his roots shall bear fruit. The Assyrian forest will be left without a hint of life in it; in contrast, the house of David, although brought low, will revive in a Branch growing out of the roots of a stump that remains. The Branch will bear glorious fruit unto God, and from this lowly beginning will grow the mighty conquering power of God's King and kingdom.

2   *The spirit of Jehovah shall rest upon him.* This is a reference to the Holy Spirit's coming upon Jesus at His baptism (Matt. 3:16; Mark 1:10; Luke 3:22; John 1:32). While Isaiah will discuss and enlarge upon this theme in later passages, here he lists six characteristics of the Spirit, characteristics with which He endows the Branch. He is (1–2) *the spirit of wisdom and understanding,* two concepts that are closely related. *Wisdom* is insight into all underlying causes and consequences of things, whereas *understanding* is ability to form a proper judgment in response to wisdom's insight. He is (3–4) *the spirit of counsel and might,* another closely related pair of characteristics. *Counsel* is direction in determining a plan or formulating a solution; *might* is the power to carry the plan or counsel through to achievement. He is also (5–6) *the spirit of knowledge and of the fear of Jehovah.* This *knowledge* entails full and complete comprehension of God and man; it is always governed and directed in *the fear of Jehovah,* that is, in reverence and with due regard for Him, His will, and His glory. The Branch would rule in the fullness of this spirit.

3   *His delight shall be in the fear of Jehovah.* It will be the delight and joy of the Branch to render full and complete service in compliance with Jehovah's will and under His guidance. Nothing will be done under compulsion, except under the compelling force of love and reverence. When Jesus renders judgment, it will not be *after the sight of his eyes, neither* (will He) *decide after the hearing of his ears;* that is, He will judge not by outward appearance, perceived by only the eyes and ears, but by His wisdom, a true knowledge of the facts and the inner spirit of those or that which is being judged.

4   *But with righteousness shall he judge the poor, and decide with equity,* that is, in favor of what is right, *for the meek,* the godly, *of the earth.* There will be neither inequity in His judgment nor acceptance of bribes. Every judgment will be right and fair. Moreover, the poor

121

and the meek will be His special concern, for of such will His kingdom consist. In contrast to His disposition toward the poor and meek, those of His own spirit, *He shall smite the earth* ("earthly-minded," Leupold) *with the rod of his mouth; and with the breath of his lips shall he slay the wicked.* (Isaiah is fond of doublets and triplets which give emphasis to his message and arouse one's attention.) John recognized this characteristic in the glorified Christ: "Out of his mouth proceeded a sharp two-edged sword" (Rev. 1:16), and again, "Repent therefore; or else I come to thee quickly, and I will make war against them with the sword of my mouth" (Rev. 2:16). And once more, "Out of his mouth proceedeth a sharp sword, that with it he should smite the nations: and he shall rule them with a rod of iron: and he treadeth the winepress of the fierceness of the wrath of God, the Almighty" (Rev. 19:15). The "sword of his mouth" in John's writings is *the rod of his mouth* of Isaiah. It is by the rod of the Branch's mouth, the sword that proceeds out of His mouth, that He rules the nations and smites them in judgment. What Isaiah saw in prophetic vision of the future, John saw in vision as fulfilled in the present. Paul likewise declares that the lawless one shall be slain "with the breath of his mouth" (II Thess. 2:8). In Isaiah we have a prophecy of the Messiah's twofold realm: the poor and the meek, who make up His kingdom (Matt. 5:3, 5), and the earthly-minded and the wicked, who are in opposition to Him. In one realm He rules by moral suasion in righteousness and equity; in the other He rules by the rod of destruction according to His righteous judgment.

5   In anticipation of His conflict with the wicked, this Shoot of Jesse comes thoroughly prepared. *Righteousness*—conformity to God's divine standard in all things—*shall be the girdle of his waist,* which will support Him in every contest. *And faithfulness*—firmness and stability from which He never wavers—shall be *the girdle of his loins.* In the confidence and strength of these attributes He challenges and meets the wicked.

The Character of the Citizens (vv. 6–10)

6–9   From a characterization of the King and His rule, the prophet passes to a description of the character of the subjects of His kingdom. *And the wolf shall dwell with the lamb, and the leopard shall lie down with the kid; and the calf and the young lion and the fatling together; and a little child shall lead them. And the cow and the bear shall feed; their young ones shall lie down together; and the lion shall eat straw like the ox. And the sucking child shall play on the hole of the asp, and the weaned child shall put his hand on the adder's den. They shall not hurt nor destroy in all my holy mountain; for the earth shall be full of the knowledge of Jehovah, as the waters cover the sea.* All of these hereditary foes now dwell together in peaceful co-existence. It is noteworthy that the prophet places side by side a wild animal and a tame or domesticated one: a wolf and a lamb, a leopard and a kid, the young lion and the fatling, the cow and the bear. Furthermore, a little child shall lead them. Here is a picture of peace and tranquility, but it is to be found only among those inhabiting God's holy mountain.

This description of peace and harmony drawn from the animal kingdom can no more be taken literally than can the description of a rod proceeding out of the mouth of Jesus. The prophet is not looking to a time when animals of the natural world will be living without enmity, but he is describing the peace of those in Jehovah's holy mountain, the kingdom of God, who have undergone a spiritual and moral transformation. It is in the holy mountain (cf. Isa. 2:2–4; Zech. 8:3; Heb. 12:18–28) that men shall not hurt or destroy each other. Neither is the prophet speaking of a time when the nations of the world will no longer be at war with one another. The prophet is describing the "animal" (carnal) nature of man as it is brought under subjection to the spirit and will of Christ. Old things have passed away; men and women have become new creatures in Christ (cf. II Cor. 5:17). The old man has been crucified in Christ, and the new man is led by a childlike spirit, a simple alertness to hear and learn, and a readiness to obey (Matt. 18:3). Some have suggested that the wild and domesticated animals represent the Gentiles and Jews, but this is doubtful.

10 It is clearly evident from the prophet's next statement that, as we have said, verses 6–9 are descriptive of conditions in the new kingdom under the rule of Messiah. *And it shall come to pass in that day, that the root of Jesse, that standeth for an ensign of the peoples,*

unto him shall the nations seek; and his resting-place shall be glorious.
In that day refers to the time dealt with in the context, which is the
day of the Shoot (the Branch or Twig) of Jesse that bears fruit
(vv. 1–5), the day when our carnal nature is subdued, when "they
shall not hurt nor destroy in all my holy mountain" (vv. 6–9). On the
day both these prophecies are fulfilled, this Root of Jesse will stand for
an ensign, a banner serving as a rallying place for an army or the
populace. The ensign is the messianic King to come, around whom
the people will rally. Isaiah uses two plurals, *peoples* and *nations*,
indicating that the messianic King will be the rallying point for the
Gentiles as well as the Jews. Paul quotes this verse and applies it to the
present time under Christ: "And again, Isaiah saith, There shall be
the root of Jesse,/And he that ariseth to rule over the Gentiles;/On
him shall the Gentiles hope" (Rom. 15:12). Paul uses this verse to
show the right of the Gentiles of his day to the gospel of Christ. Note
carefully, *it shall come to pass in that day*—the day of the emergence
of the Root of Jesse (vv. 1–5) and of perfect harmony among animals
(vv. 6–9)—that the Root of Jesse that stands for an ensign will arise as
a ruler around whom the Gentiles rally and in whom they have hope.
According to Paul (Rom. 15:12), this verse is fulfilled in Christ now;
the Gentiles now have hope. Therefore, He is reigning or ruling now,
and if He is ruling now, the scene depicting harmony among animals
pertains to the present time under Christ, not to some future period.
The passage finds its fulfillment in the conversion of sinners since
Pentecost. If the whole passage is not now fulfilled in Christ, then the
Gentiles have no basis of hope.

The Remnant (vv. 11–16)

11 *And it shall come to pass in that day,* the same time period,
that the Lord will set his hand again the second time to recover the
remnant of his people, that shall remain, from Assyria, and from
throughout the whole earth. The first time God set His hand to
recover the remnant involved the return of the Jews under Zerub-
babel and Joshua the high priest from captivity in Babylon (see Ezra
1–6). Now in that day—the day of the reigning Branch—He would
set His hand a second time to recover the remnant from all parts of

the earth. Under the gospel God has been doing this since Pentecost (Acts 2). Paul says, "Even so then at this present time also there is a remnant according to the election of grace" (Rom. 11:5). This remnant according to the election of grace is being called and gathered under the rule of Him who arose from the root of Jesse (Rom. 15:12).

12-13 With the ensign set up as the rallying point of the nations (Gentiles), God will gather the outcasts of Israel and the dispersed of Judah *from the four corners of the earth*, a figure of speech indicating all quarters of the earth. The envy and vexation that had existed between Ephraim and Judah will be abolished; the two will dwell together as one.

14 The Philistines, former longtime enemies of Israel and Judah, will be entreated and persuaded to come along as the citizens of the new kingdom *fly down upon the shoulder* (the slope from the hills to the plain) of these neighbors to the west. Thus a new coalition of Judah, Ephraim, and converted Philistines will be formed under the Messiah. *Together shall they despoil* (conquer, take as booty) *the children of the east: they shall put forth their hand upon Edom and Moab; and the children of Ammon shall obey them.* Under its powerful spiritual King, a "shoot out of the stock of Jesse" (v. 1), "the Lion that is of the tribe of Judah, the Root of David" (Rev. 5:5), the new spiritual kingdom will include kinsmen, the descendants of Abraham, and former enemies. They will now dwell together in peace (vv. 6-9).

15 *The tongue of the Egyptian sea* probably refers to the waters that confronted Israel as the people fled from Egypt. It would be destroyed, and the River (Euphrates) would be dried up. These events signify not only the removal of all obstacles to the remnant's return, but also the removal of all tribal and national boundaries. Under this new order all barriers will be removed by the power of Jehovah; men will march dryshod over sea and river.

16 The new order will be "unto the uttermost part of the earth" (Acts 1:8), for the King's dominion will "be from sea to sea, and from the River to the ends of the earth" (Zech. 9:10). For those carried away, there will be a way of return: *And there shall be a highway for the remnant of his people, that shall remain, from Assyria; like as there was for Israel in the day that he came up out of the land of Egypt.* It

125

will be a way provided by Jehovah; it will not be a human highway, but a divine one (cf. 35:8–10).

CHAPTER 12

Rejoicing and Thanksgiving of the Remnant

1   The opening phrase, *in that day,* identifies what follows with the redemption of the remnant (ch. 11, esp. v. 16). As the deliverance from Egypt had evoked a song of rejoicing (Exod. 15), so the assurance of a highway for the redeemed and the people's deliverance is followed by a psalm, a song of rejoicing and thanksgiving. The prophet speaks in the singular, for God's people will be united under the new David; as one they will praise Him: *Thou shalt say, I will give thanks unto thee, O Jehovah; for though thou wast angry with me, thine anger is turned away, and thou comfortest me.* The Lord had concluded each of the woes against His people with the refrain, "For all this his anger is not turned away" (5:25; 9:12, 17, 21; 10:4). All this was changed now, for in their returning to Jehovah His anger was turned away from them, and He comforted them. This is the blessing of the redeemed: sin has been forgiven; the light has appeared and now shines upon the people in darkness. In this song Jehovah is recognized and praised as the source of salvation.

2   The redeemed will say, *Behold, God is my salvation; I will trust, and will not be afraid: for Jehovah, even Jehovah, is my strength and song; and he is become my salvation.* They have finally crossed the river of separation from their homeland and have passed through their sea of affliction. It is Jehovah, and He alone, who has redeemed them—"Besides me there is no saviour" (43:11). As Savior, He is now the object of their trust and the source of their courage; He is the strength and song of the redeemed. The similarity to Israel's redemption from Egypt is highlighted by the inclusion of a part of Moses' song, "Jehovah is my strength and song,/And he is become my salvation" (Exod. 15:2). What a mighty power on which to rely! This spirit of joy and thanksgiving finds constant expression in the praise and

exultation of the apostle Paul, and should reflect the mood of every redeemed member of the remnant today.

3 Since Jehovah is the salvation, strength, and song of the redeemed—the source of all spiritual blessings—*Therefore with joy shall ye* (plural, each individual) *draw water out of the wells of salvation.* Joy and rejoicing should characterize God's people at all times, causing them to travel the heavenly highway (11:16) with continuous singing and perpetual praise. Paul caught the true spirit and emotionalism of this great truth and tried diligently to impress the principle of praise upon the hearts of his brethren in Philippi; over and over he urged them to rejoice and let their joy be made known to all men. In Israel's travel from Egypt to Canaan through the terrible wilderness of drought and scarcity, Jehovah had provided water from the rock at Horeb and at Meribah (Exod. 17:6; Num. 20:11). So now, along the highway for the remnant, the Lord will provide abundance of *water out of the wells of salvation.* Wells (plural) emphasizes the abundance of spiritual water for the traveler. As the people of Israel "drank of a spiritual rock that followed them: and the rock was Christ" (I Cor. 10:4), so let the pilgrim today drink from God's *wells of salvation,* wells of grace, redeeming love, strength, and courage, and from the rock which is Christ (John 4:10, 14; 7:37–38).

4 An anonymous psalmist said, "Let the redeemed of Jehovah say so" (Ps. 107:2); that is, let him declare his thanksgiving for Jehovah's goodness and loving-kindness in redeeming His saint from the hand of the adversary. In like manner, through six imperatives Isaiah urges the redeemed to "say so":

1. *And in that day shall ye say, Give thanks unto Jehovah.* The phrase *And in that day* maintains the continuity of the message introduced in chapter 11. The redeemed should be constantly grateful to God, expressing their appreciation by continuous thanksgiving to Him (cf. Col. 3:15, 17; I Thess. 5:18; Phil. 4:6). The thankful soul acknowledges that his blessings are from a higher source than himself.

2. *Call upon his name.* In ancient times one's name was regarded as a summation of one's whole character; this was particularly true of the name *Jehovah.* Even today God's name stands for all that He is. So we call upon His name when we look to Him for guidance, blessings,

and help in all circumstances of life. Through the psalmist Jehovah said, "Call upon me in the day of trouble:/I will deliver thee, and thou shalt glorify me" (Ps. 50:15).

3. *Declare his doings among the peoples.* This command points out a weakness of God's saints today, the failure to declare His mighty doings to the heathen about us. Travelers on the highway of the remnant should declare everywhere and to everyone God's hand in the affairs of nations as He controls and determines "their appointed seasons, and the bounds of their habitation" (Acts 17:26). Saints should recognize and declare constantly His providence in the life of all His people and among the nations of the world; for He not only redeems, but He also directs, overrules, and brings to a glorious consummation all His plans and purposes.

4. *Make mention that his name is exalted.* In a world of irreverence toward all things holy and God's sacred name, the redeemed traveler should recognize and mention to others that there is no name above that of our God and His Son. "Holy and reverend is his name" (Ps. 111:9).

5 5. *Sing unto Jehovah; for he hath done excellent things: let this be known in all the earth;* "sing unto Jehovah a new song, and his praise from the end of the earth" (42:10). This is a new song that has never been sung before, for never before have men been so completely and gloriously redeemed (cf. Rev. 5:9–10). The command, *let this be known in all the earth,* lays upon every redeemed traveler the joyous task of evangelism. We must tell to all the excellent things done by our God.

6 6. *Cry aloud and shout, thou inhabitant of Zion; for great in the midst of thee is the Holy One of Israel.* Before the prophet's eye and in his mind is the spiritual Zion to which we have now come (Heb. 12:22), and upon which now stand the Lamb and His jubilant 144,000, who sing as it were a new song. They have been purchased out of the earth, and they follow the Lamb wherever He goes (Rev. 14:1–5).

Oracles of Judgment Against Individual Nations (13–23)

An Introductory Word

In this section the prophet deals with the future of ten nations, including Judah; two of the prophecies relate to Babylon (13:1–14:27; 21:1–10). Since Isaiah has spoken of the fall of Assyria (ch. 10) and the establishment of God's permanent kingdom and rule under the Sprout of David (chs. 7–11), it seems that this is a most suitable place to discuss the future of heathen nations whose history touches that of His people. Jeremiah and Ezekiel follow the same pattern set here by Isaiah, bringing prophecies concerning various nations together in a group (Jer. 46–51; Ezek. 25–32). Daniel, the fourth Major Prophet, focuses on the fortunes of the permanent kingdom of God in contrast to the kingdoms of the world, all of which will be used by Jehovah and destroyed. They must cease before God's kingdom is fully established.

Two questions arise at this point: (1) What was the date of these prophecies? and (2) Did Isaiah write them; in particular, did he write the prophecy concerning Babylon? Regarding the first, the only dates occurring in the entire section are the year of the death of Ahaz (715 B.C.), when Isaiah received the prophecy concerning Philistia (14:28), and the year of Tartan's coming to Ashdod (713 B.C.), when Isaiah was instructed to give a symbolic message to Judah. When the prophet received the remaining prophecies or when he wrote them is a matter of conjecture.

The second question is one raised by liberal critics and theologians. They point out that, inasmuch as Babylon was subject to Assyria, which was the dominant kingdom of the world at the time Isaiah wrote, there was no indication that Babylon would become a great world power. From this they reason that the prophecy concerning Babylon (13:1–14:27) must have been written years later by someone other than Isaiah. The same issue is raised regarding chapter 21, also a prophecy about Babylon; chapter 39, where the prophet says the nation of Judah will go into Babylonian captivity; and 44:28–45:7, where, long before his birth, Cyrus is named as the deliverer from Babylon. There are similar references throughout the book. Consequently, the liberal critics regard the book as an unsolvable riddle and patchwork; in fact, when they get through with it, very little remains of Isaiah. On the other hand, predictions of the future of nations or individuals by God's chosen servants present no problem to the conservative student of the Bible. In chapters 41–48 God challenges the idols to a contest and rests His claim to being the sole Deity on His ability to declare the end from the beginning. Subsequent history demonstrates Jehovah's ability to do this; therefore, He is God. Clarence McCartney once said, "One's faith in miracles depends on whether he spells his god with a capital 'G'." Since the believer does, he has no problem with Isaiah's prophecies. Furthermore, two arguments settle the question: (1) the book itself claims to be "the vision of Isaiah the son of Amoz, which he saw"; and (2) Peter further settled the matter when he said, "For no prophecy ever came by the will of man: but men spake from God, being moved by the Holy Spirit" (II Peter 1:21). We proceed, therefore, in the confidence that Isaiah is the author of all the prophecies in the book bearing his

name. No man ever lived more completely in the future than did
Isaiah.

CHAPTER 13
The Oracle Against Babylon

The Call to Arms (vv. 1–5)

1   *The burden of Babylon, which Isaiah the son of Amoz did see.*
The word translated *burden* (the Hebrew *massa*) literally means "a
load." Delitzsch prefers "oracle" (margin), indicating a "verdict of
God . . . the judicial sentence of God" (I. 285). We may conclude
that the word carries the idea of a heavy or weighty pronouncement of
doom from Jehovah. The word *burden* is applied to nine of the ten
nations which come under the doom of Jehovah in this section,
including Judah and excluding Ethiopia. In addition, it occurs in
connection with lifting the pronouncement of doom from Judah or
Jerusalem (22:25).

2   Although He is not specifically named, the command of verse
2 issues from Jehovah; it is a summons to provide an army. There are
three commands: (1) to set up an ensign or flag, a place for rallying,
upon a bare mountain where it can be clearly seen; (2) to cry out, lift
the voice high, that it may be heard afar; (3) to wave or shake the
hand, denoting an urgent beckoning. Those summoned are to enter
into the gates of the nobles, either into Babylon, the city of nobles, or
into cities ruled by nobles.

3   Those consecrated by Jehovah are called to carry out the mission of war. They are described as *mighty men, even my proudly
exulting ones,* who will execute His anger against Babylon. They are
later identified as the Medes. Note that the call and execution are
entirely from Jehovah; the army will be an instrument in His hand.

4   The tempo of the prophecy rises; excitement mounts. *The
noise of a multitude in the mountains, as of a great people!* Response
to the call is instant; Isaiah sees a tumultuous group: *the noise of a
tumult of the kingdoms of the nations gathered together!* The group is

131

a heterogeneous multitude of various nationalities marshaled together for war. All doubt as to who is in command is now removed; *Jehovah of hosts is mustering the host for the battle.*

5   Jehovah will whip this mixed group into a conquering force. Without yet naming the country from which they come, the prophet continues: *They come from a far country, from the uttermost part of heaven.* Jehovah will use them as *the weapons of his indignation, to destroy the whole land.* Babylon, the nation that would rise to world domination and carry Judah into captivity (Mic. 4:10), would in turn be brought down by the mighty hand of Jehovah of hosts.

The Terror of the Day of Jehovah (vv. 6–16)

6   The prophet describes the day of Jehovah which is to come upon Babylon. The day was at hand, but not from Isaiah's point of view, for Babylon had not reached its peak of power; it was not ready for destruction. Nabopolassar and Nebuchadnezzar had not yet built the city and empire to the point that Nebuchadnezzar could say, "Is not this great Babylon, which I have built for the royal dwelling-place, by the might of my power and for the glory of my majesty?" (Dan. 4:30). The day of Jehovah will come when Babylon is at its mightiest. *The day of Jehovah* (day of the Lord) is always a day of judgment and the fierce anger of Jehovah. As such, it is a day of destruction for those upon whom it falls, although it may be a day of deliverance for the faithful; *as destruction from the Almighty shall it come.*

7–8   Men will have a sense of utter helplessness; their hands will be feeble and their hearts will sink within them. In their dismay the doomed will feel *pangs and sorrows,* anguish like the terrible pains of a woman in childbirth. As they look at one another, *their faces shall be faces of flame.* As they see enflamed Babylon flare up into a bright red and then subside into pallid emptiness, their faces will likewise be alternately flushed and pale.

9   The day itself is now described. *Behold, the day of Jehovah cometh, cruel, with wrath and fierce anger; to make the land a desolation, and to destroy the sinners thereof out of it.* This is the *destruction from the Almighty* (v. 6). The land is left a desolation, and the sinners

are destroyed out of it. Sin brings its terrible and awesome consequences upon man and upon all things that are touched by him and his sin. Although the description which follows may foreshadow the final and ultimate judgment, the prophet does not have that in mind. Rather, he is speaking of Babylon and her destruction, the end of the Babylonian world.

10 *For the stars of heaven and the constellations thereof shall not give their light; the sun shall be darkened in its going forth, and the moon shall not cause its light to shine.* All is dark—starless and without light—not physically, but psychically. Isaiah has already introduced such a thought (5:30). We are reminded of Joel's description of the visitation of the Lord and the judgment against the nations (Joel 2:10; 3:15–16). Jeremiah (4:24–28) and Ezekiel (30:3, 18) speak of impending judgments in similar terms. Jesus uses the same kind of language in describing the destruction of Jerusalem and the end of the Jewish nation and her religion (Matt. 24:29).

11–12 Erdman describes Babylon as "the type and symbol of cruel and ruthless imperialism" (p. 49); and Smith says, "Babylon represents civilization; she is the brow of the world's pride and enmity to God" (I. 427). The prophecy now goes beyond Babylon to include all those nations which she symbolizes, those nations which are motivated by pride and arrogance to conquer and destroy. *I will punish the world for their evil, and the wicked for their iniquity; and I will cause the arrogancy of the proud to cease, and will lay low the haughtiness of the terrible.* Tyrants are cast down, and men, whether great or insignificant, become more scarce than the pure gold of Ophir. The location of Ophir is uncertain; three possibilities have been suggested by scholars: India, the east coast of Africa, and southeast Arabia. Southeast Arabia is the location most generally accepted.

13–14 The prophet continues his description of the day of Jehovah as the end of Babylon. *Therefore I will make the heavens to tremble, and the earth shall be shaken out of its place, in the wrath of Jehovah of hosts, and in the day of his fierce anger.* It is the end of the world, the final judgment, for Babylon; like all nations, it will be judged in time. As the timid roe or gazelle of the field flees in the face of danger, and as sheep, animals incapable of reassembling themselves, scatter so that no man can gather them, so will every man flee to his own land, for Babylon was made up of many peoples. Each will look out for himself.

15–16 If there should be any persons remaining, they *shall be thrust through* with the sword; and those taken shall likewise be slain. The cruelty of war knows no bounds! Men become heartless, void of sentiment and feelings. The prophet concludes: *Their infants also shall be dashed in pieces before their eyes*—what horror! *Their houses shall be rifled*—plundered—and their possessions carried away; *and their wives ravished*—raped or abducted from their families.

The Completeness of the Destruction (vv. 17–22)

17 The army which was previously called together to destroy Babylon (vv. 2–5) is now clearly designated by name: *Behold, I will stir up the Medes against them.* Media lay south and southwest of the Caspian Sea, north of the Zagros Mountains. Cyrus, of the Elamite province of Anshan, came to the throne about 559 B.C. and defeated the Median army about 549 B.C., thus uniting the Medes and the Persians. In 539 B.C., Cyrus and his army took the city of Babylon, whose citizens received him as a liberator. The buildings of the city were left intact, but Babylon's political and military power was brought to an end. Isaiah notes that the Medes *shall not regard silver, and as for gold, they shall not delight in it.* This does not mean that they were a rude or barbaric people, but that they could not be bought off; they were motivated by power and by revenge, not booty.

18 The young men would be dashed to the ground, slain by arrows from the bows of the Medes. The ruthless cruelty and heartless spirit of the Babylonians would be equaled by the Medes, for *they shall have not pity on the fruit of the womb; their eye shall not spare children* (cf. v. 16).

19 Observe the contrast! On the one hand, there is *Babylon, the glory of kingdoms, the beauty of the Chaldeans' pride*, but on the other hand, she *shall be as when God overthrew Sodom and Gomorrah.* Hammurabi, who reigned over Babylon and the Old Babylonian Empire (1728–1686 B.C.), beautified the city to the point that it was the pride of the empire. Then its glory deteriorated until the days of Nabopolassar and his son Nebuchadnezzar II (crowned 605 B.C.), who restored the city's glory. From that state of glory and pride, it would become like Sodom and Gomorrah, which were overthrown by God; Jehovah would similarly work Babylon's overthrow and destruction through the Medes and Persians (see 44:28–45:7). One might infer from this that the destruction would be immediate, but this was not the case. Delitzsch says that Cyrus left the city still standing with its double ring of walls. "Darius Hystaspis, who had to conquer Babylon a second time in 518 B.C., had the walls entirely destroyed, with the exception of fifty cubits. Xerxes gave the last thrust to the glory of the temple of Belus. Having been conquered by Seleucus Nicator (312), it declined just in proportion as Seleucia rose. . . . At the time of Strabo (born 60 B.C.) Babylon was a perfect desert" (I. 304). Alexander of Macedonia had wanted to restore the city, but he died (323 B.C.) before getting the project under way. So although not immediately, the prophecy was totally fulfilled.

20 The city's destruction would be complete and final; Babylon would never be rebuilt. *It shall never be inhabited, neither shall it be dwelt in from generation to generation: neither shall the Arabian pitch tent there; neither shall shepherds make their flocks to lie down there.* On this point Leupold observes, "Somehow even the wild Arabs will avoid the place and refuse to pitch their tent there. No shepherd of any racial background will make his flock lie down on this accursed ground" (I. 249).

21–22 Instead of being a place for human habitation, Babylon will be desolate. The prophet paints a melancholic picture of wild and doleful creatures inhabiting the ruins of the once proud city. Few of these can be identifed with certainty; the translations in the American Standard Version—wild goats dancing here and there, jackals yelping, wolves howling their mournful night cry, and other creatures slithering through the rubble—do, however, give us a fairly graphic picture. Isaiah concludes, *And her time is near to come, and her days shall not be prolonged.* As noted above (v. 6), from Isaiah's point in time the destruction was not near; but from the standpoint of Babylon's glory and the zenith of her power, it was not far distant.

CHAPTER 14

A Taunting Song over the Fall of the Tyrant
(vv. 1–27); The Burden of Philistia (vv. 28–32)

Compassion on Jacob (vv. 1–2)

1 This section (vv. 1–27), a continuation of chapter 13, concerns the fall of the great tyrant, the king of Babylon. It is a song of victory over his defeat. No one king is before the prophet's mind; Isaiah is simply personifying the whole spirit of the Babylonian rulers.

The destruction of Babylon will be followed by the restoration of Israel. The Lord's compassion on Jacob and His choosing Israel to *set them in their own land* will be an act of divine grace; they will have merited nothing from Him. Isaiah does not have in view here the old kingdom of Israel, the theocracy that was cast out, but a new people chosen by God's grace to be established in their homeland. They will not be Jews only, for *the sojourner shall join himself with them, and they shall cleave to the house of Jacob.* The extent to which foreigners joined themselves to the house of Israel is not known; however, it is recorded in the Book of Esther that "many from among the peoples of the land became Jews; for the fear of the Jews was fallen upon them" (Esth. 8:17). There were "both Jews and proselytes" among those in Jerusalem on Pentecost (Acts 2:9–11), and there were devout Greeks in the synagogues of Thessalonica and Athens (Acts 17:4, 17). Impressed by the God of the Jews, Gentiles had joined in their worship. What took place at the time of the return was a foreshadowing of that which was to come under the Messiah.

2 *And the peoples* (plural) *shall take them, and bring them to their place* (cf. 43:6; 49:22; 60:4). Cyrus issued the decree which authorized the return of the Jews and restored to them the temple vessels (Ezra 1); Darius and Artaxerxes, later kings of Persia, gave assistance in rebuilding the temple (Ezra 6); and Artaxerxes allowed Nehemiah to return and build the walls of Jerusalem (Neh. 2). The prophecy that *the house of Israel shall possess them in the land of Jehovah for servants and for handmaids: and they shall take them captive whose captives they were; and they shall rule over their op-*

pressors, was not fulfilled literally, but spiritually or figuratively. The returned Jews never actually enslaved Gentiles. The prophecy was fulfilled as they conquered foreigners by the Spirit of God through truth, "bringing every thought into captivity to the obedience of Christ" (II Cor. 10:5). Isaiah is emphasizing a reversal of the former conditions when Israel served the heathen.

The Taunting Song Against Babylon (vv. 3–11)

3 As in 12:1, these words are addressed to the Israel of the future in the Israel of the present (Delitzsch), assuring them that there will come a day of rest from their sorrow and troubles and from the hard service with which they have been made to serve their captors.

4 In this day of rest, the people, supported by the understanding that comes with reflection, will find the time to take up a parable or taunting song against the king of Babylon. This will not be a song of rejoicing at the misfortune of another, but a rejoicing in the work of God. This joy will rest upon an understanding of His marvelous purpose in history. *The king of Babylon* probably does not refer to any particular individual; rather, the term is used as "a kind of symbol of the forces hostile to God and his people" (Leupold, I. 255). There will be a rejoicing in the fall of such a power: *How hath the oppressor ceased! the golden city ceased!* Isaiah is taking us beyond his own day to the time of Babylon's fall, when the oppressor will cease to oppress and the golden city will cease. Instead of *golden city*, Young suggests "haughty city"; Leupold, "boisterous raging"; Barnes, from the Jewish commentators, "exactress of gold, or of tribute." Babylon was both an *exactress* (margin) of gold and the city where gold was stored up or reserved; hence, *the golden city* of the American Standard translation.

5 In the song the Israel of the future rejoices that Jehovah has broken both *the staff* used by the tyrant against His people and *the sceptre*, the symbol of the power by which the Babylonian king had cast down peoples throughout the world. Jehovah's power has been pitted against the power of earthly rulers and their gods, and He has conquered.

6 The power and cruelty represented by the staff and sceptre,

137

which have now been broken, formerly *smote the peoples in wrath with a continual stroke,* and *ruled the nations in anger, with a persecution that none restrained.* The king's rapacious conquests, the fierceness of his army, and the inability of the other nations to restrain him, are vividly described by Habakkuk, who relates how the Chaldeans swept everything before them (Hab. 1:5–17).

7–8 With the fall of Babylon, not only Israel, but the whole earth will be at rest—at least for a season—and break forth in a joyous song of deliverance; for the power of Babylon will be broken and gone. Isaiah brings the trees into his depiction of worldwide rejoicing; sharing in the jubilation are the fir trees and the cedars of Lebanon, the majestic giants of the forest which had suffered so violently at the hands of the Babylonian monarchs. Their song is, *Since thou art laid low, no hewer* (feller of trees) *is come up against us.*

9 In contrast to the quiet of the earth at the fall of Babylon and her power, *Sheol* (the world of the unseen spirits of the dead) is greatly agitated at the prospect of the tyrant coming to that realm. His coming stirs up the spirits of the deceased ("the shades," margin), *even all the chief ones* ("he-goats," margin; i.e., the bellwethers of former flocks), now spending a shadowy existence in Sheol. The fall of such a power has raised up the great of the unseen realm to meet him as he comes to take his place with them.

10 The inhabitants of Sheol appear bewildered at his coming and express their amazement: *Art thou also become weak as we? art thou become like unto us?* The answer is a resounding Yes! for this is the ultimate destiny of all the great who leave God out of their thinking and living. Egypt, Asshur (Assyria), Elam, Meshech, Tubal, Edom—all who terrorize and destroy with the sword—are there (Ezek. 32:17–31). Therefore, Babylon should not be surprised to find all other nations there; likewise, those who are already there should not be surprised at his coming.

11 The pomp of great Babylon is brought down to Sheol, *and the noise of thy viols,* her musical instruments by which she entertained and was entertained, is silent (see Dan. 3:5 for a list of these instruments). Instead of the kingly robes with which the monarch had been clothed and the luxury of his resting place, his pallet and covering will now be worms and maggots. What a contrast!

The Fall of the Mighty! (vv. 12–20)

12   This verse has been the ground of no little misunderstanding and controversy among Bible students. *How art thou fallen from heaven, O day-star* ("Lucifer," King James), *son of the morning!* On the basis of Luke 10:18, this verse was interpreted by some early church fathers as referring to Satan's fall and ejection from heaven together with his angels. Derived from a Hebrew word meaning "to shine," the term translated *day-star* refers to the morning star, the harbinger of a new day, which is at its brightest just before dawn. *How art thou cut down to the ground, that didst lay low the nations!* Does the prophet here change figures from a star to a tree? Since the prophet often changes figures of speech to suit his purpose, and since trees are a frequent image in his book, this is possible. The one who had laid low the nations is now felled in their midst like a great tree. On the other hand, it may be that Isaiah is likening the Babylonian to a brilliant star whose glory is cut down by a fall from the height of heaven to the ground.

13   There is no record of any Babylonian monarch's having uttered in so many words the boast now put in the king's mouth. Probably the prophet is summing up the internal pride and arrogant intentions of Babylon's kings, for the phrase, *thou saidst in thy heart,* suggests purpose or desire. In his quest for power and glory the king desired to storm and take heaven as he had stormed and taken the cities and thrones of men. He would (1) *ascend into heaven,* (2) *exalt* (his) *throne above the stars* which belonged to God, and (3) *sit upon the mount of congregation, in the uttermost parts of the north*—a probable reference to the assembly of the gods, whose dwelling was thought to be on a high mount to the north of Babylon. The king was not speaking of Zion, for that little mount in Judah whose God he had defeated when he carried the Jews into captivity would have had very little appeal to a world conqueror.

14   The king's boast is not yet complete; he would ascend above the heights of the clouds. He was probably thinking of the mount of congregation, which thrust its mighty peak above the clouds. Further, he would make himself *like the Most High.* In this state of

exaltation he would be subject neither to God nor to man; but like the Most High, he would rule in all realms. A mighty ambition, indeed!

15 What a contrast between ambition and reality! From the heights above the clouds the Babylonian is cast down to the depths of *Sheol, to the uttermost parts of the pit*—the very lowest of realms. While *the pit* is not necessarily the grave, it is a common synonym for Sheol.

16–17 The scene shifts from Sheol back to earth, where men behold the body of the fallen monarch, stricken in battle and taking his place amidst the slain soldiers who served him. He is no greater than the lowliest private. As bystanders gaze upon his body, *they shall consider thee, saying, Is this the man* (note, not Satan, but the mortal being whose ambition had reached such heights) *that made the earth to tremble, that did shake kingdoms; that made the world as a wilderness, and . . . that let not loose his prisoners to their home?* In his ambition and search for greatness, in his desire to conquer and rule the world, the Babylonian had made the earth tremble with fear at the sound of his approach. He had made a wilderness of the good earth, which should have been cultivated to serve the needs of man. He had overthrown cities, taking their citizens prisoners, transferring them to lands far from their native home. (Cyrus reversed this policy of Assyria and Babylon, allowing peoples to return home and to rebuild their temples.) Yes, this is that mighty king of Babylon. He, too, is subject to the weakness of all flesh, taking his place beside the smallest of earth.

18–19 The prophet presents another contrast. When the kings of the nations die, their bodies repose in tombs built by them, but not so with the Babylonian king. He will be cast aside from (not "out of") his sepulcher as a useless branch is cut off and cast away. Habakkuk's characterization of the Babylonian king may be a clue to the meaning here—"a haughty man, that keepeth not at home [he shall not abide at home, margin]" (Hab. 2:5). He was away conquering, trying to dominate the world instead of attending to affairs at home; this may explain the lack of a sepulcher in which to be buried. He would be *clothed with the slain* ("as the raiment of those that are slain," margin), covered with blood, like those thrust through with the sword. In other words, he would be like those whom he had slain and who had gone *down to the stones of the pit; as a dead body trodden under foot.* The mighty would be cast down, slain and trodden under foot with the common rabble.

20   The cause of the king's being cast aside, of his being prevented from joining the rest of the dead in burial, is now stated: *because thou hast destroyed thy land, thou hast slain thy people.* His thirst for conquest and glory had destroyed his land and slain his people; the resources of the land had been expended on war. This dynasty of evildoers will be brought to an end, terminated forever. Could not our own country learn from this? During the past seventy years, though no wars have been fought on our soil, we have been involved in four major wars, devastating our resources, costing billions upon billions of dollars and millions of lives. History should be a better teacher than we have allowed her to be.

It Is the Vengeance of Jehovah! (vv. 21–27)

21   The call, *Prepare ye slaughter for his children for the iniquity of their fathers,* seems to be to the Medes whom Jehovah named in 13:17. The children of the mother country have imbibed the spirit of the nation. The destruction must be such that never again will the Babylonians rise up and build cities.

22   In vengeance Jehovah will rise up against the nation, to *cut off from Babylon name and remnant, and son and son's son.* The taking of Babylon by Cyrus (539 B.C.) brought to an end the kingdom which had become a world power under Nabopolassar and his son Nebuchadnezzar. In that night Belshazzar was slain and the nation never rose again.

23   Jehovah reasserts the curse of 13:21–22; Babylon will be a place for the porcupine and pools of water, a doleful waste. The completeness of Babylon's ruin is emphasized in the words, *I will sweep it with the besom of destruction.* A besom is a small broom used to sweep out corners and clear out the trash.

So has it ever been. When a nation reaches the point of such corruption and wickedness that it is unfit to continue, God brings it to an end. This is true of John's Babylon (Rev. 18), and of the beast over which she rules (Rev. 19:20).

141

24–27   Somewhat surprisingly, Assyria is again introduced at this point. Remember, however, that at the time Isaiah was writing, Assyria was still the dominant world power. Only her destruction would allow Babylon to rise to greatness. As Jehovah had purposed, so it would be; God would break the Assyrian in the land, tread him under foot upon His mountains, and remove his yoke and burden from Israel. This destruction of Assyria would be an assurance to Jehovah's suffering people that He would likewise destroy Babylon, removing her yoke from Judah's neck (cf. Jer. 50:17–46). God carries out His purpose. Whatever comes is of His will and direction, and none can annul it or turn it back.

The Oracle Against Philistia (vv. 28–32)

Probably no Canaanite state touched and affected the history of Israel as much as did the Philistine city-states. They occupied a narrow, fertile coastal plain in southwest Canaan. The Philistines were there in the days of Abraham (Gen. 21:32, 34), of Isaac (Gen. 26), and of Moses (Exod. 13:17), and they were there when under Joshua Israel entered the land. There was constant conflict between the two nations. During the days of the judges, the Philistines oppressed Israel under both Shamgar (Judg. 3:31) and Samson (Judg. 13–14). King Saul fought numerous battles with them; it was in one of those battles that he and Jonathan were killed (I Sam. 31). Under David they were finally subdued. Jehoshaphat received tribute from some of them (II Chron. 17:11); but later Jehovah stirred up the spirit of the Philistines, and with Arabian allies they came up against Jehoram, carrying away much booty (II Chron. 21:16–17). With God's help, Uzziah conquered and destroyed the walls of several Philistine cities (II Chron. 26:6–7). Because of Edomite and Philistine victories over Judah, Ahaz appealed to Tiglath-pileser for help (II Chron. 28:16–21). However, Hezekiah rebelled against the Assyrian, refusing to serve him. Enjoying the favor of Jehovah, Hezekiah was victorious over the Philistines (II Kings 18:7–8).

In the writings of prophets after Isaiah, Philistia is still under the judgment of God. She will drink of the cup of Jehovah's wrath which is passed to all the nations (Jer. 25:15–17, 20). The ultimate result will be her complete destruction (Jer. 47). "There shall be no inhabitant" remaining (Zeph. 2:5). The reason is that "the Philistines have dealt by revenge, and have taken vengeance with despite of soul to destroy with perpetual enmity" (Ezek. 25:15). As late as the time of the prophet Zechariah, Jehovah says, "I will cut off the pride of the Philistines" (Zech. 9:6).

28 *In the year that king Ahaz died was this burden.* Ahaz died in 715 B.C. It is not indicated whether the prophet received the oracle before or after the king's death.

29 The Philistines' rejoicing over the breaking of the rod that had smitten them was premature; *for out of the serpent's root shall come forth an adder* (more venomous than the first), *and his fruit shall be a fiery flying serpent.* Several explanations of this verse are offered by commentators. Delitzsch thinks that it refers to the house of David: (1) David and Solomon ruled over Philistia; so with the breaking up of Israel and Judah, Philistia rejoiced. (2) Out of the root of David comes the adder, King Hezekiah; and (3) following him will come the Messiah, who will pronounce the final doom on the Philistines. This explanation seems to miss the mark completely. Rawlinson's view, though not absolutely conclusive, is more reasonable. He sees Tiglath-pileser, who invaded the north in 734 and 727 B.C., as the serpent who has now been broken; he sees Sargon, who invaded the land and took some Philistine cities in 711, as the adder; and Sennacherib, who took several of their cities in 702, as the flying serpent. (Rawlinson deduces all this from Assyrian texts.) But inasmuch as Jeremiah said that Philistia would drink of the cup of Jehovah's wrath (the Babylonian invasion), and Zechariah, speaking after the return from Babylon, said that the pride of Philistia was yet to be cut off (Zech. 9:6), some other solution must be sought. It seems more reasonable to this writer that the Assyrians are the rod that is broken, that Babylon is the adder, and that a third power, which is not specified, is the flying serpent that will complete the destruction.

30–31 While the poor and the needy are being fed and sleeping safely, that is to say, are spared, the root and remnant of the Philistines will be killed with famine. Therefore, *Howl, O gate; cry, O city; thou art melted away, O Philistia, all of thee; for there cometh a smoke out of the north, and there is no straggler in his ranks.* The gates of

Philistia will be stormed, and her cities will melt back into the earth—not the cities only, but the whole of the nation. The smoke out of the north is variously interpreted as the campfires of the invaders, the smoke of cities burned as they press southward, or a symbol of the coming fiery destruction. If our interpretation of verse 29 be correct, the invaders in view here are the Babylonians (the adder). They will not destroy the nation completely; that task will be left for the flying serpent, whoever that might be.

32 What shall one say to the nations? Though all the heathen nations be destroyed—and they will be—Jehovah has founded Zion. His city shall stand, *and in her shall the afflicted of his people take refuge.* This of course is spiritual Zion, where all may find safety. When the Assyrians came, Zion stood because of the faith of Isaiah, Hezekiah, and a small remnant (ch. 37).

CHAPTER 15
The Burden of Moab (1)

In Isaiah's series of prophecies against the nations (chs. 13–23), the judgment against Moab is exceeded in length only by those against Babylon and Egypt. (For additional prophecies concerning Moab see 11:14; 25:10; Jer. 48; Ezek. 25:8–11; Amos 2:1–3; Zeph. 2:8–11.) The people of Moab were descendants of Lot by one of his daughters. Their territory lay east of the Dead Sea between the Arnon River to the north and the Zered to the south, extending an indefinite distance eastward into the Arabian Desert. Of the twenty-three place names mentioned in chapters 15 and 16, the location of only about ten can be identified today. The location of the cities is not really important, but catching the spirit of the people's dejection and hopeless despair is most significant.

Although kinsmen through their common ancestor Terah, Moab and Israel were bitter enemies from the beginning of their history. Through David, Jehovah had expressed His contempt for this neighbor of Israel, saying, "Moab is my washpot [wash basin]" (Ps. 60:8), indicating the lowly status of the nation. Moab was useful only as a

144

basin in which to wash one's feet. Isaiah's prophecy of the impending judgment against Moab speaks of weeping, wailing, and howling among the people because of the destruction inflicted upon them. The picture painted by the prophet tells of flight, desolate cities, dried-up watercourses, streams made red by blood, the withering of formerly green pastures, and destroyed vineyards. Through Amos, an earlier prophet (755 B.C.), Jehovah had said, "I will send a fire upon Moab, and it shall devour the palaces of Kerioth; and Moab shall die with tumult, with shouting, and with the sound of the trumpet; and I will cut off the judge from the midst thereof, and will slay all the princes thereof with him, saith Jehovah" (Amos 2:2–3). And through Zephaniah, the last prophet to mention Moab, He said, "I have heard the reproach of Moab, and the revilings of the children of Ammon, wherewith they have reproached my people, and magnified themselves against their border. Therefore as I live, saith Jehovah of hosts, the God of Israel, Surely Moab shall be as Sodom, and the children of Ammon as Gomorrah, a possession of nettles, and salt-pits, and a perpetual desolation" (Zeph. 2:8–9).

Crying, Weeping, and Trembling over Desolation (vv. 1–4)

1 Ar (whether a city or a region is uncertain) was probably to the north on the river Arnon; and Kir, if identified with Kir-hareseth (16:7), was probably about ten miles east of the south end of the Dead Sea. Both of these would be brought to nought and laid waste in a night. It is uncertain whether in a night means they would actually be destroyed at night, or at a time when disaster was least expected. The point of certainty is the destruction.

2 The citizens of Bayith (location unknown) and of Dibon (an important city throughout Old Testament history) go up to the high places and to their pagan temple to weep and cry out to their idols, wailing over Nebo (a city on or near Mount Nebo) and Medeba, a city about sixteen miles southeast of the mouth of the Jordan. The baldness of their heads and cutting of their beards, a common practice at that time to display grief, give emphasis to their dejection and hapless condition.

3 Girded with sackcloth (a coarse, hairy garment worn next to

145

the skin in time of mourning as evidence of anguish and distress), the people are in the streets, on the housetops, and in the broad places, weeping and wailing at the complete collapse of their nation.

4 Upon their invasion of the land, the Israelites had taken *Heshbon*, about eighteen miles east of the Jordan, from Sihon, king of the Amorites (Num. 21:25–26). It was rebuilt by "the children of Reuben" (Num. 32:37), but was retaken by the Moabites at some later time. *Elealeh*, also east of the north end of the Dead Sea, lay in disputed territory during much of Old Testament history. The cry of these two cities was *heard even unto Jahaz*, the site of which is unknown, even though it is mentioned several times in the Old Testament and on the Moabite Stone. The armed men cry aloud— not in victory but in despair—as their hearts tremble within them because of their terror and distress.

The Prophet's Lament (vv. 5–9)

5 The great soul of the prophet is deeply touched by the severity of his prophecy, which wrings from his lips the lament, *My heart crieth out for Moab*, as he sees her nobles ("fugitives," margin) fleeing to *Zoar*. This city is mentioned several times in the Old Testament; its exact location is unknown, though it was probably at the south end of the Dead Sea. It is uncertain whether *Eglath-shelishi-yah* is to be considered a place near Zoar, or, as the reading of the margin of the American Standard Version suggests, "a heifer three years old." If the latter reading is correct, the thought is that Moab, like a three-year-old heifer, is unaccustomed to the yoke and chafes under oppression. Jeremiah 48:11 (see also the verses which follow) lends credibility to this reading: "Moab hath been at ease from his youth, and he hath settled on his lees, and hath not been emptied from vessel to vessel, neither hath he gone into captivity: therefore his taste remaineth in him, and his scent is not changed. . . ." *Luhith* and *Horonaim* (both locations are uncertain) cry out amidst the certain destruction which the prophet sees coming.

6 *The waters of Nimrim*, which flow into the Jordan about eight miles north of the Dead Sea and mark the northern limit of the Plain

of Moab, will be desolate. The grass will be withered; and instead of green vegetation, all will be ravaged and waste.

7   As they flee in an attempt to escape the destruction of their own land, the people will carry their possessions and precious belongings *over the brook of the willows*, the river Zered which served as the border between Moab and Edom.

8   The Moabites will be seeking refuge in Edom, *for the cry is gone round about the borders of Moab*, from north to south and from east to west. Wailing is heard from *Eglaim* (location uncertain, though possibly at the north end of the Dead Sea) unto *Beer-elim*— "well of terebinths" (location likewise uncertain, though possibly on the eastern boundary).

9   And it is no wonder that there is wailing: *For the waters of Dimon* (uncertain, but possibly the Arnon) *are full of blood.* No longer flowing clear, they are colored with blood. But this is not all. The end is not yet! For God will bring a lion—further destruction— upon the remnant of the land that escape. The judgment will continue until total destruction of the nation has been accomplished.

CHAPTER 16
The Burden of Moab (2)

As is typical of modern liberal writers, Clements is positive that "these verses [16:1–5] are not from the same hand as the preceding lament and cannot originally have belonged to it" (p. 153). In contrast to this view, conservative writers rightly claim that chapter 16 is a logical continuation of chapter 15; there is no break at this point. The chapter falls into three divisions: (1) Moab's hope (vv. 1–5); (2) Moab's rejection of this hope (vv. 6–12); and (3) the fixed time of the visitation on Moab (vv. 13–14).

Moab's Hope (vv. 1–5)

1   The verses in this section are very difficult to interpret. In fact, Alexander lists six possible interpretations. The major problem is,

Who is speaking to whom? Alexander thinks we have Moabites exhorting other Moabites to make an appeal to Judah. Young agrees. Leupold, along with Delitzsch, Rawlinson, Barnes, and others, contends that the prophet is advising or exhorting Moab to send tribute to Judah, to appeal to the daughter of Zion for refuge. In either case, the basic idea is that in her distressed condition Moab can find hope only in Zion, for Jehovah had founded Zion as the refuge of His afflicted (14:32). *Send* the tribute *from Selah* (the Semitic name for Petra ["rock or cliff"]), the capital of ancient Edom, by way of the wilderness, *unto the mount of the daughter of Zion.* But why would the Moabites send tribute from the Edomite capital? Had they taken refuge there? Had they taken their flocks there for protection? Or does the word refer to a rocky section of Moab to which the people had fled? In either case, it seems that lambs were to be sent through the Edomite wilderness to Jerusalem (cf. II Kings 3:4–8).

2   In their confusion *the daughters of Moab*, the women of the land (cf. "daughters of Judah" in Pss. 48:11; 97:8), are like birds flushed from their nests and roosting places, flitting about. They dart here and yonder at the fords or crossing places of the Arnon which are nearest the land of Judah.

3   Scholars are divided in their explanations of the expression, *Give counsel, execute justice.* Is it the plea of Moab's ambassadors before the gates of Zion, begging Judah for asylum? Is it the prophet's word to Moab, pointing the people to Judah as their only possible source of refuge? Is the prophet urging Moab to treat fugitives from Judah kindly by providing a hiding place for them so that Moab can expect similar treatment from Judah? Probably it is the prophet's advice to Moab as to how to present their plea to Zion as they bring tribute to her. Moab's representatives are to ask Judah to *give counsel, execute justice; make thy shade*—that is, protection for refugees—*as the night in the midst of the noonday*—a complete covering—*hide the outcasts; betray not the fugitive.* Moab's ambassadors are to ask Judah to take the risk of hiding or protecting her former enemies.

4   Who is the object of address in verse 4? If it is Moab, the outcasts referred to are the outcasts of Israel; if Israel is addressed, the outcasts are those of Moab. Commentators have held both views, as is evident from two recent writers: Leupold translates, "Let my [i.e.,

Moab's] neglected ones sojourn among you. Be a hiding place for them from before the face of the destroyer"; whereas Young offers, "Let mine outcasts dwell with thee, O Moab! Be thou a hiding place for them from the face of the spoiler." In the light of the context Leupold's translation is preferable. The prophet is advising Moab to make a plea to Judah, for God would then show them mercy. Further, certain events had transpired in Judah that would enable her to offer refuge: *For the extortioner is brought to nought, destruction ceaseth, the oppressors are consumed out of the land.* Our inability to identify the point in history at which this prophecy was uttered adds to the difficulty.

5   Jehovah's offer of refuge made through His prophet rests on the fact that Judah's God rules all nations and that salvation is always from Him. The offer to shelter former enemies in Zion is adroitly woven into a messianic prophecy: refuge from all enemies will ultimately be found in Jehovah's spiritual Zion under the messianic David. In the light of the promise of Amos regarding the tent of David (Amos 9:11–12) and Isaiah's words concerning the Ruler and refuge to come (7:14; 9:6–7; 14:32), verse 5 must be seen as messianic: *And a throne shall be established in lovingkindness; and one shall sit thereon in truth, in the tent of David, judging, and seeking justice, and swift to do righteousness.* By heeding the prophet's advice, a remnant in Moab will escape and thus have an opportunity to share in the messianic redemption to come under the spiritual David. Otherwise, total and complete destruction will come upon the Moabites.

Moab's Rejection of This Hope (vv. 6–12)

6   If our explanation of verses 1–5 is correct, we have in verse 6 the reasons for Moab's rejection of Isaiah's advice and Jehovah's offer of refuge: arrogancy, pride, and wrath against Judah. But Moab's *boastings are nought*; for he is not dealing with the prophet and Judah, but with Jehovah. About a hundred years later Jeremiah also wrote of Moab's arrogancy: "Because thou [Moab] hast trusted in thy works and in thy treasures, thou also shalt be taken" (Jer. 48:7); "Moab hath been at ease from his youth, and he hath settled on his lees" (Jer. 48:11); "How say ye, We [Moabites] are mighty men, and valiant men

for the war?" (Jer. 48:14); "And Moab shall be destroyed from being a people, because he hath magnified himself against Jehovah" (Jer. 48:42). Thus we understand clearly the ground of Moab's rejection of any offer of help from Jehovah. Today nations and individuals also allow pride, arrogancy, and reliance on self and human wisdom to become stumbling blocks that lead to their destruction.

7 *Therefore* introduces the consequences to come upon Moab for his pride. Moab shall wail for himself; every individual shall join in the wailing, for the basis of the nation's pride and boasting is to be taken away. As their cities have been destroyed (ch. 15), so now their luxuriant vines, the source of their highly prized raisin-cakes, shall be brought to nought. *Kir-hareseth* (probably identical with Kir; see the comments on 15:1), the ancient capital of the district which dominated the caravan route (the King's Highway) from the Gulf of Aqaba to Syria, seems to have been noted for these delicacies.

8 *Heshbon* (see the comments on 15:4) and especially *Sibmah* (probably between Nebo and Heshbon) seem to have been noted for their luxuriant and prolific vines (cf. Jer. 48:32). These vineyards extended eastward to the edge of the desert and northward to *Jazer*. This city is mentioned thirteen times in the Old Testament. It was probably located west-northwest of Rabbath-Ammon and east of the Jordan, though some dispute this. The shoots of Sibmah's famous vines *passed over the sea*. This is either a hyperbolic statement or an indication that plants were carried west of the Dead Sea into the land of Judah. All of the vineyards were to be trodden down by the lords of the nations—the Gentiles—in their destruction of Moab.

9 The prophet's heart had cried out for Moab as her cities were destroyed and her people had to flee (15:5). Another *therefore* introduces the effect of the present destruction upon the prophet. He now weeps for the ruin and desolation to come upon the beautifully terraced vineyards of the land, for vineyards are one of God's gifts to man for his enjoyment and good. Sin can bring all such bounties to an end. The prophet will share the grief of the cities mentioned; he will water them with his tears. Instead of the joyous shout at the ingathering of summer fruits at harvesttime, there will be the shout of battle as the invaders tread the vines under foot. The treading of

destruction will replace the treading of the wine vat—every planting brings its own harvest.

10　Without additional comment, the prophet describes the sad plight of the people and land: *And gladness is taken away, and joy out of the fruitful field; and in the vineyards there shall be no singing, neither joyful noise: no treader shall tread out wine in the presses; I* (Jehovah) *have made the vintage shout to cease.* The deadly quiet which has settled down on the once joyous countryside, the useless stone winepresses found here and there, and the barren, trampled vineyards all bear mute witness that pride goes before destruction and a haughty spirit before a fall. And thus it shall ever be, because Jehovah rules in righteousness; sin, when full-grown, brings forth death.

11　*Wherefore* introduces another conclusion or consequence. When the prophet realizes the full scope of his prophecy, his heart vibrates with pathos and sympathy, just as harp strings pulsate at the touch of the musician. Isaiah's organs or inward parts, the seat of emotions, are deeply moved by what is to befall *Kir-heres* (see the comments on 15:1 and 16:7).

12　The people of Moab will present themselves before the idols upon the high places, each wearying himself to exhaustion as he prays to his gods. But their efforts shall be to no avail; their deities are nonentities. The Moabites know not the true God from whom all help comes.

The Fixed Time of the Visitation on Moab (vv. 13–14)

13　Three suggestions have been offered concerning the prophet's statement, *This is the word that Jehovah spake concerning Moab in time past.* One is that Isaiah is recalling prophecies spoken in the time of Moses (Num. 21:27–30; 24:17) and by Amos (Amos 2:1–3). This is very unlikely. A second view is that the prophecy of 15:1–16:12 was originally spoken by an older prophet and has now been repeated by Isaiah. There is no evidence of this; any suggestion as to who the older prophet might have been is pure speculation. A third, and much more plausible, suggestion is that the prophecy concerning Moab had been spoken by Isaiah in the early years of his lengthy (forty to sixty years) prophetic ministry. It is now about to be fulfilled.

14 *But now Jehovah hath spoken, saying, Within three years, as the years of a hireling, the glory of Moab shall be brought into contempt, with all his great multitude; and the remnant shall be very small and of no account.* The phrase *the years of a hireling* indicates a definite period, for the hireling wants to work not a day longer than the agreement, and the one who hires him wants him to work not a day less. Therefore, without any doubt the devastation of Moab will come within three years. If we knew the date of this prophecy, we could determine whether it was fulfilled by Shalmaneser, Sargon, or Sennacherib. *The glory of Moab* is her cities, wealth, and beautiful vineyards, all of which will be brought into shame and dishonor. Of the multitude of her inhabitants only a very small remnant will be spared; Jeremiah 48:45–47 indicates that such a remnant was indeed spared and remained until the invasion of Nebuchadnezzar. Thereafter Moab would be as Sodom (Zeph. 2:9).

CHAPTER 17

The Burden of Damascus

Damascus is reported to be the oldest continuously inhabited city in the world. Its origin is uncertain, but its history reaches back to the days of Abraham (Gen. 14:15; 15:2). The city is located on a fertile plain east of snow-capped Mount Hermon, on the edge of the Arabian Desert, about 135 miles northeast of Jerusalem. The area surrounding Damascus is watered by two rivers, Abana and Pharpar, which make it a garden spot of great beauty. Until about 300 B.C. it was the capital of Syria, but at that time the capital was transferred to Antioch on the Orontes River in northern Syria.

Location on caravan routes from north to south and east to west put Damascus in conflict with competing powers, especially Israel and Judah. The conflict between Syria and Israel intensified during the reigns of Omri and Ahab. The strong enmity which developed between Damascus and Assyria eventually led to the downfall of Damascus and the Syrian power.

Isaiah's prophecy against Damascus also includes Ephraim (Israel), because the kings of these two nations had conspired against Judah in an attempt to overthrow Ahaz (see ch. 7; 8:4; 10:9, where these two powers are linked together). Ephraim's alliance with a heathen power against the city and people of Jehovah brought him under the same judgment of condemnation as that of the heathen nation. This is clearly pointed out in the prophecy. (For additional prophecies concerning Damascus see Amos 1:3–5; Jer. 49:23–27; Zech. 9:1.)

The Judgment Against Damascus (vv. 1–3)

1 *Behold, Damascus is taken away from being a city, and it shall be a ruinous heap.* The prophet is not saying the buildings of the city will be destroyed, though some may have been; he is saying that Damascus will never again be the city of importance that she once was; her glory will be as a ruinous heap.

2 Three cities bearing the name *Aroer* are mentioned in the Old Testament: one about twelve miles southeast of Beersheba (I Sam. 30:28); one near Rabbah in Ammon, the precise location of which is unknown (Josh. 13:25; Judg. 11:26); and one just north of the Arnon River, east of the Dead Sea, which is mentioned numerous times. The Aroer located in the valley of the Arnon was taken by Hazael, king of Syria, and became the southwest extremity of that nation (II Kings 10:32–33). But it was apparently regained by Moab, for Jeremiah includes Aroer in his prophecy against Moab (Jer. 48:19). It seems probable that this is the city in Isaiah's mind. With its neighboring cities, it will be so completely forsaken that the land will be a place for flocks to graze, a place where they can lie down in peace with no one making them afraid.

3 Ephraim and Damascus will both be destroyed, for *the fortress shall cease from Ephraim, and the kingdom from Damascus.* The glory of both nations will be brought to nought. And it happened to them just as the psalmist had said, "The nations are sunk down in the pit that they made:/In the net which they hid is their own foot taken"

(Ps. 9:15). As they plotted the destruction of another, their own ruin
came.

The Leanness of Jacob (vv. 4–11)

4   In the day of the fall of Syria and Israel (for Syria, 732 B.C.; for
Israel, 722—both at the hands of the Assyrians), the glory of Jacob
(Israel) will be made of small account, as of a man made lean by
either poverty or serious illness. That Damascus has not yet fallen
places this particular prophecy before 732 B.C.

5   A second figure illustrating the barren state of the nation is a
man harvesting heads of grain, leaving only a little grain for the
gleaners and the bare stalks to be plowed under. *The valley of Reph-
aim* was probably an area southwest of Jerusalem where people had
witnessed similar harvest scenes many times.

6   A third figure portraying the nakedness of the land is a man
who shakes the olive berries from the boughs, leaving only a few
berries in the uppermost and outermost branches of the tree. This
metaphor emphasizes how few will make up the remnant of Israel.

7–8   The phrase *in that day* refers to the period just described, the
period of leanness. Men will no longer look to the idols and gods of
their own imagination and creation. *Asherim* is the plural of *Asherah*,
"the Canaanite goddess represented by a carved wooden image im-
planted into the ground, usually adjacent to an altar dedicated to the
god Baal and located on a hilltop under a leafy tree."[1] Men will reject
the Asherim and the sun gods in which they have trusted. Realizing
the futility of such trust, the small remnant will look instead to their
Maker, the Creator of all things, as the only one worthy of respect and
worship.

9   Again the phrase *in that day* refers to the period of leanness
when only bare stalks and a few olive berries remain. Just as the land
is barren, so will the strong cities of Israel be like forsaken places in the
forest and on the mountain top. The land and cities will be a desolation.

---

1. *Theological Wordbook of the Old Testament*, ed. R. Laird Harris (Chicago: Moody,
1980), vol. 1, p. 81.

10   The cause of all this is now clearly stated by the prophet: *For thou hast forgotten the God of thy salvation, and hast not been mindful of the rock of thy strength.* Jehovah had instructed the Israelites to drive out the gods of the Canaanites, but they did not obey. As a result, those idols became a snare to their descendants, leading them away from God, their true rock and stronghold. The Israelites had planted what they thought would be pleasant vines, but they had been strange slips ("vine slips of a strange god," margin; that is, not of Jehovah).

11   In erecting false gods and altars, the Israelites had thought they were providing for bountiful harvests and security from outside forces, *but the harvest fleeth away in the day of grief and of desperate sorrow.* Those who reject God for the empty vanities of the world will find that, when they need the help which only God can provide, they must bear their grief and sorrow alone. Just as Wisdom refused to listen when calamity came to the foolish who had responded to her earlier calls with deaf ears (Prov. 1:24–31), so Jehovah refuses to hear those who have spurned and rejected His call.

The Destruction of the Invader (vv. 12–14)

12   The prophet now returns to the Assyrians. He has already prophesied that they will sweep over Judah like a river overflowing its banks (8:5–8) and that they will be the rod of God's anger against Israel and Judah (10:5–27). Now he vividly and graphically describes this coming of the Assyrians: *Ah, the uproar of many peoples, that roar like the roaring of the seas; and the rushing of nations, that rush like the rushing of mighty waters!*

13   Assyria will come with the destructive force of a raging sea; but it will not always be thus, for *he* (Jehovah) *shall rebuke them, and they shall flee far off, and shall be chased as the chaff of the mountains before the wind, and like the whirling dust before the storm.* God is in control! He uses the nations to accomplish His purpose and then scatters them, bringing them to an end.

14   *At eventide, behold, terror; and before the morning they are not.* The meaning of this prophecy became clear with the destruction of Sennacherib's army before the gates of Jerusalem. The Assyrians

155

caused terror in the evening but were dead bodies in the morning, as Jehovah delivered His people (II Kings 19:32–37). *This is the portion of them that despoil us, and the lot of them that rob us.* God used Assyria to destroy Ephraim and Damascus, who had thought to overthrow Jerusalem; and in turn Assyria, who likewise purposed to overthrow and destroy the citadel of God, came to a similar end. Is there any reason today for God's people to worry that humanism, Communism, Zionism, and all other "Gogs and Magogs" that try to destroy His work may ultimately prove successful? None, for all such forces shall meet the same fate at His hand and in His providence.

CHAPTER 18
Ethiopia

Biblical Ethiopia, the ancient land of Cush, lay south of Egypt. It extended southward from the neighborhood of the first cataract (modern Aswan). Although it claimed a large and indefinite desert area, its lifeline lay in a narrow fertile strip along the Nile River. The ancient country is often associated with Egypt (see, e.g., ch. 20; II Chron. 12:3). Ethiopian mercenary soldiers were in the Egyptian army when Shishak assaulted Jerusalem (II Chron. 12:2–3). An army led by Zerah the Ethiopian was defeated by Asa king of Judah (II Chron. 14:9–15). Isaiah mentions Tirhakah king of Ethiopia and his effort to check Sennacherib in Judah (37:9). The probable date of the events of this chapter is the period of the Assyrian threat to Judah (720–702 B.C.).

Undoubtedly chapter 18 is the most difficult chapter encountered thus far. From where did the ambassadors come, and to whom were they sent? What is the significance of their being *tall and smooth*? And what is the significance of their sending or bringing a present to Jehovah? Commentators give numerous and varied answers to these questions.

The Ambassadors and the Prophet's Word to Them (vv. 1–3)

1   The word *ah* focuses attention on the distance and nature of

the nation considered. It is a *land of the rustling of wings*, buzzing of wings, or "shadowing with wings" (margin); that is, a land of insects, though it is not stated whether they were tsetse flies, locusts, or any of numerous other possibilities. They probably symbolize the multitudinous army that Ethiopia could mobilize. The rivers are no doubt the White and Blue Niles with their tributaries.

2   It seems clear that the ambassadors are from Ethiopia, but to whom are these ambassadors who travel *by the sea, even in vessels of papyrus upon the waters*, sent? (Vessels of papyrus were light craft suitable for rivers and canals but not for large bodies of water.) Are they sent to Jerusalem to incite outright revolt against Assyria, or to form an alliance with Judah against that power (Clements), or at least to stir up Judah in some way against the common enemy (Leupold); or, as Barnes supposes, are they sent to form an alliance with the Assyrians against Judah (p. 324)? Barnes's theory is very improbable, since Sennacherib "heard say of Tirhakah king of Ethiopia, Behold, he is come out to fight against thee" (II Kings 19:9). Others suggest that these are messengers sent by the king of Ethiopia to his own tribes, stirring them to prepare against invasion by the Assyrians (Delitzsch, Rawlinson, Young). Alexander sees in the chapter an announcement to Ethiopia of God's overthrow of Sennacherib's army. Calvin is uncertain.

The word *saying* is an interpolation, leaving the question open as to who is speaking. Are the ambassadors asking for help? Or is the prophet speaking to them, instructing them to return to their home and to be quiet, for God is about to take care of the situation and there is no need for becoming excited (Barnes, Rawlinson)? In the light of II Kings 19:9, this interpretation seems to make the better sense. The prophet tells the ambassadors to return to their own tall, smooth people, whose history from 1000 B.C. to 663 B.C. was one of successful warfare with Egypt. The ambassadors are to return to their *nation that meteth out and treadeth down*, or to their nation "meted out and trodden down" (margin). Does Ethiopia mete out and tread down, or is she meted out and trodden down? Both are true. For some five centuries Ethiopia had been ruled by Egypt; but from 1000 B.C. she had maintained independence and for some time had ruled

Egypt.[2] She was a country *whose land the rivers divide*—or "have despoiled" (margin), for the eroding of her river banks certainly despoiled Ethiopia and enriched Egypt as the silt was carried downstream to that land.

3   The prophet now calls upon all the world to take notice of an impending event. As in 11:10, 12, the language is metaphorical: an ensign is to be lifted up on the hills of Judah, and a trumpet is to announce coming judgment. Let the peoples of the nations see and hear. From the hills and mountains in the land of Judah Jehovah is going to act, and His action will serve as a rallying point for those who worship Him and as a warning of judgment for those who do not. The prophet's call to the world introduces the word from Jehovah which follows.

Jehovah Is in Control (vv. 4–6)

4   In the midst of world foment and upheaval, Jehovah speaks through the prophet, declaring His calm control of world affairs. He will be still, seemingly indifferent, as He beholds from His heavenly dwelling what is taking place. But not so; He is intently concerned. Like the clear heat of summer and the refreshing dew of the night, which gradually ripen grapes and grain for harvest, the Lord is allowing the time of judgment to mature.

5   Before the Assyrians have garnered the harvest of their invasion or gathered together the booty of their conquest, however, Jehovah will act. Before the harvest, *when the blossom is over, and the flower becometh a ripening grape, he will cut off the sprigs with pruning-hooks, and the spreading branches will he take away and cut down.* The prophet repeatedly uses the metaphor of vines and vineyards, so the people will understand. When the time is right, Jehovah will completely destroy the enemy that threatens the world.

6   Dropping the figure of the vineyard, the prophet describes Jehovah's destruction of the Assyrian power: it will be so complete that the carcasses of the army will be food *unto the ravenous birds of the*

---

2. *International Standard Bible Encyclopedia*, ed. James Orr (Chicago: Howard-Severance, 1937), vol. 2, p. 1032.

mountains, and to the beasts of the earth. Both birds and beasts will feast on them summer and winter. The Assyrian had boasted of his greatness—he would take Jerusalem with as much ease as he had taken other cities, including Samaria (10:8–11); but he had failed to realize that he was dealing with Jehovah and not with an idol. Now Jehovah will handle the matter according to His will, not the Assyrian's.

Ethiopia's Homage to the Lord (v. 7)

7   In the time of Assyria's destruction *shall a present be brought unto Jehovah of hosts from a people tall and smooth,* the people described in verse 2. Though Jehovah does not need their help and the prophet sends their ambassadors back home, the Ethiopians will be so awed by the mighty power of Jehovah and so grateful for their deliverance when Assyria is destroyed at the gates of Jerusalem (37:36–37) that they will send a present to Him. There is no record of Tirhakah's sending a present, but it is entirely possible. It would have been brought *to the place of the name of Jehovah of hosts, the mount Zion.* Earlier, when the Lord had destroyed His enemies and had scattered the peoples that delight in war, David said, "Princes shall come out of Egypt;/Ethiopia shall hasten to stretch out her hands unto God" (Ps. 68:31). And speaking of the time when men will serve Jehovah with one consent, a later prophet says, "From beyond the rivers of Ethiopia my suppliants, even the daughter of my dispersed, shall bring mine offering" (Zeph. 3:10). Jehovah's destruction of the wicked and His gracious goodness to His own will so impress those from the farthest reaches that they will bring their gifts to His throne. Glory and honor and power belong unto our God, but shame and destruction will come to those who trust in their own vanities.

CHAPTER 19
An Oracle Concerning Egypt

The Egypt of biblical times experienced a long and varied history.

Prehistoric cultures existed from about 5000 B.C. to 3200 B.C. Writing was introduced in the predynastic age, and in time a calendar of notable accuracy was developed. The Bible student's interest spans a period of approximately two thousand years, from Abraham's sojourn in that land (Gen. 12:10–13:1) to the conversion of the Ethiopian eunuch (Acts 8:26–40). Throughout those centuries the fortunes of God's people were greatly influenced by Egypt's religion, culture, and economic conditions. Though the entire history of that marvelous country is fascinating, our concern in this study is with only the period of Isaiah and what followed.

Chapter 19 falls into two rather clear-cut divisions: threats (vv. 1–17) and promises (vv. 18–25). Although Egypt had been the great oppressor of God's people in their early history and had been a pricking thorn in their flesh through the years, the Lord closes the chapter with a glowing promise of blessing and hope for both Egypt and Assyria (v. 25). Truly, the Lord is gracious. (For additional prophecies concerning Egypt see Jer. 46; Ezek. 29–32; Joel 3:19.)

Threats (vv. 1–17)

Internal discord: The failure of idolatry (vv. 1–4)

1 For the word *burden*, see the comments on 13:1. Jehovah, the only God, will judge Egypt, demonstrating His power over her gods. He will come riding *upon a swift* (light) *cloud*, a symbol of judgment. Jehovah makes "the clouds his chariot;/[He] walketh upon the wings of the wind" (Ps. 104:3); "For he cometh to judge the earth:/He will judge the world with righteousness,/And the peoples with his truth" (Ps. 96:13). The day of Jehovah is "a day of darkness and gloominess, a day of clouds and thick darkness" (Joel 2:2); it is "a day of wrath, a day of trouble and distress, a day of wasteness and desolation, a day of darkness and gloominess, a day of clouds and thick darkness" (Zeph. 1:15). In his prophecy of judgment against Egypt, Ezekiel says, "It shall be a day of clouds, a time of the nations" (30:3); and "as for her, a cloud shall cover her, and her daughters shall go into captivity" (30:18; cf. 32:7). Her idols, "things of nought" (Lev. 19:4, margin),

shall tremble at His presence. With no source of help, the heart—life, soul, or courage—of Egypt will melt in the time of judgment.

2 Jehovah's stirring up Egyptians against Egyptians indicates a state divided by internal strife and anarchy—individuals against individuals, cities against cities, and kingdom against kingdom. There is no doubt that this is the work of Jehovah, who comes riding upon the cloud of judgment. Three times He declares that it is He who acts ("I will stir up"; "I will destroy"; "I will give over"); moreover, He concludes with the words [Thus] saith the Lord, Jehovah of hosts (v. 4). We know from history that Piankhi, a Nubian prince, raided Egypt in about 728 B.C.; his successor, Shabako, also invaded that land, successfully uniting Ethiopia and Egypt under Nubian rule (715–664 B.C.). Thereafter, Psammetichus I, a prince of Sais in the Delta, arose to gain control of all Egypt.[3]

3 In the midst of this internal strife and confusion counsel will fail, for Jehovah will bring it to nought. In praising the Creator and His controlling power over His creation, a psalmist had said, "Jehovah bringeth the counsel of the nations to nought;/He maketh the thoughts of the peoples to be of no effect" (Ps. 33:10). As in all such situations, the leaders will resort to the idols (nonentities) which abound in the land (but which are totally impotent), and to the charmers, and to them that have familiar spirits, and to the wizards, people who claim to have occult powers and a relationship with mysterious unseen forces. Actually, they are as empty and false as the idols themselves.

4 Jehovah continues the threat against Egypt: And I will give over the Egyptians into the hand of a cruel lord; and a fierce king shall rule over them. Is the Lord here speaking of one individual (Delitzsch suggests Psammetichus), or is He using the singular to signify the cruel spirit of all the overlords who will rule Egypt? After defeating the Egyptians several times, the Assyrians under Ashurbanipal sacked Thebes (the No-amon of Nah. 3:8) in 663 B.C. Later, as predicted by Jeremiah (43:10–13; 46:13–26), Nebuchadnezzar smote the land of Egypt. In 525 B.C. Cambyses led a Persian army against Egypt,

---

3. *Zondervan Pictorial Encyclopedia of the Bible*, ed. Merrill C. Tenney (Grand Rapids: Zondervan, 1975), vol. 2, p. 244.

bringing the country under Persian rule. When they revolted, they brought upon themselves the wrath of Xerxes I. When Alexander invaded Egypt (332 B.C.), he was looked upon as a deliverer from the Medo-Persian tyranny. By New Testament times Rome ruled the once proud and powerful land of Egypt, which had been reduced to the status of a Roman province. So it is possible that in verse 4 the Lord is speaking not of one individual, but of the sum of cruel foreign kings who were to rule over the land.

Natural and economic disaster (vv. 5–10)

5   The *sea* mentioned by the prophet is the Nile, the lifeline of Egypt (cf. 18:2; Nah. 3:8). The river will be wasted and become dry. This verse is not necessarily to be taken literally; it may be a symbol of the wasting and decline of the nation, the death of her empire.

6–7   With the wasting of the Nile the canals become stagnant and foul, whereupon the reeds and flags, including the papyrus plant, so important to Egyptian life, wither away. Likewise the meadows or grassy areas and all the sown fields, essential to human and animal life, dry up. The glory of Egypt is brought low.

8   Not only will agriculture suffer, but also the fishermen who depend upon the Nile for their livelihood will lament the decline and failure of their business. The fishermen of that day used hooks *(angle[s])* and, as we know from the artwork of Egyptian monuments, both large dragnets and smaller throw nets.

9   The whole economy will be affected: *Moreover they that work in combed flax*, for which Egypt was noted, *and they that weave white cloth* (cotton) *shall be confounded*.

10   *And the pillars of Egypt shall be broken in pieces*. Are these the obelisks and idols of Egypt (cf. Jer. 43:13, ASV), or are they the foundations of state—honesty, virtue, piety, good people? Rawlinson thinks the wealthy merchants and political leaders are in view. Or does the prophet have in mind the working class, on whom the well-being of a nation depends? The following phrase, *all they that work for hire shall be grieved in soul*, seems to indicate *the pillars of Egypt* are the working class. However, Isaiah may be referring to the whole economy, which is certainly the foundation of a nation's existence.

Foolish counsel (vv. 11–15)

11 The prophet returns to the subject of verse 3—foolish counsel. *Zoan* (Greek, Tanis; earlier Raamses—Exod. 1:11) was located in the northeast section of the Delta near the border. Its history prior to 1300 B.C. is obscure; but during the period between 1085 and 715 B.C., it was prominent as a capital of the pharaohs. During the period 715–644 it was used occasionally by the Nubian rulers as a royal residence.

In earlier times Egypt's wisdom was renowned. "Moses was instructed in all the wisdom of the Egyptians; and he was mighty in his words and works" (Acts 7:22). But by the time of which Isaiah is speaking, *the princes of Zoan are utterly foolish; the counsel of the wisest counsellors of Pharaoh is become brutish*, without reason, irrational, stupid. No prince (any man of the so-called nobility) can claim that he is the son of the wise, the son of the ancient kings, for his advice and its consequences will betray him.

12 Just as the prophet later challenges the idols to a contest with Jehovah (41:21–29; chs. 42–48), so he now challenges the wise among the princes to declare what Jehovah has purposed concerning Egypt—His plans for the nation.

13 But *the princes of Zoan are become fools, the princes of Memphis are deceived; they have caused Egypt to go astray.* According to legend, Memphis, located on the west bank of the Nile about thirteen miles south of Cairo, was the first capital of united Egypt. It occupied an important place in the religious history of the nation. But being deceived by their own human wisdom, the princes of Memphis have now led Egypt astray. Those who are *the cornerstone of her tribes* ("castes," Young; "classes," Rawlinson), the strong leaders of the people, instead of directing them properly, have led them on a course of destruction.

14 Whatever the immediate situation may appear to be, the Lord is in control: *Jehovah hath mingled a spirit of perverseness in the midst of her* (see the comments on v. 3); *and they have caused Egypt to go astray in every work thereof,* staggering about like a drunken man. The carefully conceived plans of the princes have led to actions comparable to the staggering of an intoxicated man who falls and wallows in his own vomit.

15   No work will be accomplished by either the leaders or the common laborers, by the *head or tail, palm-branch or rush* (cf. 9:14). When Jehovah takes away the wisdom of leaders, human plans cannot save individuals or nations. This is certainly a word of warning to the world of today.

Before leaving the theme of Jehovah's rule over the nations and His ability to turn the wisdom of men into folly, it is well to consider the need for wise rulers in every nation. The Preacher said, "Woe to thee, O land, when thy king is a child, and thy princes eat in the morning!" (Eccles. 10:16). It matters not whether "child" refers to chronological age or mental and moral immaturity. The writer has in mind a king who can be swayed by poor counsellors and princes who are more concerned with feasting and getting drunk than in wise rule of their subjects (cf. v. 17; Isa. 3:4, 12; 5:11). Indeed, "Where no wise guidance is, the people falleth;/But in the multitude of counsellors there is safety" (Prov. 11:14). Of course, this maxim assumes that the counsellors are wise men, concerned with the affairs of state. By contrast, "the counsels of the wicked are deceit" (Prov. 12:5). Job says, "He [God] leadeth counsellors away stripped,/And judges maketh he fools" (Job 12:17). Wisdom says, "By me kings reign,/And princes decree justice" (Prov. 8:15). To those who reject true Wisdom and set at nought her counsel, having none of her reproof, she says, "I also will laugh in the day of your calamity;/I will mock when your fear cometh . . . ./Then will they call upon me, but I will not answer;/They will seek me diligently, but they shall not find me" (Prov. 1:26–28). This is the lot of all who trust in their own wisdom, rejecting the wisdom that comes from above; because of their rejection of Jehovah's wisdom, He brings their counsel to nought (Ps. 33:10). By now history should have made it clear that world problems cannot be solved apart from God.

No spirit—only fear and terror (vv. 16–17)

16   Delitzsch sees verses 16 and 17 as a connecting bridge between verses 1–15 and 18–25. Leupold and Young allow that these verses may be a transition between the threats and the promises. However, verse 18 is a likelier candidate for that role. *In that day* points to the period which has just been discussed. The phrase *like* *unto women* suggests a spirit of softness and timidity in contrast to the fierce determination of male warriors to fight and defend. Women have shown themselves to be courageous and of strong will, but typically have not been aggressive brute warriors. Nahum thus described Nineveh in her declining days (3:13); Jeremiah used similar imagery in writing of Babylon (50:37; 51:30). This spirit of weakness and terror comes from the hand of Jehovah, which He shakes over Egypt, threatening the nation with judgment and recompense. No specific judgment is mentioned, but collective judgments are implied.

17   The relationships with Israel during the time of Abraham, the exodus, and the days of David and Solomon, should certainly have acquainted Egypt with Jehovah, Israel's God. At no time in history has the nation of Judah been a terror to Egypt; it is Judah's God that inspires dread. The God who can confuse the counsel of political advisors can also put fear and dread into the hearts of the people. Through Moses Jehovah had said to the Israelites, "This day will I begin to put the dread of thee and the fear of thee upon the peoples that are under the whole heaven" (Deut. 2:25). Similarly, Isaiah identifies the cause of Egypt's fear: Egypt *shall be afraid, because of the purpose of Jehovah of hosts, which he purposeth against it.* That purpose has now been clearly announced.

Promises (vv. 18–25)

The transition from threats to promises (v. 18)

18   There is a great deal of confusion and disagreement as to the meaning of verse 18; therefore, we cannot be dogmatic here. The phrase *in that day* ties the prophecy of blessings to the time period in which the prophecies of judgment will be fulfilled. Out of days of judgment come experiences of blessing. The reference to *five cities in the land of Egypt* is not to be taken literally. Those who take the number literally, disagree as to the time and the cities in view. It is better to understand the word *five* as simply signifying a small number. The words, *that speak the language* ("lip," Hebrew) *of Canaan, and swear to Jehovah of hosts*, present a major problem. Nearly

165

all commentators assume that *the language of Canaan* is the language of Israel—Hebrew—which had come to supplant the language of Canaan. They try to come up with the names of Jewish leaders who, following the time of Isaiah, could have introduced Jehovah worship into Egyptian cities. Others see in the phrase a reference to a time of spiritual unity under the Messiah. However, there is no indication in Scripture that "the language of Canaan" ever came to signify the language of national or spiritual Israel. J. Arthur Thompson recognizes a kinship between Canaanite and Hebrew— "In broad terms NW Semitic included Canaanite (Hebrew, Moabite, etc.), N Canaanite (Ugaritic) and Aramaic"—but then he says, "In Palestine the surviving Canaanites were absorbed by the Israelites."[4] Therefore, it seems unlikely that "the language of Canaan" would ever have been used to designate the language of Israel.

It appears more reasonable to think of *the language of Canaan* as the language of "the merchant people" (Isa. 23:11, margin), of traffickers (Hos. 12:7)—the language of "a land of traffic . . . a city of merchants" (Ezek. 17:4; cf. margin). These traffickers or merchant people were a people "laden with silver" who were to be cut off (Zeph. 1:11; cf. margin); for in the day of Jehovah's universal reign under the Messiah, "there shall be no more a Canaanite in the house of Jehovah of hosts" (Zech. 14:21). Jehovah Himself proclaims, "For then [i.e., following His universal judgment of the heathen nations] will I turn to the peoples [plural] a pure language ['lip' (singular), Hebrew], that they may all call upon the name of Jehovah, to serve him with one consent" (Zeph. 3:9; cf. I Cor. 1:10; I Peter 4:11). Surely this universal language of faith would never be designated "the language of Canaan"! If our line of reasoning has any merit, Isaiah has in view Jews or Egyptians who swear to or by Jehovah but retain the language of Canaan, the idolatrous merchant people; it is a mongrel speech, the expression of a mixed or impure religion.

The next phrase in verse 18 is equally difficult to interpret and is subject to varied interpretations: of the five cities, *one shall be called The city of destruction.* Leupold says, "No truly satisfactory explanation of this statement has yet been offered" (I. 319). It may be signifi-

---

4. *Zondervan Pictorial Encyclopedia of the Bible*, vol. 1, p. 705.

cant, however, that by a very slight change of one consonant the word could be translated, "City of the Sun" (Heliopolis), center of the worship of the sun god Ra. A possible interpretation is that we have here a play on words—the center of Egyptian idol worship will be completely destroyed. Jeremiah 43:13 seems to offer support for this explanation. In talking about the invasion of Egypt by Nebuchadnezzar, whom Jehovah calls "my servant" (v. 10), Jeremiah says, "He shall also break the pillars [obelisks] of Beth-shemesh [margin: *the house of the sun*   Probably, *Heliopolis*, that is, *On*], that is in the land of Egypt; and the houses of the gods of Egypt shall he burn with fire." And so Isaiah seems to be saying in verse 18 that amid idolatry and confusion there will be some who swear to Jehovah while they continue to speak the mixed language of error and truth—*the language of Canaan*—until the pure spiritual language of Jehovah comes. As they do so, the center of Egyptian idolatry in their midst will be destroyed.

Jehovah to be known to Egypt (vv. 19–22)

19   The phrase *in that day* again refers to the general period being considered in this chapter. That there shall be *an altar to Jehovah in the midst of the land of Egypt* indicates that the true worship of Jehovah will be established in the midst of that idolatrous land. An altar is a raised place where sacrifices are offered; the word may be used literally or metaphorically of a spiritual altar (Heb. 13:10). Noah was the first to build an altar to Jehovah (Gen. 8:20); he was followed by Abraham, Isaac, and Jacob, who built altars in the Land of Promise. Moses built altars outside Palestine—at Rephidim and Sinai. When Israel entered Canaan, they were to destroy all the altars, pillars, and images found there (Deut. 7:5; 12:3), and to build no local shrines to Jehovah (Deut. 12:4). The people were to bring their sacrifices and offerings only to the place where Jehovah would record His name; only there were altars to be erected (Exod. 20:24; Deut. 12:5, 11, 14). Those who offered sacrifices somewhere other than at the door of the tent of meeting were to be cut off (Lev. 17:8–9). Other than the altar erected by Noah and the two erected by Moses, there is no record of an altar's being erected to Jehovah outside the land of

Israel. This clearly prohibits us from interpreting verse 19 as an indication that an actual altar to Jehovah will be set up in Egypt.

In addition to the "altar" in Egypt, there is to be *a pillar at the border thereof to Jehovah*. It was legitimate to set up pillars as memorials but not as religious symbols, for God said, "Neither shalt thou set thee up a pillar; which Jehovah thy God hateth" (Deut. 16:22). Note that whereas the altar was to be in the midst of Egypt, the pillar was to be at the border.

20   *And it* (the pillar) *shall be for a sign and for a witness unto Jehovah of hosts in the land of Egypt*. This pillar is probably a memorial of Jehovah's promise to Abraham, "In thee [thy seed] shall all the families [nations] of the earth be blessed" (Gen. 12:3; 22:18). *For they shall cry unto Jehovah because of oppressors, and he will send them a saviour, and a defender, and he will deliver them*. Egypt had been the oppressor of God's people, but now Egypt will be the oppressed. Israel had cried unto Jehovah, and He had raised them up a deliverer, a savior. Now Egypt will cry unto Jehovah, and He will raise them up a savior and defender. *He* (God) *will deliver them*.

It is true that between Isaiah's time and the New Testament era certain Jews attempted to erect places of worship in Egypt; but in view of the prohibition referred to above, any altars set up there were not acceptable to Jehovah. Further, it is true that after the Babylonian captivity and after the time of Alexander of Macedonia, many Jews came into Egypt, establishing synagogues through which Egypt could learn of the one true God, Jehovah. It is also true that the Septuagint (the translation of the Old Testament from Hebrew to Greek) was produced in Alexandria. None of these events, however, seems to fulfill the words of the prophet.

21   The prophet continues: *And Jehovah shall be known* ("make himself known," margin) *to Egypt, and the Egyptians shall know Jehovah in that day*. But He can be known only through teaching and instruction, for Isaiah says, "All thy children shall be taught of Jehovah; and great shall be the peace of thy children" (54:13). *Yea, they shall worship with sacrifice and oblation, and shall vow a vow unto Jehovah, and shall perform it*. These words indicate a faithful adherence to the will of Jehovah and a recognition of obligation to Him. Instead of looking for some literal altar and pillar in Egypt or some work which Jews performed there in the period between the covenants, we should interpret verses 19–22 in the light of Isaiah's other teachings. He has already spoken of a time when "all nations shall flow" unto God's spiritual mountain, when many peoples shall go up to it to learn of Jehovah and His way (2:2–4). Isaiah has also told of the time when Jehovah will set up the Root of Jesse for an ensign to the peoples and the nations will seek Him (11:10). Later on in the book, Jehovah says, "I will give thee [the Servant] for a covenant of the people, for a light of the Gentiles," to bring them out of the dungeon of darkness (42:6); and "I will also give thee for a light to the Gentiles, that thou mayest be my salvation unto the end of the earth" (49:6). Concerning His relationship to redeemed foreigners, the Lord says, "Even them will I bring to my holy mountain, and make them joyful in my house of prayer: their burnt-offerings and their sacrifices shall be accepted upon mine altar; for my house shall be called a house of prayer for all peoples" (56:7; cf. Mark 11:17). The prophecy seems to look for its fulfillment in the Messiah. This is confirmed in the following verses.

22   In the salvation God provides, He will smite and heal. In the midst of chastening, which the Egyptians, like all others who are redeemed, will experience (cf. Heb. 12:4–8), the Lord will purge and cleanse. When they call upon Jehovah in the midst of affliction and chastening, He will answer by healing them. Not only will smiting and healing assure the Egyptians that Jehovah is the true God, thus bringing them to repentance, but the Lord will also use chastening to bring them back to Him should they err from the true way after they have turned to Him.

Universal worship of Jehovah (vv. 23–25)

23   In the general period which Isaiah has been discussing—*in that day*— there shall also be *a highway out of Egypt to Assyria, and the Assyrian shall come into Egypt, and the Egyptian into Assyria.* For centuries the Egyptians and Assyrians had passed through the land of Israel for the purpose of waging war on each other. But now the highway through Israel will be used for a different purpose: *the Egyptians shall worship with the Assyrians.* The prophet earlier spoke of this highway in connection with the remnant of Israel that would

169

return to Jehovah from Assyria (11:16). He now advances a step further: Assyria and Egypt will travel over this highway so that they might worship together, having been reconciled in a common faith. Revelation progresses another step when Isaiah describes the highway as "The way of holiness" for the redeemed (35:8). The climax of this glorious thought is reached when, through the prophet, Jehovah says, "Go through, go through the gates; prepare ye the way of the people; cast up, cast up the highway; gather out the stones; lift up an ensign for the peoples [plural]" (62:10; cf. 11:10). Jehovah's plan is becoming clearer and clearer. Idolatry fails; Jehovah's truth triumphs. The carnal animal spirit which has dominated and controlled all the actions of Assyria and Egypt will be brought under the power of God's Spirit (see 11:1–9).

24 *In that day shall Israel be the third with Egypt and with Assyria*—not third in rank, but one of three united in spirit and place before God—a trio forming a spiritual body, *a blessing in the midst of the earth.* Israel will realize its true destiny in uniting in one body of worshipers the destroyers and the oppressors of earth. This body, the nations and Israel, under the Servant will be the true Israel of God (Gal. 6:16). Micah, a contemporary of Isaiah, describes the blessing Israel will be to the world: "And the remnant of Jacob shall be in the midst of many peoples as dew from Jehovah, as showers upon the grass" (5:7), a life-sustaining and life-refreshing force in the midst of a spiritually dry and parched earth.

25 This blessing is the gift and work of Jehovah. Consider His claim: *for that Jehovah of hosts hath blessed them, saying, Blessed be Egypt my people, and Assyria the work of my hands, and Israel mine inheritance.* Egypt is now called *my people,* an expression which at one time was reserved for Israel (Deut. 7:6), but which can now be used of all the redeemed out of every nation (I Peter 2:9). Assyria is called *the work of my hands,* for it is God who, after His own likeness, creates anew "in righteousness and holiness of truth" (Eph. 4:24); and Israel is called *mine inheritance,* for in Christ "we were made a heritage" (Eph. 1:11)—God's inheritance, His spiritual heritage. What a glorious work God has wrought in redeeming His enemies, bringing them together into one body with His people! How clearly it was envisioned by God's great prophet.

CHAPTER 20
Egypt and Ethiopia

The prophet has already declared the destiny of Ethiopia, the land south of Egypt (ch. 18), and God's judgment on and promises to Egypt (ch. 19). In 715 B.C. Egypt was overcome by Shabako, ruler of Ethiopia, who united the two under an Ethiopian suzerainty that prevailed until 664 B.C. This general period seems to be what the prophet is discussing in chapter 20.

The Trust That Failed (vv. 1–6)

1 *The year that Tartan came unto Ashdod* was 713 B.C. Tartan is not the name of an individual but the title of the Assyrian commander-in-chief. Ashdod, which was under subjection to Assyria, was a chief city of Philistia, probably the most strongly fortified of all its cities. This is the only place in the Bible where the name *Sargon* appears. The successor of Shalmaneser V, he ascended to the Assyrian throne in either 722 or 721 B.C., ruling until 705 B.C. Although mentioned only here in the Scriptures, Sargon played an important role in the history of Israel and Judah. Apparently interpreting as weakness the fact that he conducted no major campaign in Palestine after 720 B.C., Ashdod revolted in 713 B.C., drawing others into the rebellion; Judah, however, seems not to have shared in it. Tartan fought against Ashdod and took the city. Sargon himself led a campaign against cities of the area in 711 B.C. Apparently, Egypt and Ethiopia promised help which never came.

2 Isaiah was instructed by Jehovah to act out a symbolical message to Judah, pointing out the folly of trusting in Egypt. Young observes that this is the only symbolical act recorded in Isaiah. The prophet was told to *loose the sackcloth from off thy loins, and put thy shoe from off thy foot. And he did so, walking naked and barefoot.* As noted earlier, sackcloth was a coarse, hairy garment usually worn in time of sorrow or mourning; we are not told just why Isaiah was wearing the garment. The expression *walking naked* has occasioned a discussion among Bible students. Did he go about "stark naked," as

171

we would say, or did he lay aside all of his outer garments, wearing only a short tunic or breechcloth when going about his public work as statesman and prophet? Whatever he did was out of the ordinary and intended to get the attention of the people so that a lesson might be taught. It is doubtful that he went about totally nude; Delitzsch seems to have expressed the matter well when he said, "What Isaiah was directed to do, therefore, was simply opposed to common custom, and not to moral decency" (I. 372). Probably he wore the short tunic which, according to the artwork on the ancient monuments, was usually worn by captives.

3-4 Isaiah's symbolic act was to continue for three years, *for a sign and a wonder concerning Egypt and concerning Ethiopia.* The significance of the sign is now explained: as Isaiah, Jehovah's servant, has walked for three years naked and barefoot, so the king of Assyria will lead away into exile the captives of Egypt and Ethiopia, young and old, naked and barefoot, *with buttocks uncovered, to the shame of Egypt.* Intermittent war continued between Assyria and Egypt; a decisive blow was struck against Egypt in 663 B.C. when Ashur-banipal invaded the land and sacked Thebes (No-amon, Nah. 3:8), carrying away captives and large quantities of booty.

5 Those who trust in Egypt and Ethiopia for help in the time of Assyrian invasion *shall be dismayed and confounded, because of Ethiopia their expectation, and of Egypt their glory.* Isaiah's symbolic act is intended to prevent the people from trusting in Egypt, which the king of Assyria calls a "bruised reed . . . whereon if a man lean, it will go into his hand, and pierce it" (II Kings 18:21). God's people should learn to put their trust in Jehovah only and not to lean upon weak and feeble man.

6 The people of this *coast-land,* probably the whole of Palestine, including Phoenicia, Philistia, and Judah, will lament their expectation of help from the fickle kingdoms of Egypt and Ethiopia. Having turned to these two nations for help against Assyria, they will only be disappointed. And then their question will be, *And we, how shall we escape?* Having failed to rely upon Jehovah, as they were urged by the prophet, and having failed to get help from the arm of flesh, they will not know where to turn. Unless they turn to Jehovah, there is no help. Through the judgments on the heathen nations of old and on

His own people for having relied on those nations, Jehovah is teaching men of all generations to realize that He controls the destiny of all. The wicked who forget Jehovah shall be turned into Sheol (Ps. 9:17); His people who forget Him shall suffer a like fate; the only source of help and life is in Him. This message should impress all today, both the world and the church.

CHAPTER 21
Babylon, Dumah, and Arabia

Chapter 21 comprises three burdens dealing respectively with Babylon, Edom, and Arabia. These are followed by a fourth, the burden of Judah (ch. 22). The dates of the first three are uncertain.

Babylon, the Wilderness of the Sea (vv. 1–10)

A short summary of the background may help in interpreting this rather unusual and difficult prophecy. On the death of Shalmaneser V (722 or 721 B.C.) Merodach-baladan declared Babylon's independence from Assyria; but in 710 B.C. Sargon II led a successful campaign against the city, which welcomed him as a deliverer. In 703 B.C. Merodach-baladan made another bid for power. His sending ambassadors to congratulate Hezekiah upon recovery from serious illness may have been an attempt to gain that king's support (II Kings 20:12–18; Isa. 39). In 700 B.C. Sennacherib mounted a major offensive against Babylon; a further expedition in 695 B.C. led to a nine-month siege which resulted in the conquest and sacking of the city. Following the murder of Sennacherib, his son Esarhaddon ruled the empire (681–669 B.C.). He rebuilt Babylon and gave it a somewhat stable government. But again trouble erupted between Assyria and Babylon, causing Ashurbanipal to advance on Babylon (651 B.C.) and to besiege it for three years. In despair the king of Babylon set fire to his palace and perished in the flames. In 626 B.C. Nabopolassar, a chieftain in Chaldea, cleared out the Assyrians from Babylon and was made king. In 612 B.C., Nineveh was taken and destroyed. Upon the death of Nabopolassar in 605 B.C., his son Nebuchadnezzar ascended the throne. Ruling until 562 B.C., he made Babylon one of the world's most beautiful cities. He was its last powerful king. In 539 B.C. Cyrus took the city. Although he did not destroy the city, he brought the empire to an end. Babylon continued to be a city of some importance, but it began to decline slowly. Upon the death of Alexander the Great, who had planned to rebuild it, the decline became more rapid. We do know, however, that when the apostle Peter wrote his first epistle, Babylon was still in existence (5:13).

The hard vision (vv. 1–5)

1   Although not extravagant in the use of symbolic names, Isaiah does use them occasionally. For example, Ethiopia is "the land of the rustling of wings" (18:1); Edom is "Dumah" (21:11), which is Hebrew for "silence"—the silence of death (Pss. 94:17; 115:17); Jerusalem is "Ariel," hearth or lion of God (29:1); and Egypt is "Rahab," storm or arrogance (30:7). So here Babylon is *the wilderness* (or desert) *of the sea*. Babylon's destiny of destruction has already been declared by the prophet (13:20–22; 14:23) and will be further described in chapter 47. The meaning of the phrase becomes somewhat clearer in Jeremiah's announcement of Jehovah's judgment on Babylon: "O thou that dwellest upon many waters . . . thine end is come" (51:13). John says the "many waters" on which the Babylon of his prophecy sits are "peoples, and multitudes, and nations, and tongues" (Rev. 17:15), which seems to be the meaning in Jeremiah. Jeremiah says further, "A drought is upon her waters, and they shall be dried up; for it is a land of graven images, and they are mad over idols" (50:38); and "The sea is come up upon Babylon; she is covered with the multitude of the waves thereof. Her cities are become a desolation, a dry land, and a desert, a land wherein no man dwelleth, neither doth any son of man pass thereby" (51:42–43). A desert or wilderness may be either a place dry and desolate (27:10; Deut. 32:10), or a place of discipline (the Wilderness of Sinai). In this instance the wilderness which will be the lot of Babylon is a waste and desolate place. *As whirlwinds in the South* (Negeb), those fierce winds out of southern Palestine which bring sand and destruction and with which the Jews were altogether too familiar, the burden of Babylon *cometh from the wilderness, from*

a terrible land. That which was coming was the fulfilling of the grievous or hard visions of verse 2.

2   The hard vision declared to the prophet by Jehovah will be grievous in its fulfillment. The treacherous man that deals treacherously, the destroyer that destroys, is probably Babylon (cf. ch. 47; Hab. 1:5–11; 2:4–19). The whirlwind that shall wreak the havoc on her is Elam and Media (cf. 13:17), which were either in the service of the Assyrians (see the brief résumé of history above) or in the service of Cyrus. This judgment against Babylon will cause the sighing of the oppressed peoples, especially Judah, to cease; judgment against Babylon provides deliverance for God's people.

3–4   There is a question as to whether the following two verses describe the sympathy which the vision aroused in the prophet for the besieged and destroyed people or the actual physical effect of the vision upon him. His loins are filled with anguish; pangs as of a woman in travail have taken hold upon him; he is pained so that he cannot hear and dismayed so that he cannot see. The horror of the vision so frightened him that his heart fluttered; the twilight (sunset, close of the day) which he had desired for Babylon has now turned him to trembling. The effect was not as he had anticipated. Certainly there was no glee on the prophet's part in anticipating Babylon's destruction; he must have been filled with a sense of compassion for the suffering of fellow human beings. Nevertheless, inasmuch as other men of God were affected physically by visions given to them—for example, Ezekiel (1:28; 3:23), Daniel (8:27; 10:8–9, 15–17), Saul of Tarsus (Acts 9:3–9), and John (Rev. 1:17)—it is altogether possible that Isaiah is describing the physical effect of the vision upon himself.

5   The prophet returns to the siege introduced in verse 2. The city in no way expects a siege or makes preparation for it. They prepare banqueting tables; "they spread the carpets" (margin) for the banqueters to recline upon; *they eat, they drink* in a false security. Then comes the cry: *rise up, ye princes, anoint the shield,* for the battle is at hand; prepare for conflict! Does Isaiah have in view a particular siege or several of the sieges mentioned in the résumé above? Is it a description of the fall of the city at the hands of Cyrus's army (Dan. 5)? Or is it a general picture summarizing the many attacks which culminated in

the final destruction of the city? Surely it is a vivid depiction of the ultimate destruction which came to the city.

The watchman and his mission (vv. 6–10)

6 Some difficulties are removed if one keeps in mind that the context is a vision revealed to the prophet. The prophet is to set a watchman who, in the vision, can see the affairs of Chaldea and its neighbors even from the border of Judah across the Arabian Desert. The watchman is to report what he sees, keeping the people (or the prophet) informed of what is developing.

7 The watchman is told what he is to look for: *and when he seeth a troop, horsemen in pairs*, riding two abreast, *a troop of asses, a troop of camels, he shall hearken diligently with much heed*. Not only were these animals used for riding and for conveying baggage, they were also used to confuse enemy troops and to throw them into a state of disarray. Delitzsch says, "Thus Cyrus gained the victory over the Lydians by means of the great number of his camels (Herod. 1.80), and Darius Hystaspis the victory over the Scythians by means of the number of asses that he employed (Herod. iv.129)" (I. 381). The watchman is to listen intently, straining earnestly, striving diligently to hear. But it seems that he sees only a phantom army, mute as death, silent as the night, moving like shadows across the horizon. There is an air of mystery about the scene; there is no report as to where the troops are going or where they came from. We can only infer that it is the army on its way to destroy Babylon.

8 The words *And he cried as a lion* present numerous difficulties. What is their significance? Some commentators believe that the cry of the watchman is like that of a shepherd when he sees a lion approaching. Others contend that when the watchman sees the enemy, he cries with the roar of a lion as it were. Some think the watchman is complaining to Jehovah as with a low growl: *I stand continually upon the watch-tower in the day-time, and am set in my ward whole nights*. Young (also Clements) points out that the word *lion* does not occur in the Dead Sea Scroll manuscript of Isaiah; consequently, Young omits it from his translation. The cry, *O Lord*, may indicate that the watchman is the prophet himself reporting. In

whatever way we interpret the verse, the idea that the watchman is complaining to Jehovah is most unattractive.

9   At last the watchman's vigil is rewarded, for he beholds a troop of men and horsemen. Is this what he was to look for, or is it a second contingent? It is probable that this troop is what he was to look for (vv. 6–7). If it be a second troop, it is the victorious army returning after the siege of the city. At any rate, he hears that for which he has been listening: *Fallen, fallen is Babylon; and* with her fall *all the graven images of her gods are broken unto the ground.* This does not necessarily indicate that the conqueror has destroyed the images, but that Jehovah's power has triumphed and that the powerless gods of the great heathen kingdom have been brought to nought—they are cast down. Several writers have suggested that this prophecy is a foreshadowing of the events of chapters 40–66—the downfall of the heathen idols, the deliverance of God's people, and the triumph of Jehovah's cause. It seems to be all of that.

10   There is a question as to whether *my threshing, and the grain of my floor,* refers to Babylon or Israel. Although Jehovah lays claim to everything on earth (Deut. 10:14; Ps. 24:1), and in this sense Babylon belongs to Him, and although He speaks of gathering the nations (which would include Babylon) to the threshing-floor (Mic. 4:11–13), in this passage *my threshing* seems to refer to Judah. For Jehovah said, "The daughter of Babylon is like a threshing-floor at the time when it is trodden; yet a little while, and the time of harvest shall come for her" (Jer. 51:33). After Judah has been threshed and winnowed by Jehovah, and He thus gets His grain, the floor (Babylon) will be destroyed. The prophet now declares that he has been true to his commission; he has declared the message to both Babylon and Judah.

The Burden of Edom (vv. 11–12)

11   *Dumah,* which is Hebrew for "silence" (Pss. 94:17; 115:17), the silence of death, refers to Edom, the land south of the Dead Sea. *Seir* is thought by some to be the mountainous range east of the Wadi Arabah and by others to be, or to include, the mountains west of the Arabah. The latter is probably correct. *Seir* and "the land of Seir"

came to designate the land of the Edomites. Seir, "the mount of Esau" (Obad. 8), seems to have been to Edom what Zion was to Israel (cf. Obad. 17). From this mount one cries, *Watchman, what of the night? Watchman, what of the night?* Neither the one who cries nor the watchman is identified; the crier symbolizes the deep anxiety and misery of the nation, whereas the watchman is the representative of Jehovah, the only one who can give answer to the question. Remember that this is a vision, not a literal event. A translation which better expresses the concern of the question is, "How much of the night?" (Smith), or "How far in the night?" (Delitzsch). How much of it remains? We are reminded of a sufferer or sick person who, in the restlessness of the night, continually asks what time it is or how long it is before the dawn.

12   The answer is vague, obscure: *The morning cometh, and also the night*—when the morning comes, it will still be night, or night will follow. When dawn comes, there will be a few rays of light for only a moment; night will follow. Edom is a people destined to the silence and night of death. The second phase of the answer is equally obscure: *If ye will inquire, inquire ye: turn ye, come.* Edom as a nation is destined to be "cut off for ever" (Obad. 10); only those who take refuge in Mount Zion will escape (Obad. 17). Night after night came upon the nation—Assyria, Babylon, Rome—until finally, about the time of the destruction of Jerusalem in A.D. 70, they either drifted or were driven into the desert and were lost sight of completely. Therefore, if the inquirer is to return, he will have to do so with a changed heart, seeking Jehovah in spiritual Zion. Otherwise, the silence of death will be forever.

The Burden upon Arabia (vv. 13–17)

13   *Arabia*, which means "desert" or "steppe," is the name given to the peninsula lying east of Palestine and the Red Sea. The largest peninsula in the world, it covers an area of almost one million square miles. The people of Arabia were known as "the children of the east" (Judg. 6:3; 7:12), and were renowned for their wisdom (I Kings 4:30; Obad. 8; Job and his friends). It is uncertain how much of the area is included in Isaiah's prophecy; he is probably referring to the immedi-

ate western and central area and the northern section. The times were such that due to war, probably invasions by the Assyrians, the *caravans of Dedanites* had to leave their travel routes, withdrawing for refuge into thickets along the way. The exact location of Dedan is unknown, but it was probably an oasis in west central Arabia on the trade routes of the peoples of Sheba, Tema, and Buz.

14–15   Conditions were such that the caravan drivers could not camp in a conspicuous place and manner, so the people of *Tema* cautiously brought them water for their thirst and bread to sustain life. Tema was one of the largest oases in the general district. The reason for caution is clearly indicated: *For they fled away from the swords* (plural, suggesting the overwhelming number of the invaders), *from the drawn sword, and from the bent bow, and from the grievousness of war.*

16   This aid to the fugitives will soon be cut off. The Lord reveals that the time is at hand: *Within a year, according to the years of a hireling.* This indicates a definite period, for the employer never demands less, and the employee never gives more, than the time agreed upon, an exact time. *All the glory of Kedar*—the military power, wealth, and influence—*shall fail.* Kedar is named about a dozen times in the Old Testament. A people in northern Arabia, it was at one time a powerful tribe, a force to be reckoned with; but in conflicts with Assyria and Babylonia it was greatly weakened. What the prophet has in view probably occurred during one or more of the Assyrian invasions of the west.

17   The glory will not be totally destroyed, however, for the prophet proceeds to say that the archers and mighty military men *shall be few.* The fate of Arabia was guaranteed, *for Jehovah, the God of Israel, hath spoken it.* Babylon would complete what Assyria had begun, for Jehovah would later say to Nebuchadnezzar and his army, "Arise ye, go up to Kedar, and destroy the children of the east" (Jer. 49:28). The silence of death would descend upon Arabia as it had upon Edom; the night would finally come.

CHAPTER **22**
The Valley of Vision: Jerusalem

The prophet has just declared burdens upon three heathen nations:

Babylon, Edom, and Arabia (ch. 21). Why should he now include one concerning Jerusalem, the city where he and his people reside? The relationship between the four is one of character instead of physical kinship. If God's people are going to behave like the heathen nations, they must suffer the same consequence for their behavior. This point becomes clear as we consider the prophecy.

The prophecy falls into two distinct parts: in the first, the city of Jerusalem comes under the wrath of God (vv. 1–14); the second deals with an individual ruler (vv. 15–25). The date of the judgment to which the prophecy points is very indefinite and uncertain, as is indicated by the various views held by commentators. The greater number hold that Sennacherib's attack on the city (701 B.C.) is in view (Barnes, Erdman, Leupold, Rawlinson, Smith, and Driver, who says "probably"). Alexander offers a choice between the concrete event of Assyria's capture of Manasseh (II Chron. 33:11) and the general deterioration of Jerusalem. Delitzsch thinks the prophecy points to an intermediate period when Judah hoped to break away from Assyria through an alliance with Egypt. Calvin finds the fulfillment of the prophecy in the destruction of Jerusalem (586 B.C.). In a manner typical of the liberal school, Clements believes part of the passage pertains to 701 B.C. and was written by Isaiah, and another part pertains to the fall of Jerusalem in 586 B.C. and was added by a redactor who lived after that time. Young thinks that Isaiah is describing the general decline of the nation until its fall at the hands of Babylon. In the light of such differences, it is unwise to be dogmatic.

When we consider Hezekiah's preparation for the siege by Sennacherib, such as his provision for water in the city and his repair of the walls (II Chron. 32:1–5, 30), the events of 701 B.C. seem to be in Isaiah's view. However, when other matters are examined, Young's conclusion that chapter 22 depicts the general decline and ultimate destruction of the city is equally attractive. The choice seems to lie between the siege by Sennacherib (701 B.C.) and the entire period from Sennacherib's siege to the fall of the city at the hands of Nebuchadnezzar (586 B.C.).

The two foreign invasions have some aspects in common. While Sennacherib was besieging Lachish, Hezekiah sent him a large tribute of silver and gold, apologizing for having offended him by rebelling against him (II Kings 18:7, 13–16). Sennacherib kept the tribute, which was intended to secure peace; but instead of leaving Jerusalem in peace, he tried to force Hezekiah to capitulate. Sennacherib chided Hezekiah for trusting in Egypt for help (II Kings 18:21; Isa. 36:6). When he heard that King Tirhakah of Ethiopia was coming to fight against him (II Kings 19:9; Isa. 37:9), which may have aroused false hope and rejoicing among the Jews, he redoubled his efforts to persuade Hezekiah to submit (II Kings 19:10–13). Tirhakah proved to be an ineffective threat; it was Jehovah who gave Judah the victory (II Kings 19:35–37).

In the Chaldean siege of 587–586 B.C., Nebuchadnezzar was fighting against Jerusalem, Lachish, and Azekah, the only remaining fortified cities of Judah (Jer. 34:6–7). At the word of Jehovah through Jeremiah, King Zedekiah proclaimed liberty for all Hebrew man-servants and maid-servants; but afterward he reversed the decree and caused the freed servants to be made subject again to their masters (Jer. 34:8–11). This change of heart may have been occasioned by the lifting of the siege by the Chaldeans. Why was the siege lifted? Jeremiah says, "And Pharaoh's army was come forth out of Egypt; and when the Chaldeans that were besieging Jerusalem heard tidings of them, they brake up from Jerusalem" (Jer. 37:5). As in the case of Sennacherib, news of the approach of Egypt's army gave rise to a false hope and occasion for rejoicing. But also as in the days of Sennacherib's siege, Egypt was no help against Nebuchadnezzar, for, as Jehovah said, those who had come up out of Egypt to help returned to Egypt to their own land (Jer. 37:7). This time, instead of delivering the city, as in the day of Sennacherib, Jehovah gave it into the hand of the Babylonians. That Isaiah 22 could refer to the events of either 701 or 586 makes plausible the view that the prophet is actually speaking of Jerusalem's decline during the whole general period.

Rebuke of the People's Spirit of Frivolity (vv. 1–14)

1 The expression *valley of vision* seems not to indicate a par-ticular geographical location, but rather a people shut off from the world (cf. Jer. 21:13), surrounded and protected by mountains and Jehovah (Ps. 125:1–2). As the dwelling place of Jehovah, from whom

all prophecy emanates, Jerusalem was *the valley of vision*, the seat of prophecy. The housetops were flat roofs where the people might retire for relaxation (II Sam. 11:2), for idolatrous worship (Jer. 19:13; Zeph. 1:5), or for lamentation (Jer. 48:38). None of these possibilities seems to be in accord with the prophet's charge; idolatrous worship may be part of what Isaiah sees, but the others seem not to be. Is it possible that in this instance the people have, in a spirit of false confidence, gone up to their housetops to watch the approaching army? Perhaps we have here a description of the spirit of the people—a spirit of careless confidence in the face of impending danger. This spirit characterized them throughout the entire period from Sennacherib to Nebuchadnezzar, just as it characterized Nineveh just before destruction fell upon that city.

2   The people of this tumultuous city will be slain, not in battle or with the sword, but by the treading down of the Lord (v. 5), the consequence of their rejection of Jehovah. Smith has well said, "Jerusalem appeared bent on forestalling her deliverance by moral suicide" (I. 323).

3   The rulers and judges who should defend and lead the people will fail them and be captured, bound, and carried afar off. This was ultimately fulfilled in the person of Zedekiah when the nation fell to Nebuchadnezzar (Jer. 52:7–11). Jehovah's word spoken in the beginning of Jewish history was fulfilled (Lev. 26:14–45; Deut. 28:15–68).

4   The prophet looks away from this terrible vision and reveals the emotions of his heart. He will weep bitterly, even to the point of exhaustion, not in secret, but openly that the people might realize the gravity of the prophecy. There is no use attempting to comfort him; he cannot be comforted. The cause: *the destruction of the daughter of my people*—the people themselves. What the prophet describes was not fulfilled in Sennacherib's day, but it appears to be a broad view of the spirit of the people that led ultimately to the destruction under Nebuchadnezzar.

5   In the face of the spirit described in verses 1–4, the Lord has in store a day in which there will be rout and overthrow, a treading down of that which is great (cf. 2:11–12), and perplexity—the people will not know what to do in the midst of their confusion. Their rejoicing, whether the expression of a general spirit throughout the period

(701–586 B.C.) or the reaction to a specific attack, must end in judgment from the Lord; the visions and prophecies from the Lord will be fulfilled. At the breaking down of the walls in which they have trusted, the people will cry, not to Jehovah, their only source of help, but to the mountains, natural forces which can afford no help.

6　Isaiah has already prophesied that *Elam*, a warlike people from east of Babylon who were noted for their use of the bow (Jer. 49:34–39), together with Media, will bring about Babylon's fall (21:2, 9). They will also provide archers, charioteers, and cavalry against Jerusalem. *Kir* (not to be confused with the Kir of 15:1), meaning "wall," is thought to have been located somewhere north of Elam. Amos speaks of Kir as the original home of the Syrians (Amos 9:7), and the place where Syria would be carried captive (Amos 1:5; II Kings 16:9). People from Elam and Kir may have been in both the Assyrian and Babylonian armies. What the prophet means to emphasize, however, is not the specific nations, but the great distance from which fierce warriors will come. Uncovering the shield simply indicates removing the protective covering of the shield in preparation for battle.

7　The prophet speaks in the past tense, that is, the prophetic perfect, as if the event were already accomplished; for if God decrees a thing, it is as certain to be done as if it were already executed. Isaiah sees the choice valleys in and about the city filled with chariots. Horsemen are before the gate, ready to enter. That the valleys are filled indicates that the forces bent on conquest and destruction constitute a multitudinous host.

8　*And he took away the covering of Judah.* This clause has been variously interpreted: "the covering which made Judah blind to the threatening danger" (Delitzsch); "the veil of ignorance (cf. 25:7)" (Leupold); "all that which protected the nation from shame and disgrace has been removed, so that Jerusalem now stands open to dishonor" (Young); "the reference is to God who had withdrawn his protection from Jerusalem so that no adequate defense existed to prevent the Babylonian forces from working their will of destruction" (Clements). I tend to agree with Clements, for in order to lead His people, Jehovah had "spread a cloud for a covering,/And fire to give light in the night" (Ps. 105:39). This was a symbol of His presence (Ps.

78:14; Exod. 13:21), which He would restore in the redeemed Zion (4:5). This protection by Jehovah saved the city from Sennacherib's siege, but it was eventually taken away when Nebuchadnezzar destroyed the city (cf. the withdrawal of Jehovah's presence and glory in Ezek. 11:22–25). With the withdrawal of Jehovah's presence as a covering, the people were left solely to their own means—they looked *to the armor in the house of the forest*, the armory erected by Solomon (I Kings 7:2; 10:17) where arms were stored.

9–11 Breaches developed in the city of David—both literal weaknesses in the walls themselves and decay of the moral character of the people, who had allowed the spiritual glory of Zion to weaken and tarnish. Altogether too late they began making efforts to provide for the siege by building water-storage tanks between the walls and numbering the houses, tearing down what could be spared and using the stones to repair the walls. But it was all to no avail. The people's error was in their failure to look to Jehovah, the source of protection and deliverance, the one who had determined their destruction if they turned away from Him (cf. Deut. 28:15–68).

12 Continuing in the prophetic perfect, the prophet says, *And in that day*—the "day of discomfiture" of verses 5–11—Jehovah called upon the people to repent. This repentance was to find expression in weeping, mourning, cutting off the hair or shaving the head, and in girding the body with sackcloth; all of these actions demonstrate contrition of the spirit.

13 But instead of repentance, the Lord beholds *joy and gladness, slaying oxen and killing sheep, eating flesh and drinking wine*. The call produced an opposite effect which reflected the true character of the people. Their whole attitude was, *Let us eat and drink, for tomorrow we shall die*. Delitzsch observes, "This does not imply that they feel any pleasure in the thought of death, but indicates a love of life which scoffs at death" (I. 396). Smith says, "For half a century [during the prophet's prophesying] this people had worshipped God, but they had never trusted Him beyond the limits of their treaties and their bulwarks" (I. 329). So when that in which they trusted collapsed, their religion also collapsed; they now gave way to sensual dissipation and revelry.

14 Scoffing which defies the chastening and plea of God will not

be forgiven; it brings death. The Lord Jehovah of hosts revealed to the ears of the prophet, *Surely this iniquity shall not be forgiven you till ye die.* The people had committed unpardonable sin which could be expiated only by the death of the nation.

As we suggested in the introduction of this chapter, the prophet is not describing the siege of Jerusalem by either Sennacherib or Nebuchadnezzer, but the general condition of the heart of the people between those two sieges, the urgent pleas of Jehovah, and the ultimate destruction of the nation by Babylon.

The Failure of the Stewards (vv. 15–25)

15 As has been observed by numerous commentators, this prophecy against *Shebna* is Isaiah's only prophecy against an individual (unless we consider the last part of this section a prophecy against Eliakim). From the form of his name and the fact that his father is not mentioned, Driver suggests that Shebna was probably a Syrian (p. 102). He exemplifies the fleshly spirit of the period: luxury, ostentation, and the desire for personal glory. Although he was a historical character, he also personifies the general spirit of the politically ambitious of the time (the spirit of the people during this period has already been set forth in vv. 1–14). Shebna is described as the treasurer or steward *who is over the house,* apparently an office of great importance and significance which originated with Solomon's organization of his political cabinet and continued thereafter (I Kings 4:6; II Kings 15:5). Shebna's demotion is apparent in Isaiah 36:3 and 37:2, where he is spoken of as "the scribe" or chronicler, second to Eliakim. If Eliakim, who succeeded Shebna, was not in fact guilty of nepotism, he was at least strongly warned against it. Nepotism involves either looking only to one's immediate family and not to the welfare of the nation itself, or allowing members of one's family to climb by way of one's position.

16 Isaiah's language indicates strong opposition as he comes boldly to Shebna and asks sharply, *What doest thou here? and whom hast thou here, that thou hast hewed thee out here a sepulchre? hewing him out a sepulchre on high, graving a habitation for himself in the rock!* The language seems to challenge Shebna's right to hold high

185

office. By hewing out a memorial to himself, an elaborate tomb *on high*, in a most conspicuous place, he has sorely misused his office. What is believed to be the lintel of Shebna's tomb contains "the third longest monumental inscription in archaic Hebrew."[5]

17   The old saying, "Man proposes, but God disposes," is true in the case of Shebna. He had thought to be buried in Jerusalem in splendor; Jehovah had other plans. The introductory word *Behold* emphasizes the importance of what follows. Like a strong man, Jehovah will lay firm hold on him and violently hurl him away.

18   As one might wind an object into a ball that can be grasped, Jehovah will wind Shebna and cast him out of the land into *a large country*, a foreign country, a country in which he will roll like a ball and die. The clause *and there shall be the chariots of thy glory* refers to Shebna's ostentatious and flashy manner of driving about the city and country in elaborate chariots, as today one might give more concern to flashy automobiles than to doing his job. He has gloried in chariots, but shame will come to him as he has been the shame of his master's house. Although there is no record of when or to what country he was cast out, we do know that unless he repented, thus avoiding the penalty, he was surely cast out.

19   Once more Jehovah emphasizes that it is He who casts out Shebna: *And I will thrust thee from thine office; and from thy station shalt thou be pulled down.* Repeatedly it is demonstrated in Scripture that Jehovah raises up and debases men; all are in His hand.

20–21   When Jehovah removes Shebna, He will have a man ready to assume the role Shebna should have filled. Continuing to address Shebna, the Lord speaks of Eliakim, the son of Hilkiah, as *my servant*, a title of honor which designates one who was already a servant of Jehovah, habitually carrying out the will of the Master. When as the king's envoy Eliakim later meets with Rabshakeh (a high-ranking officer in Sennacherib's army), he is spoken of as one "over the household" whereas Shebna is referred to as "the scribe" (36:3; 37:2). It is uncertain whether the expression, *I will clothe him with thy robe, and strengthen him with thy girdle,* which is addressed to Shebna, refers to a particular type of garment worn by one of his

---

5. *Zondervan Pictorial Encyclopedia of the Bible*, vol. 5, p. 381.

rank or is a metaphor—God will clothe Eliakim with Shebna's position of nobility. The girdle suggests that Eliakim will be secured (or tightened) in office; Jehovah will give the governing power exercised by Shebna into the hand of Eliakim. Furthermore the Lord says, *He shall be a father to the inhabitants of Jerusalem, and to the house of Judah*. Being a father to the people suggests a protecting care exercised by love and concern for those entrusted to one's keeping. As Joseph was a father to Pharaoh (Gen. 45:8), and Job was "a father to the needy" (Job 29:16), so will Eliakim be to the people and the nation.

22   It is doubtful whether the expression, *And the key of the house of David will I lay upon his shoulder,* has reference to a literal key to the palace of the king or to the city; more probably it refers to Eliakim's responsibility to exercise the power of the office entrusted to him. His decree shall be final; when he opens none shall shut, and when he shuts none shall open—an indication of the power of his office to make conclusive decisions. The prophecy seems not to be messianic, although Jesus used the phrase concerning Himself (Rev. 3:7). Both Jesus and Eliakim have authority to bind or loose which no one has the right to alter. Jesus' authority is absolute; Eliakim's, however, is subject to the king.

23–24   Eliakim was Jehovah's choice for the office, His servant whom He would clothe with power and to whom He would commit the key of David. To this point Jehovah seems to be speaking to Shebna; the remainder of the chapter may also be spoken to him, but it is definitely spoken for Eliakim's benefit. It is a warning of the danger that he will encounter from his family. *And I will fasten him as a nail* (or peg) *in a sure* (firm) *place*. Pegs are driven into sturdy walls to hold clothing or vessels. Eliakim will occupy an important place and have responsibility on which people will lean heavily. *And he shall be for a throne of glory to his father's house*. The honor of his father's house, which hitherto seems to have been insignificant, will be reflected in him and will attract many relatives to him. Against this he is warned to be on guard at all times. Because of the glory to him and to his father's house, *the offspring and the issue*, the worthy and unworthy, *every small vessel, from the cups even to all the flagons*, from small cups to large wine-bottles or jars, will seek to attach themselves to him. They will seek to share in and profit from his honor and glory by hanging themselves upon him.

25 It seems altogether unlikely that the prophet has Shebna in mind (as some suggest), for Eliakim is the nail fastened in a sure place. It is not certain that Eliakim yielded to the pressure of his family's efforts to rise to distinction on the basis of his position. He is simply warned of the danger of nepotism. It is more probable that what Jehovah is stressing here is that the entire system of which Shebna and Eliakim are parts (some serve in this system honorably and others dishonorably) will eventually come to an end. *And the burden* (cf. v. 1) *that was upon it shall be cut off; for Jehovah hath spoken it.* With the coming of Messiah, who will claim what was given to Eliakim (Rev. 3:7), the old will be removed and give way to the new. Messiah will secure the kingdom and everything in it for Jehovah.

It thus appears that the burden of chapter 22 is generic: it deals with the nation and city as a whole. It pictures the final judgment of Jerusalem (vv. 1–14) and the end of all of its rulers, those of no account and those who are honorable. When Jehovah's purpose is accomplished in His Servant to come, all will pass away.

CHAPTER **23**
The Burden of Tyre

Chapter 23 is the concluding prophecy against individual heathen powers, both small and great. The prophet deals with three great forces in the world: military force exercised in conquest, false and decadent religion, and commerce. Isaiah began with Babylon, the great imperial power which through military might would destroy Assyria, spreading its wings of conquest over the whole world of that day even to Egypt, which previously had been a dominant world power. Egypt, along with others, would be judged and brought to an end. The false religions of the heathen, bound up in their idols and temples, would fail in time of need, destroyed by the overwhelming power of Jehovah. And Jerusalem, *the valley of vision*, the seat of

Jehovah worship, which had come to be characterized by indifference to the Lord of hosts, would be judged and destroyed because of its apostasy. And now the prophet turns his attention to Tyre, the world capital of commerce. It too will be judged and brought to nought.

Tyre, founded between 2750 and 2500 B.C., located twenty-five miles south of Sidon and thirty-five miles north of Mount Carmel, was the chief city-state of Phoenicia. The main city was located on the mainland, and a fortress was located on an island a short distance offshore. Isaiah speaks of Tyre as the daughter of Sidon (v. 12); he is either thinking of Sidon as the symbol of Phoenicia or indicating that Tyre was founded by the people of Sidon. Because of the very narrow coastal plain between the sea to the west and the Lebanon Mountains to the east, the Phoenicians were prohibited from becoming an agricultural people. Consequently, they turned to the mountains for mining and to the sea for commerce, becoming the greatest commercial power of the day. Their ships plied the waters westward to north Africa, where they founded the colony of Carthage, and to Spain, where they founded Tarshish. They extended their trade beyond the Straits of Gibraltar to Atlantic coastlands and from Ezion-geber on the north end of the Gulf of Aqaba to the Indian Ocean.

Commerce per se is good; it contributes to the well-being of the people of the world by distributing both the necessities and the luxuries of life and providing jobs for every class. However, commerce is concerned only with material gain—profit. Unlike certain other occupations, it has no higher and nobler goals. This is in no way to suggest that the profit system is wrong, for it is not. The businessman must earn a profit on his investment and for his labor if he is to remain in business. But commerce is to be condemned when it develops the mercenary spirit of lust, covetousness, and greed that leads to moral and spiritual decay and to corruption in the political structure of a nation. Smith sums up the place of Tyre in history: "There is not throughout history a more perfect incarnation of the mercenary spirit than the Phoenician nation" (I. 300). It is from this point of view that Tyre, the symbol of world trade and intercourse, is likened to a harlot who sells her soul and honor for sensual pleasures and the material riches of the world (vv. 15–17; cf. the great harlot ["Babylon"] of Rev.

189

17–18, who symbolizes the commerce and lusts of Rome). The judgment of God falls on a nation with such an attitude. The earliest friendly association between Tyre and Israel developed during the days of David of Israel and Hiram of Tyre. These two kings became friends, transacting business deals with each other. This friendly relationship intensified during the reign of King Solomon, who carried on extensive trade and shipping enterprises with the king of Tyre. Assyria and Babylon were both threats to Tyre during the period of their power, but it was not until the invasion of Alexander the Great that the city was destroyed (332 B.C.). The period of Tyrian history covered by Isaiah extends from the Assyrian and Babylonian oppression, especially that of Babylon, to the restoration of prosperity after the Chaldean domination. Destruction occurred under Alexander's conquest. A major lesson in chapter 23 is that Jehovah controls and determines the destiny of nations; and when they become unfit to live, He removes them. (For additional prophecies concerning Tyre, see Jer. 25:22; Ezek. 26:1–28:19; Amos 1:9–10.)

The Judgment of Tyre and the Effect of Her Fall (vv. 1–7)

1 As mariners are returning from Tarshish, a Phoenician colony in southern Spain, they hear of the calamity that had befallen their home port of Tyre. The *ships of Tarshish*, either fleets of ships in general that ply the heavy seas (cf. I Kings 10:22) or special Mediterranean fleets, are called upon to *howl*, for the city of Tyre is laid waste. The houses are destroyed and there is no entering the port. They hear the news either when other ships approach them near Kittim (the island of Cyprus) or when they anchor there. The news is sad indeed, for their homes are destroyed, their port is closed, and there is no market for their goods.

2 The inhabitants of the coast are the people of the Mediterranean area. They are greatly astonished at the fall of Tyre, but are told to *be still* or silent. They had been made prosperous by *the merchants of Sidon, that pass over the sea*. Sidon either stands for all of Phoenicia or refers specifically to the mother city, which, through Tyre, had trafficked with others. All had been fully supplied and enriched by the commercial ventures of the Phoenicians.

190

3   The *great waters* include the Mediterranean Sea and the oceans beyond. *The Shihor* is thought by some to be either a canal or an eastern branch of the Nile; others (e.g., Leupold) think it was a western branch of the Nile; still others believe it was a synonym for the Nile itself (cf. Jer. 2:18, where it is compared to the Euphrates). *The seed of the Shihor* is the grain of Egypt which was provided by the overflow of the Nile and shipped throughout the Mediterranean world of that day. It provided revenue for both Tyre and Egypt and food for needy peoples.

4   Instead of condoning the pride which had characterized Tyre and her sisters, the Lord says, *Be thou ashamed, O Sidon.* Again Sidon possibly refers to the whole of Phoenicia. The sea is personified and speaks for Tyre, the stronghold of the sea: *I have not travailed, nor brought forth, neither have I nourished young men, nor brought up virgins.* Tyre has never borne children. When finally slain or destroyed, she will leave nothing permanent; she has provided nothing of a lasting nature, for the gain of commerce or commerce itself is of the world and passes away.

5   When this report of Tyre's fall reaches Egypt, she shall be greatly pained; for if the buffer state of Tyre falls, the destroyer will soon reach Egypt. Or perhaps Egypt is pained because the export of her commodities will be cut off, and thereby economic disaster will be brought to the nation.

6   From Egypt, *Pass ye over to Tarshish*, the westernmost Tyrian colony, and wail or prolong your mourning there. This may indicate that during the siege of Tyre, some of the people were transported to Tarshish just as some were transferred to Carthage during Alexander's siege. Wherever they went, there would still be wailing for the fallen nation.

7   In the light of the destruction of the city, the Lord asks, *Is this your joyous city,* the city of the hustle and bustle of commerce? The prophet recognizes her as an ancient city of long establishment, *whose feet carried her afar off to sojourn.* In the pursuit of trade many of her people had sojourned in distant lands, leaving her without a permanent posterity anywhere. (For a different interpretation of this last clause, see the margin.)

To summarize these verses: the Lord calls upon the ships of Tarshish to *howl*, upon the inhabitants of the coastlands to *be still*, and upon Sidon to *be thou ashamed*; Egypt will *be sorely pained*, and those who flee to Tarshish will *wail*. The fall of a commercial power affects not only itself, but also all the nations associated with or dependent upon it.

Jehovah, the Executioner of the Judgment (vv. 8–12)

8   Who would dare plan the overthrow of a nation as great and important as Tyre, *the bestower of crowns, whose merchants are princes, whose traffickers are the honorable of the earth?* In her greatness she had bestowed crowns on the heads of monarchs, not by military conquest but by commercial and economic power. These monarchs are probably the governors of her colonies, but they could be rulers crowned by economic manipulation. Her merchants were princes in the emporiums of trade, and her traffickers were among the honorable or great of the earth.

9   The question raised by the prophet is now answered: *Jehovah of hosts hath purposed it*; only He would dare to plan the overthrow of such a nation at the zenith of its glory. The divine object was to stain or profane all earthly glory by bringing it into disgrace, for He is able to "exalt that which is low, and abase that which is high" (Ezek. 21:26).

10   As the Nile flows unobstructed through Egypt, so the people of Tarshish, which probably represents all of the colonies of Tyre, are urged to pass freely through the land. There is now no "girdle" (margin) or *restraint* from the mother city; it has been removed.

11   Just as Jehovah through Moses had in ancient times stretched out His hand, causing the sea to bring Pharaoh's army to an end (Exod. 14:21–48), and just as Isaiah has prophesied, He will stretch it out upon all the nations in judgment (Isa. 14:26), He now stretches it out *over the sea*, the realm of Tyre's wealth and glory. He is shaking the kingdoms and has *given commandment concerning Canaan* (the merchant people), *to destroy the strongholds thereof.* Although it is possible that Isaiah is making a play on words, referring to Tyre as Canaan (the merchant people), it is more probable that he is speaking of shaking the whole land of Canaan, bringing her strong-

holds down by the invaders who will execute His judgment against Tyre.

12   *And He said,* resuming the note sounded in verse 7, *Thou shalt no more rejoice*—the days of rejoicing for Tyre and Sidon are over. The shame of the people of the coastland will be like that of a sexually abused virgin. They are told to arise and pass over to Cyprus, where a Phoenician colony dwelt, but *even there shalt thou have no rest*; there is no escaping the judgment of God and the consequences of pride.

The Fate of Phoenicia: Though Cast Down, Tyre's Prosperity Shall Be Restored (vv. 13–18)

13   Without question verse 13 is the most difficult in this chapter; it is fraught with problems. Young thinks the prophet is not speaking of the physical origin of the Chaldean nation when he says, *This people was not; the Assyrian founded it for them that dwell in the wilderness*; rather, he is saying that the Babylonians were brought to power by Assyrian aggression. This could well be. In the early quarter of the first millennium B.C. Assyria was drawn into the politics of Babylon. Numerous attacks by Assyrian rulers led to Assyrian control of the city. This continued until Nabopolassar cleared Chaldea of the Assyrians in 626 B.C., becoming king of Babylon shortly thereafter. Nineveh was soon destroyed (612 B.C.) and Egypt was defeated by Nabopolassar's son Nebuchadnezzar at the battle of Carchemish (605 B.C.). Thus it was the constant conflict with Assyria which brought Babylon to the position of the dominant world power.

In spite of the difficulties of verse 13, since Tyre is the object of Isaiah's burden, it seems that its ruin at the hands of the Babylonians, a people from the desert (wilderness), is his topic here. Nebuchadnezzar besieged Tyre for thirteen years,[6] but was successfully withstood by the Tyrians. For the services rendered to Jehovah against Tyre, the Lord gave Egypt to Nebuchadnezzar (Ezek. 29:18–20). The following verses bear out this view.

14–15   With the palaces in ruin, the prophet again (as in v. 1)

---

6. *Zondervan Pictorial Encyclopedia of the Bible,* vol. 4, p. 396.

calls upon the returning ships of Tarshish to howl in lamentation over the destruction. Beginning with Nebuchadnezzar's siege of Tyre, that mighty commercial power *shall be forgotten*, lie dormant, during the seventy-year period of one king, probably the time of Chaldean domination (cf. Jer. 25:11–12; 29:10; II Chron. 36:22). From Daniel's equating of "king" and "kingdom" ("These great beasts, which are four, are four kings. . . . The fourth beast shall be a fourth kingdom"—Dan. 7:17, 23), we conclude that when Isaiah speaks of *the days of one king*, he means "the days of one kingdom."

16   At the end of the period Tyre shall sing the song of a harlot. Like an old harlot who has been forgotten for years, she will take a harp and go about the streets or in the taverns playing and singing in an effort to revive her business by enticing her former customers. What a pathetic picture! As we said above, commerce can be noble; but when it is prostituted for the purpose of sordid gain and material pleasures, it is base and distasteful to the Lord. The symbol of a harlot well illustrates the evil excesses to which commerce can lead.

17   Will Tyre have learned her lesson? By no means; *she shall return to her hire, and shall play the harlot with all the kingdoms of the world upon the face of the earth.* Her success at this time will be of the Lord for *Jehovah will visit Tyre*, not to bring judgment against her, but to restore her commercial role. So, as judgment is of Jehovah, so also is a nation's prosperity of Him; all is in His hand. He controls the destiny of nations and of men.

18   There have been numerous unsatisfactory explanations of verse 18. There is no evidence that Tyre used her gain to help Israel when the people returned from the Babylonian captivity, nor is there any evidence that the prophecy applies to events in the New Testament. Inasmuch as Jehovah judges and brings to an end and also restores and builds up, might not the prophecy mean simply that whatever the motive of tradesmen, Jehovah uses commerce for the good of mankind, consecrating it to that purpose? What we know of God and of His ways tends to make this view seem reasonable.

World Judgment and Deliverance of God's People (24–27)

An Introductory Word

Chapters 24–27 form a distinct unit in Isaiah's book, yet the four chapters are closely related to the previous section, serving as a fitting conclusion to it. There are at least two indications that the prophet is not discussing specifically the fall and destruction of Babylon or a judgment upon the land and nation of Judah: (1) the fall of Babylon is dealt with in chapters 13–14, 21 (vv. 1–9), and 46–47, and the fall of Judah throughout the book; (2) the scope of the four chapters extends far beyond just one nation, either Babylon or Judah; it includes the whole world.

Having dealt with individual nations and their judgment, the prophet now looks to the coming of a universal judgment upon the entire heathen world, including his own apostate people. Actually, it is judgment upon that which the world adores and in which it trusts: power, the lusts of the eye and the flesh, and the vainglory of life. In the midst of this judgment Jehovah's true Israel will stand forth protected and cared for and victorious. Out of universal judgment will come a universal salvation. These four chapters present a contrast between the true and the false, the lofty (proud) and the holy. De-

195

litzsch suggests that chapters 24–27 stand in relationship to chapters 13–23 as chapters 11–12 stand to chapters 7–10; he also refers to this section as the grand finale to the previous chapters.

The contrasts in chapters 24–27 are so striking that they afford an excellent introduction to the section. *The earth*, its foundations trembling (24:18), is utterly broken, rent asunder, and shaken violently (v. 19); it will stagger like a drunken man (v. 20) and its kings will be punished (v. 21) when God's judgments fall (26:9). In contrast, Jehovah will reign in *mount Zion*, the spiritual world (24:23). In Zion Jehovah will make a feast of good things for all peoples who will come to His holy mountain (25:6). There He will destroy the darkness covering their hearts (v. 7), and there His hand will rest (v. 10).

A second contrast is that of the *peoples* (plural) and the *people* (singular). The peoples shall be shaken like an olive tree (24:13) and the inhabitants of the earth shall be punished for their iniquity (26:21). By contrast, Jehovah will wipe away the reproach of His people (25:8); their enemies will behold the Lord's zeal for His own (26:11). In the midst of the storm of judgment His people shall be hidden until the indignation be past (26:20).

A third contrast is that of the *nations* and the *nation*. The prophet pictures a city of terrible nations (25:3) which will be brought low (v. 5); a veil of ignorance is spread over them (v. 7). In contrast, Jehovah's nation is a righteous nation (26:2); it shall be greatly increased and its borders enlarged (v. 15).

A fourth contrast is between the cities described. The *world city* is a lofty city (26:5) for a lofty people (24:4), a waste city that is broken down (24:10) and left in desolation (v. 12), a fortified city left a heap and a ruin (25:2), a city of terrible nations (v. 3) to be brought low (v. 5). In contrast, *the city* of Jehovah's people is a strong city with salvation as its walls and bulwarks (26:1); the righteous nation will enter this city (v. 2). In this strong city (Jerusalem), Jehovah of hosts will reign (24:23).

A fifth contrast is between *lords* and *the Lord*, and a sixth is between *death* and *life*. There have been many lords, that is, heathen idols and their foreign worshipers who have ruled over Israel; but they are dead; all remembrance of them has perished (26:13–14). But the dead of Jehovah shall live; they shall arise and sing (v. 19).

196

It must be emphasized that the cities and nations of chapters 24–27 are not to be identified with specific cities and nations of a particular time, with the possible exception of Jerusalem (27:10); they symbolize the world of the profane. The exact time when Isaiah spoke or wrote the prophecies in these chapters cannot be determined, but the time is immaterial to their content and purpose. Theologians who deny inspiration and therefore divine revelation of future events variously date this material anywhere from the time of Isaiah to the middle of the second century B.C. They ascribe parts of his prophecy to unknown writers. They are hampered by presuppositions that will not allow them to admit the prophet's ability to see God's hand clearly in present and future history. But for us who accept Peter's explanation of prophecy—"men spake from God, being moved by the Holy Spirit" (II Peter 1:21)—there is no problem. We will consider Jehovah's purpose and His majesty, as well as His control of the world and power to carry out that purpose, as underlying premises as we interpret these four chapters.

CHAPTER **24**

A World Judgment

Desolation of the Earth and the World City (vv. 1–13)

1 *Behold* is a characteristic Isaian introduction of an important or weighty theme (cf. 3:1; 17:1; 19:1; 26:21). It usually, but not always, indicates something in the immediate future. An exception is Isaiah's use of the word in reference to the coming of the Son to be born of a virgin (7:14), which was centuries in the future. In 24:1 the word focuses attention upon Jehovah, who *maketh the earth empty*. The word translated *earth* may refer to the whole earth (e.g., Gen. 1:1, 10–12), or it may be translated "land," for example, the "land" of the nation Israel (Isa. 2:7–8). It seems here to be used in the cosmological sense. It is the whole earth which is made empty; it is made waste and turned upside down, as one would empty a vessel by turning it upside down. Moreover, Jehovah scatters the inhabitants of

the earth; thus a distinction is made between the earth itself and its inhabitants. The prophet does not indicate just how this judgment is to be executed.

2   The judgment is to be universal in its scope, including all classes of people; none shall escape; all are brought to a common level. *As with the people, so with the priest,* the religious leader. In that day religion itself will save neither the priest (leader) nor the individuals who follow him. *As with the servant, so with his master;* social distinctions make no difference in such an hour. *As with the maid, so with her mistress;* differences in household status are taken away. *As with the buyer, so with the seller*—business collapses; no one has anything to buy or sell. *As with the creditor, so with the debtor; as with the taker of interest, so with the giver of interest to him;* complicated business pursuits will not escape, for breakdown and failure in business will be universal. Young observes that when social and economic differences cease to be recognized and socialism takes over in a society, anarchy follows. This should challenge present socialistic trends.

3–4   The dwelling place of the ungodly, who live only for the flesh, shall be wiped clean, for *the earth shall be utterly emptied, and utterly laid waste.* In strong and emphatic language Isaiah states the result of the judgment. He is positive and explicit, leaving no doubt of what is coming, *for Jehovah hath spoken this word.* As a result of the divine decree, *the earth mourneth and fadeth away,* like a flower (28:1), becoming languid, lifeless and weary, the consequence of man's sin (cf. Amos 1:2; Joel 1:15–20). None are exempt; *the lofty people of the earth,* the great and the mighty, the elevated and haughty, suffer with the rest; they *do languish* being brought low.

5   The judgment is not limited to Palestine, but is universal: *The earth,* the inhabitable earth as a whole, *is polluted under the inhabitants thereof.* The earth is defiled, desecrated, and made unclean by its inhabitants (cf. Gen. 3:17–18; Num. 35:33). It is sad, but true, that everything man touches becomes polluted. From the beginning God had put man under law; God gave him laws, statutes, and a covenant which Isaiah calls the everlasting covenant.[1] Man disregarded and violated them.

---

1. For a discussion of this everlasting convenant see Appendix A, pp. 531–38.

6 Inasmuch as God made and gave the laws and the covenant, it is He who pronounces the curse of judgment upon the world and its inhabitants for rejecting and violating them. Infliction of the curse upon the whole world apparently harks back to Genesis 3:17–18 (cf. also Gen. 5:29). Sin (the transgression of divine law) always brings its blighting effects upon the land and its inhabitants. *Therefore the inhabitants of the earth are burned, and few men left.* They are burned by the fire of Jehovah's fierce anger (cf. Deut. 32:22), which goes before His face to burn up His adversaries (Ps. 97:3); for God is a consuming fire (Deut. 4:24; Heb. 12:29). Note, however, that a fire which consumes may, and often does, develop from within those it consumes (26:11, margin).

7–9 *The new wine mourneth;* it portrays its kinship with the land by partaking of its sorrow. With the curse upon the land the vine fails, fading, withering, and losing its vitality and force. *The merryhearted do sigh;* their expressions of joy were no more than the noise of revelers—a shallow joy that disappeared when the wine was gone. We are reminded of Amos's cry against the revelers of Samaria, whose conduct brought upon them the woe of captivity (Amos 6:5–7). Like the Samaritans, the people of the world were giving themselves over to light, frivolous music, hemming themselves in by it. Note Isaiah's arrangement: *the mirth of tabrets—the noise of them that rejoice—the joy of the harp;* these are all to be brought to an end. The picture reminds us of our modern society in which we are constantly being bombarded with the senseless noise of hard-rock music. But it too shall end one of these days (v. 8). *They shall not drink wine with a song,* either because wine will be scarce, or because in the midst of judgment there will be no song to be sung. Those who try to drown their sorrows in strong drink find that it brings only bitter remorse (cf. Prov. 20:1); in the end wine bites like a serpent (Prov. 23:32). The picture is one of sensuous pleasure brought to an end by divine judgment.

10 The prophet looks away from the earth and its lofty people, languishing and being devoured by the curse, to *the waste city,* bare, dreary, and gloomy, a city of confusion and emptiness. Instead of a particular or specific city, Isaiah sees a conglomerate of hetero-geneous peoples given over to sin, bound together both in their rejection of God and His laws (cf. v. 5) and by their enjoyment of the world. Young points out that the word *waste* (*tohu*, Hebrew) occurs eleven times in the Book of Isaiah and only nine times in all the rest of the Old Testament; it is variously translated "waste," "confusion," "vanity," "vain thing," and "thing of nought." This city lies *broken down*, that is, defeated and destroyed; every house is shut up so that no man can come in, an indication of the ultimate destiny of the world city. Eventually the world with its lusts must pass away (I John 2:15–17), as must the city that personifies it.

11   With the breaking down of the waste city (v. 10), *there is a crying in the streets because of the wine*. This is the third time that the prophet has made mention of wine (cf. vv. 7, 9), an indication of how much the world depends on artificial stimuli for its false joys and good times. With these stimuli gone, there is wailing in the streets, *all joy is darkened, the mirth of the land is gone*. The world depends on alcoholic drinks, sports, revelings, sensuous music and entertainment for its pleasures and joys; when these are gone, its shallow joy likewise perishes.

12   *In the city*, the waste city, the world city, *is left desolation*— ruin and gloom. It is a place forsaken, like a dreary desert or a ghost town. *The gate is smitten with destruction*—that which once protected the people within is destroyed. There is no one left in the desolate city, nor would anyone outside it care to enter such a dreary heap.

13   The prophet concludes this prophecy of doom upon the earth, the lofty people, and the waste city with a word of certainty: *For thus shall it be in the midst of the earth among the peoples*. Inasmuch as the peoples have rejected the laws, statutes, and everlasting covenant of God, He has now declared a judgment which must surely come to pass. *Peoples* is plural, designating the heathen peoples in contrast to God's own people. The earth or world, including its inhabitants, will be the object of this judgment. It will be *as the shaking of an olive-tree, as the gleanings when the vintage is done*. When the olive tree has been shaken and the grapes gathered, there will be *few men left* (v. 6). The entire prophecy has an air of finality about it. Whoever opposes God and His standard of right must eventually face Him and His righteous judgment and be destroyed.

Premature Rejoicing and More Judgments (vv. 14–23)

14 *These,* apparently "the gleanings" (v. 13), the "few men left" (v. 6) who have come through the terrible judgment, now realize the purpose of the judgment and the mercy of God that spared them. In gratitude for having been spared, the survivors now lift up their voice with shouting; they cry aloud. They recognize the majesty of Jehovah; their salvation from His judgment is an expression of His mercy and grace. *From the sea* is explained in the following verse.

15 *Wherefore glorify ye Jehovah in the east* (literally, "in the lights" or "fires"). This unusual expression, which evidently means the direction from which light dawns, stands in contrast to *the isles of the sea,* the western coastlands and beyond. So the shout extends from the far east to the Mediterranean Sea (the far west), including all the lands in between. The object of praise is the majesty of Jehovah, for He has shown His majestic greatness both in judgment and in mercy. This praise is offered by a remnant who have begun to see and realize God's hand in the control of world affairs.

16 The prophet identifies himself with those who have begun to show spiritual perception, as he says, *From the uttermost part of the earth have we heard songs,* indicating the universal sweep and influence of the judgment which has produced the songs being heard. The theme of the songs, *Glory to the righteous,* poses a question: is this glory or praise intended for Jehovah, the Righteous One, or is it offered in recognition of the righteous persons who have triumphed in the judgment? Most commentators, as well as the King James and American Standard versions, take it as referring to righteous persons; a few commentators (e.g., Calvin) and the New American Standard Bible take it as referring to God. It seems better to think of the praise as directed to those who now glory in that righteousness by which they have escaped. They rejoice because they are considered righteous before the Lord.

The prophet breaks in with a groan or moan, expressing sorrow or grief: *I pine away, I pine away, woe is me!* ("Leanness to me," margin; "My leanness, my leanness," King James). The rejoicing has been premature; the condition continues to warrant more judgment, judgment which will be even more severe than that which has been experienced. *The treacherous have dealt treacherously; yea, the treacherous have dealt very treacherously.* Delitzsch translates this sentence, "Robbers rob, and robbing, they rob as robbers" (I. 431); Young renders it, "For the plunderers plunder; even with plunder do plunderers plunder" (II. 170). The point seems to be that in spite of the remnant that rejoices, the prophet sees no real conversion of the world about him. The wicked will continue to prey upon all whom they can; they will deal treacherously and cruelly with all who would do right.

17–18   The inhabitant of the earth has no place of escape from the treacherous persecutors, for *fear, and the pit, and the snare are upon thee, O inhabitant of the earth.* He who would flee from the noise of the pursuers who instill fear and terror *shall fall into the pit.* If he succeeds in climbing out of the pit, he *shall be taken in the snare* or trap; there shall be no escaping the dangers which beset him. As in the time of the great flood when "all the fountains of the great deep [were] broken up, and the windows of heaven were opened" (Gen. 7:11), and none were able to escape, so will it be again. There will be no place to flee; the wicked will cover the earth, searching out all. Nonetheless, Jehovah's judgment will follow them.

19–20   As earlier the earth was utterly emptied, and utterly laid waste (v. 3), so now *the earth is utterly broken, the earth is rent asunder, the earth is shaken violently.* Throughout the chapter we have seen a progressive development of the great world-judgment; now it reaches its climax. The prophet continues, *The earth shall stagger like a drunken man, and shall sway to and fro like a hammock.* Consider the verbs used to describe the cataclysmic event: the earth is utterly broken, rent asunder, shaken violently; it staggers and sways to and fro. The cause is clearly stated: the transgressions and wickedness of man have become so heavy upon the earth that it cannot bear the weight. Jehovah will not tolerate further violation of His law: The earth *shall fall, and not rise again.*

The terrible note of finality throughout the prophecy raises the question of whether we have here a description of the final destruction of the present order, the end of the world toward which the New Testament points. Many commentators so construe the language; however, in the judgment of this writer, Isaiah is not pointing to the final destruction of the world, but to the total and complete collapse of pagan powers, to the failure and destruction of the heathen world, to the defeat of lust and the forces governed by it. Several evidences which support this interpretation will be suggested in our comments on the following verses.

21   The phrase *in that day* always looks to the event or events being discussed in the context. Hence, in the day of the breaking up of the earth (vv. 19–20), *Jehovah will punish the host of the high ones on high*, who apparently are "the spiritual hosts of wickedness in the heavenly places" (Eph. 6:12) responsible for the spiritual upheavals of man since Eden (Gen. 3:1–15). This conflict and the subsequent defeat of Satan's forces are set forth in the vision of John: Satan and his forces are cast down from the high position that they formerly held (Rev. 12:7–10).[2] *And the kings of the earth upon the earth* shall likewise suffer punishment; for with the casting down of Satan and the defeat of his forces, the kings of earth are destined for defeat (Rev. 17:14; 19:19–21).

22   Our interpretation of the particular events in view seems to be further confirmed in verse 22: *And they shall be gathered together, as prisoners are gathered in the pit, and shall be shut up in the prison.* With the defeat of Satan at the hands of Jesus (Rev. 19:19–21), Satan was cast into the abyss (Rev. 20:1–3), which is called "his prison" (v. 7). *And after many days shall they be visited* ("punished," margin). At the end of many days (the symbolic thousand years of Revelation 20:1–6) Satan and his angels and those who served him received the final punishment in the lake of fire (Rev. 20:10, 15; Matt. 25:41, 46). Satan's judgment and defeat by Jesus (cf. John 12:31; 14:30; 16:11; Rev. 12:7–10) truly shook the earth (i.e., the world of the ungodly) to the point that it could "not rise again" (v. 20) to its former power. John therefore concludes, "Now is come the salvation, and the power, and the kingdom of our God, and the authority of his Christ: for the accuser of our brethren is cast down" (Rev. 12:10). These events took place with the defeat of Satan and his forces at the hands of Christ.

23   Here we find a third support for our position. *Then*, either at

---

2. See Homer Hailey, *Revelation: An Introduction and Commentary* (Grand Rapids: Baker, 1979), pp. 272–76.

the same time or immediately following, the light of the moon and the sun shall wane into insignificance when compared with the brilliant glory of the Lord, *for Jehovah of hosts will reign in mount Zion, and in Jerusalem.* This reign of Jehovah in Zion will follow the judgment and imprisonment of both the host on high and the kings of earth. According to Micah, Isaiah's contemporary, when the lame and the castoff are made a strong nation, "Jehovah will reign over them in mount Zion" (Mic. 4:7). This is to occur in the latter days (Mic. 4:1–4; cf. Isa. 2:2–4), the age of the Messiah. The writer of Hebrews tells us that the saints have now come to this Zion: "But ye are come unto mount Zion, and unto the city of the living God, the heavenly Jerusalem . . . and to God the Judge of all . . . and to Jesus the mediator of a new covenant" (Heb. 12:22–24). The clause *and before his elders shall be glory* not only looks back to the seventy elders of Israel (cf. Exod. 24:1, 9–10), but it also looks forward to the elders or overseers of the church, to whom Jehovah promises "the crown of glory that fadeth not away" (I Peter 5:1–4).

CHAPTER 25
Hymns of Thanksgiving for the Divine Mercy

Chapter 25 is made up of three hymns of praise and thanksgiving to Jehovah for victory over the world forces that stood in opposition to His spiritual people. Jehovah is likewise praised for His mercy toward and offer of salvation to the heathen nations as well as for His reward to those who wait for Him. A fourth song follows in chapter 26. The prophet continues to speak in terms of spiritual forces rather than actual cities or particular nations. God's people are thought of as a spiritual remnant redeemed and spared by mercy and grace, not as a political nation. The triumph of righteousness grows out of the great and terrible judgment described in the previous chapter.

A Hymn of Thanksgiving for Victory over the Terrible Ones (vv. 1–5)

1   Prior to the earth-shaking judgment at the end of chapter 24

there had been premature songs of praise. But with this judgment past and Jehovah now reigning in Mount Zion before His elders, the prophet breaks forth in praise, exalting God's mighty name: *For thou hast done wonderful things, even counsels of old.* God had executed judgments against the heathen nations for transgressing His laws and everlasting covenant, and against His own people for disregarding His covenant given at Sinai; these laws and covenants had been given after the counsel of His will (cf. Eph. 1:11), according to His eternal purpose (Eph. 3:11). All that He has done has been done *in faithfulness and truth;* Jehovah has been absolutely faithful to Himself and His purpose, and has always acted according to His true character. As Paul said of Jesus, "If we are faithless, he abideth faithful; for he cannot deny himself" (II Tim. 2:13); and again, with regard to the promise of eternal life, "God . . . cannot lie" (Titus 1:2). God can neither deny Himself nor lie; He can act only according to faithfulness and truth.

2   In working toward the fulfilling of His eternal purpose, Jehovah has exercised His mighty power among the heathen, making *of a city a heap,* a pile of rubble, and *of a fortified city a ruin*—massive bulwarks are no protection when God determines the judgment of a city or nation. He has caused *a palace of strangers to be no city.* Consider the great palaces of Nineveh, Babylon, Persepolis, and scores of other cities which were erected as monuments to the pride and power of man. They now lie in ruin as monuments to man's folly, not his greatness. Righteousness is the first line of defense of a nation (Prov. 14:34); where there is no righteousness, destruction follows. *It shall never be built;* what God brings to an end, man cannot rebuild.

3   Because of this demonstration of divine power destroying human cities and palaces, *shall a strong* ("powerful," Leupold, Young; "wild," Delitzsch) *people glorify thee; a city of terrible nations shall fear thee.* As they recognize the strength and power of Jehovah manifested in judgment, they will be brought to honor and reverence Him. This is not to say that they will submit to Him in righteousness, but that they are impressed with Jehovah's power and control over His creation.

4–5   Another expression of Jehovah's character that encourages honor and reverence among the strong nations is His care for the poor and needy. He is a stronghold in time of distress, *a refuge from the storm, a shade from the heat.* The blast of the strong against the people protected by the Lord is like fierce rain against a wall; it washes the wall but cannot destroy it. As the fierce heat in a dry place can be subdued and brought to nought by a cloud, so the Lord can silence the noise of foreigners and drive them away. *The song of the terrible ones shall be brought low.* When the strong people, the city of terrible nations, recognize the power of God's judgments (v. 3) but fail to change their character, they, too, shall be brought low.

Jehovah's Feast for the Nations (vv. 6–8)

6   Having sung of Jehovah's power in destroying the mighty structures of man and of His being a stronghold to the poor and needy in distress, turning the storm away as a wall deflects rain and providing a covering from foreigners in the time of extreme heat, the prophet now sings of the feast which Jehovah provides in Mount Zion for all nations. *And in this mountain* (Zion) in which Jehovah reigns (24:23), He will provide for *all peoples*—nations—*a feast of fat things* and of wine *well refined.* The wine upon its lees is wine that remains upon its settlings until it is well matured. It is then poured off and strained to provide the best wine possible. The picture is of the great spiritual feast that God will provide for all, Gentiles and Jews, in His Mount Zion. This adds additional beauty to the description of the mount unto which all the nations flow (2:2–4).

7   What is the *covering . . . and the veil* which Jehovah will remove in this mountain? Some have suggested the veil or covering of sorrow, hopelessness, and pessimism. But Isaiah says later, "For, behold, darkness shall cover the earth, and gross darkness the peoples; but Jehovah will arise upon thee, and his glory shall be seen upon thee. And nations shall come to thy light, and kings to the brightness of thy rising" (60:2–3). Removal of this veil of darkness seems more consistent with Isaiah's theme and is confirmed by New Testament teaching. Paul says that the Gentiles, "being darkened in their understanding, [are] alienated from the life of God, because of the ignorance that is in them, because of the hardening of their heart" (Eph. 4:18). When they come to the mount of God, His spiritual Zion, this

veil is removed. The same apostle says that when Jews whose minds are hardened "turn to the Lord, the veil is taken away" (II Cor. 3:14–16). The *veil* or *covering* seems to be ignorance and hardening of the heart against God.

8 Having made provision for the great spiritual feast and having removed the covering or veil of ignorance and unbelief, the Lord makes a third provision: *He hath swallowed up death for ever.* This was achieved through Jesus Christ. The apostle Paul says that God's "purpose and grace . . . was given us in Christ Jesus before times eternal, but hath now been manifested by the appearing of our Saviour Christ Jesus, who abolished death, and brought life and immortality to light through the gospel" (II Tim. 1:9–10). In Christ's victory over death our victory is guaranteed, for death will be swallowed up in victory (I Cor. 15:54). He will wipe away tears from the faces of His people and provide them comfort in the midst of affliction (cf. Heb. 13:5–6). And in their victory over all forces by the strength which He gives, their reproach is taken away. Isaiah's seal of certainty is now stamped upon the promise: *for Jehovah hath spoken it.* There can be no higher guarantee.

The Joy of Those Who Wait and the Destruction of the Proud (vv. 9–12)

9 The phrase *in that day* identifies what the prophet now points out with what he has just said (vv. 6–8). Those who have waited for or expected Jehovah now realize the object of their expectation, *he will save us.* The expectation of the past will be realized in the future when salvation is provided in the mountain of Jehovah, for the Lord says, "I will place salvation in Zion for Israel my glory" (46:13). Those who have waited *will be glad and rejoice in his salvation* (cf. 61:3). This is what the law and the prophets have pointed to and the faithful have waited for. When their hope is fulfilled, the redeemed will sing, "This is Jehovah's doing;/It is marvellous in our eyes./This is the day which Jehovah hath made;/We will rejoice and be glad in it" (Ps. 118:23–24)—the day of salvation.

10 *For in this mountain,* the mountain of 24:23 and 25:6, Jehovah's holy mountain (11:9), *will the hand of Jehovah rest*; it will

207

settle there permanently. The helping and protecting hand of the Lord will rest in His holy city, continuing to care for His own at all times. Also, His hand of judgment shall rest there, for it is while ruling in Zion that He "will judge between the nations, and will decide concerning many peoples" (2:4).

The abrupt introduction of judgment against Moab, in addition to that already revealed (see chs. 15–16), has given problems to liberal commentators, leading them into unreasonable positions. But when the character of Moab as set forth by the prophets is considered, it becomes evident that the nation stood as a symbol of pride and arrogance which must be completely destroyed before anyone can share the salvation in Mount Zion. Moab is characterized as very proud, arrogant, and boastful (16:6; Jer. 48:29–30), holding Israel in derision, magnifying himself against Jehovah (Jer. 48:27, 42), and holding the dignity of man in contempt (Amos 2:1; Zeph. 2:8, 10). As a consequence, *Moab shall be trodden down in his place. In his place* seems to stand in opposition to *this mountain*, where the hand of Jehovah rests. In his place of pride, arrogancy, and obstinacy against Jehovah, Moab will be trodden down, *even as straw is trodden down in the water of the dunghill.* This passage does not indicate that God hates Moab, but that the humiliation of and judgment against Moab will be complete. A century later in Jeremiah's prophecy against Moab, Jehovah held out a promise of hope to the proud nation: "Yet will I bring back the captivity of Moab in the latter days [the messianic age], saith Jehovah" (Jer. 48:47). But before Moab (or people of any nation) can participate in salvation, the spirit of haughtiness against Jehovah and His people has to be destroyed. This appears to be the point of the prophecy.

11–12 The last two verses confirm the view we have suggested. As a swimmer spreads forth his hands in order to keep from drowning, so Moab will endeavor to keep from being destroyed. *But Jehovah will lay low his pride,* that which was leading to his destruction, *together with the craft of his hands,* the cunning and skill by which he sought to escape the judgment. Jehovah will bring down, lay low, *even to the dust* all that in which the nation trusted and on which it had built its pride. This verifies the proverb, "Pride goeth before destruction,/And a haughty spirit before a fall" (Prov. 16:18).

CHAPTER 26
Glory to God for His Righteous Deeds!

A song of triumph is to be sung in Judah to celebrate the completion of Jehovah's work in preparing the strong city for occupancy. The strong city has triumphed over the lofty city. No specific city, such as Jerusalem or Nineveh or Babylon, is in view, for the prophet is continuing to reveal his message concerning the ages. He sees the defeat of that which is proud and lofty, and the glorious victory of God's cause of righteousness. In fact, most of the chapter may be considered a song of praise for Jehovah's strength and His exercise of that strength to overthrow His enemies and to redeem all who put their trust in Him (vv. 1–19). His people are urged to seek refuge in their individual chambers till the storm is past (vv. 20–21).

Praise for the Strong City (vv. 1–6)

1   *In that day* tells us that the *strong city* is simultaneous with the salvation of those who have waited for Jehovah and with the fall of Moab, the symbol of pride and arrogance (25:9–12). In contrast to Moab and what it symbolizes is the *strong city* in the land of Judah. Jehovah has "washed away the filth of the daughters of Zion" and has purged Jerusalem by the blast of judgment and of burning (4:4); He now dwells in the midst of this newly cleansed Zion-Jerusalem (24:23). This spiritual city needs no massive walls of stone for protection, for *salvation will he* (Jehovah) *appoint for walls and bulwarks*. Violence and desolation shall be unknown within her borders, for her walls shall be called *Salvation* and her gates *Praise* (60:18). Complete security from alien forces is guaranteed, for Jehovah says, "I . . . will be unto her a wall of fire round about, and I will be the glory in the midst of her" (Zech. 2:5). Now the song can be sung.

2   As yet, the city is vacant, uninhabited, for the gates have not been opened (cf. 24:12, where the gate of the waste city has been smitten with destruction). God is working out His eternal purpose, "after the counsel of his will," which will ultimately be summed up in Christ (Eph. 1:3–11). With the preparation complete, now comes the

cry, *Open ye the gates, that the righteous nation which keepeth faith may enter in.* The theme of those songs which have been heard from the uttermost part of the earth—"Glory to the righteous" (24:16)—is now being realized. This refers especially to those who have waited for Jehovah (25:9), those who have kept faith. When the proper time finally comes, they are always given preference; the gospel came to the Jews first, then to the Greeks also (Rom. 1:16; 2:8–10; Acts 3:26), including all nations and peoples (25:6–7; 2:2–4). Two characteristics of those who enter in are righteousness and steadfastness—keeping faith with God.

3   A beautiful and comforting assurance is given to those righteous ones who enter in faith: *Thou* (Jehovah) *wilt keep him in perfect peace, whose mind is stayed on thee; because he trusteth in thee,* that is, he keeps faith with God (v. 2). This reflects the description of the righteous by an unnamed psalmist: "He shall not be afraid of evil tidings:/His heart is fixed, trusting in Jehovah" (Ps. 112:7). *Perfect peace* ("peace, peace," Hebrew) signifies complete happiness, total well-being. This is the blessing of those whose mind is stayed on God.

4   This implicit trust in Jehovah is reemphasized: *Trust ye in Jehovah for ever,* not only when all goes well but also when the end of the tunnel seems dim and far away. Trust is assured reliance on another's integrity, absolute confidence in his abilities and attributes (cf. Prov. 3:5–8). Isaiah uses a phrase which occurs only here and in 12:2, *Jah, Jehovah* (translated *Jehovah, even Jehovah*). Delitzsch comments, "It is the proper name of God the redeemer in the most emphatic form" (I. 444). In Jehovah *is an everlasting rock*—a Rock of ages. Beginning with Moses' use of "rock" in reference to Jehovah (Deut. 32:4), several writers have used the word to describe certain characteristics of the Lord: Jehovah is a fortress and deliverer in whom one can take refuge (II Sam. 22:2–3); the Rock of salvation (II Sam. 22:47); a house of defense, a fortress (Ps. 31:2–3). Thus He offers shelter from the stormy winds and fierce oppressions of life. Jehovah gave Israel water from a rock in the desert; Paul uses this rock as a symbol of Christ (I Cor. 10:4).

5–6   The lofty people (24:4) are again brought into view—*them that dwell on high, the lofty city,* the proud and arrogant who exalt themselves. As Moab, the symbol of pride, was trodden down like

210

straw in the dunghill (25:10), so shall all that is lofty and high be brought down, even to the dust, becoming a "waste city" (24:10), "a heap . . . a ruin" (25:2). In contrast, the righteous nation of the strong city (vv. 1–2), whose defense is Jehovah, the Rock of ages that endures eternally, will abide as everlastingly as its Rock. God's overthrow of the lofty world-city of wickedness is progressive. The stronghold of all that exalts itself against God must be brought down (II Cor. 10:3–5). The prophet continues even more emphatically: *the foot shall tread it* (the pride and arrogance of the lofty city) *down*. The poor and the needy shall walk where pride once exulted.

The Effects of Jehovah's Judgments (vv. 7–10)

7   It is uncertain whether verse 7 serves as a conclusion to verses 1–6, or as an introduction to 8–10. We associate it with the latter because *the way of the just* is parallel with *the way of thy judgments* (v. 8). The reading of the margin better conveys the idea of the prophet: *the way of the just* (righteous) *is a right way; the path of the just thou directest aright*; it is a right and straight way. The emphasis seems to be on the rightness or straightness of the way and on the fact that Jehovah levels it. He removes the obstacles and makes the way straight. The wise man said, "For the ways of man are before the eyes of Jehovah;/And he maketh level all his paths" (Prov. 5:21).

8   *Yea*, God directs not only the steps of the just (v. 7), but also the way of His judgments. The righteous wait for Jehovah and His judgments, for they know that His judgments must come and that through them come deliverance and salvation (cf. 25:9). The desire of the soul looks to His memorial name; all that He is—all that He has done, is doing, and will do—is summed up in His name (cf. Exod. 3:15b; Hos. 12:5). Those who wait for Jehovah's righteous judgments and trust in the all-inclusiveness of His memorial name, which sums up the desire of the righteous soul, shall find the true path.

9   The prophet speaks in the first person, thus identifying himself with the faithful who have waited: *With my soul have I desired thee in the night. In the night* signifies either the night of affliction (21:11; Amos 5:8) or the darkness of ignorance and sin in which the world was steeped (60:2). With his spirit the prophet will seek Jehovah

211

earnestly, "night and day" (Alexander), with intensity and seriousness of mind, even unto the day. *Soul* and *spirit* used parallelly refer to the whole inner man. If the two terms are intended to express independent thoughts, *soul* refers to the whole being (cf. Gen. 2:7) whereas *spirit* indicates the life principle in man which relates him to God. The prophet now introduces a fresh thought concerning judgment: *for when thy judgments are in the earth, the inhabitants of the world learn righteousness*. Judgments may not turn the nations to righteousness, but they learn that Jehovah rules and that "Righteousness exalteth a nation;/But sin is a reproach to any people" (Prov. 14:34). This verse points clearly to the fact that the prophet is dealing with a world judgment and principles by which the nations should live and act.

10   The prophet continues by stating a contrast to the preceding thought: *Let favor be showed to the wicked, yet will he not learn righteousness*. Continued prosperity tends to turn the heart away from God, causing it to forget the source of blessings. The history of our nation demonstrates this. When the wicked prosper, they will take advantage of the righteous and deal wrongfully with them. In their blindness they *will not behold the majesty of Jehovah*, though He has not left Himself without witness to His majesty and benevolence (Acts 14:17).

The Lord Jehovah Versus "Other Lords" (vv. 11–15)

11   The uplifted hand of Jehovah should attract attention to His mighty power and rule among both the nations and His own people. Yet, though His hand continues to be lifted in judgment of the world and in the protection of the faithful, the peoples refuse to see and to be impressed with His being and greatness. However, one thing will stand out clearly: Jehovah's zeal is for *the people*—His own—in contrast to "the lofty people," who will languish (24:4). This zeal for His people and His wrath against the proud and rebellious will bring the nations to shame. The fire of His wrath shall devour His adversaries (cf. Ps. 97:3–4). Or, if the reading of the margin be correct, *the fire of thine adversaries shall devour them*. The adversaries will be devoured by a fire from within themselves, as so often happens. Then "Surely

the wrath of man shall praise thee;/The residue of wrath shalt thou gird upon thee" (Ps. 76:10). "The very passions which excite men to rebel against God shall be used as instruments and means of coercion" (Alexander). The fierce wrath of the Assyrian served Jehovah as His instrument of judgment, though the Assyrian did not mean to serve Him (10:5–7); likewise, the violent rage of the Chaldean involuntarily served Him (Hab. 1:5–11); Cyrus the Persian, whose ambition was to conquer the world, was Jehovah's instrument of judgment against the world of that day (45:1–7). This burning fire of ambition, pride, and conquest within the worldly consumes them.

12   In the whole of this particular stanza or paragraph the prophet continues to behold and extol the power and work of Jehovah. In the midst of the devouring fire that overtakes the adversaries of Jehovah's purpose and rule, He in His zeal for His people will provide and establish peace—full and complete happiness—for them. *For thou hast also wrought all our works for us.* The people, leaning on their own understanding and following their own ways, had failed. But the Lord had plotted their course, and all that had been achieved—their deliverance, preservation, and accomplishments—had been wrought by Jehovah.

13   Again the prophet addresses Jehovah, progressing to an even greater expression of adoration and personal relationship: *O Jehovah our God.* Isaiah looks back over the past and in shame confesses, *Other lords besides thee have had dominion over us.* Two views are held regarding the term *other lords.*

One is that they were foreign rulers who, at various times beginning with the period of the judges, had held sway over Israel. This view is in harmony with the curse pronounced in Leviticus 26:15–17: If God's people did not hearken unto Him, He would set His face against them, and "they that hate you shall rule over you." The second view is that the prophet is referring to the idol-gods which the people had served repeatedly throughout their history (cf. 2:8; Amos 5:25–26). Although scholars are divided in their views, it seems that the latter is correct. Jehovah's promise of the blessings which would follow obedience and the curses which would follow disobedience is introduced with the command, "Ye shall make you no idols . . . for I am Jehovah your God" (Lev. 26:1). Idolatry had been Israel's weak-

ness and their curse even before they entered Canaan. Behind
Jehovah's controversy with the people, the real warfare had been
between Him and the idols. When idols became the lords of the
people, the nation was brought under the lordship of heathen rulers
and thereby into even greater service of foreign gods (cf. Deut. 28:36).
But now, with Jehovah's victory demonstrated, there will be a new
relationship. Realizing the vanity of manmade deities, the people
will recognize Jehovah alone as God.

14 *They are dead, they shall not live; they are deceased* (they are
shades or shadows), *they shall not rise.* The idol-gods or lords continue to be in the prophet's view. They were lifeless works of men's
hands; they could not speak, see, or hear. There was no breath in
them; and they who made them were like them, also lifeless and dead
within (Ps. 135:15–18). Once they have been visited by Jehovah and
crushed or destroyed, they will never be raised; He makes *all remembrance of them to perish.* If the prophet is speaking of the heathen
tyrants who had ruled over Israel, the same could be said of them:
they would rise no more, and their memory would be forgotten. Of
the nations among whom Jehovah scattered the Jews, He said, "I will
make a full end" (Jer. 30:11; 46:28). And in Daniel's vision, the
dominion of the four great empires is taken away (Dan. 7:12); the
dominion of the fourth is taken away to be consumed and destroyed
"unto the end" (Dan. 7:26; cf. Rev. 17:16; 19:3, 20).

15 In contrast to the destruction of the nations that served idols,
Jehovah in His zeal has *increased the nation*—His people (cf. v. 11).
And in contrast to the destruction of the impotent idols, God is
glorified. In His increase of the nation Jehovah has enlarged all the
borders of the land and expanded the tent in which His people dwell
(54:2–3). Under His rule from the midst of purified Zion, "his dominion shall be from sea to sea, and from the River to the ends of the
earth" (Zech. 9:10).

From Failure to Victory (vv. 16–19)

16 Jehovah is certainly the central figure and power in this chapter; the word *Jehovah* occurs eleven times and *Jah* once. The prophet
addresses Him: *Jehovah, in trouble have they visited thee.* In time of

trouble and affliction the heathen "howled"—Babylon (13:6), Moab (15:2–4), and the sailors and people of Tyre (23:1, 6). The rebellious sinners of Judah made many prayers which Jehovah did not hear (1:15); they lamented "with a doleful lamentation" (Mic. 2:4). They looked not unto Jehovah (22:11); and when He called them to repentance, they ignored Him, turning to feasting and revelry instead (22:12–13). But those who waited for Jehovah (25:9) and looked for peace (26:12) poured out prayer unto Him in time of chastisement. Literally, *they poured out a whisper*, not a chirp or mutter as of a wizard (cf. 29:4), but a quiet prayer of hope, such as that of Hannah, who "spake in her heart; only her lips moved, but her voice was not heard" (I Sam. 1:13).

17–18 Like a pregnant woman who is in pain and anxious to be delivered, *so we have been before thee, O Jehovah.* Though the people have been with child and in pain, they have accomplished practically nothing, bringing forth only wind, a symbol of failure and disappointment and emptiness (cf. 41:29; Hos. 8:7; 12:1). When out of the pain of travail a child is born, there is joy to the mother (John 16:21); but the people have wrought no *deliverance in the earth*, only wind. Lacking faith and trust in God and dependence upon Him, they have accomplished little if anything toward achieving the purpose of Jehovah. *Neither have the inhabitants of the world fallen* ("been born," margin). The inhabitants of the earth, the heathen, have neither fallen to (been destroyed by) Israel nor been turned to God by them; Israel has failed.

19 In the midst of this failure and depression of spirit, a cry of hope and encouragement bursts forth. Jehovah speaks. There will yet be victory, but it will come not from man, but from God—a work of His purpose, power, and grace. *Thy dead shall live*, those whom Jehovah had given to the prophet and for whom he had been especially concerned (8:16–18); *my dead bodies shall arise*, for they are Jehovah's as well. There are three views concerning the precise resurrection being considered here: (1) the figurative resurrection of the Jewish nation and their return to their land; (2) the final resurrection of the body at the end of time; (3) a spiritual resurrection in the messianic age. We must try to determine which of these is in the prophet's mind.

1. From the context it is clear that Isaiah does not have Israel's return to the homeland in view. We have just read that in His zeal for the people Jehovah will ordain peace for them (v. 12). By bringing idolatry to nought, He will increase the nation and enlarge all the borders (v. 15). This will be accomplished, not by a resurrection and return of the Jewish nation to their land (cf. Ezek. 37:1–14), but by a spiritual resurrection.

2. The idea of a resurrection of the body had been indicated from the time of Moses. For Jesus said, "That the dead are raised, even Moses showed, in the place concerning the Bush." Quoting God's words to Moses in Exodus 3:6 ("I am the God . . . of Abraham, the God of Isaac, and the God of Jacob," all of whom had died long before the time of Moses), Jesus drew the following conclusion: "Now he is not the God of the dead, but of the living: for all live unto him" (Luke 20:37–38). David likewise pointed to the resurrection of the dead: "For thou wilt not leave my soul to Sheol;/Neither wilt thou suffer thy holy one to see corruption" (Ps. 16:10). However, Isaiah's use of "in that day" in the following chapter (vv. 1, 2, 12, 13), identifying certain events with this verse (26:19), confirms that he is not dealing with the resurrection at the last day, though the language might be so construed. Furthermore, Jesus says that everyone will arise at the last day (John 5:28–29; cf. Acts 24:15). Therefore, the language of verse 14, where we are told that the heathen lords "shall not rise," must be symbolic. If the language is symbolic there, then it is here also.

3. Viewing the resurrection of verse 19 as a spiritual resurrection is consistent with the context of the chapter. Out of the judgment and destruction of heathen nations and the spiritual forces of evil there will arise a new nation; this involves a spiritual resurrection. Jesus said, "The hour cometh, and now is, when the dead shall hear the voice of the Son of God; and they that hear ['hearken,' margin] shall live" (John 5:25). Those who hear His voice through the gospel will be made alive (cf. Eph. 2:1–6). Daniel also spoke of this spiritual resurrection: "And many [note that he does not say 'all'] of them that sleep in the dust of the earth shall awake, some to everlasting life, and some to shame and everlasting contempt" (Dan. 12:2). Of those who hear and are made alive by the gospel, some will remain faithful unto

everlasting life and some will turn back to everlasting contempt (see Matt. 24:12; Heb. 6:1–8; 10:26–31). Indeed, Simeon realized that Jesus was "set for the falling and rising of many in Israel; and for a sign which is spoken against" (Luke 2:34).

Awake and sing, ye that dwell in the dust; the dust indicates lowliness (cf. 25:12; 26:5), from which Jerusalem is to arise and shake itself free (52:2). A similar thought is expressed by Paul: "Awake, thou that sleepest, and arise from the dead, and Christ shall shine upon thee" (Eph. 5:14). *For thy dew*—the refreshing from Jehovah—*is as the dew of herbs,* sustaining life; or "the dew of light" (margin), causing the dead to shine, as Paul has indicated. Either makes sense. *And the earth shall cast forth the dead;* through the preaching of the gospel, the dead shall be brought to spiritual, and thus eternal, life by the Lord.

The view that Isaiah is speaking of spiritual resurrection is consistent with the theme and scope of the Book of Isaiah, with the particular context of chapters 24–27, and with the New Testament teaching. It seems, therefore, at least to this writer, that this view is the most plausible of the three suggested.

Wait for Jehovah (vv. 20–21)

20 The time for fulfilling the promises and hope of verse 19 was not yet at hand. Therefore through His prophet, the Lord calls, *Come, my people*—narrowing the exhortation to the faithful, those who are His—*enter thou* (His people as a unit) *into thy chambers, and shut thy doors about thee.* As in Matthew 6:6, the chamber in view here is an inner chamber where the faithful are to continue in a life of faith, prayer, and dependence on Jehovah. Where can more secure chambers be found than in Jehovah, the "everlasting rock" (v. 4)? *Hide thyself for a little moment* (time is no factor with God; a thousand years in His sight "are but as yesterday when it is past, and as a watch in the night," Ps. 90:4; cf. II Peter 3:8), *until the indignation be overpast,* the judgments of destruction which must come upon the world of the ungodly before the spiritual nation appears.

21 The indignation is executed in Jehovah's coming *forth out of his place to punish the inhabitants of the earth for their iniquity.* The language is accommodative as is that used to refer to His going down to see the tower of Babel (Gen. 11:5), or His going down to investigate the wickedness of Sodom and Gomorrah (Gen. 18:21). From His habitation in heaven He comes forth in judgment. The crimes of society shall be clearly disclosed before Him, and the penalty against such crimes shall be executed. The law had been violated (24:5), and the penalty must be carried out. Job had prayed that his blood be not covered, but that his righteousness, which was challenged by his accusers, be vindicated (Job 16:18; cf. Ezek. 24:7–8).

Since the time of the flood the death penalty for murder had evidently been included in the eternal covenant (Gen. 9:6). The law declared that the blood of the murdered could be expiated only by the blood of him that shed it (Num. 35:33). Murder unpunished by a society must be expiated by the death of that society. This was demonstrated in the case of the Jewish nation. For in demanding the murder of Jesus—"His blood be on us, and on our children" (Matt. 27:25)— they brought themselves under the death penalty which they paid a few decades later with the destruction of Jerusalem. This is the judgment which has been kept before the people in these three chapters. During this period of judgment let the people of God hide themselves from the storm.

CHAPTER 27

The Overthrow of World Power and Ingathering of Israel

The New Vineyard (vv. 1–6)

1   Some commentators consider this verse to be the conclusion of chapter 26; others consider it to be the introduction to chapter 27. In either case, it stands as the transition between the two and may be considered separately from the following verses. It deals with Jehovah's destruction of world power, an act which must precede the flourishing of the new vineyard. *In that day* identifies the work of Jehovah in this chapter as an expanding of His work set forth in

26:19–21 (cf. also vv. 2, 12). The Lord's sword is described as *hard and great and strong*—*hard*, unbreakable, well-tempered, able to retain its keen cutting edge; *great*, mighty, powerful; *strong*, not susceptible to wear, but ever able to execute God's punitive and destructive judgment. With it He *will punish leviathan the swift* ("gliding or fleeing," margin) *serpent, and leviathan the crooked* ("winding," margin) *serpent; and he will slay the monster that is in the sea.* Besides its appearance in this verse, the word *leviathan* occurs four times in poetical settings (Job 3:8; 41:1; Pss. 74:14; 104:26), apparently referring to an imaginary or mythical creature. The term was well known and understood in that day. (For a fuller discussion of the word see Young, II. 233, note 3.) Some writers claim the creatures in this verse represent three great world empires, probably Assyria, Babylonia, and Egypt; however, in the three previous chapters the prophet has dealt with universal forces of evil. In this light it seems better to think of the creatures here as symbolizing all the powers which serve Satan's efforts to defeat God's purpose. Similarly, in the Book of Revelation the beast out of the sea symbolizes world power, the beast out of the earth embodies false religion, and the harlot sums up all that is lustful and seductive. Here in Isaiah the total of these evil forces is depicted as three monsters. God's sword is stronger than all of them. With it He is able to punish them.

2   *In that day*, in the same period of time as verse 1, the Lord will plant another vineyard, but the result will greatly differ from that of a former planting (5:1–7). In the former case Isaiah sang a song to or about Jehovah ("my well-beloved"), whereas here the prophet sings about the vineyard. Some writers consider verses 3–5 to be the song. However, it appears more probable that the song is not recorded; rather, it is to be spontaneous praise from the heart. In the former case, the vineyard is destroyed because of its unfruitfulness; in this case the vineyard is praised for its rich production of grapes.

3   The care of this vineyard will not be left to frail, fallible men: *I Jehovah am its keeper.* Thus it will be well cared for and its needs provided. In contrast to the former vineyard of which Jehovah said, "I will also command the clouds that they rain no rain upon it" (5:6), He says of this one, *I will water it every moment*, constantly, regularly, even before severe need, not only with showers, but no doubt also

219

with the dew of 26:19b. Further, no one will be able to hurt it, for *I will keep it night and day*, protecting it continuously like a wall of fire about it (see the comments on 26:1).

4   That this is a difficult passage is indicated by the many paraphrases offered in an effort to get at the meaning. Alexander renders, "I am no longer angry with my people; O that their enemies (as thorns and briars) would array themselves against me, that I might rush upon them and consume them." Young explains that with His wrath gone, the Lord will now protect His people; He will meet the briars and thorns, set forth as enemies, burning them together. The thought seems to be: now that God's wrath against His people has been expended, let the enemies, once allowed to grow in the vineyard as briars and thorns (5:6), come against Him; He will march upon them and burn them with fire. As protector of His people, the new vineyard, the Lord will suffer no enemy to destroy them.

5   If the enemy wishes to escape destruction in the battle with Jehovah, *let him take hold of my strength*. Let him come over to God's side, yielding to the superior power of Jehovah. Let him make peace, be reconciled to the Lord. God is always ready to have His enemies make peace with Him, but it must be on His terms, not man's.

6   The prophet looks to the future when the vineyard will be exceeding fruitful, filling the earth with its abundance. *In days to come* ("in the generations that come," margin; that is, in the distant future when God's purpose is realized in the new vineyard) *shall Jacob take root; Israel shall blossom and bud*. The two, Jacob and Israel, occur here in poetic parallelism to sum up the whole of spiritual Israel. There will be no distinction; they will be firmly established, rooted, and grounded in Him. *And they shall fill the face of the world with fruit*, a metaphorical expression for the spiritual influence of the new vineyard. It will be like leaven, effecting a salutary result throughout the world, even to the end of time. The first vineyard was national Israel in the past; the new vineyard is spiritual Israel.

Expiation and Desolation (vv. 7–11)

7   Not only must the forces of the world be slain by the sword of Jehovah (v. 1) before the vineyard can be planted and bear fruit (vv.

2–6), but also national Israel itself must be judged and punished for its idolatry and wickedness. The judgment upon the nation is to be no mere slap on the wrist; it is a severe expression of Jehovah's hatred of sin and a judgment upon those who have rejected Him for idols. Yet He will not smite them as He smote their enemies who smote them. *Hath he* (God) *smitten them* (Israel) *as he smote those* (the enemies) *that smote them* (Israel)? The question is repeated from a slightly different angle: *Or are they* (the enemies) *slain according to the slaughter of them* (Israel) *that were slain by them* (the enemies)? The answer is no; for Jehovah had promised that even when His people are in the land of their enemies, He will not reject them or "abhor them, to destroy them utterly" (Lev. 26:44). Though Israel will not be brought to a full end, God will destroy those among whom His people will be scattered (Jer. 30:11; 46:28). A remnant of Israel will be spared (1:9) and later return unto Jehovah (10:21–22).

8   The judgment of Jehovah will be *in measure*—commensurate with the sins committed (see the comments on 40:2) and proportionate to Judah's shame (see the comments on 61:7) as determined by the Lord. Before sending them away, *thou dost contend with them*. God had met their rebellion with a serious effort (as in a debate or a lawsuit) to turn them back to Himself. When His striving against their opposition failed, He *removed them with his rough blast in the day of the east wind*, which would be temporary but severe. The east wind, the sirocco, was a fierce dry wind dreaded by the Israelites because of its destructive character; but however severe it might be, it was not as harsh as the four winds that scattered Elam (Jer. 49:36), or the destroying wind against Babylon (Jer. 51:1).

9   The word *Therefore* introduces a conclusion drawn from what has just been said (vv. 7–8). *By this shall the iniquity of Jacob be forgiven* ("expiated," margin; "purged," King James). We are not to conclude that by the judgment or removal of the people their sin is forgiven, for in the law it is said, "I have given it [the blood] to you upon the altar to make atonement for your souls: for it is the blood that maketh atonement by reason of the life" (Lev. 17:11). The writer of Hebrews likewise says that according to the law, "apart from shedding of blood there is no remission" (Heb. 9:22).

Actually, what happens in expiation or atonement is that the offense "is covered from the eyes of the holy God. . . . The sin is dealt with so effectively that it no longer remains as the object of God's condemnation."[3] The fruit or achievement of the severe judgment will be the abolition of idolatry: through the judgment *he maketh all the stones of the altar as chalkstones that are beaten in sunder,* pulverized and completely destroyed. Idolatry must be destroyed in Jacob as among the heathen. The Asherah (plural, Asherim) forbidden by Jehovah (Deut. 16:21) was a goddess worshiped by the Canaanites (the word may also have reference to a tree associated with her cult or to a grove in which an altar to her was erected). The Asherim, together with the sun images, must be so completely destroyed that they will never rise again (see the comments on 26:14). After the captivity, idolatry never appeared again among the people. Though they were corrupted by Greek philosophy, they never again yielded to the worship of idols. The purpose of God's judgment was accomplished in the removal of idolatry, the sin of sins among His people.

10   What city is *the fortified city,* now *solitary, a habitation deserted and forsaken, like the wilderness?* Writers are divided in their views. Alexander is uncertain, wavering between Babylon and Jerusalem. Leupold holds that it is Samaria, and Clements suggests the cities of Judah or Samaria. Calvin, Delitzsch, Rawlinson, and Young think that it is Jerusalem. The most probable view is that it is Jerusalem, once the center of Jehovah worship but now a city of idolatry. As the people must be judged for and cleansed of their idolatry, so Jerusalem, defiled and polluted, must be purged "by the blast of justice and by the blast of burning" (4:4, margin). Once the impregnable fortress of Israel and the dwelling place of Jehovah among them, Jerusalem will be deserted by the Lord and destroyed by fire (see Ezek. 11:23; 16:41). In the midst of the rubble of the desolate city calves will feed and lie down and, for lack of better herbage, eat the branches or twigs of vines or trees.

11   The prophet has spoken of a new vineyard (vv. 2–6) in contrast to the old (5:1–7). The old is worthless, of no value for anything

---

3. *Zondervan Pictorial Encyclopedia of the Bible,* ed. Merrill C. Tenney (Grand Rapids: Zondervan, 1975), vol. 2, p. 452.

except for firewood to be gathered and burned by women (see the description of the vine-tree in Ezek. 15). The prophet is painting a picture of complete desolation and weakness—women do not fear to come hither to find something to burn. As a *people of no understanding* (cf. 1:3; 5:13; Hos. 4:6), they seem never to have understood the true nature and character of Jehovah—His righteousness and holiness, which demand obedience to His divine will, and His judgment and destruction of that which is contrary to them. Jehovah had formed the nation, bestowing upon its people His love and favor. He had given them the land, made them His own, and sought to mold them after His own image. In their utter rejection of all this they can now have no compassion or favor from Him. They will have to suffer the consequence of their folly.

The Ingathering of the Outcasts (vv. 12–13)

12   The great prophet's characteristic of moving from a message of gloom and depression to one of encouragement and hope emerges again in these two verses. The clause *And it shall come to pass in that day* links the events being introduced with the period of history described in 26:19 and thereafter. The beating out of Jehovah's fruit from the river Euphrates to the brook of Egypt (as one would beat an olive tree [17:6] or beat out grain [28:27; Ruth 2:17]) metaphorically describes His gathering of those who are His—the remnant. The territory from the Euphrates to the Wadi el-Arish, the boundary between Canaan and Egypt, was the largest area ruled over by any king of Israel (I Kings 4:21); however, we are not to think of a literal area but should regard the phrase as symbolic of the world over which God rules. To be *gathered one by one* indicates the care with which the remnant will be gathered—not en masse but as individuals.

13   From the figure of a harvest ingathering, the prophet turns to another metaphor well understood by the people of his day. At the time of the ingathering a great trumpet will be blown, bringing those about to perish, from Assyria to Egypt, to God's holy mountain in Jerusalem for worship. A trumpet was used to call an assembly together or to introduce a feast (Num. 10:7, 10; Joel 2:15). The Day of Atonement was announced by loud trumpets sounded throughout

the land (Lev. 25:9). The sounding of this trumpet might be both a call to assemble on the mountain for worship and an announcement that atonement for sin has been perfectly provided in the sacrifice to which the law points. The idolatry of Jacob has been expiated, that is, removed from God's view (v. 9); atonement for sin has been made. The outcasts from the two extremes (as in v. 12), from Assyria to Egypt, are now being called that they might *worship Jehovah in the holy mountain at Jerusalem* (cf. 24:23; 25:6–7, 10). The writer of Hebrews says that it is to this mountain, the heavenly Jerusalem, and to the blood of Jesus that we have now come (Heb. 12:22–24).

Jerusalem-Zion: Warnings and Promises (28–35)

An Introductory Word

Delitzsch calls chapters 28–35 "The Book of Woes"; Leupold (after von Orelli) calls them "The Book of Zion." Both are appropriate. The section contains a series of prophetic discourses dealing especially with Judah's relationship to the heathen nations Egypt and Assyria, and its own sins and weaknesses (chs. 28–33). In these chapters the prophet pronounces six woes against the sins of drunken rulers in Samaria and Jerusalem, against the errors of Judah, and against an unnamed destroyer, probably Sennacherib of Assyria. (See also the six woes of 5:8–23.) In the midst of chaos God points to the stone in Zion as a place of refuge and a foundation on which to build. The section closes with a prophecy against Edom, symbol of the world (ch. 34), and a promise of Zion's future glory (ch. 35). Interspersed throughout these chapters of woes and doom, promises of glorious days to come flash brilliantly. These days will be realized under the rule of a righteous King, described in later chapters as the Servant of Jehovah.

Students of Isaiah are generally agreed that as chapters 7–12 deal with the period of Ahaz's reign, so chapters 28–35 pertain to the period of Hezekiah. The prophecies are a clear, graphic reflection of the political, moral, and religious temper of the people with whom Isaiah had to deal; they give special emphasis to the predilection of looking to Egypt for help. Isaiah's battle at this time was with the pro-Egypt party within the nation. He strongly urged, instead, dependence upon Jehovah.

The woe directed against the drunkards of Samaria (28:1–6) points to a time prior to the fall of that city to the Assyrians (721 B.C.). This raises a question concerning the date of Hezekiah's reign. According to the data in II Kings 18:1, 9, Hezekiah began to reign in 727 B.C. The prophecy in 28:1–6 could, then, have been directed against the rulers of Samaria during the early years of his reign. Young accepts 727 as the year of Hezekiah's accession (II. 540–42). Thiele, applying his theory of accession and nonaccession years and of dual dating, concluded that 715–686 B.C. are the dates of Hezekiah's reign.[1] Thiele's conclusion seems to be substantiated by the accounts of Hezekiah's religious reforms and the great Passover in the first year of his reign (II Chron. 29–30). The king sent an urgent invitation to the people of Israel to attend this Passover, but no mention is made of the rulers of Samaria (30:1–6, 11, 21). This omission suggests that by this time Samaria had fallen to Assyria. Dogmatism for either date (727 or 715 B.C.) would be unwise. The date used in this work is 715 B.C. (The process of reaching conclusions as to the date of various parts of the book is discussed at some length by Leupold [I. 19–27].)

It is clear that the prophecy against the drunkards of Ephraim was spoken before the fall of Samaria. If we accept Thiele's date for Hezekiah's reign, then two alternatives lie before us: either all of chapter 28 was delivered before the fall of Samaria and hence before the reign of Hezekiah, or the Ephraimitic prophecy was spoken before his reign and repeated later as a warning to Jerusalem. If drunken

---

1. Edwin R. Thiele, A Chronology of the Hebrew Kings (Grand Rapids: Zondervan, 1978), pp. 52–54, 65–67.

rulers contributed to the fall of one nation, they would contribute to the fall of others as well. The prophecy against and subsequent fall of Samaria would have been a powerful warning to her sister Judah, and should be to nations today also.

CHAPTER 28
Drunkards—and the Stone in Zion

Woe to the Drunkards of Ephraim (vv. 1–6)

1 *Woe*—a mournful-sounding word of doom which focuses attention on an impending disaster and portends tragedy—is used throughout these several chapters. Although not named, the city of Samaria appears clearly to be in the prophet's view. The pride of this people was pointed out earlier (9:9–10), and both Amos (4:1; 6:6) and Hosea (4:11; 7:5, 14) describe them as hard or heavy drinkers. Samaria, built by Omri the father of Ahab, was located on a hill at the head of a beautiful, luxuriant valley that extended westward to the Plain of Sharon; the Mediterranean Sea could be seen from its summit. The walls of the city extending around the crest of the hill gave the impression of a crown or chaplet of flowers on a head. This flower of Ephraim's beauty, the glory of the nation, was now fading away; like a wreath of flowers on the head of a drunken reveler, it was withering and ready to be cast under foot.

2 *Behold*—the word arrests attention—*the Lord* (Hebrew, *Adonai*—the title indicates the Master of all, whom everyone must obey), who had appeared to and called Isaiah to His service (6:1), *hath a mighty and strong one*—one of absolute power to carry out the divine will. Though not named, this *strong one* appears to be the Assyrian army, which would be used by Jehovah to humble this proud, arrogant, and drunken people (cf. 9:11; 10:5–11). His conquering and devastating power is suggested by three figures: *as a tempest of hail, a destroying storm, as a tempest of mighty waters overflowing.* This army will come upon the city of drunken revelers, sweeping up through the valleys and ravines like a terrible hailstorm,

a howling wind of hurricane force, and waters of an overwhelming flood that carries everything before it to destruction. This mighty force will cast down to the earth *with the hand*, or "with violence" (margin). This mighty power (Assyria) being wielded by God will cast down violently the drunken rulers and those whom they rule. The picture is one of savage destruction controlled only by the hand of God.

3 In this storm *the crown of pride of the drunkards of Ephraim*, that in which their hearts gloried and of which their tongues boasted, *shall be trodden under foot*, brought low by the conquerors. The mighty hand will cast down (v. 2), and the feet of invaders will trample the land (v. 3). The ruins of the once proud city and nation have continued to be trampled under foot through the ensuing centuries.

4 This fading flower of Samaria's once glorious beauty, located at the head of the luxuriant and productive valley, *shall be as the first-ripe fig before the summer.* Fig trees in Palestine produce two crops of fruit yearly: the first, referred to here, is in May or June, and the second crop in August and September. The early figs are eagerly awaited by those who have had no fresh fruit during the winter. The invader—the conqueror—will regard the city as an early ripened fig. *While it is yet in his hand he eateth it up*; he will eagerly seek it and, having found it, will hungrily devour it (cf. Nah. 3:12). The prophet has used three figures to describe the destruction: the city of drunkards shall be destroyed by the terrible forces of nature (v. 2), trodden under foot in utter helplessness (v. 3), and devoured like a first-ripe fig (v. 4).

5 Those who are cast down are not left without a word of hope, for the Lord gives to His remnant a word of encouragement that shines like a beam of light through a rift in the black and lowering clouds. *In that day*, the day of adversity, humiliation, disgrace, and shame, *will Jehovah of hosts become a crown of glory, and a diadem of beauty, unto the residue* (remnant) *of his people.* The people must be brought to a complete realization of the utter folly and failure of that which is human and worldly. With that in which they had gloried now swept away by the blast of judgment, Jehovah can become their

true crown, glory, and joy. The remnant consist of those few from both Ephraim and Judah who will return to Him.

6 When the remnant recognize Jehovah as their true crown and glory, He will be a spirit of justice to those who sit in judgment and of strength to those who defend His cause against the enemy, turning them back at the gate. This residue will be governed by the Spirit of Jehovah, not by the spirit of drunkenness and debauchery; they will be strengthened by His power, not by heathen allies.

Woe to the Drunken Rulers in Judah (vv. 7–13)

7–8 With the words, *And even these*, the prophet turns from the drunkards of Ephraim to the priests and prophets of Jerusalem. The phrase indicates that the two groups are alike in character and obnoxiousness to Jehovah. The picture is vivid, as though one has broken suddenly into the room where the priests and prophets are assembled; it is as repulsive and nauseous as if one were there smelling the stench of their vomit. In lucid and impressive language Isaiah exposes their wicked and sinful practices: *These reel with wine, and stagger with strong drink; the priest and the prophet reel with strong drink, they are swallowed up of wine, they stagger with strong drink; they err in vision, they stumble in judgment.* We can visualize a prophet rising to speak, stammering and staggering about in the assembly, and a besotted priest attempting to teach or minister to the things of God. What a mockery of spiritual service—a travesty of true religion! The priest is a teacher of God's word and the people's representative before Him; drinking wine is forbidden in this service (Lev. 10:8–11). The prophet is God's spokesman to the people, charged to speak His word as given to him by the Lord (Deut. 18:18). (For the extent to which the prophets had departed from this standard, read Mic. 2:11 and ch. 3.) In drunken stupor they err in vision and stumble in judgment. The loathesomeness of the scene is further depicted by the prophet: *For all tables are full of vomit and filthiness, so that there is no place clean*, no place in which to serve anything wholesome. If *table* is used here by metonymy for the serving of spiritual food (as it appears to be in

Ps. 69:22; Rom. 11:9), the service of the prophets and priests was totally lacking in wholesome spiritual teaching from God.

9–10 The response of the intoxicated priests and prophets to anything a true prophet from God (like Isaiah) might say takes the form of a scornful or contemptuous sneer intended to cast ridicule upon what they consider his small and insignificant speech. In a drunken monotone, they ask, *Whom will he teach knowledge? and whom will he make to understand the message* ("report," margin)? Surely, he cannot teach them anything; they are prophets and priests and rulers. Sarcastically spoken, the question continues. Would he teach us as *them that are weaned from the milk, and drawn from the breasts*? Does he think of us as babes, just weaned, who cannot think for themselves? The drunken sots continue to mock the prophet with sarcasm: *For it is precept upon precept, precept upon precept; line* (or "rule," margin) *upon line, line upon line; here a little, there a little*, as a tutor instructs a child by rote. Rawlinson has well summarized their view of the prophet's teaching: "a perpetual drizzling rain of petty maxims and rules, vexatious, cramping, confining . . . narrow, childish, and wearisome" (I. 449). "And in the repetition of the short words we may hear the heavy babbling language of the drunken scoffers" (Delitzsch, II. 7). They are completely steeped in the intoxicants of the day and so overwhelmingly stupefied thereby that they cannot discern between true and false prophecy. In their slumbering indifference they cannot detect the warning from God. These prophets and priests of God's own people see themselves as being beyond the need of God's revelation.

11 Many preachers, teachers, and hearers today have a tendency to consider parts of God's word insignificant and indifferent, and therefore they select for themselves what they will observe and what they will disregard. But to despise or disregard the Lord's word and His continuous emphasis upon the simple principles of faith, trust, and obedience is to bring upon one's self the dire consequence of ruin. The drunken spiritual leaders of Judah had charged the Lord's servant with stammering monosyllabic, childish platitudes. The prophet is ready with a stinging response: *Nay, but by men of strange lips* ("with stammering lips," margin) *and with another tongue will he speak to this people*. Moses had earlier forewarned the people of Israel that if

they failed to respect Jehovah and His word, He would "bring a nation against thee from far, from the end of the earth, as the eagle flieth; a nation whose tongue thou shalt not understand; a nation of fierce countenance, that shall not regard the person of the old, nor show favor to the young" (Deut. 28:49–50). Ahaz's appeal to Tiglath-pileser of Assyria and submission to him (II Kings 16:7–16) instead of relying on Jehovah are now bearing fruits of terror and threats of destruction. The word of Jehovah through Moses will be fulfilled.

12 The *rest* and *refreshing* that God had promised the nation were to have been found in faithfulness to Him and in observance of His covenant (Deut. 28:1–14). This word concerning *rest* and *refreshing* sums up in a sentence what Isaiah had been preaching to all, both rulers and people (cf. 1:18–19; 7:4; 30:15). *Yet they would not hear;* consequently, the Assyrians, men of strange lips, had been threatening their land for a number of years and were even now either approaching or already in the land. However, faith saved the day (ch. 37); it would be left for the Babylonians, also men of strange lips, to bring about the destruction and captivity (39:6).

13 The prophet returns to the thought of verses 10–11. Jehovah had spoken to the nation in word; now He shall speak to them in deeds, and *it shall be nought but terror to understand the message* (v. 19). As the drunken prophets and priests had charged the true prophet, so it shall be to them: *Therefore shall the word of Jehovah be unto them precept upon precept, precept upon precept; line upon line, line upon line; here a little, there a little; that they may go, and fall backward, and be broken, and snared, and taken.* In their rebellion against God, trusting in their own strength and the help of Egypt, they rose up against Assyria. Falling backward, they were eventually broken as a nation, snared in a trap of their own setting, and taken captive by Babylon. They learned slowly; however, a remnant did eventually learn, but it was precept upon precept, line upon line, little by little. The thundering message of deeds and judgment is the only language that some—whether nation, individual, or the church of God—will hear or understand. The school of experience is a hard one, but it is God's only alternative when ears are closed to His message in word. The Lord had told Isaiah that the people would not

give heed to his message; nevertheless, he was to continue to preach (6:9–10).

The Rulers' Covenant with Death and Jehovah's Foundation Stone in Zion (vv. 14–22)

14 Having addressed his message of stern rebuke and warning to the priests and prophets of Jerusalem, the prophet of God now directs his attention to the scoffing political rulers of the city. Earlier he had addressed these men as "rulers of Sodom . . . people of Gomorrah" (1:10); he now refers to them as scoffers of Jehovah and His word. It would seem from this that Hezekiah, in spite of his personal religious integrity, had surrounded himself with unbelieving and irreligious aides and counsellors. However, there were probably only men of this kind to choose from after the wicked rule of Ahaz.

15 The rulers of Judah scoffed at the idea that judgment would come to them: *We have made a covenant with death, and with Sheol are we at agreement; when the overflowing scourge shall pass through, it shall not come unto us; for we have made lies our refuge, and under falsehood have we hid ourselves.* Having made a covenant and agreement with death and the nether or unseen world, they have no fear of either. The word *scourge* (literally, a whip used to inflict punishment) is sometimes used metaphorically. Here *the overflowing scourge* is the invasion of the Assyrians (cf. 8:7–8). Whether the scoffers said these very words is of little moment; it is doubtful whether they would have been so honest. But these words do express their arrogant self-confidence and reliance upon themselves to connive a way of avoiding the overflowing scourge that threatened them, either by coming to an agreement with Assyria or by forming a league with Egypt (or some other power). They had no fear of death or of destruction from Assyria, for their own ingenuity, not trust in God, would save them. However, political treaties based on deception, lies, and falsehood, "playing both ends against the middle," at which the rulers of Judah were most adept, make a very poor refuge under which to hide in time of trouble.

16 In the midst of this vaunting self-confidence and impending doom, Jehovah announces another of His precious messianic proph-

ecies: *Therefore thus saith the Lord Jehovah, Behold, I lay* ("have laid,"
margin) *in Zion for a foundation a stone, a tried stone, a precious
corner-stone of sure foundation: he that believeth shall not be in haste.*
Both Delitzsch and Young point out the similarity between this
prophecy and the promise by which Ahaz had been rebuked. Each
begins with *therefore* and *behold,* followed by a specification of
Jehovah's deed: *The Lord himself will give you a sign* (7:14), and *I lay
in Zion for a foundation a stone.* In God's purpose this stone had been
laid in Zion from before the foundation of the world. Peter identifies
the stone laid in Zion as the Lord (I Peter 2:3–8); Christ "was fore-
known indeed before the foundation of the world, but was manifested
at the end of the times for your sake" (I Peter 1:20). This stone, tried,
tested, and proved genuine, is the firm, immovable, and permanent
foundation of salvation and safety. Precious—of great spiritual and
moral value—it is the cornerstone on which the walls are firmly
joined together. The believer who builds on this stone shall never be
put to shame by hasty and rash actions; for example, attempts to
provide against the day of judgment by making an alliance with Egypt
or some other foreign force. This stone stands in contrast to the false
foundation on which the rulers of Judah relied.

Although this passage is messianic, realized in Christ, to the
people of Isaiah's day Jehovah was the tried stone in whom alone they
could fully trust and on whom they could build for permanence.
From the earliest time of Israel's history, He had been their rock, a
fortress of security (Gen. 49:24; Deut. 32:4; Isa. 8:14–15). About a
century after Isaiah, Nahum very beautifully said, "Jehovah is good,
a stronghold in the day of trouble; and he knoweth them that take
refuge in him" (Nah. 1:7). In Jehovah the people of the Old Testament would find that which He was working toward—the Messiah,
the proved and enduring stone in God's spiritual Zion.

17   The Lord continues with His architectural metaphor: He will
make *justice the line,* the rule in all His dealings with Judah, *and
righteousness the plummet,* the standard by which they should live.
This line and plummet guarantee a straight and perpendicular wall
which, being built on the sure foundation, will stand the test of all
storms (cf. Matt. 7:24–25). But in contrast, the rulers' covenant with
death and agreement with Sheol will be utterly swept away. These

233

refuges and hiding places of lies erected by the prophets, priests, and political rulers were still relied upon by the false prophets in Ezekiel's day, a hundred years later; he calls them walls daubed with untempered mortar. These also the Lord will level to the ground with stormy wind and great hailstones (Ezek. 13:8–16). At that time the Babylonians will be the overwhelming flood.

18 Since the covenant with death and agreement with Sheol were made by the *scoffers, that rule this people that is in Jerusalem* (v. 14), the nation is involved as well. Hiding behind this sham or false protection, the nation is without fear; yet when the overflowing scourge passes through, *then ye shall be trodden down by it.* This double figure of a flood passing through and of an army treading the people under foot gives double emphasis to the hopelessness and terror of the moment.

19 *As often as it passeth through, it shall take you.* The whole land is involved, for "in the fourteenth year of king Hezekiah did Sennacherib king of Assyria come up against all the fortified cities of Judah, and took them" (II Kings 18:13). The prophet had said earlier that the Assyrian army would overflow its channels: "And it shall sweep onward into Judah; it shall overflow and pass through; it shall reach even to the neck" (8:8). It would come to the walls of Jerusalem, but not take the city (ch. 37). As word came to Jerusalem that the Assyrians were taking city after city, it would *be nought but terror to understand the message.* Note in particular the wordplay here. As the prophets and priests had mocked Isaiah, "Whom will he make to understand the message?" (v. 9), God would make them understand the message of judgment and destruction delivered by men of strange lips and stammering tongue.

20 It matters not whether this verse is a proverbial saying, as thought by some; it dramatically teaches the lesson. To stretch oneself on a short bed, attempting to cover oneself with a blanket too narrow, is not only extremely uncomfortable, but it also could result in death if the weather is cold. So, too, the rulers of Judah will find their covenant and agreement of lies too short and too narrow for protection when the overflowing scourge passes through.

About seven-and-a-half centuries later the descendants of these mockers made a similar error. They made a covenant with death and an agreement with Sheol when they declared Caesar to be their king and demanded the death of Jesus, asking Pilate to set a guard by the tomb. But every effort failed. On the morning of the third day the bars of death were broken asunder, the tomb was opened, and the body of Jesus was raised from the dead. Four decades later the Roman army swept across the land like an overwhelming flood, destroying the city and temple, slaying thousands and selling other thousands into slavery. The hail swept away their refuge of lies, for their bed was too short, their blankets too narrow. Millions since have failed to learn the lesson, continuing to make covenants with death and agreements with Sheol and hiding themselves under the lies of atheism, evolution, humanistic theories, religious errors, false faiths, and nominal Christian commitment. All efforts to hide from God and yet soothe the soul with a false sense of security are shams—walls of untempered mortar. When the overflowing scourge of divine judgment passes through, *it shall be nought but terror to understand the message. For the bed is shorter than that a man can stretch himself on it; and the covering narrower than that he can wrap himself in it.*

21   The word *For* introduces the immediate cause of this tragedy: *Jehovah will rise up as in mount Perazim, he will be wroth as in the valley of Gibeon.* This judgment will be an expression of the divine wrath, as when God broke the enemies of David at Baal-perazim (II Sam. 5:20; I Chron. 14:11), and the Philistines at Gibeon (II Sam. 5:25; I Chron. 14:16). At Gibeon, in the days of Joshua, Jehovah had also slain the Amorite kings and their armies with great hailstones from heaven (Josh. 10:10–11). The prophet calls what Jehovah will now do *his strange work . . . his strange act.* The strangeness is that Jehovah will act against His own people, who have become His foes.

22   The prophet closes his speech with a final warning: *Now therefore*—in the light of what has been said—*be ye not scoffers;* change your attitude from scoffing to faith, *lest your bonds be made strong.* The rulers may be beyond reach; but if the people hearken to God instead of them, mercy can yet be found and judgment averted. *For a decree of destruction have I heard from the Lord, Jehovah of hosts, upon the whole earth.* This decree of destruction upon the whole earth which the prophet had heard is probably the one an-

nounced in chapters 24–27. *From the Lord*, the Master and Ruler of all realms, *Jehovah of hosts*, who controls and directs to His own service and glory the armies of earth, had come this decree. This is not the stammering of the prophet, but a message which he had heard from God.

A Parable from Agriculture (vv. 23–29)

In a parable from agriculture the prophet teaches that Jehovah's judgments have a purpose; God always acts according to divine wisdom. Whatever He does looks to the bearing of spiritual fruit according to His eternal purpose.

23–24 By the use of four imperatives the prophet calls upon the people to hear his voice and harken to his parable. As the farmer plows, plants, and threshes, he keeps in mind the nature of the seeds and the desired end. The husbandman plows, then harrows to break the clods; he does not continue the process indefinitely, but only until the ground is sufficiently prepared for planting.

25–26 With the land thus prepared, the farmer then plants the seeds according to their various characteristics. Fitch (black cummin), the pods of which produce large quantities of tiny black seeds, is used in bread to make it more wholesome. The farmer *cast(s) abroad the fitches, and scatter(s) the cummin*, an aromatic herb, the seeds of which were valued to spice stewed meat and to add flavor to bread. Each of these is planted according to the wisdom of husbandry. Wheat and barley are planted in the appropriate places in rows, and spelt (a kind of wild wheat, or a kind of vetch used as camel fodder) is planted as a border around the wheat and barley. We do not know why the spelt was planted as a border, but the farmers of Judah knew and to them it made sense. This wisdom or common sense came from God, who so endows man.

27 The same kind of common sense or wisdom is likewise used in threshing. The fitches and the cummin, both small and delicate plants, are not threshed with unsuitable equipment such as a sharp instrument or a cart wheel rolled over the pods. Instead, they are beaten out by a rod or staff; this is common sense.

28 Likewise in threshing the bread grain, the agriculturist will use proper judgment. The margin seems to give the sense of this verse: *Is bread grain crushed? Nay, he will not ever be threshing it, and driving his cart wheels and his horses over it; he doth not crush it.* The farmer does not keep on threshing, or driving the horses and threshing instruments over the grain until it is crushed and unfit for bread. He knows when the threshing is complete.

29   This wisdom shown by the husbandman is from God, *who is wonderful in counsel, and excellent in wisdom.* Jehovah is far more than an unlimited power exercising vengeance; He ever acts according to His infinite wisdom and after the counsel of His divine will (cf. Eph. 1:11). As the husbandman plows and harrows, plants according to the nature of the grain, and then threshes according to common sense and wisdom, so Jehovah has been plowing, planting, and threshing according to His wisdom and counsel so that His eternal divine purpose may be accomplished. In the midst of judgment we should recognize His eternal purpose and then act in faith.

CHAPTER **29**

Woe to Ariel—and to Those Who Hide Their Counsel from God

The blighting influence and effect of the drunken prophets, priests, and rulers in Jerusalem took a grievous and bitter toll on the spiritual life of the people in Zion. After Jehovah's judgment of the scoffers who ruled the people (ch. 28), the theme of chapter 29 is the unhealthy spiritual condition in Ariel (Jerusalem-Zion), the depth to which it brought the people, and Jehovah's judgment against the foes of the true spiritual faith. Many commentators see in this chapter the siege of Jerusalem by Sennacherib (701 B.C.); admittedly, there is ground for this view. But it seems to this writer that there is evidence that the chapter centers on a deeper spiritual conflict symbolized by the Assyrian assault. The depth to which the nation is brought (vv. 1–4), the description of Judah's foes as "the multitude of all nations" which will be destroyed by Jehovah (vv. 5–8), the drunkenness of the people, but not with wine, and their drawing nigh to Jehovah with

237

the mouth but not with the heart (vv. 9–15), all point to the conclusion that we are dealing with spiritual conflicts and their consequences. This view seems to be confirmed by the second woe of the chapter, which is directed against the effort to hide counsel from Jehovah (vv. 15–16), and by the subsequent change in understanding, which issues in a rejoicing in Jehovah, the regeneration of the nation, and their sanctifying Jehovah's name and person (vv. 17–24).

Though thought by many to have been uttered in the period 705–701 B.C., Isaiah's prophecies in chapters 29–33 cannot be conclusively dated. Even if he did speak them in this period, it need not follow that what he said pertained only to the siege of Jerusalem by Sennacherib and the conditions surrounding it. Isaiah's visions involve a world view and include the coming of the Messiah and the establishment of His kingdom. They take into account the various heathen nations of the entire period, their opposition to Jehovah's purpose, Jehovah's use of them, and their destruction at His hand. Isaiah's visions also include Jehovah's judgment of idolatry in general, the spiritual condition and fruits of His own unfaithful city and kingdom, and His judgments against them. In the light of the long-range view of the Book of Isaiah and its stress on the eternal purpose of God, some of the statements which could be construed as referring to a specific siege may actually be a metaphorical description of the moral and spiritual conditions in Judah and the Lord's providential work over a very long period. This does not mean, however, that the Assyrian invasion and Jehovah's judgment of that nation are not in view here. Indeed, they are twice referred to specifically in these chapters (30:31; 31:8). The Lord is teaching that man is to look not only to His word, but also to His deeds, and to see Him at work in the events of history. Zion will be threatened and brought low, but not destroyed; Jehovah is in control as He works out His eternal purpose in and through man.

Woe to Ariel (vv. 1–14)

1 *Ho Ariel, Ariel, the city where David encamped.* Having criticized and denounced the drunken prophets, priests, and rulers of Jerusalem who scoff at the word of Jehovah, the prophet now pro-

nounces a woe upon the faithless city, rebuking the empty religious life in Zion. From the references to *the city where David encamped* and *mount Zion* (v. 8), we know that *Ariel* is a symbolic name for Jerusalem-Zion. However, the exact meaning of *Ariel* is not so clear. As the margin indicates, it may mean "the lion of God" or "the hearth of God." As the stronghold of Jehovah's people, Jerusalem had thus far resisted all foes. By continuing to resist all foes and to fiercely contend for the true faith, bringing forth the Messiah, it would in the end be a "lion of God." However, evidence is stronger for "hearth of God." The word *Ariel* occurs in Ezekiel 43:15, where it is translated "altar" (King James) and "altar hearth" (American Standard, New American Standard, New International Version). Through Moses Jehovah had said that in the place where He would choose to put His name, there the people were to offer sacrifices and observe the feasts (Deut. 12:5, 11–13; 16:2). He chose Zion for His habitation and resting place among the people (Ps. 132:13–14), and Jerusalem as the city in which His house should be built and His name placed (II Kings 21:7; II Chron. 33:4, 7). It was there that the Lord dwelt among His people, the sacrifices were offered, and the feasts observed. His "fire is in Zion, and his furnace in Jerusalem" (31:9). In this light, "hearth of God" seems to be the better understanding.

Another problem presents itself: Shall we interpret *add ye year to year; let the feasts come round* to mean that within the course of a year added to the present year, as the cycle of feasts comes around, the Assyrians will besiege the city? Or does the content of the chapter justify a broader meaning, suggesting that as year is added to year and the cycle of feasts rolls round (not once, but any number of times), Jehovah will bring Ariel low, but eventually bless her? If, as many commentators think, Isaiah has Sennacherib's invasion in mind, the former is preferable; but the content of the chapter seems to point to the total period from Isaiah to the coming of the Messiah, in which case the second view is preferable. This writer finds it difficult to restrict the time period to less than two years. The broader interpretation does not limit Jehovah's total work involving the Assyrians to their invasion of the land and siege of Jerusalem.

2   David had besieged and taken Jerusalem, making it his stronghold; he had brought the ark of the covenant into the city and thus

made it a hearth of God—Ariel. But since that time the land had become filled with idols (2:8); Ahaz had defiled the temple, setting up an altar patterned after one in Damascus (II Kings 16:10–11), and had burned his children in the fire as sacrifices (II Chron. 28:3). In spite of Hezekiah's great reforms, conditions were still in a sordid state (cf. ch. 28). At the appropriate time—indicated by the words "add ye year to year; let the feasts come round"—Jehovah will encamp about the city and distress it, causing mourning and lamentation. Before she can be a true hearth of God again, she must be brought down from her present state of pride and empty formalism. Through this distress Zion will be purged of her moral dross and spiritual filth, becoming unto Jehovah a true Ariel—a worthy altar-hearth: *she shall be unto me as Ariel.*

3 Jehovah makes it plain that the distress which will befall the faithless city is His work. Note the triple occurrence of the personal pronoun: *then will I distress Ariel* (v. 2); *I will encamp against thee round about, and will lay siege against thee with posted troops, and I will raise siege works against thee.* In an earlier prophecy the Lord had said that He would use the Assyrians against Zion and Jerusalem (10:5–12); later He says that He will bring the Chaldeans against the city (Hab. 1:5–11). Jehovah's hand is definitely in the history of nations and of His own people, controlling their destinies.

4 In the siege brought against the city by Jehovah's *posted troops* (v. 3), the people will be brought down from their self-exalted position. They will speak out of the ground, low out of the dust, gasping like a dying person or chirping like one with a familiar spirit. The latter is a medium who claims to summon and consult with the dead. Mediums deceive their clients by speaking in a weak, thin voice, or sometimes by ventriloquism, as though the words come from the ground. Jerusalem will be brought so very low that her speech will be a whimper. Sennacherib's siege did not bring Jerusalem to this state, though it did contribute to Judah's eventual downfall. A century after Assyria's invasion and devastation of the land, Babylon destroyed the city and captured the people. This was followed by Persia's rule, affliction by the Seleucids of Syria, and finally the humiliation by Rome. All of these oppressions resulted from the impotent spiritual state of the people; if they had continued strong in the Lord, these

oppressions would never have occurred. It was the low spiritual condition that brought about Judah's destruction and not the other way around.

5   We have just studied a threatening announcement from Jehovah Himself of what the future holds for the people of Jerusalem. The following four verses (5–8) present a contrast: Jehovah will bring low the heathen idolatrous nations and spiritual forces that fight against Ariel, His altar-hearth. The use of the word *multitude* four times in this passage is significant. *The multitude of thy foes* ("strangers," Hebrew) *shall be like small dust* which whirls before the storm (cf. 17:13), carried away by Jehovah. They shall be *accounted as the small dust of the balance* (40:15), to be blown away by a puff of one's breath, or wiped away by a small dustcloth. *The multitude of the terrible ones* will pass away like the chaff of the threshing floor. Chaff is used metaphorically for anything which is worthless, weak and helpless before the wind, carried away by it, vanishing forever. *Yea, it shall be in an instant suddenly,* just as the prophet earlier indicated, "At eventide, behold, terror; and before the morning they are not" (17:14). God's ability to smite suddenly was demonstrated in the destruction of that portion of Sennacherib's army sent against Jerusalem (II Kings 19:35–37). This did not exhaust Jehovah's action against the multitude of foes and terrible ones. When He so determines, physical nations and spiritual deceptions all vanish before Him.

6   This verse continues the description of the destruction introduced in verse 5. But who is to be visited, Jerusalem or the foes? The textual difficulty is indicated by the various translations: "She" (American Standard); "Thou" (King James); "You" (Leupold); "It" (Young). Probably the margin of the American Standard best suggests Isaiah's thought: *There shall be a visitation from Jehovah.* This could be a visitation of judgment or blessing, the meaning to be determined from the context. The visitation seems not to be upon Jerusalem but upon the multitudes, for *the multitude of thy foes,* the terrible ones, is the subject of the preceding verse. The prophet employs the terrifying elements of nature to describe the destructive power and forces at Jehovah's command (cf. 50:3; Jer. 4:23–26). The picture is vivid: *with thunder, and with earthquake, and great noise, with whirlwind and*

241

tempest, and the flame of a devouring fire. Who or what can withstand the fierceness of such forces when they break forth? None can withstand Jehovah's fierce judgments when they erupt like an exploding volcano.

7   The prophet continues Jehovah's judgment against Zion's foes: *And the multitude of all the nations that fight against Ariel, even all that fight against her and her stronghold, and that distress her, shall be as a dream, a vision of the night.* The prophecy is not limited to one nation (i.e., Assyria), but includes *all the nations* that war against Ariel. Those that distress Zion, seeking her destruction, shall be like a dream or an illusion that fades away. They will have visions of grandeur, thinking to conquer, but they will not succeed. A dream or a vision of the night vanishes with waking or the coming of day; so will vanish the dreams of conquering or destroying Jehovah's Ariel.

8   This verse continues the metaphor, speaking specifically of a dreamer. Whoever (be it an individual, a nation, or a school of philosophers) undertakes to thwart God's purpose by destroying His people and His truth will, like a hungry man who dreams of food, dream of victory and booty, only to awaken with the realization that the soul is empty; he will be disappointed and still hungry. A similar figure is a thirsty man who dreams that he is drinking deeply, quenching his thirst at a cool fountain, only to discover upon awakening that it was but a dream; he is still beset with a burning thirst. The application of the metaphor is not restricted to one nation; it applies to all the enemies of God. *So shall the multitude of all the nations be, that fight against mount Zion;* all are doomed.

9   The prophet has told the people of the destruction of Zion's enemies, but they are unimpressed. In their stupid spirit of dull apathy they look at him in bewilderment. Since they have rejected Jehovah and His word, the prophet now commands them to continue in that condition. He has known all along that this is what they would do (cf. 6:9–10). Smith points out that this verse is composed of four imperatives, which he translates, "Be astounded and wonder! Blind yourselves and be blind! Be drunk though not with wine! Stagger though not with strong drink!" (I. 220). Though the people are not physically drunk as were the rulers of Ephraim and the prophets and priests of Jerusalem (28:1, 7), their condition of spiritual drunkenness

is equally as bad, if not worse. Go ahead and be amazed; in your blindness continue to give yourselves to pleasure; be drunk and see nothing clearly; stagger about in an uncontrolled manner. This is what you desire; this do.

10 The prophet states the immediate cause of the condition of the people (the fundamental cause is set forth in v. 13): *For Jehovah hath poured out upon you the spirit of deep sleep.* The spirit of deep sleep and the drunken condition are the same. The people were responsible for their drunkenness, but Jehovah had sent the spirit of deep sleep. These two factors merge into one. As Jehovah can give life, wisdom, and understanding, so can there come from Him an evil spirit that troubles a man and makes him do evil (I Sam. 16:14–15; 18:10–11; 19:9), or a lying spirit that entices him to destruction (I Kings 22:20–23). This means that when we reject God and His truth, God has no alternative but to give us up to error and evil. This doctrine is clearly enunciated in the New Testament. Paul said of the Gentiles, "And even as they refused to have God in their knowledge, God gave them up unto a reprobate mind, to do those things which are not fitting" (Rom. 1:28). And of those deceived by the lawless one, he said, "They received not the love of the truth, that they might be saved. And for this cause God sendeth them a working of error, that they should believe a lie: that they all might be judged who believed not the truth, but had pleasure in unrighteousness" (II Thess. 2:10–12). The Jews of Isaiah's prophecy had given themselves up to a drunken spiritual stupor; therefore, God sent them a spirit of deep sleep.

The prophet turns from the people to consider the prophets again: God *hath closed your eyes, the prophets; and your heads, the seers, hath he covered.* As if smearing something over the eyes to prevent their seeing anything, Jehovah has closed the eyes of those who should have been the eyes of the people to guide them by His word. The Lord has covered *your heads, the seers* (another name for prophets; see I Sam. 9:9), who should have directed your thinking. So the people are left to stumble about in spiritual darkness, the blind leading the blind.

11–12 The spiritual blindness resulting in inability to see and grasp true revelation is compared to inability to read. The books of

243

that day were scrolls written on long pieces of material rolled from one stick to another. When the scrolls were rolled up and sealed, no one could read their contents. The spiritual vision of the people of Isaiah's day is likened to a sealed book or writing delivered to them with instructions to read. (It is immaterial whether an actual writing like that of 8:16–18 is in view, or whether we have here a metonymy for the word declared by the prophet.) When the book is offered to a learned and educated man, he declines, saying, I cannot, for it is sealed. Any word from God is, for the people of Judah, like this sealed book, for in their spiritual blindness and hardness of heart they cannot comprehend it. When the book is then delivered to an unlearned man with instruction to read, he likewise declines, saying, I am not learned, that is, "I do not know how to read." In this tragic picture, the learned and the unlearned are all brought under condemnation because of their sottish and brutish hearts, blinded and hardened to what God says. This condition has developed within them in spite of all that God has done for them. Young aptly remarks, "This is perhaps as sad a picture as is to be found anywhere in the Old Testament" (II. 318). How tragic!

13   The words Forasmuch as introduce a situation which is answered by the therefore of verse 14. Hypocrisy was a fruit of the people's spiritual darkness and deep sleep; they substituted empty formalism in their public worship for true service from the heart. In the law it was written, "Thou shalt love Jehovah thy God with all thy heart, and with all thy soul, and with all thy might" (Deut. 6:5); and further, "Thou shalt fear Jehovah thy God; and him shalt thou serve" (Deut. 6:13). But now, instead of worship and service from the heart, the honor the people offer is with the mouth and lips; the heart is far removed from Him. Consequently, they cannot read the book; they have no spiritual perception.

Samaria's idolatry had been open and glaring (II Kings 17:7–18); in Judah idolatry was hidden under a cloak of hypocrisy. Hezekiah had destroyed the external objects of pagan worship (II Kings 18:3–4), but it was even now as it was later when, after Josiah's reformation, Ezekiel charged, "These men have taken their idols into their heart" (Ezek. 14:3). Their fear was a fear taught by man, whereas true fear is of God. As the wise man said, "Keep thy foot when thou goest to the house of God; for to draw nigh to hear is better than to give the sacrifice of fools" (Eccles. 5:1); and again, "Fear God, and keep his commandments [not man's]; for this is the whole duty of man" (Eccles. 12:13).

Hypocritical worship prevailed again in Jesus' day; therefore, He applied Isaiah 29:13 to the people before Him: "In vain do they worship me,/Teaching as their doctrines the precepts of men" (Matt. 15:9). It was then, and always will be, the height of hypocrisy and folly to honor God with the lips, while the heart is far from Him, substituting the precepts of men for truth.

14   The prophet continues the thought of verse 13 (introduced by *forasmuch as*) with the consequence of the flagrant hypocrisy. *Therefore*, Jehovah will add a marvelous work to all that He has done (see the comments on 28:21), a work that will cause astonishment among the beholders. In the midst of this marvelous work of Jehovah and to the amazement of the people, *the wisdom of their wise men shall perish, and the understanding of their prudent men shall be hid.* As Jehovah mingled a spirit of perverseness in the midst of the counsellors of Pharaoh (19:14), so He will now take away the wisdom of Judah's leaders. Not only will the false wisdom that encourages attempts to hide from God (28:14–15) be taken away, but also all that substitutes formalism and precepts of men for true worship (v. 13), or that seeks to hide plans from God (v. 15). Paul applies the thought of this passage to all human wisdom that omits God and His way (I Cor. 1:19). In his own wisdom apart from God's wisdom, man is bound to fail; this failure will be exposed.

Woe to Those Who Hide Their Plans from God (vv. 15–24)

15   Isaiah here states a general principle which he later specifically applies to the issue of alliance with Egypt (ch. 30). It may be that at this time such an alliance was brewing. The prophet had opposed all alliances, whether with Assyria in the time of Ahaz or with Egypt in the time of Hezekiah. The prophet's counsel was to wait for and trust in Jehovah; He is in control. How foolish to think men can hide their counsels from God, the omniscient one! In their foolish reasoning and lack of true wisdom, they ask, *Who seeth us? and who knoweth us?* Who knows what we are doing? This is always the reasoning of the wicked: "They say, How doth God know?/And is there knowledge in the Most High?" (Ps. 73:11; see also Pss. 10:11; 94:7). They are underhanded in their planning, acting in the dark as they carry out their schemes. Any nation that thinks it can plan and act apart from God is doomed to failure because He knows and controls.

16 *Ye turn things upside down!* you pervert things, or act perversely, with absurdity. Your perversion of truth reverses the real order of things. You would probably say the potter is no more than the clay which he molds with his hands. But can a thing that has been made say that it has no maker—*He made me not?* Can a thing say that the person who formed it had no understanding of what he was doing or why he was doing it? Those who hide their counsel from God are in effect charging that God has no more understanding than they have; this is blasphemy. Echoing Isaiah, Paul asked the Jews of his day, "Nay but, O man, who art thou that repliest against God? Shall the thing formed say to him that formed it, Why didst thou make me thus?" (Rom. 9:20). If God is infinite, then man has no ground on which either to plan apart from God or to argue with Him and His way. The reasoning of the self-sufficient Jews sounds like the vaporous philosophy of modern evolutionists who say, We are not made, we just happened. (Isaiah will later return to this thought of the potter and the clay [45:9; 64:8]).

17 As those who tried to hide their counsel from God had thought to reverse the order of the created and the Creator, so will Jehovah actually reverse conditions. Barnes thinks that this verse quotes a proverbial expression; putting it in the form of a question presupposes an affirmative answer. The phrase *a very little while* is, of course, expressed from God's viewpoint of time; hence from our viewpoint it is indefinite and may be long or short. Turning Lebanon into a fruitful field and esteeming the fruitful field as a forest seems to be a comparison not between the high and the low, that is, between Assyria and Judah, but between what is wild and what is cultivated. The comparison seems to be between national Israel and spiritual Israel; national Israel will become an uncultivated wilderness, but spiritual Israel will become a productive field.

18 The phrase *And in that day* indicates that what the prophet is about to describe is simultaneous with the events of verse 17, the day when Lebanon becomes a fruitful field. In contrast to those who could not read and consequently could not grasp the words of the book or writing handed to them (vv. 11–12), the people now in view will be able to read, to understand the word of the Lord. *And the eyes of the blind shall see out of obscurity and out of darkness;* those who had been blind to truth, salvation, and the work of God will be able to see and understand (cf. 35:5; 42:7). This is a reversal of former conditions.

19 *The meek* are those who are oppressed or afflicted, those who suffer. The word is generally associated with endurance of oppression and a spirit or attitude of patient submission to the will of God. Endurance of affliction will be turned into constantly increasing joy in the Lord. *And the poor among men shall rejoice in the Holy One of Israel.* It matters not whether these poor be poor as to this world's goods, of whom the Lord said, "I will satisfy her [Zion's] poor with bread" (Ps. 132:15; cf. Matt. 6:33), or the poor in spirit, to whom belongs the kingdom of heaven (Matt. 5:3). Both will rejoice in their God. This joy will not be fully attained until the coming of the Messiah.

20 The word *For* introduces a clause explaining why the field will be fruitful (v. 17), why the deaf will hear and the blind see (v. 18), and why the meek and poor will rejoice (v. 19). Three enemies of truth and righteousness, three obstacles to spiritual development, are suppressed, if not vanquished. *The terrible one,* the tyrant or oppressor who undertook to destroy the people of God by force, *is brought to nought. The scoffer,* who ridiculed and sneered at the word of God (cf. 28:14), *ceaseth. And all they that watch for iniquity,* that look for an occasion to accuse righteous people, *are cut off.* Righteousness and truth will be triumphant; Jehovah's cause will be victorious.

21 The work of these three classes of opponents is likened to that of a prosecuting attorney who seeks the conviction, indeed the destruction, of the person being tried. Three procedures are followed by these prosecutors. They *make a man an offender in his cause;* either by direct accusation or by cross-examination they try to trap him.

They *lay a snare for him that reproveth in the gate*; they try to ensnare the man who reproves wickedness, seeking his destruction. As the wise man said, "He that reproveth a wicked man getteth himself a blot" (Prov. 9:7). And they *turn aside the just with a thing of nought*; they hinder legal justice on a technicality or a pretense. They seek not justice and the cause of the righteous or innocent, but a conviction condemning the righteous.

22   *Therefore thus saith Jehovah*: the hearers' thoughts are turned forward to a conclusion resting on what has just been said (vv. 17–21). As the Redeemer of Abraham, Jehovah now speaks *concerning the house of Jacob* (Abraham's descendants). The Lord had redeemed Abraham by delivering him from the service of idol-gods and from the influence of his family and environment, which might have induced him to return to those idols (Josh. 24:2; Acts 7:2–3). Jehovah had made Abraham His friend (41:8). And now, Jacob, who so earnestly desired and sought the birthright, will not be ashamed of the true children of Abraham (consequently his also), who have inherited that birthright. He will behold them as a fruitful field, people who both see and hear God's revelation (vv. 17–18). His face will not wax pale either from disappointment in them or from fear that the promise will not be fulfilled.

23   *But when he seeth his children*, his true spiritual descendants, Jacob will recognize them as *the work of my* (God's) *hands*. Though Jacob had sought to help God in achieving His purpose, he had failed; his becoming the father of the heirs of the birthright was the work of God. Likewise the spiritual accomplishment of his descendants was the work of God (44:24; 60:21); they are His workmanship, created anew after His image (Eph. 2:10; 4:24). The children Jacob sees *in the midst of him* (Jacob) are his spiritual children, the remnant, in the midst of the physical nation. Though the physical nation has failed to do so, the remnant will sanctify God's name and being, recognizing the power of both His name, which stands for all that He is, and His person—the Holy One of Jacob. By Him they were formed; recognizing the failure of idolatry and the absolute powerlessness of idols, they will stand in awe of the God of Israel, the only God (cf. 44:6).

24   As Delitzsch suggests, though the "new church" is neither

perfect nor sinless, its people have *come to understanding*. Those who once erred in spirit, being blind and deaf, now understand the word and will of God and what He seeks in and through them. And those who murmured now receive instruction. There are two Hebrew words for *murmur*. One is commonly used of the Hebrews' complainings in their early history; the other, which is found here, "suggests the malicious whispering of slander."[2] The prophet may have in mind people who once hid their counsel from God, doing their works in the dark, maliciously slandering Him and asking, "Who seeth us?" (v. 15). At any rate, these people now understand for they have received instruction. As Isaiah says later, "And all thy children shall be taught of Jehovah; and great shall be the peace of thy children" (54:13).

CHAPTER **30**

Woe to the Pro-Egyptian Policy

Isaiah has announced a general woe upon those who hide their counsel from God (29:15), and now he makes a specific application of the principle as he pronounces a woe upon the pro-Egyptian party who send presents to Egypt in an attempt to gain that nation's aid against Assyria. Jehovah has already announced the weakness and ultimate fall of Ethiopia and Egypt (chs. 18–20), warned against seeking refuge anywhere except in the stone laid in Zion (28:14–22), and declared that the multitude of nations that fight against His altar-hearth will be swept away (29:5–8). Therefore, to seek Egypt's aid is to ignore God and what He has said. Although the message of the prophet is directed to the situation of that day, the principle involved is timeless: it is always a fatal error for God's people to rely on the world of the ungodly instead of trusting in the Lord for help in emergency. Because Judah ignores God, judgment will befall the nation (vv. 1–17).

---

2. *International Standard Bible Encyclopedia*, ed. James Orr (Chicago: Howard-Severance, 1937), vol. 3, p. 2094.

Next the prophet presents the basis on which Judah should proceed: wait for Jehovah. The nation will be delivered and blessed not because of Egypt's help, but through Jehovah's grace and mercy. The blessing will be realized fully in the messianic age (vv. 18–26).

In the meantime Assyria will be destroyed, not by a political coalition of Judah and Egypt, but by the rod of Jehovah. A place of burning, deep and large, will be provided for the Assyrian king (vv. 27–33).

Any Alliance with Egypt Is Bound to Fail (vv. 1–17)

1   The third woe is pronounced upon the rebellious children who take counsel, but not of Jehovah; these children are persistently disobedient. In their dealings with Jehovah, they act like stubborn, rebellious children who refuse to obey their parents, thereby becoming worthy of death (Deut. 21:18–21). The first charge that Jehovah made against the people through Isaiah was, "I have nourished and brought up children, and they have rebelled against me" (1:2); a second charge was, "Thy princes are rebellious, and companions of thieves" (1:23). And now, the whole nation, led by the princes, is involved in the plan to appeal to Egypt, and thus is guilty of rebellion against Jehovah. They are making agreements or covenants (literally, "weaving a web" [Young]) without consulting the Lord or considering His prophet, who spoke by His Spirit. The phrase *make a league* can be translated "pour out a drink-offering" (margin). This refers to the libation offered when binding an agreement; but the translation in the text, referring to the covenant itself, is preferable. In doing this the rebellious children are adding *sin to sin*, piling up additional sin on top of all former sin (cf. Jer. 2:13).

2   The children of Judah have *set out to go down into Egypt, and have not asked at my mouth.* To ask at Jehovah's mouth is to consult Him before making decisions (cf. Num. 27:21). Throughout their history they had invited trouble by failing to inquire of Jehovah before acting (e.g., Josh. 9:14). Their purpose in appealing to Egypt was to strengthen themselves in Pharaoh, who promised much but provided little. To take refuge in his shadow was to look to him for protection; but the Spirit of Jehovah had said, "He that dwelleth in

the secret place of the Most High/Shall abide under the shadow of the Almighty" (Ps. 91:1). The leaders of Judah were forsaking this principle as they turned to Egypt for help. Years prior to this, Isaiah had demonstrated his opposition to any dependence on Egypt or Ethiopia by walking barefoot and wearing only undergarments for three years (ch. 20).

3 The word *Therefore* introduces the consequence of looking to Egypt rather than Jehovah for help. Instead of finding strength in Pharaoh and Egypt, Judah will find shame, a sense of sin and guilt with the added embarrassment of failure. Taking refuge in Pharaoh's shadow will lead to confusion (emptiness and waste) instead of solid protection. The nation is doomed to utter disappointment.

4 Even now the prophet envisions the princes on their mission. Though they are men of royal dignity and position, they are not necessarily men of royal blood. He sees them reaching Zoan, a city located in the northeast part of the Delta (see 19:11). *And their ambassadors are come to Hanes.* These are representatives of the ruler or the government. Hanes, mentioned only here in Scripture, is thought by some to have been Heracleopolis Magna in Upper Egypt. It is thought by others to have been Tahpanhes (Jer. 43:7), located not far from Zoan. Actually, the identity and location are unknown. It is not specifically stated whether Hezekiah was involved in this shameful undertaking, but it is difficult to think that the ambassadors could have embarked on such a mission without the king's knowledge and blessing (see 36:4–6).

5 The result of the appeal to Egypt will be more than an embarrassment to the nation; the prophet repeats that it will prove to be a shame and a reproach, a disgrace. In the end dependence upon Egypt proved utterly fruitless.

6 *The burden of* (oracle concerning) *the beasts of the South*—for the word *burden* see the comments on 13:1. Delitzsch thinks *the beasts of the South* refers to the hippopotamus, a symbol of Egypt; but this is very doubtful. The prophet probably has in mind the beasts that pass through the Negeb ("South") into the wilderness of Zin and Shur bearing the gifts to Egypt. This may indicate that at this time the coastal route had been cut off by the Assyrians. In poetical language the prophet describes the terrible land through which the beasts must

251

travel, portraying the dangers incurred on this useless and wasted journey.

Isaiah uses three pairs of words to describe the austerity of the land and the dangers encountered: (1) *the land of trouble and anguish*, probably a reference to the unrest and agitation, distress and despair, experienced by those who pass through the area; (2) *from whence come the lioness and the lion*, entailing danger to man and beast; (3) *the viper and fiery flying serpent*, highly poisonous snakes, which add to the perils of that desolate land. We do not know exactly what Isaiah means by *flying serpent*.

Rich gifts and treasures upon the shoulders of young asses and on the humps of camels suggest a rather large caravan carrying the wealth of Judah into Egypt. It was through this same "terrible wilderness, wherein were fiery serpents and scorpions, and thirsty ground where was no water" (Deut. 8:15), that Jehovah had led the Israelites many years before, delivering them from the very oppressors whose shadow they now seek. But they are making their appeal to a people that shall not profit them. A sad picture, indeed.

7   *For Egypt helpeth in vain*; she offers some token expression of help, but it is to no avail. It is not clear whether the name *Rahab that sitteth still* is given by Jehovah or the prophet, but it is most appropriate. The word means "storm, arrogance," a fitting emblem of Egypt, "the boaster that sitteth still." Leupold translates it, "a Big-mouth that is a Do-nothing." Four times in poetic books or passages the word is used of a monster (arrogance, pride, or power) with which Jehovah is in conflict (Job 9:13; 26:12; Ps. 89:10; Isa. 51:9). It occurs twice where Egypt is clearly in view (Ps. 87:4; Isa. 30:7). Like the Sphinx, Egypt looked strong but was helpless to act. She was a nation that could not live up to her past glory and power; she boasted in that past glory but did nothing.

8   The prophet receives a command from the Lord: *Now go, write it before them on a tablet, and inscribe it in a book*. The prophet had been instructed before to write a message for future testimony (8:1, 16), and now he is to write again. Is that which is to be written verses 6–7, verses 1–7, or the entire chapter? Probably the instruction included only verses 6–7, which would serve as a reminder of the folly of God's people in going down to Egypt instead of trusting in

Him. Some think that Isaiah wrote both on a tablet and in a book; others believe that the two terms refer to only one writing. It seems, however, that there were probably a tablet for the public to see and read, and a book to preserve the message for all time to come, *for ever and ever*. Even as we read it today, we are impressed with the absolute sureness of Jehovah's way and word. It thus serves "for a witness for ever" (margin).

9   Jehovah makes three charges against the people: *For it is a rebellious people*, a charge He had laid against them at the beginning (v. 1); *lying children*—their very lives are a lie, their refuges a lie (28:15), their worship hypocrisy (29:13); *children that will not hear the law* (or teaching) *of Jehovah*. They refused to hear what God had said through Moses in the law, and now they are refusing to hear what He is saying through His prophets.

10–11   Isaiah reveals the true spirit of the people toward the words Jehovah utters through His prophets. The rebellious children *say to the seers, See not; and to the prophets, Prophesy not unto us right things, speak unto us smooth things, prophesy deceits*. Surely they were not so honest as to come right out and say these things; but this verse very graphically reveals their true feelings. (For *seers* and *prophets* see the comments on 29:10.) Speak not right things, that is, things of truth and uprightness, for they condemn our wicked ways. Speak smooth things, things palatable and pleasing to the ear—things that entertain us. *Prophesy deceits*, that is, give us false hope, make us believe that all is well even when it is not. A modern version would be, Give us religion but not the truth of the gospel. To the true prophet the people say, *Get you out of the way*; do not hinder us in that which we have determined to do. *Turn aside out of the path*, the path of rectitude and true revelation. *Cause the Holy One of Israel to cease from before us*. No doubt this is in derision of Isaiah's constant use of the glorious title *Holy One of Israel*, which occurs about thirty times in his book. Each time the prophet mentions that name, it would cut deeply into their sinful and rebellious souls.

12   *Wherefore*—in the face of such rebellion against God and His word there is an inevitable consequence which the Lord is now ready to announce. *The Holy One of Israel*, whom the people have tried to thrust out of their lives, but who will not be thrust out, now speaks.

253

Because ye despise this word—because you hold in contempt the word of the Holy One of Israel which is being spoken by the present prophets—judgment is on its way. Another reason for the judgment is that the people *trust in oppression and perverseness, and rely thereon.* There are three thoughts on the meaning of *oppression* here. Some see it as a reference to oppressive methods used to finance the presents or bribe being sent to Egypt. Others see it as oppressive methods resorted to by the people to silence the prophets, stifling their voice. The third view is that the prophet is referring to a disposition of character that manifests itself in both. This third view seems preferable. Perverseness is a deviation from the right or true way, the demonstration of an obstinate will. It manifests itself in crooked practices in business and politics. The people rely upon falsehoods instead of truth and honesty.

13   The word *therefore* introduces the punishment for the rebellious hearts and wicked practices of the people. Jehovah uses two similes to stress the nature of this impending judgment: a crashing wall and the shattering of a clay vessel. *This iniquity shall be to you as a breach ready to fall, swelling out in a high wall.* A breach or crack may cause a wall to bulge out and eventually collapse. The problem could arise from a fault in the wall, a shift from the foundation, or a faulty foundation. In this case the problem is probably that instead of building on the sure foundation of Jehovah and His word, the people have built on a foundation of lies (28:15–16). Further, they have used their own standards in building their wall of national security. The collapse will come suddenly, without warning.

14   *And he* (Jehovah) *shall break it as a potter's vessel is broken*—an indication of total destruction—*breaking it in pieces without sparing.* The picture is clear: *there shall not be found among the pieces thereof a sherd wherewith to take fire from the hearth, or to dip up water out of the cistern.* The demolition of the Jewish kingdom will be like the smashing of a clay pot with an iron rod. The pot is so completely shattered that there is no piece large enough to carry a coal of fire from the hearth or to dip up a drink of water from a cistern. Destruction was averted in Isaiah's time because Hezekiah pleaded to Jehovah and because Jehovah's honor was at stake (37:14–29). Also, no doubt the preaching by Isaiah and Micah and the influence of

their lives turned enough hearts to the Lord that He could spare the city for their sakes. Destruction did come, but at a later time.

15 Smith captions verses 15–17 "Not Alliances, but Reliance" (I. 233), which well summarizes the prophet's message. The Lord extends a means of escape from the terrible destruction just described. *For thus said* (saith) *the Lord Jehovah, the Holy One of Israel,* the one who bears that majestic name from which the people would get away (v. 11), but which gives authority to what is promised. *In returning and rest shall ye be saved*—this is similar to the exhortations given to Ahaz (7:4) and to Jerusalem (28:12). Instead of going down into Egypt to make an alliance with that idolatrous people, return unto Jehovah in whom is salvation, for only in the old paths, the good way, which He has ordained can one find rest for his soul (Jer. 6:16). In place of that faithlessness which had caused Judah to send to Egypt, let there be quietness of trust and confidence through faith in God and His might. In this way Judah will find the strength needed to meet the emergency. This had been the basis of Hebrew power throughout their history, yet they often failed to rely solely on the Lord: *and ye would not.* Those who have learned this lesson have been and ever will be the towering rocks which enable society and the church to withstand the shifting sands of destructive intellectual and social movements.

16 *But ye said, No, for we will flee upon horses.* Smith aptly comments, "If you wish to reform the politics, you must first regenerate the people" (I. 230). Bent on following the dictates of their own rebellious ways, the people and their rulers are in deep need of spiritual regeneration. Their desire to flee upon horses probably refers to pursuing the enemy on war-horses obtained from Egypt. In the law Jehovah had forbidden returning to Egypt to secure horses (Deut. 17:16), but Judah is completely ignoring this command. Since you wish to flee upon horses, *therefore shall ye flee*; and inasmuch as you say, *We will ride upon the swift; therefore shall they that pursue you be swift.* Jehovah will grant their desire, but not in the way they intend. They will indeed fly—but as the pursued rather than the pursuer.

17 In the law Jehovah had assured His people that if they remained faithful to Him, "five of you shall chase a hundred, and a hundred of you shall chase ten thousand" (Lev. 26:1, 8). The order of this promise is now reversed; for instead of five chasing a hundred, *One thousand* (of you) *shall flee at the threat of one; at the threat of five shall ye flee.* Of course, as is often the case in Scripture, this is a strong hyperbole. It indicates the complete weakness and inevitable defeat of anyone who acts against God's will and purpose. In defeat, instead of the strong nation it could and should be, Judah will be like a tree or pole on the top of a mountain, stripped of its branches and leaves. The survivors will be lonely and few in number. But as an ensign this remnant will be the rallying point around which a new nation will emerge (1:9; 10:21–22).

Prosperity Through God's Grace (Messianic) (vv. 18–26)

18   In the midst of this bleak picture of judgment, defeat, and loneliness, Jehovah encourages the people with a word of hope and assurance, based on His grace and mercy. The word *And* connects the thought of the following passage with the preceding judgment (vv. 1–17), and the word *therefore* introduces what Jehovah will do and the basis of His action. The Lord will wait until the judgment is executed; through it the people will be put into such a frame of mind and disposition of heart that He may be gracious unto them. *Therefore will he be exalted,* lifted up in the eyes of the people and recognized as Jehovah God, *that he may have mercy* upon them (cf. 2:11, 17). Mercy is the expression of His gracious character (cf. Ps. 103:8). But, as the judgment shows, *Jehovah is a God of justice* also, just and righteous in all His ways. That justice is part of His essential nature is clearly expressed by two psalmists: "Righteousness and justice are the foundation of thy throne:/Lovingkindness and truth go before thy face" (Ps. 89:14); and "Righteousness and justice are the foundation of his throne./A fire goeth before him,/And burneth up his adversaries round about" (Ps. 97:2–3). So then, the loving-kindness and mercy of God as well as the fire of judgment reflect the inherent nature of God and the very foundation of His throne and rule. It is as consistent with His divine character to punish wickedness as it is to show mercy to the penitent. Thus, *blessed are all they that wait for Him;* instead of taking matters into their own hand, they allow Jehovah to act on the ground of His infinite righteousness and justice.

Isaiah beautifully expresses this in a later prophecy, "They that wait for Jehovah shall renew their strength; they shall mount up with wings as eagles; they shall run, and not be weary; they shall walk, and not faint" (40:31).

19 *The people,* that is, those who wait for Jehovah, shall enjoy His gracious mercy (v. 18) and *shall dwell in Zion at Jerusalem.* For the sake of emphasis, this phrase is sometimes translated "Zion, even Jerusalem." Both readings give the same sense. Zion-Jerusalem is the dwelling place of God among His people; there they shall be with Him. *Thou* is singular; the prophet is either addressing the people as a whole or addressing each member of his audience as an individual, for those who wait and receive the blessings do so as individuals. For them the days of weeping are past; they now enjoy the graciousness of Jehovah's presence and the answer to their cry. *When he shall hear, he will answer thee*—to receive an answer we must cry unto the Lord earnestly, in faith and confidence; when we do so, God answers.

20 But before the blessings come, there will be a time of affliction, the judgments mentioned above. Most commentators omit the word *though,* and translate, "The Lord will give you the bread of adversity and the water of affliction." This is nourishment provided in time of extreme need and scarcity, the opposite of food and drink in abundance. In carrying out His divine plan, the Lord will not let His people completely perish. In the time of extreme oppression and scarcity He will provide for the preservation of a remnant. An unnamed psalmist said, "We went through fire and through water;/But thou broughtest us out into a wealthy place ['abundance,' Hebrew]" (Ps. 66:12). Before the abundance came the fire and water.

The last half of this verse is difficult to translate; is it *teachers* (plural) or *teacher* (singular)? Smith opts for "Teacher," applying it to God, who for a time had hidden His face from His people, but now instructs them. Most commentators opt for "teachers," and apply it to the prophets and Levitical instructors who hid themselves during the time of severe oppression. The prophet's statement, *but thine eyes shall see thy teachers,* suggests human teachers whom the people can see, though this is not conclusive.

21 *And thine ears shall hear a word behind thee*—here is an additional difficulty. If the eyes of those who have waited for Jehovah

257

see the teachers, how can the word be heard from behind them? Numerous explanations have been given. Note, for example, that the teachers are saying, *This is the way, walk ye in it; when ye turn to the right hand, and when ye turn to the left*. It is possible that the teachers are directing people who have deviated from the right way. Having turned to the right or left, their backs are now toward the teachers. Support for this interpretation can be found in the law which says, "Ye shall not turn aside to the right hand or to the left" (Deut. 5:32), and also in the word of the wise man, "Turn not to the right hand nor to the left:/Remove thy foot from evil" (Prov. 4:27). So, with eyes to see and ears to hear, the people shall be instructed in the right way; and when it is pointed out that they have erred from that way, they will hear and return.

22   Those who now dwell in Zion, having come through the tribulation, will recognize the polluting and destroying influence of idols; therefore they will defile their idols, accounting them as filthy. Images were molded from an inferior metal or carved from wood, then overlaid with silver or gold (cf. 40:19; 44:9–20). *Thou shalt cast them away as an unclean thing; thou shalt say unto it, Get thee hence*—Be gone! Get out of my sight! Probably the idols are ground to powder and then scattered. After the destruction of Jerusalem and the Babylonian captivity the people were apparently cured of idolatry, for no more do we hear of their making or serving images.

23   Verses 23–26 are filled with the promise of rich and abundant gifts from God. He gives rain so that the seed which has been sown will sprout. From it will come bread, nutritious and in full measure. In the day of this bounty the cattle will find abundance of grass in large pastures, a great contrast to their former narrow and straitened quarters.

24   The domesticated animals—the oxen and young asses used for tilling the ground—shall eat *savory* (or salted) *provender*. The word *savory* may indicate a mash or a fermented mixture like our silage. Their food shall be of unusual and excellent quality, mixed and salted. That the provender has been *winnowed with the shovel and with the fork* suggests that, like grain intended for humans, it is cleansed of the chaff and purged of foreign substances.

25   And instead of the high hills and lofty mountains being bare,

there will be brooks and streams of water. They will provide further blessings for man and beast, furnishing water for lush meadows, for irrigation, and for household use. What a boon in a land where streams are scarce and precious (cf. 41:18)! In a rather startling manner the prophet injects a contrasting thought: *in the day of the great slaughter, when the towers fall.* There are at least two possible explanations of the passage: (1) the great slaughter when the towers fall will precede these blessings (cf. vv. 13, 18); or (2) there will be slaughter and collapsing towers in the world of the ungodly even while those in Zion-Jerusalem enjoy abundant gifts from God. In the light of the context, and especially the following verse, the second seems preferable.

26 Having described the abundance of physical provisions for man and beast, the prophet now speaks of the glorious light of that period. *Moreover the light of the moon shall be as the light of the sun, and the light of the sun shall be sevenfold, as the light of seven days* (cf. 24:23; 60:19–20). In such light all things will be clear, seen as they are. This verse provides the key to understanding the entire passage. Sunlight *as the light of seven days* is the light of one week concentrated into one brilliant day. Such brilliance in the physical world would be disastrous to life, both plant and animal. But in that day *Jehovah bindeth up the hurt of his people, and healeth the stroke of their wound.* In that day His blessings of abundance will be provided.

There can be no doubt that God intended to bless the people richly upon their return from the captivity when He would gather the remnant back into their own land. He had promised that upon this return, He would "do thee good, and multiply thee above thy fathers" (Deut. 30:5); but this was conditional upon their returning to Him with their whole heart and keeping His commandments (Deut. 30:8–10). He would "do better unto you than at your beginnings" (Ezek. 36:11). Even as late as the days of Malachi, God said that He would "open you the windows of heaven, and pour you out a blessing, that there shall not be room enough to receive it" (Mal. 3:10). But in every instance these blessings were contingent on the people's faithfulness to the Lord (cf. the "if" construction in Jer. 18:7–10). If the people did not abide by the conditions, God would not do for them what He could have. The divine blessings would not be given in complete fullness, however, until the messianic age when God poured out His spiritual blessings in rich abundance. We must understand that the language of Isaiah prefigures the glorious blessings in Christ (see Eph. 3:19; Col. 2:8–10).

Jehovah's Vengeance on Assyria (vv. 27–33)

In a speech of brilliant and glowing imagery, Isaiah depicts Jehovah's sifting of the nations and the destruction of Assyria by the strength of His arm. The prophet has already introduced the judgment of the drunkards of Ephraim (28:1–2), the overflowing scourge against Jerusalem (28:15; 29:13–14), and the destruction of the multitude of Jerusalem's foes by mighty forces directed by Jehovah Himself (29:6). He now deals especially with the destruction of Assyria, combining two metaphors which depict the coming of Jehovah as a mighty storm, fierce and fiery in its destructive force, and as a man filled with wrath and indignation.

27 *Behold, the name of Jehovah cometh from far.* The *name of Jehovah* stands for all that He is—His being, revelation, and action. Apparently the Lord had left the people to themselves, but now like a storm lighting the sky He comes to deliver them. He comes in the burning anger of righteous indignation and wrath, *in thick rising smoke,* like clouds boiling up in a terrible storm. *His lips are full of indignation* against His enemies; *his tongue is as a devouring fire,* going before Him, burning up His adversaries round about (cf. Ps. 97:2–3).

28 *And his breath is as an overflowing stream, that reacheth even unto the neck.* As the overflowing waters of the River (Assyria) had swept over Judah, coming even to the neck (8:8), so now the flood of God's wrath reaches even to the neck of Assyria. The prophet uses three metaphors to depict the agents of this judgment: an overwhelming flood, a sieve of destruction, and a bridle that directs in the way Jehovah determines. Unlike the sifting of Israel, wherein not a grain falls to the earth, but all is saved (Amos 9:9), in the sifting of the nations all are shuffled about together and destroyed (cf. Jer. 30:11). The bridle *that causeth to err* leads away to destruction. As Jehovah

mingled a spirit of perverseness among the Egyptians, causing them to go astray to their ruin (19:14), so He will lead the nations.

29 In contrast, those whose hurt Jehovah has bound up and whose wound He has healed *shall have a song as in the night when a holy feast is kept.* Though not specified, the Passover is probably referred to—"a night to be much observed unto Jehovah" (Exod. 12:42; cf. Matt. 26:30). So while the heathen nations and the Assyrian power are being destroyed, there will be a song among the redeemed as when a holy feast is being kept. There will be not only rejoicing in song, but there will also be *gladness of heart,* as when, with musical instruments, the people stream up to Jerusalem, the mountain of Jehovah, where there is protection in the Rock of Israel (see the comments on 26:4). The redeemed will praise Him who has provided for their protection and care.

30 In causing His glorious and majestic voice to be heard, Jehovah will fulfill His word and thus vindicate His righteousness. In *the lighting down of his arm* He manifests in action the judgment He has announced. In this highly figurative and symbolic language, the Lord Himself is the center of the picture, the executor of His will. The grandeur of the prophecy transcends language; to describe what Jehovah is doing, the prophet draws from all the fury of nature. The bringing down of His arm is *with the indignation of his anger, and the flame of a devouring fire.* It is like a blast (or crashing) with a terrible rain and pounding hailstones. With these images flashing before his eyes, Isaiah envisions the awful destruction of the heathen world.

31 The special object of God's fury is now specified: *For through the voice of Jehovah shall the Assyrian be dismayed.* By the decree of the God who both saves and destroys, the oppressor will be judged and brought to an end. As Jehovah had used Assyria as the rod of His anger and judgment (10:5), so now He will use a rod to smite Assyria (cf. 10:25). Babylon was that rod by which Assyria was smitten.

32 With every stroke that falls upon the cruel nation by the Lord's appointed staff (Babylon), there shall be *the sound of tabrets and harps,* musical instruments associated with joy and festivity. *With the brandishing of his arm will he* (Jehovah) *fight with them;* with the staff of His choice Jehovah will battle against the object of His indignation. There is rejoicing not because nations are being

261

destroyed and people are suffering, but because idolatry, wickedness, and cruelty are being judged and the righteous delivered (cf. Rev. 19:1–2). As it was then, so shall it ever be.

33 *For a Topheth is prepared of old;* such a place has long been provided for both kings and nations like Assyria. *Topheth* is that site in the Valley of Hinnom where children had been burned as offerings to Molech, a custom of the Canaanites which apostates of Judah adopted (II Kings 23:10). *Topheth* is also mentioned by Jeremiah, three times in chapter 7 and five times in chapter 19. After being defiled by Josiah, it became a place for the burning of refuse. The New Testament word *Gehenna*, the place of eternal burning, is derived from the Hebrew "Valley of Hinnom." Jehovah has made Topheth deep and large enough for the destruction of a nation as great as Assyria. There is much wood, and *the breath of Jehovah, like a stream of brimstone, doth kindle it.* Jehovah stands out prominently in this section as Judge and destroyer of the wicked.

CHAPTER 31
Woe to Them That Go Down to Egypt!

Judah was not just another nation—a nation among nations—but it was God's people. They had been redeemed by Jehovah, cared for and given the land of Canaan. The Lord had chosen Jerusalem-Zion as the place of His dwelling; therefore, more was expected from the people of Judah. But now they were hiding their plans from God, making alliances with their former enemy who was always God's enemy. God must rebuke such rebellion against Himself.

The problem of Judah's disposition to rely upon Egypt was so acute as to necessitate repeated prophecies against the sin. Chapter 31 appears to be an advance beyond chapter 30, but it deals essentially with the same problem. Whereas chapter 30 emphasizes Judah's disposition to leave God out of their plans and to act on their own, chapter 31 emphasizes that God's wisdom is superior to that of the politicians who made such plans and to that of the Egyptians, whose military expertise and power they sought. Also, God's fierce providence and tender care toward His people are set side by side in this chapter. Jehovah will judge and destroy Assyria without aid from Egypt.

God Also Is Wise (vv. 1–3)

1 *Woe to them that go down to Egypt for help.* The tense of the verb indicates that ambassadors have already gone down, not once, but repeatedly (Leupold). In courting Egypt's favor and help, the Jewish politicians are pitting their wisdom against that of Jehovah. Secular historians write of the vast number of horses in Egypt; the chariots, horses, and horsemen Egypt is capable of supplying give Judah a false sense of security. The people boast of their strength as they rely on the Egyptian forces for protection; *but they look not unto the Holy One of Israel, neither seek Jehovah!* As His people they should have looked to Him, but instead they would have Him desist from interfering with their plans (30:10–11). To look unto and seek Jehovah is to rely upon Him in faith and trust. This they do not do. For this attitude and their effort to secure Egypt's strategic help, Rabshakeh, the Assyrian general, sarcastically chided the people of Jerusalem (II Kings 18:21, 24).

2 *Yet he also is wise.* The prophet contrasts the wisdom of Jehovah with the wisdom of the people of Judah and that of the Egyptians on whom they rely. Of Jehovah's infinite wisdom, a wise man said, "Jehovah by wisdom founded the earth" (Prov. 3:19); and another said of His works, "In wisdom hast thou made them all" (Ps. 104:24). Imagine the weak and finite creature pitting his wisdom against that of his Creator (cf. 29:16)! In His infinite wisdom as Creator, the Lord neither makes errors in His plans nor in the words revealing them; therefore, He *will not call back his words*; He will carry out His purpose as revealed. He has said that He will punish wickedness, and in the exercise of His wisdom and great power He will do it His way. He will rise up against Judah, *the house of the evildoers, and against the help* (the Egyptians) *of them* (Judah) *that work iniquity.* God will bring His judgment both upon the evil-workers of Judah and upon those to whom they have appealed for help.

3 Pharaoh "was for his people a god among men and a man

263

among the gods." Although there were many priests, "the pharaoh was in principle the sole high priest of the gods of Egypt."[3] Is it possible that in their revolt against Jehovah the Jews were being swayed toward accepting the absurd notion of Pharaoh's deity? Were they placing his wisdom above or equal to Jehovah's? If they had any such notion, the Lord rebukes it, saying, *Now the Egyptians are men, and not God* (or gods); *and their horses flesh, and not spirit.* This is a conflict between God the Creator and man the created, between flesh that perishes and spirit that endures. It is spirit that gives life, power, and vitality; the arm of flesh fails—"Put not your trust in princes,/Nor in the son of man [men], in whom there is no help" (Ps. 146:3; cf. Isa. 30:1–7, where the same principle is set forth). The prophet enlarges on the thought of verse 2: *and when Jehovah* (who is spirit) *shall stretch out his hand, both he that helpeth* (the Egyptians) *shall stumble, and he that is helped* (Judah) *shall fall, and they all shall be consumed together.* It will then be determined beyond question who is God. Flesh fails, both the helped and the helper; spirit and divine wisdom prevail.

God's Providence: Fierce Yet Compassionate (vv. 4–5)

4 *For thus saith Jehovah unto me*— the Lord now addresses the prophet, employing two similes by which He sets forth two contrasting traits of His essential character and their expression in action: a lion that tears its prey and mother birds that hover over their young. The Lord describes a young lion at the height of its power, growling over its prey; that is, faithless Jerusalem-Zion in the hand of Jehovah. When a lion has its prey and is growling over it, shepherds may come as near as they dare, shouting and brandishing their rods, but the lion *will not be dismayed at their voice, nor abase himself for the noise of them.* Now comes the application: *so will Jehovah of hosts come down to fight upon* ("against," margin) *mount Zion, and upon* ("against," margin) *the hill thereof.* Jehovah is not fighting for, but against sinful Zion. The shepherds making the loud noise do not represent Assyria,

---

3. *Zondervan Pictorial Encyclopedia of the Bible,* ed. Merrill C. Tenney (Grand Rapids: Zondervan, 1975), vol. 4, p. 742.

for Assyria is the rod of God's anger, the staff of His indignation against Jerusalem (10:5); rather, the shepherds represent the politicians of Judah and the Egyptians. The picture is clear: the lion is Jehovah, the prey is Jerusalem, and the loud but ineffectual shepherds are the Jerusalem politicians and the Egyptians.

5   In a contrasting picture, the tender mercy and protective care of Jehovah for His own are represented through the figure of mother birds hovering over their nests, protecting their helpless young—*so will Jehovah of hosts protect Jerusalem.* While executing His fierce judgment against the wicked and faithless people of His city, He will protect and care for the remnant through whom He is to achieve His purpose. *He will protect and deliver it, he will pass over and preserve it;* the destruction will not be total. Note the four verbs: *protect, deliver, pass over, preserve.* They assure the faithful in the face of all the odds against them. The verb *pass over* calls to mind God's deliverance of His people when He passed over His own in Egypt; He destroyed the firstborn of the Egyptians but spared the firstborn of the Hebrews (Exod. 12:13, 23).

Call to Repentance (vv. 6–7)

6   The Lord now calls upon the people to repent: *Turn ye unto him from whom ye have deeply revolted, O children of Israel.* Thus they will escape the tearing as of a lion and enjoy hovering protection as of a mother bird. About one hundred years later, Ezekiel declared that Jehovah has "no pleasure in the death of the wicked; but that the wicked turn from his way and live." He then made the same plea that Isaiah made: "Turn ye, turn ye from your evil ways; for why will ye die, O house of Israel?" (Ezek. 33:11). The Lord never destroys as long as there is a possibility of repentance; but when that is gone, destruction falls. Though Judah had revolted deeply from Jehovah, apparently many did turn back to Him, for Jehovah was able to spare the city from Assyria's threat. Similarly, in Ezekiel's day He preserved a remnant.

7   *For in that day*—the day that the people turn unto the Lord—*they shall cast away every man his idols of silver, and his idols of gold, which your own hands have made unto you for a sin.* The sin of

idolatry had been Israel's downfall from the beginning of their history. Turning to Jehovah would therefore involve the destruction of idols (cf. 30:22). The idols which their hands had made were as impotent to save as were the horses and horsemen of Egypt on whom they depended; the one was lifeless material, the other merely flesh. When men turn to the Lord and enjoy the strength of His might, they realize the folly and foolishness of depending on lifeless idols, the work of their own hands.

Destruction of Assyria (vv. 8–9)

8 *And the Assyrian shall fall by the sword.* Not merely Sennacherib's army that fell before the walls of Jerusalem, but the whole Assyrian power must be destroyed. It must be clearly demonstrated that spirit, not flesh, prevails. He shall *fall by the sword, not of man; and the sword, not of men, shall devour him.* A combined force of Babylonians and Medes destroyed Nineveh (612 B.C.), but it was Jehovah who determined her end (Nah. 3:5–6). And it was Jehovah who directed Nebuchadnezzar against Egypt: "I will . . . put my sword in his [Nebuchadnezzar's] hand: but I will break the arms of Pharaoh." It was Jehovah's sword in the Babylonian's hand, it was Jehovah who broke Pharaoh's arm. And again, "I shall put my sword into the hand of the king of Babylon, and he shall stretch it out upon the land of Egypt" (Ezek. 30:24–25). As it was Jehovah's sword which Babylon wielded against Egypt, so would the instrument of the destruction of Assyria be Jehovah's sword in the hand of His servant-nation; therefore the devouring was of the Lord. Assyria's subjects would flee (cf. Nah. 3:17–18), and his young men, no longer in military service, would do regular taskwork.

9 *And his rock shall pass away.* There have been numerous suggestions as to just who or what *his rock* was. Some commentators think it was the powerful army of Assyria; others suggest that it was Assyria's idols—her gods; others think that it was the power of Assyria itself; still others think that Assyria's rock was the king. This last suggestion seems the most probable, though the gods of Assyria remain a distinct possibility. The prophet has no particular king in mind; perhaps *his rock* represents the whole of Assyria's rulers. At any

rate, the *rock shall pass away by reason of terror*, which is the terror of the Lord (cf. 10:33). That *his princes shall be dismayed* lends credibility to the hypothesis that Assyria's rock is the king. They are *dismayed at the ensign*, probably the sign of Jehovah's approaching terror. Jehovah's *fire* may signify both the fire of His altar-hearth where the sacrifices were offered, and the fire of His anger which breathed destruction (cf. 29:6; 30:27–28). For John writes that when the prayers of the saints were presented before the Lord, an angel took a censer, filled it with fire from off the altar which was before the Lord, and cast it upon the earth. Judgments of destruction followed (Rev. 8:3–5). This fire of His anger and judgment comes from before His presence, both then and now.

CHAPTER **32**

The New Order (vv. 1–8);
Warning, Judgment, and Blessedness (vv. 9–20)

The New Order (vv. 1–8)

With Judah severely chastised and Assyria out of the way, the prophet now describes the new order to come. There have been numerous allusions to the messianic period (e.g., 16:5; 28:16; 29:22–24; 30:23–26), but no direct reference to the Messiah Himself since the prophecies of Immanuel (7:14), the Son of five names who will rule on the throne of David (9:6–7), and the Branch of Jesse (11:1–10). But now Isaiah tells of the righteous and just rule of a King and His princes.

The righteous King and spiritual illumination (vv. 1–4)

1 *Behold, a king shall reign in righteousness, and princes shall rule in justice.* Diverse views are held respecting this king. Some hold that the previous chapters were written in the days of Ahaz and that Hezekiah is the king of this verse. Others believe that Josiah, the last righteous king of Judah, is the one considered. Some think the prophet is pointing to an ideal situation which will follow the fall of

Assyria. A few, not as many as one would expect, hold that the Messiah of the future ideal age is the subject of the prophet's description. It seems, however, that only the last possibility, the messianic hope which was realized in Jesus Christ, fully fits the description in this passage. Objection to this view is offered on the ground that *princes* are mentioned. Since Christ had no princes and the apostles do not appear in the prophet's vision, it is argued that Isaiah has someone other than Christ in mind.

Let us look a little more closely at the various theories as to the identity of the righteous King. Although Hezekiah is described in both Kings and Chronicles as a good man of noble character, neither he nor his princes fulfilled the anticipation of verses 1–8. Likewise, Josiah is described as a godly ruler; yet the conditions described by Isaiah did not prevail in his day. What of the suggestion that Isaiah is describing an ideal king who would rule after the fall of Assyria? David anticipated "One that ruleth over men righteously,/That ruleth in the fear of God"; but then he lamented, "Verily my house is not so with God" (II Sam. 23:3, 5). No one of his house who eventually occupied the throne of national Israel fulfilled the hope. Recall, however, that Isaiah said that the Child to be born, the Son to be given, would sit "upon the throne of David, and upon his kingdom, to establish it, and to uphold it with justice and with righteousness from henceforth even for ever" (9:7; cf. 11:1–5). Jeremiah similarly said that Jehovah would raise up unto David "a righteous Branch, and he shall reign as king and deal wisely, and shall execute justice and righteousness in the land" (Jer. 23:5; cf. 33:15). Zechariah describes the King to come as being "just, and having salvation" (Zech. 9:9). The rule of this coming Messiah, then, fits the description in this verse; He is the King who shall reign in righteousness.

And princes shall rule in justice. Princes are not necessarily of royal parentage, but they are of noble birth and royal dignity. If our contention that the King is the Messiah is correct, could not the princes be Christians? For they are "a royal priesthood" (I Peter 2:9), related to the King as brethren (Heb. 2:11) who "reign in life through the one, even Jesus Christ" (Rom. 5:17); they reign "upon the earth" (Rev. 5:10). This interpretation of both the King and the princes is in harmony with what the prophet says and what developed in the purpose of God; at the same time it does no violence to Scripture.

2   At this point there is introduced *a man* whose unique function is described by four word-pictures: (1) he *shall be as a hiding-place from the wind*, the wind of adversity and destruction; *and* (2) *a covert from the tempest*, a place of safety from the rain and hailstorms which sweep the nations (29:6); (3) *as streams of water in a dry place*—the value and great worth of water is best understood and appreciated by people living in a semiarid country like Judah; and (4) *as the shade of a great rock in a weary land*, a place of shade from the burning sun and of protection from fierce winds.

There are three possibilities as to who this man is: (1) the Messiah Himself; (2) those who are His, those princely Christians under the Messiah who have the character to serve as a hiding place from adversity; or (3) as translated by Leupold, "each of them," King and princes. The choice is probably between the first and second, though the third is not to be summarily dismissed. In favor of the position that this *man* is the Messiah is the fact that what he does is also ascribed to Jehovah (25:4). Moreover, the Hebrew word used here for *man (ish)* is also used of "the man whose name is the Branch," who will sit and rule upon His throne and serve as Priest at the same time (Zech. 6:12–13). On the other hand, those that are His have experienced a transformation of life enabling them to be a covert and shade to others, and to withstand the shifting sands of human social and religious movements.

3   The spiritual blindness and deafness of former times (6:9–10; 29:10–11) will have been taken away. In their stead there will be moral and spiritual alertness; the people will see and hear clearly (cf. 29:18; 35:5). Further, they will hearken to what they hear; rejecting the conventional morality of society, they will accept the pure morality of righteousness.

4   To the open eyes and receptive ears of verse 3, the prophet now adds the heart: *And the heart of the rash shall understand knowledge.* The eyes, ears, and heart, all of which had been insensitive to God's words (6:9–10), now are healed. The *rash* are those who in haste or recklessness disregarded what God said. They now understand knowledge; they are enlightened in the ways of the Lord. A fourth

characteristic is added: *and the tongue of the stammerers shall be ready to speak plainly*. With their eyes open that they might see, their ears unstopped that they might hear, and the heart attuned to the things of God, the subjects of the King can now clearly speak and defend their faith, "being ready always to give answer to every man that asketh [them] a reason concerning the hope that is in [them]" (I Peter 3:15; cf. 4:11; I Cor. 1:10).

Moral distinctions are now clear (vv. 5–8)

5   With their eyes, ears, and heart now illumined (vv. 3–4), the subjects of the King can judge and discern character; they are not deceived by appearances. The *fool* is one who scoffs at religion, who is empty and speaks folly. He is no longer considered noble, but recognized for what he is. The *churl* (the word occurs only here and in v. 7), a knave, "an unscrupulous opportunist" (Clements), shall not be thought of as bountiful or liberal, but as crafty and deceitful. They shall be evaluated by their character, not their claims.

6   The prophet now gives his own definition to the word *fool* (*nabal*, Hebrew; "vile person," King James). The fool speaks folly from an empty mind; his heart works iniquity, lawlessness, to practice what is contrary to God's way and standard and to utter error against Jehovah. This attitude toward God spawns a disposition of ill toward man, *to make empty the soul of the hungry, and to cause the drink of the thirsty to fail*. The fool is the complete opposite of the man described above (vv. 1–4). Rawlinson has well observed, "The prophet seems to have the portrait of Nabal [I Sam. 25] in his mind, and to take him as the type of a class" (I. 522).

7   The whole stock in trade of the churl, the knave, is evil. He spends time devising wicked purposes and ways; he employs dishonest methods in an effort to become rich. To accomplish his end he would destroy the poor, the meek who cannot resist him. He achieves his goal by lying; and even when the cause of the needy is right, he contradicts and opposes them by perversions of truth and equity. Everything about this character is evil; he is void of feeling and compassion.

8   In contrast to the churl, *the noble deviseth noble things*; he practices that which is elevating and behaves honorably toward oth-

ers. His life manifests the nobility of a prince, one related to the righteous King.

Warning, Judgment, and Blessedness (vv. 9–20)

Delitzsch considers verses 9–20 an appendix to the fifth woe (ch. 31); Young agrees, calling them a completion of that woe. Delitzsch would place this section in the Uzziah-Jotham period, which is probably too early. It is more than likely a part of Isaiah's prophecies during the period 705–701 B.C., the years of Assyria's greatest threat to Judah. Smith points out that the prophecy has the usual three stages: "sin in the present, judgment in the immediate future, and a state of blessedness in the latter days" (I. 269).

Warning to careless women (vv. 9–12)

9 The prophet charges the women with being *at ease* and *careless*, or overconfident and indifferent; they have been lulled into a condition of apathy toward the dangers that are at hand. Apparently the prophet's preaching has made no impression on them. In an earlier prophecy he charged the women with vanity and a love of display (3:16–24); now he charges them with complacency and unconcern. There is no doubt but that this disposition of the women reflected the general condition of the people as a whole. *Ye women that are at ease* and *careless daughters* are synonymous, not two separate groups. Three commands are issued: (1) *Rise up*—this is not to be taken literally as if they have been sitting haughtily, but is merely a call to be attentive; *and* (2) *hear my voice*—understand what I am saying, take it to heart; and (3) *give ear unto my speech*—respond to what I say by demonstrative action.

10 Things are about to change: *For days beyond a year* ("days above a year," Hebrew) *shall ye be troubled.* In just over a year (between one and two years from now) shall trouble come. The word translated *careless* can also mean "confident"; the probable meaning is that the women are careless and unconcerned because of overconfidence in their security. Conditions seem not to have changed since the days of Amos (Amos 6:1–6). But within the allotted time, *the vintage*, the time of harvesting grapes and making wine, *shall fail, the*

ingathering shall not come. A similar prophecy had been spoken against Moab (16:7–10); such evil shall now come upon the women of Judah.

11   The prophet restates the condition of the women, *at ease* and *careless,* no doubt for emphasis. In contrast to their present happy but indifferent state, they are called upon to *tremble,* quake, be afraid. *Be troubled,* become agitated and concerned about Judah's and your own condition, for it is not so secure as you think. The third command is to strip off the clothes of vanity and luxury, *and gird sackcloth upon your loins.* Sackcloth was a coarse scratchy garment worn next to the body in time of calamity to signify grief or penitence. The reference here may be to garments which captives wore as they were being carried away.

12   *They shall smite upon the breasts for the pleasant fields, for the fruitful vine.* Commentators agree that the language here is difficult. Young offers two possibilities, either "mourning for the breasts" or "beating upon the breasts." If the first interpretation is correct, the language is figurative. Barnes thinks *breasts* is "here used to denote that which nourishes or sustains life, and is synonymous with fruitful fields"; the women are mourning for what is no more. The second interpretation, women literally beating upon their breasts, is supported by the example of the handmaids of Nineveh when their city was destroyed (Nah. 2:7). Young suggests that there are three things for which the women are mourning: their breasts, which, if there is no food, are dry (cf. the dry breasts of Hos. 9:14); the pleasant fields now destroyed; and the once fruitful vines, now neglected and in ruin.

The judgment to come (vv. 13–15)

13   Jehovah speaks of the people as *my people,* and of the land as theirs. Instead of the pleasant fields and fruitful vineyards, there *shall come up thorns and briers* (cf. 5:6), the consequence of their sin and indifference which brought on the Assyrian attack. Yea, these shall come up where once stood the *houses of joy,* pleasant and enjoyable, *in the joyous city.* Although the city is not named, Jerusalem is no doubt in the prophet's mind. Of course, Jerusalem was not taken by the Assyrians, but the land of Judah was overrun by them. Con-

sequently, the land was no longer productive but desolate; where pleasant houses once stood in joyous cities, there was now the gloom of dejected spirits.

14 *The palace,* the dwelling place of the king, built on a grand scale, *shall be forsaken. The hill,* or Ophel, is either the hill of Zion itself or the ridge extending northeast from the original hill of David to the temple area. It and the watchtower, the identity and location of which are unknown, *shall be for dens for ever.* These once important areas shall be the dwelling places, the caves, of wild animals; and instead of the joyous and careless women, wild asses shall frolic. The area shall also be a place for the feeding of flocks. What a transition from the once proud city to a place of desolation, the habitation of wild animals! This is the price of Judah's sin.

15 The extent of *for ever* (v. 14) is now defined. It is limited to the period from the desolate and forlorn condition described in verses 13–14 until the occurrence of three events: *until* (1) *the Spirit be poured upon us from on high, and* (2) *the wilderness become a fruitful field, and* (3) *the fruitful field be esteemed as a forest.* The interpretation of the second and third events depends on the first. Elsewhere in Isaiah we read that Jehovah has poured out the spirit of deep sleep upon His people (29:10); He also pours out "the fierceness of his anger" (42:25), His wrath (Hos. 5:10), and His fury and indignation (a similar phrase occurs about ten times in Ezek.; e.g., 7:8; 14:19; 22:22, 31). By contrast we read here that He will pour out His Spirit from on high. This is subject to two interpretations:

1. In the midst of oppression Jehovah will pour out His Spirit upon the seed of Jacob (44:3). Support for this understanding is found in the fact that before their return from captivity, He says, "I will give them [the people] one heart, and I will put a new spirit within you" (Ezek. 11:19). This is later repeated in anticipation of their return to their land, with an added promise, "I will put my Spirit within you, and cause you to walk in my statutes" (Ezek. 36:26–27; 37:14). Speaking as if the return has already been accomplished, He says, "For I have poured out my Spirit upon the house of Israel" (Ezek. 39:29). In this interpretation Jehovah's Spirit signifies the ruling principle governing the seed of Jacob; the new life being lived by the people of God comes by His Spirit.

2. The second view is that the pouring out of Jehovah's Spirit was fulfilled on Pentecost (Act 2). Favoring this position is Joel 2:28–31. Dated about 830 B.C. by many, this prophecy definitely looks to the event of Acts 2, for Peter said, "This is that which hath been spoken through the prophet Joel" (Acts 2:16). Also to be noted in this connection is Zechariah 12:10: "And I will pour upon the house of David, and upon the inhabitants of Jerusalem, the spirit of grace and of supplication; and they shall look unto me whom they have pierced"—this is a messianic prophecy fulfilled in Jesus (John 19:37). It is difficult to say which of these two interpretations is correct, for the blessings from Jehovah's Spirit which were poured out upon those who returned from Babylon foreshadowed the blessings that began on Pentecost.

If the first interpretation is adopted, the two events which were to be simultaneous with the pouring out of the Spirit—until *the wilderness become a fruitful field, and the fruitful field be esteemed as a forest*—are not to be regarded as fulfilled in Judah and Jerusalem, for they never literally became a field or forest. However, Barnes says the prophecy could refer to the return from Babylon when Jerusalem, which had lain so long in ruins, was again inhabited, and Babylon, once so prosperous, became a desolate ruin. If one accepts the second view, then the language must be interpreted symbolically: the wilderness, producing scantily, will become a fruitful field of spiritual blessings, and the already fruitful field will become a rich and luxuriant forest, strong and stately. From my point of view, the second has more in its favor.

Rest and quietness at last (vv. 16–20)

16   Isaiah has declared that a King shall reign in righteousness (vv. 1–8) and the Spirit shall bring spiritual blessings (v. 15). Now he declares that the people who receive the blessing of the Spirit shall dwell in peace, quietness, and confidence (vv. 16–20). *Then*, when the Spirit has been poured upon the people, *justice shall dwell in the wilderness; and righteousness shall abide in the fruitful field*. The words *dwell* and *abide* indicate that justice and righteousness will have permanent residence in both the wilderness and fruitful field (cf. v. 15). Righteousness is conformity to a standard, man's con-

274

formity to God's standard of holiness; therefore, it entails respect for His law. Justice, virtually the same as righteousness, involves upholding the rights of others. These two principles will prevail in the new spiritual order. Only the people of God will manifest these virtues.

17 The result of righteousness and justice as they work in the heart will be real peace. Quietness and confidence will ensue forever; that is, as long as the reign of the righteous King and the blessing of the Spirit endure and the people abide in them. This is in contrast to the careless ease of verse 9. That was a false peace; this is genuine. Now are brought about the salvation to be realized in returning and rest, and the strength to be realized in quietness and confidence (30:15). God had earlier called the people to this rest, but they would not hear (28:12).

18 Jehovah designates those of whom He has been speaking: *And my people*—those that are His, the remnant. To them He now makes three glorious promises. They (1) *shall abide in a peaceable habitation, and* (2) *in safe dwellings, and* (3) *in quiet resting-places.* Note the beauty and charm of the places being described; they are peaceable, safe, quiet. What joyous words of consolation, hope, and assurance to a people who for so long had known the destructive ravages of war! The words do not characterize the life of those who returned from Babylon, but of those who became the heritage of God's people under the Messiah.

19 Suddenly, in the midst of this idyllic picture of the peace, tranquility, and security of the saints, the prophet presents a contrast: *But it shall hail in the downfall of the forest; and the city shall be utterly laid low.* Commentators differ in identifying the forest and the city. Most identify the forest as Assyria (cf. 10:18–19, 24–25). Young tends to accept this identification, but warns that it "cannot be pressed." Since hail does not totally destroy a forest, the *hail in the downfall of the forest* may refer to the suffering and loss endured by Jerusalem at the time. Commentators are not at all unanimous in their identification of the city which *shall be utterly laid low.* Since it has already been said many times that Jerusalem shall be brought low (29:1–4; 30:17, 20; 31:4), Delitzsch and others think Jerusalem is in the prophet's mind. Some scholars, including Leupold, think that the city is Nineveh, the capital of Assyria. A few think that the city is

Babylon. However, in the light of the general direction of Isaiah's prophecies in chapters 24–35, perhaps the forest designates the great conquering military powers of the period and the city represents the desolated world-cities (24:10, 12; 25:2), which would include political Jerusalem (27:10). This view seems more consistent with the total context of the Book of Isaiah.

20   Several commentators admit to having difficulty with this verse: *Blessed are ye that sow beside all waters, that send forth the feet of the ox and the ass.* They believe the meaning to be that, given the abundant harvest from copiously watered fields, the feet of the ox and ass can carry them anywhere, for what they might eat will not be missed. But this does not make good sense. Rather, the meaning is that the people, living in such peaceful surroundings (v. 17), will pursue productive occupations in the Lord. Both men and domesticated animals will be devoted to the production of good. Swords will be beaten into plowshares and spears into pruning hooks; the nations will learn war no more (2:4). This understanding is in harmony with the prophet's total message.

CHAPTER **33**

The Defeat of Assyria and Victory of Jerusalem

Smith speaks of this chapter as "the day of Isaiah's triumph," the day in which his warnings, prophecies, and promises are fulfilled. The prophet's implicit faith and trust in God are now vindicated. In this chapter there is a sharp contrast with the conditions of chapter 22. The despondency and despair that gave themselves over to fatalism and feasting (22:1–4) have now been replaced by prayer and solemnity that look to Jehovah for help. Isaiah can point to what he has said so many times: Jerusalem will not be taken; Egypt will be of no help; the rulers who scoffed at the word of God and trusted in their own wisdom have fled or failed the nation. The word of God through Isaiah has triumphed with glory to Jehovah the God of Israel instead of to the prophet.

The historical background of this chapter is recorded in II Kings

18–19 and Isaiah 36–37. Hezekiah had given Sennacherib tribute in the amount of three hundred talents of silver and thirty talents of gold, depleting the treasury and stripping the temple of its treasure. For some unrevealed reason the Assyrian immediately sent three of his chief military officers to demand the surrender of the city (II Kings 18:13–35). He may have been suspicious that Hezekiah had persuaded Tirhakah, a pharaoh of the Ethiopian dynasty, to come against the Assyrians. It is probably at this point that the prophecies of chapter 33 are declared. The details of the Assyrian's demands will be dealt with in chapters 36 and 37.

Woe to the Destroyer! (vv. 1–6)

1   Though lacking absolute proof, practically all conservative scholars consider the woe to be pronounced upon the Assyrian Sennacherib when his army threatened Jerusalem (701 B.C.). (Clements, however, along with other liberal theologians, places the chapter in the period of the Babylonian menace, and denies the ascription of chapters 33–35 to Isaiah. Such liberties with the word of God are characteristic of this school of writers.) Without provocation the Assyrians are destroying the land of Judah and her cities. The king has accepted tribute from Hezekiah, yet is demanding the surrender of the city. Leupold suggests that the prophet may have stood on the wall of the city and flung these words of defiance into the very teeth of the ambassadors: *Woe to thee that destroyest, and thou wast not destroyed. . . . when thou hast made an end of dealing treacherously, they shall deal treacherously with thee.* The destiny of the Assyrian king and his nation is not in his own hands, but in the hand of God who determines the boundaries and seasons of nations (Acts 17:26). Sennacherib received the recompense of his treachery when, some years after returning to Nineveh, his own sons slew him while he was worshiping in the temple of his god (37:38).

2   Having delivered this word of woe to the Assyrian ambassadors, the prophet turns to Jehovah in prayer: *O Jehovah, be gracious unto us.* If the city is to be saved, it will be by the graciousness of God—as the destiny of the Assyrians is in the hand of Jehovah, so also is that of Judah. *We have waited for thee;* the plural *we* probably

277

includes the prophet's disciples, the faithful to Jehovah, who, having waited with him for Jehovah (8:16–18; cf. 25:9), now pray with him and lift their voices with his (cf. 30:19). The righteous are always rewarded for waiting patiently in faith for the Lord to act in His own time and way. *Be thou our arm every morning,* our arm of strength, for there is no other source; the prayer to renew strength morning by morning indicates continuous need. Be thou *our salvation also in the time of trouble*—this plea is grounded in God's graciousness. Jonah's words while in the belly of the fish, "Salvation is of Jehovah" (Jon. 2:9), hold true in every calamity. When in a predicament like that faced by Jonah or by the people of Judah under Assyrian assault, we must readily recognize this truth.

3   Through the eye of faith the prophet beholds the answer to his prayer. He sees the peoples fleeing *at the noise of the tumult,* the thundering voice of Jehovah (cf. 30:30–31). At *the lifting up of thyself* (cf. v. 10) *the nations* (identical with *the peoples*) *are scattered.* At the sound of Jehovah's voice and His lifting Himself in action, the army, which is made up of peoples from many nations, is scattered. (Or it may be that the prophet is referring to the general dismay and dispersing which occur when heathen nations hear of Jehovah's wondrous work.)

4   Again the prophet directs his word to the Assyrians: *And your spoil,* your booty, that which you plan to carry home with you, *shall be gathered as the caterpillar gathereth. Caterpillar* in this instance refers to a developmental stage in which locusts are very destructive. Just as locusts leap from plant to plant, so shall men leap upon the booty left by the fleeing remnant of the Assyrian army, moving from item to item, greedily carrying away all they can.

5   *Jehovah is exalted; for he dwelleth on high.* Note that the prophet does not say that Jehovah "becomes exalted." His exaltation is constant, though the people, in their ignorance, may just now recognize it. In His exalted greatness, *he hath filled Zion with justice and righteousness,* demonstrating these qualities in Himself through what He is doing (cf. 32:16; Pss. 89:14; 97:2).

6   The Lord's presence among His people, and their recognition of and abiding in His righteousness and justice, shall be their stability or security. As their treasure, Israel's fear of Jehovah shall bring them

abundance of salvation, wisdom, and knowledge at all times and under all conditions. As they draw upon this treasure, the fear of Jehovah inspires faith and love which lead to obedience to His will.

The Broken Covenant and the Devouring Fire (vv. 7–16)

7   The following three verses (7–9) reveal the terrible condition of the people and the land of Judah: the weeping ambassadors (v. 7), the empty highways (v. 8), and the mourning land (v. 9). *Behold*—Isaiah calls for attention—*their valiant ones cry without.* Hebrew scholars are uncertain about the word translated *valiant.* Delitzsch renders it "heroes," and Rawlinson, "lions of God." *The ambassadors of peace,* those sent by Hezekiah to convey the tribute to Sennacherib, *weep bitterly* as they return, having delivered the gold and silver but to no avail. Delitzsch thinks the valiant ones and the ambassadors are the same group. Leupold suggests that the valiant ones are the sturdy soldiers of Judah who cry painfully at the results of rendering tribute, and that the ambassadors are the messengers sent to Sennacherib. Young, however, interprets the *valiant ones* as Assyrians who cry arrogantly; *the ambassadors of peace* who *weep bitterly* are Hezekiah's envoys. With regard to the word *valiant* Young comments, "It is quite tempting to see, and quite possibly we should see here, a reference to the haughty and overbearing language of the Rabshakeh who commanded the city of Jerusalem to give itself over to surrender."

8   *The highways lie waste,* empty; no one dares to venture upon them; wayfaring men (foot-travelers) have ceased. This is reminiscent of the days of the judges (Judg. 5:6). With their cities destroyed, probably all who are able have come to Jerusalem. The enemy's conduct is described in three categories: (1) he *hath broken the covenant,* the agreement to depart once Hezekiah had paid the tribute (II Kings 18:14); (2) *he hath despised the cities*—disdaining the covenant, he has continued to lay siege to the cities of Judah, ignoring the principles of human rights and honesty; and (3) *he regardeth not man,* paying no attention to human suffering or the protests of those who would attempt to reason with him. One historian says, "Highly gifted as a military commander, Sennacherib was ruined by an arrogant

self-consciousness which created hatred everywhere, and even alienated him from his own sons."[4]

9   With the ambassadors weeping, the highways empty, *The land mourneth and languisheth,* adding its gloom to the picture of dejection and woe. Delitzsch thinks it is autumn when the leaves are turning brown and falling and the grass is dead and dry, but this is pure conjecture. The language is figurative, suggesting that the land reflects the spirit of the people whom the invaders are overrunning and devastating. Four ordinarily flourishing sections of the country are described: *Lebanon,* the mountain range to the north, noted for its majestic beauty and mighty cedar and fir trees, *is confounded and withereth away; Sharon,* the verdant and flower-rich plain extending south from Carmel until it melts into the Shephelah of western Judea, *is like a desert; and Bashan,* extending northeast from the Sea of Galilee, noted for its oak groves and rich grazing land, *and Carmel,* the verdant mountain or hill that juts into the Mediterranean Sea, *shake off their leaves,* so that the trees are bare. The picture is one of dejection, of both people and land.

10   The time has come for Jehovah to declare Himself; He has determined that the time is now ripe for action. Three verbs emphasize His action: *Now will I arise, saith Jehovah; now will I lift up myself; now will I be exalted.* He will rise from His state of waiting; He will exert Himself in deeds; He will be exalted in the eyes of the peoples (cf. v. 5).

11   Jehovah now addresses the Assyrians: *Ye shall conceive chaff,* be pregnant with grandiose ideas, plans, and schemes. But *ye shall bring forth stubble,* the short worthless stalks of grain that remain after the harvest. Your plans to destroy Jerusalem shall come to nought, like chaff and stubble; the burning fire of your wrath and hatred shall consume you as fierce flames devour stubble (cf. 30:33).

12   *And the peoples shall be as the burnings of lime,* that is, calcium oxide. Heating calciferous material to red heat produces lime, a white powder. Moab was charged with burning the bones of the king of Edom into lime (Amos 2:1). The peoples shall also be *as*

---

4. Siegfried J. Schwantes, *A Short History of the Ancient Near East* (Grand Rapids: Baker, 1965), p. 137.

thorns cut down, that are burned in the fire. The peoples (nations) will burn like dry grass, which gives a quick heat and produces a crackling noise, but is readily consumed. Such shall be the end of *the peoples.*

13 Jehovah looks beyond Assyria to the nations of earth: *Hear, ye that are far off, what I have done.* Be warned by the display of my power upon Sennacherib's army, for what I have done to him I can do to any nation. Jehovah now turns to address His people in Jerusalem: *And, ye that are near, acknowledge my might.* Having witnessed the power of Jehovah, they should be both warned and assured by it, for a destructive force such as His can also preserve.

14 The remnant of believers is always small; in every place and period of history sinners abound. Jehovah now addresses the wicked: *The sinners in Zion are afraid; trembling hath seized the godless ones.* Sinners are those who err, who have missed the mark that God set before them. The godless are the impious people who lightly esteem that which is holy and hold nothing to be sacred. Both disregard God and His way, preferring their own. The prophet puts questions into their mouths: *Who among us* (the sinners, the godless) *can dwell with the devouring fire? who among us can dwell with everlasting burnings?* From the beginning of Israel's history, Jehovah had revealed Himself as "a devouring fire," a fire that consumes (Deut. 4:24; 9:3), a figure referred to repeatedly by Isaiah (29:6; 30:27–28, 30, 33; 31:9). The *everlasting burnings* are the wrath and anger which emanate from Jehovah's very being: "A fire goeth before him,/And burneth up his adversaries round about" (Ps. 97:3). It is very doubtful whether the idea of eternal punishment as set forth in the New Testament is in the minds of the questioners. A terror growing out of what they have seen is what prompts their questions.

15 With six brief declarative statements reminiscent of Psalms 15 and 24 the prophet answers the questions of the godless: (1) *He that walketh righteously*—walking righteously is a metaphor for the whole life of an individual who reflects the righteousness of God; *and* (2) *speaketh uprightly*—he "speaketh truth in his heart" (Ps. 15:2), with an uncompromising adherence to high moral principles, so that there is harmony between his actions and his speech; (3) *he that despiseth the gain of oppressions*—he holds in contempt the very idea

of extortion, acquiring gain by oppressing another; (4) *that shaketh
his hands from taking a bride,* that is, if a bribe is put in his hand, he
opens his hand and shakes the money out on the ground; if he is
offered a bribe, he shakes his hands to indicate his refusal to be
involved in such business (accepting bribes seems to have been especially common among judges and others in political positions in
Isaiah's day); (5) he *that stoppeth his ears from hearing of blood*—he
refuses to listen to plans or plots that involve bloodshed (young men
had been warned against becoming involved in such plans, for they
lead to destruction and death [Prov. 1:10–19]; one who refuses to
listen when such plans are being devised has taken the first step
toward protection from their consequences); *and* (6) *shutteth his eyes
from looking upon evil*—he refuses to look upon evil either favorably
or indifferently, but he keeps his eyes straight ahead (Prov. 4:25),
toward a right goal. In his answer the prophet has included righteous
conduct, upright speech, purity of heart and honesty, and ears and
eyes turned to divine principles of righteousness.

16   An individual of this character shall have no fear of the devouring fire, the everlasting burning; but rather, *he shall dwell on
high; his place of defence shall be the munitions of rocks.* His permanent dwelling-place is in the heights far above the wickedness and
fears of those who know not Jehovah. His defense shall be in the
inaccessible security of strongholds which are permanent and pass
not away, in Jehovah and that which He provides (cf. 25:4; 26:1).
Bread and water, which are not generally found in the heights of
mountains, shall be abundantly provided and made sure by the Lord.
The thought is that security is found in the stronghold of the Lord and
all necessities of life are provided by Him. The world may break the
covenant, but Jehovah is true to His word; He never fails His own, but
He is a consuming fire to the enemy. He calls upon His own to put
their faith and trust in this assurance.

The Glory of Israel's King and Jerusalem-Zion (vv. 17–24)

17   The prophet now addresses directly those of whom he has
been speaking (vv. 15–16): *Thine eyes shall see the king in his beauty.*
Alexander lists a wide range of views concerning the identity of this

king. Most, though not all, present-day commentators hold that he is Hezekiah, Jehovah, or the Messiah. The contrast between, on the one hand, Hezekiah's humiliation when he rent his clothes and covered himself with sackcloth in response to Assyria's threat (37:1) and, on the other, the days beyond Assyria's defeat, leads some scholars to believe that he is *the king in his beauty*. Jehovah's presence with His people both in the siege, when He gave them the victory, and afterward, in His majesty as Judge, Lawgiver, and King (vv. 21–22), leads others to believe that He is the King whom the righteous shall see. Although it is difficult to decide between Jehovah and the Messiah, it seems to me that the total context of the passage (vv. 17–24) points to the Messiah. Young makes an argument from the word *beauty*, noting that it is never used of Jehovah. This is true of the Hebrew word which occurs here. Although the word *noam* ("beauty") does occur twice with reference to Jehovah (Pss. 27:4; 90:17, margin), in Isaiah 33:17 the word translated *beauty* is *yophi*. Young says that *yophi* is used of the Messiah, but there is no evidence except this instance, which is the very point at issue. So, from my point of view, the word *beauty* does not prove the case either way. There is, however, a more telling piece of evidence: The clause *they* (thine eyes) *shall behold a land that reacheth afar* ("a land of far distances," Hebrew) fits well the time of the messianic reign, for "his dominion shall be from sea to sea, and from the River to the ends of the earth" (Zech. 9:10; cf. Ps. 72:8); Messiah's land reaches to all extremities.

18   When the eyes of the righteous shall see the King in His beauty and the land that reaches afar, the present suffering shall be only a memory. *Thy heart shall muse on the terror*—the mind shall meditate upon it, pondering the lesson to be learned. *Where is he that counted, where is he that weighed the tribute?* He that counted is probably the scribe (margin) who recorded the event as someone else weighed the tribute. And further, *Where is he that counted the towers?* Is this a reference to someone who looked for points of weakness at which to attack the city, or to someone who determined how many towers would be left to Hezekiah when the Assyrians took Jerusalem? In either case he, too, is gone, and the people can sing Psalm 48. They are able to "Walk about Zion, and go round about her;/[and]

Number the towers thereof" (Ps. 48:12); all the towers have survived. The Zion which God protects is unconquerable and indestructible; but when He withdraws, it is defenseless.

19   The people of Jehovah's favor will no more see *the fierce people*, the enemy; for they, too, will have been swept away. They were of a *deep* or gruff *speech*, unintelligible to the Jews (just as the Lord had promised [28:11]). And though Jehovah brought upon Judah the captains of the Assyrians to carry away Manasseh to Babylon (II Chron. 33:11), Isaiah's generation never saw them again. Any people who would thwart God's purpose by trying to destroy His own shall be swept away as the fierce Assyrians were.

20   Having beheld the King in His beauty and having seen a land of far distances, the people now have their attention directed to Jerusalem-Zion, Jehovah's permanent dwelling-place among them. Physical Jerusalem withstood the threat of Sennacherib, but it would eventually be destroyed by Nebuchadnezzar. However, the city on which attention is now focused is different. *Look upon Zion, the city of our solemnities*, the three annual festivals—Passover, the Feast of Weeks, and the Feast of Tabernacles. *Thine eyes shall see Jerusalem a quiet habitation*; its turbulent days shall be over (cf. 32:18), and the people will have quietness and confidence, the effects of righteousness (30:15; 32:17). To describe this other Jerusalem the prophet uses the figure of a permanent tent (tabernacle) unlike those of the nomadic fathers or the tent in which Jehovah had dwelt among Israel as they moved about. The eyes of the people shall see Jerusalem, *a tent that shall not be removed, the stakes* (tent pegs) *whereof shall never be plucked up, neither shall any of the cords thereof be broken*. The tent remains unmoved; its stakes are permanently driven and the cords unbroken (cf. 54:2–3). This description fits only the Zion, the heavenly Jerusalem with God in its midst, to which the saints come under the Messiah (Heb. 12:22). It became the permanent dwelling-place of God among His people after the removal of those things that were shaken and the reception of a kingdom that cannot be shaken (Heb. 12:27–28).

21   *But there Jehovah will be with us in majesty*. Dwelling in the permanent tent in the midst of His people, Jehovah will, in all the dignity of His sovereign power, preserve the righteous and repel the enemy. Calling upon his broad and extensive knowledge of world-cities such as Nineveh, Babylon, and Thebes (cf. Nah. 3:8), which were protected by rivers, canals, and moats, Isaiah uses another figure to represent the security of Jerusalem: it is a city surrounded and protected by rivers and streams. Considering the mountainous terrain of Jerusalem and Zion, this metaphor seems rather unusual, but it is filled with meaning: *a place of broad rivers and streams, wherein shall go no galley with oars, neither shall gallant ship pass thereby.* A *galley with oars* has reference to a large warship; a *gallant ship* is one that is seaworthy, or possibly a riverboat. No such vessel would pass through the waters surrounding Jerusalem to destroy the city.

22 The thought of verse 21 continues: *For Jehovah is our judge, Jehovah is our lawgiver, Jehovah is our king; he will save us.* Where He is there is safety; He is the ruler and protective power of the city. And Christ Jesus is all these things to the present Jerusalem. He has brought to us the law of the new covenant (Heb. 8:6; 12:24), and He is Judge (John 5:22) and King (Rev. 17:14). What God was to the people of Isaiah's day, Christ is to the saints now.

23 From the Jerusalem of the future, inviolable and permanent, the prophet looks to the wretchedness of the physical city. He likens it to a ship in distress, unfit for battle. In characteristic Isaianic style, the prophet speaks of three things that are faulty: the tackling, the mast, and the sail: *Thy tacklings are loosed; they could not strengthen the foot of their mast, they could not spread the sail.* Tacklings are the pulleys and cables used to hoist sails. The foot of the mast is not solidly set in the socket in the crossbeam. The sailors cannot spread the sail. Some commentators think that this refers to the ensign of the ship, but more likely it refers to the sail, without which the ship is immobile. The ship does not sink but it is helpless. Although the next expression is difficult, the prophet seems to be saying that in spite of this weak and helpless condition, there will be great spoil for the city to divide; even the lame will get his share. This indicates that even in its distress the city will not be destroyed, for Jehovah will give victory. The people will divide great spoil, but not as a result of their power.

24 Looking beyond the time of weakness (v. 23), Isaiah speaks of the time of power (vv. 21–22). Sickness is healed. *The inhabitant*

shall not say, I am sick: the people that dwell therein (the new
Jerusalem-Zion) *shall be forgiven their iniquity.* With sin forgiven,
strength is restored to those who are weak by reason of sickness. This
verse seems to look to the reign of the Messiah, the King in His
beauty; to the strong city in which God dwells, the Jerusalem to
which we have come; to the time when through the Redeemer, sins
are forgiven. Smith says, "If man is to have a future, this [the forgiv-
ing of his iniquity] must be the conclusion of all his past" (I. 341).
The prophet has progressed step by step to this point.

CHAPTER **34**

Judgments of the Nations and Edom

Chapters 34 and 35 are a unit which sets forth the judgment and
destruction of the enemies of Jehovah and His people (ch. 34), and
the redemption and glory of the ransomed (ch. 35). As we have noted
in his prophecies thus far, Isaiah is very fond of such contrasts. The
two chapters are not set in any particular period of history; they
summarize what Isaiah has been saying.

Chapter 34 is the most fiercely vivid picture of destruction and
desolation we have encountered thus far. In reading it one must
remember Edom's (Esau's) sensual and nonspiritual character, his
contempt for that which is sacred and holy, and his treatment of Israel
and scorn of Jehovah. In spite of how Israel may have felt toward his
brother nation, let it be remembered that chapter 34 is not his expression of judgment, but rather the outpouring of God's wrath against all
that is profane and antagonistic to Him and His kingdom. Esau
symbolizes the impious mind giving vent to its earthly character and
its hatred of God, His people, and everything which is spiritual.

Obadiah, thought by many to have been the earliest of the writing
prophets,[5] charges Edom with doing violence to his brother Jacob,
putting himself on the side of the destroyers of Israel, and rejoicing in

---

5. For a discussion of the date of Obadiah see Homer Hailey, *A Commentary on the
Minor Prophets* (Grand Rapids: Baker, 1972), pp. 28–29.

Jacob's calamity (vv. 10–15). Amos charges Edom with receiving from Gaza and Tyre whole villages as captives, pursuing his brother nation with the sword, casting off all pity, keeping his wrath forever (Amos 1:6, 9, 11). Ezekiel (ch. 35) charges that Edom held a perpetual enmity against Israel, delivering the people to the sword in the time of their adversity (v. 5), expressing anger, envy, and hatred against them (v. 11). Jehovah said of their attitude toward Him, "And ye have magnified yourselves against me with your mouth, and have multiplied your words against me: I have heard it" (v. 13). So, in the final analysis, all of Edom's envy, anger, and hatred against his brother was against Jehovah, for it was He who had determined which nation would receive the birthright and bring forth the Messiah. It was He who had determined their destinies. Jeremiah, echoing Obadiah, pronounced an equally strong judgment against Edom (49:7–22); and Malachi, in the closing book of the Old Covenant, pronounced the final threat against the people (1:1–5).

Knowledge of Edom's perpetual enmity and hatred toward Israel and Jehovah, despising that which is holy and sacred, helps us better appreciate the judgment pronounced by Jehovah through Isaiah. It is not the venting of the prophet's personal anger against Edom, or even of Israel's wrath against that nation; Isaiah is picturing the day of Jehovah's vengeance against all that Edom represents.

Judgment of the Nations (vv. 1–4)

1   Through the prophet, Jehovah issues a universal call to the heathen nations—the peoples—to hear and hearken, to listen and give heed to what is said. All on the earth are urged to hear and give heed to this universal judgment.

2   All nations hostile to Jehovah are the object of His indignation and wrath. Instead of learning of Him through His people and His presence among them, the heathen have tried to destroy Israel and thus rid the world of any knowledge of Jehovah. *All their host,* all the forces and peoples of the nations, will bear the brunt of His righteous indignation. The Lord speaks in the past tense as if it were already accomplished: *he hath utterly destroyed them, he hath delivered them to the slaughter.* Whatever the great God of heaven determines, is so

287

certain to be accomplished that He may speak of it as already done. In His purpose the nations have already been delivered to the slaughter by whatever means He will choose.

3   The picture of verses 3 and 4 is a gruesome one, employing hyperbole as strong as can be imagined. *Their slain also shall be cast out*, flung to the elements without burial, left to rot in the field. *The stench of their dead bodies* fills the air, rising like clouds of vapor. *And the mountains shall be melted with their blood*, a highly imaginative picture. There are landslides in the mountains caused by rivulets of blood washing away the soil. Surely, no one would think of this as literal!

4   The thought of the previous verse is continued: *And all the host of heaven shall be dissolved* ("moulder away," margin), crumble into particles, turn to dust by decay. The heavens themselves shall be rolled together like a scroll, no longer opened out to be seen and read. *All their host*, the heavenly bodies, shall fade from view as a leaf from the vine or fig tree dies, falls, and crumbles into decay.

Although the picture portrayed in these two verses may foreshadow the end of the world, the prophet does not have this in mind. Rather, he is describing in strong metaphor the end of the world for the heathen nations. When God's wrath and indignation come against the nations that oppose and fight Him, their world comes to an end (see the comments on 51:4–6, 16; 65:16–18; 66:22–24).

Judgment Against Edom—A Sacrifice (vv. 5–7)

5   Edom is singled out from among the nations. It is probably symbolic of all the heathen peoples, representing all that is profane and unspiritual. Jehovah's sword *hath drunk its fill in heaven*; it is filled with His wrath, ready to come down violently in judgment upon Edom and the people of His curse—those devoted to destruction. Jehovah's statement through Moses in Deuteronomy 32:41–42 serves as an excellent commentary on the present text: "If I whet my glittering sword,/And my hand take hold on judgment;/I will render vengeance to mine adversaries,/And will recompense them that hate me./I will make mine arrows drunk with blood,/And my sword shall

devour flesh;/With the blood of the slain and the captives,/From the head of the leaders of the enemy."

6 Jehovah is viewed as offering sacrifices. His sword is filled, dripping with blood and smeared with the fat of sacrificial animals. He begins with the smaller animals, lambs and goats and *the fat of the kidneys of rams* (the kidneys were to be burned unto Jehovah [Lev. 9:10]), and then proceeds to the larger animals (v. 7). The sacrifice is to be offered at Bozrah. This chief city of Edom, located approximately twenty-seven miles southeast of the southern end of the Dead Sea and thirty miles northeast of Petra, was strongly fortified and considered impregnable. *And a great slaughter in the land of Edom* makes clear the nature of the sacrifice—the people will be slaughtered.

7 From the smaller animals, that is, the general populace, the prophet proceeds to the greater among them: *the wild-oxen shall come down with them, and the bullocks with the bulls.* The wild ox, now extinct, was very strong and larger than ordinary cattle; its large horns accentuated its fierceness. Here associated with domesticated bullocks and bulls, the wild oxen probably symbolize the leaders of the nation who will *come down with them*, the general populace. All will fall together. As the sword of Jehovah is filled—intoxicated—with blood, so *their land shall be drunken with blood, and their dust made fat with fatness.* The whole picture is vivid, terrifying, and unmistakable. Through Ezekiel, the Lord later says, "I will prepare thee [Edom] unto blood . . . since thou hast not hated blood, therefore blood shall pursue thee" (Ezek. 35:6). Blood shed in anger and hatred will return upon the heads of those responsible.

The Judgment: Total Desolation (vv. 8–15)

8 *For Jehovah hath a day of vengeance*—a day in which punishment will be inflicted on account of injury or offense—*a year of recompense for the cause of Zion.* Delitzsch says that the phrase *for the cause of Zion*, which he translates "to contend for Zion," "is like a flash of lightning, throwing light upon the obscurity of prophecy, both backwards and forwards." It points out that judgments are imposed for the cause of Zion: "For Jehovah hath chosen Zion;/He hath

289

desired it for his habitation" (Ps. 132:13); there He dwells among the people, and there is His tabernacle where He meets with them (Ps. 76:2). Judgment is carried out in defense of Jehovah's claim and of righteousness.

9   In contrast to Zion, the beloved dwelling-place of Jehovah among His people, Edom is described as a desolate waste. Again Isaiah uses a trio of phrases to describe the devastation of the land: (1) *the streams of Edom shall be turned into pitch*, probably bitumen, a substance which occurs naturally in crude oil, tars, and asphalt; *and* (2) *the dust thereof into brimstone*—a blue sulphurous flame covers the land; *and* (3) *the land thereof shall become burning pitch*, an oily inflammable material of petroleum base. This picture of complete ruin, waste, and worthlessness is a fairly good description of hell itself, fitted only for the devil and his angels.

10   The fire of destruction burns perpetually: (1) *It shall not be quenched night nor day*, but is an eternal (agelong) flame; (2) *the smoke thereof shall go up for ever,* a constant reminder of the punishment for sin, the consequence of rejecting the spiritual life and embracing the fleshly; (3) *from generation to generation it shall lie waste; none shall pass through it for ever and ever.* Truly, here is a description not only of physical desolation, but also of the waste, desert, and deadness of the soul without God. Though Edom said they would rise and build again, Jehovah responded, "They shall build, but I will throw down; and men shall call them The border of wickedness, and The people against whom Jehovah hath indignation for ever" (Mal. 1:4). There is no life or true achievement apart from God, for "Except Jehovah build the house,/They labor in vain that build it" (Ps. 127:1). Edom had thought to build without God, but failed. This has always been, and will ever be, the lot of the godless.

11   The land of Edom shall be an eerie, ghostlike habitation for the wild creatures of the desert. Its inhabitants shall be the pelican (or screech owl) and the porcupine, a very large rodent which can sometimes weigh forty pounds or more. *The owl* (the exact identity of this creature is unknown) *and the raven shall dwell therein.* In contrast to the means by which God will construct the walls of Zion—"I will make justice the line, and righteousness the plummet" (28:17), God will stretch over Edom *the line of confusion (tohu, Hebrew) and the*

plummet of emptiness (*bohu*, Hebrew—translated "void" in Gen. 1:2 and Jer. 4:23; wherever this word appears in Scripture, it is accompanied by *tohu*—"waste and void"). Instead of being instruments for building up, the line and plummet are here used for tearing down and destroying (cf. Amos 7:7–9; II Kings 21:13).

12 In this land of confusion and emptiness, *They shall call the nobles thereof to the kingdom, but none shall be there.* Clements translates, "They shall name it No Kingdom There" (p. 274). The kingdom having ceased to exist, neither nobles nor princes can respond to a call. It is to be a land for wild animals, not for people.

13 Thorns shall come up where once palaces stood; nettles and thistles shall abound among the ruins of the strong fortresses which once challenged the enemy and protected the inhabitants of the land. The place where princes and nobles held court shall be a habitation for jackals and a court for ostriches.

14 The description of the total abandonment of the land to creatures of the wild is not yet complete. *And the wild beasts of the desert* (cf. 13:21) *shall meet with the wolves* ("howling creatures," Hebrew), *and the wild goat shall cry to his fellow.* The prophet emphasizes the untamed and the unrestrained character of these animals—wild beasts, wild goats, howling creatures. Commentators can only conjecture as to the identity of several of these creatures. *The night-monster* (*Lilith*, a Hebrew term which occurs only here) seems to have been an imaginary creature which, according to popular legend, inhabited waste places. It should not be assumed that the prophet believed in such creatures; rather, he used the word to complete his description of utter desolation. In the landscape he describes, such creatures of human fancy would find a proper resting place.

15 There are yet other creatures to complete the melancholy picture of desolation and emptiness. Such a place would be incomplete without some member of the snake family. *There shall the dart-snake*, sometimes translated "arrow snake," *make her nest, and lay, and hatch, and gather under her shade.* This is thought to be a sand viper that hides itself in the sand and, when disturbed, strikes out at whatever has agitated it. There also the *kites* (hawks or falcons, sometimes translated "vultures") gather with their mates.

291

The description of a waste and desolate land is complete. But it is more than the description of a land; it portrays the life which God has abandoned to its sin. There is nothing beautiful or pleasant in this chapter; virtually all the animals and birds listed are categorized by the law as unclean. (A possible exception is the wild goat, the identity of which is uncertain.) Neither is there anything lovely in the life committed to Satan and to sin; it is characterized by confusion and emptiness. Such a life burns as with the fires of hell; it is a place fit only for the unclean and loathsome, an abomination to God and the righteous.

The Certainty of This Devastation (vv. 16–17)

16 Like the certainty of the promised deliverance and blessings, the sureness of punishment and destruction rests on the infallible word of God. *Seek ye out of the book of Jehovah, and read;* this is doubtless the book Isaiah was writing (cf. 8:16; 30:8), which he claimed from the beginning to be the word of Jehovah (1:10). As time passes and one reads this word, he will find that not one detail spoken by the prophet concerning this destruction has failed to come to pass. Jehovah's mouth has spoken the things written therein, and by His Spirit He has gathered the various creatures into the land of ancient Edom. There one will find them all and even sense the demon spirit of the night-monster *(Lilith)* in the sighing of the wind through the ruins.

17 Jehovah Himself has cast the lot determining that this land shall belong to the wild animals. He has divided it by His own measuring line unto them. *They shall possess it for ever; from generation to generation shall they dwell therein.* For lo these two thousand years the land of ancient Edom has been the possession of creatures which inhabit the desert and ruins left by man. Since Jehovah has spoken, it is certain that Edom shall be theirs until the end of time.

CHAPTER 35
The Way of Holiness

The value of contrast—the setting of one condition or situation against another—has long been recognized by instructors. It was Isaiah's favorite method of teaching. In chapters 2–4 he contrasted the ideal Zion of the messianic age with the moral corruptions of the real Zion of his day. In chapters 9–11 he set the terrible treatment of Israel and Judah at the hands of Assyria over against the future glory and permanence of the redeemed remnant under the Root of Jesse. And now he contrasts the desolation of the nations and Edom (ch. 34) with the future glory of Zion (ch. 35).

The prophet has described Edom as a burning desert fit only for the wild, unclean animals that inhabit waste places. The description is not only of a land forsaken by the Lord, but of the soul without God, of the profane, unspiritual person. In contrast to this dreadful picture of Edom, which symbolizes the unending desolation of heathen nations, Israel, though passing through a wilderness of trials and devastation, will someday be glorious, representing the beauty of a soul which, formerly desolated by sin, has now been redeemed. The wilderness through which the redeemed come singing unto Zion is not the road from Babylon to Judah, but the spiritual desert which led to the Babylonian captivity, and eventually to the coming of the Messiah. For after Babylon came the Medo-Persian rule and oppression; it was followed by Alexander, whose empire was totally void of spiritual values. Then came the Egyptian Ptolemies and the Syrian Seleucids oppressing the people and at times desolating the land. There followed the Maccabean wars and the rise of the Pharisees and Sadducees, religious leaders who corrupted the spiritual life of the nation. In the midst of these troublous times the Romans overtook the country. It is obvious that the glorious picture in chapter 35 was not realized in the period between Babylon and the coming of Jesus. Only a messianic interpretation of the chapter fits the text.

The New Song (vv. 1–4)

1 The wilderness and the dry land which are to be glad are not, as some think, the Arabah, located south of the Dead Sea; nor are they the Arabian Desert between Babylon and Jerusalem, which the weary travelers had to circumvent on their return from captivity. The description seems to fit best the religious life of both Jews and Gen-

tiles, which had become like a wilderness and a dry land, waste and void (cf. 27:10; 32:15; 64:10). *The desert shall rejoice, and blossom as the rose*, producing both beauty and moral fragrance. The exact flower indicated by the Hebrew word (which occurs only here and in Song of Sol. 2:1) is uncertain; of the various possibilities suggested by commentators, *rose* serves as well as any. The point is that from unsightly spiritual life there will come beauty of character and sweet incense of the spirit.

2   The former wilderness and dry land will now *blossom abundantly, and rejoice even with joy and singing*, a picture of spiritual beauty and gladness as what was desert now sings the praise of Him who effected the transformation. In contrast to the blight (33:9), *the glory of Lebanon shall be given unto it, the excellency of Carmel and Sharon*. According to promise, Jehovah will lift Himself and restore the glory of these areas. To illustrate the spiritual beauty and joy of Zion's glorious redemption, Isaiah makes mention of the magnificent splendor of Lebanon—with its snow-covered peaks, massive cedars, and fir trees—wooded Carmel, and verdant Sharon carpeted with flowers. *They*—the former wilderness and dry land, and Lebanon once withered away, Sharon like a desert, and Carmel bare of leaves (33:9)—*shall see the glory of Jehovah, the excellency of our God*, demonstrated in their present productivity and restored splendor.

3   The statement of the cause for rejoicing is followed by an exhortation to strengthen the weak hands and to make firm the feeble or tottering knees. Weak hands and feeble knees are symbols of unbelief and defeat, but now in Jehovah and in the new vibrant life He bestows is to be found the strength needed for victory and triumph.

4   There are now a new relationship and responsibility; each individual must encourage his fellows: *Say to them that are of a fearful heart, Be strong, fear not*. We have here another of Isaiah's trios—the hands, the knees, the heart. The heart is the workshop in which all our deeds are wrought. The heart must be bold and courageous, fearless and strong, if the hands are to be strengthened and the knees made firm. *Behold, your God will come with vengeance, with the recompense of God; he will come and save you*. Fear is a sign of unbelief. Today's fears of spiritual failure, of Satan's power, of economic collapse, and of moral defeat must be overcome. We need not

fear, "for [God] himself hath said, I will in no wise fail thee, neither will I in any wise forsake thee" (Heb. 13:5), and "The Lord is at hand" (Phil. 4:5). The Lord will avenge the wrongs done to Zion and His people; He will render commensurate judgment upon those who afflict His people (II Thess. 1:6). At the same time He will provide salvation for those who are disposed to accept it.

Cause for the Rejoicing (vv. 5–7)

5 The similarity between verses 5–7 and Jesus' response to John the Baptist's question from prison, "Art thou he that cometh, or look we for another?" has led many to the conclusion that Jesus had Isaiah's words in mind when He sent reply to John (Matt. 11:2–6). The strong likeness is sufficient reason to conclude that Isaiah's words clearly point to the Messiah who would come and to His work. Although Jesus' reply to John refers to His physical works among men as evidence that He is the one to come, there can be no doubt that Isaiah is looking to the great spiritual work of some future time. The eyes that have been closed to God's appeal will be opened to see the salvation offered by Him; the ears that have been deaf to His call will be unstopped to hear and heed His word (cf. 6:9–10).

6 *Then*—at that time—the spiritually lame will *leap as a hart*, a strong male deer; for Jehovah "will make that which was lame a remnant, and that which was cast far off a strong nation" (Mic. 4:7). And the tongue of those who have been speechless *shall sing*; the way to Zion and the city itself will resound with their songs of rejoicing. There will be a sweeping change in the lives of the people as they are transferred from a desolate wilderness to a luxuriant garden, *for in the wilderness shall waters break out, and streams in the desert*, reviving life and transforming character.

7 *And the glowing sand*, the mirage that deceived many a weary desert-traveler struggling onward in hope of finding a life-sustaining stream, *shall become a pool*, a real lake; *and the thirsty ground springs of water*. The spiritual mirages which have disappointed the people for so many years, leaving their bones to bleach in the burning sand of life, will vanish, and there will be thirst-quenching springs in their stead. But only Jesus can provide the water that transforms the arid

desert life of sinners into a garden of beauty and productivity. He Himself said, "Whosoever drinketh of the water that I shall give him shall never thirst; but the water that I shall give him shall become in him a well of water springing up unto eternal life" (John 4:14); and "If any man thirst, let him come unto me and drink. He that believeth on me, as the scripture hath said, from within him shall flow rivers of living waters" (John 7:37–38). Truly, the thirsty ground of hearts that have come to Him has become springs of water whereby others are refreshed and society made better. In the area fitted only for a habitation of jackals that destroy and for a court of ostriches (34:13), shall be a meadow of lush grass, reeds, and rushes.

Let us review the total picture: majestic cedars of Lebanon, the wooded slopes and dells of Carmel, and the verdant, flower-decked Plain of Sharon. The scene is further enhanced by bubbling springs and a crystal-clear, inviting lake surrounded by lush gardens of grass, reeds, and rushes. It was never intended that this promise be fulfilled in the physical world, but in the spiritual. This glory is given to Zion and is experienced today by those under the blessings of the Messiah.

The Highway (vv. 8–10)

8 *And a highway shall be there, and a way.* The prophet is not speaking of two roads, the broad and the narrow (cf. Matt. 7:13–14), but is emphasizing the character of this way. It is a highway leading to the Zion of God and a way of holiness for the travelers. That only one road is in view is indicated by the singular *it* and *The way* in the following clause: *and it shall be called The way of holiness.* Isaiah has already mentioned God's highway for His people—"And there shall be a highway for the remnant of his people" (11:16)—over which the redeemed of the nations—Assyria, Egypt, and Israel—will travel as a united whole (19:23–24).

This highway is limited to a select few: *it shall be called The way of holiness; the unclean shall not pass over it; but it shall be for the redeemed.* The law specifies two kinds of uncleanness: moral and ceremonial. The prophets give special emphasis to the morally unclean. This passage bars the morally unclean from the highway, leaving only the redeemed. Jesus spoke of the way as narrow and straitened, limited and strict or rigorous, and concluded, "And few are they that find it" (Matt. 7:13–14).

The wayfaring men, yea fools, shall not err therein. Are *the wayfaring men, yea fools,* to be identified with *the redeemed;* and is the prophet then saying that they shall not err (make a mistake, violate an accepted standard of conduct) in the way? Or are they to be identified with the ravenous beasts (v. 9) which shall not be found on the road? Many commentators have thought that the phrase indicates that the way will be so simple that a fool cannot miss it. Just as the highway and the way are one road, so the wayfaring man (a foot-traveler) and the fool are one; both terms are used of the same person. This raises the question whether fools can travel on the way. Leupold explains *fool* as an inexperienced person; others think the term refers to an ignorant or unlearned one. If either of these explanations of the word *fool* be correct, then the passage excludes only the immoral and would allow the interpretation that the way is so simple that a fool cannot miss it. But is the word ever so used? *Fool* translates the Hebrew term *evil* (or *ewil*), which occurs twenty-six times in the Old Testament; in no instance is it used of an inexperienced or an uneducated or unlearned person. The word is used of the despiser of wisdom (Prov. 1:7), of the person for whom wisdom is too high (Prov. 24:7). It is used to describe one who is foolish of lips (Prov. 10:8, 10, margin), in whose mouth is a rod of pride (Prov. 14:3), and whose way is right in his own eyes (Prov. 12:15). The fool despises his father's correction (Prov. 15:5); he is quarrelsome (Prov. 20:3); his foolishness cannot be pounded out of him (Prov. 27:22), and there is no resolving ("rest") of controversy with him (Prov. 29:9). Isaiah uses the word to describe the princes of Zoan, whose counsel had become brutish, dull, erroneous (19:11); and God uses the word to describe His people who "know me not; they are sottish children, and they have no understanding; they are wise to do evil, but to do good they have no knowledge" (Jer. 4:22). The false prophets in Israel are called fools (Hos. 9:7; cf. Mic. 2:11). Surely, such people will not walk in *The way of holiness.* It seems, therefore, that the prophet is not saying that the way will be so simple that an inexperienced or unlearned person cannot miss it, but that the man who despises wisdom, being wise in evil instead, will not make the mistake of walking on it.

9   Again making use of contrast, Isaiah continues his description of those barred from the way and those who travel upon it. *No lion shall be there, nor shall any ravenous beast go up thereon; they shall not be found there.* Not until these fierce destroyers have been regenerated, transformed, their whole nature brought under submission (cf. 11:1–10), will they be found on the way. Fools will not be found there, nor will lions and ravenous beasts until they are changed. Only *the redeemed shall walk there* (cf. v. 8).

10   In this climactic verse, the prophecy reaches its highest point of development. The closing thought of verse 9 is continued: *And the ransomed of Jehovah*, those redeemed by Him, who are traveling over the way of holiness, *shall return, and come with singing unto Zion; and everlasting joy shall be upon their heads: they shall obtain gladness and joy, and sorrow and sighing shall flee away.* What a glorious description of those who have passed through the wilderness of affliction and are now experiencing the ecstatic delight and joy of redemption. They have exchanged sorrowing and sighing, which have fled away, for gladness and joy, which are everlasting and shall not be taken away. In the grandeur of this prophecy we have a foreshadowing of the glories that were to come under the Messiah. The prophets knew that these glories were not for their day, but for ours (I Peter 1:10–12). Under the Messiah we now come unto Zion (Heb. 12:22; cf. Rev. 14:1) by this very way, a new and living way (Heb. 10:19–20). And as we come, let us come in that spirit of rejoicing and thanksgiving so beautifully pictured by Isaiah; for we are heirs of all that to which the prophets pointed (Acts 3:24–26; Heb. 1:2). Let us not be deceived by a materialistic mirage of a sensuous millennial period here on earth.

Historical Link (36–39)

An Introductory Word

For almost forty years Isaiah waged a relentless war against the idolatry and idolatrous leaders of Judah, trying hard to turn enough people to God that destruction might be averted. The climax was reached when Sennacherib besieged Jerusalem (701 B.C.), and the king and other leaders in the city looked to the prophet to appeal to Jehovah that they might be spared from the Assyrian's destruction. Judah turned to Jehovah, at least temporarily. Chapters 36–37 deal with the conflict between Jehovah, the only God, and the gods of Assyria and the nations. Jehovah's victory was devastating.

All commentators recognize that there are problems of authorship and chronology in this section. Second Kings 18–19 is almost identical with Isaiah 36–37. Any noticeable difference in Kings will be indicated by the notation (K.). Delitzsch and Young argue that the account in Kings is from Isaiah, not the other way around. For a rather thorough presentation of the issue see Young's discussion (II. 556–65). The evidence is strong that these chapters were authored by Isaiah rather than by the compiler of Kings. It is possible that Isaiah edited his book late in life, and that this may account for the differences between II Kings 18–19 and Isaiah 36–37.

A more difficult problem concerns the date of Tirhakah, king of Ethiopia, who is mentioned in Scripture only twice, in Isaiah 37:9 and II Kings 19:9. His age at the time of the siege by Sennacherib has led some scholars to conclude that there were two invasions and attacks on Jerusalem by the Assyrian, in 701 B.C. and sometime in the period 689–686 B.C. However, for lack of sustaining evidence, most commentators accept only the invasion of 701. Young concludes, "The chronology is difficult, and we must await further light to understand the solution of many problems" (II. 555). We shall proceed on the assumption of one invasion (701).

CHAPTER 36
The Threat to Jerusalem

The Emissaries Sent by Sennacherib (vv. 1–3)

1 According to most modern writers, the fourteenth year of Hezekiah's reign would be 701 B.C. (see p. 37, n. 1; and p. 226). Confident because Jehovah was prospering him, Hezekiah "rebelled against the king of Assyria, and served him not" (II Kings 18:7). Sennacherib succeeded his father as ruler of Assyria in 705 B.C., and immediately began to settle uprisings in the east. When these matters had been attended to, he moved westward to put down rebellion there. The writer of II Kings inserts here, "And Hezekiah king of Judah sent to the king of Assyria to Lachish, saying, I have offended; return from me: that which thou puttest on me will I bear" (II Kings 18:14). The king of Assyria imposed upon him a tribute of three hundred talents of silver and thirty talents of gold. To raise this amount Hezekiah depleted his treasury and also stripped the gold from the doors and pillars of the temple. Sennacherib boasts that he sacked forty-six towns and villages in Judah, taking away 200,150 (Young says 200,140) prisoners and much spoil.[1]

2 *And the king of Assyria sent* (K.: "Tartan and Rab-saris and") *Rabshakeh from Lachish* (about twenty-five miles southwest of Jerusalem) *to Jerusalem unto king Hezekiah with a great army. And*

---

1. *Zondervan Pictorial Encyclopedia of the Bible*, ed. Merrill C. Tenney (Grand Rapids: Zondervan, 1975), vol. 5, p. 340; cf. Young's translation of Sennacherib's account (II. 566–69).

he (K.: "And they went up and came to Jerusalem. And when they were come up, they came and") *stood by the conduit of the upper pool in the highway of the fuller's field.* Tartan, Rab-saris, and Rabshakeh are not the names of individuals but represent three offices in the Assyrian army. Isaiah names only one, the spokesman, but the word *servants* in 37:24 (cf. II Chron. 32:9) indicates that there were others. It is interesting to note that Rabshakeh was standing on the very spot where Isaiah had told Ahaz not to fear the kings of Syria and Israel (7:3–4). Ahaz's decision to appeal to Assyria for help was now bearing its full harvest.

3 *Then came forth unto him* (K.: "And when they had called to the king, there came out to them") *Eliakim,* who had been appointed to Shebna's position as treasurer or steward (22:20–22); Shebna, who was now the scribe or secretary; and Joah, the recorder or chronicler. The exact function of these offices is not known. The three men who represent Hezekiah complement the three sent by Sennacherib.

Rabshakeh's Defiant Speech (vv. 4–10)

4 Rabshakeh shows a marvelous insight into Jewish faith and life as well as a rude and arrogant contempt for both. He begins his speech by casting aspersions upon the faith of Judah and ridiculing their God. He addresses his message to Hezekiah, but intimidates and belittles him by not recognizing him as a king and by referring to his own king as *the great king, the king of Assyria.* We know from various monuments that this is the title assumed by Assyrian kings. Contemptuously Rabshakeh asks, *What confidence is this wherein thou trustest* against such a mighty one?

5 *I say, thy counsel and strength for the war are but vain words* (K.: "Thou sayest [but they are but vain words], There is counsel and strength for the war"). Rabshakeh is charging Hezekiah with deceiving himself and his people by rebelling against the Assyrian, for where is there any strength to withstand the mighty Assyrian army? He reminds Hezekiah that he has only two sources of strength, Egypt and Jehovah, both of them futile.

6 The ambassador charges that to trust in Egypt is like leaning upon a weak, bruised reed for a staff (cf. 42:3); it will pierce one's hand, leaving him more handicapped than before. This experience will not be peculiar to Hezekiah, for *so is Pharaoh king of Egypt to all that trust on him.* On this point at least, Rabshakeh makes an accurate evaluation.

7   The next statement is probably addressed to the people. But if you trust in Jehovah, He will not help you; for Hezekiah has destroyed and taken away His altars. With all his knowledge of the Jews and their faith Rabshakeh erred here, mistakenly believing Hezekiah's reforms in cleansing the temple and destroying idols to be acts against Jehovah. In truth, they were the opposite; for Hezekiah had said, *Ye shall worship before this altar* (cf. II Chron. 29–31).

8   Having pointed out the futility of trusting in Egypt or Jehovah, Sennacherib's representative urges Hezekiah to renew his pledge and payments of tribute to his master. Rabshakeh cannot refrain from another taunt of contempt for Judah's weakness by offering two thousand horses in return, *if thou be able on thy part to set riders upon them.*

9   Now if you are unable to provide two thousand horses with horsemen, how dare you think you can *turn away the face of one captain of the least of my master's servants?* How dare you *put* (your) *trust on Egypt for chariots and for horsemen?* The man was a master at calumny! By contempt and ridicule he would break the spirit of Hezekiah and the people.

10   Rabshakeh makes one final bold argument which is a real thrust at Judah's faith: Jehovah will not help you, for He sent us. *Am I now come up without Jehovah against this land to destroy it? Jehovah said unto me, Go up against this land, and destroy it.* The claim was partly true; Jehovah had brought the Assyrians against Jerusalem (10:5–6), but whether Jehovah had spoken to Sennacherib on the matter is very doubtful. It seems, rather, that Rabshakeh's words are a daring and audacious stroke of genius based on his knowledge of the Jews and their religion (see the comments on 10:7). Whatever the case, the speaker makes no secret of the Assyrian intention to destroy the land. You cannot save yourselves, Egypt cannot save you, and Jehovah will not save you, for He is on our side; He sent us; your only hope is to capitulate to the Assyrian power. Smith has aptly said that

the envoy sought "to snap each cord of faith in God, honor to the king and love of country" (I. 362).

The Jews' Request (vv. 11–12)

11   The three representatives of Hezekiah request that Rabshakeh speak to them not in the Jewish language, but in Syrian (Aramaic), the diplomatic language of the period, which the three men understand. For fear of weakening the soldiers' courage, Hezekiah's representatives do not want the soldiers and the others on the wall to understand what is being said.

12   As would be expected, Rabshakeh's retort is one of scorn and contempt; his master had sent him to deliver a message to the whole people. He would have them believe that to refuse submission would lead to such a siege that they would be forced to eat their own dung and drink their own urine—a horrible prospect!

Rabshakeh's Second Speech (vv. 13–20)

13   In a more arrogant and scornful demonstration of his contempt for the Jews, Rabshakeh steps forward and in a loud voice addresses the people in their own language, in which he seems to have been very fluent. Again he appeals to the awesomeness of his *great king, the king of Assyria.*

14   Rabshakeh seeks to undermine the people's confidence in and loyalty to their king by asserting that Hezekiah is deceiving them into thinking that he will be able to deliver them (K.: "out of his hand," the hand of the Assyrian).

15   Since Hezekiah your king will not be able to deliver you, let him not deceive you into trusting that Jehovah will prevent the city from being delivered into the hand of the Assyrians. Earlier Hezekiah had spoken with assurance, promising that Jehovah would deliver Judah out of Assyria's hand (II Chron. 32:6–8). But as Leupold suggests, "The statement reflects not so much faith as unwarranted confidence." Hezekiah's claim is about to be tested, and the king will be humbled before Jehovah acts. Rabshakeh is a master at the art of diplomacy, which in reality is the art of deception and intrigue.

Destroy a nation's faith in their ruler, their God, and then themselves, and there is not much left. This is Rabshakeh's objective.

16 The Assyrian ambassador continues his effort to undermine the people's confidence in Hezekiah. He urges them to make their peace with the king of Assyria. The Hebrew expression is, "Make with me a blessing" (margin), which seems to indicate the idea of sharing a blessing—a benefit to both. Rabshakeh then assumes a more positive approach, appealing to the blessings of plenty as opposed to the famine of a siege. To eat of one's own fig tree and vine and to drink water out of one's own cistern is a figure of security, peace, and tranquility (cf. I Kings 4:25; Mic. 4:4; Zech. 3:10). The people will enjoy these pleasures in their own land, but only until Sennacherib completes his siege of the cities and his war with Egypt; they will then be carried away.

17 *Until I come and take you away to a land like your own land, a land of grain and new wine, a land of bread and vineyards* (K.: "a land of olive-trees and of honey, that ye may live and not die: and hearken not unto Hezekiah, when he persuadeth you, saying, Jehovah will deliver us")—very cunningly the speaker softens the concept of being carried away from one's homeland. He ignores the rigors and suffering incurred.

18 Rabshakeh makes a new approach: he warns anew against listening to Hezekiah and then points boastfully to the weakness of various gods in defending their respective nations against the Assyrians. Have any of these gods been able to withstand Assyria?

19 Rabshakeh asks, *Where are the gods of Hamath and Arpad* (see the comments on 10:9)? Although several places have been suggested, the location of Sepharvaim is unknown. We do know that Sargon II settled captives from Sepharvaim in Samaria (II Kings 17:24). Rabshakeh's boast is not quite accurate, for it was Sargon II, not Sennacherib, who had destroyed Hamath (720 B.C.);[2] Arpad was overrun by Tiglath-pileser (740 B.C.) and destroyed by Sargon (720 B.C.).[3] Also, Samaria was destroyed by either Shalmaneser or Sargon (722 or 721 B.C.).

---

2. *Zondervan Pictorial Encyclopedia*, vol. 3, p. 22.
3. Ibid., vol. 1, p. 328.

20   In spite of his knowledge of the Jews and their religion, the Assyrian does not know Jehovah; he confuses the idols of the nations with the true God of the Jews. Little does he realize that Jehovah is using him as the staff of His indignation, and that when his work is accomplished, Jehovah will set His hand to his destruction (10:5–6, 25–27).

The Report to Hezekiah (vv. 21–22)

21–22   *But they* (K.: "the people") *held their peace*, for they had been so instructed by King Hezekiah; they *answered him* (Rabshakeh) *not a word*. Faith seems to lie prostrate at the feet of infidelity. Then with their clothes rent, indicating disgrace, sorrow, and grief—and horror at the blasphemy—the three envoys of the king reported to Hezekiah the words of Rabshakeh. The nation had been humiliated and their God insulted. What shall we do? To whom shall we go?

CHAPTER 37
Victory Through Faith

Desperation, and an Appeal to Isaiah (vv. 1–7)

1   When King Hezekiah heard the report from the three men, he not only rent his clothes, but in the anguish of his soul he also put on an inner garment of sackcloth. Desperate because of the nation's condition and conscious of need for divine help, he went into the house of Jehovah, a place of prayer and reflection. The king's bold words of assurance spoken earlier (II Chron. 32:7–8) were now put to the test.

2   While in the temple, the king sent an impressive embassy of dignitaries to Isaiah: Eliakim, Shebna (see 22:15–25), and the elders of the priests, covered with sackcloth. The prophet's unwavering faithfulness to Jehovah and the fulfillment of a number of his prophecies through trying years were now recognized by the king and his men of state. Truly he was a prophet, a spokesman for Jehovah, worthy of respect.

3   In his plea to Isaiah, the king recognizes the failure of his dealings with the Assyrians and of his looking to Egypt for help, and no doubt he is conscious of his sin in not looking to Jehovah. The people are in a straitened condition, the king is rebuked, and the God of Israel has been blasphemed by an arrogant Assyrian. The nation's condition is like that of a woman who has come to the time of giving birth but does not have enough strength, a figure symbolizing great difficulty (cf. Hos. 13:13).

4   In speaking to Isaiah of *Jehovah thy God*, Hezekiah and his envoys are not indicating that they do not acknowledge Him as theirs also; rather, they are recognizing Isaiah's faithfulness to the Lord and their own occasional wavering in the faith. For Jehovah to *hear* is for Him to take note of and to act upon the blasphemous words of Rabshakeh, who has defied and challenged the omnipotence and absolute deity of the living God—living, in contrast to the lifeless idols of the nations. Hezekiah prays that Jehovah will rebuke the words of Rabshakeh which He has heard. Hope rests only in Jehovah; there is no other source. Hezekiah urges Isaiah to pray for the remnant, probably those remaining in Jerusalem.

5–6   Apparently Isaiah has already been praying, for when the embassy from the king arrives, he has an answer from Jehovah. As he had said to Ahaz, "Fear not" (7:4), so he says to the present king, *Be not afraid of the words that thou hast heard, wherewith the servants of the king of Assyria have blasphemed me.* The word *servants* is actually a disparaging term which Leupold translates "lads" or "young chaps." It is Jehovah whose name and character have been blasphemed, and He is able to handle the matter.

7   Jehovah will put a spirit (a rumor or fear) in the heart of the Assyrian king; Sennacherib will "hear a hearsay" (Delitzsch) which will cause him to return to his own land. What the tidings were is not stated; it could have been tidings of Tirhakah's plan (v. 9), or it could have been tidings of internal problems at home or of adversities here in the west. More probably it was the sense of defeat after the death of his 185,000 men, the realization that he could not cope with Israel's

God (cf. vv. 36–38). And back in his own land God would cause him to fall by the sword.

Sennacherib's Renewed Effort to Persuade Hezekiah (vv. 8–13)

8   Instead of attacking the city, Rabshakeh reported to his king. He went to Libnah, for he had heard that Sennacherib had departed from Lachish and was warring against Libnah, ten miles north. On a relief discovered in Sennacherib's palace at Nineveh, captives from Lachish are pictured bowing before the throne of the king and bringing tribute to him.

9   Having heard that Tirhakah, king of Ethiopia, was coming to fight against him, Sennacherib intensified his efforts to persuade Hezekiah to give up the city into his hands. He preferred not to wage war on two fronts. This may be the *spirit* that Jehovah put in the king (v. 7), for the rumor does agitate him. As we suggested in the introduction to this section, there are unresolved questions concerning Tirhakah, especially regarding his age at the time of the siege. Some think that he was no more than ten years of age, others that he was probably twenty or twenty-one. Until contrary evidence is provided, we will assume that he was of sufficient age to have become king of Ethiopia and to lead an expedition against Sennacherib. He is mentioned in Scripture only here and in II Kings 19:9.

10–13   Sennacherib's letter to Hezekiah is a slightly expanded duplication of Rabshakeh's speech to the people in 36:18–20. He points out the weakness of Hezekiah's God, urging the king and his people not to let Jehovah deceive them, for Jerusalem will be taken (v. 10). He again stresses the destructive power of the kings of Assyria, and reminds Hezekiah that no nation has been able to stand before them. Can you (Hezekiah) expect anything better (v. 11)? To make his letter more impressive, Sennacherib lists six additional cities whose gods were unable to save them from Assyrian destruction. Gozan, located some two hundred miles east of the northeast tip of the Mediterranean Sea, was one of the areas to which the Israelites had been deported (II Kings 17:6; 18:11). Haran, located on the river Balikh, a tributary of the Euphrates, was the city in which Terah and

Abraham settled after leaving Ur of the Chaldees and from which came the wives of Isaac and Jacob. It was destroyed by the Assyrians in 763 B.C. because of a rebellion. Rezeph, an important trade center in Old Testament times, was located between Hamath and the Euphrates. Today the site is occupied by the modern city of Rasāfa. The locations of Telassar, Hena, and Ivvah are unknown.

Hezekiah's Prayer Before Jehovah (vv. 14–20)

14   It appears that both speech and writing were used by Sennacherib's messengers (cf. II Chron. 32:16–19). Upon receiving the letter from him Hezekiah went up again into the house of Jehovah where he spread it before the Lord, not for Jehovah's information, but that He might look with pity on the plight of the king and the people. Delitzsch calls this act "a prayer without words—an act of prayer."

15–16   The king's prayer to Jehovah is expressed in lofty, pure, and devout language, breathing reverence and respect in every phrase. Throughout the prayer the king manifests a firm trust in God and total dependence upon Him. The address is majestic, *O Jehovah of hosts, the God of Israel.* In this exalted title Jehovah is acknowledged not only as Israel's God, but also as the God who controls the armies (hosts) of heaven and of nations. The clause *that sittest* ("art enthroned," margin) *above the cherubim*—probably the two angelic forms above the mercy seat which covered the ark of the covenant within the Holy of Holies—points to Jehovah's place above all angelic beings and identifies Him as the God of the national covenant with Israel. The address is climaxed by recognition of Jehovah as the only God of all the kingdoms of the world and the Maker of heaven and earth. Thus, He is able to save His people from all powers at enmity with Him or them.

17   The king sets forth the petitions of his prayer in five imperative requests: (1) *Incline thine ear, O Jehovah, and* (2) *hear;* (3) *open thine eyes, O Jehovah, and* (4) *see; and* (5) *hear all the words of Sennacherib, who hath sent to defy the living God.* The language is accommodative, attributing human characteristics to God. Actually, Jehovah sees, hears, and knows all. Although Hezekiah and the people have been humiliated and insulted, it is really Jehovah the living God

who has been mocked, scoffed at, and blasphemed. The honor of Jehovah is being taunted, and this is of deep concern to the pious king.

18–19 Hezekiah acknowledges the claim of Sennacherib that *the kings of Assyria have laid waste all the countries* (K.: "nations"), and have burned or destroyed their idol-gods, which were helpless to save themselves and the people who served them, for they were fashioned by man from physical material. Shall Jehovah, the living and all-powerful God, be numbered among such nonentities? The contest is clearly between Jehovah and the heathen deities.

20 Having unburdened his heart before Jehovah in such a reverential manner, the king now makes his earnest request for the people: *O Jehovah our God, save us* (K.: "I beseech thee, out of") *from his hand*; he continues with a plea for Jehovah's honor: *that all the kingdoms of the earth may know that thou art Jehovah, even thou only* (K.: "that thou Jehovah art God alone"). The prayer exalts Jehovah above all creation and heavenly beings, recognizes His eternal Godhood, and reverently acknowledges the dependence of both king and people upon Him for salvation in this trying hour.

Jehovah's Response—An Answer to Sennacherib (vv. 21–29)

21–22 Delitzsch says that this passage "is in all respects one of the most magnificent that we meet with" (II. 99). In response to Hezekiah's prayer, Jehovah says, "I have heard thee" (II Kings 19:20), and then directs His answer to Sennacherib's letter and the ranting of his officers. *The virgin daughter of Zion* and *the daughter of Jerusalem* are parallel expressions, each referring to the city and its people. Isaiah also refers to the "virgin daughter of Sidon" (23:12) and the "virgin daughter of Babylon" (47:1). In each instance he is referring not to the purity of the people themselves, but to the fact that these cities have not been cast down or "raped" by a conqueror. Like a virgin, Jerusalem-Zion has not been defiled by Assyria. She now despises and laughs in scorn at her would-be seducer. She shakes her head in contempt as she looks at ("after," Hebrew) him in retreat.

23 Jehovah challenges the Assyrian with two questions. (1)

Whom hast thou defied and blasphemed? He is not an idol-god, such as you have been wont to cast into the fire, but the great eternal God to whom you are indebted for your very life and who is now using you for His purposes. (2) *And against whom hast thou exalted thy voice and lifted up thine eyes on high?* Sennacherib's voice had been lifted up in arrogant boast and his eyes in haughty defiance, *even against the Holy One of Israel.*

24 *By thy servants* (K.: "messengers"), probably Tartan, Rabsaris, and Rabshakeh (II Kings 18:17), the Assyrian had defied the Lord with the arrogant boast of his inflated pride. He bragged that with the multitude—he loved that word—of his chariots he had *come up to the height of the mountains, to the innermost parts of Lebanon.* No land or height had stood in his way; he overcame them all. He then boasted of what he would do; he would *cut down the tall cedars thereof, and the choice fir-trees thereof; and I will enter into its farthest height* (K.: "lodging-place"), *the forest of its fruitful field.* Although he may have ascended into the Lebanon range, he seems here to be speaking figuratively of Judah and Jerusalem. In spite of his previous conquests, the Assyrian was determined to have all Judah and Jerusalem lying at his feet, completely conquered. (For Lebanon as a symbol of Jerusalem and Judah, see Jer. 22:6 and Ezek. 17:3.) The *forest of its fruitful field* apparently refers to the fruit-bearing trees, the vineyards and gardens of Judah.

25 The vaunting heathen continues to describe what he has done and what he will do. When wells were lacking, he had *digged and drunk* (K.: "strange" [foreign]) *water,* "water supplied by a region which had none at other times," which belonged not to the soil (Keil). He then vaunts of what he will do; there will be no barrier to taking Egypt. The Nile with its canals and tributaries will be no hindrance to him, for with the sole of his feet he will dry them up—certainly an extreme hyperbole.

26 Jehovah continues His reply to the heathen king, making it clear that what had been done was of Jehovah's predetermined purpose and not by the king's power. God asks, *Hast thou not heard how I have done it long ago, and formed it of ancient times?* As early as the time of Moses Jehovah had declared that if His people rejected His law, He would bring a nation against them from afar. This nation would not regard the life of young or old (Deut. 28:49–50), eventually carrying Israel into captivity (Deut. 28:41), and scattering them from one end of the earth to the other (Deut. 28:64). The Lord added to this threat, "And I will make your cities a waste, and will bring your sanctuaries unto desolation" (Lev. 26:31). Jehovah is now using the Assyrians to accomplish the purpose (cf. 10:5–12) which He long ago determined. So the laying waste of fortified cities, turning them into ruinous heaps, is not an accomplishment over which the Assyrian king can boast, for he is only an instrument in Jehovah's hand. Complete destruction was averted at this time by the long-term efforts of Isaiah and by the king's fervent intercession; the foretold devastation had to await the Babylonian invasion.

27   Therefore, because Jehovah was at work through the heathen nation, *their inhabitants* (the residents of the destroyed cities) *were of small power, they were dismayed and confounded*, helpless to resist. Jehovah now uses three figures to illustrate their weakness and inability to withstand: (1) they were like green grass or herbs of the field, just waiting to be devoured; (2) they were like grass which springs up on a flat housetop in the wet season, but withers when the rains pass; and (3) they were like *a field of grain* (K.: "blasted") *before it is grown up*. Sennacherib like all rulers needed to learn, "The king's heart is in the hand of Jehovah as the watercourses:/He turneth it whithersoever he will" (Prov. 21:1); and "The horse is prepared against the day of battle;/But victory is of Jehovah" (Prov. 21:31).

28–29   Nothing in the ruler's life is hid from the eyes of Jehovah; God knows his every move, the entirety of his life, and in particular his raging, his anger against the God of heaven. Because of Sennacherib's intense feeling against God and because of his arrogancy, which is fully known to the Lord, *therefore will I put my hook in thy nose, and my bridle in thy lips*, cruel devices by which captives were dragged away. The bridle is probably a ring put in the lips—certainly a heinous means of torture. As captives are led away by the will of their captor, so Sennacherib will return to his homeland by the will of Jehovah.

A Message of Assurance to Hezekiah (vv. 30–35)

30   Through the prophet, Jehovah has addressed Sennacherib,

declaring His own involvement in the king's victories and now in his defeat. That word finished, the Lord addresses Hezekiah with a message of assurance. As He had given Ahaz a sign, "even the king of Assyria" (7:17), so now, after the coming of the Assyrians, He gives Hezekiah a sign. The sign given is that in spite of the devastation inflicted by the invaders, *ye shall eat* until things return to normal. The sign does not involve a miracle, but assurance that by divine providence the people of Judah will have food until they can once again plant and harvest. This year and next, because of the war, they shall eat that which springs up from kernels which have been spilled. Then the third year they shall return to the normal activities of planting and harvesting. The planting of fields and replacing destroyed vineyards the third year will be the divine assurance that the Assyrian invasion is over and that Hezekiah and his people need fear Assyria no more.

31–32 Not only shall there be the restoring of fields and vineyards, but there shall also be the replenishing of the depleted population; for the escaped remnant of the nation *shall again take root downward, and bear fruit upward.* Without those who will have perished in the war and the thousands carried away as captives, the population will be greatly diminished. It appears that the bulk of those who will escape are the ones who will have taken refuge in Jerusalem-Zion. This remnant shall now return to their ruined homes, villages, and lands to rebuild them. God gives assurance of their ability to succeed: *The zeal of Jehovah of hosts will perform this.*

33 The Lord gives Hezekiah a final word of assurance concerning the king of Assyria: *He shall not come unto this city.* When I turn him back from whatever city he may be besieging, he will return home. The basic implements of siege are all mentioned—the archers who seek to clear the wall, those who follow protected by the shield, and finally, if necessary, those who cast up mounds or earthworks about a city. Hezekiah can be sure Jerusalem will be saved, for *thus saith Jehovah.*

34–35 Wherever Sennacherib may be, at the time Jehovah determines, *By the way that he came, by the same shall he return.* In his haste he will not turn aside to attack Jerusalem. No greater assurance of this can be given than the word, *For I will defend this city to save it.*

312

Isaiah had been preaching this message from the beginning, but before God could act, the people had to be brought to realize their need for His help. He will defend the city for His own sake—for the sake of His honor and absolute Godhood—and for the sake of David, whose seed He had sworn to preserve till the coming of Him who would fulfill the promise (of II Sam. 7:11–16).

It Is Done (vv. 36–38)

36 The writer of the Chronicles tells us that upon receipt of the letter from Sennacherib both Hezekiah and Isaiah "prayed because of this, and cried to heaven" (II Chron. 32:20). The parallel account in II Kings 19:35 adds, "And it came to pass that night," indicating that the smiting of the Assyrian came immediately after the delivery of Isaiah's message. The place of execution is not stated. Was the king still at Libnah, having sent a detachment against Jerusalem? Was he on his way toward Egypt to meet Tirhakah? Was he himself with his army on his way to Jerusalem? Or were they some other place? We do not know. Nor are we told how the destruction was effected. It is simply stated, *And the angel of Jehovah went forth, and smote in the camp of the Assyrians a hundred and fourscore and five thousand.* It is folly to attempt a human explanation. Two similar instances in Israel's history present parallels. In the case of the death of the first-born of the Egyptians, the executor of Jehovah's will is called "the destroyer" (Exod. 12:23); in the case of the death of the seventy thousand following David's sin, he is called "the angel of Jehovah" (II Sam. 24:16). In all three instances the deaths were supernaturally inflicted. Further evidence of the miraculous nature of the slaughter of the Assyrians is that those in the camp who were not slain were ignorant of what happened until morning, for it is said, *And when men arose early in the morning, behold, these were all dead bodies.* Of course there is the question of whether the men who arose were Assyrian soldiers who were not slain or people in the neighborhood. Seemingly they were the surviving soldiers, including Sennacherib; in either case the incident was of such a nature that none knew what was happening until the work was done.

37–38 The remaining history of Sennacherib is related very briefly. The king and the remnant of his army departed immediately for Nineveh. Although twenty years elapsed before the king was murdered by two of his sons, Isaiah passes over the intervening period. The two sons who slew their father fled for refuge to the land of Ararat to the north. Sennacherib's son Esar-haddon ruled in his stead. Young aptly observes that Hezekiah prayed unto his God, and his God heard and answered him; Sennacherib prayed unto his god, but his god did not hear. Instead, death came to the king in a violent manner.

It is not impossible for Isaiah to have added this historical point. If he began his prophetic work at about twenty years of age, he could have lived until the murder of Sennacherib, which was about sixty years from the beginning of Isaiah's ministry. The account was probably added as he edited his book before his death.

Two facts stand out clearly before us: (1) Through Isaiah's many prophecies, Jehovah had declared what He would do, and (2) He did it. But how soon was this wonderful deliverance by Jehovah forgotten! Manasseh, Hezekiah's son, was one of Judah's most wicked kings, leading the people into an apostasy of such magnitude that even righteous Josiah's reforms could not overcome it. Destruction would eventually come. In this history there is an enormous lesson for people of every land and age. The people of Judah soon forgot it. We must not be like them!

CHAPTER 38

Hezekiah's Sickness and Recovery

Hezekiah was twenty-five years old when he began his twenty-nine-year reign (II Kings 18:2). Since God added fifteen years to his life at the time of his sickness, it occurred in the fourteenth year of his reign. If he died in the year 686 B.C., as most (though not all) scholars hold, his sickness occurred in 701 B.C., the year of Sennacherib's effort to take Judah and Jerusalem. The events of chapter 38 are simultaneous with (or immediately prior to) chapters 36–37. Second Kings 20:1–11, which runs parallel to the first eight verses of our present chapter, bears out the view that the Assyrian siege and Hezekiah's illness were simultaneous. We will continue to use the notation (K.) to indicate notable differences in the account in II Kings.

Hezekiah's Sickness and Prayer (vv. 1–8)

1 The phrase *In those days* indicates that Hezekiah's illness occurred in the days of the Assyrian invasion. That he was *sick unto death* means that death was inevitable, at least from the human point of view. Jehovah sent Isaiah to tell the king, *Set thy house in order; for thou shalt die, and not live.* The statement as recorded is very blunt. To set one's house in order is to make a will or some other provision ensuring that one's affairs will be properly taken care of after death. It is possible that what is recorded is simply the substance of the prophet's message; it may have been presented in a more compassionate tone. However, at times God's word can be almost curt.

2–3 The king turned his face to the wall, apparently to shut out the world from before him as he prayed; for, being a devout man, he would naturally turn to God. His plea is based not on self-righteousness, but on his life of faith. He had lived before Jehovah in truth and with a pure heart, striving always to do what was right in Jehovah's sight. He may have erred in the matter of Egypt, but, unlike his father Ahaz, his error was a matter of judgment, not rebellion. Though there is always the desire of an individual to continue to live, Hezekiah's petition was not altogether selfish, for he was concerned about his nation as well. The world was in turmoil. Judah was at war with Sennacherib, and once that was over, there would be the problems of postwar reconstruction. Also, at that time, with no heir to the throne (cf. II Kings 21:1—Manasseh was born three years after Hezekiah's illness), the Davidic line was in jeopardy.

4 (K.: "And it came to pass, before Isaiah was gone out into the middle part of the city ['the middle court,' margin], that") *Then came the word of Jehovah to Isaiah*—this is an indication that there was only a short time-lapse between Isaiah's delivery of the message and God's reversal of His decree. (Whether Isaiah was in the middle of the city or the middle court, the time lapse would have been brief.) Here is a positive example of the mighty power of prayer, illustrating that "the

supplication of a righteous man availeth much in its working" (James 5:16).

5   *Go* (K.: "Turn back"), *and say to Hezekiah* (K.: "the prince of my people"), *Thus saith Jehovah, the God of David thy father, I have heard thy prayer, I have seen thy tears: behold* (K.: "I will heal thee; on the third day thou shalt go up unto the house of Jehovah. And") *I will add unto thy days fifteen years.* The God of David will give Hezekiah time to sire a son through whom the promise made to David will be fulfilled. Manasseh was born three years later (II Kings 21:1).

6   The promise that Jehovah will defend the city and deliver the king and the city out of the hand of the king of Assyria further indicates that the events of this chapter occurred during the period of Assyrian aggression. Although Isaiah does not here include "for my servant David's sake," as in 37:35, the reference to David in verse 5 and the inclusion of the phrase in the parallel passage in II Kings (20:6) make it clear that the promise to David is a part of Jehovah's motivation in saving Jerusalem.

7   (K.: "And Isaiah said, Take a cake of figs. And they took and laid it on the boil, and he recovered. And Hezekiah said unto Isaiah, What shall be the sign that Jehovah will heal me, and that I shall go up into the house of Jehovah the third day? And Isaiah said") *And this shall be the sign unto thee from Jehovah, that Jehovah will do this thing that he hath spoken.* This is probably the correct place for verses 21–22; however, since II Kings does not include Hezekiah's psalm of thanksgiving (Isa. 38:9–20), it may be that their placement after the song is correct (see the comments on verses 21–22).

8   At this point, between verses 7 and 8, the account in II Kings introduces additional material. The question is asked: "Shall the shadow go forward ten steps, or go back ten steps? And Hezekiah answered, It is a light thing for the shadow to decline ten steps: nay, but let the shadow return backward ten steps. And Isaiah the prophet cried unto Jehovah; and he brought the shadow ten steps backward, by which it had gone down on the dial of Ahaz" (II Kings 20:9–11). Jehovah caused the shadow to return ten steps or degrees on the dial. Efforts to reconstruct the dial which Ahaz used for keeping time have been rather fruitless. Likewise, efforts to determine the manner in which the shadow was caused to return ten steps or degrees have been

vain. If we acknowledge that it was a miracle, and certainly it was, then it cannot be explained; for an explained miracle is nonsense. One either accepts a miracle or he rejects it; he does not and cannot explain it. Apparently, the sickness (boil or carbuncle) of Hezekiah was providentially cured by Jehovah through the natural means suggested by Isaiah. However, the sign given to the king that he would be healed was a miracle performed by Jehovah through a supernatural intervention.

Hezekiah's Psalm of Lamentation and Thanksgiving (vv. 9–20)

9 Some commentators question Hezekiah's authorship of the psalm on the grounds of certain difficulties of language and material. but the text states that it is the writing of Hezekiah king of Judah following his sickness, and there seems to be no valid reason for rejecting the claim. The poem falls into three divisions: (1) lamentation (vv. 10–14); (2) the blessings of affliction (vv. 15–18); and (3) rejoicing (vv. 19–20). The account in II Kings omits the psalm.

10 *The noontide* ("tranquillity," margin) or quiet period *of my days* is that time when Hezekiah should have been enjoying the prime of life and the excellency of his rule. But instead he must go *into the gates of Sheol* (for Sheol see the comments on 5:14), and once those gates have closed, one cannot return. The glory of the state of the righteous dead as revealed through Christ was not yet known in Hezekiah's day. In death he would be deprived of years of life here.

11 Hezekiah will not see Jehovah in the land of the living; he knows not what awaits him in the unseen world beyond death. Likewise, he will no more see man *with the inhabitants of the world.* His thought is that he will be completely separated from God and man, from life as he has known it.

12 Like a shepherd's tent which is transferred from one place to another when the pasturage is consumed, so will Hezekiah's earthly dwelling, his life, be removed. A second figure further illustrates life's transitoriness. Like a weaver, he has rolled up his life, and now God will cut it off from the loom ("thrum," Hebrew), the weaving being complete. From the morning when the weaving had begun, God

controlled his life; and at evening when it is completed, He will make an end of it.

13 This verse is difficult, but the thought seems to be that in his sickness Hezekiah, faced with the reality of approaching death, had quieted himself through the long night. Then came the terrible realization: *as a lion, so he breaketh all my bones.* Possibly this realization came when Isaiah delivered to him the devastating message, *Set thy house in order; for thou shalt die, and not live* (v. 1). Though Hezekiah had looked death in the face as he contemplated its meaning, there had been hope that he might recover. But now with this message from God, the hope was taken away; he was left crushed at the prospect of impending death.

14 Now, like a chattering crane or swallow making an incomprehensible melancholy noise, or a dove with its mournful song, Hezekiah moans. Lifting his eyes heavenward until they fail, he cries, *O Lord, I am oppressed,* a strong word meaning "to be crushed, trampled by an abuse of power;"[4] *be thou my surety,* take responsibility for my defense, protect me. Though death seems certain, Hezekiah in faith holds on to God, asking that He be his assurance.

15 At this point there is a noticeable change in tone. From lamentation over his confrontation with death, the poet shifts to the blessings that have come out of his sufferings. The tone is now one of surprise at his unexpected deliverance and of the joy of life: *What shall I say?* Hezekiah seems to be at a loss for words. Jehovah had spoken, promising him fifteen additional years of life and also deliverance from Assyria. He had spoken and acted. In saying, *I shall go softly,* the king employs the same word used by the psalmist when he said, "I went with the throng, and led them to the house of God" (Ps. 42:4). Like one in a procession to the house of God, Hezekiah will walk humbly and solemnly all the days of his life because of the bitter memories of the sickness from which the Lord had delivered him. However, he apparently forgot this vow when Merodach-baladan's embassy arrived to congratulate him on his recovery (cf. ch. 39).

16 *O Lord, by these things men live*—what things does the poet

---

4. *Theological Wordbook of the Old Testament,* ed. R. Laird Harris (Chicago: Moody, 1980), vol. 2, p. 705.

have in mind? Apparently he is thinking of experiences such as he had just passed through, the promises and providence of God at such times, and the blessings that accrue from trials. The true life of the spirit is realized through affliction and its blessings. Which is correct, *Wherefore recover thou me*, or the alternate reading, "So wilt thou recover me" (margin)? Probably the latter, for God had so promised. *And make me to live*, that is, to find the true life through fellowship with thee.

17   Through suffering Job found a new concept of God: "I had heard of thee by the hearing of the ear;/But now mine eye seeth thee" (Job 42:5). He had something he could never have had apart from the experience through which he had passed. Similarly, Hezekiah had found a new concept of life; through the bitterness of his experience he had found peace. Also, he saw Jehovah's love in a new light; for through love God had delivered his soul from the grave, *the pit of corruption*, and had cast all of the king's sins behind His back. He had forgiven and blotted them out of His memory.

18   The king uses three words to denote that from which he had been delivered: Sheol, death, and the pit. Death is the soul's departure from this life and entrance into the realm of Sheol, the place of departed spirits. The pit is the grave, where the body sees corruption and must lie until the resurrection. The words *Sheol* and *death* are here used metaphorically for those who are there. We must in this instance not think of them from the Christian point of view, but from the Hebrew point of view. Hezekiah cannot imagine the dead praising or celebrating the Lord's glory, nor does he envision God's truth reaching them in Sheol. Though Hezekiah certainly had a belief in life beyond death, yet to him the gates of Sheol (v. 10) completely sealed off a realm where praise, celebration of fellowship, and truth cannot be found. On the other hand, through the victory of Christ the Christian concept of the dead transcends the Old Testament concept just as the heavens are higher than the earth.

19   The full measure of the king's rejoicing now finds expression. In contrast to the inability of those whose souls are in Sheol and whose bodies have gone down into the grave, he cries, possibly shouts, *The living, the living, he shall praise thee, as I do this day*. Experiencing the exuberance of life, he not only expresses his own

praise of Jehovah, but also calls upon all who truly live, that is, those who are in right relationship to God, to join him in paying homage to God. It matters not whether he is speaking of himself (that Hezekiah's heir was not born until three years after his sickness does not necessarily mean he was childless—sons may have died, or he may have had daughters) or is echoing a principle from the law (Deut. 4:9; 6:6–7) when he urges that the father pass truth on to his children. It is in this way that truth is transferred from generation to generation and that the righteousness whereby a nation shall be exalted prevails.

20   The psalm closes with an exultant word of assurance: *Jehovah is ready to save me.* He stands ready to save at any time from any grievous or deathly situation, not only Hezekiah, but also all who will turn to Him in faith and obedience. *Therefore we will sing my songs with stringed instruments/All the days of our life in the house of Jehovah.* Ahaz had closed the doors of Jehovah's house, setting up altars to false gods throughout Jerusalem (II Chron. 28:24); but Hezekiah had restored proper worship, including the songs and music which both David and he had introduced (II Chron. 29:25–28). With his life extended, the Assyrians defeated, and true worship restored, Hezekiah's life could now be what it should be.

Hezekiah's Healing (vv. 21–22)

21–22   Many commentators and several translations follow the account in II Kings, inserting these two verses between verses 6 and 7, where they logically belong. The Hebrew has it, "Isaiah said," not "had said," and "Hezekiah said," not "had said." By making the verbs past perfect, the present translation appears to be an effort to allay the difficulty of the rather strange location of the passage. However, since we do not know why it occurs here in Isaiah's text, it is the wisest course simply to say so, and leave the matter as it stands.

CHAPTER 39
Not Assyria, but Babylon

This chapter could bear several titles, for example, "The Embassy from Merodach-baladan," "Pride That Led to a Fall," or "Pride's Penalty." But inasmuch as the chapter serves as a transition from the Assyrian threat to preparation for the Babylonian captivity, the title selected seems to be most appropriate.

The most severe difficulty facing the commentator at this point is dating the passage. It is impossible to pinpoint the exact time of the messengers and letters from the Babylonian king. For a brief discussion of Merodach-baladan's rule see the introduction to chapter 21, and for the time of Hezekiah's sickness see the introduction to chapter 38. It is possible that Hezekiah's sickness occurred earlier than we suggested in the preceding chapter, but this raises other problems. At this point, determining dates with certainty is beyond our ability.

Prophet Versus King (vv. 1–4)

1   At *that time*, the time of Hezekiah's recovery, or shortly thereafter, *Merodach-baladan the son of Baladan*, of the house of Yakin (apparently the founder of the dynasty), sent letters and a present to Hezekiah. Merodach-baladan is remembered as a clever and ambitious king and a bitter enemy of the Assyrian kings Sargon and Sennacherib. Sending embassies from one country to another for political reasons was not unusual (cf. 18:1–3; 30:1–7); however, this one was. It was most unusual for a king to send congratulatory letters and a present to a far distant king on his recovery from sickness. Also, there was the difference in worldly stature and rank between the king of Babylon and Hezekiah of Judah. There are two probable reasons for the embassy. One was to investigate the miracle of the sundial, for they came "to inquire of the wonder that was done in the land" (II Chron. 32:31); the other reason, which is generally assumed by Bible students, was that the king of Babylon needed all the assistance against Assyria that he could get.

2   There can be no doubt that Hezekiah was flattered by this attention, for it is said, "his heart was lifted up" (II Chron. 32:25), and he *was glad of* (K.: "hearkened unto") *them*. Seemingly he had forgotten that it was Jehovah who had spared his life and the city, and that he had vowed to go *softly* all the days of his life (38:15). As his forefather David had succumbed to the lust of the flesh, and Sol-

321

omon had yielded to vanity and pomp, so Hezekiah, one of Judah's most admired kings, yielded to flattery and pride. The flesh is terribly weak! Apparently, since paying the heavy tribute to Sennacherib, he had accumulated considerable wealth, the extent of which is indicated in II Chronicles 32:27–29. Much of this may have been gifts sent to him following his sickness (II Chron. 32:23). By showing the men from Babylon all his wealth, silver, gold, aromatic spices, precious oil (used in anointing), and the armor among his treasures, it appears that he was trying to impress them that he was a king worthy of high regard. *His dominion*, meaning "rule" or "realm," probably refers to his government. It is doubtful that he took them on a tour of Judah, but likely he showed them the working of his governmental system. It is difficult to imagine a king gladly showing a potential enemy his whole arsenal and wealth, but such is the power of flattery.

3   The emphasis on *Isaiah the prophet* and *king Hezekiah* focuses attention on the positions of the two men: one is the spokesman for Jehovah, the other His vicegerent in political affairs. Whatever may have been the personal feelings or regard each had for the other, the prophet is in no way awed or intimidated by the king or apprehensive of possible results. He asks three questions: (1) *What said these men?*—Hezekiah does not answer; (2) *and from whence came they unto thee?*—Hezekiah's answer smacks of worldly pride. They came from a far country, even from Babylon, *unto me*. This last word is an obvious boast.

4   The prophet fires the third question: (3) *What have they seen in thy house?* The king responds with admirable honesty; he hides nothing: *All that is in my house have they seen.* Without reserve he admits to having shown the Babylonians all his treasures. Here we have another tragedy of acting irresponsibly on human intuition and fleshly motivation without asking guidance from Jehovah (cf. Josh. 9:14).

The Word of Doom (vv. 5–8)

5   Apparently the prophet had been charged with the divine message before he came to the king; for straightway he said, *Hear the word of Jehovah of hosts.* Isaiah had denounced the alliances of Ahaz with

Assyria and of Judah's politicians with Egypt, and now he is ready to denounce any alliance or relationship of Hezekiah with Babylon. In the mind of the prophet all such associations of God's people with the world are a rejection of dependence on the Lord and, therefore, sin. Such relationships sound the death knell for truth and right.

6   The prophet begins his message with his customary call to attention, *Behold*. He continues, *The days are coming* (he gives no intimation as to when), *when all that is in thy house*—all that Hezekiah has acquired or gathered together—*and that which thy fathers have laid up in store until this day, shall be carried to Babylon*. This is Isaiah's first unmistakable reference to Babylon as the land of captivity. *Nothing shall be left*; this is guaranteed, for thus *saith Jehovah*. Again the lesson is taught that as we look on the fruits of our labor, we are obliged to say, "And, behold, all [is] vanity and a striving after wind, and there [is] no profit under the sun" (Eccles. 2:11); and also, "the world passeth away, and the lust thereof" (I John 2:17). In Hezekiah is illustrated the vanity of all things earthly!

7   Not only will Hezekiah's treasured possessions be carried into Babylon, but also his descendants will be taken there and serve as eunuchs in the king's house. Whether *eunuchs* refers merely to mutilated individuals or to officers in key positions of government (cf. Dan. 1:3) is uncertain. It is more probable that in this case the latter is the meaning.

8   Hezekiah humbly submits to the will of God, grateful for any mercy shown him by the Lord: *Good is the word of Jehovah which thou hast spoken*. The prophet has been true to his mission, Jehovah has shown mercy, and now the king expresses his feeling of gratitude and thanks: *For there shall be peace and truth in my days*. Though there may be an element of selfishness in his response, the king should be given credit for his gratitude that the nation will now have peace and that he can end his reign in tranquility. Note that the nation is not named in Isaiah's prophecy of deportation and captivity; only the king's house is singled out. But because of Manasseh's sins and his influencing the nation to evil beyond that of the heathen nations (II Kings 21:9–15), Judah became worse than Israel and Sodom (Jer. 3:11; Ezek. 16:46–47). Consequently, it was declared

323

that the nation would be carried away for fifty years, after which a remnant would return (Mic. 4:10). (We use the figure of fifty years since the deportations covered a period of twenty years. The captivity lasted seventy years, but Jerusalem was empty of Jews for only fifty.)

Hope for Troublous Times (40–66)

Introduction (40)

40:1–11. A Prologue
40:12–31. The Incomparable Greatness of Jehovah

An Introductory Word

The prophet Isaiah is incontrovertible proof of the power of one man who stands with God in a crisis. Under the influence of his preaching and his unfaltering faith in Jehovah, Judah weathered the storm of the Assyrian invasion (734–701 B.C.); but the time came when the nation was carried away into Babylon, the dominant kingdom of the world following Assyria. The prophet closed Part One of his book (chs. 1–39) with a prophecy to Hezekiah: *Behold, the days are coming, when all that is in thy house, and that which thy fathers have laid up in store until this day, shall be carried to Babylon: nothing shall be left, saith Jehovah* (39:6). Such a prediction could have been made only by divine inspiration.

The subject of Part Two (chs. 40–66) is the preparation of the people for captivity in Babylon. They are assured of their return and of Jehovah's care for them until the coming of the Seed of Abraham. Confidence in their eventual return from exile would of course depend upon their faith in God and in His ability to keep His promise; therefore, the first major section of Part Two (chs. 41–48) is devoted to God's claim to power, which rests on His sole deity and Godhood. As proof of His power and sole deity, He points to His ability to foretell events and then bring them to pass. Of all evidence for the inspiration of the Bible there is none more convincing than the declaration of events to come and their fulfillment as foretold. This also affords grounds for faith in every crisis; God is a promise-keeping God.

This section is not restricted to the raising up of someone who will deliver the people from the Babylonian exile, but it looks beyond to a superior Deliverer who will free all peoples from a greater bondage—the Servant of Jehovah who will deliver from spiritual captivity. Out of the Servant's work will emerge a spiritual kingdom destined to endure forever, a kingdom that will overcome all political kingdoms. Anything human or physical is foredestined to pass away; only that which is spiritual will endure.

From the beginning in Eden there was continuous conflict between the spiritual and the fleshly. God was working toward bringing forth a spiritual kingdom which would have His own qualities of holiness and eternal endurance. It should not be surprising that this purpose was constantly before Him and that it should have been flashed before His people throughout the Old Covenant period. Isaiah was given special insight into this work; he was one of God's major instruments to set it forth in prophecy. In his time the conflict between the world and the divine kingdom was intense. The great Assyrian power represented the world of lust and conquest, which opposed the spiritual kingdom of God. It was flesh against spirit, human versus the divine. Out of the defeat and destruction of the physical and human the spiritual would arise.

It should not, therefore, seem strange that the Messiah and His kingdom come to the forefront over and over in the Book of Isaiah. The message had meaning to the people of that day and is also of consequence for all succeeding generations. One must be careful not to see the Messiah in passages where Isaiah did not intend to refer to Him, but one should be equally careful not to overlook references to Him when they are present. The Book of Isaiah is more than a chronicle of history with moral principles attached; it is a book of messianic hope and redemption.

Because of its strong predictive element, Part Two has been ascribed by many commentators to one or more authors who lived during or after the period of the captivity. R. N. Whybray, a modern scholar, goes as far as to say, "Chapters 40–66 are unintelligible if interpreted as a product of the eighth century B.C., but yield excellent sense if seen against the background of later periods."[1] Understand-

---

1. R. N. Whybray, *Isaiah 40–66*, New Century Bible Commentary (Grand Rapids: Eerdmans, 1981), p. 20. For a brief but comprehensive summary of the liberal and conservative views, see John T. Willis, *Isaiah* (Austin: Sweet, 1980), pp. 20–30.

ing God's purpose in this section, however, I believe that the chapters are perfectly intelligible if the Isaianic authorship is accepted.

Of Isaiah's word concerning Cyrus, which Whybray attributes to a second Isaiah (Deutero-Isaiah), this modern scholar further says, "It is a paradox that his influence should have made itself felt despite the fact that in his basic prediction he was to a very large extent mistaken." And in regard to his prophecies of the return from captivity, his promise "of a future of unalloyed happiness and political power remained entirely unfulfilled."[2] Such statements utterly ignore the fact that Jehovah was speaking through the prophet; they also ignore the conditions attending His promises. Moses had laid down the conditions of the return from exile and the blessings to follow; before their return from captivity the people were (1) to return unto Jehovah, and (2) to obey His voice in all that He had commanded them, "thou and thy children, with all thy heart and with all thy soul" (Deut. 30:2–3). Upon their compliance with Jehovah's terms, He would bring them back into their land, "and he will do thee good, and multiply thee above thy fathers" (v. 5; Ezek. 36:8–10). Moses then repeated God's demands of the people: "thou shalt return and obey the voice of Jehovah, and do all his commandments which I command thee this day" (Deut. 30:8). The conditions of the blessings are summed up in two "if"-clauses: "If thou shalt obey the voice of Jehovah thy God, to keep his commandments and his statutes which are written in this book of the law; if thou turn unto Jehovah thy God with all thy heart, and with all thy soul" (v. 10). These conditions must not be overlooked in interpreting the second part of Isaiah's prophecy.

Jehovah is more specific and equally as emphatic on this point as He speaks through Jeremiah (again notice the "if"-clauses): "At what instant I shall speak concerning a nation, and concerning a kingdom, to pluck up and to break down and to destroy it; if that nation, concerning which I have spoken, turn from their evil, I will repent of the evil that I thought to do unto them. And at what instant I shall speak concerning a nation, and concerning a kingdom, to build and to plant it; if they do that which is evil in my sight, that they obey not

---

2. Whybray, *Isaiah 40–66*, pp. 37–38.

my voice, then I will repent of the good, wherewith I said I would benefit them" (Jer. 18:7–10). The first of these principles is illustrated in Jehovah's threat that Zion would be plowed as a field, Jerusalem would become heaps, and the mountain of the house as the high places of a forest (Mic. 3:12). The people repented; therefore Jehovah did not carry out this threat. The second principle is illustrated in the remnant that returned from exile. They did not rebuild the house of Jehovah until twenty years after the return, and then only at the insistence of the prophets Haggai and Zechariah; and it was a hundred years from the time of their return before the walls were completed under Nehemiah. According to both Ezra and Nehemiah, the men of the returning remnants, acting contrary to the law, put away their wives and married foreign women; and in his book Malachi paints a dark picture of the religious and moral conditions of the people after their return. Because the people did not comply with God's conditions, He could not fulfill the promises He had made concerning blessings when they returned to their homeland. It is totally unfair to the Lord and His word given through the prophet to say that His promises failed or that He was mistaken. It is important, also, to remember that the Book of Isaiah is a deeply spiritual book and that many of the prophet's promises of fullness and completeness look for their fulfillment in spiritual Zion, in a spiritual kingdom under the spiritual Servant. We will point out in the commentary that this principle is implicit in the promises.

CHAPTER 40

A Prologue (vv. 1–11); The Incomparable Greatness of Jehovah (vv. 12–31)

The first nine chapters of Part Two are devoted primarily to the test of deity. Jehovah challenges the idols of all peoples to a contest. Who is able to declare the end from the beginning and the things to come as if they already are? Only Jehovah! The idol is powerless to predict anything, either good or evil; he is impotent to declare anything, either to come or already past. These chapters are filled with challenges to and satire on the folly of all idolatry. The conflict between Jehovah, the Creator of heaven and earth, and the idols, inanimate creatures of human folly, is in view throughout this section.

A Prologue (vv. 1–11)

Verses 1–11 of chapter 40 serve as a prologue to the remainder of the book. Part One (chs. 1–39) closed with the dark anticipation of captivity; and now in contrast, Part Two opens with the joyous assurance of comfort and redemption. The prophet speaks to the people who will find themselves in Babylonian exile over a hundred years in the future. They will be oppressed under the heel of a powerful tyrant, their beloved city will be in ruins, and the temple razed to the ground.

Comfort: Pardon through grace (vv. 1–2)

1   In former times the prophetic voice had been primarily one of doom, but now it is one of comfort: *Comfort ye, comfort ye my people, saith your God.* The voice of God speaks to the remnant. This verse is the theme of the remainder of the book. Although Isaiah will speak again in threatening tones of accusation and judgment, yet above the lightning flashes of judgment and the peals of thundering condemnation of sin, there will be the song of comfort in hope.

2   *Speak ye comfortably to Jerusalem*—Jerusalem stands for the surviving remnant, for at the time in view the physical city will lie in ruins and the people will be in captivity. The word of comfort is spoken "to the heart" (margin), the center of emotions which has long lain crushed under the consequence of sin and rebellion. It is now to be comforted by the God who has been spurned and rejected for empty vanities of wood and stone, the God who has sent faithless Judah into captivity for discipline. Three words of comfort are offered, each introduced by *that.* Cry unto Jerusalem (1) *that her warfare is accomplished,* finished. Her long period of bondage and misery brought on by sins is now at an end; night is giving way to the dawning of a new day. Cry unto Jerusalem (2) *that her iniquity is pardoned.* This expression of divine grace presupposes repentance; for there can be no pardon, either then or now, apart from the sinner's

repentance. It may be inferred that the conditions which Jehovah through Moses had long before stipulated as prerequisites to fulfillment of the promise (Deut. 30:2–3, 8–10) have been met. And cry unto Jerusalem (3) *that she hath received of Jehovah's hand double for all her sins*; the term *double* does not mean that Jehovah has rendered double punishment for their sins, but that the scales have been balanced. The sin on the one hand of the scales has been balanced by ample judgment and suffering on the other. Similarly, in Messiah's Zion Jehovah will recompense another double, balancing the scales of sorrow with joy (Isa. 61:7). Jeremiah uses the same figure (16:18; 17:18) as does Zechariah (9:12).

Make preparation (vv. 3–5)

3   In this verse the speaker is left unidentified. The prophet simply says, *The voice of one that crieth, Prepare ye in the wilderness the way of Jehovah.* The message must receive the emphasis; the speaker is secondary. The voice is not that of Jehovah, for the way is to be made level for Him. Shortly before Jerusalem was destroyed, Ezekiel saw a vision in which Jehovah withdrew from the temple and city, removing toward the east (Ezek. 11:23). And now through the trackless wilderness and desolate desert (cf. 21:1), He is returning to Jerusalem with His people after an absence of fifty years, the period of the captivity (586–537 B.C.). The voice cries that the way for His return be prepared. Using the figure of preparation for the journey of a great king, the prophet says, *Make level in the desert a highway for our God.*

4   *Every valley shall be exalted, and every mountain and hill shall be made low; and the uneven shall be made level, and the rough places a plain.* The voice is not speaking literally of road building, but figuratively of the hearts of the people. They are to remove every barrier and fill every hindering depression, so that they will be prepared for a new relationship with Jehovah and for the rich outpouring of blessings that He has promised.

5   *And the glory of Jehovah shall be revealed, and all flesh shall see it together.* All peoples will marvel when Jehovah raises up Cyrus to deliver His people out of Babylon (as Isaiah foretold over one hundred years before the event). The remnant will go back to Jerusalem,

where they will rebuild the temple and settle. But a greater wonder is in store for all flesh when John the Baptist comes crying in the wilderness, "Make ye ready the way of the Lord" (Matt. 3:1–3). He will claim to be only a voice (John 1:23), and his mission will be to introduce Him in whom the glory of God will be revealed (John 1:14, 18). What assurance did the people have that all this would come to pass? *The mouth of Jehovah hath spoken it;* that was sufficient; nothing more was needed. The ability of Jehovah to fulfill His word is one of the central themes of the following chapters.

The enduring word (vv. 6–8)

6   The voice that urges preparation is followed by a voice saying, *Cry;* to which another voice answers, *What shall I cry?* The reply is, *All flesh is grass, and all the goodliness thereof is as the flower of the field*—a declaration of the weakness and perishable nature of all flesh, even great military leaders who have conquered the world. What is going to be done will not be accomplished by human achievement or by fleshly power. Human strength (goodliness) is inadequate for such a work, for it is like grass, and its glory like a flower that is only for a moment. This is a striking illustration of the impotence and transitoriness of flesh.

7   *The grass withereth, the flower fadeth, because the breath of Jehovah bloweth upon it; surely the people is grass.* When Jehovah blows upon human strength and glory, they wither and fade away like grass which today is green but withers and passes away when a blistering wind from the desert blows upon it. Whether Judah in her vaunting pride and independence from God, or heathen Babylon, or a present-day nation, every people will wither, die, and fade away when the breath of God blows upon them.

8   The voice now expresses the truth to which it has been leading: *The grass withereth, the flower fadeth; but the word of our God shall stand forever.* What a glorious claim and assurance! In the midst of a decadent society and a crumbling world, pressured on every hand by human power and diabolic wickedness, what a sustaining assurance it is to know that there is something permanent, something enduring! The character of God, the word of God, and the promises of God shall never fail but shall endure eternally. *The mouth of Jehovah hath*

spoken it (v. 5) and *the word of our God shall stand forever*; this is the only real ground of hope.

Declare the tidings! (vv. 9–11)

9   The voice of grace has given assurance of pardon; the voice of hope has looked to the coming of the glory of God; the voice of faith has declared that His word stands forever. Now the voice of evangelism speaks: Tell the glad story. But who is to tell the glad tidings? Is Zion the recipient or the announcer of the good news? The text has it, *O thou that tellest good tidings to Zion* (and in the next clause, *to Jerusalem*), *get thee up on a high mountain*; the margin has Zion-Jerusalem doing the announcing, "O Zion, that bringest good tidings . . . O Jerusalem, that bringest good tidings." From the general context it seems that the latter rendering is preferable. Jehovah has returned to Zion-Jerusalem; and now that He has returned, let Zion-Jerusalem get up on a high mountain and shout the message to all the people and cities of Judah. The prophet continues, *Lift up thy voice with strength; lift it up, be not afraid; say unto the cities of Judah, Behold, your God!* Let Zion-Jerusalem shout to all the daughter cities the glad tidings that God's word has stood; He has returned to Zion and His promise is fulfilled. There is now no power of which to be afraid. Fulfillment of this promise is so certain that the prophet speaks as if it were already accomplished.

10   The theme of the good news is now made known: when Jehovah fulfills the prophecy, (1) He *will come as a mighty one*, as a conqueror exerting infinite power as opposed to the limited power of man, which is like *grass* (v. 7); (2) *his arm will rule for him*—Jehovah's arm is the power by which He overthrows His enemies, redeems His people, and exercises His rule; and (3) *Behold, his reward is with him, and his recompense before him*—He rewards the redeemed, and the redeemed are His reward.

11   The simile now changes. From a figure of power and rule, Isaiah turns to a figure of tenderness and compassion, a shepherd tending his flock: *He will feed his flock like a shepherd, he will gather the lambs in his arm*. With His arm, that is, His strength and power, He both gathers and then protects and provides for them. He will *carry them in his bosom, and will gently lead those that have their*

334

young. What a beautiful and appropriate picture with which to close this prophecy that began with comfort and hope. And what a wonderful way to introduce the trials and victories which lie before the people, and to foreshadow the redeeming work of God through Cyrus and ultimately through the Messiah.

The Incomparable Greatness of Jehovah (vv. 12–31)

There is no more appropriate title to sum up the theme of this passage than that in the American Standard Version: "The Incomparable Greatness of Jehovah." The assurance that God would visit His people in Babylon, redeem them, and care for them, rested on one ground—"the mouth of Jehovah hath spoken it" (v. 5), and "the word of our God shall stand forever" (v. 8). Their God was the author of this word. The prophet makes no argument for God's existence because he was writing for people who should long have accepted that fact. Rather, Isaiah's task was to get the people to recognize God for who He is, to realize that His being is His pledge.

Having seen their city and temple destroyed, and having experienced terrible indignities at the hand of the Babylonian tyrant—the tortures of hunger, the pain and fatigue of travel, and the humiliation of exile, bondage, and servitude—the people of Judah would find their faith strained to the breaking point. They would stumble into one of two pitfalls: they would either trust in false gods, which would only add to their state of hopelessness; or their imperfect knowledge of the true God would sink them in a state of despondency. In either case, they would need assurance and a refreshing of faith. They would need to be reminded of God's infinite greatness, His unfaltering love, and His unwavering care for His own.

Too often we ascribe to Jehovah our own weaknesses and shortcomings. When we are impotent to help ourselves, we decide that God is impotent to intervene and act on our behalf; when weariness overcomes us, we infer that God is weary and has withdrawn from us; in the midst of our failures and frustrations, we conclude that God has no purpose and that everything is in the hands of blind fate. But Jehovah knows what is in man; and anticipating our every need, He makes provision for us. Over a hundred years before Judah went into captivity, Jehovah made provision through Isaiah His prophet for their spiritual needs. Having declared the basis of their hope to be His own word (vv. 5, 8), the Lord impressed His faltering people with His incomparable greatness, an indisputable guarantee of His word. *To whom then will ye liken me, that I should be equal to him? saith the Holy One* (v. 25), is, then, the theme of this section (vv. 12–31).

Jehovah and creation (vv. 12–14)

12   The prophet begins by speaking of Jehovah and His creation, not to emphasize the magnitude and greatness of the universe, but to show by comparison how exceedingly much greater is its Creator. The prophet selects five divisions of God's universe to impress his point: (1) *Who hath measured the waters in the hollow of his hand?* Imagine the vastness of all the oceans and seas of earth, yet He is able to measure them in the palm of His hand. (2) Next the writer points to the heaven and asks, Who has *meted out heaven with the span? Span* here refers to the distance between the end of the thumb and the tip of the little finger. God determined the expanse of heaven by the span of His own hand.[3] (3) Transferring the reader's attention from heaven back to earth, the prophet inquires, And who *comprehended* (determined the exact amount of) *the dust of the earth in a measure?* As we might measure a quantity in a measuring cup, so God measured out the dust of the earth. And (4) who *weighed the mountains in scales*— as one would weigh a bale of hay or cotton— *and* (5) *the hills in a balance*—as a pharmacist weighs small quantities in a delicate balance? The symbolism exalts the greatness of God and staggers the imagination of man.

13–14   As the prophet meditates on the creation, his mind goes behind it to the wisdom of its Creator: *Who hath directed the Spirit of Jehovah, or being his counsellor hath taught him?* Who taught Him in the way of justice, and who gave Him the wisdom and insight to plan so perfectly a universe of such magnitude? The answer: no one.

---

3. For a suggestive article on the magnitude and immensity of the universe, see Rick Gore, "The Once and Future Universe," *National Geographic*, June 1983, pp. 704–49. However, the author's hypothesis as to origin is far-fetched and totally lacking in validity. Only the biblical answer to this question is satisfactory.

When we come to Jehovah, we have reached the absolute; for He is absolute in wisdom, absolute in knowledge, absolute in power. There was none to show Him the way of understanding; it was and is inherent with Him. The elders about the throne sing the song of creation: "For thou didst create all things, and because of thy will they were, and were created"(Rev. 4:11). Here we reach the ultimate; the creation is the product of God's own purpose, plan, and execution. He had no counsellor. This is the Supreme and Holy One in whom Jehovah would have His people trust. Surely, such a glorious Creator can watch over and deliver His people!

Jehovah and the nations (vv. 15–17)

15   What about the power of great military nations which would invade the land and carry away the people? Can they hold Judah against God's will? *Behold*—give attention! *The nations are as a drop of a bucket;* they are as utterly insignificant as a drop which is spilled from a bucket, which runs down the side, or which remains in the bucket after it has been emptied. They *are accounted as the small dust of the balance,* to be blown or wiped off as of no account. This is not to say that Jehovah has no concern for the nations, but that they are utterly powerless in comparison to Him.

16   Now the prophet turns to the failure of earth to provide an adequate sacrifice for God. If all the wood of Lebanon were piled together and all the animals thereof were sacrificed upon it as a burnt-offering, that would be entirely inadequate for the Creator of all things.

17   *All the nations are as nothing before him; they are accounted by him as less than nothing, and vanity*—they are as nought. God's power has not diminished and that of the nations has not increased; the relative power of each is now as it was then. Nations have risen, exulted in their glory, and vanished; but Jehovah and His power remain infinite and eternal.

Jehovah and the idols (vv. 18–21)

18   At this point is introduced the theme of the contest between Jehovah and the idols. In scorn, which at times is one's most effective weapon, He laughs them into oblivion. *To whom then will ye liken*

God? or what likeness will ye compare unto him? Can a manmade image really represent God, who is spirit? Only man is fashioned in the divine likeness.

19 With keen irony the prophet describes the idol as a workman's casting overlaid with gold by the goldsmith and decorated with silver chains fashioned by a silversmith; all of the work is by human hands.

20 If a man cannot afford an idol fashioned of metal, he chooses a tree and has a workman make of it a graven image that cannot move but must be carried about; if made from a stump in the ground, it cannot even be moved about. The absurdity of the whole picture is evident in the fact that man could not create the gold and silver or the tree from which the idol is fashioned; all have been created by the infinite God. Yet man fashions images from these materials and worships them.

21 *Have ye not known* (this)? *have ye not heard? hath it not been told you from the beginning?* At this point an appeal is made to history. From their beginning Israel had been warned against idolatry (Exod. 20:4–6; Deut. 5:8–10); time and again they had seen the impotency of idols to save them from disaster. The lesson is hard to learn; men continue to make and to worship as gods images patterned after the figments of their imagination. They will eventually rue the day of such folly (Rom. 1:20–25).

Jehovah and the princes of earth (vv. 22–25)

22 The infinite and eternal glory of God continues to occupy the prophet's thoughts. Jehovah, who sits above the circle or dome of the earth, looks down upon its inhabitants as grasshoppers, insignificant and totally dependent upon Him. (The prophet does not mean to suggest here that the earth is round.) Jehovah is described as stretching out the heavens as one would spread out a tent.

23 *That bringeth princes to nothing; that maketh the judges of the earth as vanity*—the incomparably great God can make earth's greatest as nothing. They sink into oblivion; they are but confusion and chaos, an empty space. Think back upon the so-called great men of our own age who strove for high place and tried to hold on for dear life, only to fall, victims either of their own or someone else's caprice or the infirmities of the flesh.

24 The great of the earth are like the grass when blown upon by the dreaded east wind from the desert: they are carried away like stubble before a storm. Scarcely are they planted, with their stock not yet deep rooted, when Jehovah blows upon them like the blast of a furnace, *and they wither, and the whirlwind taketh them away as stubble.*

25 In the face of the contrast between human frailty and divine power, glory, and might, *To whom then will ye liken me, that I should be equal to him? saith the Holy One.* There is no being or creature in the universe with whom God can be compared; He is in a class all His own. He transcends His creation; nations are like a drop of a bucket in His sight; rulers and judges are raised up, serve briefly, and then are removed—all at His pleasure; and man's idols, which are shaped out of things God created, are powerless nonentities. He and His Messiah are the sole beings in the universe that are worthy of man's worship and devotion.

Jehovah and the glorious assurance (vv. 26–31)

26 There come times in the life of man when he needs to lift up his eyes to the stars, not to worship them as did the ancients, nor to look for guidance as do modern astrologers, but to see behind them the face of their Creator. To those of His people who will find themselves in Babylon, feeling that He has forgotten them, Jehovah says, *Lift up your eyes on high, and see who hath created these, that bringeth out their host by number; he calleth them all by name; by the greatness of his might, and for that he is strong in power, not one is lacking.* Night after night each star is brought out by its Creator; not one is overlooked. If God, who loves His children as a devoted Father, looks after each inanimate heavenly body, will He not care for His sons and daughters? At times we may feel that God has forgotten and that He does not care. When this feeling comes, let the discouraged one lift up his eyes and beyond the stars see a God of infinite power and a Father equally infinite in love; He cares and never forgets.

27 In Babylon the captives will charge Jehovah with being indifferent to their condition. But in the light of the divine greatness, power, and tender care for each individual, how can one say, *My way* *is hid from Jehovah,* and the just treatment *due to me is passed away from my God?*

28–29 There now follows a summary of God's greatness, on which each can rely: He is (1) *The everlasting God, Jehovah,* the eternally existent, all-provident One. He is (2) *the Creator of the ends of the earth.* He (3) *fainteth not, neither is weary.* Because we grow weary, we are prone to ascribe the same weakness to our God; but frailty is totally foreign to His being. (4) *There is no searching of his understanding;* His omniscience is as wonderful as His omnipotence; He knows the thoughts and needs of each. (5) *He giveth power to the faint; and to him that hath no might he increaseth strength.* Appropriation of this great power will lie within reach of every discouraged Jew in Babylon if he will but look up and lay hold on it. The same power is offered the child of God today (Eph. 1:19–23; 3:14–21).

30–31 The Lord now presents a contrast: *the youths,* those who are in the prime and strength of manhood, *shall faint and be weary, and the young men shall utterly fall. But,* in contrast, *they that wait for Jehovah* (another favorite expression of Isaiah), they that let Him lead, who rely upon Him for help, *shall renew their strength.* They shall find sustaining power in Jehovah, who gives strength to the faint. In the joy of that strength and hope, *they shall mount up with wings as eagles; they shall run, and not be weary; they shall walk, and not faint.* In faraway Babylon there will come the news of Cyrus's decree that the Jews may return home. At this news those who have waited for Jehovah shall soar to heights of joy as they anticipate returning to their homeland. A rush of preparation for the journey will follow; but before they arrive home, there will be the long trek from Babylon to Jerusalem. And so shall it ever be. The joyous enthusiasm and hope we experience with conversion, soaring on high as with wings of an eagle, are followed by eager preparation, learning and building a foundation of faith, and running without growing weary; but before the heavenly home is reached, there is yet the long journey of trials and testings—a walk on which the sojourner of faith shall not faint. In the wearisome and monotonous everyday walk of life faith may at times become dull and hope dim; in such hours look up and grasp anew the vision of God and heaven.

The Contest Between Jehovah and the Idols (41–48)

An Introductory Word

In chapters 41–48 Jehovah introduces three characters whom He calls to His service: Cyrus, His shepherd, whom He will raise up from the east to deliver His people from Babylon; Israel, His blind and deaf servant; and the ideal Servant, the one in whom His purpose will be fulfilled. The word *servant* is not used in a derogatory sense, but refers to one to whom a solemn responsibility has been entrusted. Smith comments, "The Hebrew word for *servant* means a person at the disposal of another—to carry out his will, do his work, represent his interests" (II. 272). The captivity and return of Judah, the raising up of Cyrus over a hundred years hence, and the appearance of the messianic Servant several hundred years in the future will be proof of Jehovah's Godhood and sole deity; only an infinite being can foretell and bring such things to pass. The utter impotence of the heathen gods will also be proved, for they will be helpless to aid the nations or to hinder Jehovah in His purpose.

341

Jehovah begins revealing His purpose by introducing Cyrus, through whom He will deliver His people from Babylon (41:2–7, 25; 44:26–45:7; 46:11; 48:15). Next Israel is introduced as Jehovah's chosen servant whom He will not cast away, though blind and deaf (41:8–10; 42:18–25; 43:8–13; 44:1–5, 21–28; 45:4; 48:20–22). The third, and by far the greatest, is the ideal Servant, who holds a prominent place in the remainder of the book (42:1–9; 49:1–13; 50:4–11; 52:13–53:12). And finally, there are the "servants" (plural), the redeemed of Jehovah, who are of significance in the latter part of the prophecy (54:17; 56:6; 63:17; 65:8–15; 66:14, etc.).

Jehovah's conflict with and victory over the heathen gods is the major theme of chapters 40–48. He challenges the idols to a contest of Godhead and claims victory on the grounds that only He can foretell the end from the beginning. Having proved His eternal deity, He then asserts to Israel His right to their faith and trust.

The Hebrew names for God in this section attest His uniqueness. Three names in particular declare His sovereign deity. *El* (which is used fifteen times) means "the mighty one," the personification of strength and power. Though occasionally used of heathen gods, the word also refers to the true personal God. *Eloah* (used once in Isaiah), which occurs almost exclusively in poetic books (forty-one times in Job), is an ancient word for God which sometimes appears in parallel construction with *Rock* (44:8; cf. Deut. 32:15; Ps. 18:31). As the appellation *Rock*, which indicates permanence, attests to God's ability to protect His people, *Eloah* in Isaiah 44:8 sets Him apart as Israel's only true Rock of refuge. As such Jehovah is a terror to the wicked and a comfort to His people (Pss. 50:22; 114:7; 139:19). *Elohim* (which occurs twenty-one times) is translated in various passages as "gods," "judges," "angels." "The plural ending is usually described as a plural of majesty and not intended as a true plural when used of God." It conveys "the unity of the one God [while] allowing for a plurality of persons."[1] The plural indicates fullness and completeness of strength.

Among the other names found in chapters 40–48 is, of course,

---

1. *Theological Wordbook of the Old Testament*, ed. R. Laird Harris (Chicago: Moody, 1980), vol. 1, p. 44.

Jehovah (*Yahweh*—sixty-six occurrences), which designates Him as Israel's covenant God, the "I Am," the eternally existent one—"before me there was no God formed, neither shall there be after me" (43:10). The term *Lord* (*Adonai*—40:10; 48:16) emphasizes His rule over all (the King James translation of *Yahweh* as "Lord" is confusing). *The Holy One (of Israel)* (which occurs ten times) sets Him in contrast to Israel's sins; He is absolutely separated from them. As the Holy One of Israel, He is Israel's *Creator* and *King* (43:15), his *Maker* (45:11), who formed him as His servant (44:21). He is Israel's *Redeemer* (six occurrences), a just God and *Saviour* (43:3; 45:21) who *blotteth out thy transgressions*, remembering sins no more (43:25; 44:22). These names, which express His essence, clearly set Jehovah apart from the idols; only He can make genuine claim to these titles and to what they signify.

CHAPTER 41
Jehovah's Confrontation with the Idols

Jehovah Addresses the Nations (vv. 1–7)

1 Chapter 40 opened with an address from Jehovah to Israel; in contrast, the present chapter begins with an address to the nations. The peoples of the *islands*, the faraway coastlands surrounding the Mediterranean Sea, are charged to be silent before Jehovah, and listen. In words reminiscent of the last verse of chapter 40, where we are told that those who wait for Jehovah shall renew their strength, the nations are charged to renew their strength by turning to whatever the object of their trust might be, so that they might come before Jehovah in a court contest. After they have heard Him, then let them speak, have their say. The *judgment* to which they are to come may refer to the decision in a case of litigation or to establishment of the just claims of God.[2] Young explains it as "the passing of a sentence." Possibly there is an element of all three in the word—the decision of a

---

2. These are two of thirteen possible meanings of the Hebrew word *mishpat* (*Theological Wordbook of the Old Testament*, vol. 2, pp. 948–49).

court case in which the just claims of God are established and sentence is passed upon the nations and their gods.

2 Jehovah challenges the nations and their gods: *Who hath raised up one from the east?* He speaks as if it were already done, though it will be some one hundred and fifty years in the future before it is accomplished. Although the deliverer is not named until later (44:28; 45:1), it appears almost certain that Cyrus is in view here. He was stirred up to let the Jews return (cf. II Chron. 36:22). Persia was east of Babylon, hence, *from the east.* The phrase *in righteousness,* which the King James mistranslates "a righteous man," is tricky. In accordance with His righteous standard, God will raise up a deliverer; He will stir up Cyrus to serve His righteous cause. Young has it that God will raise up someone whom "righteousness calls to its foot." However, Smith translates the phrase, "him on whose footsteps righteousness [i.e., success or victory] waits" (II. 120, 238). Jehovah will give him to rule over kings, casting them down to the dust with his sword and pursuing them with his bow like helpless stubble. (For more on Cyrus see 44:28–45:6.)

3 The deliverer will be unhindered as he pursues his enemies; he *passeth on safely, even by a way that he had not gone with his feet.* In his uninterrupted conquest he pursues a course which he has never before taken. He will act with such speed and completeness that there will be no need to return.

4 The deliverance will be the accomplishment of Jehovah, who determines the destiny of generations. This determined destiny is according to the people's choice of faith and obedience or unbelief and disobedience. Jehovah was with the first generation and He will be with the last; He is the everlasting absolute, the eternally existent one.

5 The speed and victory of the conqueror whom Jehovah will raise up will throw the nations into a state of fear and terror. *The ends of the earth tremble*—those in the most remote areas of the then known world. They respond to Jehovah's call (v. 1), drawing near to give heed.

6–7 In what seems to be complete confusion, each tries to encourage his neighbor. Something must be done in defensive preparation, but what? The answer is to build larger and more elaborate idols, so each workman encourages the other. Working furiously together the carpenter cheers on the goldsmith, the man who smoothes with the hammer aids the forger of iron, and all encourage the solderer. When finished, the idol is nailed fast so that it can neither move itself nor be moved. Such fervor reminds us of the present-day arms race—more and greater arms, warheads, and ships, even though God still controls. As He was with the first generation, so will He be with the last and with all those between.

Jehovah Addresses Israel: What He Will Do (vv. 8–20)

8   In this word of encouragement Jehovah reminds the people of the great honor which had been bestowed upon the nation. This honor is indicated in the names which they bore from their father. As descendants of your illustrious father Israel, you have power; for of him it was said, "Thou hast striven with God and with men, and hast prevailed" (Gen. 32:28), and so can you. As Jacob, the "heel-snatcher" or "supplanter," he had gained the birthright from his brother; and Jehovah chose to make the covenant with Jacob (Exod. 19:3–5). Through this famous and distinguished father the people are the seed of Abraham, *my friend* and also "my servant" (Gen. 26:24), to whom God made the promise of a great nation, both physical and spiritual (Gen. 12:1–3). Though they are now cast down, this promise is their heritage. As the people *whom I have chosen*, they will not fail.

9   Jehovah had called Abraham out of Ur of the Chaldees (Gen. 11:31; 12:1), and in Abraham He had chosen His nation. From the Judean point of view, Abraham was called *from the ends of the earth.* Since they are Jehovah's by divine choice, He will not cast them away. The selection of Cyrus as deliverer (he is never called God's "servant," though he served as such, but is referred to as Jehovah's shepherd and His anointed [44:28; 45:1]) will not alter God's relationship to Israel, His servant; for the Lord has different purposes in mind for each.

10   In the light of Jehovah's election and purpose, He will encourage His people with the richest of promises. As His chosen nation they are told to *fear . . . not, for I am with thee*—with this assurance, what is there to fear?—and to *be not dismayed* ("look not

345

around thee [with anxiety]," margin), *for I am thy God.* Jehovah makes three promises: (1) *I will strengthen thee;* (2) *I will help thee;* (3) *yea, I will uphold thee with the right hand of my righteousness.* The right hand had long been considered a symbol of strength and power and the source of blessings. In His righteousness Jehovah will call Cyrus to do His bidding; He will also uphold Israel, that is, make the nation to stand in the strength and power of that same righteousness, accomplishing His purpose through them.

11–13   With assurance of God's power in righteousness, there is no reason to be discouraged. *Behold,* listen, give attention to the word of the Lord. In three categories Jehovah sums up the heathen nations that oppose Israel: (1) *they that are incensed against thee;* (2) *they that strive with thee;* and (3) *they that war against thee. Incensed* indicates a burning anger that would seek to consume Israel; to *strive* usually indicates physical combat, but here it probably refers to verbal confrontation, to quarrel; and *they that war against thee* indicates military encounters. Those who so oppose Israel shall be put to shame, fall into disgrace, be confounded, confused, and humiliated; they shall be frustrated in all their plans. They shall become as nothing, perishing as though they have never existed; and when sought, they shall not be found. The guarantee of these promises is the fact that Jehovah is the God of Israel. He will hold their right hand, guiding and directing them amidst the opposition of their enemies. He will say, *Fear not; I will help thee.*

14   For the third time Jehovah urges Israel, *Fear not* (cf. vv. 10, 13); be not afraid or frightened. *Thou worm Jacob, and ye men of Israel,* do not allow the dread of your enemies to be upon you. *Worm* signifies lowliness and helplessness, the present condition of Judah and the condition they will experience in Babylon and following their return. But though brought low and reduced to only a handful, they are still *men of Israel,* heirs of the promises made to their father Jacob. The promise, *I will help thee,* is repeated (cf. v. 10), with an added emphasis, *saith Jehovah, and thy Redeemer* (the one who shall redeem thee) *is the Holy One of Israel.* Under Old Testament law the nearest of kin was to serve as "redeemer"; that is, he was obligated to avenge murder, to deliver from slavery, and to restore to the original owner property which had fallen into the hands of creditors. The

Holy One of Israel will act as the Redeemer of His people, avenging wrongs done against them, delivering them from their captors, and returning to them their heritage.

15 From their lowly state as a worm and the furnace of affliction through which they must pass, Jehovah will bring the nation forth as *a new sharp threshing instrument having teeth.* The teeth are the spikes underneath the sled or heavy board which is pulled over piles of grain to sever the wheat from the chaff. Judah will *thresh the mountains* (strong nations), beating them to dust, and *make the hills* (the smaller powers) *as chaff.* The Lord is not speaking of physical conquests by the Jewish nation, but of spiritual conquests by the faithful ones. Through Jehovah and the strength of His righteousness they will survive and triumph as all world powers are brought to nought.

16 Like chaff winnowed and carried away by a strong wind, the heathen nations will be scattered throughout the earth regardless of how high and mighty they may have been. In contrast to the threshed, winnowed, and scattered nations, Israel in triumph will rejoice in Jehovah her God and *glory in the Holy One of Israel.* Again, the prophet continues to emphasize the superior power and enduring triumph of spirit and righteousness over the weakness of flesh, a principle as eternal as is God Himself.

17 The language of the following paragraph (vv. 17–20) is highly figurative; any effort to interpret it literally misses the point. There is nothing in the passage that would limit the promises to the period of captivity and the return of the remnant from Babylon. God is emphasizing His abiding concern, care, and provision for His own; His purpose will not fail. Having assured Israel of power to overcome and vanquish their enemies, the Lord now promises that out of His gracious love He will provide for their personal needs. Because they are *poor and needy,* in both physical and spiritual want, the Lord will make due provision of necessities. Because they are in danger of perishing from physical and spiritual thirst, Jehovah will provide life-sustaining water. He provided in the wilderness as His people traveled to Canaan, and He will continue to provide unto the end. He will not forsake those that are His.

18 On bare heights where water is not ordinarily found (cf.

30:25), rivers will be made to flow, and in the valleys fountains will abound. Although the word *wilderness* may refer to a pastureland or an uninhabited region, in this instance it probably refers to a desert-like area. Jehovah will make the desolate waste a pool of water, and in dry places He will cause springs to flourish (cf. 35:6–7). Apart from Jehovah and His spiritual provision, all life is a desert. Although the language here certainly has reference to the Babylonian captivity and the return, it also looks far beyond.

19 Besides the precious water that Jehovah will supply in abundance, He will also provide trees for both shade and building material. There are seven (the number of completeness) varieties named. The cedar, acacia, and fir (possibly cypress) are trees well known to us. The myrtle tree, an evergreen that grows to a height of thirty feet, is found in abundance in Palestine. The box-tree, a hardwood, reaches a height of about thirty-five feet. The oil-tree (oleaster) and pine are uncertain.

20 Four verbs identify God's purpose in providing water and trees: (1) *that they may see*—look upon and thereby discern, comprehend; *and* (2) *know*—through acquaintance with Jehovah the people will become aware of and recognize truth; *and* (3) *consider*—the Hebrew word used here sometimes means "to assign something to someone"; hence, they will assign to God a new position in their thinking; *and* (4) *understand*—they will realize who their benefactor is. God's supreme purpose is that they *together*, united as one, might realize *that the hand of Jehovah hath done this*, and that the ultimate realization of their objectives will be His doing.

The nation was soon to face a period of exile from their homeland, the result of their low spiritual and moral state. And the return from captivity would in turn be followed by a long period of subjection to foreign powers. It seems, therefore, to this writer that the Lord was preparing His people for the coming ordeal by assuring them that He would care for them throughout it all. As we said above, giving this passage a literal interpretation misses the point. The physical and material references (water and trees) are merely incidental; God's supplying of spiritual needs and His guarantee of victory are the basic themes here.

Jehovah Challenges the Idols: What Can You Do? (vv. 21–29)

Jehovah has declared what He will do; He now challenges the idols to prove themselves. He rests His claim to be the only God on His knowledge of the future. If they are Gods (with a capital "G"), declaring the future should be easy for them too.

21 Jehovah had first challenged the nations, calling them to appear with Him in a court of law to determine who is God. Terrified at the report of "one from the east" who would overrun everything in his path, they had turned to manufacturing idols which they thought would protect them (vv. 1–7). In the second stage of the court trial, Jehovah now challenges the idols themselves. *Produce your cause*, your case before a legal court, *your strong reasons*, a defense for your existence or being, *saith the King of Jacob*—that Jehovah was viewed as the actual King of Israel is evident in the fact that all the human rulers of the nation were said to sit on His throne (see, e.g., I Chron. 29:23).

22 In bringing forth their cause and strong reasons, let the idols *declare unto us what shall happen . . . that we may consider them.* The plurals *us* and *we* probably refer to Jehovah the King and the people over whom He rules, rather than to Jehovah and His heavenly court. Jehovah had declared that He would bring forth one from the east; now let the gods declare *the former things* and *the latter end of them.* The idols are not necessarily being challenged to make some pronouncement regarding Cyrus; rather, they are being challenged to tell of any purpose they might once have had (or may now have) for their subjects. Surely, the idols must have had some purpose which they have already revealed and which can now be evaluated as to whether it has been fulfilled. If not, they should make known at the present time any purpose of theirs which will have some bearing on the future.

23 Indeed, if the idols be gods, they can declare what will happen to the nations that serve them, whether deliverance or judgment is in store. *Do good, or do evil*—reveal what you purpose to do for your worshipers and what evil will befall other nations. Tell us of evil to befall Israel that we may consider it and be dismayed. Surely any true deity can reveal his plans and carry them through.

24   A pause follows the challenge in verse 23—the idols remain dumb. Jehovah breaks the silence by a scornful charge of contempt: *Behold, ye are of nothing*; neither your origin nor nature is divine. *Your work is of nought*, totally worthless, serving no good purpose. Those who choose you as their objects of worship are abominable, contemptible in the sight of God.

25   Jehovah returns to the man from the east who was introduced in verse 2. But now Jehovah calls him *one from the north*, and speaks as if he has already come. (We earlier observed that when Jehovah determines to do a thing, it can be spoken of as already accomplished, for it is certain to be fulfilled.) He then adds, *from the rising of the sun.* Cyrus was of Anshan, a region of eastern Elam, which was east of Babylon. After becoming king of Persia, he conquered Media to the north; uniting the Medes and Persians, he attacked Babylon. So he was from both the east and the north. That he is characterized as *one that calleth upon my name* does not imply that he was a convert to Judaic monotheism. Rather, he recognized that it was Jehovah who gave him all the kingdoms of the earth and that he should rebuild the temple of Jerusalem (Ezra 1:2). In contrast to the silence of the idols, Jehovah declares that the one whom He will raise up will *come upon rulers*—deputies or subordinate rulers, "probably a loan word from Akkadian."[3] In that day he will trample them as one tramples mortar and the potter treads clay.

26   As though present during the coming captivity, Isaiah asks the question, *Who hath declared it from the beginning?* Who told us about it *beforetime, that we may say, He is right* (correct)? No idol had so spoken; no word had been heard from them. Only Jehovah had spoken, and so clearly that all could hear and know.

27   Jehovah had been the first to say to Zion, *Behold, behold them,* evidently referring to the words which He had spoken concerning Zion's deliverance. He had spoken them before the captivity. And in view of His purpose and promise, He *will give to Jerusalem one that bringeth good tidings.* The referent is either Isaiah, God's

---

3. *Theological Wordbook of the Old Testament*, vol. 2, p. 617.

messenger of the good news more than a century beforehand, or Cyrus, who will announce the good news that the Jews may return to Zion.

28 Again there seems to be a hushed silence over the courtroom. There is no one to accept the challenge, no man to answer, and no prophet of the idols to offer counsel. They answer not a word.

29 The verdict is rendered: *Behold,* consider what has taken place; *all of them,* the idol-gods and their worshipers, *are vanity,* emptiness, *and nought,* nothing, nonentities. Further, *their molten images are wind and confusion,* moral and spiritual emptiness. The victory for Jehovah is complete; the defeat of idolatry is crushing.

CHAPTER 42
Jehovah's Servant and Israel's Punishment

Jehovah's Ideal Servant (vv. 1–9)

1 As in chapter 41, Jehovah speaks in the greater part of chapter 42. There is no explicit statement as to who is being addressed. Leupold's suggestion, "to all who will take heed," is probably correct. *Behold*—Jehovah invites special attention to what is to be said—*my servant, whom I uphold; my chosen, in whom my soul delighteth.* Jehovah's Servant holds a high and noble position and is entrusted with a divine responsibility by the eternal God. Jehovah will *uphold* or sustain the Servant in all of His career. He has been chosen by God for a redemptive work, and Jehovah's soul will delight in Him as He carries out this work.

The Servant has been variously identified. Cyrus has been suggested, as have been the prophets (collective) of God. Whybray holds that Deutero-Isaiah, whom he assumes to have been the writer of chapters 40–66, is in view, whereas Willis suggests Israel, the nation. The vast majority of conservative commentators support the view that the Servant is the Messiah, the Lord Jesus of the New Testament. When the Servant's mission is considered (vv. 1–9), it becomes clear that only the Christ fulfills the assignment; all others fall short. He alone is the instrument of Israel's restoration and redemption, a light to the Gentiles, and the establisher of justice on the earth. Also, the means He used in accomplishing His mission sets Him apart from any of the other suggestions. Matthew settles the question when he quotes the opening verses of Isaiah 42 and applies them to Jesus (Matt. 12:15–21). Leaving for a moment His declaration concerning Cyrus, Jehovah turns to the ultimate Redeemer.

Choosing the Servant for a special mission, Jehovah says, *I have put my Spirit upon him;* the Spirit will fully endow the Servant for all His work (see the comments on 11:2; 61:1; cf. Matt. 3:16–17; 17:5). Among other things, *he will bring forth justice to the Gentiles* (nations) (cf. vv. 3–4). *Justice* is preferable to the King James rendering "judgment." The Hebrew word means "law, rule, or government," which includes judgment but is not restricted to it. Since God is the absolute Sovereign, and the foundation of His throne is justice and righteousness (Pss. 89:14; 97:2), it follows that the rule initiated by the Servant will be just and right, based on Jehovah's own character. Unlike the law which God gave to the Jews at Sinai, it will be universal in scope. It will include the Gentiles, who have long refused to have anything to do with God and His law.

2–3 The means the Servant will use in accomplishing His task is set forth under three negatives: (1) *He will not cry, not lift up his voice, nor cause it to be heard in the street.* The Servant will reject sensationalism, boisterous harangue, rabble-rousing, and noisy demonstrations in the streets. When Messiah came, He presented truth as the conquering power over men's souls, letting it transform the lives of believers. In Him was fulfilled the prediction, "Thy people offer themselves willingly/In the day of thy power, in holy array" (Ps. 110:3). (2) *A bruised reed will he not break, and a dimly burning wick will he not quench.* Instead of breaking and casting aside as useless the weak life which has been bruised and bent, the Servant will strengthen and succor it that it might become straight and strong. And instead of quenching the smoking wick of a dimly burning lamp, extinguishing its faint and flickering flame, He will add oil, protect the flame, and fan it into a brilliant and glowing light. Life will be precious in His sight. *He will bring forth justice in truth;* Jesus came to "bear witness unto the truth," and to reign over a kingdom founded on truth (John 18:36 –38). Truth presented in humility was the controlling and guiding power in His work, the basis of rule in His kingdom. His life demonstrated a meek and lowly spirit (Matt. 11:29).

4   The third negative setting forth the means by which the Servant will accomplish His task regards Himself: *He will not fail* ("burn dimly," margin) *nor be discouraged* ("bruised," margin) *till he have set justice in the earth.* Although the Servant will face many seemingly impossible obstacles and severely trying problems in His work, He will not succumb. Unlike those whom He comes to redeem, He will be free from weakness. He will accomplish His task; He will set justice, a right government, on the earth; He will not fail as the servant Israel has. To realize justice on earth, the isles, the coastlands of the Gentiles, will have to wait for His law, for only in it will they find a just government, redemption, and hope; *law* and *justice* are parallel. His law will not be the one which Jehovah gave to Israel at Sinai, but a new one.

5–6   To achieve the end for which He has been called, the Servant will be given the strength of God Jehovah, by whose power heaven and earth were created. The prophet now speaks: *Thus saith God Jehovah, he* (God) *that created the heavens, and stretched them forth; he that spread abroad the earth and that which cometh out of it; he* (Jehovah) *that giveth breath unto the people upon it, and spirit to them that walk therein.* One of Isaiah's favorite means of emphasizing the certainty of a prophecy is to call attention to the incomparable greatness of Jehovah, whose power underlies and is expressed in creation. *I, Jehovah,* is God's personal name to His people (Exod. 3:14; Hos. 12:5). The root of the name *Jehovah* means "to be," "I am"; hence the eternally existent one. The name itself "connotes God's nearness, his concern for man, and the revelation of his redemptive covenant."[4] It is the God of creation (hence of power) and the personal "I Am" of Israel's covenant who speaks: *I, Jehovah, have called thee in righteousness* (cf. 41:2), a moral and ethical standard in accordance with the nature and will of God, that is, in accordance with truth. Since Jehovah has called the Servant, Jehovah will also sustain

---

4. *Theological Wordbook of the Old Testament,* vol. 1, p. 212.

Him: (1) *I will hold thy hand, and will keep thee,* thereby sustaining and protecting at all times (John 8:29); (2) *and give thee for a covenant of the people,* and (3) *for a light of the Gentiles* (nations). Some hold that *the people* (singular) is parallel with and equivalent to *the Gentiles* (the heathen nations). However, this interpretation is contrary to the general usage of the two words; *the people* signifies Israel, and "the nations" or *Gentiles* refers to the heathen. The prophet is saying that the Servant is given for a covenant to Israel and for a light to the Gentiles; He will be the mediator of the covenant and the light of the nations. In the words of Delitzsch, the Servant will be "the personal bond which unites Israel and its God in a new fellowship" (II. 265); this new Israel will include the Gentiles.

7   The Servant's mission to be *a covenant of the people* and *a light of the Gentiles* (v. 6) is spiritual. He will open the eyes of the spiritually blind that they may behold the glory of Jehovah's redemptive work (cf. 29:18; 35:5). He will bring out those held in spiritual bondage, delivering them from the power of idolatry; and He will set free those imprisoned in moral darkness (cf. John 8:31–36; Gal. 4:8).

8   Jehovah is Himself the guarantee that what He has foretold will be accomplished; His name is His bond. The glorious honor that is due Him for redeeming both Israel and the Gentiles will not be given to another; He will not share His praise with inanimate idols which can neither speak nor act.

9   The idols failed to meet Jehovah's challenge to declare things past or future; He now adds additional evidence of His being the only God. *The former things are come to pass,* the former prophecies are fulfilled. Does the prophet project himself into the Babylonian period and stand with the exiles, calling attention to the prophecies that foretold the captivity and the raising up of Cyrus? Or is he speaking from the viewpoint of his day, calling attention, for example, to God's promise to make a great nation of Abraham, to the kingdom established in David, and to the prophecy to Ahaz concerning the coming of the Assyrians and their later defeat? Or is he referring to numerous other prophecies that had been fulfilled? Prophecies fulfilled before Cyrus seem to fit the entire context better. For the last part of the verse— *and new things do I declare; before they spring forth* (sprout) *I tell you of them*—seems to refer to Cyrus and the remaining proph-

ecies of the book, including the Servant's work. On the basis of prophecies which have been fulfilled, the people can believe that the new things which God is declaring will come to pass. This principle is vital today. On the ground of the promises God has already fulfilled, we can believe what He says concerning the future. We can put our trust in Him to carry out His promises.

A New Song of Praise to Jehovah (vv. 10–17)

10   An unnamed psalmist at an unknown time said, "Oh sing unto Jehovah a new song;/For he hath done marvelous things" (Ps. 98:1). Now too, marvelous things have been done. The new relationship to Jehovah through the new covenant, which includes Gentiles as well as Jews, calls for a new or fresh song (cf. Rev. 5:9–10). Let this new song of praise be sung *from the end of the earth,* for light, justice, and God's law have been extended to the Gentiles and set in the earth (vv. 4, 6). *Ye that go down to the sea,* sailors, merchants, and all who ply the oceans of earth for trade or travel, *and all that is therein,* the isles and coastlands and their inhabitants—let all these praise Jehovah. Although it is through the Servant that a universal blessing has been bestowed upon the inhabitants of the earth, the purpose of this blessing is and will continue to be the glory and praise of Jehovah.

11–12   *Let the wilderness,* the sparsely inhabited desert lands, *and the cities thereof,* often walled enclosures (the Hebrew word "refers to a permanent settlement without reference to size or claims"),[5] *lift up their voice* in praise. Also included are *the villages,* the unenclosed inhabited areas, often just a camp of Bedouins, *that Kedar doth inhabit* (for *Kedar* see the comments on 21:16–17). Turning from the isles of the sea and the regions of northern Arabia, the Lord looks next to the south and includes *the inhabitants of Sela,* the rock city in Edom, later known as Petra. Let them sing Jehovah's praise, shouting it from the top of their mountains. Only the work of the ideal Servant made possible this shout and song of universal joy and praise to Jehovah the true God.

---

5. *Theological Wordbook of the Old Testament,* vol. 2, p. 664.

Verse 12 is a recapitulation of what is said in verses 10–11. Let all peoples who sail the seas, who dwell on the coastlands, in desert areas, or somewhere in between, *give glory unto Jehovah, and declare his praise in the islands,* the remote areas of earth.

13 It has been observed by other writers that this is the most warlike word in the song. Once the Servant has provided light and justice to the Gentiles and a new covenant bond for a new Israel, Jehovah will declare war on the enemies of His spiritual cause and people. *Jehovah will go forth as a mighty man,* often translated "warrior," a hero or champion among armed forces. He will stir up His zeal for His cause and jealousy for them that are His, *like a man of war* who fights against his oppressors and in defense of his homeland. He will shout ("roar," King James) like a man going into battle. He will be mighty, that is, have strength, be great *against his enemies.* This is the cry of an all-out universal war waged by Jehovah; but as we will point out later, it will be waged through the victorious Servant.

14 The Lord now declares some of the new things which will come to pass (v. 9). The question arises, Is He referring in verses 13–17 to the captivity and His struggle against Babylon which will result in the return of His people? Or does He have here a larger, world-inclusive view that looks beyond the captivity to the Servant's appearance and what He will do? The latter appears to fit the context better. Dropping the figure of a warrior, the Lord depicts Himself as a woman in the throes of childbirth. The Lord says, *I have long time holden my peace.* For a long period Jehovah has held in check His purpose against idols, idolaters, and wickedness. But now, like a woman in the pangs of childbirth, He will gasp and pant, indicating an intense effort to achieve His purpose; He will destroy idolatry and bring forth a new age or era. He has overlooked certain times of ignorance (Acts 17:30), "passing over . . . the sins done aforetime" (Rom. 3:25), but no longer—His pent-up anger is about to explode.

15 Jehovah will (1) *lay waste mountains and hills,* (2) *dry up all their herbs,* and (3) dry up the rivers so that islands will appear, the result of the receding waters; He will also dry up the remaining pools. Views differ as to the Lord's meaning here, but in the light of the context it seems that He is not speaking of governments and great political or military powers, but of spiritual forces. In the war that He

will wage following the Servant's mission, the old idolatrous religions of the heathen peoples will be brought to nought (cf. v. 17). This is in stark contrast to what He will do for His own (cf. 35:7).

16   Having laid waste the heathen religions and their idol-gods (v. 15), Jehovah will bring those who have been blind to Him by a way hitherto unknown to them (cf. I Cor. 2:9), but known to Jehovah. *In paths that they know not will I lead them*, paths of God's appointment, paths of righteousness (Ps. 23:3) that go forth out of Zion (2:3). The darkness in which they once walked will be made light, and the crooked and twisted places of life—the difficulties confronted—the Lord will overcome. He will do these things; and He will not forsake those who were once blind, but will continue with them to the end.

17   This verse confirms our position that we are dealing here with Jehovah's war against idolatry and against its demoralizing consequences, a spiritual conflict. They *that trust in graven images, that say unto molten images, Ye are our gods*—those who walk in darkness and do not know Jehovah's way—*shall be turned back, they shall be utterly put to shame*. Both the Gentiles who have always been given over to idolatry and those of Israel who have succumbed to it, together with the idols themselves, will be cast down. Because of their failure and complete defeat at Jehovah's hand, both the idols and their worshipers shall fall into disgrace, ultimately to pass away.

Israel, Jehovah's Blind and Deaf Servant, to Be Punished (vv. 18–25)

18   Jehovah resumes the theme of Israel the servant, which He introduced in 41:8–16. He will continue with this theme—Israel's failure, punishment, and eventual restoration—through chapter 45. The charge, *Hear, ye deaf; and look, ye blind, that ye may see*, indicates that the condition was willful and self-imposed, for they could see if they would but look. Since they are responsible for the condition, they must correct it.

19   Although the Gentiles are blind to truth and righteousness, none are so blind as Israel, Jehovah's servant and messenger. As Jehovah's servant, Israel had been given a divine responsibility to

357

represent Him to the world; as Jehovah's messenger he had been sent to deliver words from God to the inhabitants of earth. Israel's mission had been to make known to the world the righteousness and rule of Jehovah as the Creator and only God. To this mission they had been both blind and deaf. *Who is blind as he that is at peace with me?* (The King James translation, "as he that is perfect," is incorrect.) The word translated *as he that is at peace with me* signifies completeness, a state of wholeness, which should have been the result of the covenant of peace which Jehovah had made with His people. But Israel was blind to the real nature of his relationship with God and to the blessings and responsibilities that grew out of that relationship.

20   With the physical eye Israel had seen many things, but had not comprehended their spiritual significance. He *observest not*—he did not take full cognizance of them so as to do them carefully or diligently. He was without excuse, for while his ears were open, his heart was not; he did not hear, grasp, and respond.

21   Jehovah's righteousness must be upheld and His word vindicated. Therefore, it pleased Him *to magnify the law, and make it honorable.* The *law* (teaching or instruction) is viewed here in its broadest sense, embracing the commands given at Sinai and the word spoken through the prophets, the psalmists, and the wise men. The law included commands, promises, and penalties; and if Jehovah is to magnify it, that is, to exalt its importance and greatness, to make it appreciated, then the penalties for violating it must be executed. Otherwise it is meaningless. Because of its source it is superior to all other laws and must be respected.

22   The state of the people as it is now described is due to their blindness and deafness to Jehovah's purpose and mission for them; it is the result of their sins against the worthy and honorable law of Jehovah. They are allegorically depicted as a people being robbed and plundered, snared in holes and hid in prison-houses; they are homeless and bitter. Further, they are a prey to those stronger than they, because they are weakened by unbelief and sin, and have none to deliver them from the plunderer, for Jehovah has withdrawn from them. They are *for a spoil*, or booty, *and none saith, Restore.* The Hebrew word literally means "return." No one tells them to return to Jehovah to be restored to a proper relationship with Him that their

rightful possessions may be returned. Although this picture is most often viewed as applying to the captivity in Babylon, it need not be so narrowly restricted; for in their blind and deaf spiritual state, the people in Isaiah's days were already in bondage and prison-houses of sin and wickedness, as are all those today who have not responded to God and His word.

23–24 The Lord calls upon the people as individuals to consider carefully what He is saying. He asks two questions: (1) Who will give attention to what He has said and thus come to recognize the nation's plight as a righteous judgment, as the consequence of past deeds? And (2) who will give ear that from past experiences he may profit in time to come? Though some might think so, it was not by the power of heathen idols that the people were given over to spoilers and robbers. It was of Jehovah, *against whom we* (the present generation) *have sinned, and in whose ways they* (the past generation or generations) *would not walk, neither were they obedient unto his law* (teaching). Israel had only their rebellion against Jehovah, their disregard for His law, and their blindness and deafness to His mission to blame for their present state of exile. For Jehovah must establish His righteousness in the earth and magnify His law, making it honorable. According to Paul, "whatsoever things were written aforetime were written for our learning" (Rom. 15:4); they "were our examples . . . and they were written for our admonition, upon whom the ends of the ages are come" (I Cor. 10:6, 11). Therefore let us learn from them.

25 When, in the righteousness of Jehovah, His long-suffering reached the limit beyond which it could not be extended, He *poured upon him the fierceness of his anger, and the strength of battle. The fierceness of his anger* is righteous indignation at Israel's disregard for and gross violation of God's law as well as their indifference to the majesty of God Himself. Jehovah outpoured His anger by bringing the Babylonians to carry His people away into exile. Though set on fire by these divine judgments, Israel never understood what the Lord was doing; they laid not to heart the fact that all He did was for their salvation. Truly, the heart of man often becomes so deadened and calloused by sin that it recognizes neither the grace and mercy of God

in the outpouring of blessings nor the chastening judgments which
He sends for correction.

CHAPTER 43

"Ye Are My Witnesses. . . . Besides Me There Is No Saviour"

A Renewed Promise to Israel of Deliverance and Protection (vv. 1–7)

1   The words *But now* introduce a contrast; the tone changes
from reproof and rebuke to encouragement and consolation. Previously Jehovah had said, "Fear thou not, for I am with thee" (41:10),
and "Fear not; I will help thee" (41:13); now He adds, *Fear not, for I
have redeemed thee*. He has paid the price for Israel's redemption (see
v. 3). He gives them four reasons why they should not fear: (1)
Jehovah had *created* Jacob, that is, He had brought forth something
new—a new creation—at Sinai. (2) He had *formed* Israel, fashioning
the princely people out of Jacob, a supplanter. What a contrast between the heathens' fashioning insensate materials into idols that
could render no service and God's fashioning Israel into a nation that
could serve Him! (3) Jehovah had *redeemed* or ransomed the people
from Egypt; and when they suffer in Babylon, He will act as their
avenger. And (4) He had *called* them by their name "Israel" to be His
own peculiar people and nation (Exod. 19:5–6), giving them a special
task as His servant and messenger (41:9).

2   Because *thou art mine*, because Israel has been called and
redeemed by Jehovah (cf. v. 1), He will protect and care for them.
There are yet many trials before the people; but though they should
pass through the floods of affliction and the rivers of adversity, they
will not be overwhelmed for Jehovah will be with them. And when
they walk through the fires of tribulation, testing, and judgments,
they will not be burned (cf. Ps. 66:12; also Dan. 3:27, where God
gives a literal demonstration of this lesson), for Jehovah will sustain
and protect them.

3 The guarantee stamped on these promises is the name of the Lord Himself: *For I am Jehovah*—the personal name by which He is known to the people of the covenant—*thy God*—the God of power and strength, the only God—*the Holy One of Israel*—set apart from the sins of Israel, absolute in holiness—*thy Saviour*—the Lord delivers His people from distress and oppression to safety and peace. *Ransom* is payment to redeem someone or something that has been captured. Israel was Jehovah's and for it He would give up the rest of the nations, including Egypt, Ethiopia, and Seba, which include all that was known of Africa at the time. Whether, as some scholars think, this has reference to the conquest of Egypt in 525–522 B.C. by Cambyses, son of Cyrus, is uncertain.

4 The first word in this verse *(Since)* gives trouble to several commentators. It is variously translated: "from the time" (Alexander); "because" (Delitzsch, Leupold); "due to the fact that" (Young); "inasmuch as" may be the most representative rendering. *Thou hast been precious in my sight,* of great value; therefore Jehovah will redeem Israel at great cost. There are also various translations of the Hebrew word which the American Standard Version renders *honorable*: "thou hast been honored" (Alexander, Young); "[you are] honored" (Leupold); "highly esteemed" (Delitzsch). In spite of the uncertainties in this verse, however, the thought is clear. Israel's special position with God and the responsibility that goes with that position have made the nation honorable, worthy of honor. (To receive that honor, they must, of course, live in proper relationship to Him.) The clause *I have loved thee* traces God's favors "down to their deepest root—the love of God" (Leupold). Because the people of Israel are honorable and precious to Him, Jehovah, in His love for them, places them above all nations, giving up others in exchange for them.

5–6 The Lord reiterates the word with which he introduced this prophecy: *Fear not; for I am with thee* (cf. v. 1; 41:10, 13, 14), for the waters and the fire (cf. v. 2) are yet to come. He is looking ahead to that time when the people will be scattered to the four corners of earth. Alexander observes that God does not say, "I will bring back," as of a restoration, but *I will bring thy seed,* offspring or descendants, from the four directions—east, west, north, and south. It is God who

361

will bring them together, gathering them into one. To the *north* He says, *Give up; and to the south, Keep not back; bring my sons from far, and my daughters from the end of the earth.* All of His children are included. No particular individual or group is being addressed or commanded to bring God's people together. Rather, the thought is, "Suffer all my people to come unto me; let no one or nothing hinder." The remnant that will return from Babylon or come together under the Servant will be those who "return unto me with their whole heart" (Jer. 24:7).

7   Included among those that are to be brought and gathered is *every one that is called by my name,* God's sons and daughters, spiritual Israel. They were created—brought into existence—for Jehovah's own glory, which is the ultimate objective of all of God's work. To be gathered together are all those *whom I have formed*— those upon whom God acted in history that He might bring forth a peculiar nation—*yea, whom I have made.* God shaped or formed Israel as a special reflection of His glory (cf. v. 1). Though this passage speaks of the return of the remnant from the exile, it certainly also looks beyond to the gathering together of all people called by God's name. This was accomplished only under the Servant Jesus Christ, whom God appointed to the task.

A Fresh Challenge to Israel and the Nations (vv. 8–13)

8   Jehovah previously called the gods of the nations to a court of inquisition to examine their claims to deity (41:1–7, 21–24). He now calls *the blind* and *deaf* servant Israel to meet Him in a similar court of inquiry. Though blind and deaf, Israel has eyes and ears with which they can see and hear if only they will; the Lord seeks to open their eyes and ears by pointing out the wondrous works He has performed in and through them.

9   Jehovah also calls the heathen nations to attend the session, challenging them as He had their idols (41:21–24) to declare something that was foretold and has been fulfilled among them. *Let them bring their witnesses, that they may be justified,* that their confidence in and worship of idols may be vindicated. God challenges the nations to *declare this, and show us former things,* that is, to point out

various events which their gods foretold and then brought to pass. If the nations cannot meet this challenge, *let them hear* (what Jehovah has to say), *and say, It is truth.* When an honest person examines his suppositions and finds no evidence on which to accept them, he should be willing to hear the other side. When sufficient evidence is presented in favor of the other side, he should say, "It is truth." Today, as then, this principle needs to be recognized in all religious investigations.

10   The Lord now addresses Israel: *Ye are my witnesses, saith Jehovah, and my servant whom I have chosen.* As God's special people, Israel is His servant and messenger (42:19), and now also His witness. The word *witness* is common in court circles; a witness is one who has firsthand knowledge of an event and can bear accurate testimony thereto. The people of Israel can bear testimony that Jehovah is God, not only to the nations, but also to their own skepticism. By comparing Jehovah's work with that of the idols, and the witness of the heathen with their own, Israel can clearly distinguish the power of Jehovah and the powerlessness of idols. Thus they can come to *know and believe me;* they will become firmly established in their faith, no longer wavering between the two. They will *understand that I am he;* that is, they will recognize Jehovah as the only God. For *before me there was no God formed, neither shall there be after me.* While impressing upon the heathen the vanity of their gods, Jehovah here impresses upon His own vacillating people the truth that He alone is the eternal God.

11   Jehovah continues to emphasize His point: *I, even I, am Jehovah,* the "I Am," the eternally existent and all-provident one; *and besides me there is no saviour.* When the people find themselves in exile in Babylon, they will realize that there is salvation in none other. Jonah learned this lesson in the belly of the fish; he cried out, "Salvation is of Jehovah" (Jon. 2:9). When men reject God, any hope of finding release from bondage is forfeited; there is no other source of salvation.

12   Jehovah claims that He Himself has accomplished what He has challenged the nations to do (v. 9): He has *declared,* has made known what He will do in the future; He has *saved,* that is, He has delivered His people from Egypt and from Sennacherib, and He will

deliver them from Babylon; and He has *showed*, has reported in a clear and unmistakable way the fulfillment of what He earlier foretold. When He says, *And there was no strange god among you*, He does not mean that there was no idolatry among the people, but that there was no other god with whom Jehovah collaborated or who foretold anything that would be done; Jehovah stood and acted alone. *Therefore ye are my witnesses*, testifying to Jehovah's absolute Godhood. He has so clearly shown that He is able to declare the end from the beginning and then bring it to pass, that it cannot be denied. As Jehovah and God, He is both the eternally existent one, the covenant God, and the Lord of power and strength who is able to carry out His purpose. (Several centuries later, Israel would similarly be a witness of the deity of Christ.)

13   Shall we follow the text, *Yea, since the day was I am he*; or the reading of the margin, "From this day forth I am he"? Although commentators are divided over which to accept, it is preferable to follow the text; for since time began, God has been present in His creation and in history. He was present with the first generation and will be present with the last (41:4). None can snatch away a person or a nation that is in His hand. And when He purposes a work, no god can hinder it.

Jehovah's Power to Remove Obstacles in Redeeming His People (vv. 14–21)

14   As Redeemer, Jehovah acts in a manner consistent with His own holiness, which is constantly emphasized in the phrase *the Holy One of Israel*. He had created Israel for His glory (v. 7), and He now acts toward that new creation in such a way "that they might set forth my praise" (v. 21). *For your sake I have sent to Babylon*, an apparent reference to Cyrus, whom He will raise up and send against Babylon (41:1–7; 44:28–45:7; 48:14; cf. 13:17; 21:2). Note that once again Jehovah speaks of a future action as if it were already done. The people of that proud and mighty city and nation will be brought down like fugitives, that is, like a people fleeing from an enemy. They will be brought down *in the ships of their rejoicing*, the ships of commerce that had brought great rejoicing through the wealth which had en-

riched the city. The ships of which the Babylonians are so very proud will become the means of their humiliating flight before their enemies. Jehovah is hereby declaring His control over the nations, both mighty Babylon and him whom He will send against her.

15 Jehovah not only controls the heathen powers, sending Cyrus against Babylon; but also, as the Creator of Israel, He exercises control over her destiny. The nation may be in exile in Babylon, but He is still their King and will not forget; He will deliver them at His own pleasure.

16–17 The Lord not only determines the destiny of nations and molds and fashions Israel towards a definite end, He also exercises His creative and controlling power over nature. He opened a way in the Red Sea and a path in its fierce and strong waters that His people might pass through. Further, it is only by His overruling decree and the exercise of His divine power that armies can act. Chariots and horses, armies and mighty men are destroyed at His will, as when Pharaoh's forces attempted to pursue Israel and perished when the waters returned to their original location (cf. Ps. 76:5–6). All these mighty human forces *lie down together, they shall not rise. They are extinct, they are quenched as a wick.* They are like a lamp whose light is snuffed out. The verb used here always relates to the act of putting out a fire, whether figurative or literal;[6] it vanishes from sight.

18–19 The people are urged to cease looking to and appealing to the past (except to learn from its examples and warnings), and to look to the future instead. Jehovah promises that He will do a new thing which they will see and know. In pointing to what He will do through the ideal Servant, Jehovah has already said, "New things do I declare; before they spring forth [sprout] I tell you of them" (42:9); these things are in the distant future. But the new thing presently before Him is more immediate: *now shall it spring forth;* the generation addressed will share in it. As He redeemed Israel out of Egypt, so will He *make a way in the wilderness, and rivers in the desert* for a new exodus. By His providence and power He will provide a path for the exiles' return journey and will supply water for their thirst. Though He probably

---

6. *Theological Wordbook of the Old Testament*, vol. 1, p. 428.

did not cause literal rivers to spring miraculously into existence, He did provide for the people's needs.

20–21 In highly poetic language similar to that used by Job, "When the morning stars sang together" (38:7), and by a psalmist, "the trees of the wood sing for joy/Before Jehovah" (Ps. 96:12–13; cf. Isa. 55:12—"the trees of the field shall clap their hands"), the prophet says that the animals of the field and the wild creatures of the desert areas shall honor Jehovah. As the animal world suffered because of judgment upon man for his sins (see, e.g., Jer. 14:6; Hos. 4:3; Joel 1:18), so now in some way will they partake of God's blessings bestowed upon a redeemed people. The people formed by Jehovah for Himself will be brought forth that they might praise Him; this should ever be the aim of His people.

Israel's Indifference—Jehovah's Grace (vv. 22–28)

22 In spite of Jehovah's concern for Israel and His desire to act on their behalf, the people have been indifferent to Him and His lovingkindness. He has power to deliver and provide for their needs, but they have not called upon Him. Instead they have become weary of His ways and the exertion necessary to serve Him.

23 The second charge directed against the people concerns the ritual of sacrifice: *Thou hast not brought me of thy sheep for burntofferings; neither hast thou honored me with thy sacrifices.* What is the meaning here, the precise nature of the offense? Has the nation failed to sacrifice because they have turned to idolatry? Is it a matter of indifference to the Mosaic ritual? Or is God angry because the captives in Babylon do not perform the rites? The first two possibilities are ruled out; for though the people may serve idols, they are not indifferent to the offering of sacrifice; as a matter of fact, they are profuse in it (see 1:10–16). The third possibility is ruled out on the ground that all sacrifices were to be offered in Jerusalem; Jehovah would not hold the people responsible for not offering sacrifice if they were in Babylon. The most plausible explanation is that their offerings are not from the heart; the ceremony is there but lacks the true spirit and meaning. They offer sacrifices to secure protection from the Lord and to try through formal ceremonies to escape His wrath.

The people have missed the point of sacrifice. It is not intended to be a burden from the Lord, but a means of joyous fellowship with Him.

24 The *sweet cane* which the people have not bought for Jehovah is thought by most commentators to be an aromatic plant imported from another country rather than the sugar cane with which we are acquainted. It was probably used in incense or anointing oil. This point is uncertain. At any rate, instead of bringing the sweet cane and satisfying God with conscientious offering of the fat which belonged to Him, the people burdened Him with their sins and wearied Him with their iniquities. This attitude, which characterized their lives in general, nullified any possible worth of their offerings. It seems not to have been restricted to a specific period but was a persistent problem in the nation's history.

25 Although omnipotent, as demonstrated in His power over Babylon, over Cyrus and the Medes whom He used to destroy Babylon, and over both animate and inanimate nature (vv. 14–21), Jehovah could do good for Israel only if the people turned from their sins. *I, even I, am he that blotteth out thy transgressions;* this is an act of pure grace on His part and not the result of any merit on theirs. Forgiveness comes through faith in Him and not through ceremonial sacrifices performed as mere formalities. God says he blots out transgressions *for mine own sake,* that is, so that He might demonstrate the proper combination of divine mercy and justice, expressed in love, judgment, and grace. When blotted out, sins are remembered no more—"As far as the east is from the west,/So far hath he removed our transgressions from us" (Ps. 103:12).

26 The Lord now urges Israel to put Him in remembrance, to call to mind His infinite being and holy character (as set forth in ch. 40), His holy laws which were given them for their good, His loving care and tender mercy, and His willingness to forgive and receive back into His bosom those who hearken to Him. He now makes a plea reminiscent of both the invitation which He issued at the outset of the book (1:18) and His call to the nations (41:21–24): *let us plead together: set thou forth thy cause, that thou mayest be justified.* If there is any ground or merit in you to warrant your deliverance, bring it forth; Jehovah stands ready to listen. If there is no ground in you which merits God's deliverance, then your deliverance will be based on His love and unmerited favor.

27   Israel cannot plead excellence on the ground of their ancestry, for *Thy first father sinned.* Scholars have variously interpreted this reference: Adam, Abraham, Jacob, and even David; but it seems that Jacob is the father herein considered, for he had gained the blessing and birthright by deceit and an unbrotherly bargain. *And thy teachers* ("interpreters," Hebrew) *have transgressed against me;* that is, prophets, priests, and others who should have given proper instruction in the law sinned by giving false teaching instead. So, from their father Jacob to the present the people have been encouraged by example and precept to transgress the divine law.

28   However, the people are still responsible for their departure from God; for as there have been unfaithful teachers, there have also been faithful prophets and teachers among them. But the people did not listen to them. *Therefore,* consequently or in the light of this, Jehovah *will profane the princes of the sanctuary.* The word *princes,* which may refer to royal rulers, also denotes chieftains or leaders in the sanctuary; they should have been holy, consecrated to their ministry. The Lord will desecrate them by sending them to Babylon, a profane or unclean land and kingdom. Eventually He will *make Jacob a curse,* that is, consign him to destruction, *and Israel a reviling,* an object of abusive speech. Although this judgment was in part fulfilled by the Babylonian captivity, the curse and reviling have continued throughout the history of Israel; they continue to live under the ban.

CHAPTER 44
The Folly of Idolatry

Israel's Blessings in Spite of the Curse (vv. 1–5)

1   In sharp contrast to the ban and curse under which Jehovah had placed the nation (43:25–28), He now pronounces a blessing upon them, a blessing so rich that it will attract the heathen. *Yet now*

hear, for in spite of the eventual destruction of the nation, Jehovah will accomplish His purpose through them. From out of all the peoples of the earth Jehovah had chosen the nation Jacob-Israel to be His own (cf. 41:8). As His elect, His purpose for and through them will not fail.

2   Again Jehovah addresses the people as their Creator and Maker (cf. 43:1, 7), adding that He had formed them *from the womb*—from birth. Though some commentators think that this reference looks back only to Sinai, the phrase probably looks back to the call of Abraham and to the promise given him which continued in Isaac and Jacob, even to the forming of the nation at Sinai. Although the nation will be carried into Babylonian exile and eventually destroyed, God gives encouragement: *Fear not,* a constantly recurring exhortation in this section, *O Jacob my servant; and thou, Jeshurun, whom I have chosen.* The name *Jeshurun,* which occurs only here and in Deuteronomy 32:15; 33:5, 26, is thought to have come from a root word meaning "upright," hence, the "upright one"; the real meaning of the word, however, is obscure and uncertain. The name may suggest what Jacob should have been, for it is used instead of *Jacob* where the patriarch had failed to live up to the standard of his calling (Deut. 32:9, 15). The name is now applied to the nation Jacob which likewise had failed to live according to the upright standard of Jehovah's code. But in spite of Jacob's conduct, the Lord will use him because He had chosen him.

3   The reading of the margin is preferable to the text, for it maintains a balance of thought: *I will pour water upon him that is thirsty* ("the thirsty land," margin), *and streams upon the dry ground.* The nation will experience a period of spiritual drought and thirst which Jehovah will remedy by an outpouring of water and streams. The Lord explains what He will do: *I will pour my Spirit upon thy seed, and my blessing upon thine offspring.* Water and *streams* are parallel as are *thirsty* ("land") and *dry ground;* so also are *Spirit* and *blessing,* and *seed* and *offspring.* As water poured out upon a dry and arid land brings to life its dormant seed, so the pouring out of Jehovah's Spirit upon Israel's seed will bring spiritual life and blessings upon his offspring. Spiritual life and blessings emanate from the energizing power of the Spirit, who, of course, comes from God.

4   *And they,* the seed and offspring (v. 3), *shall spring up among the grass.* From dormant seed or a withered plant, they will spring up among the lush grass, *as willows by the watercourses.* The word *grass* is from a word that means "to be green," hence, "alive, growing." There are several kinds of willows that grow in Palestine, and the specific kind in view here is uncertain. Some think it may be the poplar which grows along Israel's streams. Under the providential provision of God's Spirit and spiritual blessings, individuals will spring to life; a new nation will come forth.

5   This new spiritual life and its attendant blessings will attract individuals from among the heathen. Their turning to the new life will not be a mass movement, but individual—*one* and *another* and *another.* That one says he is Jehovah's and others name themselves after Jacob or Israel does not indicate a divided state reminiscent of the world's division into many nations. Rather, what is indicated is that each accepts all that is involved in belonging to Jehovah, in the promise made to Jacob, and in the name *Israel,* which each individual takes as his surname in truth, not as an empty title. Subscribing one's hand unto Jehovah probably reflects the custom of signing a pledge of loyalty, a contract, or a covenant. The thought here may be that the individuals in view name and honor the God of Jacob with their lips and serve Him with their hands. (Verses 1–5 seem to serve as a conclusion to chapter 43, rather than as an introduction to chapter 44.)

Israel's King—The Only God (vv. 6–8)

6   The Lord resumes the court scene of 43:8–21, contrasting His own absolute deity (vv. 6–8) with the utter folly of idolatry (vv. 9–20). In presenting His majesty and glory in contrast to the idols, Jehovah uses three titles which occur repeatedly in this section: (1) *Thus saith Jehovah, the King of Israel* (Jacob) (cf. 41:21; 43:15)—at any given time any human ruler over Israel ruled only as Jehovah's representative; Jehovah was King over His people at all times; (2) *his Redeemer* (cf. 41:14; 43:1, 14)—Jehovah had always been the Redeemer of Israel and would be to the end; (3) *Jehovah of hosts* (this title recurs throughout Isaiah), Ruler over all created beings, forces, and powers,

which are subject to Him and used by Him as He carries out His divine purpose. To these titles the Lord adds two characteristics of His absolute deity: (1) *I am the first, and I am the last* (cf. 41:4; 43:10; 48:12); *and* (2) *besides me there is no God* (cf. 43:11; 44:8; 45:5–6, 21). This is the platform on which Jehovah stands and from which He challenges the idols and individuals of all nations. He is eternal, omnipotent, and the complete Master of His universe.

7   The Lord now issues a challenge to a simple but all-determining contest: let anyone (idol or man) declare something he foretold in the past and point to its fulfillment either in the past or in the present. Who will set himself beside Jehovah to call, declare, and set in order? Who has changed anything since God set the nations and His own in their proper state? Or, since God is now declaring future things that pertain to the nations and Israel, let the heathen deities declare things of the future which we can recognize when they are fulfilled. The challenge rings throughout this section (chs. 40–48), but it is never taken up. Jehovah remains the only God, His claim uncontested; besides Him there is no other.

8   The word translated *fear* here and in verse 11 differs from the word usually used by Isaiah. It signifies a more intense fear, a terror, or a dread. The object of this fear is not specified; but since the nation will be captive in Babylon, it probably refers to fear of idols. Be not in terror of them, for they are powerless. Of old, Jehovah had declared what He would do and He did it. You, Israel, *are my witnesses* to this. *Is there a God besides me?* None, *there is no Rock; I know not any.* There is no stronghold, fortress, or place of refuge other than Jehovah; only He is permanent. And being omniscient as well as omnipotent, He would know.

The Shame and Folly of Idolatry (vv. 9–20)

The prophet interrupts his line of thought in verses 6–8 to deal with the idols and their makers, the would-be rivals to Jehovah's claim to be the sole God and only being worthy of man's worship. To provide further evidence of Jehovah's claim of being the only God, Isaiah sets forth the shame and folly of idolatry. In language that bristles with pointed and withering scorn, he exposes the vanity of human wisdom that stoops to the manufacture and worship of objects born of man's imagination. The passage is a classic unmasking of the emptiness and impotence of all human religions. As Leupold observes, it took courage to cry out so boldly against a way of life that had become deeply entrenched among all mankind.

9   The prophet begins with the makers of the idols: *They that fashion a graven image,* they are all of them *vanity* (*tohu,* Hebrew— void, waste, emptiness; cf. Gen. 1:2). And the false gods, the idols that *they delight in,* that they adore and look to, shall bring them no profit or gain. They are as empty as their makers. *And their own witnesses,* the worshipers of the idols who come forth to testify on their behalf, neither see nor comprehend the extent of their folly. In their blindness and ignorance they shall *be put to shame;* they shall be confused, embarrassed, and dismayed at the total failure of their gods.

10   *Who hath fashioned* such *a god?* Only the blind and senseless, who will find that their labor is futile; they make a *nothing.* God created the dust and from it made man. Can that dust now take created material and form a God? The very thought is preposterous.

11   The phrase *his fellows* (i.e., those with whom one is closely united, sharing with them a community of spirit) probably has reference to the worshipers of the idols—in worshiping idols they have fellowship or communion with them (cf. I Cor. 10:19–20). However, the workmen who made the idols will likewise be put to shame; for what is human cannot create something which is divine. Therefore, when they stand up together, the workmen and worshipers, *they shall fear* (see the comments on v. 8), *they shall be put to shame together* (see the comments on v. 9).

12   It is not clear whether Isaiah is describing the making of an axe with which the carpenter cuts the wood and shapes the idol or the shaping of iron into an idol; he is probably describing the former. In either case the lesson is clear: the work is hard and the strong arm of the smith grows weary; the man becomes hungry and must eat; he becomes thirsty and must have water. The idol-maker is subject to human frailties and needs, for which the idol can make no provision. Everything—the metal for the tools, the food and water for the man—has to be provided from another source.

13 The carpenter takes a piece of wood provided by a source outside both himself and the idol he wishes to fashion; and with a pencil ("red ochre," margin) and a compass, he marks out a pattern on the wood. With a plane, also made by man, he shapes the idol *after the figure of a man*, giving to it his own image and beauty. When completed, it must have a dwelling place. In the whole procedure the idol is passive, providing no aid to its maker and exercising no control over its appearance, dwelling, or destiny.

14 The prophet moves back a step from the situation depicted in verses 12–13 to the procuring of the wood from which the idol is made. Using the axe forged by the smith (v. 12), the idol-maker selects and hews down trees which are helpless to resist (the various trees named are not clearly identifiable today). In their stead he plants a fir tree which must be nurtured from the soil beneath and watered with rain from above. Note that it is totally dependent on external forces over which the idol and the idol-maker have no control.

15 The felled tree then serves several purposes, all of them subject to the whims and providing for the needs of the man. It may be burned so that the man is warmed; that portion of the wood is consumed. With another part of it he makes a fire on which to bake bread and cook meat for his own needs; that portion also becomes ashes. He then takes a part of the trunk and with his own hands makes a graven image. Though it, too, is subject to decay, he falls down before it in adoration. All that God created on the earth was intended for man's use. When the man burned part of the wood for warming himself and for cooking his food, he used it properly and it served its divine purpose. But when he made it an object of worship, he made it an abomination, misusing that which had been entrusted to him. No creature is ever to be an object of worship; only the eternal Creator is worthy of our veneration.

16–17 The prophet now summarizes how the wood was used. The man burned part of it to prepare food to satisfy his hunger and part of it to provide warmth for his body. Then he said, *Aha, I am warm, I have seen the fire*. With the remainder he made a god before which he fell and prayed, *Deliver me; for thou art my god*. This inanimate matter was utterly powerless to deliver itself from being felled by the woodsman's axe, from being partially burned, and from

373

being carved into whatsoever shape the maker desired, yet it is expected to deliver the man from danger or destruction. What folly!

18   Though the craftsman has seen the fire, he has not seen that his reasoning and conduct are irrational. Now is described the idol-worshiper's true spiritual condition, to which he is insensible. He neither understands nor gives thought to the emptiness and worthlessness of his practice. God has *shut* ("daubed," margin) *their eyes, that they cannot see; and their hearts, that they cannot understand.* From one point of view, God may be said to have closed their eyes and hearts; but this is not an arbitrary act on God's part. They themselves are responsible (Rom. 1:20–28). In their self-imposed darkened state idolaters cannot understand their folly.

19   None of the idolaters call to mind or consider what they are doing. With part of the wood they have kindled a fire and warmed themselves; they have baked bread and roasted meat upon its coals. In the light of these uses of the wood they should have asked, *Shall I make the residue thereof an abomination,* a thing to be loathed and detested? Of course, the idolater would not call it *an abomination,* for he is blind and insensible to what he is doing.

20   The poor deluded soul is trying to feed his spiritual life on the ashes of idolatry, which are totally void of life and of life-sustaining qualities. Deception, which has ever been a powerful tool in Satan's hand, has turned man's heart aside from God who alone can satisfy the soul's hunger. When man refuses knowledge of God, exchanging the truth of God for a lie, man attempts to fill the void by turning to creature-worship. A moment's serious reflection would show him that idols cannot deliver him and would cause him to say, *Is there not a lie in my right hand?* In giving up God man has given to an idol the place of honor at his right hand, the place which rightly belongs to the Creator. In the belly of the fish Jonah made a comment pertinent to the present situation: "They that regard lying vanities/Forsake their own mercy" (Jon. 2:8). What a reflection on human wisdom! God created; the idol is an inanimate creature. God is eternal life; the idol is dead matter. God delivers; the idol is helpless. God foretells; the idol is dumb. Yielding to the vanity of idols, Israel had been taken into Assyrian captivity; soon Judah would go into Babylonian captivity.

Pardon and Praise (vv. 21–23)

21 Having pointed out the folly and emptiness of idolatry (vv. 9–20), the prophet resumes the Lord's declaration of His care for Israel and of their deliverance from Babylon (cf. vv. 6–8). *Remember these things*, Jehovah's redemption and provision for you on the one hand, and the total impotence and lie of idolatry on the other. Jehovah is active—He formed man. Idols are passive—they do not form man, but are formed by him. Jehovah will not forget the one He formed to be His servant and to carry out His purpose.

22 Sin and iniquity had separated Israel from their God (59:2); now these obstacles have been blotted out, wiped away as Jehovah might clear the sky of clouds. The Lord speaks as if this were already accomplished, for by His grace it will be done. Therefore, *return unto me; for I have redeemed thee* (cf. 43:1); Jehovah has given heathen nations as a ransom (43:3). No doubt this verse looks beyond the redemption of the nation to the ransom price that God would pay for the complete blotting out of sins (Heb. 9:15).

23 The prophet breaks forth in a shout of praise to Jehovah for what He has done, for He has redeemed Israel. Using three imperatives, he urges all creation to join him: (1) *Sing, O ye heavens, for Jehovah hath done it;* (2) *shout, ye lower parts of the earth;* (3) *break forth into singing, ye mountains, O forest, and every tree therein: for Jehovah hath redeemed Jacob, and will glorify himself in Israel.* Everything is included—from the greatest height (heaven) to the lowest cave, canyon, and crevice of earth, and the mountains, forests, and trees in between. Beyond the redemption of Jacob which Jehovah has accomplished, He will glorify Himself in the spiritual Israel, a reference to the salvation which Christ was to offer to the world.

Cyrus the Deliverer is Named (vv. 24–28)

24 Before naming the coming deliverer, Jehovah again declares His own eternal greatness on which rests the fulfillment of the prophecy. In His greatness He had formed Israel; in His love He had redeemed him. He is the Maker of all things in the universe; by His word they were brought forth (Ps. 33:6), and by His wisdom they were set in order (Prov. 8:22–31). It is He who stretched forth the heavens from infinity to infinity and who spread out the earth from the east to the west. There was no god with Him; He did it alone. In His infinite power He controls the destiny of history.

25 Being God, He is able not only to create and control, foretell and bring to pass, but also to frustrate or confuse the efforts by the idolaters to prove their claims by signs. He *maketh diviners mad;* men who seek information about the future from a supposedly divine source are made mad by the results. (For an example of the diviner's methods in determining a matter, see Ezek. 21:21–22). The Lord likewise confuses the knowledge of the wise men, turning it to nought and leaving them in a state of perplexity.

26 In contrast to confusing and reversing the efforts of idolaters, Jehovah *confirmeth*, that is, establishes or makes to stand, *the word of his servant, and performeth the counsel of his messengers.* The servant may be Israel (41:8; 42:19), but this is unlikely; it is probable that Isaiah is the servant and that the messengers are God's prophets or others whom He may send to accomplish a divine purpose. But whoever is in view, the Lord fulfills His purpose and word through them. He has challenged the idols to do likewise, but they have failed to respond. He now proposes to accomplish His purpose through Cyrus. Through Isaiah Jehovah now says that Jerusalem shall be inhabited, the cities of Judah shall be rebuilt, and the waste places, so numerous during the captivity, shall be raised up. In this particular case, the *messengers* would include the prophets Jeremiah, Ezekiel, Haggai, and Zechariah, as well as Cyrus, through whom the return was effected.

27 The Lord not only reveals through His servant, the prophet, what He will do about restoring the Jews to their country and cities, but He also further declares His power: I am Jehovah, *that saith to the deep, Be dry, and I will dry up thy rivers.* One view of this passage is that God is referring to the dividing of the Red Sea that allowed Israel to pass through on dry land, and to the crossing of the Jordan, which "rose up in one heap" (Josh. 3:16), providing dry ground on which the Israelites could cross. A second opinion is that the reference is to the taking of Babylon when Cyrus diverted the flow of the Euphrates River in such a way that he was able to use the dry riverbed as a passageway under the wall into the city. A third thought is that the prophet is speaking metaphorically of God's power to overcome all obstacles which might stand in opposition to the carrying out of His will; there are no obstacles which He cannot remove. This third view is preferable.

28   To this point the deliverer has not been specifically identified. But now Jehovah does a thing unheard of among the nations: He names the one whom He will raise up to deliver His people some one hundred fifty years hence: I am Jehovah, *that saith of Cyrus, He is my shepherd, and shall perform all my pleasure, even saying of Jerusalem, She shall be built; and of the temple, Thy foundation shall be laid.* In this announcement the prophet reaches the climax toward which he has been moving since his prophecy in 41:1–7. A shepherd is one who tends or pastures a flock. Cyrus will act as Jehovah's shepherd, seeing that Jerusalem and the temple are rebuilt and His flock restored to their proper homeland. Deliverer and deliverance are determined in the secret counsel of the Almighty, which is fulfilled in His own time. The naming of Cyrus more than a century in advance is a stumbling block to modern theologians; therefore, they date the prophecy to the time of Cyrus. But it would require no greater inspiration to announce an event one hundred fifty years in advance than to announce it six months prior to its occurrence. Even if Cyrus had already taken Babylon when the prophecy was spoken, how could one know that he would allow the Jews to return and that Jerusalem would be rebuilt? Without hesitation or apology, this writer stands with the older Bible commentators who ascribed the entire book to but one man, the prophet Isaiah, and believed that by the inspiration of Jehovah's Spirit he foretold events far in the future.

CHAPTER 45
"Unto Me Every Knee Shall Bow"

Jehovah Addresses Cyrus: His Mission (vv. 1–7)

1   Jehovah has addressed the nation Israel, naming Cyrus as His

shepherd who will do all His pleasure; now He addresses Cyrus himself, calling him His anointed and announcing the divine mission to which he is called. As shepherd Cyrus will care for God's flock; as Jehovah's anointed he is designated by the Lord to carry out His purpose of deliverance. The word *shepherd* (44:28) has no reference to the character of the king and does not suggest that he was a worshiper of Jehovah. It is worthy of note that Isaiah does not refer to a single moral or religious virtue in the character of Cyrus, though tradition depicts him as an honorable and good man. When Isaiah uses the term *righteousness* in connection with Cyrus, it is the righteousness of Jehovah and His purpose which is in view. Cyrus is simply an instrument in Jehovah's service; the emphasis is on Jehovah's carrying out His plan through him. The Cyrus Cylinder clearly indicates that he was a polytheist and not a monotheist. In it he refers to Marduk, chief of the Babylonian deities, as "the great lord," and to several lesser deities as gods.[7] Holding Cyrus's right hand, Jehovah led him and controlled his movements and destiny that he might subdue nations. His world conquest was not his own doing, but the work of Jehovah. Through Jehovah, Cyrus was able to loose the loins of kings, to strip them of their power, reducing them to weakness. The doors that opened before him and the gates that would not be shut are the doors and gates of cities which Jehovah gave into his hand. The power by which Cyrus conquered was the power of Jehovah; God was doing what He had said He would do. Idols were powerless before Him.

2 Jehovah now reveals Himself as a mighty and powerful one going before Cyrus, opening the way by removing all obstacles. He will *make the rough places smooth*, that is, make level the hills or mountains (the word seems to so indicate). He will *break in pieces the doors of brass*, the mighty bronze doors or gates of cities (the gates of Babylon were especially famous). He will *cut in sunder the bars of iron*, the heavy iron bars that bolt the doors shut. The emphasis is not on Cyrus, but on Jehovah, who will give him the cities and nations of earth. By His mighty power Jehovah will remove every barrier that

---

7. For a translation of the inscription, see George A. Barton, *Archaeology and the Bible*, 7th ed. (Philadelphia: American Sunday-School Union, 1937), pp. 484–85.

stands in the way of Cyrus's conquest and the return of His people to their own land.

3   Further, Jehovah will give Cyrus the treasures of kings which are laid up in dark vaults or subterranean storehouses, *and hidden riches of secret places*. Under the hand of Jehovah Cyrus conquered Croesus of Lydia, whose very name is synonymous with wealth, taking his riches as booty. Babylon and her great wealth, and the treasures of other cities and nations, also fell to him. This was not because of any righteousness in Cyrus or because of his power, but *that thou mayest know that it is I, Jehovah, who call thee by thy name, even the God of Israel*. Jehovah is vindicating His previous claims of absolute Godhood.

4   Jehovah will give strength to Cyrus for the sake of Jacob His servant and Israel His chosen. In captivity because of their sins and iniquities, the Jews will be delivered by the grace and power of God; Cyrus will be the instrument of that deliverance. It is to this end that God calls and surnames Cyrus, *though thou hast not known me*. As Jehovah used the Assyrians (10:5–11), the Babylonians (Hab. 1:5–6), and Cyrus, though they knew Him not, so He uses the nations and rulers of all time (Dan. 4:17).

5   As Jehovah had repeatedly said to Israel and the nations, so now He declares to Cyrus the eternal truth that He alone is God and besides Him there is no other. In saying, *I will gird thee*, Jehovah means that He will provide Cyrus with the essentials necessary to conquer nations and to allow Israel to return (the girdle or waistband is an essential part of the soldier's equipment). Here the Lord repeats the clause *though thou hast not known me*. This is a proper place to raise the question of how, if Cyrus did not know Jehovah, he was able to assert that Jehovah had given him his victories and had charged him to return the Jews to Judah and rebuild the temple (II Chron. 36:22–23; Ezra 1:1–2). The most reasonable answer is that, given his interest in religion and the Jewish writings, he had himself read this passage in Isaiah, or it was pointed out to him by Daniel, the counsellor of kings, who continued into the third year of his reign (Dan. 10:1). (Cf. Josephus, *Antiquities* XI. 1–2.) Either of these explanations is possible, but the latter is more probable.

6   Jehovah will gird Cyrus not only that Cyrus may know that

Jehovah alone is God (v. 3), but also that the nations may know, *from the rising of the sun, and from the west* (from the east to west), *that there is none besides me.* He is Jehovah, *and there is none else.* The raising up of Cyrus, his conquests, and the return of the Jews to their homeland will stand for all time as a monument to the power and Godhood of Jehovah. And more significantly, the return of the Jews to their land will ensure that the coming Ruler will be born in Bethlehem (Mic. 5:2). This will be further verification of the claims of Jehovah.

7 Jehovah's claim that He forms the light and creates darkness presents no problem, for darkness is simply the absence of light. He created—initiated—the darkness; He then fashioned or formed the light, dispelling the darkness by His creative ability and action. As in the physical world, so in the moral; where no light is fashioned, darkness prevails as the consequence of the absence of light; when light is formed, darkness is dissipated. The clause *I make peace, and create evil,* presents some difficulty, for we know that God is not the author of moral evil. The Hebrew word translated *make* "frequently emphasizes God's acts in the sphere of history."[8] And though *peace* connotes prosperity, completeness, and fulfillment of one's undertakings, it also means the absence of strife. This is probably the meaning here; God intervenes to end strife. His claim to *create evil* should be interpreted accordingly. This is not moral evil, but the judgments which Jehovah sends into history. He is speaking of the distress and disaster which men experience from God as a consequence of their sin (cf. Amos 3:6).

Heaven's Cooperation Invoked (v. 8)

8 Heaven and earth are summoned to join hands in the glory of Israel's redemption and restoration. Let the skies pour forth righteousness like rain from heaven, and let the earth open her bosom to receive it, that the fruit of salvation may spring forth. The *righteousness* to be established in the world seems to be an ethical and moral standard in accordance with God's nature and will. "Salvation"

---

8. *Theological Wordbook of the Old Testament*, vol. 2, p. 701.

is deliverance, safety, freedom from distress. Righteousness and salvation shall spring up together. *I, Jehovah, have created it*—I have made ample provision for this union; therefore, my work to this end will be done. And indeed, idolatry in Israel was abolished to a marked degree, the deliverer was raised up, and the people brought home; but the results were disappointing. Israel's failure after the return of the Jews is revealed in the prophetic books of Haggai, Zechariah, and Malachi; the historical books Ezra and Nehemiah; and Daniel's prophecy of events to occur between the Covenants (chs. 10–12). Consequently, the commands in this verse were not fully carried out until the coming of the ideal Servant.

Jehovah's Response to Israel's Complaint (vv. 9–13)

9   Jehovah now responds to Israel's complaint (real or anticipated) about being delivered by a heathen king: *Woe unto* (or, Alas for) *him that striveth with his Maker!* The word translated *striveth* may refer to verbal controversy or to complaining; it may also have a legal-judicial significance. In this instance it probably means "to complain about what God is doing." A *potsherd* is a potter's product, a vessel made of clay. Or the reference may be to a fragment large enough to bear water or fire (30:14). The point made by the prophet is that man, a vessel of clay, is as completely out of line when he complains to God about His work, as a clay pot would be in criticizing the potter who fashioned it (cf. 29:16; Rom. 9:20). The complaint is about God's raising Cyrus, a heathen, to deliver Israel or about handling Israel as He has. He has acted as if He has no hands, bungling the job.

10   In a metaphor which depicts Israel's action as even more offensive, the prophet parallels Israel's contention with Jehovah to a child's criticizing his parents for making him what he is. You should have made me different or not at all.

11   Jehovah now replies to the faultfinder's criticism of what He is doing. As the Holy One and Maker of Israel, Jehovah has the wisdom and the right to make of him a vessel after His pleasure and for His divine purpose; therefore, Israel should inquire of Him and learn of His purpose before criticizing His work. Jehovah urges, yea, commands, the critics to ask Him concerning the things that are to come;

what are the Lord's long-range plans for His people? And inasmuch as they have insinuated that He has no hands by which to accomplish His work (v. 9), they should ask Him what He seeks to accomplish. As their Father, Jehovah stands ready to reveal His plans to them and in fact does so in later prophecies.

12   In His wisdom and by His power Jehovah created the earth, made and placed man upon it, and with His hands (in response to the charge of v. 9) stretched out the heavens; *and all their host have I commanded. Their host* may refer to the sun, moon, and stars, which God controls, or it may refer to the angelic host that serves His purpose at His command. In either case, as Creator He directs their actions and gives the orders; He is neither directed in His actions, nor does He take orders.

13   There is no ground for Israel's anxiety concerning Cyrus, nor is there ground for complaint against Jehovah's work. As the Maker of Israel and Planner of his destiny, as the Creator of earth and heaven and Commander of the host of heaven, He will raise up Cyrus *in righteousness* (cf. 41:2). That is, Jehovah will raise up Cyrus to carry out His own righteous purpose; all of Cyrus's conquests will be to this end. Jehovah *will make straight all his ways*—God will direct Cyrus's paths of conquest and remove all obstacles that stand in the way. Because Cyrus allowed the exiles to return home and rebuild the city, it could be said that he built it. This action was *not for price nor reward*, but of Jehovah's own will, power, and grace. So Israel has no just reason to complain. This is the way God has planned it, and this is the way it will be done.

The Effect of Israel's Redemption upon the Gentiles (vv. 14–17)

14   Israel's victory and redemption under Jehovah, through Cyrus, will have a profound effect upon the Gentiles. Three nations (cf. 43:3) which seem to be representative of the heathen generally, are named. *The labor of Egypt* stands for the fruit of her labor; *the merchandise of Ethiopia* represents the wealth gained by commerce. Whybray thinks these phrases refer to the people themselves—"the toilers of Egypt; the traders of Ethiopia" (p. 109). Together with the

Sabeans, men of stature and strength, they *shall come over unto thee,* an indication of free choice in the matter—they "offer themselves willingly/In the day of thy power" (Ps. 110:3). They shall become a part of Israel and go after him *in chains* like bondservants. *They shall fall down unto thee,* not to worship Israel, but to make supplication, saying, *Surely God is in thee; and there is none else;* there is no deity or god besides the God of Israel. The Gentiles will offer themselves and what they have, they will go after and bow down to Israel, because of the God who is in the midst of Israel. Just as He will be the power that draws and uses Cyrus, so will He be the power that draws the heathen.

15   Commentators differ as to who now speaks. Some think the redeemed heathens of verse 14 are the speakers, asking why Jehovah has so long hid Himself from them. Others, with greater probability, hold that it is the prophet speaking, expressing his astonishment and wonder at what has been done. The clause *Verily thou art a God that hidest thyself* probably means that Jehovah "reserves the right to veil some of His purposes."[9] The full effect of Israel's redemption upon the heathen has been veiled. It is now clearly manifested, however, that Israel's God is *the Saviour* of Gentiles as well, for there is no other.

16   Beholding what God has done for Israel and what influence that action has had on the idolatrous nations, the makers and worshipers of idols are put to shame and thrown into a state of confusion. Together they are disgraced and humiliated at the exposure of their folly, for their whole cause is defeated and lost—permanently and eternally.

17   Israel's state is boldly contrasted with that of the idolaters, and Jehovah's power with that of the idols: *Israel shall be saved by Jehovah with an everlasting salvation.* The word *everlasting* is subject to several interpretations, but here it indicates a permanent and endless salvation. The everlasting salvation which emanates from Jehovah will bear His likeness; it, too, will be endless. This is confirmed by the assurance that, unlike the idolaters, Israel shall not be put to shame nor confounded, *world without end* (from the same Hebrew word as

---

9. *Theological Wordbook of the Old Testament,* vol. 2, p. 636.

everlasting). Israel's freedom from shame and from confusion and their salvation will be coexistent; both are without end.

It seems evident that the prophet is not looking for a literal coming of the three nations in chains, bowing before Israel and accepting Jehovah as God upon the return from Babylon. This did not happen; nor can Israel's deliverance from Babylon be deemed an *everlasting salvation*, for they were under some kind of bondage until the Christ came. But with their return under the command of Cyrus the way was being opened for the full realization of the promises in this passage. These prophecies were fulfilled in a spiritual sense under the Messiah, whom Cyrus foreshadowed (see the comments on 41:17–20; 42:1–13; 43:4–7, 18–21; 44:1–5). Throughout Part Two Jehovah is working and pointing toward the coming of the spiritual Servant, the Redeemer and Deliverer from sin.

Jehovah's Purpose in Creation (vv. 18–25)

18   In verses 18–19, Jehovah appeals to His two great witnesses: creation and revelation. First He declares that He is God in the fullest and most absolute sense and that as the Creator of heaven and earth He had before Him a divine purpose. He did not create the earth to be a waste (*tohu*, "chaos"), but to be a suitable habitation for living creatures. Although in the beginning it was a waste (*tohu*, Gen. 1:2), it was not created to remain in such a condition; this is Isaiah's point. The ability of God's created earth to sustain life as we know it, to be a fit dwelling-place for man, and to provide for his every physical need, testifies to His absolute Godhood; He alone is God. The earth was *established*, permanently fixed, for this purpose.

19   The second witness supporting Jehovah's claim to sole deity is revelation. Unlike the spokesmen for heathen idols who reveal their messages from the dark recesses of caves or the inner sanctums of temples, or by alleged communications from the spirits of the dead, He speaks openly. At Sinai He spoke to the people in a thundering voice, clear and distinct; then He put His words in the mouth of prophets who were to declare them to the people (Deut. 18:18–19). As the people were not to live in a physical chaos, so were they not to live in a moral void. God did not say, *Seek ye me in vain* (*tohu*, "chaos" as in v. 18); they were not to live in spiritual and moral confusion and emptiness. As they lived in an all-sufficient physical world where every need was provided, so were they to live in an all-sufficient spiritual world. When Jehovah speaks, He reveals only righteousness. Like the wonders of creation, the fulfillment of all spiritual needs through Jehovah's word of revelation testifies that He is God.

20 Having provided an all-sufficient world in which He would have men live, Jehovah addresses the heathen: *Assemble yourselves and come; draw near together, ye that are escaped of the nations.* The Lord does not limit His call to those who would escape the upheavals consequent upon Cyrus's conquest of the world, but includes all who would escape the judgments to come; for all nations will be judged. Isaiah earlier said, "When thy judgments are in the earth, the inhabitants of the world learn righteousness" (26:9); the Lord would now have them learn the righteousness of His revelation. As only a remnant of Israel will escape and return to Jehovah, so amidst the Gentiles only a remnant will escape to hear God's call and come. They who serve idols of wood which must be carried about *have no knowledge,* that is, they do not have the knowledge provided by Jehovah, and they *pray unto a god that cannot save.* Those who serve a god that cannot save them live in a chaos, a world of spiritual and moral confusion.

21 Once again the Lord challenges the heathen to declare something and then bring forth its fulfillment (cf. 41:22–23; 43:9). As time progresses and the prophecies concerning the nations (chs. 13–23), Cyrus and Babylon, and Israel and the Servant are fulfilled, Jehovah's case will be incontestably established. The heathen will recognize Him as the only God and the Savior of all—Jews and Gentiles.

22 With the evidence clearly presented, Jehovah makes an appeal to all men, even to the ends of the earth, to look unto Him. All gods have failed; only Jehovah's claims have stood. Therefore, look to Him that you may be saved. Though all are invited, it is only as individuals that men will respond.

23 *By myself have I sworn*—Jehovah could swear by none greater (cf. 62:8; Gen. 22:16; Jer. 22:5; Rom. 14:11; Heb. 6:13–20)—*the word is gone forth from my mouth,* that is, the word of the oath, *that* *unto me every knee shall bow, every tongue shall swear.* To swear is to give one's solemn unbreakable word that he will perform some deed, be loyal to some individual, or hold to some truth. In this instance the individual bows the knee in complete submission to the Lord and pledges with his most solemn word to do His will. Shall we follow the text, *the word is gone forth from my mouth in righteousness, and shall not return,* or one of the alternative readings? The first of the translations in the margin—"righteousness is gone forth from my mouth"— may best comport with the Lord's statement in verse 19. Regardless of which reading is followed, it is clear that the word God utters is one of righteousness and that it shall not be taken back; it shall stand.

24 It is an established truth that only in Jehovah are righteousness and strength, and all who seek these virtues must come to Him. But not everyone seeks righteousness and truth, for there have been and will be those who are antagonistic to His work in His people. There has been opposition from the time of the return to Judah to the time of the Messiah and following. But all the enemies of God will eventually be put to shame, for His cause will prevail and theirs will fail.

25 This verse cannot apply to physical Israel, for some of its members neither are justified nor glory in Jehovah. But in spiritual Israel, the remnant redeemed under the Servant, this verse is realized to the full. The return under Cyrus pointed to a greater and more glorious deliverance and redemption under the Messiah, a deliverance which would include both Jews and Gentiles.

CHAPTER 46

Jehovah and the Gods of Babylon

Chapters 46 and 47 reveal the impending doom of Babylon. Cyrus's call and mission have been set forth, and now Jehovah is ready to make known the fall of the great heathen city. The prophet begins by describing the impotence of her gods. Unable to carry their worshipers or save themselves, the idols of Babylon must be borne on beasts of burden. In contrast, Jehovah is not borne by His people, but bears them.

The Shame of Babylon's Gods (vv. 1–2)

1   The name *Bel*, which is cognate with the Canaanite term *Baal* and means "lord" or "possessor," was given as an honorific title to the Babylonian god Marduk. It gradually became the common name for Marduk. [10] *Bel boweth down;* he kneels or sinks down to his knees, an indication of helplessness. *Nebo*, son of Marduk, was "the god of wisdom and writing, and the patron-god of the Babylonian rulers." [11] His name appears as an element in the names Nabopolassar, Nebuchadnezzar, and Nabonidus. He *stoopeth*, bends down or crouches. The reference to *their idols*, the idols of Bel and Nebo, indicates a distinction between the deities themselves and their idol representations. These inanimate objects are heavy loads on the backs of beasts and domesticated cattle which wearily trudge along. The weariness of the beasts suggests that the idols are being carried away into some distant place.

2   *They*, Bel and Nebo, as well as the images that represent them, *bow down together*. Being unable to deliver the people, the idols must go into captivity. The Cyrus Cylinder (see p. 378, n. 7) depicts the conqueror accepting Babylon's gods and doing homage to them. Thus their time extended beyond the fall of Babylon. Nevertheless, Isaiah's word holds fast, for they were eventually cast down and carried into oblivion.

The Glory of Israel's God (vv. 3–11)

3–5   Jehovah addresses three urgent admonitions to the house of Jacob, now reduced to the remnant of Israel: *Hearken* (v. 3), *Remember* (v. 8), and *Hearken* (v. 12). To *hearken* is to give ear or attention to what is about to be said; in this instance, behold and

---

10. *Zondervan Pictorial Encyclopedia of the Bible*, ed. Merrill C. Tenney (Grand Rapids: Zondervan, 1975), vol. 1, p. 511.
11. Ibid., vol. 4, p. 394.

consider the difference between the idols and Jehovah. The heathen idols must be borne upon beasts, whereas Jehovah has borne Israel from their birth (from the selection of Abraham or from Sinai). He has borne them "on eagles' wings," bringing them to Himself (Exod. 19:4; Deut. 32:11); as a father bears his son (Deut. 1:31), so He bore them through the wilderness. In His care for them He "gather[s] the lambs in his arm, and carr[ies] them in his bosom" (40:11). In the highest and most divine sense, the prophet says that God carries them upon His heart, for "in all their affliction he was afflicted, . . . in his love and in his pity he redeemed them; and he bare them, and carried them all the days of old" (63:9). And even now, He is not ready to give them up, but will carry them to venerable old age. Smith has fittingly said, "It makes all the difference to a man how he conceives his religion—whether as something he has to carry, or as something that will carry him" (II. 198). This is one of the distinctions between the idols and Jehovah. He so transcends every other being known to man that there is none with whom to compare Him.

6   The prophet again points out the folly of idolatry and idols, the making of which begins with a profuse pouring or shaking out of gold from a bag and a weighing of silver in the balances. The gold and silver are then turned over to a metalsmith who is hired to make a god. For him this is just a way to earn a living; he may have no regard for the deity. The manufacture of idols grew out of a materialistic concept of deity and a realization of man's need for an object of worship. They who furnished the material and paid the idol-maker now fall down and worship the inanimate object he has fashioned. Is it proper to compare this abomination with the man who fashioned it (let alone with Jehovah, who created the material that went into it)? Surely human intelligence, even if not properly directed, and will are greater than material substance.

7   Now that it has been made, the idol must be borne on the shoulders of man or beast to whatever place has been chosen for it. There it remains, staring lifelessly into space; it cannot remove itself. In their folly men cry to it, pressing their appeals for help in time of need or for deliverance from oppression; their cries are to no avail, for the idol remains silent, helpless to respond. Even today man continues to fashion idols which are first conceived in hearts that know

not God, only to find that in time of need they utterly fail him, leaving him in a chaos of confusion.

8 Jehovah issues a second admonition to those wavering between Himself and the idols: *Remember this,* what He has said about idols and Himself—they cannot save, only He can. Remembering is a faculty of man which enables him to store facts in his mind for future use, and then, through reasoning, to act upon them. *Show yourselves* (to be) *men,* not vacillating weaklings, but strong individuals able to reason and respond in a sensible manner. *Bring it again to mind*—make use of what I have said—*O ye transgressors.* The Hebrew word translated *transgressors* is used of people who have cast off their allegiance or rebelled against their rulers. Wavering Israel, or those among Israel who waver in choosing between Jehovah and the idols, are charged with rebellion against their sovereign King (cf. 1:28). For this they will find themselves in Babylon.

9 Remember not only what Jehovah is saying of things present, but also *Remember the former things of old,* what He said and did in the distant past. These things will confirm what He is about to say. God repeats His claims to absolute deity: I am *El,* the mighty God of strength, and *Elohim,* "the Being who unites in Himself all divine majesty by which reverence is evoked" (Delitzsch, II. 235). There is no one like Him; He stands alone.

10 Israel is called to look back upon ancient times and learn; they are to consider God's ability in contrast to that of heathen idols and to cease wavering between the two. Jehovah declares *the end from the beginning, and from ancient times things that are not yet done.* Some things declared of old have been carried out; some have not. Those that have come to pass stand as a guarantee that the things *not yet done* will be done. And further, *My counsel,* that is, God's purpose and will, *shall stand,* be established, *and I will do all my pleasure.* Only Jehovah is able to do this. Israel can test this assertion for themselves. They need simply look back to the call of Abraham with its promise of a great nation and then see the fulfillment through the driving out of the Amorites and a whole host of other events down to the present. All of them were declared before they were done.

11 Now for that which is not yet done: *calling a ravenous bird* (literally, "a bird of prey") *from the east, the man of my counsel* (or

selection) *from a far country*. Cyrus the Persian is again referred to as the man of God's choice (41:1–7; 44:28–45:7). Persia lay to the east of Babylon, a far country in relationship to Jerusalem. Jehovah has spoken; He will bring to pass what He has said. When Cyrus arises, overthrows Babylon, and allows God's people to return, Jehovah's claim to being the sole deity will be even further established.

Salvation Is Drawing Near (vv. 12–13)

12   Jehovah has called upon the house of Jacob—the remnant of Israel—to hearken (v. 3), and upon the transgressors to remember (v. 8). He now addresses the *stout-hearted*, the stubborn of heart, probably the transgressors of verse 8, to listen and take heed to what He is saying. In this condition, they *are far from righteousness*, God's moral, ethical, and spiritual standard. In their state of transgression and stubbornness of heart, they will suffer Jehovah's righteous judgment—the destruction of their city and temple, and captivity in Babylon. Likewise, His raising up Cyrus to overthrow Babylon will be a righteous judgment against that city's sinful condition. Allowing a remnant to return home will be an act in accordance with His own immutable standard, character, and will. His every act is absolute right.

13   Jehovah brings forth His *righteousness*; as the basis of all His actions, it is never far off. Accompanying His righteousness is His salvation, which shall not tarry. It should be noted that both righteousness and salvation are the provision of God; neither idols nor man can provide them. The Hebrew word translated *salvation* is from a root meaning "to make wide," which connotes a freeing from distress, deliverance from that which restricts.[12] Inasmuch as Jehovah's deliverance is based on His righteousness, *righteousness* and *salvation* are here parallel. But in a state of transgression and stubbornness of heart one cannot experience deliverance; there must be a change of affection, mind, and will. This change is expressed in repentance and a genuine faith in God which impels one to implicit obedience to His will as set forth in His word. The salvation provided

---

12. *Theological Wordbook of the Old Testament*, vol. 1, p. 414.

by Jehovah's righteousness shall be in Zion, to which those who are delivered will have returned. There, Israel shall be for Jehovah's glory, the glory of His name, power, and absolute deity.

CHAPTER 47
Jehovah's Judgment Pronounced on Babylon

From near the dawn of human history to its sunset, Babylon has been and will continue to be a symbol of pride and enmity against the eternal God and His standard of righteousness. The tower erected at Babel (forerunner of Babylon) after the flood (Gen. 11:1–9) was an expression of man's desire to have his own god and a religion molded after the imagination of his own heart. The Babylon of Chaldea, characterized by the same spirit, symbolized the cruelty and haughtiness of man without God, the pride of man when left to his own devices. The Babylon of Revelation (chs. 17–18) represented Rome, the center of world power, conquest, commerce, and wealth, with all their attendant vices. John's Babylon thus became a permanent symbol of all that is lustful, seductive, and enticing—all that appeals to the flesh. Each of the Babylons either has been or will be brought to an end by divine judgment. God rules in history, and His ways cannot be flouted without dire consequence.

In chapter 14 Isaiah dealt with the arrogant boast and fall of the Babylonian king; in chapter 46 he revealed the divine judgment against the idols of Babylon; now he points to the fall of the queen city herself. All arrogant, proud, cruel, and immoral cities that leave God out of their thinking will suffer a similar fate.

The Humiliation of Babylon (vv. 1–7)

1 Although there have been other suggestions, it seems that except in verse 4, Jehovah is the speaker throughout this chapter. He begins by addressing Babylon as the former queen of a great empire. From this position of glory and grandeur she is cast down to the place of a slave girl. *Sit in the dust . . . sit on the ground*—what humilia-

tion and shame! The form of address—O *virgin daughter of Babylon*—does not refer to moral chastity, but to the fact that since Babylon became a world power, neither city nor land has been humbled; she has long been inviolable. The Chaldean Empire extended northwest from the Persian Gulf to the Mediterranean Sea. The queen city would no longer be called *tender and delicate* (cf. Deut. 28:56), the consequence of profligate living; the period of luxury would be over.

2 Babylon is told to *Take the millstones*, which were two stones used to grind grain. The lower stone was larger and remained stationary; the upper stone was moved back and forth over grain to grind it into flour. Grinding grain was a menial task usually performed by women; this is to be the lot of voluptuous Babylon. *Remove thy veil, strip off the train*—lift the skirt, thereby uncovering the leg—an action preparatory to crossing streams. The undressing of Babylon and the exposing of the proud woman's body will be most humiliating. As Babylon had humbled nations, stripping them of their glory and carrying them into captivity, so will she be humbled in the presence of others.

3 Stripped of her power, wealth, and glory, Babylon will appear before the nations in her nakedness and shame, to be stared at and mocked by men. The assertion *I will take vengeance, and will spare no man*, must be understood in the light of Jehovah's holiness and justice, the foundation of His throne—a fire goes before Him and devours His adversaries (Ps. 97:2–3). He had long before said, "Vengeance is mine, and recompense. . . ./I will render vengeance to mine adversaries,/And will recompense them that hate me" (Deut. 32:35, 41). The very foundation on which rests His throne—the throne of the universe—demands an avenging of all unrighteousness, a vindication of His righteous and holy Godhead and laws. He will neither withdraw this declaration of judgment nor make exceptions to it.

4 It is uncertain whether this exclamation is voiced by the prophet as he rejoices in Jehovah's power and will to accomplish the downfall of Babylon, or by the captives who shout praise at the Lord's assurance of Babylon's fall. In either case, it can be said, "This is Jehovah's doing;/It is marvelous in our eyes" (Ps. 118:23).

5   Humiliated by the shame of her fall, the proud queen is now told to sit in the silence of her grief, no longer boasting of her greatness but slinking away into the darkness of obscurity and oblivion. *For thou shalt no more be called The mistress of kingdoms*, the ruling lady of nations. Although Babylon is not specifically referred to as a harlot, comparison of this general description with Nahum's characterization of Nineveh, the "well-favored harlot, the mistress of witchcrafts" (Nah. 3:4), suggests that she falls into the same category.

6   The Lord explains the reason for the severity of His judgment against Babylon. He was indignant against Israel because of their disregard for Him and for the dignity of their calling. Therefore, He allowed His people to be profaned—defiled, considered unholy instead of holy—by committing them to the hands of Babylon for punishment and correction. Babylon showed them no mercy, disregarding all principles of humane consideration by cruelly placing heavy burdens upon all, even the aged. But the fact that "in the image of God made he man" (Gen. 9:6) renders respect for the dignity of life and human rights obligatory. This duty was totally disregarded by Babylon.

7   Confident of her power to withstand all opponents permanently, Babylon had boasted in vaunting pride, *I shall be mistress for ever*. She gave no thought either to her actions or to the divine law of retribution. She considered herself beyond God's reach; she placed herself in the realm of deity.

Babylon's Blasphemous Claims and Their Consequences (vv. 8–11)

8   *Now therefore* introduces a series of claims made by Babylon and the consequent judgments determined by Jehovah. The mistress was living *securely* ("carelessly," King James), in a state of unconcern. In her arrogant heart she said, *I am, and there is none else besides me*, a claim which Jehovah alone can make and which He had made repeatedly (e.g., 45:5–6, 18; 46:9). In making this claim Babylon exalted herself to a place of deity (cf. Nineveh's boast in her period of greatness—Zeph. 2:15). Blissfully ignoring any force or power outside herself, she makes a further boast that she will not experience

widowhood nor the loss of children. Her destiny is safely in her own hands. Widowhood and the loss of children are great calamities in the life of any woman. The expression is used metaphorically of one who is left helpless and lonely, reduced to the status of a slave.

9   But both of the calamities from which the queen feels secure shall come upon her *in a moment in one day,* very suddenly, *in their full measure,* to an extent commensurate with her blasphemous boast. They will come despite the multitude and abundance of her magical arts, which will be unable to save her. Babylon was noted for her magical arts: astrology originated there, and witchcraft of every sort abounded. *Sorceries* were a form of witchcraft, the casting of a spell over either an individual or a nation. *Enchantments* were means used to charm and influence people in devious ways.

10   Babylon has already been charged with cruelty and arrogance; now a third sin is laid at her feet: *Thou hast trusted in thy wickedness.* The *wickedness* in which she trusts is probably a characterization of the whole course of her life; however, some aspects of it are specified. Among them are self-deification, which makes her feel secure and indestructible, and the use of the occult arts to seduce others. And now is added the boast *None seeth me.* What Babylon deems wisdom and knowledge has actually caused her heart to turn aside from true wisdom and knowledge. She ignorantly claims to be divine and therefore responsible to no one. Pride and arrogance are truly deceptive (cf. Obad. 3–4).

11   Babylon's wickedness brings upon her God's evil, the distress and disaster of judgment (for *evil* see the comments on 45:7). It is difficult to determine which is correct: the reading in the text—*thou shalt not know the dawning thereof,* or the reading of the margin— "how to charm it away." Either suits the context. If the former is accepted, the point is that the consequence of wickedness comes so gradually that man is unconscious of its power until it is too late; then the full brunt hits suddenly, in a moment. If the latter is accepted, then the prophet is saying that all of Babylon's magical arts are unable to avert the evil. In either case, she does not see it coming until it is upon her; and when she does see it, all her magical arts are unable to charm it away. *Mischief*—calamities—will come upon her unexpectedly; *desolation*—devastation, a day of ruin such as results in a desert

waste—*shall come upon thee suddenly.* As Paul put it, "When they are saying, Peace and safety, then sudden destruction cometh upon them" (I Thess. 5:3). Here is a lesson for all time.

The Failure of Babylon's Occult Arts (vv. 12–15)

12 The Lord has declared that destruction is on its way (v. 11), and now He calls upon the great imperial city to stand with her multitude of enchantments and sorceries (cf. v. 9), and to put them to the test. Her wise men had not attended to these subjects as amusing pastimes, but had labored as seriously to learn their secrets as do devoted students of a science. An opportunity to challenge the entire system is now at hand. Apparently in a sarcastic vein the Lord adds, *If so be thou shalt be able to profit, if so be thou mayest prevail* ("strike terror," margin; i.e., in Jehovah or His people).

13 Throughout history man has desired to look into and know the future. All occult systems are efforts toward this end, but this prerogative belongs only to God. Babylon has wearied herself in the multitude of her counsels, consulting with the various orders of the magical arts, receiving advice and various plans from them. Three types of advisors are named: *astrologers* ("dividers of the heavens," Hebrew—the word occurs only here), who make an effort to determine hidden mysteries; *star-gazers*, men who study the movements of the stars to discover messages from and the will of their gods; and the *monthly prognosticators*, "men who knew the omens of the new moon."[13] These groups are called to stand up (with those of v. 12), *and save thee* (Babylon) *from the things that shall come upon thee.*

14 Unable to save others, the occultists are also powerless to save themselves from the flame, and they shall all perish like dry grass or chaff in a quick blaze. The fire will be a flash, burning brightly for a moment and subsiding as quickly. It will provide nothing beneficial, not even *a coal to warm at, nor a fire to sit before.*

15 This will be the end of those pursuits upon which Babylon has expended her labor and in which she has placed her trust; they

---

13. *International Standard Bible Encyclopedia*, ed. James Orr (Chicago: Howard-Severance, 1937), vol. 1, p. 297.

will fail in time of need, for all things earthly are vanity and a striving after wind. Also, the merchants and tradesmen with whom she has done business from her beginning will likewise fail her in time of necessity. They shall each go to his own particular place. When the judgment falls, Babylon's gods will prove impotent, her wisdom and cunning will be ineffectual, her host of specialists in the field of magic shall come to nought, and her commercial connections will all fail her. *There shall be none to save thee.* Since the day in which this prophecy was fulfilled, the history of Babylon has been repeated over and over in the annals of nations; and yet men fail to learn!

CHAPTER 48

Assurance of Deliverance

Chapter 48 concludes this section, which has dealt primarily with Jehovah's controversy with the heathen idols, His plan involving Cyrus, and the destruction of Babylon. His purpose has been twofold: to strengthen Israel's faith in Him and to show the folly of worshiping or fearing idols, for they are impotent and the gods they represent are nonentities. Commentators acknowledge several difficulties with regard to this chapter; there are questions concerning authorship, date, and division. We shall proceed on the assumption that the prophet Isaiah is the author. He projected himself into the time of the Babylonian captivity; from that vantage point he looked back at the cause of the captivity, and forward to the deliverance by Cyrus as being at hand. Jehovah is speaking through Isaiah, revealing that which is to come.

Rebuke of Israel's Hypocrisy and Stubbornness (vv. 1–11)

1   Jehovah addresses the exiles as the *house of Jacob, who are called by the name of Israel,* indicating that their life reflected the cunning supplanter (Jacob) rather than the prince of God (Israel). Their coming *forth out of the waters of Judah* points out that their tribe of origin is Judah, the headwaters of the nation. National hypoc-

risy is clearly indicated by their appeal to Jehovah, *the God of Israel*, in an oath. They recognize a relationship to Him, but their oath is *not in truth*, the root meaning of which is "firmness," "certainty," "fidelity." Their oath is not according to the standard of right.

2 The exiles claim citizenship and residence in *the holy city*, Jerusalem (cf. 52:1), where Jehovah dwells, giving it the quality of holiness. They lean upon Jehovah, looking to Him for support, but neither in faith and true confidence nor in a way to merit that support.

3 Jehovah again affirms that He has done what He has challenged the heathen and their gods to do. He has *declared the former things from of old* (cf. 41:22; 42:9; 43:18; 44:7–8; 45:21; 46:9–10)—He announced them and then brought them to pass. Are *the former things* events in the earlier history of Israel, or are they the Babylonian captivity and the raising up of Cyrus? Since we hold the view that the prophet Isaiah himself wrote the entire book in the period 740–700 B.C., the *former things* are the promises concerning, for example, Abraham, Egypt, the exodus, and the development of Israel, which were fulfilled prior to 740. Numerous events had been declared in advance and fulfilled by that time. The people could examine the evidence—the prophecies and their fulfillment—for themselves.

4–5 God's reason for declaring in advance what He will do is Israel's rebellious attitude. He lists three of their characteristics: (1) they are *obstinate*, stubborn, and rebellious against the yoke laid upon them; (2) their *neck is an iron sinew*—a stiff-necked people, their tendons are iron rather than human tissue—and (3) their *brow brass*—they are hardheaded. Knowing of their disposition against Him and their devotion to the gods of their own creation, the Lord anticipated that they would ascribe His actions to their idols, that they would say their idols *commanded* these actions and brought them forth.

6 As Jehovah's people who had heard the words of His prophets and had seen them brought to pass, Israel should have been anxious to confess Jehovah as God and herald this truth to the heathen. Instead, they had refused. Since they had failed to benefit by the former prophecies and their fulfillments, Jehovah will now show

397

them *new things from this time, even hidden things, which thou hast not known.* Are these *new things* the raising of Cyrus, the destruction of Babylon, and the Jews' return from exile? This is unlikely, since these events have been the theme of chapters 40–47. It is more probable that the *new things* are Jehovah's work set forth in the remainder of Isaiah's prophecy, especially the new concept of the Servant, who by suffering will deliver both the Jews and Gentiles (49:1–13; 53). The *new things* also include the enlargement and glory of redeemed Zion (e.g., ch. 54), and a completely new order, a new heaven and new earth (65:16–17, 25). Though foredetermined in the mind of God, these things have heretofore been hidden or kept from the nation's view.

7 *They are created*—brought into being or initiated—*now, and not from of old.* This raises another question: In what sense are these coming works of God created now? It is clearly revealed in both Isaiah (e.g., 46:10) and the New Testament (Rom. 8:28; 9:11; Eph. 1:9–11; 3:11; II Tim. 1:9; I Peter 1:10–12, 20) that God's plan—His scheme of redemption, which includes the suffering Servant—was in His mind as a divine purpose from of old. In His present activity of returning and restoring the Jews through Cyrus, Jehovah is working out this purpose and bringing it into effect. *Before this day* it had not been made known unto Israel what the Lord was doing, lest they should say that they knew it all the time, that their idols had made it known to them. Having told His people this much, the Lord will proceed with fulfilling His plan.

8 Israel has neither heard nor known from of old what God's ultimate purpose is, for their *ear was not opened* to understand. They heard the word, but they did not hear the message, for they could not understand until their ear was opened by Jehovah to reveal His purpose to them (cf. I Cor. 2:8–13). He was unable to make His plan known to them because He was aware of their treachery and unfaithfulness; like an unfaithful spouse, they had disregarded the terms of God's covenant from the time of their beginning.

9 Although Israel's hypocrisy (v. 1), obstinacy (v. 4), devotion to idols (v. 5), general deafness to His word, treachery, and transgression have aroused Jehovah's anger and indignation, yet for His name's sake and for His praise He will defer the full expression of His anger. To cut

the nation off at this time would defeat His purpose of bringing in the Servant Savior through Israel; therefore, He will not cut the nation off. However, when the Servant came and they crucified Him, Jehovah did cut them off.

10   This verse is subject to several translations, and consequently to as many interpretations. Of the numerous interpretations suggested by commentators, the most plausible is presented here. Silver is refined that the metal might be separated from any impurities. But when Jehovah placed Israel in the furnace of affliction, He did not try them with the intensity of heat which is necessary to refine silver. The results are disappointing: there is no pure silver; dross remains in the nation.

11   Jehovah now reiterates what He said in verse 9. The phrase *For my own sake* is repeated for emphasis. He defers His anger for His own sake; to make sure that His name will not be defiled, dishonored, or desecrated by the heathen, He will not destroy Israel as they deserve. If He did, the heathen would probably ascribe to their deities the glory that is His, just as Israel had put Him on a level with idols. This He will not allow. Nor will He allow weakness to be charged against Him on the ground that He has overlooked their sins. Consequently, He rebukes the nation for its hypocrisy, but does not destroy it.

Jehovah's Faithfulness (vv. 12–16)

12   If any among His people yet question Jehovah's will and ability to bring them back to their homeland, let them hearken to what He has to say. He has "chosen" (44:1) and "called" Israel; their return is guaranteed by the eternal God—*I am he; I am the first, I also am the last.* When time began, He was there; and He will be there when time fades away into eternity; in between He has never ceased to be and to be in control. The word of such a God is the guarantee of their return.

13   Jehovah's *hand hath laid the foundation of the earth.* This is probably a reference to its being firmly established, for Job said, "He . . . hangeth the earth upon nothing" (Job 26:7), an indication that there is no material substance upon which it rests. And the psalmist

said, "The world also is established that it cannot be moved" (Ps. 96:10). Thus the *foundation* is that which holds the earth in its position in space. In addition, with His right hand Jehovah *hath spread out the heavens*, the great expanse. So both the earth, which was created to be inhabited (45:18), and the heavens, with their multiplied millions of stars, planets, and galaxies, are the work of His hands. And they are all subject to His command, for when He calls unto them, *they stand up together*; they stand at attention to do His bidding.

14   The command, *Assemble yourselves, all ye, and hear*, is addressed to Israel (cf. v. 12). Jehovah's question to them is in reference to the idolaters and their deities (cf. 45:21). What have they declared concerning the things now taking place? Jehovah said that He would raise up one from the east (41:2), a ravenous bird "from a far country" (46:11), who would do His bidding. From the vantage point of the captivity, Jehovah is either doing those things now or will soon do them. The reference to Cyrus as *he whom Jehovah loveth* does not signify the love which brings salvation, but means that Jehovah saw fit to choose Cyrus to faithfully work His will and pleasure upon Babylon; this is the sense in which the Lord loved Cyrus.

15   Israel's hope of deliverance rests upon their faith in Jehovah, the God who has spoken to them. He is the first and the last, that is, He is beyond time; He is the Creator of all that fills space; He is the Controller and Director of history. He has spoken; how can one not believe? Jehovah makes three assertions regarding Cyrus: (1) *I have called him*; (2) *I have brought him*; and (3) *he shall make his way prosperous*. As the heavens and earth stand up at the call of Jehovah, so also does man. Cyrus has responded to the Lord's call; by performing Jehovah's pleasure against Babylon, he shall make his way prosperous, that is, he shall succeed by doing what Jehovah has called him to do. This is the last mention of Cyrus.

16   The Lord calls upon His hearers, *Come ye near unto me, hear ye this*. This seems to indicate that He is about to introduce an important new subject. But first He prepares them for what He is about to say. *From the beginning*, from the time of His choice and call of Israel, Jehovah had spoken to them through His prophets. Therefore He could say, *I have not spoken in secret* (cf. 45:19); He had made

known His will in a clear and understandable way. *From the time that it was*—from the time that He began to communicate with His people through His prophets—*there am I*, always present, always working for Israel, doing "nothing, except he reveal his secret unto his servants the prophets" (Amos 3:7).

The following affirmation is an abrupt intrusion which raises the question of the speaker's identity. Of the many suggestions offered by commentators, only two are in keeping with the context: the speaker is either the prophet Isaiah or the ideal Servant who will come. Although recognizing the difficulties involved, I accept the latter, for *the Lord Jehovah hath sent me, and his Spirit*, is one of the new truths now to be made known. The Servant was introduced earlier in this section (42:1–13), is prominent in the next section (49:1–13; 50:4–11; 52:13–53:12), and appears in the final section (61:1–3). Old Testament prophecy looked to His coming when He would carry out the purpose and work of Jehovah. The Spirit would accompany Him and then complete the work after His return to the Father. If there is objection that this savors too much of New Testament teaching, let it be remembered that Jehovah is declaring new things to come, even beyond Cyrus and the return of the exiles. The coming of Jesus is the chief theme of prophecy; He is the one for whom the Jews were taught to look.

What Might Have Been and What Will Be (vv. 17–22)

17 Although Jehovah might be accused of harshness in allowing Israel to go into captivity, it must be remembered that He is also their *Redeemer, the Holy One of Israel*; what He has done and will do is right. He is also their Teacher, instructing them both by His law and by His judgments on their sins, judgments which are for the benefit of His people. Dependence on Egypt had been of no profit (30:5); likewise, making and serving idols were "profitable for nothing" (44:9–10). By contrast, Jehovah *leadeth thee by the way that thou shouldest go*; He guides His people by His teaching. In order for the teaching to be of profit or benefit, however, they have to walk according to its direction. This principle is as true now as it was then; there

401

can be no right conduct apart from proper teaching of right and adherence to that teaching.

18–19 From the heart of God there now bursts forth a cry expressing His holy desire for His people—not captivity and affliction, but blessings: *Oh that thou hadst hearkened to my commandments,* my teaching, "For all [God's] commandments are righteousness" (Ps. 119:172). What a difference that would have made! This puts the responsibility for their captivity and suffering upon the nation itself, for Jehovah had taught them, giving them "right ordinances and true laws, good statutes and commandments" (Neh. 9:13). The Lord makes known to them four special blessings that would have been theirs had they hearkened: (1) *then had thy peace been as a river—* their yearnings would be fulfilled; their lives would flow full and calm; *and* (2) *thy righteousness,* the fruits of their purity of life, would be as innumerable and constant *as the waves of the sea;* (3) their posterity would be as uncountable as the grains of sand on the seashore, just as Jehovah had promised Abraham (Gen. 22:17); and (4) their name would not be cut off, for faithfulness to the commandments of God's law was the condition on which their name and relation to Him depended. But now their name has been cut off; the Jews are no longer God's people. Though they shall always exist as a race (Jer. 30:11; 46:28), they are cast out from Him as a people (Gal. 4:24–31).

20 We now see the silver lining to the dark cloud that has so long hung over Israel. Jehovah urgently exhorts the people, *Go ye forth from Babylon, flee ye from the Chaldeans.* Basically the word *flee* means to run away from an enemy, but here it means to leave, to go out from a place of exile and return to one's homeland. The people had entered Babylon with weeping and had hung their harps on the willows, being unable to sing in a foreign land (Ps. 137:1–4). But now they are to leave the land *with a voice of singing,* declaring their deliverance to the ends of the earth, saying, *Jehovah hath redeemed his servant Jacob.* The Lord had executed His threatened judgment. Having carried out His purpose, He now fulfills His promise of deliverance. This is the prophet's last mention of Babylon.

21 Leaving the land of their captivity with singing, Israel will enjoy Jehovah's protective care and provision for their needs throughout the journey home. The prophet's language describing this provision is reminiscent of the deliverance from Egypt and Jehovah's care through the wilderness of Sinai. There is no historical account of the returning exiles' cleaving a rock from which waters gushed forth. This prophecy, then, was not intended to be taken literally. The Lord is saying that He will provide for His peoples' needs and bring them home (cf. 43:19; Ezra 8:21–23).

22 In contrast to the blessings of deliverance, peace, and protection for the righteous, *there is no peace, saith Jehovah, to the wicked.* These are the godless in Israel who violate the law of Jehovah. In their hearts and in their relationships with their neighbors, they show absolutely no regard for Him and His commands. For such people there is only chaos.

The Servant and the Glory of Zion (49–57)

An Introductory Word

In the previous section (chs. 40–48) the court scene between Jehovah and the heathen idols; Cyrus, the anointed of Jehovah, who will deliver Israel from captivity; and the fall of Babylon were in the forefront. The prophet also expounded on the majesty of Jehovah and Israel's relationship to Him as His servant and witness in the midst of a heathen world. These subjects now fade into the background. The present section sets forth the character, mission, and achievement of the divine Servant, and the glory of redeemed Zion. These are Isaiah's chief themes.

CHAPTER 49
The Servant and Despondent Zion

Before making detailed comments on chapter 49 let us first deter-

405

mine who the Servant is. Willis says, "The speaker is the Lord's 'servant' (vv. 3, 5, 6), 'Israel' (vs. 3), rather than the Lord or the prophet" (p. 398). Whybray assumes that the Servant is "Deutero-Isaiah," the prophet-spokesman of chapters 40–55 (pp.44–55). Driver contends that the Servant is ideal Israel, realized in Jesus Christ (p. 180). Smith holds the view that the Servant is the faithful in Israel; they reach their ideal in the Christ (the Servant of chapter 53 must be a person). Smith sees a development in the Servant passages—from (1) the nation to (2) Israel within Israel (the few) to (3) a person who he says can be none other than the Messiah (II. 269–93). By far the greater number of commentators, however, and especially the conservative writers, consider the Servant to be the Christ of the New Testament (e.g., Alexander, Barnes, Calvin, Delitzsch, Leupold, Rawlinson, Robinson, Young); this is the view held by the writer of the present study and the basis on which the passage will be interpreted. An array of names does not prove the point, but study of the four chief passages that deal with the Servant strongly indicates that *Servant* is not a collective noun, but a reference to an individual, and that only the Messiah fulfills the prophecies. The second of the "Servant Songs" (49:1–13), for example, presents the Servant as an individual with a worldwide mission of redemption.

Endowments for His Work (vv. 1–4)

1   The Servant calls those who are afar off, the Gentiles, urging them to heed the message about to be announced. The *isles* are the islands and coastlands of the Mediterranean Sea (cf. 42:4, 10, 12), and generally, "the ends of the earth" (41:5). The message involves all the peoples (nations) of earth. The womb, even *the bowels* of His mother, from which Jehovah called the Servant, is neither the nation nor the virgin Mary, but the spiritual remnant that returned from Babylon. Though giving emphasis to the nation to be born, Isaiah says that Zion will bring forth a man-child (66:7–8). Micah says that the travailing "daughter of Zion," who will "go forth out of the city" into Babylon but eventually be rescued and redeemed, will bring forth the "ruler in Israel; whose goings forth are from of old, from everlasting" (Mic. 4:10; 5:2–3; cf. Rev. 12:1–5). This is Jesus (Matt.

2:6), whose name Jehovah mentioned even before His birth. These passages indicate that the mother is spiritual Zion. The emphasis of the present passage is not upon Messiah's kingship, but upon His servanthood. Isaiah has already called Him by His kingly names: "Immanuel"; "Wonderful, Counsellor, Mighty God, Everlasting Father, Prince of Peace" (7:14; 9:6). The two offices, King and Servant-Redeemer, are united in Jesus Christ.

2   The Servant continues to speak, setting forth the forces by which He will conquer. Jehovah, who controls everything and provides all power, will make the Servant's *mouth like a sharp sword*. *Mouth* is a metonymy for the words which the Servant will speak, for it is by words that He will conquer, bringing the peoples of the world under His dominion (cf. 2:3; John 7:16; 8:28; 12:49; Eph. 6:17; Heb. 4:12). As for the heathen nations that will not hearken, He will rule and break them with a rod of iron (Ps. 2:9; Rev. 12:5), smiting them with the sharp two-edged sword that proceeds out of His mouth (Rev. 1:16; 19:15). *And he hath made me* (the Servant) *a polished shaft*—the Servant is the arrow by which Jehovah will penetrate the heart of His enemies, either bringing them under His dominion or spreading a judgment of death and destruction (cf. Pss. 45:3–5; 110; Hab. 3:11–13). With the sword of His words and as a powerful arrow fashioned and shot by Jehovah, the Servant will go forth "conquering, and to conquer" (Rev. 6:2). In the meantime, *in the shadow of his hand hath he hid me . . . in his quiver hath he kept me close*. The Messiah and His mission will remain hidden, unrevealed, until God's appointed time (64:4; I Cor. 2:9–13; Gal. 4:4).

3   The speaker is now identified as the Servant of Jehovah: *and he said unto me, Thou art my servant; Israel, in whom I will be glorified*. From this identification of the Servant as Israel, some commentators have concluded that the Servant of this passage is the nation itself, or ideal Israel. Two arguments refute this conclusion: first, the following verses indicate otherwise; and second, Paul applies verse 6 specifically to the Christ, the Redeemer of the Gentiles; the apostle identifies himself and Barnabas as participants in Christ's work of extending salvation to the nations—"For so hath the Lord commanded us" (Acts 13:47). The use of Israel as a personal name should present no problem, for it was first given to Jacob (Gen. 32:28), the father of the

twelve-tribe nation, and later passed to the nation itself. The name signifies conquest by faith, one who wrestles or strives and prevails, but both the first Israel (Jacob) and the nation that carried his name had failed to strive and prevail. Calling the Servant Israel points to His victory: He will redeem both Jews and Gentiles and become the head of the new Israel. In Him and His work Jehovah's ideal will be achieved and God glorified.

4 With the words *in vain, nought*, and *vanity*, the Servant expresses disappointment with the results of His work. *But I said, I have labored in vain*, without results; *I have spent my strength for nought and vanity*, a vapor or breath. He will come unto His own, and they that are His own will not receive Him (John 1:11); they will reject and crucify Him (cf. Ps. 22:11–21; Isa. 53). However, the outcome of His work will be left with the Lord: *yet surely the justice due to me is with Jehovah, and my recompense with my God*. God will determine the measure of defeat or victory, justify and vindicate the Servant, give the increase and accomplish the desired end.

The Enlarged Mission (vv. 5–7)

5 The Servant's sense of failure and disappointment at not reaching Jacob, His own people, is answered by assurance from the Lord to whom He belongs. The Servant is honorable in the sight of Jehovah and derives strength from Him. The Servant has done His part nobly, and His achievement is glorious. The special object of His commission was the restoration of Israel, and His labor does in fact recover a remnant (11:11–16); but God has a wider mission for Him, a mission which includes all nations.

6 *Yea, he saith, It is too light a thing that thou shouldest be my servant to raise up the tribes of Jacob, and to restore the preserved of Israel*. Scattered and fallen, Jacob and Israel needed to be raised up and restored. *The preserved of Israel* are not the entire nation, but those who survived the punishment of destruction and were held guiltless. The Servant's enlarged mission is to become Jehovah's light and salvation to the Gentiles, even to the end of the earth (cf. 42:1, 6). Neither the nation nor the faithful remnant had ever been or could ever be the light to the Gentiles. The Servant will bring the light of

truth to those whom He called to *listen* (v. 1). It is strange that the Jews did not understand (and have not yet understood) that the Servant's mission included the Gentiles. It is equally strange that dispensational groups today cannot see that His mission was spiritual, not political and material.

7   Although the Servant's work is to raise up and restore Israel and to serve as a light and provide salvation for the nations, Jehovah points out that the Servant will not be well received. Man in general will despise Him, disdaining and holding Him in contempt as of little worth. *The nation abhorreth* Him; Israel will loathe Him, regarding Him with the same detestation with which the Lord views idols. He will be *a servant of rulers*; rulers will look upon Him with the same disdain with which they look upon a servant who is far beneath them. But all this will change! The one so despised will triumph over all obstacles. His victory will be so complete that kings will be forced to acknowledge Him as Jehovah's Servant and Prophet; they will rise up and do Him homage. Princes also will recognize His greatness and bow before Him in reverence. His victory is attributed to Jehovah's power and faithfulness to His promises. We see this victory in the Messiah set forth in the New Testament.

Salvation and Succor (vv. 8–13)

8   Jehovah continues to speak to His Servant (the exiles in Babylon are not in view). In the day when Jehovah provides salvation for His people, He will come to the aid of His Servant. He will do so at *an acceptable time*—a time favorable to Jehovah, in accordance with His pleasure and will. Paul confirms that we are correct in identifying this day as the messianic period, for he quotes the first part of verse 8 and then adds his own inspired comment, "Behold, now is the acceptable time; behold, now is the day of salvation" (II Cor. 6:2). The acceptable time, the day of Jehovah's salvation, is *now*, the gospel age. Jehovah *will preserve* the Servant, guard His life from danger until the appointed hour comes (John 8:20; 12:23; 13:1). It was earlier said (42:6) that the Servant will be given "for a covenant of the people, for a light of the Gentiles; to open the blind eyes. . . ." Here it is said that He will be given *for a covenant of the people, to raise up the land*, a

place for the new Israel, enlightened Jews and Gentiles. In 44:26 to "raise up the waste places" referred to the restoring of Jerusalem and the waste places of Judah upon the return from Babylon. Here, in view of the messianic context, *to raise up the land* is to make it stand up, to extend it as far as is possible, which would be "from sea to sea, and from the River to the ends of the earth" (Ps. 72:8; Zech. 9:10). The Servant will also *make them inherit the desolate,* devastated or deserted, *heritages;* that is, the spiritual power to overcome opposition will be restored (54:17).

9–11   As Jehovah had assured Jacob-Israel that He would provide for them (41:18), so now He assures the new Israel under the Servant that He will care for them also. To those who are bound in the dungeon of sin, He says, *Go forth;* and to those who sit in spiritual darkness, *Show yourselves,* declare yourselves to be on God's side—take your stand. Assuming the role of a shepherd, He will lead His flock where pastureland and water abound. And further, He will be their protection from the burning heat of opposition, persecution, and judgment, for they will respond to His offer of abundant mercy. As the mountains are Jehovah's by creation, and hence subject to His will, He will be able to remove them, fill up the valleys, and thus provide a way over which His redeemed people can travel (cf. 35:8; 40:4). This, of course, means that He will make a way for them.

12   Those whom the Servant will lead are not the returnees from Babylon, for they will long since have been delivered; rather, those for whom He will provide are from a dominion that is worldwide: *these from the north and from the west; and these from the land of Sinim.* Because of the similarity between "Sinim" and "Syene," some commentators have concluded that *Sinim* refers to the city of Syene, which was in the extreme south of ancient Egypt. Others reason that *Sinim* is China, to the far distant east. This is also improbable. Whatever *Sinim* denotes, it appears safe to conclude that the name refers to a faraway land. The people from all parts of the earth will respond to the Servant's call.

13   The worldwide response to the Lord's charge, "Go forth . . . Show yourselves" (v. 9), evokes Isaiah's characteristic call for universal rejoicing and praise (cf. 44:23). Let the heavens, the earth, and the mountains break forth into singing, for through the Servant, *Jehovah*

hath comforted his people, and will have compassion upon his afflicted. It is obvious that verses 1–13 transcend the Jewish return from exile. They look to a universal ingathering of Jehovah's people, Jews and Gentiles, under the Lord Jesus, and to His provision and care for them (see the comments on 66:18–24).

Zion's Complaint and Amazement (vv. 14–21)

14 Again we are faced with an oft-occurring question. Is the prophet dealing with Zion-Jerusalem during the Babylon captivity or with the spiritual desolation which would exist until the Servant appeared? Certainly the desolation of Zion during the period of exile until the return of the remnant is a phase of the entire period of Zion's spiritual depression which looked forward to restoration under the Messiah. But the limited period of Babylonian exile does not fully satisfy the prophecy which follows. Zion's complaint of feeling forsaken and forgotten of the Lord reflects a despondency which could be relieved only by the coming of the Christ.

15 Jehovah's response to this cry is among the most tender expressions to be found in the Old Testament. He compares His love for Zion to the love of a mother for her infant, the fruit of her womb, whom she affectionately nurtured at her own breasts. Can a mother forget her baby or fail to show compassion for the child when it has gone astray? Though there are a few mothers who may become so worldly, calloused, and hardened of heart as to forget, it is not so with the very great majority. And it is not so with Jehovah: *yet will not I forget thee;* for His love is infinite, transcending that of mankind as far as the heavens are higher than the earth.

16 Zion and her walls are continually before Jehovah. When the Lord gave Israel His law, He instructed the people to bind the laws as frontlets upon their foreheads, so they would always have His commands in mind, and as signs upon their hands, so they would always see His commands in action (Deut. 6:8). In this way the law was ever before them. Metaphorically, in like manner Jehovah has graven Zion and her walls upon the palms of His hands; thus, *thy walls are continually before me.* From the beginning (Gen. 3), Jehovah had a plan of which He never lost sight—the building of spiritual Zion

411

according to His eternal purpose (Eph. 3:11). In Christ we have come to that spiritual Zion (Heb. 12:22–24; I Peter 2:5–6; Rev. 14:1–5).

17 Zion is now likened to a mother whose wayward children are returning to her. When God's eternal purpose is fulfilled and the walls of spiritual Zion are erected, her *children* (will) *make haste* to come home. We cannot determine whether the destroyers who overthrew Zion and broke down her walls, leaving her desolate and waste, are Assyria and Babylon from without, or her wicked children from within. Perhaps both are in view, for both will have withdrawn from her. She is ready to receive those who come in faith, having forsaken wickedness and unrighteousness (55:7) and having been redeemed by Jehovah (35:10; 44:22).

18 Zion is urged to lift up her eyes and look round about, for her children (v. 17) are gathering themselves together to come home; her despondent days are over. On the surest of all guarantees—His own being *(As I live)*—Jehovah pledges that the children shall return and that with them Zion shall beautify herself just as jewels enrich a bride's attire. If there was any realization of this prophecy upon the return from Babylon, it was only minimal; the full realization was under the messianic Servant.

19–20 As her children return home, Zion will find the *waste* and *desolate places* and the *land that hath been destroyed* too strait, too small, for their habitation; they will need a broader land in which to dwell. *And they that swallowed thee up shall be far away*—the probable meaning of this rather oddly positioned clause is that the destroyers shall be far away (cf. v. 17), leaving those who return completely free from opposition such as they once experienced. The children are now secure enough to dwell in cities without walls, for Jehovah "will be unto her a wall of fire round about" (Zech. 2:4–5; cf. Ezek. 38:11). *The children of thy bereavement*, those of whom she had been bereft, will return in great numbers. The increase will be too much for old Zion, for Gentiles will also be included (v. 6). The children shall say, either to Zion or in her hearing, that the place is too narrow; they need more space wherein to dwell. And additional space shall be amply provided as they "enlarge the place of thy tent," spreading abroad on every hand (54:2–3).

21 Zion is amazed at this turn of events and asks herself, *Who* *hath begotten me these?* Apparently the large influx of Zion's children is swelled by Gentiles who are likewise coming to make Zion their spiritual home. The Jewish children were not a great number, for she had been barren, *solitary, an exile, and wandering to and fro.* She had suffered the pangs of loneliness during that time because her wayward children had deserted her and the Gentiles would not arrive until the Servant had come.

Jehovah's Assurance to Zion (vv. 22–26)

22 Jehovah describes the manner in which the children of Zion shall be gathered. He will lift or wave His hand either to signal those nearby or to point to the ensign; He will set up His ensign, a standard or banner, to indicate the rallying point to those who are at a distance (cf. 11:10, 12). The Hebrew word translated *ensign* is a favorite of Isaiah, occurring eight times in Part One and twice in Part Two. The combination of lifting or waving the hand and setting up an ensign occurs only here and in 13:2; this is testimony to the unity of the book. The *nations* and *peoples* are the Gentiles, all those outside of Israel; they will come bringing Zion's sons and daughters *in their bosom*, that is, in their arms, close to their heart, or upon their shoulders, an indication of tender care for them.

23 From the *nations* and *peoples* on one hand, and the *sons* and *daughters* of Zion on the other, Jehovah now shifts His attention to the kings and queens of the world on one hand, and Zion herself on the other. *Kings shall be thy nursing fathers;* the term *nursing fathers* is also translated "foster-fathers" (Delitzsch), "tutors or attendants" (Whybray), "supporters" (Young); "it expresses the basic concept of support."[1] The description of kings and queens serving as nurses to Zion is metaphorical; it indicates a reversal of circumstances. From the lowly state of being forced to serve others, Zion has now come to be served by kings and queens. That they bow down *with their faces to the earth, and lick the dust*, indicates that the royalty of Zion and her children is of a superior quality—they are "a royal priesthood" (I Pe-

---

1. *Theological Wordbook of the Old Testament*, ed. R. Laird Harris (Chicago: Moody, 1980), vol. 1, p. 51.

ter 2:9) and brethren to the supreme King (Heb. 2:11–12). When this comes to pass, it will be evident that Jehovah is God; *and they that wait for me* (to complete this work) *shall not be put to shame.*

24   Zion raises a skeptical question as to whether what God has just promised will indeed be accomplished. Though the question is in two parts, it is actually one. Can the prey or booty, captives seized by the mighty, be taken from him? Can captives be retrieved from *the mighty*—royal conquerors, powerful warriors, men of great strength? The second phase of the question is more difficult, though it carries the same general idea. Can *the lawful captives* ("the captives of the just," Hebrew) *be delivered?* Are these righteous captives, or are they captives taken by righteous conquerors? Or should the phrase "captives of the just" be translated, as one of the Qumran Scrolls has it, "captives of the tyrant"? (For a discussion of this possibility, see Whybray, who accepts it, and Young, who questions it.) Possibly the meaning is that the captivity of the Jews was just or righteous. Because of their wickedness the judgment in itself was just, though it was executed by terrible men.

25   Jehovah's answer to the question is emphatic. The captives of the mighty shall indeed be taken away, *and the prey of the terrible*— mighty or violent oppressors—*shall be delivered.* Fulfillment of this promise is guaranteed by God's determination to deliver them. Anyone who would interfere will find himself contending, at war, not with man but with Jehovah. The conflict could take the form of a verbal battle or physical force. Actually, both then and now, a quarrel with Jehovah's people, purpose, or word, is a quarrel with Him. The result is inevitable: *I will save thy children.*

26   In a gruesome picture Jehovah describes the consequence of contending with Him, oppressing His people, or hindering the accomplishment of His purpose. Those who do so will, like cannibals, eat their own flesh, and *be drunken with their own blood.* It is doubtful whether, as some scholars suggest, this means the people will be brought to such dire straits that they will literally eat one another; rather, it means that in the judgments brought upon them, they will destroy one another—"every man's sword shall be against his brother" (Ezek. 38:17–21; Zech. 14:12–13). As Jehovah through His Servant redeems, protects, and provides for His spiritual Israel, *all flesh shall* *know that I, Jehovah, am thy Saviour, and thy Redeemer, the Mighty One of Jacob.* Only a Servant sent by Jehovah could accomplish this worldwide mission. The fulfillment of His purpose and the steadfastness of His word are incontrovertible evidence of His eternal Godhood and unfailing promises.

CHAPTER 50

The Servant as a Suffering Prophet—A Soliloquy

Rather than try to determine whether verses 1–3 are a conclusion to chapter 49, an introduction to chapter 50, or a short detached prophecy, it seems best to think of the passage as a link between the chapters. Remember that the entire section we are now studying is a unit, developing the general theme of the Servant and the glory of Zion.

Rebuke to the Exiles for Thinking Themselves Rejected (vv. 1–3)

1   Having addressed Zion as if she is a mother (49:14–22), Jehovah now addresses the exiles as if they are children. He returns to the charge made against Him in 49:14, answering it by challenging the exiled children to produce a bill of divorcement proving that He had cast off their mother, or to produce a receipt proving that they had been sold to a creditor. The word *divorcement*, which occurs only in Deuteronomy 24:1, 3; Jeremiah 3:8; and the present verse, is from a root meaning "to cut off." It is used of a husband's dismissal of his wife. Jehovah had given no such bill to Zion; if He had, He could not have taken her back as His wife (Deut. 24:1–4).

The case of the northern kingdom was different. Israel was destroyed (Amos 9:8), caused to cease (Hos. 1:4), given a bill of divorcement by Jehovah (Jer. 3:8). Therefore, the kingdom of the ten tribes could never be taken back as Jehovah's wife, but from among them He could and would receive individuals (Jer. 3:14) after the disappearance of the ark of the covenant from the temple (Jer. 3:16), and

415

Jerusalem would be called "the throne of Jehovah" (Jer. 3:17). By contrast, a bill of divorcement was never given to Judah.

It was legally permissible to sell one's children to pay a debt (Exod. 21:7), but Jehovah was not in debt to Babylon, nor did He receive money for the Jewish captives (52:3). He did not sell them into captivity. They alone were responsible and to blame for their enslavement; because of their deviation from the right way, their crooked behavior, and their rejection of Jehovah's authority and rule over them, *was your mother put away.*

2   By reason of the people's blindness, deafness, and the hardening of their hearts (6:9–10; 42:18–20), there were *none to answer,* none who gave heed, when Jehovah came to them, speaking through His prophets. He repeats the exiles' charge against Him: *Is my hand shortened at all?* Is He powerless to redeem and deliver them from their bondage? In His reply to this charge, whether vocalized or tacit, Jehovah points to the exercise of His power in the natural world. He dries up the seas, makes rivers a desert, causing the fish to die of thirst and stink. If Jehovah can exercise such control over the created forces of His natural world, can He not exercise that same mighty power for the good of His people, delivering them from bondage? But because they lack knowledge of God, they have no faith.

3   Jehovah points to another expression of His infinite power: *I clothe the heavens with blackness* (the word occurs only here and carries a connotation of mourning; cf. Jer. 4:28),[2] *and I make sackcloth their covering* (a further indication of grief). A God of such power can bring Babylon or any other opposing force to nought and distress, thereby delivering His people from that which holds them. If He can deliver from Babylon, can He not also deliver from Satan and sin?

The Servant's Soliloquy (vv. 4–9)

In the second of the "Servant Songs" (49:1–13), the Servant was represented as a prophet with a worldwide mission. In this the third song, He contemplates His preparation and qualifications for pro-

---

2. *Theological Wordbook of the Old Testament*, vol. 2, p. 786.

phetic work and His reception by the people. In the present soliloquy He represents Himself as totally submissive to and completely dependent upon Jehovah for His message and the power to deliver it. This ideal attitude, which Jehovah desired of the nation, individuals, and, of course, His prophets, was realized to its fullest extent only in Jesus Christ, the Prophet who delivered God's final word.

Throughout her history Israel had resisted Jehovah's prophets, treating them shamefully and receiving their message with scorn. Repeatedly Jehovah says that He rises up early, sending His servants the prophets and speaking through them to the people; but they neither hear nor incline the ear.[3] Micaiah was smitten on the cheek and his prophecy rejected (I Kings 22). Israel was blind to Isaiah's message (29:9–10). Jeremiah was imprisoned in the court of the guard and put in a dungeon (pit); the scroll containing his message was burned in the fire (Jer. 32:2; 38:6; 36:23). Ezekiel was regarded not as a prophet, but as a "speaker of parables," a singer of lovely songs—his message was rejected (Ezek. 20:49; 33:31–32). Amos was told by Amaziah to go home and preach in Judah, but not in Bethel (Amos 7:12–13).

Jesus charged that the fathers of His contemporaries "slew the prophets" (Matt. 23:31). Stephen asked, "Which of the prophets did not your fathers persecute?" (Acts 7:52). The Jews whom Jesus addressed were not interested in His message, but instead "took counsel how they might ensnare him in his talk" (Matt. 22:15). The people's attitude toward Jesus as a prophet, and toward prophecy in general, is well summed up in the sneering remark made by those who smote Him in the house of Caiaphas: "Prophesy unto us, thou Christ: who is he that struck thee?" (Matt. 26:68). To these hypocritical Jews, prophesying was little more than a magical art. Smith has fittingly said, "There is something in the mere utterance of truth, that arouses the very devil in the hearts of many men" (II. 345). In this soliloquy we find a clear description of the ideal prophet (which was realized in Christ) and the typical human response to the prophetic message.

4 It is from *the Lord Jehovah* that the Servant receives His qualifications to serve as a prophet: the tongue of the learned (those

---

3. Cf. Jer. 7:25; 26:5; 29:19; 35:15; 44:4; Ezek. 38:17; Dan. 9:6, 10; Amos 3:7; Zech. 1:6.

who have been taught) and the ear of a ready listener. Back of the teacher's tongue must be the listening ear of the disciple. A prophet must be ready to hear what Jehovah his Teacher says. Jehovah had said to Moses of the Prophet whom He would raise up, "I will put my words in his mouth, and he shall speak unto them all that I shall command him" (Deut. 18:18; cf. Acts. 3:22–23). Thus equipped, the Servant is prepared *to sustain with words,* that is, to uphold and encourage with words of truth, *him that is weary.* The weary include both Jews and Gentiles. The Jews were weary with sin, a burden the law could not lift; and the Gentiles were laden down with idols and all the evils that typically accompany them (cf. 46:7; Matt. 11:28; John 8:31–36; Gal. 4:8). The source of the Servant's sustaining words is constant, for Jehovah wakens His ear *morning by morning;* thus He is being constantly taught by the Fountainhead of all truth. The teaching is ever fresh, coming directly from Jehovah; it never grows stale or fails to satisfy the hungry soul that will listen. The Servant's tongue is ever ready to speak to the open ear, a principle to be followed by all who would teach truth.

5   To *the Lord Jehovah* who opened the Servant's ear to hear and understand the divine will, the Servant says, *I was not rebellious, neither turned away backward.* Even Moses shrank from his call (Exod. 4:1, 10, 13), Jonah fled from the responsibility imposed upon him (Jon. 1:3), and Jeremiah complained of his task and lot (Jer. 15:15–18; 20:7–18); but the Servant is of no disposition to rebel, turn away, or back off from His mission. He is totally submissive to the will and instruction of His Teacher (John 6:38; Luke 22:42); He speaks what He is instructed to teach (cf. John 7:16; 8:28b; 12:49). The true prophet or teacher speaks only that which is revealed from God.

6   In response to Jehovah's gift to Him (v. 4), the Servant deliberately and willingly gave His back to the smiters, His cheeks to them that plucked off the hair, and *hid not* (His) *face from shame and spitting.* The inveterate hatred of mankind for the teacher of truth and the willingness of the teacher to suffer for truth are vividly set forth in this verse. "The plucking out of (a portion of) the hair was the expression of violent wrath or moral indignation."[4] In indignation

---

4. C. F. Keil, *Ezra, Nehemiah, Esther,* Commentaries on the Old Testament (Grand Rapids: Eerdmans, 1950 reprint), p. 117.

Ezra plucked out his own hair (Ezra 9:3); in a similar spirit Nehemiah plucked out the hair of Jews who intermarried with the heathen (Neh. 13:25). The Servant submitted to just such an outrage, but one of unrighteous rather than righteous indignation. To spit upon another was an act of ritual defilement and contempt (Lev. 15:8; Num. 12:14; Deut. 25:9). The Servant hid not His face from this dishonor and undeserved humiliation (cf. Matt. 26:67; 27:30).

7   As *the Lord Jehovah* has given the Servant the tongue of the learned with which to speak and the open ear with which to hear, so now will Jehovah be the Servant's support, rendering help and assistance in every time of need. Because He receives such help the Servant will not be *confounded*, a strong word indicating that He will not be thrown into confusion or perplexity by shameful treatment. He will not fail to live up to the trust bestowed upon Him. Because of Jehovah's help, the determination of His own heart—for He has *set* (His) *face like a flint*, a very hard stone—and His complete submission to the Lord, He can confidently affirm, *I know that I shall not be put to shame*. Whatever others might charge or do, in His heart He knows that with Jehovah's help, and with His own determination and submission, He will be victorious. Any teacher can have this same assurance to the degree that he follows the Servant.

8   Jehovah serves as Judge of the Servant's behavior and teaching and the consequent wrath of His enemies. He who is the Servant's help is also near to justify Him, defending and vindicating the righteousness of both Him and His cause. Appearing before such a Judge the Servant issues a challenge: *Who will contend with me*, that is, Who will cross swords with me in a forensic contest? *Let us stand up together.* He continues with a parallel challenge: *Who is mine adversary?* Who will challenge or accuse me in a court trial? *Let him come near to me.* Jesus flung this very challenge into the teeth of His enemies: "Which of you convicteth me of sin?" (John 8:46), a challenge which was met neither then (Mark 14:55–56) nor since.

9   Once more the Servant declares the source of His help, *the Lord Jehovah*, and repeats the challenge to His enemies, *Who is he that shall condemn me?* The Servant has violated neither Jehovah's former teaching in the law nor His own teaching; He has not mistreated any fellow man. The Servant concludes by saying of those

who would condemn Him, *Behold, they all shall wax old as a garment; the moth shall eat them up.* Enemies of the Servant, of His truth, and of all the faithful, shall fade away and come to nought like a garment consumed by moths.

Light for Believers, Sorrow for Unbelievers (vv. 10–11)

10 Two groups are now examined: those who fear Jehovah (v. 10), and those who reject the true light (v. 11). Commentators differ as to whether the speaker is Jehovah, the Servant, or the prophet; but of course it is Jehovah, whether He speaks directly or through the prophet or the Servant. The speaker addresses those who fear Jehovah and obey the voice of the Servant, who has spoken as a prophet of the Lord. Note the clear distinction between the faithful and the Servant, establishing our point that the Servant is a person, not the nation of Israel nor a group composed of believers from various nations. To fear Jehovah is to hold Him in such holy reverence as to obey what He says. Yet even though one both fears Jehovah and obeys the voice of His Servant, he may find himself in darkness, unable to see the end of the tunnel and not understanding some aspects of his faith and life. When this occurs, one should follow the example of the Servant: *let him trust in the name of Jehovah,* which stands for all that Jehovah is, *and rely upon his God,* the God in whom the Servant trusted and on whom He leaned.

11 The speaker next addresses unbelievers, the disobedient people who reject the light revealed in the Servant and kindle their own fire. They gird themselves about with firebrands (missiles or sparks),[5] creating light by which to walk. These firebrands prove to be as destructive to those who reject the divine light as idolatry is to the heathen. *This shall ye have of my hand;* Jehovah turns this type of folly back upon the disobedient, just as He turns back all other efforts of man to devise his own way. *Ye shall lie down in sorrow,* be brought into terror (literally, "a place of pain";[6] "torment," Revised Standard).

---

5. *Theological Wordbook of the Old Testament,* vol. 1, p. 249.
6. Ibid., vol. 2, p. 688.

This is the end of all who reject the light of truth and devise their own way of life.

CHAPTER 51
Encouragement for Prostrate Zion (1)

Hearken! An Exhortation to the Faithful (vv. 1–8)

1   In the midst of those who kindle a fire and walk therein to their own destruction (50:11), there is yet a faithful remnant, though they may be very few at times. The Lord addresses this small group as those who *follow after righteousness*, who *seek Jehovah*; the two descriptions complement each other. He urges the faithful to *Hearken to me* (v. 1), *Attend unto me* (v. 4), and again, *Hearken unto me* (v. 7)—hear, listen, and pay attention to His word. Righteousness can be attained only by listening attentively to what God says and by seeking after Him. Those addressed are probably despondent because they are few in number; so He says, *Look unto the rock whence ye were hewn, and to the hole of the pit* (quarry) *whence ye were digged.*

2   The despondent faithful are to look to Abraham and Sarah, the source from which they sprang. Why look to them? The Lord had called Abraham, the father of all the faithful, when he was but one. To Abraham and Sarah was born Isaac, a son of promise, through whom would come the seed that would bless all nations and tribes (Gen. 12:1–3; 18:18; 21:12; 22:18). The remnant are the children of Isaac, the children of faith (Gen. 15:6; Heb. 11:11), the seed which is to be as numberless as the stars of heaven and the sand upon the seashore (Gen. 15:5; 22:17). They should remember Jehovah's word to Sarah when she laughed at the idea that she would be the mother of nations: "Is anything too hard [wonderful] for Jehovah?" (Gen. 18:14). If Jehovah could bring forth the great nation of Israel from Abraham and Sarah, when she was past age and he was "as good as dead" (Heb. 11:11–12), can He not through this small remnant carry out His purpose of building a great spiritual nation in which all peoples shall be blessed (Gen. 12:3; 22:18)? Jehovah is telling the

discouraged few to remember the promise to Abraham and Sarah and their faith, and to realize that they are the children of that promise and faith.

3   In His promise to Abraham before Isaac was born, Jehovah said, "The father of a multitude of nations have I made thee" (Gen. 17:5), speaking as if the promise were already fulfilled. Paul quoted this text and added that God "giveth life to the dead, and calleth the things that are not, as though they were" (Rom. 4:17). Just as on many other occasions in Isaiah's prophecy Jehovah speaks of things not yet done as though they were (cf. 46:10), so He speaks now: *For Jehovah hath comforted Zion* (cf. 40:1; 49:13). He has purposed to comfort Zion together with her waste and desolate places, and so it shall be done. The mighty God who can dry up seas and rivers, making them a wilderness (50:2), can reverse the order and restore to their former state the waste and desolate ruins of Zion, whether physical or spiritual. He has made her *waste places, and . . . her wilderness like Eden, and her desert like the garden of Jehovah,* luxuriant and fruitful, as was man's original home. This work of Jehovah results in the restoring of *joy and gladness . . . thanksgiving, and the voice of melody.* However, due to the failure to hearken and attend to Jehovah and His word, this prophecy was fulfilled to only a very limited extent when the Jews returned from exile; full realization of the promise was experienced only with the appearance of the Servant.

4   *Attend unto me, O my people; and give ear unto me, O my nation*—with a view to obedience, pay close attention to what I say. Note the parallel constructions: *Attend unto me* and *give ear unto me; O my people* and *O my nation.* Jehovah is exhorting His nation and people. The law establishing justice will go forth as *a light of the peoples*—the nations or Gentiles; a clear distinction is thus made between *my people* and *the peoples.* This is very definitely a messianic prophecy to be fulfilled in the Servant (cf. 42:6; 49:6); the law of justice here in view will go forth out of Zion-Jerusalem (2:3) under the Servant (42:1–4). It will be a "law of faith" (Rom. 3:27), "the law of the Spirit of life" (Rom. 8:1–2).

5   *My righteousness is near, my salvation is gone forth*—again note the parallel construction. Is *my righteousness* the principle on which God acts and His throne rests (Ps. 89:14; 97:2), or is it the

justice to be established by the new law which shall go forth from Him? Also, is *my salvation* deliverance from Babylon, or deliverance from sin through the new law? It could be both, for deliverance from both Babylon and sin rests on righteousness; however, it seems clear to this writer that we are dealing with a definite messianic prophecy fulfilled only in Christ, the Servant of the songs already presented (42:1–13; 49:1–13; 50:4–9). Let us go back for a moment to verse 2, where the faithful were urged to look to Abraham and the promise to him, "In thee shall all the families of the earth be blessed" (Gen. 12:3). Paul quotes this promise and declares it fulfilled in the Gentiles' salvation by faith in Christ (Gal. 3:8). Moreover, in his second recorded sermon, Peter says, "Yea and all the prophets from Samuel and them that followed after, as many as have spoken, they also told of these days [the days of and following Christ's redemptive work]. Ye are the sons of the prophets, and of the covenant which God made with your fathers, saying unto Abraham, And in thy seed shall all the families of the earth be blessed." The apostle then explains that this Old Testament promise (Gen. 12:3; 22:18) was fulfilled when "God, having raised up his Servant, sent him to bless you, in turning away every one of you from your iniquities" (Acts 3:24–26). Here we have an inspired confirmation that in this particular passage of Isaiah *salvation* means deliverance from sin. Zion was not truly comforted nor her waste places built up until the coming of the Servant. Note further that Jehovah says that when His righteousness and salvation go forth, He will *judge the peoples* (cf. 2:4). This He has done since spiritual Zion was established by Messiah's work (Heb. 12:22–24). *The isles shall wait for me*, as they wait for His law (42:4); they were earlier urged to listen to the Servant (49:1). When the Servant and His law appear, the isles will "sing unto Jehovah a new song" (42:10). Those from the isles, the Gentiles from the remote parts of earth, will trust in Jehovah as they lean upon His arm for support, a metonymy for His redeeming power.

6   As the old pagan systems of the nations will pass away, bringing the heathen world to an end (see the comments on 34:4), so also will the Jewish order pass away—*the heavens shall vanish away like smoke, and the earth shall wax old like a garment*. The prophet is not describing the end of the world as set forth in the New Testament, but the

end of the world of Judaism (cf. 65:16–17 and comments). Judaism's heaven vanishes, its world waxes old, *and they that dwell therein shall die in like manner.* Some commentators prefer as an alternative translation "shall die like gnats," but the "meaning is dubious."[7] The thought is that the old system shall pass away; its world shall come to an end. No one shall continue to live under that system and sustain a relationship to God through it. In contrast, says Jehovah, *my salvation shall be for ever,* as long as the age lasts, *and my righteousness shall not be abolished;* it shall abide as long as time endures. Both the doing away with the old and the establishing of the new are the work of the Servant.

7   Jehovah continues to address the discouraged remnant: *ye that know righteousness,* that is, who practice it ("follow after righteousness," v. 1), in whose heart is the law which goes forth from Him (v. 4). Only as the law abides in the heart (the mind and affections), expressing itself through the will and actions, can one know righteousness. Although Jehovah said that He would make "Jacob a curse, and Israel a reviling" (43:28), He urges the citizens of redeemed Zion, the new order, to *fear ye not the reproach of men, neither be ye dismayed at their revilings. Reproach* is blame, scorn, contempt; *revilings* are injurious words, abusive language expressing scorn. The righteous are to lean upon the arm of Jehovah (v. 5b), neither fearing nor being dismayed by such treatment, and to follow the example of the Servant (50:6–9).

8   The destruction pronounced upon the adversaries of the Servant (50:9) is also pronounced against those who berate the followers of the Servant: they shall be consumed like a garment eaten by moths or wool by a worm. The word translated *worm* occurs only here; it is uncertain whether it means a worm or a species of moth. In contrast to the destruction of the enemies of the faithful, Jehovah's righteousness and salvation are everlasting. They will not pass away but will endure unto all generations.

An Appeal to Jehovah and His Reply (vv. 9–16)

9   The Lord's word to His people has been encouraging and assur-

---

7. *Theological Wordbook of the Old Testament*, vol. 1, p. 444.

ing (vv. 1–8). In response, the prophet cries to the *arm of Jehovah*, a symbol of His power, for immediate action. *Awake, awake,* arouse Thyself from inactivity, and be clothed in strength, actively using Thy mighty power in behalf of the nation. The double use of *awake* shows that the prophet's plea is particularly fervid and urgent, whereas the third occurrence implores Jehovah to take action *as in the days of old.* Time after time in ancient days Jehovah had come to rescue and deliver His people; the prophet pleads for a repeat of such action. Jehovah had *cut Rahab in pieces* and had pierced *the monster.* The Hebrew word *rahab* "denotes a tempestuous, and then arrogant, attitude," proud and boisterous behavior.[8] Earlier the prophet used *Rahab* in speaking of Egypt: in pride and arrogance Egypt lay still like a crocodile (30:7). Again he has in mind Egypt, the sea monster or serpent of the Nile. Jehovah had exercised His strength by cutting Egypt, the arrogant monster or enemy, the noisy one, in pieces, piercing and wounding the power on which he relied. There is nothing in the biblical use of the word to indicate, as suggested by many modern commentators, that Isaiah is using a figure from pagan mythology.

10   The prophet recalls Israel's deliverance from Egypt, a work of Jehovah's mighty power. He had opened the Red Sea, dried up the water that Israel might cross on dry land, and thereby provided a way for His people's redemption. What Jehovah had done in the past He can do in the present. Therefore Isaiah cries, *Awake, put on strength* (v. 9). He calls on God to deliver the exiles from Babylon by exercising the same power He had demonstrated in delivering the nation from Egypt.

11   Once this power has been freshly exercised, *the ransomed of Jehovah shall return, and come with singing unto Zion.* This entire verse is a word for word repetition of 35:10. In the former instance the shout occurs in a messianic context (see comments), whereas here it expresses the joyous spirit of the people's return from Babylonian exile and foreshadows the messianic deliverance and joy that are to come.

12   Use of the double *I—I, even I—*recalls and emphasizes

---

8. *Theological Wordbook of the Old Testament,* vol. 2, p. 834.

Jehovah's claim to be the sole deliverer and source of Israel's comfort. If His people recognize and acknowledge this fact, then who is there for the faithful to fear? Man will die, but Jehovah is eternal; *the son of man*, the offspring of man, all who are to come, *shall be made as grass*, but Jehovah and His word endure forever (cf. 40:6–8). Which is stronger and more to be feared, the temporal which passes or the eternal which endures?

13 Israel's fear of man is the consequence of their having forgotten Jehovah and His mighty power. The Lord resorts to a favorite illustration of His power: He is their *Maker, that stretched forth the heavens, and laid the foundations of the earth* (see 37:16; 40:22; 42:5; 45:12, 18; 48:13). This creative might reveals His ultimate and absolute power. Having forgotten God's power (such forgetfulness is a weakness of all sons of men), His people are in constant fear *because of the fury of the oppressor*, that is, the hot displeasure of one who brings distress by exerting pressure from without in an attempt to destroy. The contest is between the God whose power is manifested in creation and the fury of man, who like grass will be brought to nought. When Jehovah blows upon the strong of earth, they are carried away like stubble (cf. 40:24).

14 In Jehovah's own appointed time, *The captive exile* ("He that is bent down," margin) *shall speedily* (quickly) *be loosed*. The one bent down under the yoke of Babylonian captivity shall be released, as from bonds or chains. *He shall not die and go down into the pit.* The word *pit* differs from the term used in verse 1; the word here means the grave, destruction, ruin or corruption. He will be delivered from the pit, and furthermore, his necessities of life will be provided. Jehovah will surely care for him.

15 The people's assurance of their deliverance is the word of Jehovah their God. He who stirs the sea and causes the waves to roar, who is the power behind the terrifying force of hurricanes and gigantic tidal upheavals, has declared it. Jehovah, the God of all powers heavenly and earthly, *is his name*.

16 This great God who creates and by His providence controls all forces both in nature and in the nations, has put His words in the mouth of the prophet (cf. Deut. 18:18); they shall not fail because they are from Him. He protects both His prophet and His word by covering them in the shadow of His hand, defending them by His infinite power. This guarantees the planting of *the heavens* and the laying of *the foundations of the earth*. Having spoken of the old order that will pass away (v. 6), Jehovah speaks now of the new order to be brought forth—new heavens and a new earth (cf. 65:16–17 and comments). This will be fulfilled under the Messiah, the Servant, who will *say unto Zion, Thou art my people*. This new world, the new spiritual Zion, the city of the new spiritual people, has been realized under Christ in the present age.

Jerusalem, Awake! Stand Up!—Her Tragic Plight (vv. 17–20)

17   The prophet sets forth one of those sad, tragic, and pitiable pictures often found in Scripture (e.g., Ezek. 16:23–43). In this instance the picture is that of a woman in a drunken stupor whose children are incapable of helping her. In verse 9 the double imperative "Awake, awake," was spoken *to* the Lord; in this instance it is spoken *by* the Lord. Jehovah calls to Jerusalem, the symbolic mother of His people, to *awake* and *stand up*. At that time she lay prostrate in ruins, having *drunk at the hand of Jehovah the cup of his wrath*, a metaphor also used by later prophets. Jehovah will send the cup of His wrath to all the nations and force them to drink of it (Jer. 25:12–29). This includes Jerusalem (Ezek. 23:31–35), who has now drained it. The cup Jerusalem has drained is Babylon (Jer. 51:7), whom Jehovah will likewise require to drink the cup of His wrath someday (see v. 23). Having drunk of this cup, Jerusalem staggers, stumbles, and falls, for she has been forced to drain it even to the dregs, an indication of the completeness of her judgment.

18   Of all the sons whom Jerusalem had borne, there is none to guide her back to a sober, upright, and useful path. Not one can take her by the hand and say, "This way," for all her children have departed from the Lord's way and forgotten her, therefore becoming subject to the same judgment as their mother. Only Jehovah can restore Jerusalem and her children; this He intends to do.

19   *Who shall bemoan thee* in this fallen condition? That is, who will comfort you or be sorry for you? The word translated *bemoan*

means "to move to and fro"; it is used of the movement of the head when one falls asleep or nods sympathetically.[9] Young translates it literally, "who will nod (the head) for you?" in expressing sympathetic grief (III. 321). Two things had befallen Jerusalem: (1) *desolation and destruction*, which, it seems, pertained to the devastation of the land and city; and (2) *famine and the sword*, which had come to her children, the inhabitants of Jerusalem and its environs. The question *how shall I comfort thee?* is variously translated and interpreted by expositors. But since there are none to bemoan her, the thought seems to be, "Only I, Jehovah, can comfort thee, and I will do so."

20   The prophet now presents a more graphic description of the cup of wrath that has left Jerusalem in ruins. Like an antelope entangled in a net, her sons are helpless, having fainted. The meaning of the clause *they lie at the head of all the streets* is uncertain. It could suggest that they perished trying to defend the city at various sites where roads enter into it, or it could mean that they perished there trying to flee. We prefer to think it was the former. In any case, they were draining the cup of Jehovah's wrath, imbibing to the fullest the fury of His judgment.

Jehovah's Gracious Promise (vv. 21–23)

21   In view of Jerusalem's condition and inability to save herself, Jehovah says, *Therefore hear now this*—listen to what I have to say. The mother and her children are afflicted, suffering physical distress: Jerusalem is destroyed and her inhabitants exiled. They are drunken "not with wine" (cf. 29:9), but with Jehovah's cup of wrath.

22   The God of Israel, *thy Lord Jehovah*, who pleads *the cause of his people*, speaks. Formerly, as their accuser, He had called His people to a court of law (e.g., 43:8–13, 26); but now He who had given to Jerusalem *the cup of staggering* stands as their defender to plead their cause. He who had determined the judgment now determines the extent of its duration and the time of restitution. He will take the cup out of their hand; since the judgment for their former sins is complete, they shall drink of that cup no more.

---

9. *Theological Wordbook of the Old Testament*, vol. 2, pp. 560–61.

23   The cup of wrath and of staggering will be put *into the hand of them that afflict thee.* Babylon had been Jehovah's golden cup by which all the nations had been made drunken (Jer. 51:7). After they have drunk, the cup will be given to Babylon that she might drink (Jer. 25:26 [Sheshach = Babylon; cf. Jer. 51:41]). Jehovah's recompenses of judgment shall come upon her (Jer. 51:54–56). The *soul* to which Babylon said, *Bow down, that we may go over,* is the totality of the life of the people of Jerusalem. They were subjected to cruel and harsh treatment of both body and mind (47:6), forced to *bow* to indignities inflicted by a heartless people. But Jehovah, "a God of recompenses," will bring destroyers upon Babylon (Jer. 51:54–56; Hab. 2:15–16), for there is always a day of reckoning.

CHAPTER 52:1–12
Encouragement for Prostrate Zion (2)

The first twelve verses of chapter 52 are a continuation of chapter 51; there is no special reason for a break at this point.

Awake, Jerusalem! Put on Your Beautiful Garments (vv. 1–6)

1   This is the third time that the prophet has used the double imperative, *Awake, awake* (see 51:9, 17). Zion has lain prostrate, weak and helpless, like a woman in a drunken stupor, having drained the cup of Jehovah's fury; but the time has come for her to arise and take her rightful place as a queen. She is to put on strength instead of weakness, her *beautiful garments,* even the beauty of holiness (I Chron. 16:29; Pss. 29:2; 110:3). Such garments, unlike those polluted by sin (64:6), befit her relationship to the Lord. The robe she is to put on may be her redeemed children gathered about her (49:18), or it may be her own garment of salvation and righteousness (61:10). Whichever it may be, Zion will be so clothed only when the people clothe themselves in the beauty of holiness. *The holy city* is the city where Jehovah had dwelt among His people (cf. 48:2), and to which

He will return when she is properly cleansed (vv. 8–10; Ezek. 43:1–2). It is highly unlikely that the Lord is speaking of physical and political Jerusalem when He says, *For henceforth there shall no more come into thee the uncircumcised and the unclean.* Willis explains this to mean that the uncircumcised and the unclean "will not attack and overthrow the city as the Babylonians had done" (p. 413). However, this interpretation is not in harmony with either history or Scripture, for after the return from Babylon and the division of Alexander's empire, Jerusalem became a kind of buffer football kicked back and forth between Syria and Egypt during the third and second centuries B.C. Although neither kingdom destroyed the city, Antiochus Epiphanes subdued it, desecrated the temple and its worship by offering swine's flesh on an altar to Zeus, and forbade circumcision, observance of the Sabbath, and the possession of copies of the Scriptures.[10] Later pagan Rome entered the city and destroyed it. Willis's literalistic explanation is obviously wrong. Also indicating that verse 1 applies to spiritual Jerusalem and the Messiah are similar statements of Jehovah which appear in other prophetic books: "No foreigner, uncircumcised in heart and uncircumcised in flesh, shall enter into my [new spiritual] sanctuary" (Ezek. 44:9); and "So shall ye know that I am Jehovah your God, dwelling in Zion my holy mountain: then shall Jerusalem be holy, and there shall no strangers pass through her any more" (Joel 3:17; cf. Isa. 35:8 and comments, and Zech. 9:8–10). All who enter spiritual Zion, the city of God, will have been circumcised with a circumcision not made with hands (see Col. 2:11; Rom. 2:28–29; Gal. 6:15); no others shall enter into it.

2   In the beginning of his ministry Isaiah had said Jerusalem-Zion "shall be desolate and sit upon the ground" (3:26) and "whisper out of the dust" (29:4). The prophet now presents a contrast between Babylon, who will "come down, and sit in the dust . . . without a throne" (47:1), and Zion, who is told (1) to *shake thyself from the dust*, (2) *sit on thy throne*, and (3) *loose thyself from the bonds of thy neck*, the rope or cord which bound captive to captive. The status of the two

---

10. *Zondervan Pictorial Encyclopedia of the Bible*, ed. Merrill C. Tenney (Grand Rapids: Zondervan, 1975), vol. 1, pp. 192–93; Charles F. Pfeiffer, *Between the Testaments* (Grand Rapids: Baker, 1972), p. 81.

cities is reversed: one is reduced from worldly glory to humility and shame; the other is exalted from shame to divine glory.

3 Jehovah has the right to release His captive people, freeing them from their oppressors, for they *were sold for nought*. They were Jehovah's people, and nothing had been paid to Him for them; therefore, He can redeem them without payment (cf. 45:13; 50:1). Neither Jehovah nor Judah owes Babylon anything, for Judah had not sinned against Babylon but against Jehovah.

4 Israel had gone down into Egypt as the guests of that nation through the invitation of Pharaoh (Gen. 45:16–20; 47:5–6), but they were later enslaved there. Likewise, Assyria had no cause to invade and oppress Israel; though she was used by Jehovah as the instrument of His judgment (10:5–10), she was prompted by the lust of conquest. Therefore, Jehovah had the right to judge both Egypt and Assyria and to deliver from them whomever He chose.

5 Neither does Babylon have any claim on Judah or ground on which to justify invading the land and carrying away the people as captives and their possessions as booty (cf. Hab. 1:5–11). Since they were *taken away for nought* and Jehovah is no more in debt to Babylon than to Egypt or Assyria, He asks, *Now therefore, what do I here?* Under these conditions, why should He remain silent and inactive? Why not do something? Why should He not take them back to their homeland? Their rulers, the Babylonians, *do howl*, speak harshly to them, ridiculing their God for His weakness, thus blaspheming His name. So why not act? It was because of Israel's sins before the captivity that they were in Babylon, and it was their conduct while there that evoked this blasphemy of Jehovah's name (Ezek. 36:20, 23), blasphemy which continued even unto the day of the apostles (Rom. 2:24).

6 However, it will not always be this way; for when Zion is redeemed and purified, *my people* in truth, clothed in salvation and righteousness (v. 1; cf. Zech. 8:8), these *shall know my name*. They shall know it in its fullness, for it stands for all that He is—His might and power, His wrath and fury, His righteousness and justice, His love and mercy, His fatherhood and providence—the totality of His being, character, and purposes. *In that day*, the day of Zion's strength and beauty, God's people will know that it was Jehovah who spoke and that He keeps His word, fulfilling it in His own time.

The Herald of Good News, and an Exhortation (vv. 7–12)

7   By prophetic inspiration Isaiah sees God's promise fulfilled, His power exerted, the people redeemed, and the messenger bringing the good news (cf. 40:9; 41:27). *How beautiful,* or suitable, befitting the glory of the messenger, *are the feet of him that bringeth good tidings; the feet* symbolize the messenger himself. Nahum uses almost the same words when he proclaims the fall of Nineveh (Nah. 1:15). As the messenger heralds Zion's redemption, Isaiah sees him *upon the mountains,* not only of Judah but also of the whole world. He *publisheth peace,* peace between God and His people through redemption. He *bringeth good tidings of good,* that is, of moral good or moral blessings (for this use of the word *good,* cf. 7:15–16; 38:3). He *publisheth salvation,* deliverance from oppression, both individual and national, spiritual and political (this salvation will be "unto all generations," 51:8). *He saith unto Zion, Thy God reigneth!* This is the basis of the tidings. Although the message included the deliverance and return of the exiles, it need not—in fact, it cannot—be limited to that event. Its universality is indicated by Paul's application of this verse to the apostles whom the Lord prepared and sent into all the world with the good news of salvation (Rom. 10:15).

8   Though the walls are in ruins and the city a waste, yet in the continuation of his vision the prophet sees watchmen upon the walls of Zion anxiously waiting for the bringer of good tidings. The watchmen need not be thought of as either angelic watchers (as in Dan. 4:13, 17, 23) or prophets (Ezek. 3:17; 33:7; Hab. 2:1), though they may be the latter; but they should be seen as entrusted with the responsibility of guarding the city and keeping the people informed. As they see the herald approaching with the good tidings, they break forth in unison, singing praises to God who reigns and has redeemed Zion. The phrase *eye to eye* occurs only here and in Numbers 14:14, where it is translated "face to face." It probably means that they will closely observe the realization of God's purpose and work *when Jehovah returneth to Zion.*

9   The waste places of the city also are called upon to break forth in joyous singing, *for Jehovah hath comforted his people, he hath redeemed Jerusalem.* The Lord has fulfilled His promise to restore and to raise up the waste places (44:26; 51:3); therefore, rejoice!

10   In baring *his holy arm* Jehovah has responded to the cry, "Awake, awake, put on strength, O arm of Jehovah" (51:9). He has uncovered His arm, unencumbering it from any garment that might restrict movement; and in holiness and righteousness, *in the eyes of all the nations,* He has delivered Zion. This work of Jehovah in delivering Zion through Cyrus foreshadows what will be completed by the Servant. The last clause poses a question. Does the expression *all the ends of the earth have seen the salvation of our God* mean that people at the ends of the earth have beheld salvation in the return of the exiles and heard it in the joyous message of their restoration (48:20)? Or does it mean that they have shared in it themselves (45:22)? The former is probably the meaning; but the latter is not to be completely ruled out, for it was in the ultimate plan of God (cf. 42:10; 51:5).

11   A period of fifty to seventy years is a long time in the life of an individual or a nation. The people have been in Babylon for that period; and during that time, many changes have taken place among them. Whatever may have been the cause of the people's hesitation, the prophet's call to depart is urgent and imperative: *Depart ye . . . go ye out from thence.* There are two ways in which the exodus from Babylon differs from the one from Egypt. In leaving Babylon the people are to lay hands on nothing Babylonian in character; they are to make a clean break from the worldly spirit and possessions of the land which had held them captive. In contrast, as they left Egypt the Israelites were to ask for jewels, gold, and other precious items, thus despoiling their neighbors (Exod. 3:22; 11:2–3; 12:35–36). It seems that the priests and Levites are addressed next: *cleanse yourselves, ye that bear the vessels of Jehovah.* Just as many other coming events were revealed to the prophet, so it was also made known to him that the vessels of the temple which would be carried away by Nebuchadnezzar would also be returned to the Jews by Cyrus (for the fulfillment of this prophecy see Ezra 1:5–11). The bearers of the sacred vessels are to cleanse themselves for this holy task (cf. Lev. 22:3–4).

The call to depart extends beyond the physical captivity to the spiritual out of which Paul and John called the saints centuries later (II Cor. 6:17; Rev. 18:4).

12   A second difference between the two exoduses is that the people were to leave Egypt in haste, being thrust out (Exod. 12:33, 39), whereas they are to leave Babylon neither in haste nor in flight. The Egyptian Pharaoh had pursued the fathers in an attempt to retain them, but Cyrus issued the decree that sent the Jews home. Furthermore, Jehovah will lead in the front and protect at the rear. Thus the returnees will be surrounded by His presence, and there will be no need for haste or fear.

CHAPTERS 52:13–53:12
Victory Through Vicarious Suffering

It is generally acknowledged by students of the prophets that in this the fourth of the Servant Songs is attained the loftiest height of prophecy. It was pointed out in the third song (50:4–11) that the Servant will suffer in obedience to the word of God, but the purpose of His suffering was not explained. This final song deals with both purpose and achievement. The Servant is to conquer as a sufferer, not as a warrior (cf. Rev. 5:4–6). From His shameful suffering and inhumane treatment He is to emerge in triumph and glory.

In this song the Servant neither appears in person nor speaks, but He is the central figure in the message of both Jehovah and the prophet. No time factor is found in the song. It deals with the past, present, and future; its theme embraces the whole of time. A question may be posed as to whether 52:13–15 is a conclusion to 52:1–12, which deals with the deliverance of Israel, a transition from 52:1–12 to chapter 53, or a part of chapter 53, serving as the introduction. Although the three verses build upon 52:1–12, they are best regarded as the introduction to the following chapter, the first of five stanzas in the final Servant Song (52:13–53:12).

Exaltation of the Servant (52:13–15)

In Isaiah 52:13–15 the themes of chapter 53 are condensed, but appear in reverse order. Exaltation is followed by suffering, whereas in chapter 53 suffering is followed by exaltation. In this stanza the prophet speaks in the future tense, in 53:1–9 he uses the past tense (what is to be is spoken of as if already accomplished), and in verses 10–12 he returns to the future.

13 Isaiah begins the song characteristically: *Behold* (cf., e.g., 7:14; 42:1)—attention is focused on the Servant. He *shall deal wisely*—He shall act with such divine insight and understanding as to produce effective and successful results (cf. Jer. 23:5). The prophet uses three terms *(exalted, lifted up,* and *very high)* which, though similar in meaning, suggest a progressive development: *He shall be exalted and lifted up, and shall be very high.* Delitzsch translates, "He will rise up, he will raise himself still higher, he will stand on high," indicating the commencement, the continuation, and the climax of the exaltation (II. 305). The climax was reached when Christ was raised from the dead and exalted to God's right hand (Acts 2:32–33; Phil. 2:5–11).

14 But before the exaltation the Servant will be subjected to the basest of treatment and severest of suffering. Many will be astonished, struck with amazement or shock at what they see. The cause is stated in the parenthetical statement: *(his visage was so marred more than any man, and his form more than the sons of men).* The emphasis is on His suffering and the disfigurement which was brought on by it. What the people found was utterly contrary to what they were looking for. In contempt, men turned away in disgust. Note that neither this description nor the one in 53:2 has reference to the Servant's facial features or stature, but to the humiliation, suffering, and shame to which He was subjected.

15 Many people will be astonished, many nations will be sprinkled (or startled), and kings will not speak in the presence of such a one. The clause *so shall he sprinkle* ("startle," margin) *many nations* has two basic interpretations; scholars are about evenly divided as to whether the reading should be *sprinkle* or *startle*. *Sprinkle* is a technical term occurring many times in the Old Testament; blood, water, ashes, and oil are sprinkled in rites of cleansing, purifying, and consecrating. Accordingly, many commentators believe the prophet has in mind the cleansing and purifying of nations through the Servant's suffering (e.g., Alexander, Barnes, Young). Others hold that those who were astonished at what they had seen of His marred visage are now startled, caused to leap up in amazement, trembling with awe as they behold His exaltation (e.g., Delitzsch, Leupold, Rawlinson, Smith). Though the first view has much to its credit, the latter seems to be verified by what follows: *For that which had not been told them shall they see; and that which they had not heard shall they understand.* Kings, possibly from among the Gentiles, will be startled and spring up in amazement, though they will keep silent, when they see and understand what they have not previously been shown or told. As for the Jews, they have long heard wonderful words and seen marvelous deeds, but they have been deaf and blind to the underlying meaning. They should have recognized the Servant-Messiah when He came, but they did not.

Acquaintance with Grief (53:1–3)

   1   *Who hath believed our message?*—the plural *our* raises a question as to who the proclaimers are. This question is answered by the apostles John and Paul. After reporting that the people who heard Jesus "believed not on him," John quotes this verse and comments, "These things said Isaiah, because he saw his glory; and he spake of him" (John 12:37–41). And Paul likewise quotes the verse, applying it to the failure of the Jews to hearken to the glad tidings preached by the apostles (Rom. 10:16–21). Thus, *our message* is to be identified as the messianic message from God through Isaiah, Jesus, and the apostles which generally was rejected by the people. *The arm of Jehovah* is a metonymy for the power of God which is revealed in the message and exerted in the salvation which results from believing it (cf. 51:5; 52:10). By both word and power God revealed Himself and the salvation He would provide.
   2   So certain is Jehovah of what will be done that He speaks of coming events in the past tense. They are as if already accomplished: *For he grew up before him as a tender plant, and as a root out of a dry*

ground. As a tender plant or twig, the Servant will grow up in the constant presence and care of Jehovah (cf. John 8:29). The *dry ground* out of which He will grow is the fallen lot of the house of David; for the Edomite Herod, whose ancestors were enemies of God's people, was on the throne of Judah, and Rome ruled over him. The corrupt priesthood was greatly influenced by the Sadducean philosophy of unbelief, and the people were bound by tradition rather than committed to truth. Out of such a dry political, religious, and moral desert, God will make a twig, "a dry tree" according to Ezekiel (Ezek. 17:22–24), to flourish. Horribly disfigured by the treatment at His trials and the crucifixion, He will be repulsive to look upon. There will be *no beauty,* no regal adornments such as the people desire, but only an unimposing peasant carpenter from a small obscure village in Galilee. He will have none of the human glory that men look for and desire.

3 A man humble in background and unimpressive in appearance by the world's standard, *He was despised, and rejected of men; a man of sorrows, and acquainted with grief* (sickness): *and as one from whom men hide their face he was despised; and we esteemed him not.* To despise is to ascribe little worth to someone or something, to hold in contempt, as Esau despised his birthright and sold it for a mess of pottage (Gen. 25:34). The grief or sickness with which the Servant was acquainted was not His own bodily illnesses, but the spiritual sickness of the human race, the fruit of their sin (cf. 1:4–6). This caused Him deep concern and mental anguish, sorrow of soul under which He groaned with grief. Men, calloused by sin and steeped in their own iniquities, despised such a tender and holy spirit, failing to see in Him the true Servant of God who could lift them to solid spiritual health and right relationship with their Creator. Doing nothing but good, He came to save God's people, but they repaid Him by doing nothing but evil and bad. *We,* the nation, even all men, *esteemed him not;* all failed to see the spiritual beauty of His life and teaching and therefore failed to set a proper value upon Him. How blind man must be not to have recognized then, nor to recognize even now, the greatest Benefactor and Benefit ever offered by God to the human family!

Ill Treatment: The Servant's Vicarious Suffering (53:4–6)

4 The griefs (sicknesses) which the Servant bore and the sorrows (mental anguish) which He carried were not His, but ours, those of the world. The Servant willingly took these burdens upon Himself. But because of His painful sufferings and afflictions, His sorrows and acquaintance with grief, the people regarded Him as smitten by the Lord, punished for His own sins.

Physical diseases and infirmities result from Satan's work (Luke 13:16); according to the general biblical teaching, they are the consequence of man's violation of God's physical and spiritual law. For this reason Matthew (8:17) can apply this verse to the Messiah's healing of diseases and infirmities. But more is involved. For in healing physical maladies Jesus was foreshadowing His expiatory work of healing our spiritual sicknesses and their evil effects (I Peter 2:24; Heb. 9:28). The vicarious character of His sacrifice is emphasized throughout this section. He was smitten of God only in the sense that God allowed Him to suffer; God provided Him as an offering for man's sin. Little did the people realize that He was being subjected to such indignities for their sins, not His own.

5 The prophet corrects the misconception: *But he was wounded for our transgressions, he was bruised for our iniquities; the chastisement of our peace was upon him; and with his stripes are we healed.* Instead of *wounded*, several commentators (e.g., Alexander, Delitzsch, Leupold, Young) suggest *pierced*, which more accurately reflects what is said in other passages. Not only were the Servant's hands and feet pierced with nails (Ps. 22:16) and His side pierced with a spear (John 19:34), but Zechariah prophesied (12:10) that one day the inhabitants of Jerusalem would look unto Him whom they had pierced (John 19:37). *He was wounded for our transgressions,* our acts of rebellion against God's authority and law; bringing a breach between man and God, such acts must be either punished or pardoned. *He was bruised,* a strong word meaning "to crush," which emphasizes the emotional and spiritual suffering of the Servant as He became sin on our behalf. The word *iniquities* is derived from a verb meaning "to bend, twist, distort";[11] hence, *iniquities* are perversions or violations

---

11. *Theological Wordbook of the Old Testament*, vol. 2, p. 650.

of what is right. *Chastisement* usually indicates disciplinary measures which aim at correction or instruction, but in this instance the word refers to punishment. The punishment for our transgressions and iniquities which had broken the unity, the relationship, between man and God, was laid upon the Servant; *and with his stripes we are healed*, restored to a complete harmony with God. In bearing the guilt of man's sins, the Servant also bore the punishment for them. The punishment of sin is (eternal) separation from God (II Thess. 1:9). Jesus experienced (though not eternally) this very punishment when He was on the cross (Ps. 22:1; Matt. 27:46; cf. also Eph. 2:14–18; I Peter 2:21–25).

6 *All we like sheep have gone astray*; not just a few individuals, but the whole of mankind wander in the wilderness of sin, having rejected Jehovah as their Shepherd. *We have turned every one to his own way*; though the whole flock goes astray, we do so as individuals. Each of us is personally responsible for his own conduct. The iniquity laid on Him is the propensity of every individual to turn *to his own way*. This is an excellent commentary on the word *iniquity* (cf. v. 5), for it indicates the character of the action as well as the action itself—rejecting God's way for man's way.

Total Submission of the Servant (53:7–9)

7 The suffering, death, and burial of the Servant are foreshadowed in this stanza. *He was oppressed*, subjected to ill treatment such as a tyrant might inflict upon a captive (cf. 9:4; 14:3–4), *yet when he was afflicted*, suffering the physical and inner pain to which He willingly submitted for others, *he opened not his mouth*. As a lamb that is slaughtered or a sheep that is shorn remains silent, so did the Servant react to His tormentors. When He was accused by the chief priests and questioned by Pilate, "he gave [them] no answer, not even to one word" (Matt. 27:1–14); and when He was questioned by Herod, "he answered him nothing" (Luke 23:9). Delitzsch says, "All the references in the New Testament to the Lamb of God . . . spring from this passage in the book of Isaiah" (II. 325).

8 The unfair judicial treatment of the Servant is now graphically foreshadowed. *By* ("From," margin) *oppression and judgment he was*

taken away; from a violent miscarriage of justice He was led away to death. Delitzsch comments, "Hostile oppression and judicial persecution were the circumstances out of which He was carried away by death" (II. 324). Young suggests, "It is best to understand *he was taken* as referring to a being taken away by death from an unjust trial. . . . From the midst of his suffering he was taken away by death" (III. 351–52). Pilate's verdict that Jesus was innocent ("I find no crime in him"), which he repeated three times (John 18:38; 19:4, 6), was in effect reversed when "he delivered him unto them [the Jews] to be crucified" (John 19:16). The Servant was cut off from *his generation,* His contemporaries. *He was cut off,* snatched away, *out of the land of the living,* an indication of the violent nature of His death. Who among those living at the time of His crucifixion had any idea that His death was for the transgressions of God's people, *to whom the stroke was due?* The people of His generation saw Him as a blasphemer deserving death. Actually, in view of His life and theirs, they should have realized that they themselves were worthy of death and that He was the Servant who came to reveal God and His redemptive love.

9   Having revealed the violent nature of the Servant's death executed by those to whom the stroke was due, Isaiah next points to the Servant's burial: *And they made his grave with the wicked, and with a rich man in his death.* Barnes interprets the passage impersonally, "And his grave was appointed with the wicked; but he was with a rich man in his death" (II. 276). The thought is that although it was intended that He be buried with the wicked—either with His cross according to Roman custom (Rawlinson) or at an ignominious site according to Jewish custom (Young)—He was instead buried in the tomb of a rich man. Delitzsch concurs, "They assigned Him His grave with criminals, and after He had actually died a martyr's death, with a rich man" (II. 328). Jehovah could by His providence prevent His beloved Servant from experiencing ignominious burial. The prophecy was fulfilled in the request of the wealthy Joseph of Arimathaea that the body be given to him for burial. Pilate granted the request and thus provided a burial with dignity in a new tomb (Matt. 27:57–60). Christ's life was ever above reproach, His speech always sincere and true. He had done no criminal act and had not

failed in His work and mission; therefore, His Father saw to it that the faithful Servant received an honorable burial.

Victory and Reward (53:10–12)

Isaiah began this song with a declaration of the Servant's exaltation (52:13); but before the exaltation, He must be subjected to extreme humiliation. Having shown the depth to which He will stoop for others, the prophet returns to the subject of the Servant's reward and triumph.

10 *Yet it pleased Jehovah to bruise him; he hath put him to grief.* Jehovah was *pleased*, "experienced an emotional delight,"[12] not in seeing the Servant suffer (for He momentarily turned His face from the awful scene of Calvary—Matt. 27:46), but in providing a sacrifice adequate for the redemption of man. His delight was in the achievement of the Servant; it would prosper in His hand. Man's putting the Servant to death was not by accident or by a miscarriage of God's plan, but according to "the determinate counsel and foreknowledge of God" (Acts 2:23). Jehovah was pleased to *bruise* the Servant, to crush Him with excruciating pain and put Him to heart-rending mental anguish, though He Himself had done no sin. This was the cost of salvation. The *soul*, the life Christ poured out, was an adequate, perfect, and complete offering in every respect. In Him all sin-offerings, trespass-offerings, burnt-offerings, peace-offerings, and offerings for cleansing find their fulfillment; all point to Him (Heb. 9:13–14; 10:10; etc.).

Three results follow the offering of this sacrifice: (1) *He shall see his seed;* the Servant shall see His spiritual posterity, the new spiritual Israel born of His sacrifice, spread abroad and possess the nations (54:3; cf. Rom. 2:28–29; Gal. 6:15–16; Phil. 3:3). (2) *He shall prolong his days,* extend His years into the infinite future. Clearly this is a reference to the resurrection, for His death has been plainly announced (vv. 8–9). He was dead, but is now alive forevermore and holds the keys of death and Hades (Rev. 1:17–18). (3) *And the pleasure of Jehovah shall prosper in his hand.* It pleased Jehovah to bruise the

---

12. *Theological Wordbook of the Old Testament,* vol. 1, p. 310.

Servant (v. 10) so that His purpose might be satisfactorily achieved. It was God's good pleasure that in Him all fullness would dwell (Col. 1:19), and that through His victory the new Israel would prosper, its destiny resting in His hand. It may be further observed that He now occupies the throne of God (Rev. 3:21) as "KING OF KINGS, AND LORD OF LORDS" (Rev. 19:16). All things have been put in subjection under His feet, and He is the head of the redeemed body (Eph. 1:22). Through His sacrifice and suffering, He has acquired the right to hold the book of God's plan for human redemption (Rev. 5:4–7). The saints are given power to overcome Satan through the blood of Him who made sacrifice (Rev. 12:11). This is *the pleasure of Jehovah* that continues to prosper in the Servant's hand.

11   *He shall see of the travail of his soul*, the dark side of the Servant's mission. Though the experience through which the Servant passes is painful, He (Jehovah or the Servant) shall be abundantly satisfied with the achieved results. For *by the knowledge of himself shall my righteous servant justify many; and he shall bear their iniquities*. Jehovah is speaking, but to whose knowledge does He refer? Is it the Servant's knowledge of Jehovah and of His purpose to justify His people? Or is it the sinner's knowledge of the Servant and the redemption that He offers? Inasmuch as the Servant is the Savior, it appears that the meaning is that the sinner is justified by his knowledge of the Servant and His sacrifice and work. Later the prophet says, "And all thy children shall be taught of Jehovah" (54:13); Jesus says that only as people are taught of Jehovah and learn can they come unto Him (John 6:44–45); Paul says that the faith by which men are justified comes only by hearing the word of God (Rom. 10:17). As they come to knowledge of Him, the righteous Servant will justify many by bearing their iniquities.

12   By His sacrifice and conquest over sin and death, the Servant will not only justify many, but will also triumph in victory over Satan: *Therefore*, because of His victory, *will I divide him a portion with the great, and he shall divide the spoil with the strong*. To His Servant who stooped so low, Jehovah will give a place among the great; and in His conquest the Servant will divide the spoil with the strong, the mighty or powerful one. This points to the Servant's conquest over Satan (the strong one) and the deliverance of many of those whom he holds

captive; the Servant divides the booty with him. On this point Jesus said, "When the strong man fully armed guardeth his own court, his goods are in peace: but when a stronger than he shall come upon him, and overcome him, he taketh from him his whole armor wherein he trusted, and divideth his spoils" (Luke 11:21–22; cf. Matt. 12:29). In this parabolic statement Satan is "the strong man" and Jesus is the "stronger than he." The Lord further said, "Now is the judgment of this world: now shall the prince of this world be cast out" (John 12:31); "he hath nothing in me" (John 14:30)—Satan cannot hold back the Servant. The writer of Hebrews confirms the interpretation that the Servant will deliver many from Satan, the strong one: "Since then the children are sharers in flesh and blood, he also himself in like manner partook of the same; that through death he might bring to nought him that had the power of death, that is, the devil; and might deliver all them who through fear of death were all their lifetime subject to bondage" (Heb. 2:14–15). His sacrifice covers God's people of the Old Testament ("a death having taken place for the redemption of the transgressions that were under the first covenant, they that have been called may receive the promise of the eternal inheritance"—Heb. 9:15), and all those who have lived since. The ground of His victory is again declared: *because he poured out his soul unto death, and was numbered with the transgressors: yet he bare the sin of many, and made intercession for the transgressors.* The pouring out of the Servant's soul indicates that it was deliberate, a willful or willing act on His part; it was not accidental. His being numbered with the transgressors identifies Him with the whole fallen race He came to redeem. Not only is it the case that the Servant *made intercession for the transgressors,* but He "maketh" (margin) intercession. Not only did He pray from the cross for His tormentors (Luke 23:34), but He ever lives to make intercession for all transgressors who draw near unto God through Him (Heb. 7:25).

The five glorious stanzas of Isaiah's final Servant Song consider various features of the Servant's character, life, and mission: (1) His exaltation; (2) His acquaintance with grief; (3) His ill treatment and vicarious sufferings; (4) His total submission to Jehovah's will; and (5)

His victory and reward. On these hang the whole of New Testament preaching and the salvation of all mankind.

CHAPTER 54
The Future Splendor of Zion

There is a close relationship between the fourth Servant Song and chapter 54—the undertone of grief, sadness, and suffering which characterized 52:13–53:12 gives way to joy, singing, and assurance. In the song the suffering and victory of the Servant were portrayed, whereas in the present chapter the glorious redemption accomplished by His suffering is foretold. All attempts to interpret this chapter as a prophecy of the exiles' return from Babylon and the rebuilding of physical Israel as a nation and of physical Jerusalem as a city are extremely weak. Rather, the subject here is the glorious results of the Servant's sacrificial work redeeming a spiritual people. Chapter 54 reveals God fulfilling His ultimate plan. This interpretation is in perfect harmony with the Old Testament prophecies, the work of Christ, and the teaching of the apostles. The church as a part of God's eternal purpose was no accident or afterthought; it was very definitely in His plan (Eph. 3:9–11) and was foreshadowed in Isaiah.

Although neither Zion nor Jerusalem is named between chapter 52, where both terms occur four times, and chapters 59 and 62 respectively, it is evident that the symbolic wife of Jehovah in chapter 54 is Jerusalem-Zion. Fallen and disgraced like a drunken woman with no one to guide her (51:17–18), she is restored under the Servant and raised to a state of unparalleled glory.

The Joy and Enlargement of Zion (vv. 1–8)

1   Verses 1–5 are a development of chapter 49:14–23. Zion was barren during the time of her captivity, which was a period of separation, not divorcement (50:1), from Jehovah her husband. But now this desolate period of devastation and barrenness, the result of judgment, is over. Zion is to break forth in joyous singing, for she who did

not *travail* in childbirth (a different word from that used in 53:11) is now to bear profusely. From Paul's allegory involving Sarah and Hagar, where he quotes this verse (Gal. 4:21–31), we conclude that the prophet is speaking of the children to be born of the spiritual promise (Gen. 12:3) rather than those born of the fleshly promise (Gen. 12:2). This promise of a spiritual posterity through Abraham's seed (Gen. 22:18) was held in abeyance until the coming of the Seed. That Seed has now come (ch. 53), and Zion, which has passed through a terrible crisis, learning the tragedy of sin, will now be taken back by her husband to bear spiritual children unto Him. The spiritual offspring will be far greater in number than the fleshly family.

2   With the huge increase in her family, Zion will need larger living quarters (cf. 26:15; 33:20; 49:19–20). Her tent will be enlarged to cover the area "from sea to sea, and from the River to the ends of the earth" (Zech. 9:10). So she is told to *stretch forth the curtains*, the panels of cloth which make up the tent, *of thy habitations* (from the Hebrew word for "tabernacle," this is the dwelling where the children will abide). Though God's dwelling-place among His people will be permanent (33:20), it is possible that the figure of a tent is used because of the nomadic condition of spiritual Israel. They are "sojourners and pilgrims" in the world (I Peter 2:11–12), and like the apostles, they have "no certain dwelling-place" here (I Cor. 4:11). Zion is to *spare not*, holding nothing in restraint, but to lengthen the ropes which support or hold the tent in place and to strengthen the pegs which are driven into the earth to hold the ropes. The picture is of a tent sufficient in size to accommodate the large family and strong enough to withstand any storm.

3   Zion will *spread abroad on the right hand and on the left*, that is, in every direction. *Thy seed*, those redeemed by the Servant (53:10), *shall possess the nations*, that is, conquer the Gentiles, bringing them into submission to the Lord (cf. 49:6), not by military triumph but by spiritual conquest. In this way the spiritually devastated cities will be inhabited by a spiritually renewed citizenry, a holy nation (I Peter 2:9).

4   Zion is not to be in fear or terror of any external force, for there is none that can overcome her in her new relationship with God. Neither shall she *be put to shame*, fall into disgrace and humiliation

445

because of a baseless trust or unholy life. She will not be embarrassed by the shame of idolatry or by defeat at the hand of enemies. The shame of her youth which she will forget is not, as some commentators think, the Egyptian bondage or the many times she has been assaulted and overrun by her enemies. Rather, it is the shame of her idolatry which began already in Egypt, the period of her youth (Ezek. 20:6–8; 23:2–4, 19). The idolatry which began in her youth eventually brought Jerusalem-Zion to the reproach of widowhood in the Babylonian captivity (49:21), which likewise will be forgotten (cf. 65:16).

5   The widowhood of Zion is only a temporary aberration, for Jehovah is still her husband. He is not only her husband, but also her Maker. He had made the people a nation and Jerusalem the holy city of His presence. *Jehovah of hosts is his name;* He is the eternally existent Lord to whom the hosts of heaven and earth are subject. Three other titles reflect His greatness: (1) He is *the Holy One of Israel,* the revelation and standard of absolute holiness; as such He was forced to put Jerusalem away. (2) He is Israel's *Redeemer;* as Israel's Maker, He can both put her away and redeem her again unto Himself, but to be redeemed she must abandon her unholy ways. And (3) He is, and has always been, *the God of the whole earth;* now He will be recognized as such by all of the inhabitants of the world (cf. Rom. 3:29).

6   The relationship which has been temporarily interrupted by a separation will be renewed by Jehovah, who has summoned Israel to be His wife. Jehovah had departed from her (Ezek. 11:23), leaving her with her deep grief of spirit. She was abandoned by a husband who could no longer dwell with her. Jehovah loved her, but hated her wicked ways. A *wife of youth* is a wife taken in her youth, not necessarily one who is still youthful.

7–8   The thoughts of these two verses run parallel. God abandoned Zion *for a small moment.* Her Babylonian exile or widowhood was but a brief time (fifty years) in comparison with the total history of Jehovah's relationship to the people (cf. 26:20). Though *in overflowing wrath* He had hid His face for this small moment, with great mercies and *with everlasting lovingkindness* He will gather her to Himself, for God's tenderness manifested in His love is everlasting—

"For his anger is but for a moment;/His favor is for a life-time:/Weeping may tarry for the night,/But joy cometh in the morning" (Ps. 30:5). This is an eternal principle with God.

"As the Waters of Noah" (vv. 9–10)

9   In His holy wrath against the exceeding wickedness of ancient man, Jehovah had destroyed the earth with a flood; but after cleansing the earth by the great waters, He made a covenant (the equivalent of an oath) with Noah that never again would He destroy the earth in such a manner (Gen. 9:11). And now once more, with overflowing wrath against the sins of His people He has purged them, and restored a remnant as His wife. To these survivors He swears that never again will He be wroth with or rebuke them as He has fleshly Israel and her city Jerusalem. This promise is not made to national Israel or physical Jerusalem, for both experienced the vent of His indignation from soon after the return from exile until the destruction by the Romans. Rather, the promise is made to spiritual Israel. It does not mean that she will not be severely tested. What it does mean is that though she might be unmercifully persecuted by her enemies and forced to pass through the floods and fire of tribulation, the true spiritual Zion and Jerusalem (the church) will never be the object of God's wrath and judgment of destruction (cf. Hag. 2:6–7; Zech. 14:1–5; Heb. 12:22–28).[13] Jehovah has kept his oaths that He will not destroy the earth with another flood nor pour out His wrath against spiritual Jerusalem. The earth has not been destroyed by water again, and the true people of God have endured through the centuries. There have always been a faithful few.

10   Not only will Jehovah's wrath never be demonstrated against His spiritual people, but also His loving-kindness and covenant of peace will never depart from them. The mountains and hills, which man considers permanently fixed features of earth, may be removed from sight, and the world become a plain; but Jehovah's loving-kindness and *covenant of peace*, a covenant that brings peace to man

13. See the comments on Zech. 14:1–5 in Homer Hailey, *A Commentary on the Minor Prophets* (Grand Rapids: Baker, 1972), pp. 394–96.

(cf. Jer. 31:31; Ezek. 37:26; Heb. 13:20–21), will abide forever (cf. Matt. 24:35). And so, in the midst of a changing, crumbling, and passing world where new theories are ever being substituted for tried and true values, there are some things that are permanent, unshakable, and immovable. God's being and character are fixed; the deity, victory, and rule of Christ are permanent; a kingdom that cannot be shaken has been received (Heb. 12:28); a firm foundation stands, having the seal of God (II Tim. 2:19); the constitution of that kingdom, the covenant of peace sealed by Christ's blood (Matt. 26:28), shall not pass away (Matt. 24:35).

Jerusalem's Glory and Permanence in the Messianic Age (vv. 11–17)

11–12 Jehovah addresses the city in her present condition, *afflicted, tossed with tempest, and not comforted*—the result of having drunk the cup from His hand (51:17–21). She is afflicted, suffering the pain of destitution, driven and tossed like chaff before a wind or waves by a storm, with no one to comfort or console her as a mother would her child. But in loving-kindness Jehovah, who alone has the capability, will change all this. The Lord continues to speak of the city as a bride. In lavish terms He describes the beauty of the new community of redeemed people: *Behold, I will set thy stones in fair colors*. The *fair colors* ("antimony," margin) may be a property of the stones themselves, or of a substance which glazes or binds them (here and I Chron. 29:2); the word also refers to eye paint used by Oriental women to enhance their beauty (II Kings 9:30; Jer. 4:30). The thought seems to be that the precious stones of which the city is to be built will be embedded in a setting that emphasizes their beauty, as eye paint emphasizes the beauty of a woman's eyes. The foundations will be laid with blue sapphires—the city will be both beautiful and permanent. An emphatic point is that the restoration of the city and its beauty are Jehovah's work, not the work of man. Zion's *pinnacles* Jehovah will make of rubies. The word translated *pinnacles* is actually the plural form of a Hebrew term meaning "sun."[14] The numer-

---

14. *Theological Wordbook of the Old Testament*, vol. 2, p. 940.

ous translations which have been suggested indicate the difficulty in determining the meaning here: "windows" (margin and King James), "minarets" (Delitzsch), "battlements" (Young), "the upper fringe of the battlements" (Leupold). Whatever object is in view, it shines with the brilliance of a precious gem. Each gate will be made of *carbuncle*, probably a stone giving off a fiery glow. This term, like *rubies* in the preceding phrase, cannot be identified with certainty. Alexander observes that it is not important to be able to identify the particular gems; the point being stressed is their sparkling brilliancy (II. 316). It is likewise uncertain whether the term *border* refers to the walls of the city, its physical boundaries, or the farthest limits of its territorial possessions; whatever the case, the *border* consists of precious stones or jewels which reflect the glory of its Maker. The picture portrays "the riches of the glory of his inheritance in the saints" (Eph. 1:18), the church.

13   As verses 11 and 12 set forth the glory of the church as viewed from without, this verse describes the beauty within. *And all thy children shall be taught of Jehovah*; knowledge of and from God is a prerequisite for citizenship in the new Zion—"For they shall all know me, from the least of them unto the greatest of them, saith Jehovah: for I will forgive their iniquity, and their sin will I remember no more" (Jer. 1:34). This knowledge belongs only to those who are "taught of God" (cf. John 6:44–45; I Thess. 4:9). The source of this learning is not human wisdom or the philosophies and traditions of men, but the word of God. On the foundation of this knowledge and the forgiveness of sin (cf. 53:11), the spiritual city, the church, will be built. *And great shall be the peace of thy children* (cf. John 14:27; Phil. 4:7; Col. 3:15); in contrast to their former distress and desolation and to the state of the wicked, for whom there is no peace (48:22), the children of spiritual Zion will enjoy a state of total well-being.

14   Righteousness is the foundation of Jehovah's throne (Pss. 89:14; 97:2), and His righteousness and salvation will be "for ever" unto all generations, never to disappear (51:6, 8). We know that the city He has fashioned is similarly fixed and permanent, for He says to her, *In righteousness shalt thou be established*. Although the word translated *established* basically means "to bring something into being

with the consequence that its existence is a certainty,"[15] in this instance it probably means "fixed" or "permanent," no longer "tossed with tempest" (v. 11), as indestructible and immovable as is the foundation of God's throne. Jehovah's righteousness is the basis of the righteousness and salvation of the citizens of spiritual Zion, for He says, "Their righteousness . . . is of me" (v. 17), and the standard of life they follow is set forth in His word (v. 13). The city will thereby attain the ideal sought by Jehovah, "The city of righteousness, a faithful town" (1:26). Since parallelism is such a popular device with Isaiah, we regard the following clause not as an imperative ("Be thou far from oppression," margin), but as a promise: *Thou shalt be far from oppression, for thou shalt not fear; and from terror, for it shall not come near thee.* The Lord is not instructing His people to refrain from oppressing others, but He is promising that by virtue of their righteousness in Him, they need fear no oppression that might threaten them. Alexander's paraphrase conveys the idea: "When once established by the exercise of righteousness on my part and your own, you may put far off all dread of oppression, for you have no cause to fear it, and of destruction, for it shall not come nigh you" (II. 318–19).

15   *Behold, they,* those who would come against God's people and city to oppress and destroy them, *may gather together* (note that the possibility of a conspiracy does exist), *but not by me.* In the past Jehovah had brought hostile nations against His people in judgment (10:5–11; 47:6; Hab. 1:5–11), but He will not do so again. If they should come against the new city, they will do so without His will or sanction, and they will therefore be doomed to *fall because of thee,* that is, because the citizens of Zion "know righteousness" and God's law is in their heart (51:7–8). When God's righteousness and law prevail among men, there can be no defeat (vv. 16–17); this is the victory of the redeemed people under the Servant.

16   All enemies shall fail and fall when they come against the righteous, because Jehovah is their Protector. God created the smith, whose work it is to produce weapons. As He controls the smith, so in His providence Jehovah controls the manufacture of weapons and their use (cf. 13:5; 42:13). He also created the waster, whose work is to

---

15. *Theological Wordbook of the Old Testament*, vol. 1, p. 433.

destroy. Inasmuch as God is the Creator of the destroyer, He can and does control him as well.

17   With the smiths, the weapons, and the wasters under God's power and subject to His will, no weapon that is formed against His city can defeat or destroy her. Furthermore, every tongue that accuses her shall be condemned by the truth abiding in His people. This assurance of divine protection and victory over their enemies is a permanent possession of God's servants. These servants are partakers of the salvation purchased by the Servant, and accept their responsibility to service as did He. The righteousness by which they triumph and by which they receive justice is of Jehovah. The guarantee of their victory is God's word—*saith Jehovah*. That all the powers which have sought to destroy God's spiritual city and people have failed and fallen (among them are the Jews and Rome) assures victory throughout time. Clearly the prophecy points to the church and the spiritual Jerusalem of the New Testament.

CHAPTER 55

The Great Invitation: Free Mercy for All

Many titles have been ascribed to this chapter, but the one we have selected seems to emphasize its total content best. The Servant has come, providing salvation for the whole human race (52:13–53:12); the glory of Zion has been enhanced, the "tent" enlarged to accommodate a large influx of children, and Jehovah has received Jerusalem back as His wife (ch. 54). Now the Lord invites dispersed Israel and the cast-off nations to come and partake of the spiritual life which He has provided through the Servant. To limit this chapter to exiled Judah in Babylon, or even to give the Babylonian exiles major prominence, is to restrict the call to confines entirely too narrow. For chapter 55 foreshadows the invitation of Jesus to come unto Him and find rest (Matt. 11:28–30), the invitation to the marriage feast (Matt. 22:1–14), and the abundant offer of God's grace to Jews and Gentiles (Acts 15:11). The invitation is both urgent and universal.

Come and Partake Without Price (vv. 1–5)

1   Jehovah earlier promised that He would provide abundant water for the thirsty (41:17–18) and that in the purified Zion "with joy shall ye draw water out of the wells of salvation" (12:3). He has now provided that water, and beckons, *Ho, every one that thirsteth, come ye to the waters* (plural, suggesting abundance), and drink enough to quench the soul's thirst for God (cf. Pss. 42:2; 63:1). The invitation is universal, *every one*; all are invited to come and buy *without money*. This appears to be contradictory, for how can one *buy* without money? However, the emphasis here is on the free grace of God who abundantly provides and graciously invites all to come and eat and drink freely. The invitation to *eat* indicates that the spiritual bread which satisfies the soul's hunger (cf. Deut. 8:3; Matt. 4:4) has also been provided. The water refreshes as it quenches spiritual thirst, the wine "maketh glad the heart" (Ps. 104:15), and the milk provides food for growth (I Peter 2:2). All are free gifts of divine grace.

2   The folly of the people's desire for that which is material and perishable is reproved by a question: Why do you labor and *spend money for that which is not bread*, that which will not satisfy? The world has expended its energies in search of commodities which fail to satisfy spiritual hunger and thirst, leaving the soul to dry up and perish. So *hearken diligently*, listen closely as Jehovah speaks, and act upon what He says. *Eat ye that which is good*, spiritual foods of worth and value which permanently satisfy life's deepest yearnings. *Let your soul*, your complete person or self, *delight itself in fatness*, in the sustenance, the completeness, provided through the Servant, "that ye may be filled unto all the fulness of God" (Eph. 3:19).

3   *Incline*, extend or stretch out, *your ear* with the intent of paying heed to the Lord's words, *and come unto me: hear, and your soul shall live*. Only by coming to the Lord and hearing what He says, with the intent of doing it, can man live. These are also the conditions for entering into the covenant about to be introduced: *And I will make an everlasting covenant with you, even the sure mercies of David*. A *covenant* is a "legally binding obligation, especially of God for man's redemption."[16] In the Scriptures *everlasting* often means "age-last-

---

16. *Zondervan Pictorial Encyclopedia of the Bible*, vol. 1, p. 1000.

ing," that is, for the duration of a particular age or period. Several Old Testament covenants are referred to as "everlasting"—the covenants Jehovah made with Noah and every living creature (Gen. 9:16), with Abraham and his seed (Gen. 17:10, 13; I Chron. 16:16–17; Ps. 105:9–10), with Isaac (Gen. 17:19), with Israel (Lev. 24:8), with David (II Sam. 23:5), and with the inhabitants of earth (ch. 24:5). Israel so thoroughly violated the covenant made at Sinai (Ezek. 16:59) that God fashioned a new and different one "with the house of Israel, and with the house of Judah" (Jer. 31:31–34). When the people violated the old covenant, Jehovah annulled (broke) it that He might make a new one (Zech. 11:10).

Jehovah will make a new and everlasting covenant of peace (Ezek. 37:26) with those who incline their ear and come to Him (cf. 61:8; Ezek. 16:60, 62). He had earlier promised that He would set one of David's line upon his throne. Jehovah would be Father to this Seed, and the Seed would be Jehovah's Son. Moreover, the kingdom and throne of the Seed would be established forever (II Sam. 7:11–14; Ps. 89:3–4). Fulfillment of this covenant was as certain as the covenant of day and night; only if day and night were to fail would Jehovah fail to fulfill the promise He made to David (Jer. 33:19–21).

It is abundantly clear that the phrase *the sure mercies of David* looks to the establishment of David's Seed, the Messiah, upon his throne under an everlasting covenant of peace. We know that a political king is not in view, for Jehovah said with regard to the carrying off of Coniah (Jeconiah or Jehoiachin) into Babylon, "No more shall a man of his seed prosper, sitting upon the throne of David, and ruling in Judah" (Jer. 22:30). He was the last divinely approved king in Judah, for his successor Zedekiah was a puppet king set up by Nebuchadnezzar (II Chron. 36:10). Furthermore, when the crown was removed from Zedekiah, and his rule overturned, Jehovah said, "This also shall be no more, until he come whose right it is; and I will give it him" (Ezek. 21:27). The earthly kingdom and temporal throne of David came to an end with Coniah and Zedekiah, never again to be established as a political entity. Christ the Servant is the one "whose right it is." The promise of a throne and kingdom that would endure forever was fulfilled at His coming.

The second David is referred to by at least three other prophets.

Hosea, who was contemporary with Isaiah, said that after the devastation "shall the children of Israel return, and seek Jehovah their God, and David their king"; this will occur "in the latter days" (Hos. 3:5), which is always a reference to the messianic period. Jeremiah speaks of "David their king whom I [Jehovah] will raise up unto them" (Jer. 30:9). Jehovah will cause "a Branch of righteousness to grow up unto David." In that day Judah will be saved and Jerusalem will dwell safely (Jer. 33:15–18). Ezekiel says that Jehovah will raise up His "servant David" to be shepherd and prince among His people (Ezek. 34:23–24), and that while David is their king and prince, He (Jehovah) will make with them "a covenant of peace," "an everlasting covenant" (Ezek. 37:24–26). *The sure mercies of David* include all these promises made through Hosea, Jeremiah, and Ezekiel, the blessings to be bestowed by the Seed of David, the Messiah, who will be a light and salvation to the nations (49:6). All of this will be achieved through sacrifice (ch. 53) and not through arms (Zech. 9:10). Paul in fact quotes Isaiah 55:3 and declares it fulfilled in Christ, through whom are proclaimed the blessings of remission of sins and justification for all who believe (Acts 13:34–39). It is noteworthy that in his next sermon Paul specifically includes the Gentiles by quoting Isaiah 49:6 (Acts 13:47). In Christ the throne and kingdom of David have now been permanently established, and the sure mercies of an everlasting covenant of peace provided.

4   Jehovah has *given him for a witness to the peoples*, that is, God has given the world someone who can bear firsthand testimony to the truth. Some commentators think that the prophet has David in mind—his victories gave a witness of Jehovah's power and being to the heathen nations. However, it is much more probable that Isaiah is speaking of the new or second David (v. 3)—Jesus Christ "the faithful witness" (Rev. 1:5), who was sent into the world to bear witness to the truth (John 18:37). The witness will also be *a leader and commander*. A leader is a ruler or captain, usually the one at the top; a commander is one who gives orders. The witness will be both a leader and commander *to the peoples*, that is, to all mankind.

5   Evidently, Jehovah is addressing the David of verse 4, the Messiah. He will call a nation into being that He has not previously known, even "a holy nation" (I Peter 2:9). By means of the gospel,

this nation will be called from among "the nations" (Matt. 28:18–20; Mark 16:15–16). People who have not known Him will hasten unto Him; they will flow unto God's holy mountain from which Messiah will reign (2:2–3). All this will be because of Jehovah His God, *the Holy One of Israel*, who will have glorified the Messiah with His own self (cf. John 17:4–5; Acts 3:13–15), having received Him "up in glory" (I Tim. 3:16).

"Seek Ye Jehovah While He May Be Found" (vv. 6–13)

6   In the light of what Jehovah has done for the salvation of Jews and Gentiles, the prophet urgently calls upon both to *Seek ye Jehovah while he may be found*. Though the invitation includes the Jewish exiles in Babylon, it extends far beyond them. To seek Jehovah is to inquire after Him and His will with care and concern (cf. Amos 5:4, 6, 14). It has always been God's will that man seek after Him to the end of finding and serving Him (Acts 17:27). The clause *while he may be found* indicates a time limit; for though He may call today, the door may be shut tomorrow (Luke 13:25). The time to seek is now! Though He may be near at hand, He can withdraw Himself so that He cannot be found (cf. Hos. 5:6).

7   The *wicked* and the *unrighteous* are not to be distinguished from one another. They are the same class of people—men who act contrary to God's character and will and whose thoughts are to do evil. Response to Jehovah's call involves a complete change of both lifestyle and heart. Completely renouncing evil activities and thoughts, one must return unto Jehovah, from whom he has been separated by sin and iniquity (59:2). When one turns and returns, Jehovah promises to *abundantly pardon* him (cf. 1:18), to completely forgive the sin committed and the penalty incurred. This is divine grace, mercy, and loving-kindness in action.

8   The word *For* occurs four times in the following verses, introducing four reasons to seek Jehovah and change one's ways. The first is: *For my thoughts are not your thoughts, neither are your ways my ways, saith Jehovah.* Man should heed the admonition of verses 6–7, because though he is created in the image of God, man fails to achieve the ideal of Jehovah's thoughts and ways. Indeed, "the imag-

ination of man's heart is evil from his youth" (Gen. 8:21), affecting his ways and leading him to do things which never come into the mind or thought of God (Jer. 19:5; 32:35). Man makes the mistake of thinking that God is down on his level. As Jehovah charges, "Thou thoughtest that I was altogether such a one as thyself" (Ps. 50:21). But Jehovah's thoughts toward His people, unlike man's, have always been "thoughts of peace and not of evil" (Jer. 29:11). Such were His thoughts even before He sent them to Babylon.

9   A second *For* introduces a second reason for man to change his ways: God's ways and thoughts are greatly superior to those of man. The difference is illustrated by the height of the heavens above the earth, an infinite measure. Jehovah is exalted above the heavens (Ps. 57:5, 11), which He stretched out as a dwelling place for Himself (40:22). And His thoughts and ways are commensurate with His surroundings (cf. 57:15).

10–11   Here we find the third cause for seeking Jehovah and changing our ways and thoughts. Rain and snow come down from heaven, nourishing the earth and sustaining life. They cause vegetation and life to flourish, providing seed to the sower and bread for food. The water does not return until it has accomplished its purpose; it then returns in the form of vapor to begin the cycle again (cf. Eccles. 1:7). And *so shall my word be that goeth forth out of my mouth.* As the rain and snow accomplish God's purpose in the earth, so His word will fulfill His purpose in the hearts of those who draw near to hear, give heed, and change their ways and thoughts. *It shall accomplish that which I please,* fashion anew the thoughts and ways of those who seek after God. His word shall never return unto Him empty, but *it shall prosper in the thing whereto I sent it.* As the pleasure of Jehovah prospers in the hand of the Servant (53:10), so shall His word effect the results which He desires. When heeded, His word completely changes the life of men, fulfilling God's desires.

12   The final *For* introduces a fourth reason for giving heed to Jehovah's call and developing new ways and thoughts—the joy of the exodus. Whether Isaiah has in view the Jewish exiles as they go out from literal Babylon and look toward Jerusalem, or the redeemed of Jehovah as they are freed from spiritual Babylon and their captivity in sin, they *go out with joy* and are *led forth with peace.* In this exodus

there is no evidence of hurry or fear as in the flight from Egypt, but rather there is a manifestation of exuberance, gladness, and rejoicing of heart. In highly poetic language the prophet describes the praise of all nature sharing in the grand occasion. *The mountains and the hills,* symbols of permanence and duration, *shall break forth . . . into singing; and all the trees of the field shall clap their hands.* The image of nature sharing in the joy of people who have been delivered is popular with the prophet (cf. 35:1–2; 41:17–20; 44:23; 49:13).

13   When Jehovah uprooted His vineyard, taking away its hedge, breaking down its wall, and laying it waste, He said, "There shall come up briers and thorns" (5:5–6; cf. 32:13). But now, in their stead, there will come up the fir tree and the myrtle tree. Both of these are evergreens, symbols of life. The branches of the myrtle were used in making booths for the Feast of Tabernacles (Neh. 8:15); and the fir tree, whose roots run deep into the earth and whose branches spread to provide shade and protection, is a symbol of Jehovah, the source of all strength, protection, and fruitfulness (Hos. 14:8). The Lord's redemptive work and deliverance of His people will be *for an everlasting sign that shall not be cut off.* Other signs might be cut off or fail, but the deliverance of the Jews from Babylon and the Servant's deliverance of the redeemed from among all nations stand, and will ever stand, as testimonies to Jehovah's being and power.

CHAPTER **56**

Consolation for the Rejected;
A Rebuke of the Blind Watchmen

The prophet has comforted the people who will find themselves in Babylonian exile by assuring them of Jehovah's concern and care for them. Through Cyrus He will deliver them from their captivity. This deliverance foreshadows a greater redemption and deliverance by the Servant from a more severe bondage. It also foreshadows the glorification of redeemed Zion beyond all previous splendor. Although verses 1–8 are variously interpreted, it seems that this passage looks to the removing of restrictions which have hindered certain groups from God's assembly; it looks to a time when God will accept people from throughout society. If this interpretation be correct, these eight verses serve as a conclusion to the preceding chapters and deal with the transition (through the synagogues) from the old to the new dispensation.

Consolation for Foreigners and Eunuchs (vv. 1–8)

1   Jehovah's command, *Keep ye justice, and do righteousness,* grows out of His own character and conduct, for "Righteousness and justice are the foundation of his throne" (Ps. 97:2). Justice denotes equitable dealings and impartial decisions in civil and religious government; righteousness is behavior in accordance with Jehovah's ethical and moral standard. The people are to keep justice and do righteousness in preparation for the fulfilling of Jehovah's promise that in righteousness He will call Cyrus the deliverer (41:2; 45:13) and thus bring near both deliverance and salvation (46:13). And now Jehovah pledges, *My salvation is near to come, and my righteousness to be revealed.* From the divine point of view the time of deliverance is drawing near, while from the human standpoint, there must be preparation to participate in it.

2   The Hebrew word translated *Blessed* can also be rendered "happy" (I Kings 10:8), but *Blessed* is the better reading here (and in 30:18; 32:20). *Man* and *the son of man* are synonymous—man and the offspring of man. In order to be blessed, a man must meet three conditions: (1) He must prepare for the salvation and righteousness which are to appear; that is, he must hold fast the commandment of verse 1.·(2) Blessed is he *that keepeth the sabbath from profaning it.* While in captivity the people could not possibly keep a number of their laws. For example, being separated from the temple and the altar in Jerusalem, they had no opportunity to offer proper sacrifices. But inasmuch as the synagogue and its worship service originated while they were in Babylon, it is probable that the Sabbath could be observed to an acceptable extent. There were three basic reasons for setting aside the seventh day: (a) the Sabbath was sacred to Jehovah, the Creator of the universe, for He Himself rested on the seventh day following the six days of creation (Gen. 2:2); (b) to the Jew the Sab-

bath was a reminder of the mighty power by which Jehovah had delivered the nation from Egyptian bondage (Deut. 5:15); (c) the Sabbath was a sign between Jehovah and the children of Israel that He had sanctified them unto Himself as His special possession (Exod. 31:12–17; Ezek. 20:12). Thus observance of the Sabbath signified recognition of Jehovah's power in creation, in the deliverance of the Israelites from Egypt, and in their special relationship to Him. (3) In order to enjoy blessedness, a man must keep his hand (a metonymy for the whole man) from doing anything contrary to God's will.

3 Barriers that formerly separated certain classes of persons from Jehovah's assembly are to be removed. *The foreigner* ("the son of the stranger," King James) was a non-Israelite, one of another nationality; *the eunuch* was a man who had been mutilated. Under the law of Moses the stranger was permitted to "offer an offering made by fire, of a sweet savor unto Jehovah" (Num. 15:14); and at the dedication of the temple Solomon prayed that Jehovah hear the words of any foreigners who might come to the temple to pray (I Kings 8:41–43). Herod's temple provided a Court of the Gentiles; if they ventured beyond it, however, they were liable to the death penalty. [17] But here Jehovah gives the instruction that the foreigner who joins himself to Jehovah and returns with the exiles is not to say, *Jehovah will surely separate me from his people.* There is no historical evidence that any foreigners joined themselves to Jehovah and returned with the Jews, but it is evident from the New Testament that in the intertestamental period many from among the nations did seek Him. Jehovah also includes the eunuch: *Neither let the eunuch say, Behold, I am a dry tree.* Jehovah will receive him also. In accepting the eunuch Jehovah is either revising the law of Deuteronomy 23:1, where the eunuch is forbidden to enter the assembly, or looking to the messianic period when eunuchs receive special attention (Acts 8:26–39).

4 The word of Jehovah in verses 4 and 5 indicates that He now sees fit to accept eunuchs under certain conditions. *The eunuchs that* (1) *keep my sabbaths, and* (2) *choose the things that please me, and* (3) *hold fast my covenant* (the covenant made at Sinai, for only that

---

17. *Zondervan Pictorial Encyclopedia of the Bible*, vol. 5, p. 650.

particular covenant included the Sabbath regulations), will receive the following blessings:

5 *Unto them will I give in my house and within my walls a memorial and a name better than of sons and of daughters*—the reference to the house and walls does not mean that a plaque of some sort will be set up in the temple, but that within Jehovah's spiritual family the eunuch will be given a memorial and a name that will perpetuate his memory. The Hebrew word here rendered *memorial* is most often translated "hand"; it may, then, be an indication of power and might within God's family. One's *name* signifies all that one is. Because of their enduring spiritual and moral quality, the eunuch's power (memorial) and name within Jehovah's family will be *better than of sons and of daughters.* Jehovah's assurance of *an everlasting name, that shall not be cut off,* will be the eunuch's reward for service. A name passed on to sons and daughters can be cut off, but a name which Jehovah gives to a member of His spiritual family cannot be cut off, for only He can blot it out of His book. The account of the Ethiopian nobleman in Acts 8 indicates that it was not uncommon for a eunuch to respond to Jehovah's invitation to worship in Jerusalem.

6 Having given assurance to the eunuchs, Jehovah turns to address the foreigners with a similar word. His blessing will be upon those who of their own desire and will *join themselves* to Him in a true spiritual relationship (1) *to minister unto him,* that is, to render service in His house; (2) *to love the name of Jehovah,* holding it in reverence; and (3) *to be his servants,* assuming and faithfully carrying out the responsibilities entrusted to them. As in the case of the eunuchs, the foreigners also must keep and respect the Sabbath, holding fast the covenant which binds them to the Lord.

7 Although foreigners and eunuchs were formerly rejected, Jehovah will now bring to His holy mountain all those of their number who will join themselves to Him. The Lord will Himself return to Jerusalem-Zion, His *holy mountain,* and dwell in the midst of her (Zech. 8:1–3). To this mountain we also have come (Heb. 12:22–24). Thus the promise finds fulfillment both in the return from Babylon and under the Messiah. It may be concluded from Jesus' quotation of this verse, "My house shall be called a house of

prayer for all the nations" (Mark 11:17), that from the time of the return from Babylon a new emphasis was given to receiving all who would seek after Jehovah (cf. Acts 17:26–27). Jehovah here promises that no one who comes according to His will shall be rejected (cf. John 6:37). In this spiritual relationship there shall be a gladsome spirit, the privilege and joy of prayer, and sacrifices to Jehovah, which shall be graciously accepted.

8   The Lord has a special interest in *the outcasts of Israel*, but His love extends beyond them to include the outcasts of the Gentiles as well. It is uncertain to what extent the outcasts of the nations came to Him after Israel's return from captivity. But we do know that when the Servant came, He said, "Other sheep I have, which are not of this fold: them also I must bring, and they shall hear my voice; and they shall become one flock, one shepherd" (John 10:16), and that the Gentiles have indeed responded in great numbers to His invitation.

A Rebuke of the Blind Watchmen (vv. 9–12)

Commentators hold two different opinions on the passage 56:9–57:21. Some believe that Isaiah's condemnation of the blind watchmen and rampant idolatry has in view the conditions after the exile; others hold that he is speaking of his own generation. The theory that this passage portrays conditions after the exile is difficult to harmonize with the text. Probably the strongest argument for this view is found in the character of the nobles and rulers who were the recognized leaders during the rebuilding of Jerusalem and her walls. Having money to lend they were given to greed and usury (Neh. 5:7); they failed to pay their tithes, forsook the house of God, and desecrated the Sabbath (Neh. 13:10–18). It is highly significant, however, that they are never spoken of as watchmen or shepherds.

The evidence within the passage is far stronger for the view that Isaiah has turned from prophesying of the captivity, the return under Cyrus, and the coming of the Messiah, to speak to the people of his own day, summarizing the causes that will lead to the captivity. The portrayal of watchmen and shepherds who fail in their responsibility, giving themselves to drink (56:9–12), fits the period before the captivity, as does the charge that the people are children of sorcery, adultery, and harlotry. Furthermore, we have no records of a general idolatry (57:3–8) or the sending of ambassadors (57:9) after the return. Accordingly, we will interpret this passage as a description of conditions prior to the captivity.

9   *All ye beasts of the field . . . yea, all ye beasts of the forest*—this is apparently a parallel construction. The wild beasts of the field and forest are being called to come and devour. But whom or what are they to devour? This prophetic word of Isaiah is expanded in Jeremiah. Having forsaken His heritage (house, family) because they have been a lion against Him, Jehovah says, "Go ye, assemble all the beasts of the field, bring them to devour" Judah. He then charges that the shepherds are responsible for the disastrous situation (Jer. 12:7–10; cf. Ezek. 34:5). Young notes (III. 395) another possible construction of this verse: "All ye beasts of the field, come to devour all the beasts in the forest"; that is, the beasts of the field are the enemies, and the beasts of the forest are Israel. However, the former reading is preferable.

10   *His watchmen*, those of Judah, *are blind.* Watchmen are guards stationed on a wall to warn of approaching danger. They keep check on developments (21:6–9) and occasionally announce good tidings (52:7–8). Prophets are sometimes referred to as watchmen, for they give warning to the people (Ezek. 3:17–21; 33:7–9; Jer. 6:17). These watchmen are to serve Jehovah as leaders; their concern should be for the people. Jehovah has raised up watchmen, but many of them are blind to the dangers; they are without knowledge of Jehovah and their responsibility to Him. *They are all dumb dogs, they cannot bark*; thus they fail to warn the people. Refusing to face reality, they prefer idleness, sleeping, dreaming. They are "at ease" in Zion, putting the evil day far away and living in a fool's paradise of revelry (Amos 6:1–7).

11   *Yea, the dogs*—the watchmen who are shepherds of God's flock—*are greedy* (the Hebrew here is "strong of appetite"). They are never satisfied with their position before God and His remuneration, but turn aside to gain. The term *shepherds* often refers to the rulers or protectors of a nation (Nah. 3:18), to a king like Cyrus who served Jehovah's purpose (44:28), or to the kings of Judah (Jer. 22:1–23:8; Ezek. 34:1–10). The prophet Jeremiah similarly refers to his being a

shepherd after Jehovah (Jer. 17:16), but the word primarily has reference to kings. Lacking understanding of Jehovah and failing to walk
in His paths, *they have all turned to their own way, each one to his
gain, from every quarter,* that is, they greedily grasp at everything
within their reach. This covetous spirit extends from the kings down
to the least of their subjects, and even includes prophets and priests
(Jer. 6:13).

12   At this point the prophet is clearly speaking to his own generation. Earlier he pronounced a woe upon all those who give themselves to drink (5:11), to the men in high places (5:22–23), to the
rulers, prophets, and priests who, staggering under its baneful influence, err in judgment (28:7–8; cf. Mic. 2:11). He now points at those
who cover their woes and stimulate false hopes through drink, living
only from day to day, with no concern for the future.

CHAPTER 57
A Rebuke of the Wickedness of Isaiah's Day

"Blessed Are the Dead Who Die in the Lord" (vv. 1–2)

1   In contrast to the indifferent and faithless watchmen and shepherds who give themselves to dreaming and drinking (56:9–12), *The
righteous perisheth, and no man layeth it to heart.* The word *perish*
can indicate either a violent or natural death. In perishing the righteous man dies unobserved, and his influence on the ungodly world
is lost. When the merciful or godly man is taken away, no one
considers that his being removed *from the evil to come* upon the
nation is actually a blessing for him: he will be spared from the
calamity. Micah's parallel description of people in the pre-exilic period (Mic. 7:2; cf. II Kings 22:20) confirms that this passage does not
refer to postexilic conditions.

2   *He entereth into peace;* not only will the righteous man escape
the evil which is to come upon the people, but he will also partake of
that well-being, wholeness, and completeness for which the soul of
the righteous yearns. *They rest in their beds*—this is not to say that the

righteous man ceases from labor, but that he experiences the eternal rest of victory and redemption which the Lord intends for His people (Heb. 4:9; cf. Ps. 95:11). In the light of the context, *beds* apparently signifies the resting place of the deceased, as when David said, "If I make my bed in Sheol, behold, thou art there" (Ps. 139:8). Eternal rest in Jehovah is the reward for the man who walks *in his uprightness*, or "straight forwardly," the man who "has walked a straight path through life" in accordance with the ethical and moral standard of Jehovah.[18] His future will be peace and rest. This concept of the future of the righteous foreshadows the full revelation in the New Testament.

Idolatry and Faithlessness Severely Rebuked (vv. 3–13)

3 The word *But* introduces a contrast between the righteous and godly man of verses 1–2 and the idolaters of verses 3–13. The *sons of the sorceress, the seed of the adulterer and the harlot*, are instructed to draw near and hear what Jehovah has to say through His prophet. Here we have a description of the spiritual character of the nation, a recapitulation of the charges made in chapters 1 and 2. The citizens of Judah are children of idolatry, the offspring of people who forsook Jehovah for the witchcraft of the heathen, and the posterity of spiritual adulterers who went whoring after false gods. The rejection of Jehovah and of true worship has resulted in apostasy and excessive wickedness (cf. 1:4, 21; 2:6).

4 In showing contempt for any righteous persons among them by opening wide the mouth and putting out the tongue, both signs of derision (Ps. 22:7), the people of Judah are actually scorning Jehovah. In transgressing God's law and serving idols they, not the righteous, are the contemptible ones: *are ye not children of transgression, a seed of falsehood?* They are the spiritual offspring of idolatry, which is a lie (44:20), and of the goldsmith's "molten image [which] is falsehood" (Jer. 10:14). We are the children and servants of him whose will we do and serve (John 8:44; Rom. 6:16).

5 The following verses are a graphic description of the idolatry

---

18. *Theological Wordbook of the Old Testament*, vol. 2, p. 579.

which was strongly condemned before the exile. There are no records of such practices after the return from Babylon. Idolatrous worship was carried on *among the oaks, under every green tree* (cf. 1:29); these heathen shrines should have been destroyed (Deut. 12:2), but were not. In such places Israel "played the harlot" (Jer. 3:6; Hos. 4:13–14); Judah and her King Ahaz did likewise (I Kings 14:23; II Kings 16:4). Altars were erected "upon every high hill, on all the tops of the mountains, and under every green tree, and under every thick oak, the places where they offered sweet savor to all their idols" (Ezek. 6:13). Here the idolaters were inflamed, emotionally and sexually heated, for sexual perversions were a part of the Canaanite worship adopted by the people (cf. Amos 2:7). The abomination of sacrificing children to Molech, which was condemned by Moses (Lev. 18:21; 20:1–5), was practiced by the kings of Israel (II Kings 17:17), by Ahaz and Manasseh, kings of Judah (II Kings 16:3; 21:6), and also by the people. They practiced this abomination *in the valleys*, especially the Valley of Hinnom, which Jehovah would make totally desolate (Jer. 7:31–34), and *under the clefts of the rocks*, probably hidden sites or places difficult to find.

6   The phrase *Among the smooth stones of the valley* presents difficulty, for the word *stones* is not in the original text. The reference may be to smooth stones of which altars to Molech were constructed or to the idols themselves. Since the Hebrew word translated *smooth* can also mean "slippery," the reference may be to a place where one might slip and fall, the deceitful stones of error. At any rate, here the idolaters will find their portion, their lot, a barren and unproductive inheritance or reward; for here they have made drink- and meal-offerings to idols. Jehovah will take vengeance upon those who make such offerings; they will be left to the emptiness of their false gods. This will be their portion.

7   The prophet shifts his attention from the valleys below to the heights—*a high and lofty mountain* where altars were erected. This suggests that idolatry was practiced everywhere in those days—in the valleys, in the mountains, and in between. Rebellious idolaters sought not the bed of rest and peace found by the righteous (v. 2), but the bed of idolatry upon a high mountain: *thither also wentest thou up to offer sacrifice*. The rugged nature of the terrain indicates that

Isaiah is speaking of the land of Judah, not Babylon; the condemnation of idolatry indicates that the period before the exile, not
after, is in his view.

8   Behind the doors or posts of his house the idolater has set up a
memorial, probably an image which brings to mind the deity whom
he serves and audibly invokes. *For thou hast uncovered thyself to
another*; Judah is behaving like an unfaithful and adulterous wife
who forsakes her covenant with her husband and embraces another
man. Judah has thrown off her loyalty to Jehovah, giving herself to
idolatry and committing spiritual adultery. As a woman of unseemly
character makes preparation for her illicit love, so Judah has taken the
initiative by enlarging her bed for her sin. While yet married to
Jehovah (50:1), she has entered into a covenant with others; she loves
the bed of the heathen wherever she sees it. In this, Judah has
followed the example of her wicked sister Israel, who "committed
adultery with stones and with stocks" (Jer. 3:9). Instead of turning
away in abhorrence wherever she sees foreign gods and heathen ways,
she loves and embraces them, striking hands with foreigners (see
2:6–8).

9   Any form of idolatry erodes faith in God; therefore, it is only
natural that the idolatry described by the prophet has led Judah to
look for help from someone other than Jehovah. Some commentators picture the people of Judah as anointing themselves with oil. It
seems more likely, however, that they are carrying oil as a present to
some unnamed king and are making themselves more appealing by
applying perfume to themselves. No particular king is specified, but
we do have an account of Ahaz's sending a message to Tiglath-pileser,
king of Assyria: "I am thy servant and thy son: come up, and save me
out of the hand of the king of Syria, and out of the hand of the king of
Israel" (II Kings 16:7). And in the days of Hezekiah ambassadors
bearing treasures were sent to Egypt in an attempt to form an alliance
with Pharaoh (30:1–6). The prophet's declaration that the people
have thus debased themselves *even unto Sheol* indicates the depth to
which they have stooped in their departure from God.

10   Although becoming weary in the way she has chosen and in
her search for help, Judah has never recognized or admitted, *It is in
vain*—to no avail. Instead of renewing their strength in Jehovah

(40:31), the people have found a momentary false quickening of strength in their idols. *Therefore thou wast not faint* (sick), did not completely give up. Human nature does not change; today, instead of finding satisfaction for spiritual needs and strength in the Lord, multitudes are seeking help in the cults and false religions. Such recourses may serve for the moment, but in the end they are doomed to failure.

11   *Of whom hast thou been afraid and in fear?*—the word *afraid* connotes anxiety and worry; *in fear* suggests terror or reverential awe of idol-gods. If one has a proper attitude toward Jehovah, there is no place for anxiety, for fear of idols or of foreign kings, for reverence of heathen gods. But the people's attitude toward the Lord has been one of negligence and indifference, if not actual flagrant rebellion. They have lived a lie before Him, practicing a false righteousness; they have not remembered Him in times of crisis; and they have not laid to heart the power of God to deliver, the greatness of their sin against Him, and the terror of His judgments. For a long time He has held His peace, restraining judgment against them; but His long-suffering has availed nothing. They have refused to hear Him and to render that awe of reverence due His holy name.

12   *I will declare thy righteousness*—Jehovah will tell or make known that which is not righteousness at all. Judah's righteousnesses are "as a polluted [or filthy] garment" (64:6), and Jehovah will expose them for what they actually are. All of Judah's zealous works in making and serving idols and their fervent appeal to kings will be for nought; these activities will only bring judgment and destruction upon them.

13   The time will come when the nation will cry to Jehovah for help, but it will be too late. Let them cry to the idols that they have gathered and served, and to the kings to whom they have appealed; let foreign gods and rulers help them. But both idols and kings are impotent before Jehovah, for they are all vanity and confusion (41:29), to be taken away by the wind and brought to nought by the breath of Jehovah's mouth (cf. 11:4; 40:24). *But he that taketh refuge in me shall possess the land, and shall inherit my holy mountain* (cf. Nah. 1:7). What a contrast to the lot of the idolaters (v. 6)! Israel's original possession of the land was unconditional; it was given to

Israel in fulfillment of the promise made to Abraham (Gen. 12:7, etc.), and it was intended to be theirs permanently, "for ever" (Exod. 32:13). But the retaining of the land was conditional (Lev. 26:14–45); if they turned away from Jehovah and kept not His covenant, but served idols, they would be plucked off the land and scattered (Deut. 28:63–64). When Isaiah prophesied, there was yet a possibility of escaping the captivity. If the people would renounce idols and trust in Jehovah rather than in some foreign power or in themselves, they would possess the land in perpetuity and hold His holy mountain as a heritage.

The Condescending Love of God (vv. 14–21)

14 The opening words of this paragraph, And he will say ("it shall be said," margin), leave the heavenly voice unidentified; but the phrase my people makes it clear that Jehovah is the speaker. The Lord calls for the casting up of a highway: prepare the way for God's people to return to Him (cf. 11:16; 35:8). Take up the stumbling-block out of the way; remove out of the road by which the people will return, everything that has caused them to stumble—the sin of idolatry and unbelief, the hard and closed heart, evildoers who give occasions of stumbling. Remove these obstacles and cast up the way for the journey.

15 Having uttered this call, Jehovah identifies Himself as the high and lofty One, the only being who has the right to issue such a command and the ability to guarantee the promise that follows. In previous chapters Jehovah has repeatedly appealed to His people on the ground of His greatness and the greatness of His name. He is the high and lofty One that inhabiteth eternity—He transcends His creation and is eternal in His being. One's name sums up all that he is; Jehovah's name Holy sums up the perfection of His being and sets Him apart from all that is profane. He dwells in the high and holy place, in heaven itself (cf. I Kings 8:27; Hab. 2:20; Zech. 2:13). Though He is so infinitely great and high, He condescends to dwell with him that is of a contrite and humble spirit. The contrite spirit is the brokenhearted person who is crushed beneath the weight of sin; the humble spirit is the person who bows before Jehovah, acknowledging his sinfulness and total dependence on the Lord. Jehovah will condescend to abide with such a one; His presence will revive the contrite spirit and humble heart. The spirit is the immaterial consciousness of man, the seat of his conscience; the heart is the mind, the seat of understanding, emotions, and will. This is Jehovah's gracious offer to those who will accept chastening for sin and submit to His will.

16 Jehovah will not continue to reprove in anger forever, *neither will* (He) *be always wroth*; for if He should put no restraint on His wrath, all would be utterly consumed. Therefore, "for my name's sake will I defer mine anger . . . that I cut thee not off" (48:9). If this were not done, man's whole inner life would be overwhelmed by hopeless despair, and God's purpose in making man would fail. Consequently, let man "account that the longsuffering of our Lord is salvation" (II Peter 3:15), both then and now.

17 To the sins of idolatry (vv. 3–8), faithlessness shown by appealing to foreign kings (vv. 9–10), lies and forgetting God (v. 11), there is now added the sin of covetousness: *For the iniquity of his covetousness was I wroth*. The word translated *covetousness* means literally "to cut off what is not one's own,"[19] greed and lust for personal gain. The greedy oppressors of Isaiah's day are described by Micah as cannibals who skin people alive and eat them; they spend their time thinking up ways to get that which belongs to another (Mic. 2:1–2; 3:1–4). This greed took the form of usury even in the days after the return from exile (Neh. 5:8–11). The general spirit of covetousness brought down God's wrath and judgments upon the nation: He *smote him*. The singular used here probably refers to the nation collectively. Hiding His face, Jehovah withdrew His presence and withheld His blessings from the people (cf. 8:17; 54:8). In spite of Jehovah's judgments, the nation went on *backsliding in the way of his heart*, walking in the way of an apostate.

18 Notwithstanding the nation's ways which Jehovah has seen, for the people's sins have been flagrantly committed before Him, He will yet *heal him*, Israel. *I will* indicates future action, what He will do after the day of wrath. First, Jehovah promises healing—forgiveness

---

19. *Theological Wordbook of the Old Testament*, vol. 1, p. 122.

of sins and restoration to a proper relationship with Himself (cf. 43:25). Second, He will lead the people, directing their paths aright (40:11; 52:12). And third, He will restore the spiritual comforts which have been withdrawn because of sins, comforts which result from His presence (Ps. 23:4). Mourning is often associated with death, but here it is probably an expression of grief over the condition of the nation (cf. Ezek. 9:4)—they mourn over their sinful ways (cf. 22:12). They will be comforted, for Jehovah's anger is not forever—"Weeping may tarry for the night,/But joy cometh in the morning" (Ps. 30:5).

19 *I create the fruit of the lips*—the word *create* emphasizes initiation, bringing something new into existence. The Lord will make it possible to say, *Peace, peace* (cf. 26:3: "perfect peace"; "peace, peace," Hebrew), *to him that is far off and to him that is near.* The terms *far* and *near* may refer to Hebrews in their homeland and in exile, but in the light of New Testament preaching, they may also designate Gentiles and Jews (Eph. 2:17). The false prophets had preached peace when there was no peace (Jer. 6:14; 8:11; Ezek. 13:10); but now Jehovah will create a new *fruit of the lips*, the message and joyous refrain of peace which follows Jehovah's healing the nation.

20 In contrast to the serenity of mind and heart of those who are healed, *the wicked are like the troubled sea; for it cannot rest.* In its frenzied state, *its waters cast up mire and dirt*, only filth, nothing that is good. Probably only the wicked Jews are in the prophet's mind, but his words are an excellent description of all the wicked. For in their restless and unregenerated condition they contribute nothing to moral and spiritual life. They are proof of the Lord's statement, "He that is not with me is against me" (Matt. 12:30).

21 The second major section of Part Two closes on the same note as did the first: *There is no peace, saith my God, to the wicked* (cf. 48:22). They find neither rest nor peace in their separation from God, but their "wild waves [foam] out their own shame" (Jude 13).

National Sins, Redemption by Jehovah, and Future Glory (58–66)

An Introductory Word

Although a new section begins at chapter 58, a close relationship exists between chapter 57 and chapters 58 and 59, making it difficult to distinguish clearly where one section ends and the next begins. There is also a problem in determining the precise point in history to which the new section belongs. Is Isaiah writing of the sins of and hope for the people of his own day, or is a "Deutero-Isaiah" writing during the captivity, or is a "Trito-Isaiah" writing in the period following the exile? Since the weight of evidence overwhelmingly points to a unitary authorship rather than to a Deutero- or a Trito-Isaiah, we shall proceed on the premise that the prophet Isaiah is the author of this section and is speaking to the people of his day. Furthermore, while we do not know enough about the Jews' condition during the exile to say that the abuses Isaiah here condemns were prevalent at

471

that period, we do know that Micah, Isaiah's contemporary, said of his day, "For it is an evil time" (Mic. 2:3). Having revealed the captivity to come, the assured return of a remnant, salvation in the Servant, and the glory of future Zion, Isaiah now addresses his thoughts to present conditions. The most reasonable theory is that at some time following Sennacherib's defeat and return to his homeland (ch. 37) and the prophecy of the Babylonian exile (ch. 39), Isaiah compiled various prophecies which he had spoken during his ministry. These he preserved in the last major section of his book.

CHAPTER 58

Right and Wrong Observances of Fasts and Sabbaths

Cry Out! Spare Not! (vv. 1–2)

1   The prophet is instructed by Jehovah to *cry aloud*, not in a sneering nor screaming voice, but "with the throat" (Hebrew), that is, with a powerful voice that commands attention. He is to cry without restraint and withhold nothing as he exposes the sins of the people. The trumpet sounds an alarm, to warn the people of danger (Num. 10:9; Hos. 5:8; Joel 2:1; Amos 3:6); with such a voice Isaiah is to warn *the house of Jacob*, which is parallel with *my people*, of their transgression and its consequence.

2   The nation is guilty of the sin of formality and hypocrisy; the people sin against Jehovah and transgress His laws, yet *they seek* (Him) *daily*, professing to delight in the knowledge of His ways. They act as if they have done righteousness and have not forsaken the ordinance of their God. They ask of Jehovah righteous judgments and feign delight in formally drawing near unto Him. All the show and pious cant, all the affected outward appearance of religion without sincerity, are an abomination to Him (cf. 1:11–14). The Lord charges the prophet to expose the hypocrisy.

Hypocritical Formalism Versus True Fasting (vv. 3–12)

3 The people raise the question, *Wherefore have we fasted . . .
and thou seest not?* Fasting had been a part of the nation's life from its
beginning; it was usually practiced out of a genuine sense of need and
accompanied by weeping, confession of sins, and prayer. Occasionally it might be insincere, as in the case of Jezebel, who proclaimed a
fast as part of her plot to slay Naboth (I Kings 21:9, 12); in contrast,
Ahab truly humbled himself and fasted (v. 27). All Israel wept and
fasted before Jehovah at Bethel (Judg. 20:26), and they gathered
together at Mizpah to fast and confess their sins (I Sam. 7:6). The
men of Jabesh-gilead buried Saul and the bodies of his sons and fasted
seven days (I Sam. 31:13); David also wept and fasted for Saul
(II Sam. 1:11–12). Later he fasted in hopes that his child by Bath-
sheba might live (II Sam. 12:16). When threatened by his foes,
Jehoshaphat proclaimed a fast and prayed (II Chron. 20:3–6). Twice
during times of destruction Joel called upon the people to "sanctify a
fast, call a solemn assembly" (Joel 1:14; 2:15). Even the people of
heathen Nineveh fasted when they heard Jonah and believed Jehovah
(Jon. 3:5). However, in the period before the captivity Israel's fasts had
become meaningless (Jer. 14:12), being for themselves rather than for
Jehovah (Zech. 7:5). This spirit continued to characterize the people
during the years of captivity. If they had listened to the word of the
prophets, then there would have been no need to fast (Zech. 7:7).
Moreover, as they fast insincerely, they ask, Why *have we afflicted our
soul, and thou takest no knowledge?* The answer is simple; they have
acted selfishly. In their concern for their own pleasure and profit, they
have exacted heavy work from the laborers. They have not sought
Jehovah's aid and glory.

4 The people are making their fasts occasions of strife and contention among themselves, even to the extent of smiting *with the fist
of wickedness.* Barnes sees a dramatic and vivid parallel in the attitude
of denominations and sects of our day (II. 330). Instead of the
humble spirit of a contrite heart, Israel gave vent to the passions of
their soul. Consequently, their voice was not heard on high. God
does not accept such fasts nor does He hear contentious voices raised
in sham praise or prayer.

5   In response to the question, "Wherefore have we fasted?" (v. 3), Jehovah now asks, *Is such the fast that I have chosen? the day for a man to afflict his soul?* The only fast ever ordained by Jehovah was that of the annual atonement: "In the seventh month, on the tenth day of the month, ye shall afflict your souls, and shall do no manner of work . . . for on this day shall atonement be made for you, to cleanse you; from all your sins shall ye be clean before Jehovah. . . . ye shall afflict your souls; it is a statute for ever" (Lev. 16:29–31). The affliction of the soul is a self-inflicted inner pain expressing contrition; it is accompanied by fasting. Jehovah had appointed no other fast. Formally bowing the head like a rush or spreading sackcloth (a coarse hairy cloth) and ashes without the spirit of remorse, humility, and sincere petition to Jehovah, is hypocrisy. Only the spiritually blind, ignorant, and indifferent would conclude that such actions, which in no way meet God's requirement, constitute an affliction of the soul, *and an acceptable day to Jehovah.*

6   The Lord challenges the hypocritical people with the question, *Is not this the fast that I have chosen?* He then proceeds to review several of His demands. Obeying these demands is what is really meant by fasting and carries with it gracious promises of God's blessing. Having given special emphasis to principles concerning the people's relation to God, the Lord now sets forth ethical principles of His law which deal with the people's relationships to one another. The fast that He requires is not so much an abstinence from food as the humble spirit enjoined in the second great commandment, "Thou shalt love thy neighbor as thyself" (Lev. 19:18; cf. Matt. 22:39).

The three exhortations, (1) *loose the bonds of wickedness,* (2) *undo the bands of the yoke,* and (3) *let the oppressed go free,* indicate that some of the Jewish people were being unjustly and wickedly treated by their fellows—even to the point of illegal enslavement. The law demanded that in the seventh year every Hebrew servant should be liberated (Exod. 21:2; Deut. 15:12; cf. Lev. 25:39). When King Zedekiah made a covenant to release all the Hebrew servants, but then retracted, Jeremiah pointed to the law which had been violated: "At the end of seven years ye shall let go every man his brother that is a Hebrew . . . but your fathers hearkened not unto [Jehovah], neither inclined their ear" in this matter (Jer. 34:14). Among the "fathers" who violated this command were the people of Isaiah's day. It was God's eternal command that the people were to liberate their brethren from social and economic fetters imposed upon them and from every figurative yoke of oppression.

7   "The fast that I have chosen" (v. 6) involves certain other demands: (1) sharing food with the hungry; (2) opening one's home to destitute and distressed brethren who have been cast off (cf. Lev. 25:35); and (3) providing clothing for the unfortunate. These exhortations serve as an excellent summation of what the virtue of hospitality entails (cf. Heb. 13:1–2). Though all men are descended "of one" (Acts 17:26), Isaiah emphasizes that the people must in particular not shirk their responsibilities to those of the house of Israel: *Hide not thyself from thine own flesh.*

8   The word *Then* is significant: it points to the blessings that reward just conduct. When a fast is in accord with Jehovah's requirements, then His blessing will break forth like the morning light and dispel the darkness through which the people have been passing. And healing of their national and personal wounds *shall spring forth speedily*, without delay. At that point their righteousness will go before them like a guiding light to steer them from the pitfalls of destruction and to lead them in the paths of peace. At the same time, the glory or brightness of Jehovah will be their rearward, ever accompanying them as had the pillar of fire in their exodus from Egypt (cf. 52:12).

9a   The richest reward of all is that when the people call, Jehovah will answer; when they cry out unto Him, He will say, *Here I am.* This will not be the case if they feign righteousness and practice hypocrisy, for "He that turneth away his ear from hearing the law,/ Even his prayer is an abomination" (Prov. 28:9).

9b   Verses 9b–12 recapitulate and enlarge upon what has already been said (vv. 1–9a). The Lord continues to deal with social and ethical sins, making His blessing conditional upon change. The people must remove the yoke of affliction imposed upon their brethren; they must desist from pointing the finger of accusation and scorn at others, for such action cuts deeply; they must cease from *speaking wickedly* of their fellows. These injustices all spring from evil hearts which must be cleansed if the people are to please Jehovah (cf. 1:16–17).

10 Jehovah lays down one other condition: *if thou draw out thy soul to the hungry, and satisfy the afflicted soul.* The word *satisfy* often refers to appeasing one's hunger for food, but here it seems to indicate more than simply feeding the body (cf. Ps. 22:26). It seems to indicate a sharing of one's self by sympathizing, comforting, and bearing the burden of those afflicted with inward pain. When this condition, as well as those of verse 9b, is met, the darkness which has hidden the way vanishes; for "Unto the upright there ariseth light in the darkness" (Ps. 112:4), and "They walk, O Jehovah, in the light of thy countenance" (Ps. 89:15).

11 Three additional blessings are pronounced upon the upright: (1) They will have assurance of Jehovah's continual guidance; therefore, they will not stumble. (2) As they have satisfied the hungry soul of the afflicted (v. 10), so Jehovah will comfort and fill their souls in times of spiritual drought. (3) He will *make strong thy bones. Bones* signifies the whole person (cf. Ps. 6:2), and to *make strong* is to equip one for fighting. Further, the righteous one will be as productive as a well-watered garden; he will be an unfailing spring, possibly a wellspring of wisdom (Prov. 18:4) or a spring of spiritual water by which others are refreshed (cf. John 7:38).

12 *And they* (plural) *that shall be of thee* (singular), individuals who come out of either the nation or God's ideal people regarded collectively, *shall build the old waste places.* This may refer to the physical rebuilding after the return from captivity or to the rebuilding of the spiritual waste places of Isaiah's time. The latter seems more probable, for the conditions specified by Jehovah for reception of His blessings point to a spiritual rebuilding of places laid waste by sin. The time at which this work of spiritual restoration will occur is left indefinite: it could take place in Isaiah's day, after the return, and even today. And indeed, a spiritual remnant does raise up the foundations on which every generation builds; they repair the breaches in the walls of Zion and restore the old paths, the good way in which to travel and dwell (cf. Jer. 6:16).

Proper Observance of the Sabbath (vv. 13–14)

13 It is clear from Jehovah's earlier charge (1:13–14) that in

476

Isaiah's day the people had become lax in properly regarding the Sabbath. (For the significance of the Sabbath, see the comments on 56:2.) This disrespect continued, probably increased, into the time of Jeremiah, who charged the people with disregarding the day. He pointed to the origin of the Sabbath and to the law regulating it: "Hallow ye the sabbath day, as I commanded your fathers. But they hearkened not" (Jer. 17:21–23). The fathers who hearkened not would include the time of Isaiah (over a hundred years previous). Had Isaiah's charge at this point been observed, it would not only have served his generation, but would have been a strong force holding the people together as one and binding them to the Lord during the exile.

Isaiah instructs the people to turn away the foot from Jehovah's Sabbath; that is, they are to refrain from *doing thy pleasure on my holy day . . . doing thine own ways*, thus profaning it. The figure of the foot also appears in the Preacher's injunction, "Keep thy foot when thou goest to the house of God" (Eccles. 5:1), and in the wise man's advice, "Remove thy foot from evil" (Prov. 4:27). Instead of keeping the Sabbath as a day of rest, the people engaged in secular pleasures. They should have observed it as a day of "exquisite delight,"[1] holy and honorable because Jehovah had sanctified it for their good. Three ways of honoring it are set forth: (1) *Not doing thine own ways*—we should forsake our own ways and thoughts, and stress those of Jehovah (55:7–8); (2) *Nor finding thine own pleasure*, but seeking that which pleases the Lord; (3) *Nor speaking thine own words*— engaging in trivial conversation or even empty words during worship (cf. Eccles. 5:2–7). When one learns this lesson, the Sabbath will be a delight, for it will be a day of withdrawal from the secular and a day filled with spiritual enrichment.

14 *Then*—out of this delight, a second follows—*shalt thou delight thyself in Jehovah*. The Sabbath was not only a rest day but also a holy day, a day for spiritual refreshing and fellowship with God. Jehovah now promises to His faithful Israel a blessing reminiscent of Moses' song concerning Jacob, "He made him ride on the high places of the earth" (Deut. 32:13). Faithful Israel shall soar above the purely

---

1. *Theological Wordbook of the Old Testament*, ed. R. Laird Harris (Chicago: Moody, 1980), vol. 2, p. 679.

mundane and find delight in God and His ways. Further, Jehovah will feed him with the true heritage of Jacob, the full wealth of the Promised Land. This blessing is guaranteed, *for the mouth of Jehovah hath spoken it.*

CHAPTER 59

Sin: The Wall of Separation

Jehovah had given Isaiah the responsibility of declaring unto the people their transgressions and sins (58:1), and the prophet has partially carried out his mission by condemning their disregard for the laws concerning fasting and observance of the Sabbath. He now continues by rebuking the nation's sin of wickedly ignoring God's law in general. The Book of Micah is probably the best available commentary on this chapter; accordingly, we shall make numerous references to it.

Jehovah's Charge Against the People (vv. 1–8)

1–2   Why have the people not realized the salvation so often promised by the Lord? The Lord responds that the reason is not a shortened hand (lack of power on His part—cf. 50:2) nor a deaf ear (i.e., He is not ignorant of their desires and needs); indeed, He has repeatedly revealed both His omnipotence and omniscience. As Smith aptly says, "In the Infinite there is a heart to throb for men and a will to strike for them" (II. 457). What separates them from Jehovah, causing Him to hide His face from them, is their disregard for the covenant (their iniquities) and transgression of the law (their sins). In this condition they cannot find Him, and their prayers are an abomination in His sight (Prov. 28:9).

3   Sinful actions and words are charged against the people: (1) Their hands are defiled with the blood of murder and their fingers with iniquity (cf. Mic. 7:3: "Their hands are upon that which is evil to do it diligently"). This charge was made earlier by Isaiah (1:15): because the people's hands are full of blood, God will not hear their

prayers. They are charged not only with literally shedding blood (cf. 1:21), but also with robbing and crushing the poor as to bring want and death to them (cf. 3:14–15; 10:2). Micah says, "They all lie in wait for blood; they hunt every man his brother with a net" (Mic. 7:2). He further charges that while upon their beds they make evil plans against the helpless, carrying them out when it is day (Mic. 2:1–3). (2) *Your lips have spoken lies, your tongue muttereth wickedness;* in political, economic, social, and religious matters, the people have uttered wicked lies which make "empty the soul of the hungry, and . . . cause the drink of the thirsty to fail" (32:6). Micah says, "If a man walking in a spirit of falsehood do lie . . . he shall even be the prophet of this people" (Mic. 2:11). And further, "For the rich men thereof are full of violence, and the inhabitants thereof have spoken lies, and their tongue is deceitful in their mouth" (Mic. 6:12). These things Jehovah hates (Prov. 6:16–19), and in the hail of judgment He will sweep away "the refuge of lies" (28:17).

4   Both social and judicial injustice characterized society at the time. Though here the Lord may be dealing specifically with injustice in the courts, the accusation is more inclusive, incorporating social injustice also. The heads and rulers of the house of Jacob, they "that abhor justice, and pervert all equity" (Mic. 3:9), set the example and pattern for the people. When they go to court (or try to settle matters privately), they do not seek due legal process and justice, nor do they present their case in truth, but they pursue it by speaking lies. Mischief and dark deeds begin with the false and lying heart; thus conceived, the fruit or offspring is iniquity, never righteousness.

5   To impress the lesson He is teaching, the Lord uses a strong simile: Out of the union of vanity and lies, conceived in the heart of the wicked and practiced among them, are hatched *adders' eggs.* Neither the adder nor the viper of this verse can be positively identified, but it is clear that they are venomous serpents known to the people of Isaiah's day. If eaten, the *adders' eggs* bring death; and when crushed, they produce another deadly snake equally destructive of life. Lies and lack of moral integrity and of righteousness are bound to poison a society and ultimately bring it to death. As then, so now; for principles never change.

6   The wicked weave flimsy and worthless spider's webs which

shall not become garments; similarly, their works cannot cover them. Both their webs and works are futile and empty. The webs probably are plots for trapping the unwary, for Micah says of the evil plans of the prince, the judge, and the great man, "Thus they weave it together" (Mic. 7:3; cf. 2:1–2). The works are *works of iniquity* which condemn and bring to destruction. Acts of extreme violence and wickedness are in their hands to be committed at their pleasure. As Micah observes, "Their hands are upon that which is evil to do it diligently" (Mic. 7:3).

7　The wicked do not enter leisurely into evil; but their feet run, rushing precipitously into it and making haste to shed innocent blood. Their violence is planned beforehand—*their thoughts are thoughts of iniquity*. Their paths are highways of *desolation and destruction*, the fruit of such thinking. The condition of Noah's day seems to be repeating itself; for now, as then, "every imagination of the thoughts of [man's] heart was only evil continually" (Gen. 6:5).

8　The wicked have not known the way of peace, whether with God, themselves, or their fellow men, for "there is no peace, saith my God, to the wicked" (57:21). There is no justice or sense of right in their life; they themselves have made their paths crooked, dishonest, and full of deceit. Those who enter such a life shall find not peace but its opposite—discord, tumult, and strife. Paul quotes verses 7–8 to describe the universal condition of his day (Rom. 3:15–17). They seem to fit our national condition as well.

The Prophet's Reply: A Confession of Wickedness (vv. 9–15a)

9　In response to Jehovah's accusation against the nation, the prophet answers for the people by confessing their sins. In the midst of such conditions they find only gloom, for sin has left its dire effects. There is no justice, no righting of the existing state of affairs; righteousness is never attained. They look for light, probably deliverance from the existing plight, but instead there is darkness. In their blindness they walk in obscurity instead of in the brightness of the salvation for which they yearn. Jehovah longs and certainly is able to change all of this (vv. 1–2). But in their spiritual stupor the people do not look to Him and, therefore, He cannot act.

10   The people grope about like the blind, searching for a wall which they might follow to freedom or behind which they might find protection. Even at noonday when all should be bright and clear, they stumble along as in the twilight or night, just as Jehovah, through Moses, had said they would (Deut. 28:28–29). The clause *among them that are lusty we are as dead men* is difficult since the word translated *lusty* occurs only here. The clause is variously rendered: "among the living like the dead" (Delitzsch); "among men of lusty strength, we are like dead men" (Leupold); "among those in full vigor" (Whybray); "among the stout like the dead" (Young). The margin has "we are in dark places like the dead," that is, we are like disembodied spirits moving in the shades. However the word is translated, the picture is one of utter hopelessness.

11   Malcontent, *we roar* (growl) *all like bears* in turmoil; and we *moan sore like doves*, in a low, plaintive voice expressing the melancholy of our hearts. *We look for justice, but there is none*—the complaint of verse 9 is repeated.

12   Speaking for the people, the prophet confesses the cause of their stumbling along. Both he and they can see it clearly, for it is not hid. They stumble blindly, growling like a bear in their discontent and moaning like a dove in their state of melancholy, because their transgressions are multiplied before God and their sins testify against them. Like a wall, sins separate the people from God (v. 2); and until they are removed, the blessings they desire and cry for cannot be theirs. Their transgressions are not hid; they are plainly evident, known to God and man: *we know them*. Thus, the people are without excuse for not correcting their errors.

13   The transgressions which are so evident to all are summed up: (1) *transgressing and denying Jehovah, and turning away from following our God*—continuing in what they know to be transgression, the people are denying Jehovah as their God; (2) *speaking oppression and revolt*—*oppression* is a grievous sin, for it involves misuse of power and authority, mistreating those who are without adequate protection of their rights; *revolt* involves turning away or defecting from God and His way; (3) *conceiving and uttering from the heart words of falsehood*

(cf. v. 3). The heart is the womb in which thoughts, words, and deeds are conceived (cf. Matt. 12:34; 15:19–20). It must be kept with all diligence, "for out of it are the issues of life" (Prov. 4:23). Failure to keep the heart pure has resulted in acting and speaking against Jehovah.

14 Again justice and righteousness appear in combination, as they do so often in this book. Justice, or right judgment, is reversed; and righteousness stands beyond reach. Injustice and unrighteousness prevail. Like a soldier felled in battle, so *truth is fallen in the street*, cast down by those who should have upheld it (cf. Dan. 8:12, where truth is "cast down" by a heathen enemy). And when truth is not present, *uprightness cannot enter.*

15a When truth has been cast down in the street and trodden on by the people and falsehood has become the standard, then *he that departeth from evil maketh himself a prey.* In such an environment, he who turns away from evil and seeks to do right is oppressed, harassed, and destroyed by evil men (cf. 5:23; 10:2; 32:7; Mic. 2:1–2).

Jehovah's Response: Vengeance and Deliverance (vv. 15b–21)

15b Whatever distress Israel may have experienced at the hands of the heathen, the greater part of her suffering was self-inflicted, coming from within. *And Jehovah saw it,* the results of the nation's rejection of truth, *and it displeased him that there was no justice,* right dealing, among the people.

16 As Jehovah was displeased upon seeing the lack of justice, so He also *wondered* when He saw *that there was no man,* no intercessor. He was appalled, so to speak, by the spiritual desolation which He beheld; and He was shocked that no man acted as intercessor, championed His cause, or made contact with Him on behalf of the oppressed people. *Therefore,* in consequence of this situation, *his own arm* (power) *brought salvation unto him.* Until the coming of the Servant, who would "bring forth justice in truth" (42:3), Jehovah would act personally, depending on none other than Himself and His own arm of strength to intercede and bring His people into a right relationship with Him. His own absolute righteousness and the righteousness of His purpose would uphold Him in His actions—rendering vengeance upon His enemies and redeeming His people from their transgressions.

17 In the conflict with injustice, transgression, and sins, Jehovah assumes the role of a warrior prepared to enter the field of battle (cf. Exod. 15:3; Deut. 1:30; Isa. 42:13). The armor with which He arrays Himself is spiritual, suitable for the nature of the conflict at hand. His breastplate or coat of mail is the righteousness which sustains Him; the salvation for which He fights is a shining helmet upon His head; He wraps Himself in a garment of vengeance against His enemies; over all He clasps a mantle or cloak of zeal, a strong and fervent passion for spiritual battle and righteousness.

18 *According to their deeds, accordingly he will repay;* in this battle there will be a fair and just judgment for all. They will receive according to their attitude toward God and the deeds which follow therefrom. There will be a just balancing of the scales (see the comments on 40:2). The distinction between *his adversaries* and *his enemies* is not altogether clear. It seems, however, that the *adversaries* are God's own people and *his enemies* are the heathen. This conclusion rests on the phrase *to the islands* (coastlands), which refers to the regions inhabited by "the peoples," foreigners or Gentiles. In this case it appears to be parallel with *his enemies.*

19 *From the west, and . . . from the rising of the sun,* that is, from the remotest regions of earth—everywhere—men will respond to Jehovah's great judgment and offer of deliverance. From among both Jews and Gentiles, and especially the latter, those who behold the work of His own arm shall *fear the name of Jehovah,* turn to Him, and revere *his glory. Name* and *glory* are probably used synonymously. The second half of the verse is more difficult. If we follow the text, Jehovah will come against His enemies *as a rushing stream,* driven by His own breath, His mighty power as exhibited in creation (cf. Ps. 33:6). If we accept the reading of the margin, it is the enemy who will come like a mighty flood; in the midst of this turbulence Jehovah will *lift up a standard against him,* thus providing a place of refuge for His saints and a rallying point from which to defeat His enemies. Whatever the translation and the situation in view—be it Jehovah's work of redemption, His work of judgment, or the oppres-

sion inflicted by the enemy—the thought is that God is in complete control. In the past He saved Israel "for his name's sake,/That he might make his mighty power to be known" (Ps. 106:8), and He will continue to exert that power on behalf of His people.

20 In the Old Testament, the next of kin had the right and responsibility to recover the forfeited property of a relative or to purchase the freedom of a relative who had fallen into slavery. The technical term for the person who was expected to pay the full price necessary to help his relative is *redeemer*. Isaiah uses the word in its full significance of someone who buys back or pays a ransom price for another's liberty and freedom. At least twelve times in Part Two of the Book of Isaiah, Jehovah is referred to as Israel's Redeemer. But in this instance the prophet has in mind the Servant-Messiah, who has already been promised many times and whose redemptive work has been clearly revealed. This view is sustained by Paul's application of the passage to Jesus the Christ (Rom. 11:26–27). Isaiah says, *And a Redeemer will come to Zion, and unto them that turn from transgression in Jacob*; in quoting the passage Paul says, "There shall come out of Zion the deliverer." The apparent discrepancy between the Redeemer's coming "to Zion" (Isaiah) and His coming "out of Zion" (Paul) has given rise to considerable discussion among commentators. It is not necessary for us to set forth the various solutions suggested, however. For Isaiah is speaking of the Redeemer's coming to His own—God's Zion—to offer salvation to them first (Matt. 15:24; John 1:11). When they rejected it, He turned from them to the Gentiles (Acts 13:46–48; 18:6). This is Paul's point. The Servant-Messiah came unto Zion as King and Savior (Zech. 9:9–10). Jehovah set Him up as King on the holy hill of Zion (Ps. 2:6). From there Jehovah sent forth the rod of His strength (Ps. 110:2); from there went forth the law and word of Jehovah (2:3). This explains the Redeemer's coming "to Zion." From Zion He also went forth in the gospel, conquering and to conquer. As Paul said, Christ "came and preached peace to you that were far off [Gentiles], and peace to them that were nigh [Jews]" (Eph. 2:17). In this sense, the Redeemer came forth "out of Zion."

21 *This is my covenant*—Jehovah makes the covenant. Man either accepts its terms and enters into it, or rejects it. The covenant in view here is "the sure mercies of David" (see 55:3 and comments). Established in the Servant (42:6; 49:8), it shall not be removed (54:10). The pledge, *my Spirit that is upon thee, and my words which I have put in thy mouth, shall not depart out of thy mouth,* is spoken to the Redeemer. Jehovah has put His Spirit upon the Redeemer (cf. 42:1; 61:1), and by His teaching Jehovah has supplied the Redeemer with words (see 50:4 and comments). No compromise will be made by the Redeemer; He will hold fast the truth as He has received it from Jehovah. The Redeemer "shall see his seed," His spiritual offspring (53:10). Indeed, "A seed shall serve him;/It shall be told of the Lord unto the next generation./They shall come and shall declare his righteousness/Unto a people that shall be born, that he hath done it" (Ps. 22:30–31). There will always be a seed (a remnant) holding faithfully to His word, passing it on from one generation to the next. This promise has been fulfilled in the Christ who received His words from the Father, in the gospel, and in the true church of Christ.

CHAPTER **60**
Glorious Zion! (1)

In this remarkable chapter, and the two following, there is not a critical note or rebuke of the people; here Jehovah reveals the future glory of Zion, the work of His hands. In their enthusiasm on hearing that they are free to return home, the exiles "shall mount up with wings as eagles" (40:31). Doubtless, Zion will appear exceeding glorious in their eyes. And yet, only under the Redeemer (59:20) can the glowing description of chapters 60–62 be fulfilled. The exaltation of Zion is in sharp contrast to the lowly condition of the people (chs. 58–59). Delitzsch suggests that a contrast between Babylon (ch. 47) and Jerusalem may also be intended.

From the ashes of physical Zion, which fades into the background, arises the splendor of the new city under the Messiah. In highly poetic language the prophet extols the glory of Jehovah's holy city (v. 14). As he does so, Isaiah weaves into the picture images from various realms of creation—light, man, animals, gold, incense, birds, the majestic trees of the forest.

Made Glorious Through the Light of Jehovah's Presence (vv. 1–3)

1 Zion has lain prostrate in a drunken stupor from which she is to awake (51:17) and put on beautiful garments (52:1). A barren and desolate wife, she will someday break forth in singing because of her children (54:1). She has looked for light, only to behold darkness and walk in obscurity (59:9). Now she receives a double command: *Arise, shine*. To *arise* is to get up from a prostrate position; this "word of power . . . puts new life in her limbs" (Delitzsch). Though she has no light within herself, Zion is also enjoined to *shine; for thy light is come, and the glory of Jehovah is risen upon thee*. While this light will not actually come until the future, the prophet speaks of it as if already here, for the promise is backed by the authority of Jehovah. As the sun bursts suddenly in the east, so Jehovah's glory will burst in splendor upon Zion. This light and glory will come when the Word becomes flesh, bringing life and light and revealing the Father in all the brightness of His majesty (John 1:4, 9, 14, 18).

2 The light will appear at a time when spiritual and moral darkness cover the earth, and when the peoples (plural), that is, the nations, dwell in *gross* (heavy and oppressive) *darkness*, "the deep darkness" of death (Jer. 13:16, margin). Some will be steeped in idolatry, some in Jewish traditions and prejudices, others in Greek and Roman philosophy (Acts 17:16–18), none of which shed any real light. But in the midst of this depressing condition Jehovah will rise upon Zion in the person of His Son; in Christ the glory of God will be revealed. Jehovah's Servant will be a light unto all peoples, Jews and Gentiles (42:6; 49:6).

3 The brightness of this light in a world of moral and spiritual darkness will attract the heathen. Drawn by this illuminating and guiding light, they will come to learn of Jehovah's ways and to walk in them (2:2–3; cf. 40:5). Kings will be so impressed by the brightness that they will worship Jehovah (cf. 49:7; 52:15).

Made Glorious Through the Return of Her Children (vv. 4–9)

4   Zion is told, *Lift up thine eyes round about, and see*. She is to look in all directions for her children, including adopted children from among the Gentiles (49:22; Rom. 8:15). They are coming from every quarter of the earth, both from far and near (cf. 49:18). Zion's daughters, the more delicate of her children, *shall be carried in the arms* ("nursed upon the side," margin; i.e., "carried on the hip," a typical Oriental mode of carrying small children).

5   At the sight of her returning children, Zion's face shall light up and beam for joy, and her *heart shall thrill* ("fear," King James)—be awed and excited—*and be enlarged* to receive Gentiles as well as Jews. It cannot be determined dogmatically whether *the abundance of the sea* (which) *shall be turned unto thee* refers to wealth brought by ships to enrich Zion materially or to masses of people who, in this instance, come bringing their wealth with them (cf. the references to "the sea" in Dan. 7:1–8). In the light of the history of both the nation after its return from exile and spiritual Zion under Christ, the latter is probably in the prophet's mind. For when people come from the world unto God's spiritual Zion, they bring and dedicate to Him all that they have.

6–7   As Zion looks away from the western sea to the east, she beholds nomadic traders coming from the desert lands with a multitude of camels. Ephah was a son of Midian, a son of Abraham by Keturah (Gen. 25:1–4). Sheba, whose dwelling place was the southwest tip of Arabia, was also a grandson of Abraham by Keturah (Gen. 25:1–3). Proclaiming the praises of Jehovah, they bring gold and frankincense. Kedar and Nebaioth were sons of Ishmael, the son of Abraham by Hagar the handmaid (Gen. 25:13). Kedar's land lay northeast of Jerusalem in the desert between Judah and Babylon. The location of Nebaioth's land is uncertain. Their flocks and herds will be dedicated to the praise of Jehovah; this does not mean that animal sacrifices will again be offered after the coming of Messiah, but that the descendants of Abraham by Hagar and Keturah will share with his descendants by Sarah (i.e., with the seed of Isaac) in glorifying God's spiritual house. His house will be "a house of prayer" for all nations,

487

and their sacrifices will be acceptable (56:7). God will *glorify the house of* (His) *glory* by receiving Abraham's cast-off descendants and their gifts. All are Jehovah's by creation, and creation's best belongs to Him.

8–9   Again looking toward the sea, Zion sees the white sails of ships coming toward her. They fly like clouds floating in the sky and like doves returning to their resting place. She asks, *Who are these?* Coming from *the isles,* the coastlands, they are Gentiles from the remotest regions who have long waited for Jehovah and His law (cf. 42:4; 51:5) and are now being rewarded for their wait. *The ships of Tarshish* are either vessels flying the flag of Tarshish, a trading colony located afar off in what is now Spain, or a specific type of large vessel which plies the oceans of the earth. They *bring thy sons from far,* together with their precious possessions of silver and gold. As when Israel departed from Egypt, "there shall not a hoof be left behind" (Exod. 10:26). Drawn to Zion because she has been glorified and beautified by Jehovah's presence, light, and name, multitudes of foreigners from throughout the world come bringing their all; everything they have is dedicated to Him.

Made Glorious Through Offerings (vv. 10–14)

10   Continuing to address Zion, Jehovah points out that foreigners will build her walls. (For earlier prophecies of the relationship of foreigners to spiritual Israel, see 19:21–25; 56:6–7; and comments.) Concerning Zion's walls, Isaiah also says, "Salvation will he appoint for walls and bulwarks" (26:1), and "Thou shalt call thy walls Salvation, and thy gates Praise" (v. 18). In His wrath Jehovah smote the old city, using foreigners to break down her walls; now He will use the descendants of these former enemies to build the walls of new Zion.

11   The thought of building walls while leaving the gates open seems paradoxical. Why have walls if the gates are to be always open: *they shall not be shut day nor night?* Note that this description does not apply to the conditions after the Jews returned from Babylon. When Nehemiah rebuilt the walls of Jerusalem, special emphasis was placed on repairing the gates (Neh. 3). Afterwards he instructed

the people, "Let not the gates of Jerusalem be opened until the sun be hot; and while they stand on guard, let them shut the doors, and bar ye them" (Neh. 7:3). But of the spiritual city, Isaiah said, "Open ye the gates, that the righteous nation which keepeth faith may enter in" (26:2). Now they are to be kept open, *that men may bring unto thee the wealth of the nations.* The blessings of Jehovah's spiritual Zion are open to all at all times. *Their kings will be led captive,* not in chains as prisoners of war, but as participants in Christ's triumphal march (II Cor. 2:14), with "every thought [brought] into captivity to the obedience of Christ" (II Cor. 10:5). No force is involved, for "Thy people offer themselves willingly/In the day of thy power" (Ps. 110:3).

12   Only the nations who come and build in Jehovah's city, serving the God of Zion and offering themselves willingly, shall survive; all the others shall perish. In a chapter with strong messianic overtones, Micah similarly says that Jehovah "will execute vengeance in anger and wrath upon the nations which hearkened not" (Mic. 5:15). Obviously, the time following the exile is not in view.

13   Trees are to be brought into the city not for building purposes, but *to beautify the place* of Jehovah's sanctuary (for the specific trees see the comments on 41:19). *And I will make the place of my feet glorious*—the temple is referred to as "the footstool of our God" (I Chron. 28:2), and the place of worship as "his footstool" (Pss. 99:5; 132:7), for in worship we look up to Him.

14   Jerusalem-Zion, which for so long has been afflicted and despised, shall now be honored by her oppressors. They shall recognize her relationship to God and bow at the soles of her feet. They shall do homage in honor of her God who has beautified her. And they shall call her *The city of Jehovah, the Zion*—dwelling place—*of the Holy One of Israel.*

Made Glorious Through Her Eternal Excellency (vv. 15–18)

15   Because the people of Zion had forsaken Jehovah, He gave them up to their own ways (cf. 50:1; 54:6). In taking this action, He was following a principle that He had declared long before (cf. II Chron. 12:1, 5; 15:2). Because of the desolation none dwelt in

Zion, and *no man passed through* her (cf. 33:8–9). This condition will now be changed; Jehovah will elevate Zion to a place of majestic splendor, *an eternal excellency*. The word *eternal* indicates a long time or period; Zion will last for an entire age, through *many generations*. As *a joy of many generations* Zion will maintain a just and righteous pride in her position. It is possible that her *eternal excellency* will extend beyond the messianic age into the everlasting glory of the heavenly state.

16 *Thou shalt also suck the milk of the nations*—this unusual figure, which may be drawn from Deuteronomy 33:19, must be interpreted figuratively (cf. 49:23). Recognizing Zion for what she is, the sons of former enemies have been attracted to her (v. 14). As she is sustained and built up by drawing the wealth of nations and kings from their breasts, she shall know that Jehovah is her Savior and Sustainer. He is *the Mighty One of Jacob*, able to redeem, build, and sustain the new nation of Zion just as He built and cared for the Israel and Zion of old.

17 The nature of the materials that go into Zion makes it precious in value and indestructible. This prophecy is certainly not to be taken literally; rather, it is an indication that God's house will progress from good to better: from brass to gold, from iron to silver, from wood to brass, and from stones to iron. Everything is to be better, more precious than before. The word *better (kreissōn)* occurs thirteen times in the Book of Hebrews, setting forth the superiority of the new Zion over the old. An equitable government will be established; the ruling forces will be peace and righteousness. The peace of Messiah will rule (arbitrate) in the heart (Col. 3:15). He will break the yoke of oppression (9:4); in its place He will establish the sceptre of righteousness (Heb. 1:8).

18 In the worldwide kingdom of peace ruled from Zion, *violence shall no more be heard*. Those who are drawn to Zion from among the nations will have beaten their swords into plowshares and their spears into pruning-hooks; they will learn war no more (2:2–4). There will be no desolation and destruction within the borders of Zion, for desolation and destruction pertain only to those who know not Jehovah and the joys of Zion. By contrast, those who have passed through the gates of Praise and dwell within the walls of Salvation will

continue to praise Him for His salvation and to practice peace instead of violence.

Made Glorious Through Jehovah's Everlasting Light (vv. 19–22)

19–20   This prophecy began (v. 1) with a picture of the glorious light of Jehovah's presence in His future kingdom. Having introduced this picture in earlier prophecies as well (24:23; 30:26), the prophet now returns to it. In the city here described, the sun and moon contribute no light, for *Jehovah will be unto thee an everlasting light, and thy God thy glory*. God is the light and glory of the spiritual city. Surely if the sun and moon can contribute nothing to the splendor of this city, the light of human wisdom and philosophy would add only confusion and darkness. With Jehovah as the light of Zion, neither her sun nor moon shall ever go down or withdraw their light! Further, the day of mourning in spiritual darkness and searching after the true light will have come to an end; from henceforth all will be bright.

21   A city of Zion's character demands a special type of citizen. They *shall be all righteous*, adhering to God's divine standard. Their conduct is totally governed by His law. (For a description of the residents of Mount Zion, see Rev. 14:1–5.) The righteous, not the Jews after the flesh (Gal. 4:30), are to inherit Zion's land forever (cf. 57:13b); they shall never be driven out or cast off. Earlier Jehovah's vineyard had been left to destruction (5:1–7), but the citizens of His new city are identified as *the branch of my planting*, which relates them to the Root and Branch of Jesse, the rallying point of the nations (11:1, 10). Through the Servant, Jehovah will accomplish this planting, the work of His hand, that He may be glorified (cf. 61:3).

22   The number and strength of the citizens will be multiplied: *The little one*, those of little apparent significance, the less privileged, *shall become a thousand. And the small one*, the poor, weak, or young, shall become *a strong nation* (cf. Mic. 4:7). The time at which this prophecy will be fulfilled is in the hand of the Lord; He *will hasten it in its time* (cf. Mark 1:14–15; Acts 1:7; Gal. 4:4). What has been promised will be done, for "the zeal of Jehovah of hosts will perform this" (9:7).

CHAPTER 61
Glorious Zion! (2)

It has been suggested by several writers that chapter 60 reveals the outer grandeur of Zion, whereas chapter 61 emphasizes its inner glory. In chapter 60 Jehovah is the speaker, praising the external glory of Zion, which is His own creation: "I will glorify the house of my glory" (v. 7). In our present chapter the Servant is the speaker. Through Him Jehovah will bring inner beauty to His glorious city.

The Herald of Good Tidings (vv. 1–3)

1   Athough the word *Servant* does not occur in these verses, one feels constrained by the context and likeness to the four Servant Songs previously considered to identify the speaker as the Servant-Messiah, the Lord Jesus. Some commentators identify the speaker as the prophet Isaiah, but the message and work of the speaker far transcend those of a prophet, even one of Isaiah's stature; they are characteristic of deity. The question is settled by Jesus Himself. At the beginning of His ministry, He read these verses in the synagogue and then said, "To-day hath this scripture been fulfilled in your ears" (Luke 4:16–21). Of course, it was not completely fulfilled, but was beginning to be fulfilled.

The speaker begins by declaring that the Spirit of the Lord is upon Him (cf. 42:1 [Isaiah sees the Spirit as having a developing role in the work of the one to come—11:2; 42:1; 48:16b; 49:8; 50:4]). Significantly, Peter declares that God anointed Jesus Christ "with the Holy Spirit and with power" (Acts 10:38). With this divine appointment and power, the speaker continues, He will preach the good tidings or news (cf. 40:9; 41:27; 52:7) of victory and deliverance to the meek, that is, to the humble, lowly, and gentle, who are disposed to hear. His mission will be not only to preach, but also to provide blessings. The good tidings are accompanied by divine action: (1) He will *bind up* as with a bandage *the broken-hearted*, those whose inner life is crushed by sin; (2) He will *proclaim liberty to the captives—liberty* is a technical term for the release of debtors and slaves in the fiftieth year,

the year of jubilee (Lev. 25:10; Jer. 34:8, 15); and (3) He will announce *the opening of the prison to them that are bound*, that they
may be brought out into the light of freedom. Though the return
from exile foreshadowed the Servant's work, this prophecy was not
fulfilled then, but in Him. Jesus' application of this passage to Himself indicates that it looks to a spiritual fulfillment.

2   Further, the Servant will loudly *proclaim the year of Jehovah's
favor* (grace), *and the day of vengeance*. Delitzsch calls attention to
the relative length of the two events—"a promise which assigns the
length of a year for the thorough accomplishment of the work of
grace, and only the length of a day for the work of vengeance" (II.
427). However, *year* and *day* in this case may be used simply as
general expressions meaning "time" (cf. 63:4). The vengeance is
upon whoever or whatever holds the people of God in prison. In
addition to proclaiming the year of favor and day of vengeance, the
Servant will *comfort all that mourn*. The word translated *mourn*
occurs most frequently in reference to grieving for the dead, though it
may be used figuratively, as in "the land mourneth" (33:9). Those
who grieve for the dead will be consoled, for in the Servant life
beyond death is guaranteed (53:10–12).

3   The mourners in Zion have signified their grief for her by
sprinkling ashes upon their heads. The Lord will now give them a
headpiece of beauty instead. For their mourning, He will also give
them the oil of joy, used by the ancients as a symbol of gladness and
festivity (Ps. 45:7; Eccles. 9:8; Song of Sol. 4:10). And to relieve their
heaviness of spirit, He will clothe them in a *garment of praise*, for
they are to be a praise unto Him at all times. They shall *be called trees
of righteousness*, trees being a symbol of sturdiness and endurance, of
beauty, and of fruitfulness. They are planted by Jehovah (cf. 60:21) so
that He may be glorified. Read Jeremiah's beautiful description of the
man whose trust is Jehovah: "he shall be as a tree planted by the
waters" (Jer. 17:7–8).

The Mission and Blessing of the Redeemed (vv. 4–9)

4   Those who have been blessed by the Servant's work are given a
threefold task: they are to (1) *build the old wastes* (waste places), (2)

493

raise up the former desolations, and (3) *repair the waste cities* (see the comments on 49:8; 54:3; 58:12). These desolations had not occurred overnight, but developed over many generations. The old boundaries are too small, too restricted for the new Zion; the prophet has a world-view before him (see the comments on 49:19–20).

5 *Strangers,* people who are not related to the original citizens of Zion and who have not been party to the covenants of the promise (Eph. 2:12), aliens or foreigners, shall contribute their share in building Zion (see the comments on 56:6–8; cf. Zech. 6:15). It is evident that the Lord speaks metaphorically, for there is no record that after the return from Babylon foreigners fed the flocks, plowed the fields, and dressed the vineyards of the Jews. Spiritual Israel is not concerned with flocks or plowmen or vineyards. And though the Gentile Christians helped to alleviate the physical needs of Jewish saints and the Jewish saints ministered to the spiritual needs of the Gentiles (Rom. 15:25–27; I Cor. 16:1–3; II Cor. 8:13–15; 9:12–15), it is unlikely that these services were broad enough to be what is envisioned in this verse. More probably the thought is that Jews and Gentiles worked together in building the new Zion.

6 When Gentiles and Jews come to Zion, there will be no distinction between them; all *shall be named the priests of Jehovah.* There will be no special priesthood apart from the citizens of the new city, for each is a priest (I Peter 2:5, 9; Rev. 5:9–10). Neither will there be a clergy distinct from the laity, for all will be called *the ministers of our God,* each offering "service well-pleasing to God with reverence and awe" (Heb. 12:28), and each offering "up a sacrifice of praise to God continually" (Heb. 13:15). As priests and ministers under the Messiah, *ye shall eat the wealth of the nations* (see the comments on 60:5–11), which will be provided by Him; for all is His and belongs to Him (I Cor. 3:21–23). While the world provides for the material needs, the saints will provide for the spiritual. The clause *and in their glory shall ye boast yourselves* is difficult. It may mean that true glory, which the nations once thought of as theirs, now belongs to the redeemed. This is a cause of boasting (in a good sense) for the citizens of Zion.

7 *Instead of your shame ye shall have double* (for the meaning of *double* see the comments on 40:2). The sin on the one side of the

scales has been balanced by judgment on the other. Now, instead of shame and dishonor (cf. 54:4), the scales are balanced with everlasting joy. This everlasting joy is a share of inheritance *in their land*, which is not Canaan but the realm of spiritual blessings, Jehovah's "holy mountain" (cf. 57:13b).

8 Whatever Jehovah does, whether He renders judgment or joy, He does because He loves justice, which is rightness, a quality inherent in God, for "Jehovah is a God of justice" (30:18). On the other hand, He hates *robbery*, the violent taking away of something which belongs to another, *with iniquity*, crookedness or deviation from the right. The very essence or nature of God demands that He give *recompense in truth*, that He destroy His enemies and reward the righteous. *In truth* indicates the certainty and faithfulness of His own character, the basis of His actions. He *will make an everlasting covenant with them* (cf. Ezek. 37:26), which entails assurances of reward for the faithful and warnings of judgment and punishment for the disobedient.

9 The seed of the godly, the righteous, shall be recognized among the nations because they are different. Although the heathen may not accept the truth in which the offspring of the godly live, they will recognize the righteousness of their lives and the spirit of joy and peace which they possess. These are blessings which come only from above.

Zion's Burst of Praise! (vv. 10–11)

10 Zion, not the Messiah or the prophet, breaks forth in a song of praise and rejoicing in her God. She is the recipient of the blessings listed in verses 1–3. Jehovah has clothed her with garments of salvation and thrown over her the robe of righteousness; the filthy garments of the past have been cast off. To further describe the beauty of Zion's glory, Isaiah utilizes the figure of the ornamental attire of both a bridegroom and a bride. Like a bridegroom, Zion decks herself with a headpiece or turban (cf. v. 3); and like a bride, she adorns herself with jewels.

11 That which is to be achieved in Zion through the Servant will be Jehovah's work. As He causes the plants of the earth to sprout and

grow and the seed sown in the garden to come forth, so He *will cause righteousness and praise to spring forth before all the nations.* In spite of all the opposition of the heathen, Jehovah will anoint the Servant with His Spirit, redeem and glorify Zion, establish an everlasting covenant, and make His people known among the nations. To Him be the glory and praise forever!

CHAPTER 62

Salvation Is Drawing Near

As in the last two chapters, we are again confronted with the question of whether the prophet is speaking of Israel's return from Babylonian exile or looking beyond the return to the glory of spiritual Zion, the Zion of God. Careful consideration of the content of the three chapters indicates that they are best interpreted as a prophecy of Zion's place in the messianic period rather than the postexilic period.

The New Name and Glory of Zion (vv. 1–5)

1 It is difficult to determine whether the speaker of these verses is Jehovah (Delitzsch, Leupold, Young), the Servant (Rawlinson), or the prophet himself (Alexander, Calvin, Smith, Whybray, Willis). Barnes suggests that the identity of the speaker is uncertain. Argument can be made for each view; however, verse 6 lends credence to the view that the speaker is Jehovah. The question is not too significant, for what we have here is the word of Jehovah made known through the prophet and revealing the Servant's work.

The light of *Zion* and *Jerusalem* (the two terms are used synonymously) has been obscured in the shadow of a long night. But now for her sake, that is, on her account or for her benefit, the night will be vanquished by the brilliance of her glory. Jehovah will never hold His *peace* (be quiet, refrain from speaking) nor *rest* (be still, inactive), *until her righteousness go forth as brightness, and her salvation as a lamp that burneth.* Her righteousness is her vindication or justification; it rests upon her salvation through a Savior (the Servant). This righteousness and salvation, the work of Jehovah upon Zion, will be seen as a steadily beaming light from a lamp (or torch) that will not go out. (For *righteousness* and *salvation*, see the comments on 61:10.)

2   The new standard of righteousness and the new glory of Zion will stand in such stark contrast to the heathen darkness and pseudoglory that nations (Gentiles) and kings shall see them clearly and be amazed (cf. 49:7; 52:15; 60:1–3). It is not altogether clear what the *new name, which the mouth of Jehovah shall name*, is (see the comments on v. 4); but possibly the new name is like the new song which only the 144,000 can learn and sing (Rev. 14:3). A name signifies and stands for all that the individual that bears it is. Consequently, the new name of Zion may be a name known only to Jehovah and to Zion, for only her citizens know the reality of the new relationship and life (cf. Rev. 2:17; 3:12; 19:12).

3   Let it be observed that Zion will be *a crown of beauty* and *a royal diadem* not upon Jehovah's head but in His hand. It was earlier declared that at a point in time Jehovah will "become a crown of glory, and a diadem of beauty" unto the remnant of His people (28:5), but there is no account of His wearing either. A *crown of beauty* indicates honor and glory, and *a royal diadem* signifies a mitre or turban (cf. Job 29:14; Zech. 3:5) as of a king or queen. The phrase *in the hand of thy God* probably suggests that Zion was fashioned by Him according to His will; protected by Him, its beauty and glory are in a conspicuous place where they are to be seen and admired by all.

4   *Thou* (Zion) *shalt no more be termed Forsaken*—the people of Zion had forsaken Jehovah; therefore He had forsaken her (cf. Deut. 28:15; II Chron. 15:2; Isa. 51:19–20), though only "for a small moment" (54:7). Never again will Jehovah forsake the people, because the new Zion will be "The city of righteousness, a faithful town" (1:26), faithful to Him in righteousness (62:1–2). Thus she will be made "an eternal excellency, a joy of many generations" (60:15). *Neither shall thy land any more be termed Desolate*. Note the distinction drawn between Zion and the land. Desolation and devastation had been the result of the sins committed in the land; a divine judgment had been brought upon it (cf. Lev. 26:23–24, 31–33; Jer. 12:7–13). But Zion will now be called *Hephzi-bah* ("My delight is in

497

her"), and the land *Beulah* ("Married"); *for Jehovah delighteth in thee.* Both *Forsaken* ("Azubah," Hebrew) and *Hephzi-bah* are names of women who were mothers of kings of Judah (I Kings 22:42; II Kings 21:1). *And thy land shall be married*—there will be a close and permanent relationship of possession between Zion and the land, for "he that taketh refuge in me [Jehovah] shall possess the land" (57:13).

5   *For as a young man marrieth a virgin, so shall thy sons marry thee*—the question has been raised as to whether this means the sons of Zion marry Zion or the sons of the land marry the land. Neither; the sons of Zion marry the land, that is, become intimately related to it. We read of "the children of Zion" (Ps. 149:2), "the daughter of Zion" (1:8; 62:11); Zion's sons and daughters (49:22; 60:4), and the "precious sons of Zion" (Lam. 4:2); Jehovah also "say[s] unto Zion, Thou art my people" (51:16). But we never read of "the sons of the land." The emphasis here is the joyous intimate relationship between the sons of Zion, who are Jehovah's people, and the land, which is His holy mountain (57:13; cf. 60:21; 61:7). As a young man marries a virgin and dedicates himself to protecting and caring for her honor, so the sons of Zion dedicate themselves to the honor of Jehovah's land and people—His kingdom. The relationship will be pure and chaste. *And as the bridegroom rejoiceth over the bride*, over their pure, divine love, *so shall thy God rejoice over thee*—over Zion's marriage to the land, His holy mountain.

Jehovah's Protection and Provision for Zion (vv. 6–9)

6–7   The phrase *watchmen upon thy walls* cannot refer to fallen Jerusalem while the people were in Babylon, nor to the return from the exile, for it was one hundred years before Nehemiah completed rebuilding the walls. It is much more probable that Jehovah is speaking of the spiritual Zion of verses 1–6, the walls of which will be called "Salvation" and her gates "Praise" (see the comments on 26:1; 49:16; 60:18). If this is correct, then the watchmen are not Old Testament prophets, priests and prophets, or angels, as is thought by some, but "apostles . . . prophets [New Testament] . . . evangelists . . . pastors and teachers," whose work is the perfecting of the saints (Eph. 4:11–12). They *never hold their peace day nor night*, but watch constantly in behalf of souls (Heb. 13:17). They are *Jehovah's remembrancers*, who take no rest, but ever keep petitions before Jehovah in behalf of Zion's citizens. They will not be silent before the Lord until He establishes His word concerning Jerusalem, making her *a praise in the earth*, which is a continuous work.

8–9   Earlier Jehovah swore that He would not be wroth with Zion, that His loving-kindness would not depart from her, and that the covenant of peace would not be made void (54:9–10). Now He adds to that oath. By His uplifted hand (a gesture signifying an oath) and by the mighty *arm of his strength*, He swears that no more will He give to Zion's enemies the grain and wine *for which thou hast labored*, which is to be her sustenance. Material grain and wine can neither sustain the immaterial part of man nor support an immaterial city; Zion's food will be spiritual. Jesus said, "Work not for the food which perisheth, but for the food which abideth unto eternal life, which the Son of man shall give unto you" (John 6:27); this is the food on which Zion survives. Enemies can never take it away from her. They who labor for this bread and drink shall at all times partake of it to the praise of Jehovah in the courts of His sanctuary, that is, before Him, in His presence. The world can neither appreciate this food nor rob Zion of it.

Salvation of the Daughter of Zion (vv. 10–12)

10   There is a diversity of opinion on these verses, especially the command *Go through, go through the gates*. The double charge may be for emphasis, or a double command may be intended: go out, come in. The majority of commentators think that the return from the exile is in the prophet's mind, but this interpretation is not in harmony with the remainder of the chapter. Zion's glory has been established (vv. 1–5), and Jehovah's care guaranteed by an oath (vv. 6–9); therefore, it seems that Jehovah is enjoining Zion to ⁻epare for the nations to come in. Those within are to go forth and *prepare ye the way of the people; cast up, cast up the highway; gather out the stones;* that is, they are to clear the way into Zion. Then they are to *lift up an ensign for* ("over," margin) *the peoples* (plural). The ensign or standard could be a rallying point for an army in the field or for a scattered

people. Isaiah earlier said that the Root of Jesse (i.e., the Messiah) "that standeth for an ensign of the peoples, unto him shall the nations seek" (11:10); and Jehovah promised that He would lift up His hand to the nations and "set up [His] ensign to the peoples," whereupon they would bring Zion's sons and daughters to her (49:22). It appears, then, that Zion's citizens go forth removing obstacles, making clear the way, and lifting high the banner so that those of the nations (Gentiles) can find their way to Zion and pass through the gates into the city.

11   When the Servant comes, He will come not only to Jacob, but Jehovah will give Him "for a light to the Gentiles, that thou mayest be my salvation unto the end of the earth" (49:6). Jehovah makes this proclamation to His people, who are scattered to the ends of the earth: *Say ye to the daughter of Zion* (the citizens), *Behold, thy salvation cometh*. The prophet is looking to that time when the glory of Zion will be complete through the Savior; then Jehovah's reward to the people will be a dwelling place in His presence, the wages for their patient waiting and labor (cf. 40:10).

12   Delitzsch translates the opening words of this verse, "And men will call them . . ."; Young translates the verb in the passive, "They will be called. . . ." In either case the point is that those to whom salvation comes will be called *The holy people, The redeemed of Jehovah*. They will be recognized as a people separate from all others because their redemption is of Jehovah, not man. The complaint that Jehovah has forsaken Zion (49:14), that she has been cast off as His wife (54:6), forsaken and hated (60:15), will no more be heard. Rather, *thou shalt be called Sought out*, for the Lord will have sought and called her out of the world, and A *city not forsaken* (cf. v. 4), constantly under His divine care and protection. But should the citizens of Zion lose sight of this sacred relationship, become a religious "social club" concerned primarily with political affairs and business enterprises, they will cease to be *The holy people*, separate and different from the world. They will become simply another religious body.

CHAPTER 63
Vengeance, Mercy, and a Prayer

In antiquity, national Israel stood as the symbol of Jehovah worship, representing the one true God. Edom, its brother-nation, stood as a symbol of opposition to Jehovah and the true religion, for as it opposed and hated Israel, it also hated Jehovah. Its enmity against Jacob is demonstrated throughout the history of the two nations; Edom always stood on the other side, the side of the opponents and destroyers of Israel. For this perpetual hatred of its brother-nation and Jehovah, Edom must be judged and brought to an end (see the introduction to chapter 34; Obad.; Mal. 1:2–5). No specific time is indicated for this judgment; the vision simply reveals what Jehovah will ultimately do to the nation. (Unlike Edom, whose hatred was reserved for Israel, Babylon sought to bring all nations under its dominion; only in that respect was it concerned with forcing Israel to submit. However, it too had to be destroyed [ch. 47].)

Jehovah's Vengeance on His Enemies (vv. 1–6)

1 In a vision the prophet sees a strong and mighty warrior coming from Bozrah, a chief city and probably sometime capital of Edom (though this is not certain).[2] The prophet asks, *Who is this?* and then describes the warrior as wearing *dyed* ("crimsoned," margin) *garments.* He is *glorious in his apparel,* which reflects the dignity of His own person. He marches proudly onward with the confident stride of a victor, *in the greatness of his strength.* The mighty one's response leaves no doubt as to His identity: *I that speak in righteousness, mighty to save.* It is Jehovah, who speaks truth and declares "things that are right" (45:19). In saving His people He acts consistently with His standard of righteousness.

2 The prophet responds with a second question, *Wherefore art thou red in thine apparel?* The implication is that the garments have

---

2. *Zondervan Pictorial Encyclopedia of the Bible,* ed. Merrill C. Tenney (Grand Rapids: Zondervan, 1975), vol. 1, p. 645.

been stained. Why are Jehovah's garments splattered with a red color, as if He has been treading grapes in a wine vat? In ancient times wine-makers gathered grapes in a stone which had been hewn out or in a wooden trough, and then trampled them. In the process the garments worn by those who trod the grapes were stained by spurting juice.

3   Jehovah responds to the prophet's question with a metaphor. As one treads grapes in the wine vat, so has He trodden His enemies in the winepress of His wrath, staining His raiment with their blood. He has acted alone, for *of the peoples* (plural) *there was no man with me: yea, I trod them* (plural) *in mine anger*. He has executed judgment single-handedly, not only against Edom, but against the nations (hea-then) generally. In working for the salvation of His people (cf. 59:16) and in judging His enemies, He acts alone. The anger and wrath of Jehovah is His righteous indignation in response to man's sins. Righ-teousness must be vindicated and judgment executed. In the execu-tion of judgment in the winepress of His wrath, the lifeblood of the heathen has splashed upon His garments (cf. Lam. 1:15; Joel 3:13; Rev. 14:19–20). That *all my raiment* has been stained indicates the far-reaching extent of the judgment. The New Testament counter-part is found in Revelation 19:13–15: The Word of God treads the winepress of God's wrath as He brings the heathen to their end.

4   That vengeance is the vindication of the Lord's holiness which righteousness and justice demand is evident throughout the entire passage (vv. 1–6). It was in His heart to trample the wicked. Delitzsch and Leupold hold that there is significance in the ratio suggested by the words *day* and *year*: one day of vengeance to one year of salvation; Willis and Young, however, think the two words simply mean "time" (see the comments on 61:2).

5   Jehovah looked closely and intently, expecting and desiring (cf. 5:2) that among all the peoples surely there would be an individual or a nation on His side; but there was neither, just as He had found no counsellor in Zion (41:28; 59:16). *And I wondered*, stood appalled, at the spiritual desolation. There was no response. Therefore, Jehovah's own mighty arm had to save Him in battle, and His holy wrath had to uphold Him in His execution of judgment.

6   Finding no helper, Jehovah Himself trampled the peoples (na-tions) underfoot in His anger *and made them drunk in my* (His)

wrath, reducing them to a state of total helplessness. Thus trodden down, their lifeblood (literally, "strength") was poured out upon the earth and brought to an end.

Jehovah's Enduring Love for His People (vv. 7–9)

Jehovah has assured the people of salvation through the Servant (52:13–53:12); He has urged Zion to prepare for a great influx of new citizens (54:1–3); the glory of Zion has been foretold (chs. 60–62); and the judgment of the heathen has been guaranteed (63:1–6). It is now time to count blessings and offer praise to Jehovah (vv. 7–9), to remember Jehovah's mercies of old (vv. 10–14), and to pray (63:15–64:12).

7   Although the prophet uses the personal pronoun *I*, he is probably speaking for the faithful few of his day, but this is not certain. He mentions *the lovingkindnesses of Jehovah*, His acts of tenderness based on His everlasting love. This loving-kindness is a ground for praise to the Lord, *according to all that Jehovah hath bestowed on us.* A second characteristic of Jehovah is His *great goodness toward the house of Israel*, the graciousness to which they can appeal for forgiveness. A third consideration to be declared is His *mercies*, which are *according to the multitude of his lovingkindnesses.* The Lord's mercies sum up His sympathy for His people, His deep love for them.

8   When Jehovah brought Israel out of Egypt, He claimed them as His people, among whom He would walk as their God (Lev. 26:12; Deut. 29:13). There was the condition, however, that if He was to abide among them, they must hearken unto His voice (Deut. 6:3; Jer. 7:23; Ezek. 11:20). In the light of the loving-kindnesses, great goodness, and abundant mercies shown to His people (v. 7), *Surely, they . . . will not deal falsely*, but be faithful to Him. This is what Jehovah has a right to expect, for He has chosen them as His people. Moreover, He *was their Saviour* (cf. Ps. 106:21–22) and would always be there to help when called upon. But He was disappointed in them.

9   *In all their affliction he was afflicted*—*affliction* is a straitened, pressed-in condition beset with "an intense inner turmoil." If the reading of the margin is adopted, "In all their adversity he was no adversary," the thought is, as expressed by Alexander, "in all their

503

enmity (to him) he was not an enemy (to them)" (II. 419); He did not afflict them to hurt them but to do them good. If, on the other hand, the basic translation is accepted, the thought seems to be that He shared with them the grief and hurt of their afflictions, as is indicated in Judges 10:16 as well: "And his [Jehovah's] soul was grieved for the misery of Israel." Throughout Israel's history the Lord was concerned for and shared in the people's suffering, just as the Savior is "touched with the feeling of our infirmities" (Heb. 4:15). Empathy is a characteristic of both Jehovah and the Messiah.

And the angel of his presence (the phrase *angel of his presence* occurs only here) *saved them*—the word translated *angel* may also be rendered "messenger" or "representative"; the word translated *presence* literally means "face." Jehovah promised Moses, "My presence [face] shall go with thee" (Exod. 33:14). Thus *the angel* is the representative of Jehovah's face or presence that went with Israel. Inasmuch as Christ accompanied Israel in the wilderness (I Cor. 10:4), and is "the image of God" (II Cor. 4:4, 6; Col. 1:15) and "the effulgence of his glory" (Heb. 1:3), this representative of Jehovah's presence probably is the Word of God that became flesh (John 1:14), the preincarnate Messiah. Moved by pity through Him, Jehovah *redeemed them; and he bare them, and carried them all the days of old.* Isaiah ascribes unto Jehovah the praise and glory for Israel's redemption and providential care through history.

The People's Response: Rebellion (vv. 10–14)

10 Though Jehovah had been gracious to Israel, having urged them to hear the voice of the messenger whom He would send, and having warned them not to rebel against Him (Exod. 23:21), yet they heeded not, but rebelled from the beginning (Deut. 9:7). They had *grieved his holy Spirit*, bringing sorrow and pain to Him (cf. Pss. 78:40; 106:43). Therefore, instead of being what He wished to be toward them, Jehovah became their enemy, finally abandoning or giving them up as He did the antediluvian world (Gen. 6:6–7). He fought against Israel-Judah as He fought other enemies of righteousness.

At this point an exegetical question is raised: does the *holy Spirit* refer to Jehovah Himself, to His temper or disposition, or to the Holy Spirit as a person? There are differing views on this point. The angel or representative of Jehovah (v. 9) is a personal being distinguished from Him; likewise, the *holy Spirit* is here distinguished from Jehovah. He can experience grief (cf. Eph. 4:30), a characteristic peculiar to a person. This leads to the conclusion that the prophet is speaking of the Holy Spirit as a person. If so, in these verses we have Jehovah; the angel (representative) of Jehovah, that is, the Son; and the Holy Spirit—the three persons of the Triune God all working in behalf of Israel. The rebellion of the people is therefore against the total Godhead.

11   Another question of exegesis is raised here. Shall we accept the text, *Then he remembered the days of old, Moses and his people,* or the alternate reading, "Then his people remembered the ancient days of Moses" (margin)? Five questions follow. The first, *Where is he that brought them up out of the sea with the shepherds of his flock?* seems to confirm the reading of the margin. Is the question being asked by the faithful few or by the people as a whole? It seems to be more in harmony with the context to view the nation as the questioner, although some scholars think that the prophet is speaking for the faithful few. *Out of the sea* refers to the crossing of the Red Sea (cf. Ps. 106:9); *the shepherds of his flock* are Moses and Aaron. But if the singular form *shepherd* (margin), which occurs in some ancient manuscripts, is adopted, the shepherd is Moses. In the light of the phrase *Moses and his people,* the singular is preferable.

The second question, *Where is he that put his holy Spirit in the midst of them?* probably refers to Jehovah's giving His Spirit to the seventy elders in the wilderness (cf. Num. 11:17, 25, 29; Hag. 2:5). The Spirit here, as in verse 10, is the third person of the Trinity.

12   The third question, *Where is he . . . that caused his glorious arm to go at the right hand of Moses?* points back to Jehovah's leading and strengthening Moses from the time of deliverance out of Egypt to arrival at the border of Canaan. *His glorious arm* is the mighty power (see the comments on 40:10; 51:5; 52:10; 59:16; 63:5) God exhibited in the deliverance from Egypt and the care of His people in the wilderness as He stood by Moses throughout.

The fourth question pertains to the power exhibited in dividing the waters of the Red Sea. Where is He now who formerly exercised that power when He led Israel out of Egypt, thus making for Himself *an everlasting name* both among the nations then and among all peoples since?

13   The fifth question asks, Where is He *that led them* (the people) *through the depths*, through waters in which they would have drowned, except for the exercise of His glorious power? In crossing the sea, Israel was like a sure-footed horse traveling on a smooth desert waste where it does not stumble—the crossing was without mishap to the people and their stock.

14   A final illustration or simile completes the picture. As cattle that have been grazing on the rugged slopes of a mountain go down into the valley for water and rest, so *the Spirit of Jehovah caused them to rest* in Canaan at their journey's end. By His great strength and mighty power Jehovah led His people through all these trials, making His name more glorious. Leupold has well summarized the whole point of verses 11–14, "Why 'then' and not 'now'?" Jehovah displayed His infinite power at the beginning of the nation's history; why, then, are we left as we are at the present time?

An Impassioned Prayer for Mercy and Help (vv. 15–19; ch. 64)

15   The nation has looked back at Jehovah's love, mercy, and mighty power exhibited in the deliverance under Moses. They have compared that exhibition of His presence with their current condition and now cry unto Him in prayer for help. His throne is in heaven (Ps. 11:4) where the people have looked for blessings in the past (Deut. 26:15) and have sought help in time of need (Ps. 80:14). There the fullness of His glory and holiness dwells, and the nation now appeals to these attributes. They cry, *Look down from heaven* with a favorable attitude toward us, and *behold*, consider and have regard for our condition. Where are the zeal against our enemies and the accompanying mighty power which were once promised (cf. 26:11; 42:13; 59:17)? Jehovah seems to have removed Himself, for they further ask, Why have the yearnings of His heart and His compassions been withdrawn from the nation? Though we, like the na-

tion which is here at prayer, may not perceive it at the time, there is always a purpose back of chastening.

16   The ground of Israel's appeal for help is that Jehovah is their Father, the one who brought the nation into existence (cf. Deut. 32:6). Though He had brought them up as His children, they had rebelled against Him (1:2); this is the answer to the question of verse 15. That Abraham and Israel do not know the nation does not mean that they now reject the people, or claim no relation to them, but that descent from the patriarchs cannot help them now. For although Abraham and Jacob were the physical progenitors of the nation, Jehovah is their spiritual Father and true Redeemer. To Him they must appeal.

17   At first reading this verse seems to be, as Rawlinson suggests, a "reproach that borders on irreverence" (II. 444); but God cannot be charged with responsibility for man's sins—man alone is responsible. The explanation of this difficult verse seems to be found in the charge given to Isaiah at his call. If the people hearken to Jehovah, it will be well; but if they do not, they will become completely hardened (see the comments on 6:10). They did not hearken; therefore, they were hardened by that which should have turned them to Jehovah. The plea is for God to return for the sake of Israel, whom He has chosen to be His servants, lest the tribes become extinct in the land.

18–19   The many explanations and alternative textual readings suggested by commentators and critics are evidence that we are faced here with another difficult passage. In the original, there is no direct object for the verb *possessed*, so what did the people possess? Was it the land, the mountain (as some propose), or the sanctuary? Any of these is possible. The following is offered as a probable explanation. In the beginning of Israel's history, Jehovah had said that when they "have been long in the land" and have fully corrupted themselves with idolatry, "ye shall soon utterly perish from off the land" that you go over Jordan to possess (Deut. 4:25–26). The land was woefully corrupted by Manasseh (II Kings 21:1–18); after him there was only one good king, Josiah, who attempted but failed to reform Judah. He was succeeded by four wicked kings, the destruction of Jerusalem, and the Babylonian exile. Could this not be the fulfillment of Isaiah's words that *Thy holy people possessed it* (the land) *but a little while*, for a short time? After abandoning themselves to idolatry, they perished just as Jehovah had forewarned in Deuteronomy. Those who *have trodden down thy sanctuary* could be the Babylonians (see the comments on 64:11), or the idolaters of the pre-exilic days who, despising the established faith, profaned Jehovah's sanctuary. In this condition they were like foreigners who had never submitted to Jehovah nor been called by His name.

CHAPTER 64

A Fervent Prayer

Prayer for Jehovah's Presence and Action (vv. 1–7)

1 The prayer which began at 63:15 continues through this chapter. It opened with the plea, "Look down from heaven, and behold" (v. 15), which is now repeated and expanded: *Oh that thou wouldest rend the heavens, that thou wouldest come down.* Look and observe, then act. The prophet continues to speak for the nation; it is their prayer that Jehovah rend, or tear, the heavens behind which He has hidden Himself from them. The plea is for Him to come down as at Sinai when the earth quaked at His presence (Exod. 19:11, 18–20). Shall we translate the verb here *quake, flow down* (margin; King James), or *melt at thy presence?* The answer can be found in verse 3. In making this plea the people seem to have forgotten the terror of Sinai (Exod. 20:18–21; Deut. 5:25–27), for they ask Jehovah to appear again in their midst. They had refused to hear Him then; will they hear Him now?

2 The intensity of the heat of Jehovah's presence in judgment is like fire which kindles dry brushwood or causes water to boil; hence, some commentators prefer *melt* or *flow down* to *quake* (v. 1). In such a show of might He would cause His name to be recognized among His adversaries for its true greatness (cf. 63:12); the nations would *tremble at thy* (His) *presence.* They would become fully aware of His being and power.

3 The *terrible things* which Jehovah had done might better be

called "awesome" or "awe-inspiring"; however, at times some of His acts were indeed terrifying far beyond the people's imagination or anticipation. In doing them He had "come down" from heaven (Neh. 9:13–15). Now the people pray for a similar demonstration (v. 1). When He came down at Sinai, the earth quaked. Nahum uses similar language in a graphic description of the changes wrought by Jehovah's presence: "The mountains quake at him, and the hills melt; and the earth is upheaved at his presence, yea, the world, and all that dwell therein" (Nah. 1:5). The emphatic thought here is to be found at the conclusion of each of the first three verses: *thy presence*; this is what the people are praying for.

4   Jehovah had challenged the idol-gods to speak or act—to do something (41:21–24)—but they only brought shame to their devotees by their inability (44:9). Isaiah now says, *For from of old*, even from the beginning of time, men have heard no message and have seen no action of an idol-god. Only Jehovah has worked in behalf of *him that waiteth for him*. To wait connotes "an attitude of earnest expectation and confident hope" (cf. 40:31).[3]

Regarding the citation of this verse in I Corinthians 2:9 Young says, "Paul is not speaking to give an exact quotation of this verse, but rather is using the language and varying it as he will to express his own thoughts concerning the newness and uniqueness of the Gospel" (III. 494). Before all of God's words and works, whether in delivering His people of old, in rendering judgments against the wicked, or in providing the gospel of redemption, man stands in awe of His unique being and power; there is none comparable to Him.

5   Of this verse, Alexander says, "There is perhaps no sentence in Isaiah, or indeed in the Old Testament, which has more divided and perplexed interpreters, or on which the ingenuity and learning of modern writers have thrown less light" (II. 431). For a rather lengthy list of the various views, see the commentaries of Alexander and Barnes. While the text is obscure, the meaning of the verse seems to be that Jehovah meets and aids those who rejoice in Him and work righteousness. The Hebrew word translated *Thou meetest* is translated "intercession" in 53:12 and "intercessor" in 59:16; thus Jehovah

---

3. *Theological Wordbook of the Old Testament*, vol. 1, p. 282.

speaks or intercedes for those who work righteousness, those who remember, pay mental attention to, His ways (cf. Prov. 3:5–8), and act in harmony with them. Though Jehovah has been so gracious and has warned against iniquity by His wrath against sin, yet *we sinned*. In this state, *shall we be saved?* The answer is that salvation comes only by seeking Jehovah and giving heed to Him and His ways (55:6–7).

6 *For we are all become as one that is unclean*—the prophet still has in mind the question, "And shall we be saved?" (v. 5). Even the believers in Israel, with whom the prophet stands, have become affected by the national sins. Whether he is speaking of the people of his own day (as seems to be the case), of Judah immediately before the captivity, or of the Jews in the captivity, he sees the nation *as one that is unclean* (cf. Lev. 5:2). This uncleanness may be ceremonial or moral, but in either case it makes the people unfit to approach the Lord (see Hag. 2:12–14). Their righteousnesses are *as a polluted garment*, a garment soiled by a woman during her menstrual period, making her and the garment impure and untouchable (cf. Lev. 15:19–30, 33). In such an unholy state their life and strength *fade as a leaf* (cf. 1:30; 34:4); and their iniquities, *like the wind*, carry them away from Jehovah and from their true spiritual fatherland.

7 The prophet is speaking of the nation in general when he says there is none who call upon God's name. Though there were always a faithful few, it is possible that even they have ceased to pray. Either the nation has lost faith in Jehovah's willingness to answer prayer, or, in their uncleanness, they consider themselves unfit to approach Him. Perhaps both conditions exist; but at any rate, prayer has ceased among the people. In their spiritual inertia they have ignored this great privilege of prayer, failing to use its power and to take hold of Jehovah through it. Consequently, He has hidden His face from them and consumed them by means of (by the hand of) their iniquities. The basic meaning of the word translated *consumed* is "to melt," as in "My heart is like wax;/It is melted within me" (Ps. 22:14), and "mountains melted like wax at the presence of Jehovah" (Ps. 97:5; cf. Mic. 1:4). Whatever the translation, the strength of the nation is gone; for without Jehovah's aid they are weak and helpless, as shapeless as melted wax, in their iniquities.

A Renewed Cry for Mercy (vv. 8–12)

8   The words *But now* introduce a new argument or a fresh aspect of the plea. The cry of 63:16 is repeated, except that there as Father He is addressed as Redeemer, whereas here He is addressed as Creator, the Fashioner of Israel: *we are the clay, and thou our potter,* the one who fashioned us as a people (cf. 29:16). Though Jehovah is the Creator of all mankind, He is the Father of only His spiritual people. It should be remembered that a potter can mold a vessel only as the clay yields itself in his hand; if he is unable to make a vessel unto honor, then he makes one unto dishonor (Jer. 18:1–4). He seeks to make the best but may have to settle for something inferior. The people have not yielded themselves; therefore, Jehovah must make of them a vessel of dishonor.

9   As the God of the nation, Jehovah has promised for His own sake to blot out transgressions and to forget their sins (43:25). On that ground the people now make their plea, not that there be no judgment, but that He not remember their sins unto eternity. They cry, *We are all thy people* (cf. v. 8). Rephrased by Habakkuk, their entreaty is, "In wrath remember mercy" (Hab. 3:2). In Jehovah's reply (ch. 65) He separates the faithful from the unfaithful, declaring the destiny of each.

10   Some commentators think *thy holy cities* are Zion and Jerusalem. However, it is much more probable that the prophet is referring to the cities of Judah, for Judah is spoken of as "the holy land" (Zech. 2:12). The land and its people were holy unto God. The cities of Judah and Zion *are become a wilderness,* uninhabited, a desert, and *Jerusalem a desolation,* a waste.

11   Amid the desolation and waste, *Our holy and our beautiful house, where our fathers praised thee, is burned with fire.* Commentators who believe there were a second (Deutero-) and, in some cases, even a third (Trito-) Isaiah ascribe the writing of this description to the days of the exile or the period immediately following it. However, such a conclusion is not necessary; for the Bible abounds in declaring events long before they occur, speaking of them as though they have already taken place. To the Jews of His day Jesus said, "Your father Abraham rejoiced to see my day; *and he saw it,* and was glad" (John

511

8:56, italics added). David (Ps. 22) and Isaiah (ch. 53) had clear foresight of certain aspects of the trial and crucifixion of Jesus. At the beginning of Israel's national history, Jehovah told the people that if they would not hearken unto Him, "I will make your cities a waste, and will bring your sanctuaries unto desolation" (Lev. 26:31). At the dedication of Solomon's temple Jehovah warned that if they turned away from worshiping Him and keeping His commandments, "then will I cut off Israel out of the land which I have given them; and this house which I have hallowed for my name, *will I cast out of my sight*" (I Kings 9:6–7, italics added). And through Isaiah Jehovah declared to Hezekiah that all in his house, and that which had been laid up by his fathers, "shall be carried to Babylon: nothing shall be left" (39:6). In the light of the wickedness of his day and these warnings from God, Isaiah could easily have seen the temple in ruins as an accomplished fact. Remember also that Jehovah had challenged the idols to declare events to come and thereby prove their deity (41:23), and then had rested His claim to sole deity on His ability to declare the future (42:9)—"I am God . . . declaring the end from the beginning" (46:9–10). Paul similarly affirms that God "calleth the things that are not, as though they were" (Rom. 4:17). It was just as easy for Jehovah to describe the destruction of the temple as to proclaim in advance the captivity and the coming of Cyrus to deliver the people (44:28–45:7, 13). It is the conviction of this writer that Isaiah himself, being moved by the Spirit (cf. II Peter 1:21), was given the insight that the temple would soon be destroyed as a result of the people's sins. The *pleasant places* to be laid waste include the cities, the homes, and the gardens which the people esteem. Everything, including the temple and its precinct, will be in ruins.

12   The prayer closes with two questions to Jehovah. In view of the conditions just described, can He fail to act? Will He continue the affliction indefinitely? Though the questions are not answered explicitly, a negative answer seems to be implied (see ch. 65).

CHAPTER 65
Jehovah's Response to the Prayer

Some writers feel that this chapter is independent of chapter 64, but it seems obvious that it is Jehovah's response to the nation's prayer. Because of their rebellion and idolatry He cannot do what they plead for. He will cast off the fleshly nation, but will redeem or save a remnant. The present order will pass away, and He will create a new one.

Destruction of the Apostates: A Just Recompense (vv. 1–7)

1 Numerous commentators believe that in this verse Jehovah is speaking of His relationship with Israel (e.g., Erdman, p. 155; Leupold, II. 358). According to Paul's use of the passage, however, this is not what is in Jehovah's view. The nation of Israel has prayed to God for help on the ground that they are His people. Jehovah's reply is that He is rejecting them and that He will be found of a people who have not sought Him. Paul applies verse 1 to the Gentiles and verse 2 to Israel (Rom. 10:20–21). The Gentiles have not sought God, nor have they been called by His name; but He will summon the people of a nation not hitherto included (55:5), inviting them through the gospel (Matt. 28:18–19; Mark 16:15–16), as Isaiah has earlier foretold (49:6). Though Paul probably quoted from the Septuagint version and deleted part of the passage, his application of it is the surest commentary we have.

2 Jehovah now addresses Himself to Israel. To spread out the hands is a gesture of appeal; as one in prayer lifts his hands toward Jehovah, so has He stretched or reached out His hands in imploring the people to hear Him. He has done this *all the day*, continually; He will not give them up until He is forced to by their stubbornness. But they have continued to be *a rebellious people, that walk* (the verb connotes manner of life) *in a way that is not good*, but evil, *after their own thoughts*, devices, or plans—they do what they want to do (cf. 63:10). This rebellious attitude continued even into the New Testament era (Acts 7:51). Jehovah now spells out what it is that they have done *after their own thoughts*, and what His reaction is:

3 The people provoke Jehovah to anger by their continual insults before His very face, openly, in defiance of His eternal Godhood; there is no effort to hide their blasphemous deeds (cf. 3:9). They are guilty of *sacrificing in gardens*, a cause for shame (cf. 1:29). This is a

513

reference to the enclosed plots which they have turned into places of idolatrous worship (66:17). The meaning of *burning incense upon bricks* is uncertain. Alexander thinks the bricks are "altars slightly and hastily constructed." The reference could also be to altars that were built on the roofs of houses (II Kings 23:12), or to the tiles on house-tops where incense was burned to the host of heaven (Jer. 19:13; Zeph. 1:5).

4   The people also *sit among the graves* or tombs. Although uncertain, this may be an allusion to necromancy—consultation with the dead, seeking messages from them instead of from God (cf. Lev. 19:31; Deut. 18:11–12). Lodging *in the secret places* "may refer to the mysteries celebrated in natural caves and artificial crypts" (Delitzsch). The eating of swine's flesh was forbidden by the law (Lev. 11:7; Deut. 14:8); this stipulation is now being flagrantly violated. The *broth of abominable things* may have been a concoction supposed to provide some magical power or relate one to some false deity.

5   Individuals practicing such abominations consider themselves holier than the true worshipers of God. Young thinks that the command, *Stand by thyself, come not near to me, for I am holier than thou*, is spoken to God Himself. This interpretation is doubtful; but if correct, it reveals the depth to which idolatry can carry one. Those who practice idolatry *are a smoke in my* (Jehovah's) *nose*, a cause for deep anger and for a fire of divine jealousy that burns continually. Verses 3–5 well expose the terrible idolatry of the people (cf. Ezek. 8, the prophet's vision of the idolatry being practiced in Jerusalem).

6   Just as Jehovah keeps an account of the righteous and their deeds (4:3), recording the tears of His saints (Ps. 56:8), and maintaining a register of them that fear Him and think upon His name (Mal. 3:16), so does He keep an account of the wicked. Accordingly, *I will not keep silence*—He will not remain inactive toward the rebellious idolaters. The people's violation of His laws is ever before Him. He will pay them in full for their continuous disregard of Him and His law: *I will recompense into their bosom. Bosom* is a fold in an apron or garment in which goods can be carried (cf. Ruth 3:15), or a bribe concealed (Prov. 17:23). In an earlier metaphor Jehovah pledged that the sons of Zion would be brought to her in the bosom of the peoples (49:22).

7   The sin among the people, which must be recompensed in full, had continued from their fathers (Amos 2:4). The mountains and hills had been favorite places for erecting altars on which to offer sacrifices to idols. These sacrifices, accompanied with immoral practices, had blasphemed God by bringing reproaches upon His holy name (cf. 57:7; Hos. 4:13). So instead of blessing the people as they requested, Jehovah will *measure their work into their bosom*; He will balance the scales by casting off the wicked nation as they had cast Him off.

Salvation of a Remnant—Destruction of the Faithless (vv. 8–12)

8   Though the wicked will be destroyed, yet not all of Israel will be cut off, for Jehovah will spare a remnant. No one destroys a cluster of good grapes that stands out among clusters of sour or worthless ones (cf. 5:4); but it is spared, *for a blessing is in it*, that is, the blessing that God has provided in grapes for man's nourishment. *So will I do for my servants' sake*, those who have chosen to serve me, *that I may not destroy them all*. God promised a blessing to all nations in the seed of Abraham (Gen. 12:3; 22:18; cf. also the promise to Isaac and Jacob in Gen. 26:2–5; 28:14), and for His name's sake it will be fulfilled. Not everyone will be cut off (48:9; cf. Jer. 24, the prophet's vision of the baskets of good and bad figs).

9   In order to fulfill His purpose, Jehovah will bring forth *a seed out of Jacob, and out of Judah an inheritor of my mountains*. Jacob and Judah represent the people as a whole. Both Israel and Judah went into captivity, both ceased to exist as political kingdoms, and from both Jehovah will redeem His remnant. This *seed* will inherit, come to possess, *my mountains*, which is equivalent to "my land" (14:25), "the mountains of Zion" (Ps. 133:3), His "holy mountains" (Ps. 87:1). The context of the chapter makes it clear that this is not a reference to the return from Babylon, but to those who take refuge in God (57:13). There have always been moral conditions upon a people's possession of a land. The Canaanites were cast out of their land because of moral corruption (Deut. 9:3–5); Israel was to retain it on the condition of faithfulness to God's standard (Lev. 18:24–30; Deut.

515

4:37–40). If they remained faithful to Jehovah, the land was to be for an inheritance to their children forever (I Chron. 28:8). Further, the return of the remnant was conditioned on a change of heart (Deut. 30:8–10), and the rebuilding of the nation rested on conditions (Jer. 18:7–10). It seems that after their return the people never met these conditions for God's blessings, but the new *seed, my chosen*, the branch of God's planting, shall inherit His mountains (cf. 60:21); *and my servants* (the phrase is parallel to *my chosen*) *shall dwell there*. The promise that they will inherit what national Israel failed to possess was fulfilled spiritually under the Servant.

10   This verse is an expansion of the promise in verse 9: the valleys between which lie the mountains to be inherited by *my people that have sought me* will be prosperous. *Sharon* is the northwest plain between Mount Carmel and Joppa on the Mediterranean coast. *Achor* is a valley northwest of the Dead Sea; it was the place where Achan was stoned for taking the Babylonish garment and wedge of gold (Josh. 7:24–26). Jehovah will give "the valley of Achor [the valley of Troubling] for a door of hope" (Hos. 2:15). *Sharon shall be a fold of flocks*, an enclosure or pasture which offers protection and security; Achor shall be *a place for herds to lie down in*, a place of fullness and serenity. The new redeemed state and homeland of spiritual Israel will be characterized by abundance, security, and blessings.

11   The Lord turns His attention away from His chosen seed, the people who have sought Him (v. 10), to those who forget His holy mountain and forsake Him to serve idols. The translations *Fortune* ("Gad," Hebrew) and *Destiny* ("Meni," Hebrew) are preferable to the King James renderings *that troop* and *that number*. Evidently these are early Canaanitish deities, for when Israel came into the land, at least two towns bore the name *Gad*, Baal-gad (Josh. 11:17) and Migdal-gad (Josh. 15:37). Delitzsch devotes four pages to a learned discussion of these two names (II. 482–85). For our purposes we need only mention that Fortune and Destiny are heathen deities before whom Israel had spread tables (cf. Pss. 23:5; 69:22; 78:18–19) of food and offered drink oblations. Of course, there is no such thing as luck (Fortune) or fate (Destiny), for "the righteous, and the wise, and their works, are in the hand of God" (Eccles. 9:1). His providence determines the destiny of all.

12 With a play on the word *destine* Jehovah continues, *I will destine you to the sword, and ye shall all bow down to the slaughter.* The destiny and fate of the people does not rest in the hands of idols, but in the determined counsel and overruling providence of God; He will number them one by one to their slaughter. The reason for their destruction is twofold: *when I called, ye did not answer; when I spake, ye did not hear,* attend to what I said. Jehovah desires from His people goodness, knowledge of Him, and a contrite heart rather than burnt-offerings (Hos. 6:6; Ps. 51:16–17). But instead of His way, they have chosen their own, a way in which He *delighted not* and for which they must now suffer the consequence.

Blessings and Judgments (vv. 13–16)

13–14 The word *Therefore* introduces conclusions based on the foregoing promises of blessings and threats of judgment. The clause *saith the Lord Jehovah* emphasizes Jehovah's lordship and, therefore, His power to carry out what He proposes. His *servants* are those who have been spared (v. 8), the "chosen" ones who will inherit and dwell in His mountains (v. 9). God addresses those who will escape the sword of slaughter (v. 12) but whose lot, being apart from Him, will nonetheless be a hard one. Four contrasts are set forth: (1) *Behold, my servants shall eat, but ye shall be hungry;* (2) *behold, my servants shall drink, but ye shall be thirsty.* In view of the content of the chapter, it is clear that the Lord is speaking of spiritual food and drink which His servants will have, but which those who forsake Him will not have (cf. 62:8–9). The Servant came offering bread from heaven and the water of life; those who have partaken will neither hunger nor thirst (John 6:35). For in Him is "every spiritual blessing" (Eph. 1:3), and in Him dwells all the fullness of the Godhead. Those who are in Him, then, are made full (Col. 2:9–10) "unto all the fulness of God" (Eph. 3:19). Those who reject Him will be left hungry and thirsty. (3) *Behold, my servants shall rejoice, but ye shall be put to shame;* and (4) *behold, my servants shall sing for joy of heart, but ye shall cry for sorrow of heart, and shall wail*—cry out in anxiety and distress—*for vexation* ("breaking," Hebrew) *of spirit.* Apart from God and His spiritual blessings there is no fullness, no joy, and no singing.

15 One's name stands for all that he is—his being, character, and personal traits. All that fleshly, rebellious national Israel is and has been will be left for a curse. No greater judgment could be pronounced than this deserved fate which befell the nation (cf. Jer. 24:9). *And the Lord Jehovah will slay thee,* bringing to an end the idolatrous nation as it has been; this He did, casting it out (Gal. 4:30). Because of the stigma attached to the name *Israel,* Jehovah *will call his servants by another name* (cf. 62:2), namely, "My delight is in her" (62:4, margin). In the New Testament the name *Christian* summarizes all that is new about God's new people.

16 To bless means "to endue with power for success, prosperity, fecundity, longevity, etc."[4] One can be blessed only in the Lord, for apart from Him there are no blessings. They are not to be sought in Fortune and Destiny. By contrast, the commitments of *the God of truth* ("the God of Amen," margin) hold fast (II Cor. 1:20); He is "the Amen, the faithful and true" (Rev. 3:14). Further, all oaths will be sworn in the name of *the God of truth* ("Amen") and not of an idol deity. Such oaths are as binding as is the character of God in whose name they are taken. *The former troubles are forgotten;* the afflictions brought on by unfaithfulness are completely removed, blotted out. *They are hid from mine* (Jehovah's) *eyes,* not to be brought against His people again. The old order with its heavens "shall vanish away like smoke," and its "earth shall wax old like a garment" to be laid aside (51:6). At that time Jehovah will plant new spiritual heavens and lay the foundation of a new earth.

The New Heavens and the New Earth (vv. 17–25)

17 The coming of the Messiah will introduce a new spiritual and moral order or arrangement. Paul calls this new order "a dispensation [arrangement] of the fulness of the times," when all things will be summed up (brought together under one head) in Christ (Eph. 1:10). Isaiah's new heavens and new earth are the new arrangement to which Paul refers, and before which all old dispensations must pass away (read afresh the comments on 34:3–4; 51:6, 16). *For, behold—*

---

4. *Theological Wordbook of the Old Testament,* vol. 1, p. 132.

attention is focused on Jehovah and what He is about to do—*I create*. The word *create* (*bārā*, Hebrew), which was used by Moses to refer to the original creation (Gen. 1:1), emphasizes Jehovah's intention to bring something new into being. A completely new order shall be created by God, *and the former things shall not be remembered, nor come into mind.* This strong language emphasizes that the entire former system, which included a special physical nation and geographical area, animal sacrifices, and ceremonial rites, will be completely removed and abolished forever. As Paul describes it, "The old things are passed away; behold, they are become new" (II Cor. 5:17).

18–19 The people are to *rejoice for ever,* as long as the age shall last, *in that which I create,* the new heavens and the new earth—the new spiritual order. This new arrangement requires a new central city for the newly created people. Therefore, *behold, I create* (*bārā*) *Jerusalem a rejoicing,* an object and place of rejoicing, *and her people a joy* (cf. 35:10; 51:11). As Jehovah has shared the affliction of His people (63:9), so He now shares their joy. He rejoices in Jerusalem and in His people (cf. 62:5, *Jerusalem* and *my people* being equivalent. With former troubles forgotten and with joy and rejoicing in the new creation, weeping and crying are past (see the comments on 25:9).

20 The various unsatisfactory explanations made by commentators indicate the difficulty of this verse. The following may also be unsatisfactory, but it seems plausible. In Jehovah's eternal nature, time is not an element to be reckoned with, for with Him a thousand years are as a day, and vice versa (cf. Ps. 90:4; II Peter 3:8). He measures His activities by the accomplishment of the several aspects of His purpose, not by years. In the new order each citizen, whether for a brief moment (e.g., Stephen—Acts 7) or for a lengthy period (e.g., Paul, John), will fulfill his mission in God's purpose. It is not the length but the fullness of one's days that counts. And the sinner, regardless of the length of his days, is accursed. He will suffer the consequence of his deeds and die in his sins, regardless of when they were committed.

21–22 Security and permanence, together with God's providential care and supply for all needs, are indicated here (cf. v. 10, where a different figure is used to express the same idea). Jehovah's oath that the people of the new order will not be robbed of their heritage and the fruit of their labor (62:8–9) will be fulfilled. The days of Jehovah's people, His chosen, will be *as the days of a tree*, a symbol of longevity, permanence, beauty, and fruitfulness (cf. 61:3; Jer. 17:8). They shall long enjoy the fruitful works of their hands.

23 In past years the people labored for that which satisfies not (55:2) and wearied themselves in following their own way (57:10), but now it will be different. Their labor in the new order will not be in vain (I Cor. 15:58), nor will it bring *calamity*, the sudden terror of death and destruction as punishment from the Lord, as had the idolatry and faithlessness of the old nation. The reason is that *they are the seed of the blessed of Jehovah* (cf. 53:10; 61:9). An additional part of God's promise here is that their spiritual offspring will likewise share in the blessing.

24 Promising to answer prayer, Jehovah goes beyond what is pledged in 58:9 and Psalm 145:18–19: before His saints call on Him, Jehovah will know their needs (Matt. 6:8), and will have made provision for them. This assurance does not mean that there will be no need to pray, but that "The eyes of Jehovah are toward the righteous, / And his ears are open unto their cry" (Ps. 34:15; cf. I Peter 3:12). His chosen servants are never to be anxious, for the Lord is always at hand; so in everything they are to make their requests known unto Him (Phil. 4:4–7).

25 This verse confirms our position that the present passage (vv. 17–25) pertains to the messianic period. The prophet condenses what he said in 11:6–9—the wild and domesticated animals shall eat together—and adds the note that the serpent shall eat dust. (See the comments on 11:6–9, where it is pointed out on the basis of the context of the entire chapter that Isaiah is writing of the messianic period when the animal nature of man will be brought under subjection to the divine Spirit of the Branch or Root of Jesse.) The expression *They shall not hurt nor destroy in all my holy mountain* occurs both in 11:9 and here. God's holy mountain is the mountain of His house unto which all nations shall flow (2:2–4), the mountain to which foreigners shall be brought when they join themselves to Jehovah (56:6–7), and the mountain which is the inheritance of those who take refuge in Him (57:13; 66:20). (See also Appendix B, p. 538.)

The clause *and dust shall be the serpent's food* is related to Genesis 3:14, where Jehovah says to the serpent, "Dust shalt thou eat all the days of thy life." To "eat" or "lick the dust" is metaphorical for a humbled or defeated condition (cf. 49:23; Mic. 7:17). In the great spiritual conflict which began already in Eden between Satan and his angels on one side and Jehovah and His forces of right on the other, the serpent was cast down to the earth, and a great voice in heaven declared the coming of God's salvation, kingdom, and power, "and the authority of his Christ" (Rev. 12:9–10). This defeat of Satan by the Christ (Heb. 2:14; I John 3:8) guarantees the victory of the saints (Rom. 16:20). This is the holy mountain and heavenly Jerusalem to which we have come and in which we experience special blessings (Heb. 12:22).

CHAPTER 66
Jehovah's Judgments—Zion's Rejoicing

In this concluding chapter, Isaiah brings into focus Jehovah's future judgments and the enlargement, rejoicing, and glory of Zion. The Lord seems to be pointing to the final days of Judah and the coming glory of Zion in the new dispensation. There are numerous views regarding the time at which this chapter was written, the author, and the particular events being described. It is our view that the prophet Isaiah is writing of things to come which were revealed to him by Jehovah through His Holy Spirit. The prophet is looking to the climax of judgment and the glorious hope about which he has been preaching throughout his long life of service to Jehovah and His people.

Jehovah's Greatness and the Abomination of Idolatry (vv. 1–6)

1 From the beginning of his prophetic work Isaiah has spoken of the coming collapse and fall of the nation because of moral corruption within (ch. 1; 5:5–7). But out of the ruin there will be established

a new nation composed of many peoples and of a remnant which has been redeemed, cleansed, and purified (2:2–4; 4:2–6). The final chapter of the prophecy begins with the affirmation that Jehovah is speaking. In vision, Isaiah has seen the sanctuary trodden down (63:18) and the beautiful house of the Lord laid waste (see 64:11 and comments). And now, in view of the fact that the spiritual remnant and the redeemed from the nations are coming to Zion, there is need to build another temple. Jehovah says, *Heaven is my throne, and the earth is my footstool* (cf. Pss. 11:4; 103:19), and asks, *What manner of house will ye build unto me? and what place shall be my rest?* This is not, as some commentators suggest, a criticism of Haggai's zeal for rebuilding the temple upon the return from captivity, for phrases like "saith Jehovah" and "the word of Jehovah" occur about twenty-five times in his short book, affirming that the urgency was from the Lord Himself. And Zechariah, Haggai's contemporary, offers corroboration: "Therefore thus saith Jehovah: I am returned to Jerusalem with mercies; my house shall be built in it" (Zech. 1:16). A physical temple was necessary under that dispensation, but even it could not contain Jehovah (I Kings 8:27). Accordingly, the people were not to put their trust in the temple, but in Jehovah Himself. Yet they seemed to trust in the temple because it represented His presence (Jer. 7:1–4).

2   The physical material which went into the building of Solomon's temple was made by Jehovah, but it is perishable and will pass away. However, the material with which God is to build His new house will be men that are (1) *poor*—the word not only means deprived of material possessions, but often points to someone who is afflicted or distressed, a meek person (cf. 61:1); *and* (2) *of a contrite* (or smitten) *spirit*, as David's heart "smote" him when he cut off Saul's garment (I Sam. 24:5; cf. Isa. 57:15); *and* (3) *that tremble[th] at my word*, that is, have a penitent spirit and a warm respect for God's word. Such individuals will be the building material of Jehovah's new house (cf. Eph. 2:21; I Peter 2:5).

3   This verse is admittedly difficult. Is the prophet saying that one who burns incense or offers legal sacrifices (e.g., an ox, a sheep, an oblation [a meal or cereal offering]) in the wrong spirit is guilty of murder (or human sacrifice—57:5) and of offering abominable sacrifices to idols? Or is he saying that in the new temple and under the

new order, the offering of sacrifices that were formerly acceptable will be idolatry? In either case, *they have chosen their own ways, and their soul delighteth in their abominations.* What they are doing is displeasing to God, for any worship offered in the wrong spirit or unauthorized by God, both then and now, is unacceptable to Him.

4 Jehovah will determine the consequence of such actions, bringing upon those who delight in their abominations the full recompense of their rejection of His will and way. If they choose their own ways and sacrifices, Jehovah *will choose their delusions* (cf. 65:12; II Thess. 2:11–12).

5 The Lord now addresses those who hear His word, tremble at it, and yield to its instruction; He clearly distinguishes this group from *your brethren that hate you.* The phrase *your brethren* indicates that the two groups being distinguished in verses 1–6 consist of Jews. They who tremble at God's word are hated because of their righteousness and fear of Jehovah. They are cast out *for my name's sake,* that is, excluded or excommunicated as if unclean. In an ironical or sarcastic spirit, those who hate the righteous say, *Let Jehovah be glorified, that we may see your joy.* But those who fear God will not be humiliated; *it is they* (those who hate the righteous) *that shall be put to shame.*

6 The entire passage (vv. 1–6) seems to point to the close of the old Jewish order when Jerusalem and the temple were destroyed (A.D. 70). There is heard A *voice of tumult from the city, a voice from the temple.* The basic meaning of the word translated *tumult* is an uproar of a great crowd of people, or the crashing din of war (cf. 13:4). The *voice of Jehovah that rendereth recompense* is the havoc inflicted in response to His command bringing about the destruction of the city and temple in retribution for the mockers' insults. This points to the destruction of Jerusalem by either the Babylonians or the Romans, probably the latter.

But even if the Babylonian assault is in view, it foreshadows what will happen when the Jews reject the Servant, bringing swift and sure recompense upon themselves. Both Jerusalem and the temple will be destroyed at the voice (command) of Jehovah.

Blessings in the New Zion (vv. 7–14)

7–8 In the second Servant Song, Zion is portrayed as a mother who gives birth to the Servant (49:1–13). She is then portrayed as a mother who is surprised and comforted by the return of her wayward children (49:14–26). The unexpected increase of her children makes necessary an enlarged dwelling (54:1–3). The present passage gives prominence to the sudden birth of the *man-child*, the new *nation* and *land*, and *her children*. The *man-child* seems to be none other than the long-expected Servant, the Messiah born of the spiritual Zion (see the comments on 49:1; cf. Mic. 4:10; 5:2–3; Rev. 12:1–5),[5] who will "suddenly come to his temple" (Mal. 3:1). *Who hath heard such a thing?* Here is something unparalleled in history; for immediately following the birth of the Man-Child, a nation, its land, and Zion's children are brought forth. Only the entrance of Christ into the world and the events of Pentecost can be in view here; the Son was exalted, the new nation was established, and Zion's children began to multiply (Acts 2; 4:4).

9 Jehovah asks, *Shall I bring to the birth, and not cause to bring forth?* Having in His eternal purpose planned a scheme of redemption, foretold it by His prophets, and controlled history to that end, *Shall I that cause to bring forth shut the womb,* not bringing it to birth or fulfillment? This plan of redemption is the central theme of revelation; all other things are but contributors to its fulfillment. This vivid foretelling of His purpose together with its achievement is a stumbling block not to faith but to unbelief.

10–11 The Servant to come will comfort all that mourn for and in Zion (61:2–3); at His coming, mourning will cease (60:20). That time has now come; the mourners who love Zion will now rejoice. As an infant finds satisfaction and comfort at its mother's breasts, so shall those who love Zion and rejoice in her find complete satisfaction, and *be delighted with the abundance of her glory.*

12 If the people had obeyed God, Israel would have possessed "peace . . . as a river, and . . . righteousness as the waves of the sea" (48:18); all the glory of which the nations boasted (60:5; 61:6) would have then been hers. *For thus saith Jehovah, Behold, I will extend peace to her like a river, and the glory of the nations like an overflowing*

---

5. See Homer Hailey, *Revelation: An Introduction and Commentary* (Grand Rapids: Baker, 1979), pp. 267–72.

stream. As it so often does, *peace* here means welfare and prosperity, completion and fulfillment. In a beautiful picture of a suckling babe drawing nourishment from its mother's breasts, being borne upon the side in Oriental fashion (cf. 60:4), and being bounced upon the knee in a playful and affectionate manner, Jehovah describes the future innocence and blessings of His people.

13 *As one,* either a child or a man, *whom his mother comforteth* (cf. 49:15), Zion's children will be comforted in the spiritual Jerusalem.

14 *And ye shall see it*—the people will personally realize and experience the blessings of Zion in which they rejoice. *And your bones shall flourish,* grow and be made strong with freshness, vigor, and a new life such as characterized the early church and caused it to spread throughout the world. These blessings will be bestowed by the mighty hand of Jehovah, which *shall be known toward his servants.* As so often in Isaiah's writing, he presents a contrast: Jehovah will bless Zion and her children, *and he will have indignation against his enemies.* His indignation is set forth in the following verses.

Indignation Against the Idolaters (vv. 15–17)

15 Throughout the Scriptures fire is used repeatedly as a symbol of divine punishment, of Jehovah's righteous wrath and indignation. The psalmist observes, "A fire goeth before him,/And burneth up his adversaries round about" (Ps. 97:3); Jeremiah (Jer. 4:4) and Ezekiel (Ezek. 22:21) speak of the fire of Jehovah's wrath; and Nahum declares, "His wrath is poured out like fire" (Nah. 1:6). Isaiah said earlier that the enemies of Ariel "shall be visited . . . with whirlwind . . . and the flame of a devouring fire" (29:5–6), that the flame of a devouring fire will consume Assyria (30:27–31), and that Jehovah poured upon Israel "the fierceness of his anger . . . and it set him on fire round about" (42:25). Now the prophet adds, *For, behold, Jehovah will come with fire, and his chariots shall be like the whirlwind* (a storm wind); *to render his anger with fierceness, and his rebuke with flames of fire.* Here we have a vivid and dramatic picture of Jehovah's judgment against the rebellious idolaters in contrast to His blessings upon Zion.

16 By the fire of His righteous indignation, and *by his sword*, the instrument which He uses, whether Babylon (Ezek. 30:24–25) or Rome (Luke 21:20–24, esp. v. 24), Jehovah will execute His judgment *upon all flesh*. The judgment extends beyond the Jews to include all who are in rebellion against Him (for the phrase *all flesh* cf. Gen. 6:13; Lev. 17:14; Isa. 40:5–6; 49:26; Jer. 32:27). *And the slain of Jehovah shall be many*, for many rebel against Him and shall come under the judgment. Alexander and Young are probably correct in saying that the prophet is looking toward the destruction of Jerusalem by the Romans (Matt. 24:15–22; Luke 21:20–24). When the Roman Empire (the fourth beast in Daniel's vision) was itself brought to an end, it too was destroyed by a divine judgment (Dan. 7:11, 26).

17 It is difficult to determine whether the *one in the midst* is an individual leader of the sacred mysteries (Delitzsch), "one tree" (King James—the word *tree* does not appear in the Hebrew text), or the image of an idol. One thing is clear: instead of going to the sanctuary of God to worship Him in truth, the people are going into gardens of their own creation (cf. 1:29) to worship idols (cf. 65:3–5). Alexander sees this verse as a summary of the idolatry, rebellion, and spiritual temper of the Jews from the days of Isaiah to the coming of Christ (cf. v. 3), at which time *they* (the nation and the Old Testament system) *shall come to an end together*. I am inclined to agree. In language which the people of his day can understand, the prophet is describing the spiritual condition which the Servant will find in the nation and which will bring about its destruction. That condition is the result of the people's conduct throughout their entire history. Because they have acted like heathen, they must suffer the consequence of heathenism.

Jehovah's Glory Proclaimed to the World and the Response (vv. 18–24)

18 There is an ellipsis here that had to be filled by the translators. The words *know* and *the time* have been supplied. The idea seems to be that *their works and their thoughts* are cause for gathering *all nations and tongues*. All languages and dialects are to be represented (cf. Gen. 10:5, 20). The glory which they will see is Jehovah's pres-

ence and power exerted in the judgment of the idolatrous people
(v. 17) in contrast to the glory of His redeemed remnant (40:5;
60:1–3). Though many expositors think otherwise, it seems that this
verse points to the Roman destruction of Jerusalem.

19 The sign that Jehovah will set is not identified. Although it
may be a special miraculous sign as in 7:11, 14, that seems doubtful.
It could be the accomplishment of a particular deed or purpose (see
the comments on 19:19–20; 55:13). It could be the resurrection of the
Messiah and evidence confirming it. Or it could be the destruction of
Jerusalem and the temple by the Romans, for their army was composed of "mercenaries drawn from all parts of the Roman world."[6] Or
the sign could be the establishment of the church and its power in the
world. The clause *and I will send such as escape of them unto the
nations* suggests that the sign may have been the judgment of destruction which befell the apostate nation and its city and temple. From
among the survivors of the judgment, men will be sent unto the
various nations with a message. These nations include *Tarshish* to the
extreme west (modern Spain); *Pul*, probably Put, in Africa; and *Lud*,
which is either in western Asia Minor (Lydia) or in Africa. As nations
that draw the bow, Pul and Lud were probably of a warlike nature.
Tubal (modern Turkey), *Javan* (Greece), and *the isles afar off*, remote
coastlands (cf. 41:1), are symbolic of the entire world of that day; all
nations are included (cf. 49:12). Those who *have not heard my fame*,
neither have seen my glory, will hear of it through the message of those
who escape and are sent by Jehovah to the ends of the earth. It seems
that this verse points to the work of the apostles and other early
Christians who carried "the light of the gospel of the glory of Christ"
(II Cor. 4:4) to the world of their day.

20 *They*—those sent to the ends of the world—*shall bring all
your brethren out of all the nations for an oblation unto Jehovah.*
With the "middle wall of partition" broken down (Eph. 2:14), Gentiles from among all the nations will be brought with the redeemed
Jews as brethren, as one new man, unto Jehovah. They will be
brought to Him *for an oblation*, a bloodless offering (the Old Testament meal-offering). A great mixed caravan will hasten to Jehovah;

---

6. *Zondervan Pictorial Encyclopedia of the Bible*, vol. 3, p. 907.

they will come *upon horses, and in chariots, and in litters* (the Hebrew word is translated "covered wagons" in Num. 7:3), *and upon mules, and upon dromedaries* (*swift beasts*, King James; the Hebrew word occurs only here). In Isaiah's day these were the swiftest means of travel. The redeemed will be brought to Jehovah's *holy mountain Jerusalem* (cf. 56:7; 57:13), "the mountain of Jehovah's house" (2:2–4). As the children of Israel have brought their oblations to Jehovah in clean vessels, so will the redeemed from the nations be brought in cleanness to the house of Jehovah.

21 No longer will the ministers in Jehovah's house be taken exclusively from among the descendants of Levi and Aaron; but *of them also*, the Gentile converts brought to the holy mountain, *will I take for priests* (cf. 61:6). All the redeemed under Christ are "a royal priesthood" who offer spiritual sacrifices to God through Christ (I Peter 2:9). Men purchased "of every tribe, and tongue, and people, and nation," have been made "a kingdom and priests; and they reign upon the earth" (Rev. 5:9–10).

22 As *the new heavens and the new earth* (see the comments on 65:17 and Appendix B) endure, so will the seed and name of the new Israel remain. There will always be a seed, a faithful remnant who serve God (cf. Ps. 22:30–31). Confusing old national Israel with the new Israel is a chief error among religious teachers today. In his allegory based on the history of Hagar and Sarah, and Ishmael and Isaac, sons after the flesh and after the Spirit respectively, Paul says, "Cast out the handmaid and her son: for the son of the handmaid shall not inherit with the son of the freewoman" (Gal. 4:21–31). Though fleshly (national) Israel is cast off (cf. 65:15), spiritual Israel is ever before Jehovah (cf. 49:16). It is the seed and name of the new spiritual Israel that shall endure before His presence.

23 The prophet now clothes a spiritual truth in the idiom of his day. *From one new moon to another, and from one sabbath to another*—Isaiah is here referring to specific times of worship prescribed by Jehovah—*shall all flesh come to worship*. The new moons and Sabbaths of the old dispensation are taken away (1:14; II Cor. 5:16; Heb. 10:9), for they are only a shadow of things to come (Col. 2:16–17). *All flesh*, that is, all those of the new spiritual order, will come before Jehovah to worship. That all mankind will come before

Him not in physical Jerusalem, but in the new spiritual city, is clearly apparent from the impossibility of the former. Under the new order all who make up spiritual Zion will come before the Lord to worship at divinely prescribed times.

24 As the two previous sections of Part Two concluded with a dark picture of the fate of the rebellious—"There is no peace . . . to the wicked" (48:22; 57:20), so this final section ends with an even darker picture which vividly portrays the destruction of sinners. This picture is not to be interpreted in a literal manner, but in the light of its context. As gold and silver have been used to describe the glory of future Zion (60:17), so fire and worms now depict the end of the transgressors. As the faithful worshipers (v. 23) go forth from before Jehovah, they behold the terrible state of the apostates. Isaiah is probably contrasting the new spiritual Israel and old fleshly Israel. The latter are as *dead bodies* which shall never be brought to a full end as a people (Jer. 30:11). For the worms or maggots which consume them *shall not die*, and the fire of divine rebuke and judgment which torments them shall never be quenched (cf. vv. 15–16). Thus the people whom God chose, but who chose to reject Him and His Christ, *shall be an abhorring unto all flesh* (cf. 43:28). In the sight of God and of the righteous, then, there is a clear contrast between spiritual Zion and her children on one hand, and physical Jerusalem and her children on the other. This contrast foreshadows the contrast between the ultimate destiny of the worshipers of Jehovah and the wicked at the end of time. The infinite difference between the glory of God and of the righteous and the terrible doom of idolatry, sin, and the wicked is graphically set forth. What a fitting climax to Isaiah's majestically spiritual book!

Appendixes

A. The Everlasting Covenant
B. The New Heaven and the New Earth in the New Testament

APPENDIX A
The Everlasting Covenant

Isaiah affirms that judgment comes upon the heathen world *because they have transgressed the laws, violated the statutes, broken the everlasting covenant* (24:5). What were these laws, statutes, and the everlasting covenant which they violated? This is a question that has troubled many commentators. Certainly the reference is not to the Mosaic covenant given to Israel at Horeb, for the heathen nations were never under it (Deut. 5:1–3); nor is the reference to the new covenant of Christ, for it lay far in the future.

The word *everlasting*, which translates the Hebrew *ōlām* in the Old Testament (and the Greek *aiōnios* in the New Testament), literally means "age-long," "age-lasting," or "of long duration."[1] The precise meaning must be determined from the context. When one speaks of a "servant for ever" (e.g., Deut. 15:17), the phrase *for ever* means "for a lifetime"; when one speaks of a statute or a people's possession of their land as "everlasting," the word means "age-lasting," as long as the age lasts, that is, until the coming of the Christ. The "everlasting hills" will endure as long as time continues. When God is spoken of as "everlasting" or "eternal," the word is used in its

---

1. *International Standard Bible Encyclopedia*, ed. James Orr (Chicago: Howard-Severance, 1937), vol. 2, p. 1041; *Zondervan Pictorial Encyclopedia of the Bible*, ed. Merrill C. Tenney (Grand Rapids: Zondervan, 1975), vol. 2, p. 380.

strictest sense, for He antedates time and will continue beyond time, having neither beginning nor ending. In the passage before us, *the everlasting covenant* is coexistent with the laws and statutes which have been transgressed. They were to endure for an age appointed by God; they did not antedate the time of their revelation or extend beyond the period for which they were given. Accordingly, Leupold translates the phrase "the covenant of ancient times." To better understand what it entailed, we will now take a close look at a few relevant references in the books of Moses, Job, Amos, and Paul.

In the Writings of Moses

From Adam to Noah

Apparently there was a law of sacrifice by which Abel and Cain were governed in their offerings; otherwise, one would not have been acceptable and the other unacceptable (Gen. 4:3–5). John says, "Cain was of the evil one" and "his works were evil" (I John 3:12); obviously, Cain had violated God's law. In the days of Seth men began to call on the name of Jehovah (Gen. 4:26). Enoch walked with God (Gen. 5:24). By the time of Noah, the wickedness of men had become great (Gen. 6:5); the earth was exceedingly corrupt and violent (Gen. 6:11–13). Therefore God determined to send a flood of destruction. Though we are not told of any laws or covenant which had been given, the accounts of God's commendation of Abel's offering, the beginning of the practice of calling on the name of the Lord, the acceptance of Enoch, and the wickedness and corruption of Noah's time, all imply some divine standard revealed by the Lord.

Noah

In the midst of universal corruption Noah was a righteous and perfect man who walked with God and found favor with Him (Gen. 6:8–9). Noah built an ark, as the Lord instructed him (Gen. 6:22; 7:5), and after the flood he built an altar and offered acceptable sacrifices to Jehovah (Gen. 8:20–21). Noah's righteousness and perfection, his walking with God and building an altar and offering sacrifices, are indications that he acted and lived by a divine standard

532

which had been revealed to him. After the flood he was given permission to eat flesh (Gen. 9:3–4); he was also given the law of capital punishment as a deterrent to murder (Gen. 9:5–6). God then made a covenant with Noah, his seed, and all the animals of the earth that He would never again destroy the earth with a flood; and He gave the rainbow as a token of that covenant (9:8–17). This covenant was unconditional. Since it carried no conditions to be kept, it is not the covenant of Isaiah's prophecy.

Abraham

When Abraham was called upon to leave his homeland and family, he obeyed and went forth as commanded (Gen. 12:1–4). When he reached Shechem, he built an altar unto Jehovah (Gen. 12:6–7). Between Bethel and Ai he built another altar and called upon the name of Jehovah (Gen. 12:8). At the oaks of Mamre in Hebron the patriarch built a third altar unto Jehovah (Gen. 13:18). When God renewed the promise of a numerous posterity, Abraham "believed in Jehovah; and he reckoned it to him for righteousness" (Gen. 15:6). The Lord made a covenant pledging to Abraham's seed the land of the original promise (Gen. 15:18–21). Later Jehovah appeared to Abraham and said, "I am God Almighty; walk before me, and be thou perfect" (Gen. 17:1). Walking before God in perfection presupposes a standard. God then made with Abraham the covenant of circumcision: all males in his household, both those born in his house and those bought with his money, had to be circumcised (Gen. 17:9–14). Obeying this instruction of Jehovah, Abraham was circumcised with all his house (Gen. 17:23–27).

Jehovah commended Abraham for his faithfulness, recognizing his ability to "command his children and his household after him, that they may keep the way of Jehovah, to do righteousness and justice" (Gen. 18:19). When Jehovah instructed him to send out Ishmael, as Sarah insisted, Abraham bowed to the command, sending Hagar and Ishmael into the wilderness (Gen. 21:8–14). The great strength of the patriarch's faith was most strikingly demonstrated when he was told by the Lord to take his son Isaac to a mountain in the land of Moriah and there offer him as a burnt-offering. With a heavy heart, but with implicit faith that God was able to give his son back by raising him from the dead (Heb. 11:17–19), Abraham obeyed to the point of lifting the knife to take the lad's life. Only then did the Lord intervene, staying Abraham's hand (Gen. 22:1–19).

Abraham's great faith was commended by Jehovah: "Abraham obeyed my voice, and kept my charge, my commandments, my statutes, and my laws" (Gen. 26:5). Surely Jehovah's instructions to Abraham which we have just mentioned are in view here, but Abraham's conduct and actions reflect more than the specific commands recorded. They go back to a former revelation regarding altars and sacrifices, a standard of ethics and righteousness, and various principles of a right relationship with God such as were exhibited in the lives of certain antediluvians, including Noah. Although not specifically labeled a covenant, nor laid out in specific details, these principles and standards involving Jehovah and the ancients appear to be what Isaiah has in mind when he speaks of *the everlasting covenant* (24:5). Further, Isaiah's charge that "the enemy hath broken the covenant, he hath despised the cities, he regardeth not man" (33:8), seems to entail a violation of the principle set forth in Genesis 9:5.

Melchizedek

King of righteousness, king of Salem (peace), priest of God Most High, and contemporary of Abraham, Melchizedek walked across a page of history (Gen. 14:17–20), never to be forgotten. He was a type of Christ as king and priest. To him Abraham gave a tenth of the spoils. Questions arise concerning Melchizedek: How did he learn of God Most High and of his priestly duties? How did Abraham learn that a tenth belonged to Melchizedek as priest? What made Melchizedek so great that he could bestow blessings upon Abraham, the father of the faithful (Heb. 7:1–10)? We seem here to be face to face with revelation from God that evidently included laws, statutes, and, apparently, an early covenant.

Reuel (Jethro) and Balaam

In the writings of Moses the last two men we meet who have a knowledge of God apart from the Lord's revelation to Moses are Jethro, the father-in-law of Moses, and Balaam, a prophet of sorts from Mesopotamia.

Jethro is called "the priest of Midian" (Exod. 2:16; 3:1; 18:1). He presented a burnt-offering and sacrifices to God, in which Aaron and the elders of Israel partook (Exod. 18:12). He offered advice to Moses regarding his duties as judge (Exod. 18:13–27). Again we ask, From where came his knowledge of God and of offerings and sacrifices? God obviously had given him instruction.

Balaam, who is called a prophet (II Peter 2:16) and a soothsayer (Josh. 13:22), apparently had a wide reputation and some knowledge of God. His response to the messengers from Balak was, "I cannot go beyond the word of Jehovah my God, to do less or more" (Num. 22:18). God used him (Num. 22–24), but his misuse of whatever knowledge he had of the Lord led to his death (Num. 31:8). He is the last heathen mentioned in the Old Testament who had knowledge of God apart from the law.

In the Book of Job

The date of Job's life is uncertain, but most conservative scholars contend that he lived somewhere around the time of Abraham. There is no allusion to the law of Moses in the book. Yet Job said that it would be his consolation that he had "not denied the words of the Holy One" (6:10). He further affirmed, "His way have I kept, and turned not aside./I have not gone back from the commandment of his lips;/I have treasured up the words of his mouth more than my necessary food" (23:11–12). Apparently, certain portions of the divine revelation—"the commandment of his lips" and "the words of his mouth"—were known, respected, and kept by this man of God long before the days of Moses and the law.

In the Book of Amos

Amos, who prophesied approximately fifteen years before Isaiah, condemned six heathen nations before turning his attention to Judah and Israel (Amos 2:4). Since three of these nations, Damascus (Syria), Gaza (Philistia), and Tyre (Phoenicia), were not related to Abraham, they were heathen in the strictest sense; the other three, however, Edom, Ammon, and Moab, were related to the patriarch and should have known of God through their ancestors. The first three are charged with crimes of inhumane cruelty, violation of human rights, and insensitivity to human dignity. Since Jehovah accused them of transgression, they must at some time have been given some law or statute which they then knowingly transgressed. Not until the prophet comes to Judah, however, does he introduce *the law:* "They have rejected the law of Jehovah, and have not kept his statutes" (2:4). Likewise, the transgressions of Israel are transgressions of the law (2:6–8). It seems, then, that the heathen nations have violated some revelation of law or statutes separate from the law violated by Judah and Israel.

In the Writings of Paul

Romans 1

Paul's charge against the Gentiles in Romans 1 is a further argument that an everlasting covenant was made with men before the covenant at Sinai. The apostle says, "For the wrath of God is revealed . . . because that which is known of God is manifest [made known] in them; for God manifested it unto them" (Rom. 1:18–19). All that was or is known of God is a matter of revelation, however blurred and perverted that knowledge may have become through the centuries. Paul charges that "knowing God, they glorified him not as God, neither gave thanks; but became vain in their reasonings, and their senseless heart was darkened" (Rom. 1:21). Their knowledge of Him, which could have come only by revelation, did not result in their glorifying or acknowledging Him as the source of blessings. They were therefore responsible for their own condition. Further, professing to be wise, the Gentile world at some time in the past foolishly "changed the glory of the incorruptible God" for likenesses of animate creatures. "Wherefore God gave them up in the lusts of their hearts unto uncleanness . . . for that they exchanged the truth of God for a lie" (Rom. 1:23–25). Now they could not have exchanged something they did not have. So at some time they must have had some truth concerning God's being, character, and will. This truth, which had been manifested (revealed or made known) by God, they ex-

536

changed for the lie of idolatry and all that accompanies it. "For this cause God gave them up unto vile passions" (Rom. 1:26). "And even as they refused to have God in their knowledge, God gave them up unto a reprobate mind, to do those things which are not fitting" (Rom. 1:28). A list of sins follows. When the Gentiles gave God up, He had no alternative but to give them up and allow them to learn from sad experience what it means to reject Him.

It is beyond the scope of this appendix to discuss Romans 2:12–16. Let it suffice to say that whatever Paul may have had in mind when he wrote that Gentiles who, not having the law, "do by nature the things of the law . . . show the work of the law written in their hearts" (Rom. 2:14–15), it does not cover all of the Gentiles' knowledge of God which was mentioned in Romans 1. Nor is this natural consciousness a sufficient explanation of the everlasting covenant, laws, and statutes which Isaiah charges the nations with having violated. As indicated in Romans 1, there must have been some specific revelation.

The Book of Ephesians

Paul, the apostle to the Gentiles, in writing to Christians who were once heathen, says, "Ye were dead through your trespasses and sins [which involved violation of law], wherein ye once walked according to the course of this world [this is the standard that they followed after having left God], according to the prince of the powers of the air, of the spirit that now worketh in the sons of disobedience; among whom we also all once lived in the lusts of our flesh, doing the desires of the flesh and of the mind [rather than the will of God], and were by nature [practice] children of wrath, even as the rest" (Eph. 2:1–3). The apostle continues to describe the former condition of the Gentile Christians to whom he is writing: "Ye were at that time separate from Christ, alienated from the commonwealth of Israel, and strangers from the covenants of the promise, having no hope and without God in the world" (Eph. 2:12). They were completely separate from the covenants of the promise made to Abraham and his seed. Since God had given them up in view of their refusal to have Him in their knowledge (Rom. 1:28), they were without Him.

Having noted that the saints at Ephesus "no longer walk as the Gentiles also walk, in the vanity of their mind, being darkened in their understanding, alienated from the life of God," Paul explains the cause of the Gentiles' alienation: they are alienated "because of the ignorance that is in them, because of the hardening of their heart" (Eph. 4:17–18). According to Romans 1, their ignorance is willful—they have hardened their hearts against the revelation they received. Finally, Paul describes the consequence of the Gentiles' rejection of God: "being past feeling [they] gave themselves up to lasciviousness, to work all uncleanness with greediness" (Eph. 4:19).

We know that the Gentiles were never under the Mosaic covenant, and they were not under the covenant of Christ until they brought themselves under it by individual obedience to its terms. Yet we also know from Paul that they were under condemnation for willfully rejecting God's general revelation and in particular a covenant He had made with them in ancient times (Isa. 24:5). They brought themselves under the penalty of death. It appears to this writer that God made a covenant in the beginning, or at some early date, which was not recorded and has therefore been lost to history. This covenant contained laws and statutes to be kept, but the Gentiles turned away from it when they rejected God and knowledge of Him. It is hoped that this brief discussion will help in interpreting Isaiah 24–27 and in understanding the condition of the heathen today.

APPENDIX B
The New Heaven and New Earth in the New Testament

Two New Testament writers, Peter and John, speak of a new heaven and a new earth; and, like Isaiah, they refer to a new order or arrangement. But the new order of which they write is not that of Isaiah, but a new order beyond the judgment.

In his second epistle Peter writes of mockers in the last days who will ask, "Where is the promise of his coming?" and scornfully note that "all things continue as they were from the beginning of creation" (II Peter 3:3–4). But the day of the Lord, that is, the day of judgment and destruction of ungodly men, "will come as a thief; in the which the heavens shall pass away with a great noise, and the elements shall be dissolved with fervent heat, and the earth and the works that are therein shall be burned up" (II Peter 3:10). Beyond this "day of the Lord," in which the present order will pass away, "we look for new heavens and a new earth, wherein dwelleth righteousness" (3:13). Isaiah's new heavens and new earth have been realized in the present dispensation of Christ; Peter's new heavens and new earth are to be realized beyond the coming of Christ and the judgment. It is the new order in heaven.

John, the other New Testament writer to use the expression, likewise places the new heaven and the new earth beyond the judgment. Having described the thousand-year reign of Christ and the saints, which is a symbol of the present reign of Christ (Rev. 20:1–6), John speaks of the passing away of the present earth and heaven, and the judgment to follow (20:11–15). This is in agreement with Peter's description of the end and that which follows. After picturing the judgment scene, John says, "And I saw a new heaven and a new earth: for the first heaven and the first earth are passed away" (Rev. 21:1). John then offers a figurative depiction of the glorified church at home with God, the heaven of the new order to which we look.

We conclude that while Isaiah's new heavens and new earth are the present order under Christ (65:17), which followed the passing of the old heathen systems (34:3–4) and the Jewish order (51:6, 16), the new heavens and new earth of Peter and John are the eternal arrangement of God beyond the judgment. In neither of the new orders—the one prophesied by Isaiah and the one prophesied by the apostles—is there a place for a millennial reign of Christ on earth, for modern-day concepts of a "new planet earth," or for a utopian "world of tomorrow." Such theories are figments of man's imagination, illusions of error bereft of all truth. Let us rejoice in what God has provided for today, and in joyful anticipation look for that which He will provide for us in the heavenly state.

Bibliography

Introductions

Driver, S. R. *An Introduction to the Literature of the Old Testament.* New York: Meridian, 1957.

Pfeiffer, Robert H. *Introduction to the Old Testament.* New York: Harper, 1948.

Unger, Merrill F. *Introductory Guide to the Old Testament.* Grand Rapids: Zondervan, 1956.

Young, Edward J. *An Introduction to the Old Testament.* Grand Rapids: Eerdmans, 1956.

Commentaries

Alexander, Joseph Addison. *Commentary on the Prophecies of Isaiah.* Grand Rapids: Zondervan, 1953 reprint.

Barnes, Albert. *Isaiah.* 2 vols. Barnes' Notes on the Old Testament. Grand Rapids: Baker, 1963 reprint.

Calvin, John. *Commentary on the Book of the Prophet Isaiah.* 2 vols. Calvin's Commentaries. Grand Rapids: Baker, 1979 reprint.

Clements, R. E. *Isaiah 1–39.* Rev. ed. New Century Bible Commentary. Grand Rapids: Eerdmans, 1980.

Delitzsch, Franz. *Biblical Commentary on the Prophecies of Isaiah.* 2 vols. Grand Rapids: Eerdmans, 1950 reprint.

Keil, Carl F. *Kings.* Commentaries on the Old Testament. Grand Rapids: Eerdmans, 1950 reprint.

Leupold, H. C. *Exposition of Isaiah.* 2 vols. Grand Rapids: Baker, 1971.

Rawlinson, George. *Isaiah.* 2 vols. Pulpit Commentary. New York: Funk and Wagnalls, n.d.

Smith, George Adam. *The Book of Isaiah.* 2 vols. Rev. ed. The Expositor's Bible. Garden City, N.Y.: Doubleday, n.d.

Whybray, R. N. *Isaiah 40–66.* New Century Bible Commentary. Grand Rapids: Eerdmans, 1981.

Willis, John T. *Isaiah.* Austin: Sweet, 1980.

Young, Edward J. *The Book of Isaiah.* 3 vols. New International Commentary on the Old Testament. Grand Rapids: Eerdmans, 1972.

Supplementary Works

Allis, Oswald T. *The Unity of Isaiah*. Philadelphia: Presbyterian and Reformed, 1950.

Ante-Nicene Fathers. New York: Scribner, 1903.

Barton, George A. *Archaeology and the Bible*. 7th ed. Philadelphia: American Sunday-School Union, 1937.

Driver, S. R. *Isaiah: His Life and Times and the Writings Which Bear His Name*. New York: Revell, n.d.

Eiselen, Frederick Carl. *The Prophetic Books of the Old Testament*. Vol. 1. New York: Methodist Book Concern, 1923.

Erdman, Charles R. *The Book of Isaiah*. Westwood, N.J.: Revell, 1954.

Free, Joseph P. *Archaeology and Bible History*. Wheaton, Ill.: Van Kampen, 1950.

International Standard Bible Encyclopedia. Edited by James Orr. 5 vols. Chicago: Howard-Severance, 1937.

Kraeling, Emil G. *Rand McNally Bible Atlas*. Chicago: Rand McNally, 1976.

Pfeiffer, Charles F. *The Biblical World*. Grand Rapids: Baker, 1966.

Robinson, George L. *The Book of Isaiah*. Rev. ed. Grand Rapids: Baker, 1954 reprint.

Sayce, A. H. *The Life and Times of Isaiah*. London: Religious Tract Society, 1889.

Schwantes, Siegfried J. *A Short History of the Ancient Near East*. Grand Rapids: Baker, 1965.

Theological Wordbook of the Old Testament. Edited by R. Laird Harris. 2 vols. Chicago: Moody, 1980.

Thiele, Edwin R. *A Chronology of the Hebrew Kings*. Grand Rapids: Zondervan, 1978.

Young, Edward J. *Isaiah Fifty-Three: A Devotional and Expository Study*. Grand Rapids: Eerdmans, 1952.

_____. *Studies in Isaiah*. Grand Rapids: Eerdmans, 1954.

_____. *Who Wrote Isaiah?* Grand Rapids: Eerdmans, 1958.

Zondervan Pictorial Encyclopedia of the Bible. Edited by Merrill C. Tenney. 5 vols. Grand Rapids: Zondervan, 1975.

For a complete bibliography of works on Isaiah, see Edward J. Young, *The Book of Isaiah*, vol. 3, pp. 553–60.